Chapterwise DPP *for* NEET

PHYSICS

Collection of 1305+ MCQs based on NCERT

Improves your Score by at least 20%

28 Chapters based on NCERT

DAILY PRACTICE PROBLEM DPP CHAPTERWISE CP07 - PHYSICS

Scoring Grid

Total Questions	45	Total Marks	180
Attempted		Correct	
Incorrect		Net Score	
Cut-off Score	45	Qualifying Score	60
Success Gap = Net Score – Qualifying Score			
Net Score = (Correct × 4) – (Incorrect × 1)			

- **Corporate Office** : 45, 2nd Floor, Maharishi Dayanand Marg, Corner Market,
  Malviya Nagar, New Delhi-110017
  Tel. : 011-49842349 / 49842350

Typeset by Disha DTP Team

Printed at : Repro Knowledgecast Limited, Thane

For further information about books from DISHA,

Log on to **www.dishapublication.com** or email to **info@dishapublication.com**

INDEX/CHAPTERS

Date : | Start Time : | End Time :

PHYSICS $\boxed{\text{CP01}}$

SYLLABUS : Physical World, Units & Measurements

Max. Marks : 180   **Marking Scheme :** (+4) for correct & (–1) for incorrect answer   **Time : 60 min.**

INSTRUCTIONS : This Daily Practice Problem Sheet contains 45 MCQs. For each question only one option is correct. Darken the correct circle/ bubble in the Response Grid provided on each page.

1. The density of material in CGS system of units is 4g/cm^3. In a system of units in which unit of length is 10 cm and unit of mass is 100 g, the value of density of material will be
   (a) 0.4 unit   (b) 40 unit
   (c) 400 unit   (d) 0.04 unit

2. The time period of a body under S.H.M. is represented by: $T = P^a D^b S^c$ where P is pressure, D is density and S is surface tension, then values of a, b and c are

   (a) $-\dfrac{3}{2}, \dfrac{1}{2}, 1$ (b) $-1, -2, 3$

   (c) $\dfrac{1}{2}, -\dfrac{3}{2}, -\dfrac{1}{2}$ (d) $1, 2, \dfrac{1}{3}$

3. The respective number of significant figures for the numbers $23.023, 0.0003$ and 2.1×10^{-3} are
   (a) 5, 1, 2   (b) 5, 1, 5   (c) 5, 5, 2   (d) 4, 4, 2

4. Young's modulus of a material has the same unit as that of
   (a) pressure   (b) strain
   (c) compressibility   (d) force

5. Of the following quantities, which one has dimensions different from the remaining three?
   (a) Energy per unit volume
   (b) Force per unit area
   (c) Product of voltage and charge per unit volume
   (d) Angular momentum

6. The pressure on a square plate is measured by measuring the force on the plate and length of the sides of the plate by using the formula $P = \dfrac{F}{\ell^2}$. If the maximum errors in the measurement of force and length are 4% and 2% respectively, then the maximum error in the measurement of pressure is
   (a) 1%   (b) 2%   (c) 8%   (d) 10%

RESPONSE GRID					
1. ⓐⓑⓒⓓ	2. ⓐⓑⓒⓓ	3. ⓐⓑⓒⓓ	4. ⓐⓑⓒⓓ	5. ⓐⓑⓒⓓ
6. ⓐⓑⓒⓓ					

Space for Rough Work

7. The siemen is the SI unit of
   (a) resistivity
   (b) resistance
   (c) conductivity
   (d) conductance

8. An object is moving through the liquid. The viscous damping force acting on it is proportional to the velocity. Then dimensions of constant of proportionality are
   (a) $[ML^{-1}T^{-1}]$
   (b) $[MLT^{-1}]$
   (c) $[M^0LT^{-1}]$
   (d) $[ML^0T^{-1}]$

9. The least count of a stop watch is 0.2 second. The time of 20 oscillations of a pendulum is measured to be 25 second. The percentage error in the measurement of time will be
   (a) 8%
   (b) 1.8%
   (c) 0.8%
   (d) 0.1%

10. Weber is the unit of
    (a) magnetic susceptibility
    (b) intensity of magnetisation
    (c) magnetic flux
    (d) magnetic permeability

11. The physical quantity which has the dimensional formula $[M^1T^{-3}]$ is
    (a) surface tension
    (b) solar constant
    (c) density
    (d) compressibility

12. The dimensions of Wien's constant are
    (a) $[ML^0T K]$
    (b) $[M^0 LT^0 K]$
    (c) $[M^0 L^0 T K]$
    (d) $[MLTK]$

13. If the capacitance of a nanocapacitor is measured in terms of a unit 'u' made by combining the electric charge 'e', Bohr radius 'a_0', Planck's constant 'h' and speed of light 'c' then
    (a) $u = \dfrac{e^2 h}{a_0}$
    (b) $u = \dfrac{hc}{e^2 a_0}$
    (c) $u = \dfrac{e^2 c}{h a_0}$
    (d) $u = \dfrac{e^2 a_0}{hc}$

14. The dimensions of $\dfrac{1}{\epsilon_0}\dfrac{e^2}{hc}$ are
    (a) $M^{-1} L^{-3} T^4 A^2$
    (b) $ML^3 T^{-4} A^{-2}$
    (c) $M^0 L^0 T^0 A^0$
    (d) $M^{-1} L^{-3} T^2 A$

15. The density of a cube is measured by measuring its mass and length of its sides. If the maximum error in the measurement of mass and length are 4% and 3% respectively, the maximum error in the measurement of density will be
    (a) 7%
    (b) 9%
    (c) 12%
    (d) 13%

16. Which is different from others by units ?
    (a) Phase difference
    (b) Mechanical equivalent
    (c) Loudness of sound
    (d) Poisson's ratio

17. A quantity X is given by $\varepsilon_0 L \dfrac{\Delta V}{\Delta t}$ where ϵ_0 is the permittivity of the free space, L is a length, DV is a potential difference and Dt is a time interval. The dimensional formula for X is the same as that of
    (a) resistance
    (b) charge
    (c) voltage
    (d) current

18. If the error in the measurement of the volume of sphere is 6%, then the error in the measurement of its surface area will be
    (a) 2%
    (b) 3%
    (c) 4%
    (d) 7.5%

19. If velocity (V), force (F) and energy (E) are taken as fundamental units, then dimensional formula for mass will be
    (a) $V^{-2}F^0E$
    (b) V^0FE^2
    (c) $VF^{-2}E^0$
    (d) $V^{-2}F^0E$

20. Multiply 107.88 by 0.610 and express the result with correct number of significant figures.
    (a) 65.8068
    (b) 65.807
    (c) 65.81
    (d) 65.8

21. Which of the following is a dimensional constant?
    (a) Refractive index
    (b) Poissons ratio
    (c) Strain
    (d) Gravitational constant

22. If E, m, J and G represent energy, mass, angular momentum and gravitational constant respectively, then the dimensional formula of EJ^2/m^5G^2 is same as that of the
    (a) angle
    (b) length
    (c) mass
    (d) time

23. The refractive index of water measured by the relation $m = \dfrac{\text{real depth}}{\text{apparent depth}}$ is found to have values of 1.34, 1.38, 1.32 and 1.36; the mean value of refractive index with percentage error is
    (a) $1.35 \pm 1.48\,\%$
    (b) $1.35 \pm 0\,\%$
    (c) $1.36 \pm 6\,\%$
    (d) $1.36 \pm 0\,\%$

<table>
<tr><td rowspan="4">RESPONSE GRID</td><td>7. ⓐⓑⓒⓓ</td><td>8. ⓐⓑⓒⓓ</td><td>9. ⓐⓑⓒⓓ</td><td>10. ⓐⓑⓒⓓ</td><td>11. ⓐⓑⓒⓓ</td></tr>
<tr><td>12. ⓐⓑⓒⓓ</td><td>13. ⓐⓑⓒⓓ</td><td>14. ⓐⓑⓒⓓ</td><td>15. ⓐⓑⓒⓓ</td><td>16. ⓐⓑⓒⓓ</td></tr>
<tr><td>17. ⓐⓑⓒⓓ</td><td>18. ⓐⓑⓒⓓ</td><td>19. ⓐⓑⓒⓓ</td><td>20. ⓐⓑⓒⓓ</td><td>21. ⓐⓑⓒⓓ</td></tr>
<tr><td>22. ⓐⓑⓒⓓ</td><td>23. ⓐⓑⓒⓓ</td><td></td><td></td><td></td></tr>
</table>

24. If e is the charge, V the potential difference, T the temperature, then the units of $\dfrac{eV}{T}$ are the same as that of
(a) Planck's constant (b) Stefan's constant
(c) Boltzmann's constant (d) gravitational constant

25. The dimensions of mobility are
(a) $M^{-2}T^2A$ (b) $M^{-1}T^2A$
(c) $M^{-2}T^3A$ (d) $M^{-1}T^3A$

26. Two quantities A and B have different dimensions which mathematical operation given below is physically meaningful?
(a) A/B (b) A + B (c) A – B (d) A = B

27. The velocity of water waves (v) may depend on their wavelength l, the density of water r and the acceleration due to gravity, g. The method of dimensions gives the relation between these quantities is
(a) v (b) $v^2 \propto g\lambda$
(c) $v^2 \propto g\lambda^2$ (d) $v^2 \propto g^{-1}\lambda^2$

28. The physical quantities not having same dimensions are
(a) torque and work
(b) momentum and Planck's constant
(c) stress and Young's modulus
(d) speed and $(m_0e_0)^{-1/2}$

29. A physical quantity of the dimensions of length that can be formed out of c, G and $\dfrac{e^2}{4\pi\varepsilon_0}$ is [c is velocity of light, G is universal constant of gravitation and e is charge]
(a) $c^2\left[G\dfrac{e^2}{4\pi\varepsilon_0}\right]^{1/2}$ (b) $\dfrac{1}{c^2}\left[\dfrac{e^2}{G4\pi\varepsilon_0}\right]^{1/2}$
(c) $\dfrac{1}{c}G\dfrac{e^2}{4\pi\varepsilon_0}$ (d) $\dfrac{1}{c^2}\left[G\dfrac{e^2}{4\pi\varepsilon_0}\right]^{1/2}$

30. The unit of impulse is the same as that of
(a) energy (b) power
(c) momentum (d) velocity

31. If Q denote the charge on the plate of a capacitor of capacitance C then the dimensional formula for $\dfrac{Q^2}{C}$ is
(a) $[L^2M^2T]$ (b) $[LMT^2]$
(c) $[L^2MT^{-2}]$ (d) $[L^2M^2T^2]$

32. The mass of the liquid flowing per second per unit area of cross-section of the tube is proportional to (pressure difference across the ends)^n and (average velocity of the liquid)^m. Which of the following relations between m and n is correct?
(a) m = n (b) m = – n (c) $m^2 = n$ (d) $m = -n^2$

33. The Richardson equation is given by $I = AT^2e^{-B/kT}$. The dimensional formula for AB^2 is same as that for
(a) IT^2 (b) kT (c) Ik^2 (d) Ik^2/T

34. Turpentine oil is flowing through a capillary tube of length ℓ and radius r. The pressure difference between the two ends of the tube is p. The viscosity of oil is given by :
$\eta = \dfrac{p(r^2 - x^2)}{4v\ell}$. Here v is velocity of oil at a distance x from the axis of the tube. From this relation, the dimensional formula of η is
(a) $[ML^{-1}T^{-1}]$ (b) $[MLT^{-1}]$
(c) $[ML^2T^{-2}]$ (d) $[M^0L^0T^0]$

35. Given that $y = A\sin\left[\left(\dfrac{2\pi}{\lambda}(ct - x)\right)\right]$, where y and x are measured in metre. Which of the following statements is true?
(a) The unit of λ is same as that of x and A
(b) The unit of λ is same as that of x but not of A
(c) The unit of c is same as that of $\dfrac{2\pi}{\lambda}$
(d) The unit of (ct – x) is same as that of $\dfrac{2\pi}{\lambda}$

36. If L = 2.331 cm, B = 2.1 cm, then L + B =
(a) 4.431 cm (b) 4.43 cm (c) 4.4 cm (d) 4 cm

37. In the relation x = cos (ωt + kx), the dimension(s) of ω is/are
(a) $[M^0 LT]$ (b) $[M^0L^{-1}T^0]$
(c) $[M^0L^0T^{-1}]$ (d) $[M^0LT^{-1}]$

<table>
<tr><td rowspan="3">Response Grid</td><td>24. ⓐⓑⓒⓓ</td><td>25. ⓐⓑⓒⓓ</td><td>26. ⓐⓑⓒⓓ</td><td>27. ⓐⓑⓒⓓ</td><td>28. ⓐⓑⓒⓓ</td></tr>
<tr><td>29. ⓐⓑⓒⓓ</td><td>30. ⓐⓑⓒⓓ</td><td>31. ⓐⓑⓒⓓ</td><td>32. ⓐⓑⓒⓓ</td><td>33. ⓐⓑⓒⓓ</td></tr>
<tr><td>34. ⓐⓑⓒⓓ</td><td>35. ⓐⓑⓒⓓ</td><td>36. ⓐⓑⓒⓓ</td><td>37. ⓐⓑⓒⓓ</td><td></td></tr>
</table>

Space for Rough Work

38. In a vernier calipers, ten smallest divisions of the vernier scale are equal to nine smallest division on the main scale. If the smallest division on the main scale is half millimeter, then the vernier constant is
(a) 0.5 mm   (b) 0.1 mm   (c) 0.05 mm   (d) 0.005 mm

39. Which two of the following five physical parameters have the same dimensions?
(A) Energy density   (B) Refractive index
(C) Dielectric constant   (D) Young's modulus
(E) Magnetic field
(a) (B) and (D)   (b) (C) and (E)
(c) (A) and (D)   (d) (A) and (E)

40. In the eqn. $\left(P + \dfrac{a}{V^2}\right)(V - b) = \text{constant}$, the unit of a is
(a) dyne cm^5 (b) dyne cm^4
(c) dyne/cm^3 (d) dyne cm^2

41. The dimensions of Reynold's constant are
(a) $[M^0L^0T^0]$ (b) $[ML^{-1}T^{-1}]$
(c) $[ML^{-1}T^{-2}]$ (d) $[ML^{-2}T^{-2}]$

42. Which of the following do not have the same dimensional formula as the velocity?
Given that m_0 = permeability of free space, e_0 = permittivity of free space, n = frequency, l = wavelength, P = pressure, r = density, w = angular frequency, k = wave number,
(a) $1/\sqrt{\mu_0 \varepsilon_0}$ (b) n l   (c) $\sqrt{P/\rho}$ (d) ωk

43. Unit of magnetic moment is
(a) ampere–metre^2 (b) ampere–metre
(c) weber–metre^2 (d) weber/metre

44. An experiment is performed to obtain the value of acceleration due to gravity g by using a simple pendulum of length L. In this experiment time for 100 oscillations is measured by using a watch of 1 second least count and the value is 90.0 seconds. The length L is measured by using a meter scale of least count 1 mm and the value is 20.0 cm. The error in the determination of g would be:
(a) 1.7%   (b) 2.7%   (c) 4.4%   (d) 2.27%

45. The dimensional formula for magnetic flux is
(a) $[ML^2T^{-2}A^{-1}]$ (b) $[ML^3T^{-2}A^{-2}]$
(c) $[M^0L^{-2}T^2A^{-2}]$ (d) $[ML^2T^{-1}A^2]$

RESPONSE GRID					
	38. (a)(b)(c)(d)	39. (a)(b)(c)(d)	40. (a)(b)(c)(d)	41. (a)(b)(c)(d)	42. (a)(b)(c)(d)
	43. (a)(b)(c)(d)	44. (a)(b)(c)(d)	45. (a)(b)(c)(d)		

DAILY PRACTICE PROBLEM DPP CHAPTERWISE CP01 - PHYSICS

Total Questions	45	Total Marks	180
Attempted		Correct	
Incorrect		Net Score	
Cut-off Score	50	Qualifying Score	70
Success Gap = Net Score – Qualifying Score			
Net Score = (Correct × 4) – (Incorrect × 1)			

Space for Rough Work

Date : [   ]   Start Time : [   ]   End Time : [   ]

PHYSICS $\boxed{CP02}$

SYLLABUS : Motion in a Straight Line

Max. Marks : 180   **Marking Scheme :** (+4) for correct & (−1) for incorrect answer   **Time : 60 min.**

INSTRUCTIONS : This Daily Practice Problem Sheet contains 45 MCQs. For each question only one option is correct. Darken the correct circle/ bubble in the Response Grid provided on each page.

1. A particle starts moving rectilinearly at time $t = 0$ such that its velocity v changes with time t according to the equation $v = t^2 - t$ where t is in seconds and v is in m/s. Find the time interval for which the particle retards.

   (a) $\dfrac{1}{2} < t < 1$ (b) $\dfrac{1}{2} > t > 1$

   (c) $\dfrac{1}{4} < t < 1$ (d) $\dfrac{1}{2} < t < \dfrac{3}{4}$

2. The co-ordinates of a moving particle at any time 't' are given by $x = \alpha t^3$ and $y = \beta t^3$. The speed of the particle at time 't' is given by

   (a) $3t\sqrt{\alpha^2 + \beta^2}$ (b) $3t^2\sqrt{\alpha^2 + \beta^2}$

   (c) $t^2\sqrt{\alpha^2 + \beta^2}$ (d) $\sqrt{\alpha^2 + \beta^2}$

3. If a car covers $2/5^{th}$ of the total distance with v_1 speed and $3/5^{th}$ distance with v_2 then average speed is

   (a) $\dfrac{1}{2}\sqrt{v_1 v_2}$ (b) $\dfrac{v_1 + v_2}{2}$ (c) $\dfrac{2v_1 v_2}{v_1 + v_2}$ (d) $\dfrac{5v_1 v_2}{3v_1 + 2v_2}$

4. Choose the correct statements from the following.
   (a) The magnitude of instantaneous velocity of a particle is equal to its instantaneous speed
   (b) The magnitude of the average velocity in an interval is equal to its average speed in that interval.
   (c) It is possible to have a situation in which the speed of the particle is never zero but the average speed in an interval is zero.
   (d) It is possible to have a situation in which the speed of particle is zero but the average speed is not zero.

5. A particle located at $x = 0$ at time $t = 0$, starts moving along with the positive x-direction with a velocity 'v' that varies as $v = \alpha\sqrt{x}$. The displacement of the particle varies with time as
   (a) t^2 (b) t (c) $t^{1/2}$ (d) t^3

6. Figure here gives the speed-time graph for a body. The displacement travelled between t = 1.0 second and t = 7.0 second is nearest to

   (a) 1.5 m
   (b) 2 m
   (c) 3 m
   (d) 4 m

7. A particle is moving in a straight line with initial velocity and uniform acceleration a. If the sum of the distance travelled in t^{th} and $(t + 1)^{th}$ seconds is 100 cm, then its velocity after t seconds, in cm/s, is
   (a) 80   (b) 50   (c) 20   (d) 30

RESPONSE	1. ⓐⓑⓒⓓ	2. ⓐⓑⓒⓓ	3. ⓐⓑⓒⓓ	4. ⓐⓑⓒⓓ	5. ⓐⓑⓒⓓ
GRID	6. ⓐⓑⓒⓓ	7. ⓐⓑⓒⓓ			

Space for Rough Work

8. A thief is running away on a straight road on a jeep moving with a speed of 9 m/s. A police man chases him on a motor cycle moving at a speed of 10 m/s. If the instantaneous separation of jeep from the motor cycle is 100 m, how long will it take for the police man to catch the thief?

(a) 1 second   (b) 19 second

(c) 90 second   (d) 100 second

9. The displacement x of a particle varies with time according to the relation $x = \dfrac{a}{b}(1-e^{-bt})$. Then select the false alternative.

(a) At $t = \dfrac{1}{b}$, the displacement of the particle is nearly $\dfrac{2}{3}\left(\dfrac{a}{b}\right)$

(b) The velocity and acceleration of the particle at $t = 0$ are a and $-ab$ respectively

(c) The particle cannot go beyond $x = \dfrac{a}{b}$

(d) The particle will not come back to its starting point at $t \to \infty$

10. A metro train starts from rest and in five seconds achieves a speed 108 km/h. After that it moves with constant velocity and comes to rest after travelling 45m with uniform retardation. If total distance travelled is 395 m, find total time of travelling.

(a) 12.2 s   (b) 15.3 s   (c) 9 s   (d) 17.2 s

11. The deceleration experienced by a moving motor boat after its engine is cut off, is given by $dv/dt = -kv^3$ where k is a constant. If v_0 is the magnitude of the velocity at cut-off, the magnitude of the velocity at a time t after the cut-off is

(a) $\dfrac{v_0}{\sqrt{(2v_0^2 kt + 1)}}$ (b) $v_0\, e^{-kt}$

(c) $v_0/2$ (d) v_0

12. The velocity of a particle is $v = v_0 + gt + ft^2$. If its position is $x = 0$ at $t = 0$, then its displacement after unit time ($t = 1$) is

(a) $v_0 + g/2 + f$ (b) $v_0 + 2g + 3f$

(c) $v_0 + g/2 + f/3$ (d) $v_0 + g + f$

13. A man is 45 m behind the bus when the bus starts accelerating from rest with acceleration 2.5 m/s². With what minimum velocity should the man start running to catch the bus?

(a) 12 m/s (b) 14 m/s (c) 15 m/s (d) 16 m/s

14. A body is at rest at $x = 0$. At $t = 0$, it starts moving in the positive x-direction with a constant acceleration. At the same instant another body passes through $x = 0$ moving in the positive x-direction with a constant speed. The position of the first body is given by $x_1(t)$ after time 't'; and that of the second body by $x_2(t)$ after the same time interval. Which of the following graphs correctly describes $(x_1 - x_2)$ as a function of time 't'?

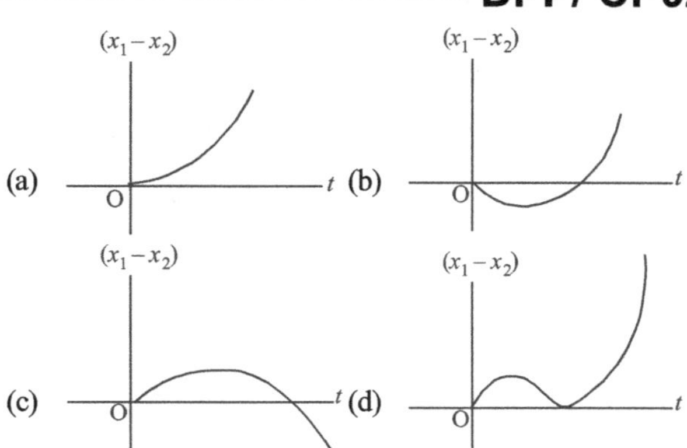

15. From the top of a building 40 m tall, a boy projects a stone vertically upwards with an initial velocity 10 m/s such that it eventually falls to the ground. After how long will the stone strike the ground ? Take $g = 10$ m/s².

(a) 1 s   (b) 2 s   (c) 3 s   (d) 4 s

16. Two bodies begin to fall freely from the same height but the second falls T second after the first. The time (after which the first body begins to fall) when the distance between the bodies equals L is

(a) $\dfrac{1}{2}T$ (b) $\dfrac{T}{2} + \dfrac{L}{gT}$ (c) $\dfrac{L}{gT}$ (d) $T + \dfrac{2L}{gT}$

17. Let A, B, C, D be points on a vertical line such that $AB = BC = CD$. If a body is released from position A, the times of descent through AB, BC and CD are in the ratio.

(a) $1:\sqrt{3}-\sqrt{2}:\sqrt{3}+\sqrt{2}$ (b) $1:\sqrt{2}-1:\sqrt{3}-\sqrt{2}$

(c) $1:\sqrt{2}-1:\sqrt{3}$ (d) $1:\sqrt{2}:\sqrt{3}-1$

18. The water drops fall at regular intervals from a tap 5 m above the ground. The third drop is leaving the tap at an instant when the first drop touches the ground. How far above the ground is the second drop at that instant? (Take $g = 10$ m/s²)

(a) 1.25 m (b) 2.50 m (c) 3.75 m (d) 5.00 m

19. The displacement 'x' (in meter) of a particle of mass 'm' (in kg) moving in one dimension under the action of a force, is related to time 't' (in sec) by $t = \sqrt{x} + 3$. The displacement of the particle when its velocity is zero, will be

(a) 2 m   (b) 4 m   (c) zero   (d) 6 m

20. A body moving with a uniform acceleration crosses a distance of 65 m in the 5 th second and 105 m in 9th second. How far will it go in 20 s?

(a) 2040 m (b) 240 m (c) 2400 m (d) 2004 m

21. An automobile travelling with a speed of 60 km/h, can brake to stop within a distance of 20m. If the car is going twice as fast i.e., 120 km/h, the stopping distance will be

(a) 60 m   (b) 40 m   (c) 20 m   (d) 80 m

RESPONSE GRID					
	8. ⓐⓑⓒⓓ	9. ⓐⓑⓒⓓ	10. ⓐⓑⓒⓓ	11. ⓐⓑⓒⓓ	12. ⓐⓑⓒⓓ
	13. ⓐⓑⓒⓓ	14. ⓐⓑⓒⓓ	15. ⓐⓑⓒⓓ	16. ⓐⓑⓒⓓ	17. ⓐⓑⓒⓓ
	18. ⓐⓑⓒⓓ	19. ⓐⓑⓒⓓ	20. ⓐⓑⓒⓓ	21. ⓐⓑⓒⓓ	

22. A particle accelerates from rest at a constant rate for some time and attains a velocity of 8 m/sec. Afterwards it decelerates with the constant rate and comes to rest. If the total time taken is 4 sec, the distance travelled is
(a) 32 m   (b) 16 m
(c) 4 m   (d) None of the above

23. The equation represented by the graph below is :

(a) $y = \dfrac{1}{2}\,gt$

(b) $y = \dfrac{-1}{2}\,gt$

(c) $y = \dfrac{1}{2}gt^2$

(d) $y = \dfrac{-1}{2}gt^2$

24. A particle moves a distance x in time t according to equation $x = (t+5)^{-1}$. The acceleration of particle is proportional to:
(a) $(\text{velocity})^{3/2}$ (b) $(\text{distance})^2$
(c) $(\text{distance})^{-2}$ (d) $(\text{velocity})^{2/3}$

25. A particle when thrown, moves such that it passes from same height at 2 and 10 seconds, then this height h is :
(a) 5g   (b) g   (c) 8g   (d) 10g

26. The distance through which a body falls in the nth second is h. The distance through which it falls in the next second is
(a) h   (b) $h + \dfrac{g}{2}$ (c) $h - g$ (d) $h + g$

27. A stone thrown upward with a speed u from the top of the tower reaches the ground with a velocity 3u. The height of the tower is
(a) $3u^2/g$ (b) $4u^2/g$ (c) $6u^2/g$ (d) $9u^2/g$

28. A particle moves along a straight line OX. At a time t (in seconds) the distance x (in metres) of the particle from O is given by $x = 40 + 12t - t^3$. How long would the particle travel before coming to rest?
(a) 40 m   (b) 56 m   (c) 16 m   (d) 24 m

29. The graph shown in figure shows the velocity v versus time t for a body.
Which of the graphs represents the corresponding acceleration versus time graphs?

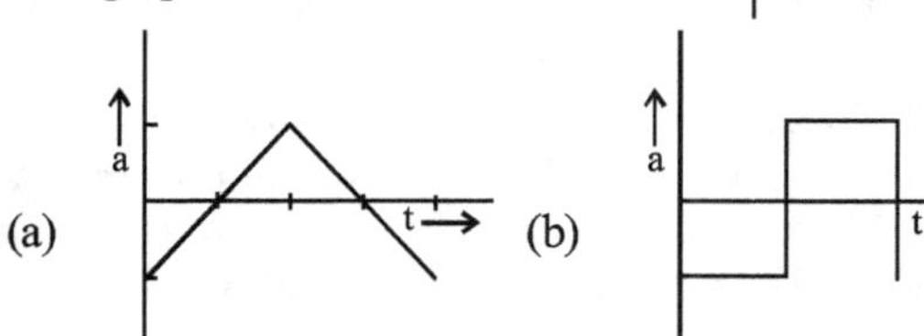

(a)   (b)

30. A particle moving along x-axis has acceleration f, at time t, given by $f = f_0\left(1 - \dfrac{t}{T}\right)$, where f_0 and T are constants. The particle at $t = 0$ has zero velocity. In the time interval between $t = 0$ and the instant when $f = 0$, the particle's velocity (v_x) is
(a) $\dfrac{1}{2}f_0 T^2$ (b) $f_0 T^2$ (c) $\dfrac{1}{2}f_0 T$ (d) $f_0 T$

31. A body is thrown vertically up with a velocity u. It passes three points A, B and C in its upward journey with velocities $\dfrac{u}{2}, \dfrac{u}{3}$ and $\dfrac{u}{4}$ respectively. The ratio of AB and BC is
(a) 20 : 7   (b) 2   (c) 10 : 7   (d) 1

32. A boat takes 2 hours to travel 8 km and back in still water lake. With water velocity of 4 km h^{-1}, the time taken for going upstream of 8 km and coming back is
(a) 160 minutes   (b) 80 minutes
(c) 100 minutes   (d) 120 minutes

33. A body starts from rest and travels a distance x with uniform acceleration, then it travels a distance 2x with uniform speed, finally it travels a distance 3x with uniform retardation and comes to rest. If the complete motion of the particle is along a straight line, then the ratio of its average velocity to maximum velocity is
(a) 2/5   (b) 3/5   (c) 4/5   (d) 6/7

34. A man of 50 kg mass is standing in a gravity free space at a height of 10 m above the floor. He throws a stone of 0.5 kg mass downwards with a speed 2 m/s. When the stone reaches the floor, the distance of the man above the floor will be:
(a) 9.9 m   (b) 10.1 m   (c) 10 m   (d) 20 m

35. A boy moving with a velocity of 20 km h^{-1} along a straight line joining two stationary objects. According to him both objects
(a) move in the same direction with the same speed of 20 km h^{-1}
(b) move in different direction with the same speed of 20 km h^{-1}
(c) move towards him
(d) remain stationary

RESPONSE GRID	22. ⓐⓑⓒⓓ	23. ⓐⓑⓒⓓ	24. ⓐⓑⓒⓓ	25. ⓐⓑⓒⓓ	26. ⓐⓑⓒⓓ	
	27. ⓐⓑⓒⓓ	28. ⓐⓑⓒⓓ	29. ⓐⓑⓒⓓ	30. ⓐⓑⓒⓓ	31. ⓐⓑⓒⓓ	
	32. ⓐⓑⓒⓓ	33. ⓐⓑⓒⓓ	34. ⓐⓑⓒⓓ	35. ⓐⓑⓒⓓ		

36. A rubber ball is dropped from a height of 5 metre on a plane where the acceleration due to gravity is same as that onto the surface of the earth. On bouncing, it rises to a height of 1.8 m. On bouncing, the ball loses its velocity by a factor of

(a) $\dfrac{3}{5}$ (b) $\dfrac{9}{25}$ (c) $\dfrac{2}{5}$ (d) $\dfrac{16}{25}$

37. A stone falls freely from rest from a height h and it travels a distance $\dfrac{9h}{25}$ in the last second. The value of h is

(a) 145 m (b) 100 m (c) 122.5 m (d) 200 m

38. Which one of the following equations represents the motion of a body with finite constant acceleration ? In these equations, y denotes the displacement of the body at time t and a, b and c are constants of motion.

(a) $y = at$ (b) $y = at + bt^2$

(b) $y = at + bt^2 + ct^3$ (d) $y = \dfrac{a}{t} + bt$

39. A particle travels half the distance with a velocity of 6 ms^{-1}. The remaining half distance is covered with a velocity of 4 ms^{-1} for half the time and with a velocity of 8 ms^{-1} for the rest of the half time. What is the velocity of the particle averaged over the whole time of motion ?

(a) 9 ms^{-1} (b) 6 ms^{-1} (c) 5.35 ms^{-1} (d) 5 ms^{-1}

40. A bullet is fired with a speed of 1000 m/sec in order to penetrate a target situated at 100 m away. If g = 10 m/s^2, the gun should be aimed

(a) directly towards the target
(b) 5 cm above the target
(c) 10 cm above the target
(d) 15 cm above the target

41. A body covers 26, 28, 30, 32 meters in 10th, 11th, 12th and 13th seconds respectively. The body starts

(a) from rest and moves with uniform velocity
(b) from rest and moves with uniform acceleration
(c) with an initial velocity and moves with uniform acceleration
(d) with an initial velocity and moves with uniform velocity

42. A particle is moving with uniform acceleration along a straight line. The average velocity of the particle from P to Q is 8ms^{-1} and that Q to S is 12ms^{-1}. If QS = PQ, then the average velocity from P to S is

(a) 9.6 ms^{-1} (b) 12.87 ms^{-1}
(c) 64 ms^{-1} (d) 327 ms^{-1}

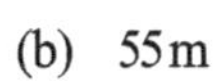

43. The variation of velocity of a particle with time moving along a straight line is illustrated in the figure. The distance travelled by the particle in four seconds is

(a) 60 m
(b) 55 m
(c) 25 m
(d) 30 m

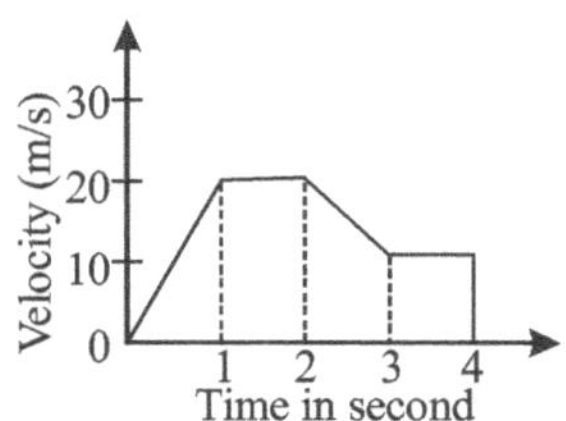

44. A stone falls freely under gravity. It covers distances h_1, h_2 and h_3 in the first 5 seconds, the next 5 seconds and the next 5 seconds respectively. The relation between h_1, h_2 and h_3 is

(a) $h_1 = \dfrac{h_2}{3} = \dfrac{h_3}{5}$ (b) $h_2 = 3h_1$ and $h_3 = 3h_2$

(c) $h_1 = h_2 = h_3$ (d) $h_1 = 2h_2 = 3h_3$

45. A car, starting from rest, accelerates at the rate f through a distance S, then continues at constant speed for time t and then decelerates at the rate $\dfrac{f}{2}$ to come to rest. If the total distance traversed is $15\,S$, then

(a) $S = \dfrac{1}{6} ft^2$ (b) $S = ft$

(c) $S = \dfrac{1}{4} ft^2$ (d) $S = \dfrac{1}{72} ft^2$

| RESPONSE | 36. ⓐⓑⓒⓓ | 37. ⓐⓑⓒⓓ | 38. ⓐⓑⓒⓓ | 39. ⓐⓑⓒⓓ | 40. ⓐⓑⓒⓓ |
| GRID | 41. ⓐⓑⓒⓓ | 42. ⓐⓑⓒⓓ | 43. ⓐⓑⓒⓓ | 44. ⓐⓑⓒⓓ | 45. ⓐⓑⓒⓓ |

DAILY PRACTICE PROBLEM DPP CHAPTERWISE CP02 - PHYSICS

Total Questions	45	Total Marks	180
Attempted		Correct	
Incorrect		Net Score	
Cut-off Score	50	Qualifying Score	70
Success Gap = Net Score − Qualifying Score			
Net Score = (Correct × 4) − (Incorrect × 1)			

Space for Rough Work

Date : ___________ Start Time : ___________ End Time : ___________

PHYSICS $\boxed{\text{CP03}}$

SYLLABUS : Motion in a Plane

Max. Marks : 180   **Marking Scheme :** (+4) for correct & (–1) for incorrect answer   **Time : 60 min.**

INSTRUCTIONS : This Daily Practice Problem Sheet contains 45 MCQs. For each question only one option is correct. Darken the correct circle/ bubble in the Response Grid provided on each page.

1. A projectile is given an initial velocity of $(\hat{i} + 2\hat{j})$ m/s, where $\hat{i}$ is along the ground and $\hat{j}$ is along the vertical. If g = 10 m/s², the equation of its trajectory is :
   (a) $y = x - 5x^2$
   (b) $y = 2x - 5x^2$
   (c) $4y = 2x - 5x^2$
   (d) $4y = 2x - 25x^2$

2. An aircraft moving with a speed of 250 m/s is at a height of 6000 m, just overhead of an anti aircraft–gun. If the muzzle velocity is 500 m/s, the firing angle θ should be:
   (a) 30°
   (b) 45°
   (c) 60°
   (d) 75°

   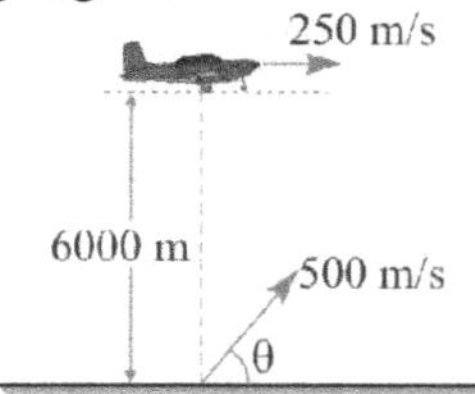

3. Two racing cars of masses m_1 and m_2 are moving in circles of radii r_1 and r_2 respectively. Their speeds are such that each makes a complete circle in the same duration of time t. The ratio of the angular speed of the first to the second car is
   (a) $m_1 : m_2$
   (b) $r_1 : r_2$
   (c) $1 : 1$
   (d) $m_1 r_1 : m_2 r_2$

4. A boy playing on the roof of a 10 m high building throws a ball with a speed of 10m/s at an angle of 30° with the horizontal. How far from the throwing point will the ball be at the height of 10 m from the ground ?
   $[g = 10\text{m/s}^2, \sin 30^o = \dfrac{1}{2}, \cos 30^o = \dfrac{\sqrt{3}}{2}]$
   (a) 5.20m   (b) 4.33m²   (c) 2.60m²   (d) 8.66m

5. A bomber plane moves horizontally with a speed of 500 m/s and a bomb released from it, strikes the ground in 10 sec. Angle at which it strikes the ground wil be (g = 10 m/s²)
   (a) $\tan^{-1}\left(\dfrac{1}{5}\right)$
   (b) $\tan\left(\dfrac{1}{5}\right)$
   (c) $\tan^{-1}(1)$
   (d) $\tan^{-1}(5)$

6. Two particles start simultaneously from the same point and move along two straight lines, one with uniform velocity v and other with a uniform acceleration a. If α is the angle between the lines of motion of two particles then the least value of relative velocity will be at time given by
   (a) $\dfrac{v}{a}\sin \alpha$ (b) $\dfrac{v}{a}\cos \alpha$ (c) $\dfrac{v}{a}\tan \alpha$ (d) $\dfrac{v}{a}\cot \alpha$

7. Initial velocity with which a body is projected is 10 m/sec and angle of projection is 60°. Find the range R
   (a) $\dfrac{15\sqrt{3}\text{m}}{2}$
   (b) $\dfrac{40}{3}\text{m}$
   (c) $5\sqrt{3}\text{m}$
   (d) $\dfrac{20}{3}\text{m}$

   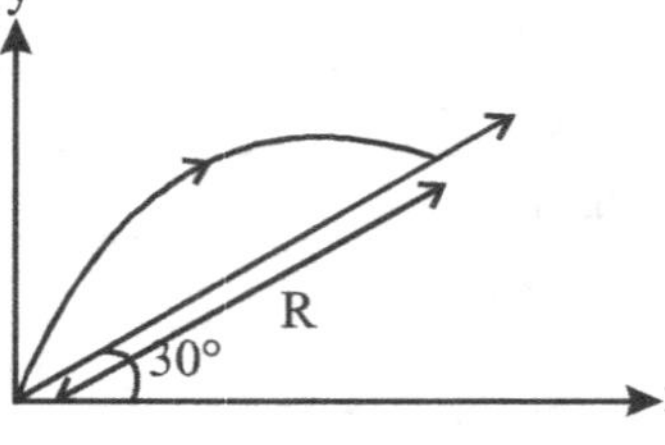

RESPONSE GRID	1. ⓐⓑⓒⓓ	2. ⓐⓑⓒⓓ	3. ⓐⓑⓒⓓ	4. ⓐⓑⓒⓓ	5. ⓐⓑⓒⓓ
	6. ⓐⓑⓒⓓ	7. ⓐⓑⓒⓓ			

Space for Rough Work

8. The position vectors of points A, B, C and D are

$A = 3\hat{i} + 4\hat{j} + 5\hat{k}, B = 4\hat{i} + 5\hat{j} + 6\hat{k}, C = 7\hat{i} + 9\hat{j} + 3\hat{k}$

and $D = 4\hat{i} + 6\hat{j}$ then the displacement vectors $\overline{AB}$ and $\overline{CD}$ are
(a) perpendicular   (b) parallel
(c) antiparallel   (d) inclined at an angle of 60°

9. A person swims in a river aiming to reach exactly on the opposite point on the bank of a river. His speed of swimming is 0.5 m/s at an angle of 120° with the direction of flow of water. The speed of water is
(a) 1.0 m/s   (b) 0.5 m/s   (c) 0.25 m/s   (d) 0.43 m/s

10. A projectile thrown with velocity v making angle θ with vertical gains maximum height H in the time for which the projectile remains in air, the time period is
(a) $\sqrt{H\cos\theta/g}$ (b) $\sqrt{2H\cos\theta/g}$
(c) $\sqrt{4H/g}$ (d) $\sqrt{8H/g}$

11. A ball is thrown from a point with a speed $'v_0'$ at an elevation angle of θ. From the same point and at the same instant, a person starts running with a constant speed $\dfrac{'v_0'}{2}$ to catch the ball. Will the person be able to catch the ball? If yes, what should be the angle of projection θ ?
(a) No, 0°   (b) Yes, 30°   (c) Yes, 60°   (d) Yes, 45°

12. If vectors $\vec{A} = \cos\omega t\,\hat{i} + \sin\omega t\,\hat{j}$ and $\vec{B} = \cos\dfrac{\omega t}{2}\hat{i} + \sin\dfrac{\omega t}{2}\hat{j}$ are functions of time, then the value of t at which they are orthogonal to each other is :
(a) $t = \dfrac{\pi}{2\omega}$ (b) $t = \dfrac{\pi}{\omega}$ (c) $t = 0$ (d) $t = \dfrac{\pi}{4\omega}$

13. A bus is moving on a straight road towards north with a uniform speed of 50 km/hour turns through 90°. If the speed remains unchanged after turning, the increase in the velocity of bus in the turning process is
(a) 70.7 km/hour along south-west direction
(b) 70.7 km/hour along north-west direction.
(c) 50 km/hour along west
(d) zero

14. The velocity of projection of oblique projectile is $(6\hat{i} + 8\hat{j})\,\mathrm{m\,s}^{-1}$. The horizontal range of the projectile is
(a) 4.9m   (b) 9.6m   (c) 19.6m   (d) 14m

15. A point P moves in counter-clockwise direction on a circular path as shown in the figure. The movement of 'P' is such that it sweeps out a length $s = t^3 + 5$, where s is in metres and t is in seconds. The radius of the path is 20 m. The acceleration of 'P' when $t = 2$ s is nearly

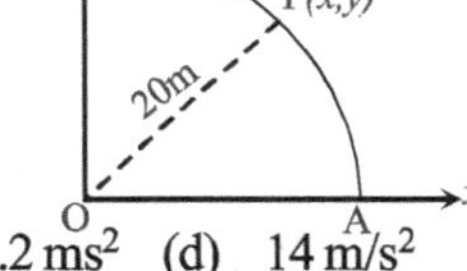

(a) 13 m/s²   (b) 12 m/s²   (c) 7.2 ms²   (d) 14 m/s²

16. The resultant of two vectors $\vec{A}$ and $\vec{B}$ is perpendicular to the vector $\vec{A}$ and its magnitude is equal to half the magnitude of vector $\vec{B}$. The angle between $\vec{A}$ and $\vec{B}$ is
(a) 120°   (b) 150°   (c) 135°   (d) 180°

17. A man running along a straight road with uniform velocity $\vec{u} = u\,\hat{i}$ feels that the rain is falling vertically down along $-\hat{j}$. If he doubles his speed, he finds that the rain is coming at an angle θ with the vertical. The velocity of the rain with respect to the ground is
(a) $ui - uj$ (b) $ui - \dfrac{u}{\tan\theta}\hat{j}$
(c) $2u\hat{i} + u\cot\theta\hat{j}$ (d) $ui + u\sin\theta\hat{j}$

18. Two projectiles A and B thrown with speeds in the ratio $1 : \sqrt{2}$ acquired the same heights. If A is thrown at an angle of 45° with the horizontal, the angle of projection of B will be
(a) 0°   (b) 60°   (c) 30°   (d) 45°

19. A projectile can have the same range 'R' for two angles of projection. If 'T_1' and 'T_2' be time of flights in the two cases, then the product of the two time of flights is directly proportional to
(a) R (b) $\dfrac{1}{R}$ (c) $\dfrac{1}{R^2}$ (d) R^2

20. A man standing on the roof of a house of height h throws one particle vertically downwards and another particle horizontally with the same velocity u. The ratio of their velocities when they reach the earth's surface will be
(a) $\sqrt{2gh + u^2} : u$ (b) $1 : 2$
(c) $1 : 1$ (d) $\sqrt{2gh + u^2} : \sqrt{2gh}$

21. If a unit vector is represented by $0.5\hat{i} + 0.8\hat{j} + c\hat{k}$, the value of c is
(a) 1   (b) $\sqrt{0.11}$ (c) $\sqrt{0.01}$ (d) 0.39

22. An aeroplane is flying at a constant horizontal velocity of 600 km/hr at an elevation of 6 km towards a point directly above the target on the earth's surface. At an appropriate time, the pilot releases a ball so that it strikes the target at the earth. The ball will appear to be falling
(a) on a parabolic path as seen by pilot in the plane
(b) vertically along a straight path as seen by an observer on the ground near the target
(c) on a parabolic path as seen by an observer on the ground near the target
(d) on a zig-zag path as seen by pilot in the plane

RESPONSE GRID				
8. ⓐⓑⓒⓓ	**9.** ⓐⓑⓒⓓ	**10.** ⓐⓑⓒⓓ	**11.** ⓐⓑⓒⓓ	**12.** ⓐⓑⓒⓓ
13. ⓐⓑⓒⓓ	**14.** ⓐⓑⓒⓓ	**15.** ⓐⓑⓒⓓ	**16.** ⓐⓑⓒⓓ	**17.** ⓐⓑⓒⓓ
18. ⓐⓑⓒⓓ	**19.** ⓐⓑⓒⓓ	**20.** ⓐⓑⓒⓓ	**21.** ⓐⓑⓒⓓ	**22.** ⓐⓑⓒⓓ

23. A particle is projected with a velocity v such that its range on the horizontal plane is twice the greatest height attained by it. The range of the projectile is (where g is acceleration due to gravity)

(a) $\dfrac{4v^2}{5g}$ (b) $\dfrac{4g}{5v^2}$ (c) $\dfrac{v^2}{g}$ (d) $\dfrac{4v^2}{\sqrt{5}g}$

24. Two stones are projected from the same point with same speed making angles $(45° + \theta)$ and $(45° - \theta)$ with the horizontal respectively. If $\theta \le 45°$, then the horizontal ranges of the two stones are in the ratio of

(a) $1:1$ (b) $1:2$ (c) $1:3$ (d) $1:4$

25. Three forces acting on a body are shown in the figure. To have the resultant force only along the y-direction, the magnitude of the minimum additional force needed is:

(a) $0.5\,\text{N}$

(b) $1.5\,\text{N}$

(c) $\dfrac{\sqrt{3}}{4}\,\text{N}$

(d) $\sqrt{3}\,\text{N}$

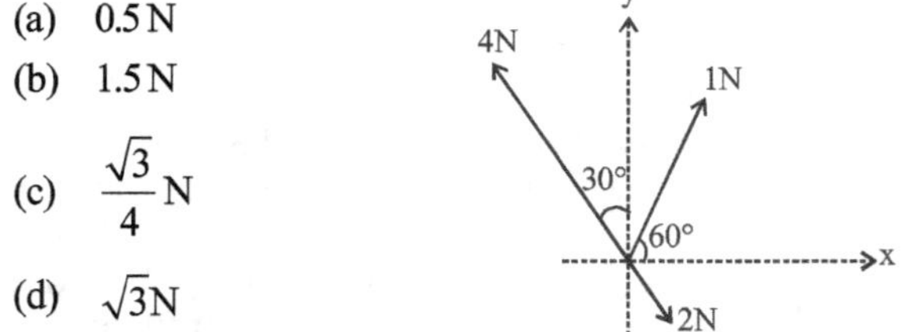

26. A particle moves in x-y plane under the action of force $\overrightarrow{F}$ and $\overrightarrow{p}$ at a given time t $p_x = 2\cos\theta$, $p_y = 2\sin\theta$. Then the angle θ between $\overrightarrow{F}$ and $\overrightarrow{p}$ at a given time t is :

(a) $\theta = 30°$ (b) $\theta = 180°$ (c) $\theta = 0°$ (d) $\theta = 90°$

27. A person sitting in the rear end of the compartment throws a ball towards the front end. The ball follows a parabolic path. The train is moving with velocity of 20 m/s. A person standing outside on the ground also observes the ball. How will the maximum heights (y_m) attained and the ranges (R) seen by the thrower and the outside observer compare with each other?

(a) Same y_m different R (b) Same y_m and R
(c) Different y_m same R (d) Different y_m and R

28. A car moves on a circular road. It describes equal angles about the centre in equal intervals of time. Which of the following statement about the velocity of the car is true ?

(a) Magnitude of velocity is not constant
(b) Both magnitude and direction of velocity change
(c) Velocity is directed towards the centre of the circle
(d) Magnitude of velocity is constant but direction changes

29. Three particles A, B and C are thrown from the top of a tower with the same speed. A is thrown up, B is thrown down and C is horizontally. They hit the ground with speeds v_A, v_B and v_C respectively then,

(a) $v_A = v_B = v_C$ (b) $v_A = v_B > v_C$
(c) $v_B > v_C > v_A$ (d) $v_A > v_B = v_C$

30. A particle is moving such that its position coordinate (x, y) are

$(2\text{m}, 3\text{m})$ at time $t = 0$
$(6\text{m}, 7\text{m})$ at time $t = 2$ s and
$(13\text{m}, 14\text{m})$ at time $t = 5$s.

Average velocity vector $(\vec{V}_{av})$ from $t = 0$ to $t = 5$s is :

(a) $\dfrac{1}{5}(13\hat{i} + 14\hat{j})$ (b) $\dfrac{7}{3}(\hat{i} + \hat{j})$

(c) $2(\hat{i} + \hat{j})$ (d) $\dfrac{11}{5}(\hat{i} + \hat{j})$

31. A particle moves so that its position vector is given by $\vec{r} = \cos\omega t\hat{x} + \sin\omega t\hat{y}$. Where ω is a constant. Which of the following is true ?

(a) Velocity and acceleration both are perpendicular to $\vec{r}$
(b) Velocity and acceleration both are parallel to $\vec{r}$
(c) Velocity is perpendicular to $\vec{r}$ and acceleration is directed towards the origin
(d) Velocity is perpendicular to $\vec{r}$ and acceleration is directed away from the origin

32. Two boys are standing at the ends A and B of a ground where $AB = a$. The boy at B starts running in a direction perpendicular to AB with velocity v_1. The boy at A starts running simultaneously with velocity v and catches the other boy in a time t, where t is

(a) $a/\sqrt{v^2 + v_1^2}$ (b) $a/(v + v_1)$
(c) $a/(v - v_1)$ (d) $\sqrt{a^2/(v^2 - v_1^2)}$

33. A projectile is fired at an angle of $45°$ with the horizontal. Elevation angle of the projectile at its highest point as seen from the point of projection is

(a) $60°$ (b) $\tan^{-1}\left(\dfrac{1}{2}\right)$ (c) $\tan^{-1}\left(\dfrac{\sqrt{3}}{2}\right)$ (d) $45°$

34. The position vector of a particle $\vec{R}$ as a function of time is given by $\vec{R} = 4\sin(2\pi t)\hat{i} + 4\cos(2\pi t)\hat{j}$

where R is in meter, t in seconds and $\hat{i}$ and $\hat{j}$ denote unit vectors along x- and y-directions, respectively. Which one of the following statements is wrong for the motion of particle?

(a) Magnitude of acceleration vector is $\dfrac{v^2}{R}$, where v is the velocity of particle
(b) Magnitude of the velocity of particle is 8 meter/second
(c) Path of the particle is a circle of radius 4 meter.
(d) Acceleration vector is along $-\vec{R}$

35. The vectors $\overrightarrow{A}$ and $\overrightarrow{B}$ are such that $|\overrightarrow{A} + \overrightarrow{B}| = |\overrightarrow{A} - \overrightarrow{B}|$ The angle between the two vectors is

(a) $60°$ (b) $75°$ (c) $45°$ (d) $90°$

RESPONSE GRID					
23. ⓐⓑⓒⓓ	24. ⓐⓑⓒⓓ	25. ⓐⓑⓒⓓ	26. ⓐⓑⓒⓓ	27. ⓐⓑⓒⓓ
28. ⓐⓑⓒⓓ	29. ⓐⓑⓒⓓ	30. ⓐⓑⓒⓓ	31. ⓐⓑⓒⓓ	32. ⓐⓑⓒⓓ
33. ⓐⓑⓒⓓ	34. ⓐⓑⓒⓓ	35. ⓐⓑⓒⓓ		

36. The velocity of projection of oblique projectile is $(6\hat{i} + 8\hat{j})\,\text{m s}^{-1}$. The horizontal range of the projectile is
(a) 4.9 m   (b) 9.6 m   (c) 19.6 m   (d) 14 m

37. An artillary piece which consistently shoots its shells with the same muzzle speed has a maximum range R. To hit a target which is R/2 from the gun and on the same level, the elevation angle of the gun should be
(a) 15°   (b) 45°   (c) 30°   (d) 60°

38. A car runs at a constant speed on a circular track of radius 100 m, taking 62.8 seconds in every circular loop. The average velocity and average speed for each circular loop respectively, is
(a) 0, 10 m/s   (b) 10 m/s, 10 m/s
(c) 10 m/s, 0   (d) 0, 0

39. A vector of magnitude b is rotated through angle θ. What is the change in magnitude of the vector?
(a) $2b\sin\dfrac{\theta}{2}$ (b) $2b\cos\dfrac{\theta}{2}$ (c) $2b\sin\theta$ (d) $2b\cos\theta$

40. A stone projected with a velocity u at an angle θ with the horizontal reaches maximum height H_1. When it is projected with velocity u at an angle $\left(\dfrac{\pi}{2} - \theta\right)$ with the horizontal, it reaches maximum height H_2. The relation between the horizontal range R of the projectile, heights H_1 and H_2 is
(a) $R = 4\sqrt{H_1 H_2}$ (b) $R = 4(H_1 - H_2)$
(c) $R = 4(H_1 + H_2)$ (d) $R = \dfrac{H_1^2}{H_2^2}$

41. The vector sum of two forces is perpendicular to their vector differences. In that case, the forces
(a) cannot be predicted
(b) are equal to each other
(c) are equal to each other in magnitude
(d) are not equal to each other in magnitude

42. A particle crossing the origin of co-ordinates at time t = 0, moves in the xy-plane with a constant acceleration a in the y-direction. If its equation of motion is $y = bx^2$ (b is a constant), its velocity component in the x-direction is
(a) $\sqrt{\dfrac{2b}{a}}$ (b) $\sqrt{\dfrac{a}{2b}}$ (c) $\sqrt{\dfrac{a}{b}}$ (d) $\sqrt{\dfrac{b}{a}}$

43. A vector $\overline{A}$ is rotated by a small angle Δθ radian (Δθ << 1) to get a new vector $\overline{B}$. In that case $\left|\overline{B} - \overline{A}\right|$ is :
(a) $\left|\overline{A}\right|\Delta\theta$ (b) $\left|\overline{B}\right|\Delta\theta - \left|\overline{A}\right|$
(c) $\left|\overline{A}\right|\left(1 - \dfrac{\Delta\theta^2}{2}\right)$ (d) 0

44. If a body moving in circular path maintains constant speed of 10 ms^{-1}, then which of the following correctly describes relation between acceleration and radius ?

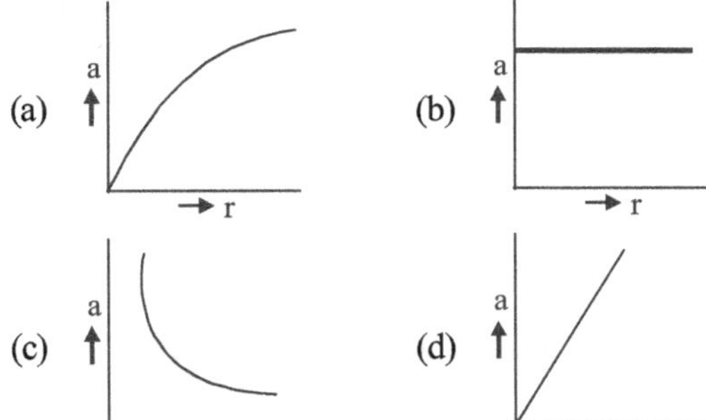

45. The position of a projectile launched from the origin at t = 0 is given by $\vec{r} = \left(40\hat{i} + 50\hat{j}\right)$ m at t = 2s. If the projectile was launched at an angle θ from the horizontal, then θ is (take g = 10 ms^{-2})
(a) $\tan^{-1}\dfrac{2}{3}$ (b) $\tan^{-1}\dfrac{3}{2}$ (c) $\tan^{-1}\dfrac{7}{4}$ (d) $\tan^{-1}\dfrac{4}{5}$

RESPONSE GRID					
36. ⓐⓑⓒⓓ	**37.** ⓐⓑⓒⓓ	**38.** ⓐⓑⓒⓓ	**39.** ⓐⓑⓒⓓ	**40.** ⓐⓑⓒⓓ
41. ⓐⓑⓒⓓ	**42.** ⓐⓑⓒⓓ	**43.** ⓐⓑⓒⓓ	**44.** ⓐⓑⓒⓓ	**45.** ⓐⓑⓒⓓ

DAILY PRACTICE PROBLEM DPP CHAPTERWISE CP03 - PHYSICS

Total Questions	45	Total Marks	180
Attempted		Correct	
Incorrect		Net Score	
Cut-off Score	50	Qualifying Score	70
Success Gap = Net Score – Qualifying Score			
Net Score = (Correct × 4) – (Incorrect × 1)			

Space for Rough Work

Date : [   ]   Start Time : [   ]   End Time : [   ]

PHYSICS $\boxed{\text{CP04}}$

SYLLABUS : Laws of Motion

Max. Marks : 180   Marking Scheme : (+4) for correct & (–1) for incorrect answer   **Time : 60 min.**

INSTRUCTIONS : This Daily Practice Problem Sheet contains 45 MCQs. For each question only one option is correct. Darken the correct circle/ bubble in the Response Grid provided on each page.

1. A player stops a football weighing 0.5 kg which comes flying towards him with a velocity of 10m/s. If the impact lasts for 1/50th sec. and the ball bounces back with a velocity of 15 m/s, then the average force involved is
   (a) 250 N   (b) 1250 N   (c) 500 N   (d) 625 N

2. For the given situation as shown in the figure, the value of θ to keep the system in equilibrium will be

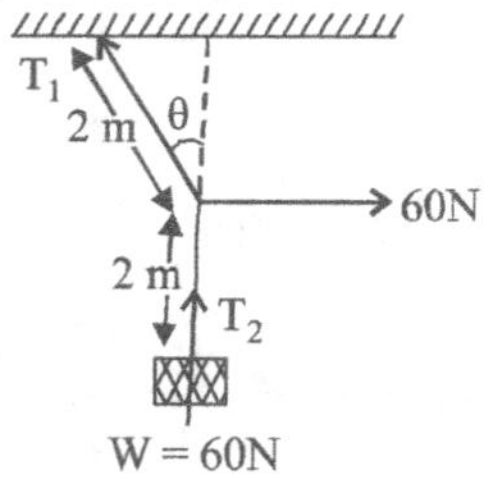

   (a) 30°   (b) 45°   (c) 0°   (d) 90°

3. A 5000 kg rocket is set for vertical firing. The exhaust speed is 800 m/s. To give an initial upward acceleration of 20 m/s^2, the amount of gas ejected per second to supply the needed thrust will be (Take g = 10 m/s^2)
   (a) 127.5 kg/s   (b) 137.5 kg/s
   (c) 155.5 kg/s   (d) 187.5 kg/s

4. Which one of the following statements is correct?
   (a) If there were no friction, work need to be done to move a body up an inclined plane is zero.
   (b) If there were no friction, moving vehicles could not be stopped even by locking the brakes.
   (c) As the angle of inclination is increased, the normal reaction on the body placed on it increases.
   (d) A duster weighing 0.5 kg is pressed against a vertical board with force of 11 N. If the coefficient of friction is 0.5, the work done in rubbing it upward through a distance of 10 cm is 0.55 J.

5. A stone is dropped from a height h. It hits the ground with a certain momentum P. If the same stone is dropped from a height 100% more than the previous height, the momentum when it hits the ground will change by :
   (a) 68%   (b) 41%   (c) 200%   (d) 100%

6. A 3 kg ball strikes a heavy rigid wall with a speed of 10 m/s at an angle of 60°. It gets reflected with the same speed and angle as shown here. If the ball is in contact with the wall for 0.20s, what is the average force exerted on the ball by the wall? 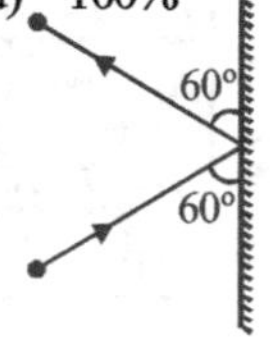
   (a) 150 N   (b) zero
   (c) $150\sqrt{3}$ N   (d) 300 N

RESPONSE GRID	1. ⓐⓑⓒⓓ	2. ⓐⓑⓒⓓ	3. ⓐⓑⓒⓓ	4. ⓐⓑⓒⓓ	5. ⓐⓑⓒⓓ
	6. ⓐⓑⓒⓓ				

Space for Rough Work

7. The upper half of an inclined plane of inclination θ is perfectly smooth while lower half is rough. A block starting from rest at the top of the plane will again come to rest at the bottom, if the coefficient of friction between the block and lower half of the plane is given by

(a) $\mu = \dfrac{2}{\tan \theta}$

(b) $\mu = 2 \tan \theta$

(c) $\mu = \tan \theta$

(d) $\mu = \dfrac{1}{\tan \theta}$

8. A block of mass m is in contact with the cart C as shown in the figure.

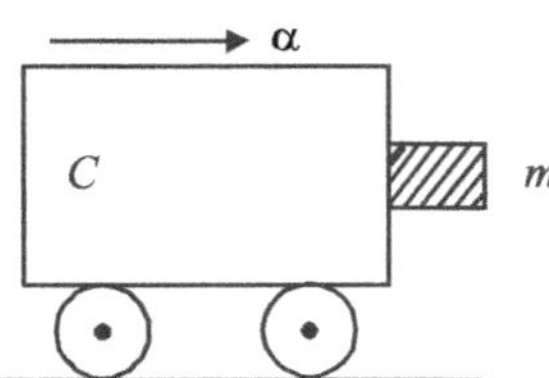

The coefficient of static friction between the block and the cart is μ. The acceleration α of the cart that will prevent the block from falling satisfies:

(a) $\alpha > \dfrac{mg}{\mu}$ (b) $\alpha > \dfrac{g}{\mu m}$ (c) $\alpha \geq \dfrac{g}{\mu}$ (d) $\alpha < \dfrac{g}{\mu}$

9. A bridge is in the from of a semi-circle of radius 40m. The greatest speed with which a motor cycle can cross the bridge without leaving the ground at the highest point is ($g = 10$ m s^{-2}) (frictional force is negligibly small)

(a) 40 m s^{-1} (b) 20 m s^{-1}

(c) 30 m s^{-1} (d) 15 m s^{-1}

10. An explosion blows a rock into three parts. Two parts go off at right angles to each other. These two are, 1 kg first part moving with a velocity of 12 ms^{-1} and 2 kg second part moving with a velocity of 8 ms^{-1}. If the third part flies off with a velocity of 4 ms^{-1}, its mass would be

(a) 5 kg (b) 7 kg (c) 17 kg (d) 3 kg

11. A monkey is decending from the branch of a tree with constant acceleration. If the breaking strength is 75% of the weight of the monkey, the minimum acceleration with which monkey can slide down without breaking the branch is

(a) g (b) $\dfrac{3g}{4}$ (c) $\dfrac{g}{4}$ (d) $\dfrac{g}{2}$

12. A car having a mass of 1000 kg is moving at a speed of 30 metres/sec. Brakes are applied to bring the car to rest. If the frictional force between the tyres and the road surface is 5000 newtons, the car will come to rest in

(a) 5 seconds (b) 10 seconds

(c) 12 seconds (d) 6 seconds

13. A spring is compressed between two toy carts of mass m_1 and m_2. When the toy carts are released, the springs exert equal and opposite average forces for the same time on each toy cart. If v_1 and v_2 are the velocities of the toy carts and there is no friction between the toy carts and the ground, then :

(a) $v_1/v_2 = m_1/m_2$ (b) $v_1/v_2 = m_2/m_1$

(c) $v_1/v_2 = -m_2/m_1$ (d) $v_1/v_2 = -m_1/m_2$

14. A plate of mass M is placed on a horizontal frictionless surface (see figure), and a body of mass m is placed on this plate. The coefficient of dynamic friction between this body and the plate is μ. If a force 2μ mg is applied to the body of mass m along the horizontal, the acceleration of the plate will be

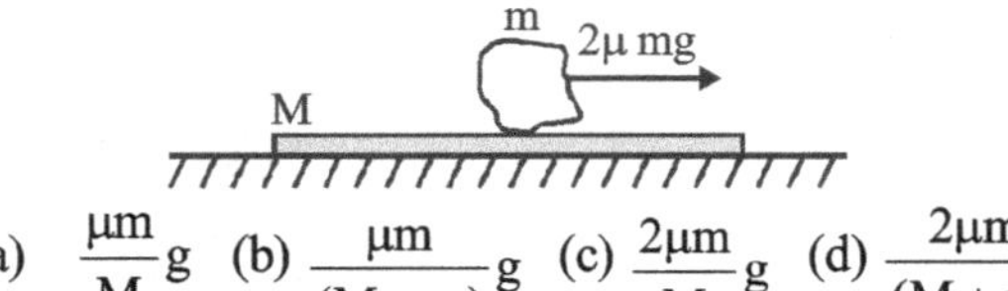

(a) $\dfrac{\mu m}{M} g$ (b) $\dfrac{\mu m}{(M+m)} g$ (c) $\dfrac{2\mu m}{M} g$ (d) $\dfrac{2\mu m}{(M+m)} g$

15. The rate of mass of the gas emitted from rear of a rocket is initially 0.1 kg/sec. If the speed of the gas relative to the rocket is 50 m/sec and mass of the rocket is 2 kg, then the acceleration of the rocket in m/sec^2 is

(a) 5 (b) 5.2 (c) 2.5 (d) 25

16. A plank with a box on it at one end is gradually raised about the other end. As the angle of inclination with the horizontal reaches 30° the box starts to slip and slides 4.0 m down the plank in 4.0s. The coefficients of static and kinetic friction between the box and the plank will be, respectively :

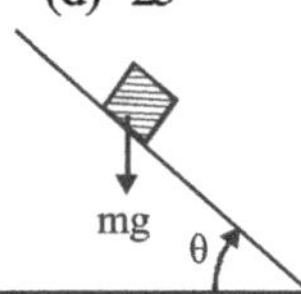

(a) 0.6 and 0.5 (b) 0.5 and 0.6

(c) 0.4 and 0.3 (d) 0.6 and 0.6

17. Four blocks of same mass connected by cords are pulled by a force F on a smooth horizontal surface, as shown in fig. The tensions T_1, T_2 and T_3 will be

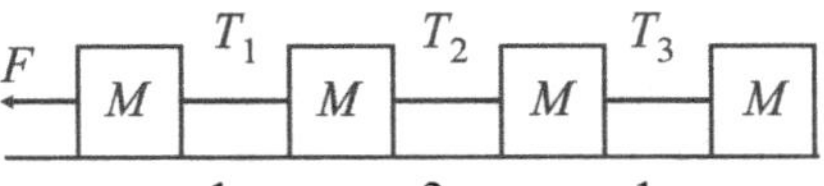

(a) $T_1 = \dfrac{1}{4}F, T_2 = \dfrac{3}{2}F, T_3 = \dfrac{1}{4}F$

(b) $T_1 = \dfrac{1}{4}F, T_2 = \dfrac{1}{2}F, T_3 = \dfrac{1}{2}F$

(c) $T_1 = \dfrac{3}{4}F, T_2 = \dfrac{1}{2}F, T_3 = \dfrac{1}{4}F$

(d) $T_1 = \dfrac{3}{4}F, T_2 = \dfrac{1}{2}F, T_3 = \dfrac{1}{2}F$

18. A body of mass M is kept on a rough horizontal surface (friction coefficient μ). A person is trying to pull the body by applying a horizontal force but the body is not moving. The force by the surface on the body is F, then

(a) $F = Mg$ (b) $F = \mu Mg$

(c) $Mg \leq F \leq Mg\sqrt{1+\mu^2}$ (d) $Mg \geq F \geq Mg\sqrt{1+\mu^2}$

Space for Rough Work

19. Which one of the following motions on a smooth plane surface does not involve force?
  (a) Accelerated motion in a straight line
  (b) Retarded motion in a straight line
  (c) Motion with constant momentum along a straight line
  (d) Motion along a straight line with varying velocity

20. A block A of mass m_1 rests on a horizontal table. A light string connected to it passes over a frictionless pulley at the edge of table and from its other end another block B of mass m_2 is suspended. The coefficient of kinetic friction between the block and the table is μ_k. When the block A is sliding on the table, the tension in the string is
  (a) $\dfrac{(m_2 - \mu_k m_1)g}{(m_1 + m_2)}$
  (b) $\dfrac{m_1 m_2 (1 + \mu_k)g}{(m_1 + m_2)}$
  (c) $\dfrac{m_1 m_2 (1 - \mu_k)g}{(m_1 + m_2)}$
  (d) $\dfrac{(m_2 + \mu_k m_1)g}{(m_1 + m_2)}$

21. The upper half of an inclined plane with inclination f is perfectly smooth while the lower half is rough. A body starting from rest at the top will again come to rest at the bottom if the coefficient of friction for the lower half is given by
  (a) 2 cos φ   (b) 2 sin φ   (c) tan φ   (d) 2 tan φ

22. A particle describes a horizontal circle in a conical funnel whose inner surface is smooth with speed of 0.5 m/s. What is the height of the plane of circle from vertex of the funnel?
  (a) 0.25 cm   (b) 2 cm   (c) 4 cm   (d) 2.5 cm

23. You are on a frictionless horizontal plane. How can you get off if no horizontal force is exerted by pushing against the surface?
  (a) By jumping
  (b) By spitting or sneezing
  (c) by rolling your body on the surface
  (d) By running on the plane

24. The coefficient of static and dynamic friction between a body and the surface are 0.75 and 0.5 respectively. A force is applied to the body to make it just slide with a constant acceleration which is
  (a) $\dfrac{g}{4}$ (b) $\dfrac{g}{2}$ (c) $\dfrac{3g}{2}$ (d) g

25. In the system shown in figure, the pulley is smooth and massless, the string has a total mass 5g, and the two suspended blocks have masses 25 g and 15 g. The system is released from state $\ell = 0$ and is studied upto stage $\ell' = 0$. During the process, the acceleration of block A will be
  (a) constant at $\dfrac{g}{9}$
  (b) constant at $\dfrac{g}{4}$
  (c) increasing by factor of 3
  (d) increasing by factor of 2

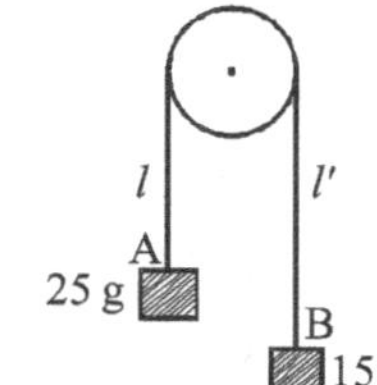

26. The minimum force required to start pushing a body up rough (frictional coefficient μ) inclined plane is F_1 while the minimum force needed to prevent it from sliding down is F_2. If the inclined plane makes an angle θ from the horizontal such that tan θ = 2μ then the ratio $\dfrac{F_1}{F_2}$ is
  (a) 1   (b) 2   (c) 3   (d) 4

27. Two blocks are connected over a massless pulley as shown in fig. The mass of block A is 10 kg and the coefficient of kinetic friction is 0.2. Block A slides down the incline at constant speed. The mass of block B in kg is
  (a) 3.5   (b) 3.3   (c) 3.0   (d) 2.5

28. Tension in the cable supporting an elevator, is equal to the weight of the elevator. From this, we can conclude that the elevator is going up or down with a
  (a) uniform velocity
  (b) uniform acceleration
  (c) variable acceleration
  (d) either (b) or (c)

29. A particle tied to a string describes a vertical circular motion of radius r continually. If it has a velocity $\sqrt{3\,gr}$ at the highest point, then the ratio of the respective tensions in the string holding it at the highest and lowest points is
  (a) 4 : 3   (b) 5 : 4   (c) 1 : 4   (d) 3 : 2

30. It is difficult to move a cycle with brakes on because
  (a) rolling friction opposes motion on road
  (b) sliding friction opposes motion on road
  (c) rolling friction is more than sliding friction
  (d) sliding friction is more than rolling friction

31. A plumb line is suspended from a celling of a car moving with horizontal acceleration of a. What will be the angle of inclination with vertical?
  (a) $\tan^{-1}(a/g)$
  (b) $\tan^{-1}(g/a)$
  (c) $\cos^{-1}(a/g)$
  (d) $\cos^{-1}(g/a)$

32. A cart of mass M has a block of mass m attached to it as shown in fig. The coefficient of friction between the block and the cart is μ. What is the minimum acceleration of the cart so that the block m does not fall?
  (a) μg
  (b) g/μ
  (c) μ/g
  (d) M μg/m

<table>
<tr><td rowspan="3">RESPONSE GRID</td><td>19. ⓐⓑⓒⓓ</td><td>20. ⓐⓑⓒⓓ</td><td>21. ⓐⓑⓒⓓ</td><td>22. ⓐⓑⓒⓓ</td><td>23. ⓐⓑⓒⓓ</td></tr>
<tr><td>24. ⓐⓑⓒⓓ</td><td>25. ⓐⓑⓒⓓ</td><td>26. ⓐⓑⓒⓓ</td><td>27. ⓐⓑⓒⓓ</td><td>28. ⓐⓑⓒⓓ</td></tr>
<tr><td>29. ⓐⓑⓒⓓ</td><td>30. ⓐⓑⓒⓓ</td><td>31. ⓐⓑⓒⓓ</td><td>32. ⓐⓑⓒⓓ</td><td></td></tr>
</table>

33. What is the maximum value of the force F such that the block shown in the arrangement, does not move?

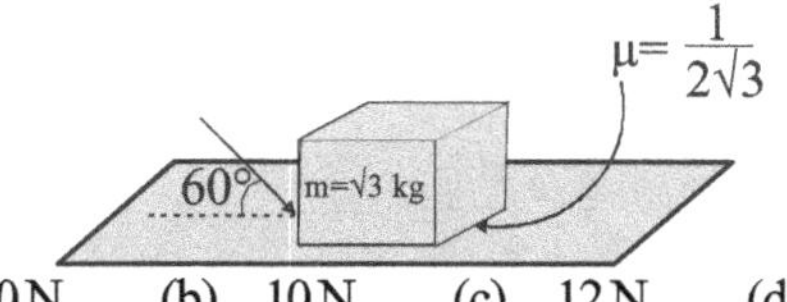

(a) 20 N   (b) 10 N   (c) 12 N   (d) 15 N

34. A block has been placed on an inclined plane with the slope angle θ, block slides down the plane at constant speed. The coefficient of kinetic friction is equal to
(a) $\sin\theta$ (b) $\cos\theta$ (c) g   (d) $\tan\theta$

35. A block of mass m is connected to another block of mass M by a spring (massless) of spring constant k. The block are kept on a smooth horizontal plane. Initially the blocks are at rest and the spring is unstretched. Then a constant force F starts acting on the block of mass M to pull it. Find the force of the block of mass m.
(a) $\dfrac{MF}{(m+M)}$ (b) $\dfrac{mF}{M}$ (c) $\dfrac{(M+m)F}{m}$ (d) $\dfrac{mF}{(m+M)}$

36. A block of mass m is placed on a surface with a vertical cross section given by $y=\dfrac{x^3}{6}$. If the coefficient of friction is 0.5, the maximum height above the ground at which the block can be placed without slipping is:
(a) $\dfrac{1}{6}$ m   (b) $\dfrac{2}{3}$ m   (c) $\dfrac{1}{3}$ m   (d) $\dfrac{1}{2}$ m

37. A ball of mass 10 g moving perpendicular to the plane of the wall strikes it and rebounds in the same line with the same velocity. If the impulse experienced by the wall is 0.54 Ns, the velocity of the ball is
(a) $27\,\text{ms}^{-1}$ (b) $3.7\,\text{ms}^{-1}$ (c) $54\,\text{ms}^{-1}$ (d) $37\,\text{ms}^{-1}$

38. A block is kept on a inclined plane of inclination θ of length ℓ. The velocity of particle at the bottom of inclined is (the coefficient of friction is μ)
(a) $[2g\ell(\mu\cos\theta-\sin\theta)]^{1/2}$ (b) $\sqrt{2g\ell(\sin\theta-\mu\cos\theta)}$
(c) $\sqrt{2g\ell(\sin\theta+\mu\cos\theta)}$ (d) $\sqrt{2g\ell(\cos\theta+\mu\sin\theta)}$

39. A 100 g iron ball having velocity 10 m/s collides with a wall at an angle 30° and rebounds with the same angle. If the period of contact between the ball and wall is 0.1 second, then the force experienced by the wall is
(a) 10 N   (b) 100 N   (c) 1.0 N   (d) 0.1 N

40. A bullet is fired from a gun. The force on the bullet is given by $F=600-2\times10^5\,t$ where, F is in newton and t in second. The force on the bullet becomes zero as soon as it leaves the barrel. What is the average impulse imparted to the bullet?
(a) 1.8 N-s   (b) zero   (c) 9 N-s   (d) 0.9 N-s

41. Two stones of masses m and 2 m are whirled in horizontal circles, the heavier one in radius $\dfrac{r}{2}$ and the lighter one in radius r. The tangential speed of lighter stone is n times that of the value of heavier stone when they experience same centripetal forces. The value of n is :
(a) 3   (b) 4   (c) 1   (d) 2

42. A 0.1 kg block suspended from a massless string is moved first vertically up with an acceleration of $5\,\text{ms}^{-2}$ and then moved vertically down with an acceleration of $5\,\text{ms}^{-2}$. If T_1 and T_2 are the respective tensions in the two cases, then
(a) $T_2>T_1$
(b) $T_1-T_2=1\,\text{N}$, if $g=10\,\text{ms}^{-2}$
(c) $T_1-T_2=1\,\text{kg f}$
(d) $T_1-T_2=9.8\,\text{N}$, if $g=9.8\,\text{ms}^{-2}$

43. Three forces start acting simultaneously on a particle moving with velocity, $\vec{v}$. These forces are represented in magnitude and direction by the three sides of a triangle ABC. The particle will now move with velocity
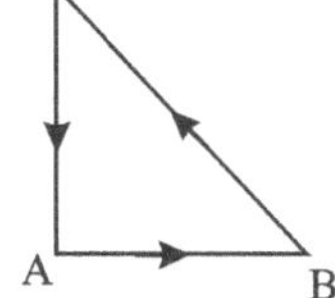
(a) less than $\vec{v}$
(b) greater than $\vec{v}$
(c) $|v|$ in the direction of the largest force BC
(d) $\vec{v}$, remaining unchanged

44. If in a stationary lift, a man is standing with a bucket full of water, having a hole at its bottom. The rate of flow of water through this hole is R_0. If the lift starts to move up and down with same acceleration and then the rates of flow of water are R_u and R_d, then
(a) $R_0>R_u>R_d$ (b) $R_u>R_0>R_d$
(c) $R_d>R_0>R_u$ (d) $R_u>R_d>R_0$

45. A stationary body of mass 3 kg explodes into three equal pieces. Two of the pieces fly off in two mutually perpendicular directions, one with a velocity of $3\hat{i}\,\text{ms}^{-1}$ and the other with a velocity of $4\hat{j}\,\text{ms}^{-1}$. If the explosion occurs in 10^{-4} s, the average force acting on the third piece in newton is
(a) $(3\hat{i}+4\hat{j})\times10^{-4}$ (b) $(3\hat{i}-4\hat{j})\times10^{-4}$
(c) $(3\hat{i}-4\hat{j})\times10^{4}$ (d) $-(3\hat{i}+4\hat{j})\times10^{4}$

RESPONSE GRID					
33. ⓐⓑⓒⓓ	34. ⓐⓑⓒⓓ	35. ⓐⓑⓒⓓ	36. ⓐⓑⓒⓓ		
37. ⓐⓑⓒⓓ	38. ⓐⓑⓒⓓ	39. ⓐⓑⓒⓓ	40. ⓐⓑⓒⓓ	41. ⓐⓑⓒⓓ	
42. ⓐⓑⓒⓓ	43. ⓐⓑⓒⓓ	44. ⓐⓑⓒⓓ	45. ⓐⓑⓒⓓ		

DAILY PRACTICE PROBLEM DPP CHAPTERWISE CP04 - PHYSICS

Total Questions	45	Total Marks	180
Attempted		Correct	
Incorrect		Net Score	
Cut-off Score	45	Qualifying Score	60
Success Gap = Net Score − Qualifying Score			
Net Score = (Correct × 4) − (Incorrect × 1)			

Date : [   ]   Start Time : [   ]   End Time : [   ]

PHYSICS [CP05]

Max. Marks : 180   **Marking Scheme :** (+4) for correct & (–1) for incorrect answer   **Time : 60 min.**

INSTRUCTIONS : This Daily Practice Problem Sheet contains 45 MCQs. For each question only one option is correct. Darken the correct circle/ bubble in the Response Grid provided on each page.

1. A spring of spring constant 5×10^3 N/m is stretched initially by 5cm from the unstretched position. Then the work required to stretch it further by another 5 cm is
(a) 12.50 Nm
(b) 18.75 Nm
(c) 25.00 Nm
(d) 6.25 Nm

2. A particle of mass 10 g moves along a circle of radius 6.4 cm with a constant tangential acceleration. What is the magnitude of this acceleration if the kinetic energy of the particle becomes equal to 8×10^{-4} J by the end of the second revolution after the beginning of the motion ?
(a) 0.1 m/s^2 (b) 0.15 m/s^2 (c) 0.18 m/s^2 (d) 0.2 m/s^2

3. A body is moved along a straight line by a machine delivering a constant power. The distance moved by the body in time 't' is proportional to
(a) $t^{3/4}$ (b) $t^{3/2}$ (c) $t^{1/4}$ (d) $t^{1/2}$

4. A ball is thrown vertically downwards from a height of 20 m with an initial velocity v_0. It collides with the ground and loses 50% of its energy in collision and rebounds to the same height. The initial velocity v_0 is : (Take $g = 10$ ms^{-2})
(a) 20 ms^{-1}
(b) 28 ms^{-1}
(c) 10 ms^{-1}
(d) 14 ms^{-1}

5. A cord is used to lower vertically a block of mass M, a distance d at a constant downward acceleration of g/4. The work done by the cord on the block is

(a) $Mg\dfrac{d}{4}$ (b) $3Mg\dfrac{d}{4}$ (c) $-3Mg\dfrac{d}{4}$ (d) Mg d

6. A rubber ball is dropped from a height of 5m on a plane, where the acceleration due to gravity is not shown. On bouncing it rises to 1.8 m. The ball loses its velocity on bouncing by a factor of

(a) $\dfrac{16}{25}$ (b) $\dfrac{2}{5}$ (c) $\dfrac{3}{5}$ (d) $\dfrac{9}{25}$

7. A ball of mass m moving with a constant velocity strikes against a ball of same mass at rest. If e = coefficient of restitution, then what will be the ratio of velocity of two balls after collision?

(a) $\dfrac{1-e}{1+e}$ (b) $\dfrac{e-1}{e+1}$ (c) $\dfrac{1+e}{1-e}$ (d) $\dfrac{2+e}{e-1}$

8. A particle of mass m is driven by a machine that delivers a constant power of k watts. If the particle starts from rest the force on the particle at time t is

(a) $\sqrt{mk}\ t^{-1/2}$ (b) $\sqrt{2mk}\ t^{-1/2}$

(c) $\dfrac{1}{2}\sqrt{mk}\ t^{-1/2}$ (d) $\sqrt{\dfrac{mk}{2}}t^{-1/2}$

RESPONSE GRID	**1.** ⓐⓑ©ⓓ	**2.** ⓐⓑ©ⓓ	**3.** ⓐⓑ©ⓓ	**4.** ⓐⓑ©ⓓ	**5.** ⓐⓑ©ⓓ
	6. ⓐⓑ©ⓓ	**7.** ⓐⓑ©ⓓ	**8.** ⓐⓑ©ⓓ		

Space for Rough Work

9. A body of mass 2 kg moving under a force has relation between displacement x and time t as $x = \dfrac{t^3}{3}$ where x is in metre and t is in sec. The work done by the body in first two second will be

(a) 1.6 joule   (b) 16 joule
(c) 160 joule   (d) 1600 joule

10. A sphere of mass 8m collides elastically (in one dimension) with a block of mass 2m. If the initial energy of sphere is E. What is the final energy of sphere?

(a) 0.8 E   (b) 0.36 E
(c) 0.08 E   (d) 0.64 E

11. Two similar springs P and Q have spring constants K_P and K_Q, such that $K_P > K_Q$. They are stretched, first by the same amount (case a,) then by the same force (case b). The work done by the springs W_P and W_Q are related as, in case (a) and case (b), respectively

(a) $W_P = W_Q$; $W_P = W_Q$ (b) $W_P > W_Q$; $W_Q > W_P$
(c) $W_P < W_Q$; $W_Q < W_P$ (d) $W_P = W_Q$; $W_P > W_Q$

12. In the figure, the variation of potential energy of a particle of mass m = 2 kg is represented w.r.t. its x-coordinate. The particle moves under the effect of this conservative force along the x-axis.

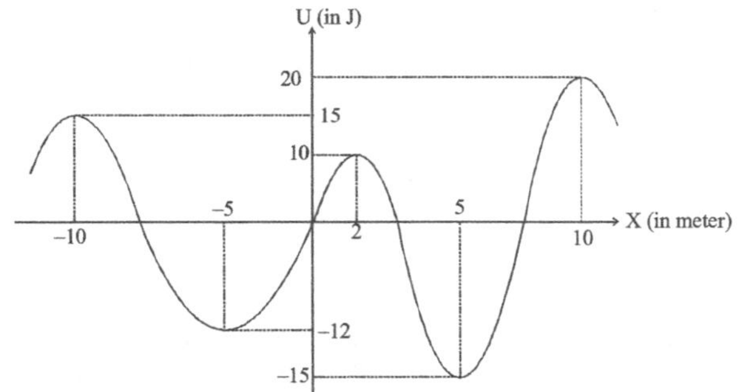

If the particle is released at the origin then
(a) it will move towards positive x-axis
(b) it will move towards negative x-axis
(c) it will remain stationary at the origin
(d) its subsequent motion cannot be decided due to lack of information

13. The potential energy of a certain spring when stretched through distance S is 10 joule. The amount of work done (in joule) that must be done on this spring to stretch it through an additional distance s, will be

(a) 20   (b) 10   (c) 30   (d) 40

14. A force applied by an engine of a train of mass 2.05×10^6 kg changes its velocity from 5 m/s to 25 m/s in 5 minutes. The power of the engine is

(a) 1.025 MW   (b) 2.05 MW
(c) 5 MW   (d) 6 MW

15. The relationship between the force F and position x of a body is as shown in figure. The work done in displacing the body form x = 1 m to x = 5 m will be

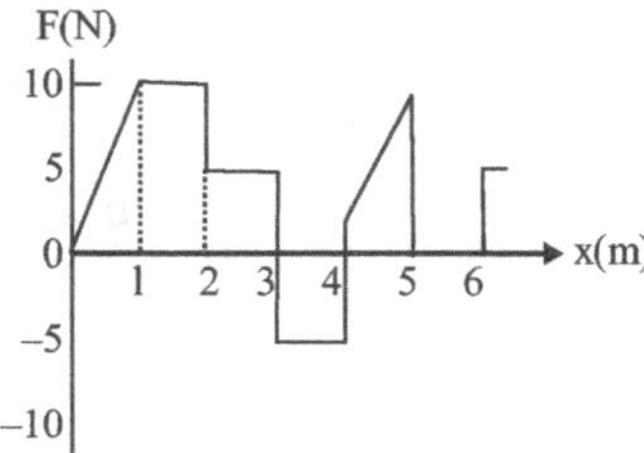

(a) 30 J   (b) 15 J   (c) 25 J   (d) 20 J

16. A body is allowed to fall freely under gravity from a height of 10m. If it looses 25% of its energy due to impact with the ground, then the maximum height it rises after one impact is

(a) 2.5m   (b) 5.0m   (c) 7.5m   (d) 8.2m

17. A block C of mass m is moving with velocity v_0 and collides elastically with block A of mass m and connected to another block B of mass 2m through spring constant k. What is k if x_0 is compression of spring when velocity of A and B is same?

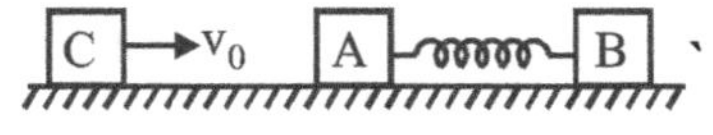

(a) $\dfrac{mv_0^2}{x_0^2}$ (b) $\dfrac{mv_0^2}{2x_0^2}$

(c) $\dfrac{3}{2}\dfrac{mv_0^2}{x_0^2}$ (d) $\dfrac{2}{3}\dfrac{mv_0^2}{x_0^2}$

18. Two springs of force constants 300 N/m (Spring A) and 400 N/m (Spring B) are joined together in series. The combination is compressed by 8.75 cm. The ratio of energy stored in A and B is $\dfrac{E_A}{E_B}$. Then $\dfrac{E_A}{E_B}$ is equal to :

(a) $\dfrac{4}{3}$ (b) $\dfrac{16}{9}$ (c) $\dfrac{3}{4}$ (d) $\dfrac{9}{16}$

19. A body of mass 1 kg begins to move under the action of a time dependent force $\vec{F} = (2t\hat{i} + 3t^2\hat{j})$ N, where $\hat{i}$ and $\hat{j}$ are unit vectors alogn x and y axis. What power will be developed by the force at the time t?

(a) $(2t^2 + 3t^3)$W   (b) $(2t^2 + 4t^4)$W
(c) $(2t^3 + 3t^4)$ W   (d) $(2t^3 + 3t^5)$W

20. A bullet of mass 20 g and moving with 600 m/s collides with a block of mass 4 kg hanging with the string. What is the velocity of bullet when it comes out of block, if block rises to height 0.2 m after collision?

(a) 200 m/s   (b) 150 m/s   (c) 400 m/s   (d) 300 m/s

RESPONSE GRID					
9. ⓐⓑⓒⓓ	**10.** ⓐⓑⓒⓓ	**11.** ⓐⓑⓒⓓ	**12.** ⓐⓑⓒⓓ	**13.** ⓐⓑⓒⓓ
14. ⓐⓑⓒⓓ	**15.** ⓐⓑⓒⓓ	**16.** ⓐⓑⓒⓓ	**17.** ⓐⓑⓒⓓ	**18.** ⓐⓑⓒⓓ
19. ⓐⓑⓒⓓ	**20.** ⓐⓑⓒⓓ			

21. A body of mass m kg is ascending on a smooth inclined plane of inclination $\theta \left(\sin \theta = \dfrac{1}{x} \right)$ with constant acceleration of a m/s². The final velocity of the body is v m/s. The work done by the body during this motion is
(Initial velocity of the body = 0)

(a) $\dfrac{1}{2}mv^2(g+xa)$

(b) $\dfrac{mv^2}{2}\left(\dfrac{g}{2}+a\right)$

(c) $\dfrac{2mv^2x}{a}(a+gx)$

(d) $\dfrac{mv^2}{2ax}(g+xa)$

22. A glass marble dropped from a certain height above the horizontal surface reaches the surface in time t and then continues to bounce up and down. The time in which the marble finally comes to rest is

(a) $e^n t$
(b) $e^2 t$
(c) $t\left[\dfrac{1+e}{1-e}\right]$
(d) $t\left[\dfrac{1-e}{1+e}\right]$

23. The potential energy of a 1 kg particle free to move along the x-axis is given by $V(x) = \left(\dfrac{x^4}{4} - \dfrac{x^2}{2}\right) J$.

The total mechanical energy of the particle is 2 J. Then, the maximum speed (in m/s) is

(a) $\dfrac{3}{\sqrt{2}}$
(b) $\sqrt{2}$
(c) $\dfrac{1}{\sqrt{2}}$
(d) 2

24. Water falls from a height of 60 m at the rate of 15 kg/s to operate a turbine. The losses due to frictional force are 10% of energy. How much power is generated by the turbine?(g = 10 m/s²)
(a) 8.1 kW (b) 10.2 kW (c) 12.3 kW (d) 7.0 kW

24. A car of mass m starts from rest and accelerates so that the instantaneous power delivered to the car has a constant magnitude P_0. The instantaneous velocity of this car is proportional to :

(a) $t^2 P_0$
(b) $t^{1/2}$
(c) $t^{-1/2}$
(d) $\dfrac{t}{\sqrt{m}}$

25. When a 1.0kg mass hangs attached to a spring of length 50 cm, the spring stretches by 2 cm. The mass is pulled down until the length of the spring becomes 60 cm. What is the amount of elastic energy stored in the spring in this condition. if g = 10 m/s².
(a) 1.5 joule (b) 2.0 joule (c) 2.5 joule (d) 3.0 joule

26. A block of mass m rests on a rough horizontal surface (Coefficient of friction is μ). When a bullet of mass m/2 strikes horizontally, and get embedded in it, the block moves a distance d before coming to rest. The initial velocity of the bullet is $k\sqrt{2\mu gd}$, then the value of k is

(a) 2 (b) 3 (c) 4 (d) 5

27. A force acts on a 30 gm particle in such a way that the position of the particle as a function of time is given by x = $3t - 4t^2 + t^3$, where x is in metres and t is in seconds. The work done during the first 4 seconds is
(a) 576mJ (b) 450mJ (c) 490mJ (d) 530mJ

28. A particle of mass m_1 moving with velocity v strikes with a mass m_2 at rest, then the condition for maximum transfer of kinetic energy is
(a) $m_1 \gg m_2$ (b) $m_2 \gg m_2$ (c) $m_1 = m_2$ (d) $m_1 = 2m_2$

29. A mass m is moving with velocity v collides inelastically with a bob of simple pendulum of mass m and gets embedded into it. The total height to which the masses will rise after collision is

(a) $\dfrac{v^2}{8g}$
(b) $\dfrac{v^2}{4g}$
(c) $\dfrac{v^2}{2g}$
(d) $\dfrac{2v^2}{g}$

30. A 10 H.P. motor pumps out water from a well of depth 20 m and fills a water tank of volume 22380 litres at a height of 10 m from the ground. The running time of the motor to fill the empty water tank is (g = 10 ms⁻²)
(a) 5 minutes (b) 10 minutes
(c) 15 minutes (d) 20 minutes

31. A particle of mass m_1 is moving with a velocity v_1 and another particle of mass m_2 is moving with a velocity v_2. Both of them have the same momentum but their different kinetic energies are E_1 and E_2 respectively. If $m_1 > m_2$ then
(a) $E_1 = E_2$ (b) $E_1 < E_2$ (c) $\dfrac{E_1}{E_2} = \dfrac{m_1}{m_2}$ (d) $E_1 > E_2$

32. A block of mass 10 kg, moving in x direction with a constant speed of 10 ms⁻¹, is subject to a retarding force F = 0.1 × J m during its travel from x = 20 m to 30 m. Its final KE will be :
(a) 450 J (b) 275 J (c) 250 J (d) 475 J

33. Identify the false statement from the following
(a) Work-energy theorem is not independent of Newton's second law.
(b) Work-energy theorem holds in all inertial frames.
(c) Work done by friction over a closed path is zero.
(d) No potential energy can be associated with friction.

34. A one-ton car moves with a constant velocity of 15 ms⁻¹ on a rough horizontal road. The total resistance to the motion of the car is 12% of the weight of the car. The power required to keep the car moving with the same constant velocity of 15ms⁻¹ is [Take g = 10 ms⁻²]
(a) 9 kW (b) 18 kW (c) 24 kW (d) 36 kW

35. A ball is released from the top of a tower. The ratio of work done by force of gravity in first, second and third second of the motion of the ball is
(a) 1 : 2 : 3 (b) 1 : 4 : 9 (c) 1 : 3 : 5 (d) 1 : 5 : 3

RESPONSE GRID	21. (a)(b)(c)(d)	22. (a)(b)(c)(d)	23. (a)(b)(c)(d)	24. (a)(b)(c)(d)	25. (a)(b)(c)(d)
	26. (a)(b)(c)(d)	27. (a)(b)(c)(d)	28. (a)(b)(c)(d)	29. (a)(b)(c)(d)	30. (a)(b)(c)(d)
	31. (a)(b)(c)(d)	32. (a)(b)(c)(d)	33. (a)(b)(c)(d)	34. (a)(b)(c)(d)	35. (a)(b)(c)(d)

36. Two spheres A and B of masses m_1 and m_2 respectively collide. A is at rest initially and B is moving with velocity v along x-axis. After collision B has a velocity $\dfrac{v}{2}$ in a direction perpendicular to the original direction. The mass A moves after collision in the direction.
(a) Same as that of B
(b) Opposite to that of B
(c) $\theta = \tan^{-1}(1/2)$ to the x-axis
(d) $\theta = \tan^{-1}(-1/2)$ to the x-axis

37. A 2 kg block slides on a horizontal floor with a speed of 4m/s. It strikes a uncompressed spring, and compresses it till the block is motionless. The kinetic friction force is 15N and spring constant is 10,000 N/m. The spring compresses by
(a) 8.5 cm   (b) 5.5 cm   (c) 2.5 cm   (d) 11.0 cm

38. An engine pumps water through a hose pipe. Water passes through the pipe and leaves it with a velocity of 2 m/s. The mass per unit length of water in the pipe is 100 kg/m. What is the power of the engine?
(a) 400 W   (b) 200 W   (c) 100 W   (d) 800 W

39. A uniform chain of length 2 m is kept on a table such that a length of 60 cm hangs freely from the edge of the table. The total mass of the chain is 4 kg. What is the work done in pulling the entire chain on the table ?
(a) 12 J   (b) 3.6 J   (c) 7.2 J   (d) 1200 J

40. A mass 'm' moves with a velocity 'v' and collides inelastically with another identical mass. After collision the 1st mass moves with velocity $\dfrac{v}{\sqrt{3}}$ in a direction perpendicular to the initial direction of motion. Find the speed of the 2nd mass after collision.

(a) $\sqrt{3}v$ (b) v (c) $\dfrac{v}{\sqrt{3}}$ (d) $\dfrac{2}{\sqrt{3}}v$

41. A spherical ball of mass 20 kg is stationary at the top of a hill of height 100 m. It rolls down a smooth surface to the ground, then climbs up another hill of height 30 m and finally rolls down to a horizontal base at a height of 20 m above the ground. The velocity attained by the ball is
(a) 20 m/s (b) 40 m/s   (c) $10\sqrt{30}$ m/s (d) 10 m/s

42. A block of mass M is kept on a platform which is accelerated upward with a constant acceleration 'a' during the time interval T. The work done by normal reaction between the block and platform is

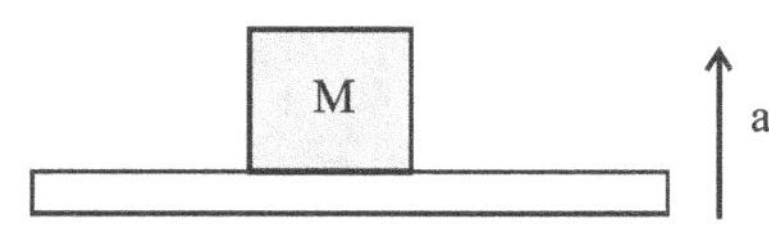

(a) $-\dfrac{MgaT^2}{2}$ (b) $\dfrac{1}{2}M(g+a)aT^2$

(c) $\dfrac{1}{2}Ma^2T$ (d) Zero

43. A spring lies along an x axis attached to a wall at one end and a block at the other end. The block rests on a frictionless surface at x = 0. A force of constant magnitude F is applied to the block that begins to compress the spring, until the block comes to a maximum displacement x_{max}.

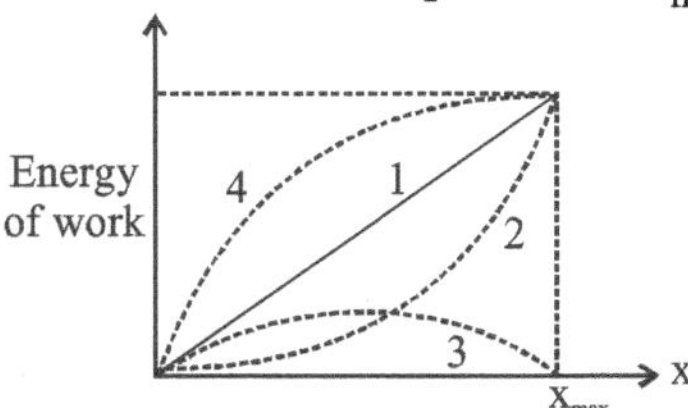

During the displacement, which of the curves shown in the graph best represents the kinetic energy of the block ?
(a) 1   (b) 2   (c) 3   (d) 4

44. The K.E. acquired by a mass m in travelling a certain distance d, starting form rest, under the action of a constant force is directly proportional to
(a) m   (b) $\sqrt{m}$
(c) $\dfrac{1}{\sqrt{m}}$ (d) independent of m

45. A vertical spring with force constant k is fixed on a table. A ball of mass m at a height h above the free upper end of the spring falls vertically on the spring so that the spring is compressed by a distance d. The net work done in the process is
(a) $mg(h+d)-\dfrac{1}{2}kd^2$ (b) $mg(h-d)-\dfrac{1}{2}kd^2$
(c) $mg(h-d)+\dfrac{1}{2}kd^2$ (d) $mg(h+d)+\dfrac{1}{2}kd^2$

RESPONSE GRID					
36. ⓐⓑⓒⓓ	37. ⓐⓑⓒⓓ	38. ⓐⓑⓒⓓ	39. ⓐⓑⓒⓓ	40. ⓐⓑⓒⓓ
41. ⓐⓑⓒⓓ	42. ⓐⓑⓒⓓ	43. ⓐⓑⓒⓓ	44. ⓐⓑⓒⓓ	45. ⓐⓑⓒⓓ

DAILY PRACTICE PROBLEM DPP CHAPTERWISE CP05 - PHYSICS

Total Questions	45	Total Marks	180
Attempted		Correct	
Incorrect		Net Score	
Cut-off Score	50	Qualifying Score	70
Success Gap = Net Score – Qualifying Score			
Net Score = (Correct × 4) – (Incorrect × 1)			

Space for Rough Work

Date :   Start Time :   End Time :

PHYSICS   CP06

SYLLABUS : System of Particles and Rotational Motion

Max. Marks : 180   **Marking Scheme :** (+4) for correct & (–1) for incorrect answer   **Time : 60 min.**

INSTRUCTIONS : This Daily Practice Problem Sheet contains 45 MCQs. For each question only one option is correct. Darken the correct circle/ bubble in the Response Grid provided on each page.

1. From a solid sphere of mass M and radius R, a cube of maximum possible volume is cut. Moment of inertia of cube about an axis passing through its center and perpendicular to one of its faces is :

   (a) $\dfrac{4MR^2}{9\sqrt{3}\pi}$ (b) $\dfrac{4MR^2}{3\sqrt{3}\pi}$ (c) $\dfrac{MR^2}{32\sqrt{2}\pi}$ (d) $\dfrac{MR^2}{16\sqrt{2}\pi}$

2. A hollow sphere is held suspended. Sand is now poured into it in stages.

   The centre of mass of the sphere with the sand

   (a) rises continuously
   (b) remains unchanged in the process
   (c) first rises and then falls to the original position
   (d) first falls and then rises to the original position

3. A body A of mass M while falling vertically downwards under gravity breaks into two parts; a body B of mass $\dfrac{1}{3}M$ and a body C of mass $\dfrac{2}{3}M$. The centre of mass of bodies B and C taken together shifts compared to that of body A towards

   (a) does not shift
   (b) depends on height of breaking
   (c) body B (d) body C

4. From a uniform wire, two circular loops are made (i) P of radius r and (ii) Q of radius nr. If the moment of inertia of Q about an axis passing through its centre and perpendicular to its plane is 8 times that of P about a similar axis, the value of n is (diameter of the wire is very much smaller than r or nr)

   (a) 8   (b) 6   (c) 4   (d) 2

5. A billiard ball of mass m and radius r, when hit in a horizontal direction by a cue at a height h above its centre, acquired a linear velocity v_0. The angular velocity ω_0 acquired by the ball is

   (a) $\dfrac{5v_0 r^2}{2h}$ (b) $\dfrac{2v_0 r^2}{5h}$ (c) $\dfrac{2v_0 h}{5r^2}$ (d) $\dfrac{5v_0 h}{2r^2}$

6. Three bricks each of length L and mass M are arranged as shown from the wall. The distance of the centre of mass of the system from the wall is

   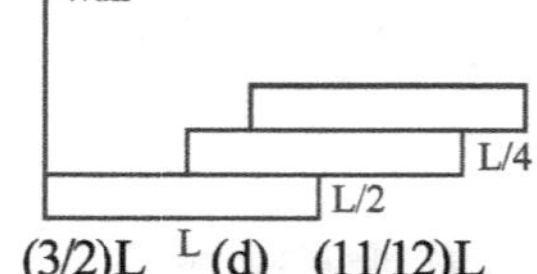

   (a) L/4   (b) L/2   (c) (3/2)L   (d) (11/12)L

7. Four point masses, each of value m, are placed at the corners of a square $ABCD$ of side ℓ. The moment of inertia of this system about an axis passing through A and parallel to BD is

   (a) $2m\ell^2$ (b) $\sqrt{3}m\ell^2$ (c) $3m\ell^2$ (d) $m\ell^2$

8. A loop of radius r and mass m rotating with an angular velocity ω_0 is placed on a rough horizontal surface. The initial velocity of the centre of the hoop is zero. What will be the velocity of the centre of the hoop when it ceases to slip?

   (a) $\dfrac{r\omega_0}{4}$ (b) $\dfrac{r\omega_0}{3}$ (c) $\dfrac{r\omega_0}{2}$ (d) $r\omega_0$

| **RESPONSE GRID** | 1. ⓐⓑⓒⓓ | 2. ⓐⓑⓒⓓ | 3. ⓐⓑⓒⓓ | 4. ⓐⓑⓒⓓ | 5. ⓐⓑⓒⓓ |
| | 6. ⓐⓑⓒⓓ | 7. ⓐⓑⓒⓓ | 8. ⓐⓑⓒⓓ | | |

Space for Rough Work

9. Two masses m_1 and m_2 are connected by a massless spring of spring constant k and unstretched length ℓ. The masses are placed on a frictionless straight channel, which are consider our x-axis. They are initially at $x = 0$ and $x = \ell$ respectively. At $t = 0$, a velocity v_0 is suddenly imparted to the first particle. At a later time t, the centre of mass of the two masses is at :

(a) $x = \dfrac{m_2\ell}{m_1 + m_2}$

(b) $x = \dfrac{m_1\ell}{m_1 + m_2} + \dfrac{m_2 v_0 t}{m_1 + m_2}$

(c) $x = \dfrac{m_2\ell}{m_1 + m_1} + \dfrac{m_2 v_0 t}{m_1 + m_2}$

(d) $x = \dfrac{m_2\ell}{m_1 + m_2} + \dfrac{m_1 v_0 t}{m_1 + m_2}$

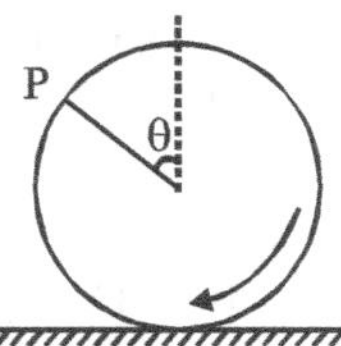

10. A body of mass 1.5 kg rotating about an axis with angular velocity of 0.3 rad s^{-1} has the angular momentum of 1.8 kg m²s^{-1}. The radius of gyration of the body about an axis is

(a) 2m   (b) 1.2m   (c) 0.2m   (d) 1.6m

11. If $\vec{F}$ is the force acting on a particle having position vector $\vec{r}$ and $\vec{\tau}$ be the torque of this force about the origin, then:

(a) $\vec{r}\cdot\vec{\tau} > 0$ and $\vec{F}\cdot\vec{\tau} < 0$

(b) $\vec{r}\cdot\vec{\tau} = 0$ and $\vec{F}\cdot\vec{\tau} = 0$

(c) $\vec{r}\cdot\vec{\tau} = 0$ and $\vec{F}\cdot\vec{\tau} \neq 0$

(d) $\vec{r}\cdot\vec{\tau} \neq 0$ and $\vec{F}\cdot\vec{\tau} = 0$

12. A thin uniform rod of length l and mass m is swinging freely about a horizontal axis passing through its end. Its maximum angular speed is ω. Its centre of mass rises to a maximum height of

(a) $\dfrac{1}{6}\dfrac{l\omega}{g}$ (b) $\dfrac{1}{2}\dfrac{l^2\omega^2}{g}$ (c) $\dfrac{1}{6}\dfrac{l^2\omega^2}{g}$ (d) $\dfrac{1}{3}\dfrac{l^2\omega^2}{g}$

13. A wheel is rolling straight on ground without slipping. If the axis of the wheel has speed v, the instantenous velocity of a point P on the rim, defined by angle θ, relative to the ground will be

(a) $v\cos\left(\dfrac{1}{2}\theta\right)$ (b) $2v\cos\left(\dfrac{1}{2}\theta\right)$

(c) $v(1+\sin\theta)$ (d) $v(1+\cos\theta)$

14. A solid sphere having mass m and radius r rolls down an inclined plane. Then its kinetic energy is

(a) $\dfrac{5}{7}$ rotational and $\dfrac{2}{7}$ translational

(b) $\dfrac{2}{7}$ rotational and $\dfrac{5}{7}$ translational

(c) $\dfrac{2}{5}$ rotational and $\dfrac{3}{5}$ translational

(d) $\dfrac{1}{2}$ rotational and $\dfrac{1}{2}$ translational

15. A ring of mass M and radius R is rotating about its axis with angular velocity ω. Two identical bodies each of mass m are now gently attached at the two ends of a diameter of the ring. Because of this, the kinetic energy loss will be :

(a) $\dfrac{m(M+2m)}{M}\omega^2 R^2$ (b) $\dfrac{Mm}{(M+m)}\omega^2 R^2$

(c) $\dfrac{Mm}{(M+2m)}\omega^2 R^2$ (d) $\dfrac{(M+m)M}{(M+2m)}\omega^2 R^2$

16. A certain bicycle can go up a gentle incline with constant speed when the frictional force of ground pushing the rear wheel is $F_2 = 4$ N. With what force F_1 must the chain pull on the sprocket wheel if $R_1 = 5$ cm and $R_2 = 30$ cm?

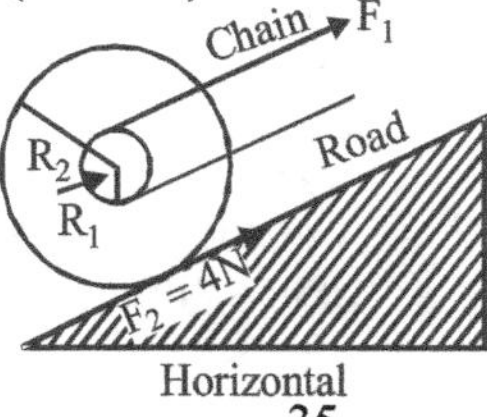

(a) 4N   (b) 24N   (c) 140N   (d) $\dfrac{35}{4}$ N

17. A wooden cube is placed on a rough horizontal table, a force is applied to the cube. Gradually the force is increased. Whether the cube slides before toppling or topples before sliding is independent of :
(a) the position of point of application of the force
(b) the length of the edge of the cube
(c) mass of the cube
(d) Coefficient of friction between the cube and the table

18. From a circular ring of mass M and radius R, an arc corresponding to a 90° sector is removed. The moment of inertia of the ramaining part of the ring about an axis passing through the centre of the ring and perpendicular to the plane of the ring is k times MR². Then the value of k is
(a) 3/4   (b) 7/8   (c) 1/4   (d) 1

19. A mass m moves in a circle on a smooth horizontal plane with velocity v_0 at a radius R_0. The mass is attached to string which passes through a smooth hole in the plane as shown.

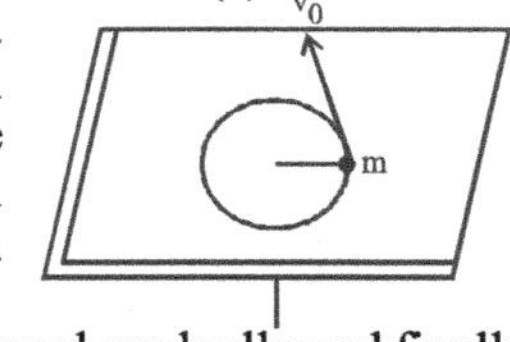

The tension in the string is increased gradually and finally m moves in a circle of radius $\dfrac{R_0}{2}$. The final value of the kinetic energy is

(a) $\dfrac{1}{4}mv_0^2$ (b) $2mv_0^2$ (c) $\dfrac{1}{2}mv_0^2$ (d) mv_0^2

20. A rod PQ of length L revolves in a horizontal plane about the axis YY'. The angular velocity of the rod is ω. If A is the area of cross-section of the rod and ρ be its density, its rotational kinetic energy is

Space for Rough Work

(a) $\dfrac{1}{3}AL^3\rho\omega^2$ (b) $\dfrac{1}{2}AL^3\rho\omega^2$

(c) $\dfrac{1}{24}AL^3\rho\omega^2$ (d) $\dfrac{1}{18}AL^3\rho\omega^2$

21. A solid sphere of mass 2 kg rolls on a smooth horizontal surface at 10 m/s. It then rolls up a smooth inclined plane of inclination 30° with the horizontal. The height attained by the sphere before it stops is

(a) 700 cm   (b) 701 cm   (c) 7.1 m   (d) 70 m

22. A hollow smooth uniform sphere A of mass m rolls without sliding on a smooth horizontal surface. It collides head on elastically with another stationary smooth solid sphere B of the same mass m and same radius. The ratio of kinetic energy of B to that of A just after the collision is

(a) $1:1$
(b) $2:3$
(c) $3:2$
(d) $4:3$

23. Two discs of same thickness but of different radii are made of two different materials such that their masses are same. The densities of the materials are in the ratio of $1:3$. The moments of inertia of these discs about the respective axes passing through their centres and perpendicular to their planes will be in the ratio of

(a) $1:3$ (b) $3:1$ (c) $1:9$ (d) $9:1$

24. A pulley fixed to the ceiling carries a string with blocks of mass m and 3 m attached to its ends. The masses of string and pulley are negligible. When the system is released, its centre of mass moves with what acceleration ?

(a) 0   (b) $-g/4$ (c) $g/2$ (d) $-g/2$

25. A ring of mass m and radius R has four particles each of mass m attached to the ring as shown in figure. The centre of ring has a speed v_0. The kinetic energy of the system is

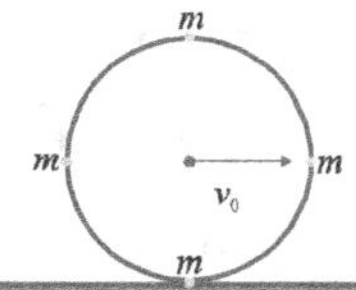

(a) mv_0^2 (b) $3mv_0^2$ (c) $5mv_0^2$ (d) $6mv_0^2$

26. Consider a uniform square plate of side 'a' and mass 'M'. The moment of inertia of this plate about an axis perpendicular to its plane and passing through one of its corners is

(a) $\dfrac{5}{6}Ma^2$ (b) $\dfrac{1}{12}Ma^2$ (c) $\dfrac{7}{12}Ma^2$ (d) $\dfrac{2}{3}Ma^2$

27. A dancer is standing on a stool rotating about the vertical axis passing through its centre. She pulls her arms towards the body reducing her moment of inertia by a factor of n. The new angular speed of turn table is proportional to

(a) n   (b) n^{-1} (c) n^0 (d) n^2

28. A uniform square plate has a small piece Q of an irregular shape removed and glued to the centre of the plate leaving a hole behind. Then the moment of inertia about the z-axis

(a) increases
(b) decreases
(c) remains same
(d) changed in unpredicted manner.

29. A circular turn table has a block of ice placed at its centre. The system rotates with an angular speed ω about an axis passing through the centre of the table. If the ice melts on its own without any evaporation, the speed of rotation of the system

(a) becomes zero
(b) remains constant at the same value ω
(c) increases to a value greater than ω
(d) decreases to a value less than ω

30. Seven identical coins are rigidly arranged on a flat table in the pattern shown below so that each coin touches it neighbors. Each coin is a thin disc of mass m and radius r. The moment of inertia of the system of seven coins about an axis that passes through point P and perpendicular to the plane of the coin is :

(a) $\dfrac{55}{2}mr^2$ (b) $\dfrac{127}{2}mr^2$ (c) $\dfrac{111}{2}mr^2$ (d) $55\,mr^2$

31. In a two-particle system with particle masses m_1 and m_2, the first particle is pushed towards the centre of mass through a distance d, the distance through which second particle must be moved to keep the centre of mass at the same position is

(a) $\dfrac{m_2 d}{m_1}$ (b) d   (c) $\dfrac{m_1 d}{(m_1+m_2)}$ (d) $\dfrac{m_1 d}{m_2}$

32. A uniform bar of mass M and length L is horizontally suspended from the ceiling by two vertical light cables as shown. Cable A is connected 1/4th distance from the left end of the bar. Cable B is attached at the far right end of the bar. What is the tension in cable A?

(a) 1/4 Mg   (b) 1/3 Mg   (c) 2/3 Mg   (d) 3/4 Mg

33. A couple produces
(a) purely linear motion
(b) purely rotational motion
(c) linear and rotational motion
(d) no motion

34. Point masses 1, 2, 3 and 4 kg are lying at the point (0, 0, 0), (2, 0, 0), (0, 3, 0) and (–2, –2, 0) respectively. The moment of inertia of this system about x-axis will be

(a) 43 kgm²   (b) 34 kgm²   (c) 27 kgm²   (d) 72 kgm²

<table>
<tr><td rowspan="3">RESPONSE GRID</td><td>20.ⓐⓑⓒⓓ</td><td>21.ⓐⓑⓒⓓ</td><td>22.ⓐⓑⓒⓓ</td><td>23.ⓐⓑⓒⓓ</td><td>24.ⓐⓑⓒⓓ</td></tr>
<tr><td>25.ⓐⓑⓒⓓ</td><td>26.ⓐⓑⓒⓓ</td><td>27.ⓐⓑⓒⓓ</td><td>28.ⓐⓑⓒⓓ</td><td>29.ⓐⓑⓒⓓ</td></tr>
<tr><td>30.ⓐⓑⓒⓓ</td><td>31.ⓐⓑⓒⓓ</td><td>32.ⓐⓑⓒⓓ</td><td>33.ⓐⓑⓒⓓ</td><td>34.ⓐⓑⓒⓓ</td></tr>
</table>

35. A solid sphere of mass M and radius R is pulled horizontally on a sufficiently rough surface as shown in the figure. Choose the correct alternative.

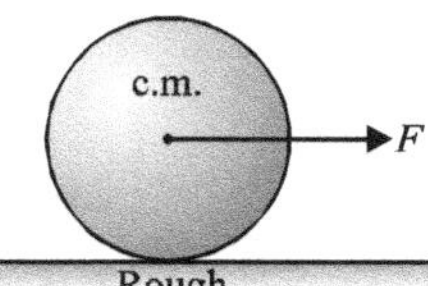

(a) The acceleration of the centre of mass is F/M

(b) The acceleration of the centre of mass is $\dfrac{2}{3}\dfrac{F}{M}$

(c) The friction force on the sphere acts forward

(d) The magnitude of the friction force is F/3

36. The moment of inertia of a body about a given axis is $1.2\,\text{kg m}^2$. Initially, the body is at rest. In order to produce a rotational kinetic energy of 1500 joule, an angular acceleration of 25 radian/sec^2 must be applied about that axis for a duration of

(a) 4 sec (b) 2 sec (c) 8 sec (d) 10 sec

37. A gymnast takes turns with her arms and legs stretched. When she pulls her arms and legs in

(a) the angular velocity decreases

(b) the moment of inertia decreases

(c) the angular velocity stays constant

(d) the angular momentum increases

38. An equilateral triangle ABC formed from a uniform wire has two small identical beads initially located at A. The triangle is set rotating about the vertical axis AO. Then the beads are released from rest simultaneously and allowed to slide down, one along AB and the other along AC as shown. Neglecting frictional effects, the quantities that are conserved as the beads slide down, are

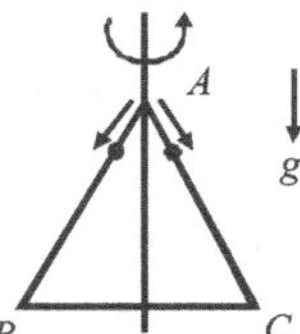

(a) angular velocity and total energy (kinetic and potential)

(b) total angular momentum and total energy

(c) angular velocity and moment of inertia about the axis of rotation

(d) total angular momentum and moment of inertia about the axis of rotation

39. The moment of inertia of a uniform semicircular wire of mass m and radius r, about an axis passing through its centre of mass and perpendicular to its plane is $\text{mr}^2\left(1-\dfrac{k}{\pi^2}\right)$. Find the value of k.

(a) 2 (b) 3 (c) 4 (d) 5

40. Initial angular velocity of a circular disc of mass M is ω_1. Then two small spheres of mass m are attached gently to diametrically opposite points on the edge of the disc. What is the final angular velocity of the disc?

(a) $\left(\dfrac{M+m}{M}\right)\omega_1$ (b) $\left(\dfrac{M+m}{m}\right)\omega_1$

(c) $\left(\dfrac{M}{M+4m}\right)\omega_1$ (d) $\left(\dfrac{M}{M+2m}\right)\omega_1$.

41. Two identical discs of mass m and radius r are arranged as shown in the figure. If α is the angular acceleration of the lower disc and a_{cm} is acceleration of centre of mass of the lower disc, then relation between a_{cm}, α and r is

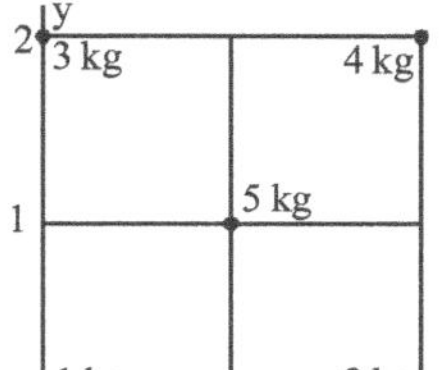

(a) $a_{cm} = \alpha/r$ (b) $a_{cm} = 2\alpha r$

(c) $a_{cm} = \alpha r$ (d) None of these

42. Five masses are placed in a plane as shown in figure. The coordinates of the centre of mass are nearest to

(a) 1.2, 1.4

(b) 1.3, 1.1

(c) 1.1, 1.3

(d) 1.0, 1.0

43. Three particles, each of mass m gram, are situated at the vertices of an equilateral triangle ABC of side ℓ cm (as shown in the figure). The moment of inertia of the system about a line AX perpendicular to AB and in the plane of ABC, in gram-cm^2 units will be

(a) $\dfrac{3}{2}\text{m}\ell^2$

(b) $\dfrac{3}{4}\text{m}\ell^2$

(c) $2\,\text{m}\ell^2$

(d) $\dfrac{5}{4}\text{m}\ell^2$

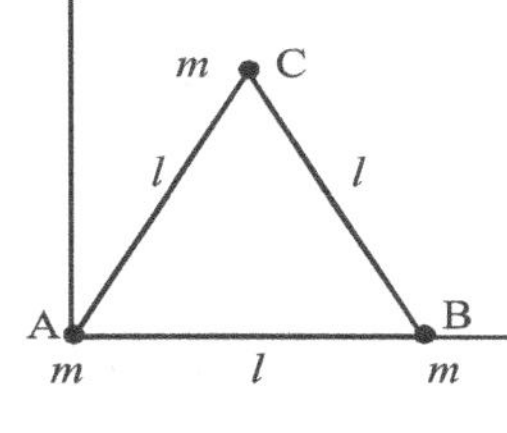

44. When a ceiling fan is switched on, it makes 10 rotations in the first 3 seconds. Assuming a uniform angular acceleration, how many rotation it will make in the next 3 seconds?

(a) 10 (b) 20 (c) 30 (d) 40

45. A solid sphere spinning about a horizontal axis with an angular velocity ω is placed on a horizontal surface. Subsequently it rolls without slipping with an angular velocity of :

(a) $\dfrac{2\omega}{5}$ (b) $\dfrac{7\omega}{5}$ (c) $\dfrac{2\omega}{7}$ (d) ω

RESPONSE GRID					
	35. (a)(b)(c)(d)	36. (a)(b)(c)(d)	37. (a)(b)(c)(d)	38. (a)(b)(c)(d)	39. (a)(b)(c)(d)
	40. (a)(b)(c)(d)	41. (a)(b)(c)(d)	42. (a)(b)(c)(d)	43. (a)(b)(c)(d)	44. (a)(b)(c)(d)
	45. (a)(b)(c)(d)				

DAILY PRACTICE PROBLEM DPP CHAPTERWISE CP06 - PHYSICS

Total Questions	45	Total Marks	180
Attempted		Correct	
Incorrect		Net Score	
Cut-off Score	45	Qualifying Score	60
Success Gap = Net Score − Qualifying Score			
Net Score = (Correct × 4) − (Incorrect × 1)			

Date :   **Start Time :**   **End Time :**

PHYSICS $\boxed{\text{CP07}}$

SYLLABUS : Gravitation

Max. Marks : 180   **Marking Scheme :** (+4) for correct & (–1) for incorrect answer   **Time : 60 min.**

INSTRUCTIONS : This Daily Practice Problem Sheet contains 45 MCQs. For each question only one option is correct. Darken the correct circle/ bubble in the Response Grid provided on each page.

---

1. The radius of a planet is $1/4^{\text{th}}$ of R_e and its acc. due to gravity is 2g. What would be the value of escape velocity on the planet, if escape velocity on earth is v_e.

(a) $\dfrac{v_e}{\sqrt{2}}$ (b) $v_e\sqrt{2}$ (c) $2\,v_e$ (d) $\dfrac{v_e}{2}$

2. A projectile is fired vertically from the Earth with a velocity kv_e where v_e is the escape velocity and k is a constant less than unity. The maximum height to which projectile rises, as measured from the centre of Earth, is

(a) $\dfrac{R}{k}$ (b) $\dfrac{R}{k-1}$ (c) $\dfrac{R}{1-k^2}$ (d) $\dfrac{R}{1+k^2}$

3. A solid sphere of uniform density and radius R applies a gravitational force of attraction equal to F_1 on a particle placed at A, distance 2R from the centre of the sphere.

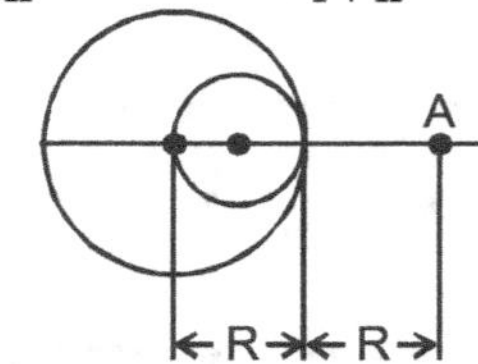

A spherical cavity of radius R/2 is now made in the sphere as shown in the figure. The sphere with cavity now applies a gravitational force F_2 on the same particle placed at A. The ratio F_2/F_1 will be

(a) 1/2   (b) 3   (c) 7   (d) 1/9

4. A geostationary satellite is orbiting the earth at a height of 5R above that surface of the earth, R being the radius of the earth. The time period of another satellite in hours at a height of 2R from the surface of the earth is :

(a) 5   (b) 10   (c) $6\sqrt{2}$ (d) $\dfrac{6}{\sqrt{2}}$

5. A satellite of mass m is orbiting around the earth in a circular orbit with a velocity v. What will be its total energy?

(a) $(3/4)\,mv^2$ (b) $(1/2)\,mv^2$

(c) mv^2 (d) $-(1/2)m\,v^2$

| RESPONSE GRID | 1. ⓐⓑⓒⓓ | 2. ⓐⓑⓒⓓ | 3. ⓐⓑⓒⓓ | 4. ⓐⓑⓒⓓ | 5. ⓐⓑⓒⓓ |

Space for Rough Work

6. The gravitational force of attraction between a uniform sphere of mass M and a uniform rod of length l and mass m oriented as shown is

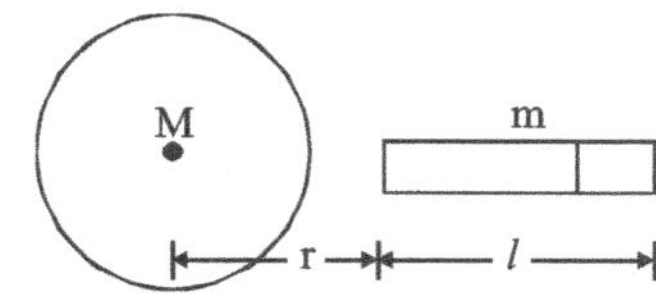

(a) $\dfrac{GMm}{r(r+l)}$ (b) $\dfrac{GM}{r^2}$ (c) $Mmr^2 + l$ (d) $(r^2 + l)mM$

7. If the gravitational force between two objects were proportional to $1/R$ (and not as $1/R^2$) where R is separation between them, then a particle in circular orbit under such a force would have its orbital speed v proportional to
(a) $1/R^2$ (b) R^0 (c) R^1 (d) $1/R$

8. A satellite of mass m revolves around the earth of radius R at a height 'x' from its surface. If g is the acceleration due to gravity on the surface of the earth, the orbital speed of the satellite is

(a) $\dfrac{gR^2}{R+x}$ (b) $\dfrac{gR}{R-x}$ (c) gx (d) $\left(\dfrac{gR^2}{R+x}\right)^{1/2}$

9. A body is projected up with a velocity equal to 3/4th of the escape velocity from the surface of the earth. The height it reaches from the centre of the earth is (Radius of the earth = R)

(a) $\dfrac{10R}{9}$ (b) $\dfrac{16R}{7}$ (c) $\dfrac{9R}{8}$ (d) $\dfrac{10R}{3}$

10. A Planet is revolving around the sun.

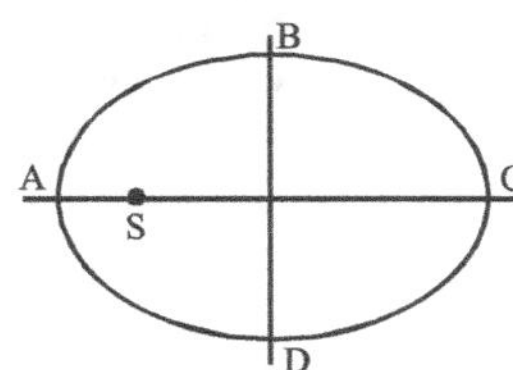

Which of the following is correct option?
(a) The time taken in travelling DAB is less than that for BCD
(b) The time taken in travelling DAB is greater than that for BCD
(c) The time taken in travelling CDA is less than that for ABC
(d) The time taken in travelling CDA is greater than that for ABC

11. The acceleration due to gravity on the planet A is 9 times the acceleration due to gravity on planet B. A man jumps to a height of 2m on the surface of A. What is the height of jump by the same person on the planet B?

(a) $\dfrac{2}{3}$ m (b) $\dfrac{2}{9}$ m (c) 18m (d) 6m

12. If suddenly the gravitational force of attraction between the earth and a satellite revolving around it becomes zero, then the satellite will
(a) continue to move in its orbit with same speed
(b) move tangentially to the original orbit with same speed
(c) become stationary in its orbit
(d) move towards the earth

13. Mass M is divided into two parts xM and $(1 - x)$M. For a given separation, the value of x for which the gravitational attraction between the two pieces becomes maximum is

(a) $\dfrac{1}{2}$ (b) $\dfrac{3}{5}$ (c) 1 (d) 2

14. The potential energy of a satellite, having mass m and rotating at a height of 6.4×10^6 m from the earth surface, is
(a) $-mgR_e$ (b) $-0.67\,mgR_e$
(c) $-0.5\,mgR_e$ (d) $-0.33\,mgR_e$

15. If the radius of the earth were to shrink by 1%, with its mass remaining the same, the acceleration due to gravity on the earth's surface would
(a) decrease by 1% (b) decrease by 2%
(c) increase by 1% (d) increase by 2%

16. Suppose the law of gravitational attraction suddenly changes and becomes an inverse cube law i.e. $F \propto \dfrac{1}{r^3}$, but still remaining a central force. Then
(a) Kepler's law of area still holds
(b) Kepler's law of period still holds
(c) Kepler's law of area and period still holds
(d) neither the law of area nor the law of period still holds

17. Four equal masses (each of mass M) are placed at the corners of a square of side a. The escape velocity of a body from the centre O of the square is

(a) $4\sqrt{\dfrac{2GM}{a}}$ (b) $\sqrt{\dfrac{8\sqrt{2}GM}{a}}$ (c) $\dfrac{4GM}{a}$ (d) $\sqrt{\dfrac{4\sqrt{2}GM}{a}}$

18. If the gravitational force had varied as $r^{-5/2}$ instead of r^{-2}; the potential energy of a particle at a distance 'r' from the centre of the earth would be directly proportional to
(a) r^{-1} (b) r^{-2} (c) $r^{-3/2}$ (d) $r^{-5/2}$

19. A particle of mass 'm' is kept at rest at a height 3R from the surface of earth, where 'R' is radius of earth and 'M' is mass of earth. The minimum speed with which it should be projected, so that it does not return back, is (g is acceleration due to gravity on the surface of earth)

(a) $\left(\dfrac{GM}{R}\right)^{\frac{1}{2}}$ (b) $\left(\dfrac{GM}{2R}\right)^{\frac{1}{2}}$ (c) $\left(\dfrac{gR}{4}\right)^{\frac{1}{2}}$ (d) $\left(\dfrac{2g}{4}\right)^{\frac{1}{2}}$

RESPONSE GRID					
	6. ⓐⓑⓒⓓ	7. ⓐⓑⓒⓓ	8. ⓐⓑⓒⓓ	9. ⓐⓑⓒⓓ	10. ⓐⓑⓒⓓ
	11. ⓐⓑⓒⓓ	12. ⓐⓑⓒⓓ	13. ⓐⓑⓒⓓ	14. ⓐⓑⓒⓓ	15. ⓐⓑⓒⓓ
	16. ⓐⓑⓒⓓ	17. ⓐⓑⓒⓓ	18. ⓐⓑⓒⓓ	19. ⓐⓑⓒⓓ	

20. The ratio between the values of acceleration due to gravity at a height 1 km above and at a depth of 1 km below the Earth's surface is (radius of Earth is R)

(a) $\frac{R-2}{R-1}$ (b) $\frac{R}{R-1}$ (c) $\frac{R-2}{R}$ (d) 1

21. The weight of an object in the coal mine, sea level and at the top of the mountain, are respectively W_1, W_2 and W_3 then

(a) $W_1 < W_2 > W_3$ (b) $W_1 = W_2 = W_3$
(c) $W_1 < W_2 < W_3$ (d) $W_1 > W_2 > W_3$

22. The period of moon's rotation around the earth is nearly 29 days. If moon's mass were 2 fold its present value and all other things remain unchanged, the period of moon's rotation would be nearly

(a) $29\sqrt{2}$ days (b) $29/\sqrt{2}$ days
(c) 29×2 days (d) 29 days

23. The mean radius of earth is R, its angular speed on its own axis is ω and the acceleration due to gravity at earth's surface is g. What will be the radius of the orbit of a geostationary satellite ?

(a) $(R^2g/\omega^2)^{1/3}$ (b) $(Rg/\omega^2)^{1/3}$
(c) $(R^2\omega^2/g)^{1/3}$ (d) $(R^2g/\omega)^{1/3}$

24. In order to make the effective acceleration due to gravity equal to zero at the equator, the angular velocity of rotation of the earth about its axis should be ($g = 10\ ms^{-2}$ and radius of earth is 64000 km)

(a) Zero (b) $\frac{1}{800}$ rad sec^{-1}
(c) $\frac{1}{80}$ rad sec^{-1} (d) $\frac{1}{8}$ rad sec^{-1}

25. A body weighs 72 N on the surface of the earth. What is the gravitational force on it due to earth at a height equal to half the radius of the earth from the surface?

(a) 32 N (b) 28 N (c) 16 N (d) 72 N

26. A body weighs W newton at the surface of the earth. Its weight at a height equal to half the radius of the earth, will be

(a) $\frac{W}{2}$ (b) $\frac{2W}{3}$ (c) $\frac{4W}{9}$ (d) $\frac{8W}{27}$

27. A shell of mass M and radius R has a point mass m placed at a distance r from its centre. The graph of gravitational potential energy U(r) vs distance r will be

(a)
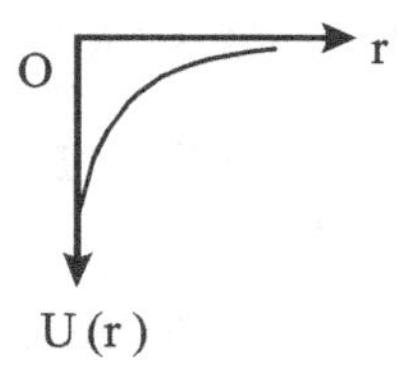

(b)
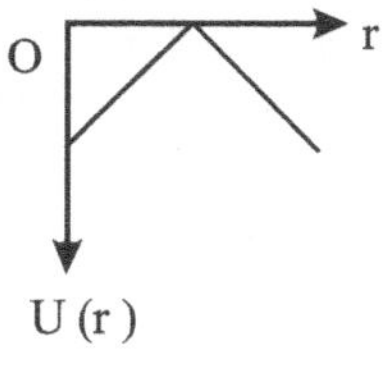

(c)
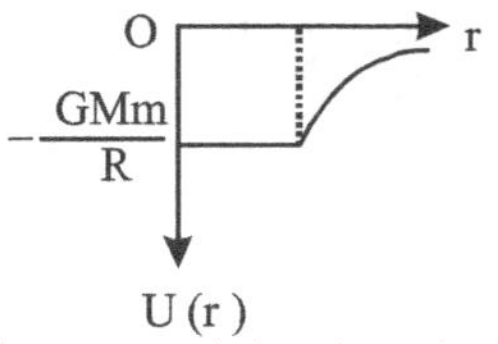

(d)
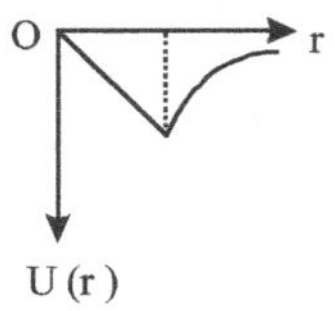

28. The largest and the shortest distance of the earth from the sun are r_1 and r_2. Its distance from the sun when it is at perpendicular to the major-axis of the orbit drawn from the sun

(a) $(r_1+r_2)/4$ (b) $(r_1+r_2)/(r_1-r_2)$
(c) $2r_1r_2/(r_1+r_2)$ (d) $(r_1+r_2)/3$

29. A planet is moving in an elliptical orbit around the sun. If T, V, E and L stand respectively for its kinetic energy, gravitational potential energy, total energy and magnitude of angular momentum about the centre of force, then which of the following is correct ?

(a) T is conserved
(b) V is always positive
(c) E is always negative
(d) L is conserved but direction of vector L changes continuously

30. The earth is assumed to be sphere of radius R. A platform is arranged at a height R from the surface of Earth. The escape velocity of a body from this platform is kv, where v is its escape velocity from the surface of the earth. The value of k is

(a) $\frac{1}{\sqrt{2}}$ (b) $\frac{1}{3}$ (c) $\frac{1}{2}$ (d) $\sqrt{2}$

31. A solid sphere of mass M and radius R is surrounded by a spherical shell of same mass M and radius 2R as shown. A small particle of mass m is released from rest from a height h [<< R] above the shell. There is a hole in the shell.

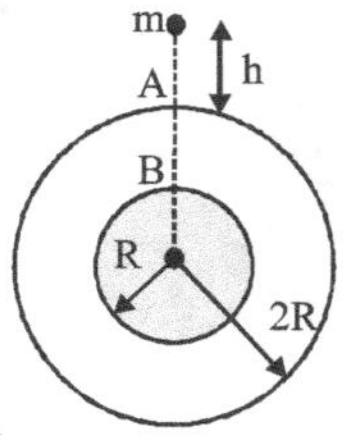

What time will it enter the hole at A ?

(a) $2\sqrt{\frac{hR^2}{GM}}$ (b) $\sqrt{\frac{2hR^2}{GM}}$
(c) $\sqrt{\frac{hR^2}{GM}}$ (d) $\sqrt{\frac{3hR^2}{GM}}$

32. A body starts from rest from a point distance R_0 from the centre of the earth. The velocity acquired by the body when it reaches the surface of the earth will be (R represents radius of the earth).

(a) $2GM\left(\frac{1}{R}-\frac{1}{R_0}\right)$ (b) $\sqrt{2GM\left(\frac{1}{R_0}-\frac{1}{R}\right)}$
(c) $GM\left(\frac{1}{R}-\frac{1}{R_0}\right)$ (d) $2GM\sqrt{\left(\frac{1}{R}-\frac{1}{R_0}\right)}$

RESPONSE GRID					
	20. ⓐⓑⓒⓓ	21. ⓐⓑⓒⓓ	22. ⓐⓑⓒⓓ	23. ⓐⓑⓒⓓ	24. ⓐⓑⓒⓓ
	25. ⓐⓑⓒⓓ	26. ⓐⓑⓒⓓ	27. ⓐⓑⓒⓓ	28. ⓐⓑⓒⓓ	29. ⓐⓑⓒⓓ
	30. ⓐⓑⓒⓓ	31. ⓐⓑⓒⓓ	32. ⓐⓑⓒⓓ		

Space for Rough Work

33. A satellite of mass M is moving in a circle of radius R under a centripetal force given by $(-k/R^2)$, where k is a constant. Then

(a) The kinetic energy of the particle is $\dfrac{k}{12}R$

(b) The total energy of the particle is $\left(-\dfrac{k}{2R}\right)$

(c) The kinetic energy of the particle is $\left(-\dfrac{k}{R}\right)$

(d) The potential energy of the particle is $\left(\dfrac{k}{2R}\right)$

34. The change in the value of 'g' at a height 'h' above the surface of the earth is the same as at a depth 'd' below the surface of earth. When both 'd' and 'h' are much smaller than the radius of earth, then which one of the following is correct?

(a) $d=\dfrac{3h}{2}$ (b) $d=\dfrac{h}{2}$ (c) $d=h$ (d) $d=2h$

35. Two identical geostationary satellites are moving with equal speeds in the same orbit but their sense of rotation brings them on a collision course. The debris will
(a) fall down
(b) move up
(c) begin to move from east to west in the same orbit
(d) begin to move from west to east in the same orbit

36. A diametrical tunnel is dug across the Earth. A ball is dropped into the tunnel from one side. The velocity of the ball when it reaches the centre of the Earth is .... (Given : gravitational

potential at the centre of Earth $= -\dfrac{3}{2}\dfrac{GM}{R}$)

(a) $\sqrt{R}$ (b) $\sqrt{gR}$ (c) $\sqrt{2.5gR}$ (d) $\sqrt{7.1gR}$

37. A satellite revolves around the earth of radius R in a circular orbit of radius 3R. The percentage increase in energy required to lift it to an orbit of radius 5R is
(a) 10%   (b) 20%   (c) 30%   (d) 40%

38. A (nonrotating) star collapses onto itself from an initial radius R_i with its mass remaining unchanged. Which curve in figure best gives the gravitational acceleration a_g on the surface of the star as a function of the radius of the star during the collapse

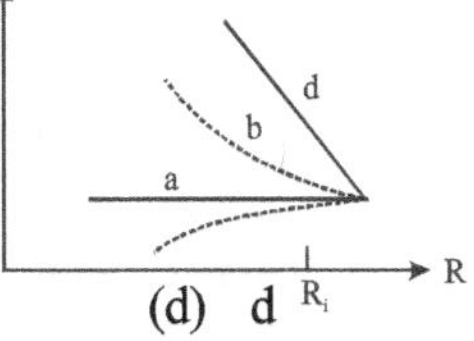

(a) a   (b) b   (c) c   (d) d

39. If the earth is treated as a sphere of radius R and mass M; its angular momentum about the axis of its rotation with period T, is

(a) $\dfrac{\pi MR^3}{T}$ (b) $\dfrac{MR^2\pi}{T}$ (c) $\dfrac{2\pi MR^2}{5T}$ (d) $\dfrac{4\pi MR^2}{5T}$

40. A satellite is launched into a circular orbit of radius R around the earth. A second satellite is launched into an orbit of radius 1.01 R. The period of second satellite is larger than the first one by approximately
(a) 0.5%   (b) 1.0%   (c) 1.5%   (d) 3.0%

41. A uniform spherical shell gradually shrinks maintaining its shape. The gravitational potential at the centre
(a) increases   (b) decreases
(c) remains constant   (d) cannot say

42. The depth d at which the value of acceleration due to gravity becomes $\dfrac{1}{n}$ times the value at the surface of the earth, is [R = radius of the earth]

(a) $\dfrac{R}{n}$ (b) $R\left(\dfrac{n-1}{n}\right)$ (c) $\dfrac{R}{n^2}$ (d) $R\left(\dfrac{n}{n+1}\right)$

43. Radius of moon is 1/4 times that of earth and mass is 1/81 times that of earth. The point at which gravitational field due to earth becomes equal and opposite to that of moon, is (Distance between centres of earth and moon is 60R, where R is radius of earth)
(a) 5.75 R from centre of moon
(b) 16 R from surface of moon
(c) 53 R from centre of earth
(d) 54 R from centre of earth

44. If earth is supposed to be a sphere of radius R, if g_{30} is value of acceleration due to gravity at lattitude of 30° and g at the equator, the value of $g - g_{30}$ is

(a) $\dfrac{1}{4}\omega^2R$ (b) $\dfrac{3}{4}\omega^2R$ (c) ω^2R (d) $\dfrac{1}{2}\omega^2R$

45. What is the minimum energy required to launch a satellite of mass m from the surface of a planet of mass M and radius R in a circular orbit at an altitude of 2R?

(a) $\dfrac{5GmM}{6R}$ (b) $\dfrac{2GmM}{3R}$ (c) $\dfrac{GmM}{2R}$ (d) $\dfrac{GmM}{2R}$

RESPONSE GRID					
	33. ⓐⓑⓒⓓ	34. ⓐⓑⓒⓓ	35. ⓐⓑⓒⓓ	36. ⓐⓑⓒⓓ	37. ⓐⓑⓒⓓ
	38. ⓐⓑⓒⓓ	39. ⓐⓑⓒⓓ	40. ⓐⓑⓒⓓ	41. ⓐⓑⓒⓓ	42. ⓐⓑⓒⓓ
	43. ⓐⓑⓒⓓ	44. ⓐⓑⓒⓓ	45. ⓐⓑⓒⓓ		

DAILY PRACTICE PROBLEM DPP CHAPTERWISE CP07 - PHYSICS

Total Questions	45	Total Marks	180
Attempted		Correct	
Incorrect		Net Score	
Cut-off Score	45	Qualifying Score	60
Success Gap = Net Score − Qualifying Score			
Net Score = (Correct × 4) − (Incorrect × 1)			

Date : ___________ **Start Time :** ___________ **End Time :** ___________

PHYSICS $\boxed{\textbf{CP08}}$

SYLLABUS : Mechanical Properties of Solids

Max. Marks : 180   **Marking Scheme :** (+4) for correct & (−1) for incorrect answer   **Time : 60 min.**

INSTRUCTIONS : This Daily Practice Problem Sheet contains 45 MCQs. For each question only one option is correct. Darken the correct circle/ bubble in the Response Grid provided on each page.

1. Two wires A and B are of the same material. Their lengths are in the ratio 1 : 2 and the diameter are in the ratio 2 : 1. If they are pulled by the same force, then increase in length will be in the ratio
   (a) 2 : 1   (b) 1 : 4   (c) 1 : 8   (d) 8 : 1

2. The load versus elongation graphs for four wires of same length and made of the same material are shown in the figure. The thinnest wire is represented by the line
   (a) OA
   (b) OC
   (c) OD
   (d) OB

3. A spring of force constant 800 N/m has an extension of 5 cm. The work done in extending it from 5 cm to 15 cm is
   (a) 16 J   (b) 8 J   (c) 32 J   (d) 24 J

4. A metal wire of length L_1 and area of cross-section A is attached to a rigid support. Another metal wire of length L_2 and of the same cross-sectional area is attached to the free end of the first wire. A body of mass M is then suspended from the free end of the second wire. If Y_1 and Y_2 are the Young's moduli of the wires respectively, the effective force constant of the system of two wires is
   (a) $\dfrac{(Y_1Y_2)A}{2(Y_1L_2 + Y_2L_1)}$
   (b) $\dfrac{(Y_1Y_2)A}{(L_1L_2)^{1/2}}$
   (c) $\dfrac{(Y_1Y_2)A}{Y_1L_2 + Y_2L_1}$
   (d) $\dfrac{(Y_1Y_2)^{1/2}A}{(L_2L_1)^{1/2}}$

5. The approximate depth of an ocean is 2700 m. The compressibility of water is 45.4×10^{-11} Pa^{-1} and density of water is 10^3 kg/m^3. What fractional compression of water will be obtained at the bottom of the ocean ?
   (a) 1.0×10^{-2} (b) 1.2×10^{-2}
   (c) 1.4×10^{-2} (d) 0.8×10^{-2}

6. The Young's modulus of steel is twice that of brass. Two wires of same length and of same area of cross section, one of steel and another of brass are suspended from the same roof. If we want the lower ends of the wires to be at the same level, then the weights added to the steel and brass wires must be in the ratio of :
   (a) 2 : 1   (b) 4 : 1   (c) 1 : 1   (d) 1 : 2

7. Choose the wrong statement.
   (a) The bulk modulus for solids is much larger than for liquids.
   (b) Gases are least compressible.
   (c) The incompressibility of the solids is due to the tight coupling between neighbouring atoms.
   (d) The reciprocal of the bulk modulus is called compressibility.

RESPONSE GRID					
1. ⓐⓑⓒⓓ	2. ⓐⓑⓒⓓ	3. ⓐⓑⓒⓓ	4. ⓐⓑⓒⓓ	5. ⓐⓑⓒⓓ
6. ⓐⓑⓒⓓ	7. ⓐⓑⓒⓓ				

Space for Rough Work

8. A copper wire of length 1.0 m and a steel wire of length 0.5 m having equal cross-sectional areas are joined end to end. The composite wire is stretched by a certain load which stretches the copper wire by 1 mm. If the Young's modulii of copper and steel are respectively 1.0×10^{11} Nm^{-2} and 2.0×10^{11} Nm^{-2}, the total extension of the composite wire is :

(a) 1.75 mm (b) 2.0 mm (c) 1.50 mm (d) 1.25 mm

9. A cube at temperature 0°C is compressed equally from all sides by an external pressure P. By what amount should its temperature be raised to bring it back to the size it had before the external pressure was applied. The bulk modulus of the material of the cube is B and the coefficient of linear expansion is a.

(a) P/Bα (b) P/3Bα (c) 3πα/B (d) 3B/P

10. The diagram below shows the change in the length X of a thin uniform wire caused by the application of stress F at two different temperatures T_1 and T_2. The variation shown suggests that

(a) $T_1 > T_2$

(b) $T_1 < T_2$

(c) $T_2 > T_1$

(d) $T_1 \geq T_2$

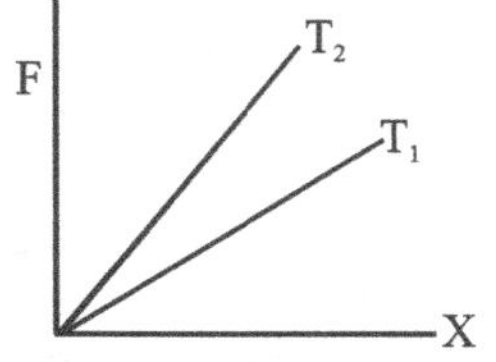

11. If the ratio of lengths, radii and Young's moduli of steel and brass wires in the figure are a, b and c respectively, then the corresponding ratio of increase in their lengths is :

(a) $\dfrac{3c}{2ab^2}$

(b) $\dfrac{2a^2c}{b}$

(c) $\dfrac{3a}{2b^2c}$

(d) $\dfrac{2ac}{b^2}$

12. The Young's modulus of brass and steel are respectively 10^{10} N/m^2. and 2×10^{10} N/m^2. A brass wire and a steel wire of the same length are extended by 1 mm under the same force, the radii of brass and steel wires are R_B and R_S respectively. Then

(a) $R_S = \sqrt{2}\, R_B$ (b) $R_S = R_B / \sqrt{2}$

(c) $R_S = 4R_B$ (d) $R_S = R_B / 4$

13. Steel ruptures when a shear of 3.5×10^8 N m^{-2} is applied. The force needed to punch a 1 cm diameter hole in a steel sheet 0.3 cm thick is nearly:

(a) 1.4×10^4 N (b) 2.7×10^4 N
(c) 3.3×10^4 N (d) 1.1×10^4 N

14. A ball falling in a lake of depth 400 m has a decrease of 0.2% in its volume at the bottom. The bulk modulus of the material of the ball is (in N m^{-2})

(a) 9.8×10^9 (b) 9.8×10^{10}
(c) 1.96×10^{10} (d) 1.96×10^9

15. A circular tube of mean radius 8 cm and thickness 0.04 cm is melted up and recast into a solid rod of the same length. The ratio of the torsional rigidities of the circular tube and the solid rod is

(a) $\dfrac{(8.02)^4 - (7.98)^4}{(0.8)^4}$ (b) $\dfrac{(8.02)^2 - (7.98)^2}{(0.8)^2}$

(c) $\dfrac{(0.8)^2}{(8.02)^4 - (7.98)^4}$ (d) $\dfrac{(0.8)^2}{(8.02)^3 - (7.98)^2}$

16. Two wires are made of the same material and have the same volume. However wire 1 has cross-sectional area A and wire 2 has cross-sectional area $3A$. If the length of wire 1 increases by Δx on applying force F, how much force is needed to stretch wire 2 by the same amount?

(a) $4F$ (b) $6F$ (c) $9F$ (d) F

17. In materials like aluminium and copper, the correct order of magnitude of various elastic modului is:

(a) Young's modulus < shear modulus < bulk modulus.
(b) Bulk modulus < shear modulus < Young's modulus
(c) Shear modulus < Young's modulus < bulk modulus.
(d) Bulk modulus < Young's modulus < shear modulus.

18. What per cent of length of wire increases by applying a stress of 1 kg weight/mm^2 on it?
($Y = 1 \times 10^{11}$ N/m^2 and 1 kg weight = 9.8 newton)

(a) 0.0067% (b) 0.0098%
(c) 0.0088% (d) 0.0078%

19. An elastic string of unstretched length L and force constant k is stretched by a small length x. It is further stretched by another small length y. The work done in the second stretching is :

(a) $\dfrac{1}{2}ky^2$ (b) $\dfrac{1}{2}k(x^2 + y^2)$

(c) $\dfrac{1}{2}k(x+y)^2$ (d) $\dfrac{1}{2}ky(2x+y)$

20. Two, spring P and Q of force constants k_p and $k_Q \left(k_Q = \dfrac{k_p}{2} \right)$ are stretched by applying forces of equal magnitude. If the energy stored in Q is E, then the energy stored in P is

(a) E (b) 2E (c) E/2 (d) E/4

<table>
<tr><td rowspan="3">RESPONSE GRID</td><td>8. (a)(b)(c)(d)</td><td>9. (a)(b)(c)(d)</td><td>10. (a)(b)(c)(d)</td><td>11. (a)(b)(c)(d)</td><td>12. (a)(b)(c)(d)</td></tr>
<tr><td>13. (a)(b)(c)(d)</td><td>14. (a)(b)(c)(d)</td><td>15. (a)(b)(c)(d)</td><td>16. (a)(b)(c)(d)</td><td>17. (a)(b)(c)(d)</td></tr>
<tr><td>18. (a)(b)(c)(d)</td><td>19. (a)(b)(c)(d)</td><td>20. (a)(b)(c)(d)</td><td></td><td></td></tr>
</table>

21. The pressure that has to be applied to the ends of a steel wire of length 10 cm to keep its length constant when its temperature is raised by 100°C is:

(For steel Young's modulus is $2 \times 10^{11}\, \mathrm{Nm^{-2}}$ and coefficient of thermal expansion is $1.1 \times 10^{-5}\, \mathrm{K^{-1}}$)

(a) 2.2×10^8 Pa   (b) 2.2×10^9 Pa

(c) 2.2×10^7 Pa   (d) 2.2×10^6 Pa

22. A steel ring of radius r and cross sectional area A is fitted onto a wooden disc of radius R (R > r). If the Young's modulus of steel is Y, then the force with which the steel ring is expanded is

(a) A Y (R/r)   (b) A Y (R−r)/r
(c) (Y/A)[(R−r)/r]   (d) Y r/A R

23. Two wires A and B of same material and of equal length with the radii in the ratio 1 : 2 are subjected to identical loads. If the length of A increases by 8 mm, then the increase in length of B is
(a) 2 mm   (b) 4 mm   (c) 8 mm   (d) 16 mm

24. A material has poisson's ratio 0.50. If a uniform rod of it suffers a longitudinal strain of 2×10^{-3}, then the percentage change in volume is
(a) 0.6   (b) 0.4   (c) 0.2   (d) Zero

25. The upper end of a wire of diameter 12mm and length 1m is clamped and its other end is twisted through an angle of 30°. The angle of shear is
(a) 18°   (b) 0.18°   (c) 36°   (d) 0.36°

26. The pressure on an object of bulk modulus B undergoing hydraulic compression due to a stress exerted by surrounding fluid having volume strain $\left(\dfrac{\Delta V}{V}\right)^2$ is

(a) $B^2\left(\dfrac{\Delta V}{V}\right)$ (b) $B\left(\dfrac{\Delta V}{V}\right)^2$

(c) $\dfrac{1}{B}\left(\dfrac{\Delta V}{V}\right)$ (d) $B\left(\dfrac{\Delta V}{V}\right)$

27. A structural steel rod has a radius of 10 mm and length of 1.0 m. A 100 kN force stretches it along its length. Young's modulus of structural steel is $2 \times 10^{11}\, \mathrm{Nm^{-2}}$. The percentage strain is about
(a) 0.16%   (b) 0.32%   (c) 0.08%   (d) 0.24%

28. A beam of metal supported at the two edges is loaded at the centre. The depression at the centre is proportional to

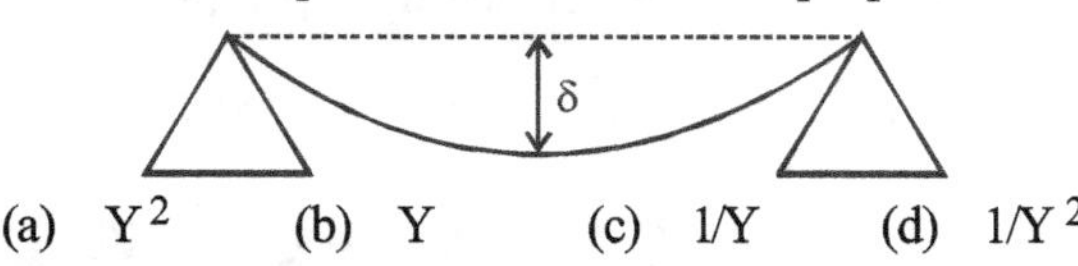

(a) Y^2 (b) Y   (c) 1/Y   (d) $1/Y^2$

29. When a 4 kg mass is hung vertically on a light spring that obeys Hooke's law, the spring stretches by 2 cms. The work required to be done by an external agent in stretching this spring by 5 cms will be (g = 9.8 m/sec^2)
(a) 4.900 joule   (b) 2.450 joule
(c) 0.495 joule   (d) 0.245 joule

30. The length of a metal is ℓ_1 when the tension in it is T_1 and is ℓ_2 when the tension is T_2. The original length of the wire is

(a) $\dfrac{\ell_1+\ell_2}{2}$ (b) $\dfrac{\ell_1 T_2+\ell_2 T_1}{T_1+T_2}$

(c) $\dfrac{\ell_1 T_2-\ell_2 T_1}{T_2-T_1}$ (d) $\sqrt{T_1 T_2 \ell_1 \ell_2}$

31. For the same cross-sectional area and for a given load, the ratio of depressions for the beam of a square cross-section and circular cross-section is
(a) $3:\pi$ (b) $\pi:3$ (c) $1:\pi$ (d) $\pi:1$

32. The bulk moduli of ethanol, mercury and water are given as 0.9, 25 and 2.2 respectively in units of $10^9\, \mathrm{Nm^{-2}}$. For a given value of pressure, the fractional compression in volume is $\dfrac{\Delta V}{V}$. Which of the following statements about $\dfrac{\Delta V}{V}$ for these three liquids is correct ?
(a) Ethanol > Water > Mercury
(b) Water > Ethanol > Mercury
(c) Mercury > Ethanol > Water
(d) Ethanol > Mercury > Water

33. The graph given is a stress-strain curve for

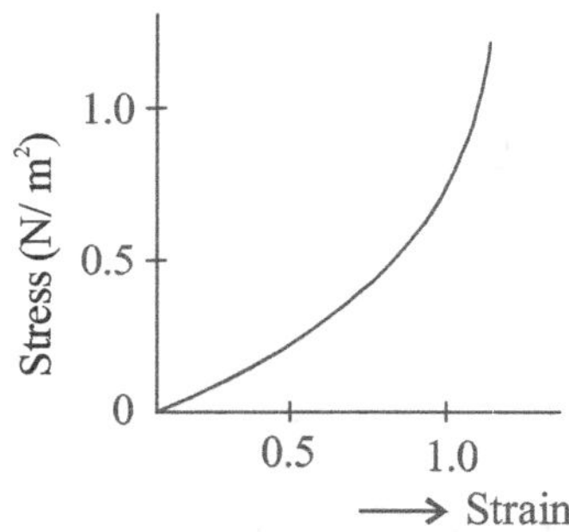

(a) elastic objects   (b) plastics
(c) elastomers   (d) None of these

34. A metal rod of Young's modulus $2 \times 10^{10}\, \mathrm{N\,m^{-2}}$ undergoes an elastic strain of 0.06%. The energy per unit volume stored in J m^{-3} is
(a) 3600   (b) 7200   (c) 10800   (d) 14400

35. Two wires of the same material and same length but diameters in the ratio 1 : 2 are stretched by the same force. The potential energy per unit volume of the two wires will be in the ratio
(a) 1 : 2   (b) 4 : 1   (c) 2 : 1   (d) 16 : 1

RESPONSE GRID					
	21. ⓐⓑⓒⓓ	22. ⓐⓑⓒⓓ	23. ⓐⓑⓒⓓ	24. ⓐⓑⓒⓓ	25. ⓐⓑⓒⓓ
	26. ⓐⓑⓒⓓ	27. ⓐⓑⓒⓓ	28. ⓐⓑⓒⓓ	29. ⓐⓑⓒⓓ	30. ⓐⓑⓒⓓ
	31. ⓐⓑⓒⓓ	32. ⓐⓑⓒⓓ	33. ⓐⓑⓒⓓ	34. ⓐⓑⓒⓓ	35. ⓐⓑⓒⓓ

36. The length of an elastic string is a metre when the longitudinal tension is 4 N and b metre when the longitudinal tension is 5 N. The length of the string in metre when the longitudinal tension is 9 N is

(a) $a - b$ (b) $5b - 4a$ (c) $2b - \dfrac{1}{4}a$ (d) $4a - 3b$

37. A force of 10^3 newton, stretches the length of a hanging wire by 1 millimetre. The force required to stretch a wire of same material and length but having four times the diameter by 1 millimetre is

(a) 4×10^3 N   (b) 16×10^3 N

(c) $\dfrac{1}{4} \times 10^3$ N   (d) $\dfrac{1}{16} \times 10^3$ N

38. A steel wire of length l and cross sectional area A is stretched by 1 cm under a given load. When the same load is applied to another steel wire of double its length and half of its cross section area, the amount of stretching (extension) is

(a) 0.5 cm   (b) 2 cm   (c) 4 cm   (d) 1.5 cm

39. The adjacent graph shows the extension (Δl) of a wire of length 1 m suspended from the top of a roof at one end with a load W connected to the other end. If the cross-sectional area of the wire is 10^{-6} m^2, calculate the Young's modulus of the material of the wire :

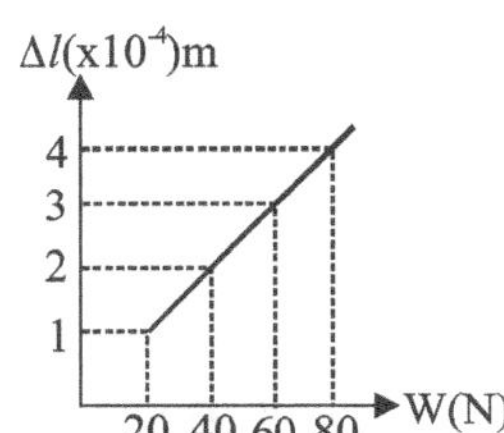

(a) 2×10^{11} N/m^2 (b) 2×10^{-11} N/m^2

(c) 3×10^{-12} N/m^2 (d) 2×10^{-13} N/m^2

40. If a rubber ball is taken at the depth of 200 m in a pool, its volume decreases by 0.1%. If the density of the water is 1×10^3 kg/m^3 and g = 10 m/s^2, then the volume elasticity in N/m^2 will be

(a) 10^8 (b) 2×10^8 (c) 10^9 (d) 2×10^9

41. A ball is falling in a lake of depth 200 m creates a decrease 0.1 % in its volume at the bottom. The bulk modulus of the material of the ball will be

(a) 19.6×10^{-8} N/m^2 (b) 19.6×10^{10} N/m^2

(c) 19.6×10^{-10} N/m^2 (d) 19.6×10^8 N/m^2

42. The diagram shows a force-extension graph for a rubber band. Consider the following statements :

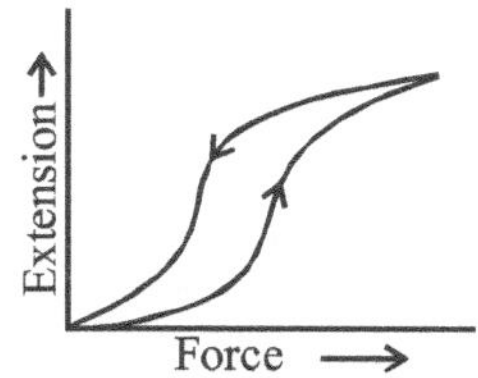

I.   It will be easier to compress this rubber than expand it

II.   Rubber does not return to its original length after it is stretched

III.   The rubber band will get heated if it is stretched and released

Which of these can be deduced from the graph:

(a) III only   (b) II and III   (c) I and III   (d) I only

43. The Poisson's ratio of a material is 0.5. If a force is applied to a wire of this material, there is a decrease in the cross-sectional area by 4%. The percentage increase in the length is:

(a) 1%   (b) 2%   (c) 2.5%   (d) 4%

44. Copper of fixed volume 'V; is drawn into wire of length 'l'. When this wire is subjected to a constant force 'F', the extension produced in the wire is 'Δl'. Which of the following graphs is a straight line?

(a) Δl versus $\dfrac{1}{l}$ (b) Δl versus l^2

(c) Δl versus $\dfrac{1}{l^2}$ (d) Δl versus l

45. When a 4 kg mass is hung vertically on a light spring that obeys Hooke's law, the spring stretches by 2 cms. The work required to be done by an external agent in stretching this spring by 5 cm will be (g = 9.8 m/sec^2)

(a) 4.900 joule   (b) 2.450 joule

(c) 0.495 joule   (d) 0.245 joule

RESPONSE	36. ⓐⓑⓒⓓ	37. ⓐⓑⓒⓓ	38. ⓐⓑⓒⓓ	39. ⓐⓑⓒⓓ	40. ⓐⓑⓒⓓ
GRID	41. ⓐⓑⓒⓓ	42. ⓐⓑⓒⓓ	43. ⓐⓑⓒⓓ	44. ⓐⓑⓒⓓ	45. ⓐⓑⓒⓓ

DAILY PRACTICE PROBLEM DPP CHAPTERWISE CP08 - PHYSICS

Total Questions	45	Total Marks	180
Attempted		Correct	
Incorrect		Net Score	
Cut-off Score	50	Qualifying Score	70
Success Gap = Net Score − Qualifying Score			
Net Score = (Correct × 4) − (Incorrect × 1)			

Date :   Start Time :   End Time :

PHYSICS $\boxed{\text{CP09}}$

SYLLABUS : Mechanical Properties of Fluids

Max. Marks : 180 **Marking Scheme :** (+4) for correct & (–1) for incorrect answer **Time : 60 min.**

INSTRUCTIONS : This Daily Practice Problem Sheet contains 45 MCQs. For each question only one option is correct. Darken the correct circle/ bubble in the Response Grid provided on each page.

---

1. The density of water at the surface of ocean is ρ. If the bulk modulus of water is B, what is the density of ocean water at a depth where the pressure is nP_0, where P_0 is the atmospheric pressure ?

(a) $\dfrac{\rho B}{B-(n-1)P_0}$

(b) $\dfrac{\rho B}{B+(n-1)P_0}$

(c) $\dfrac{\rho B}{B-nP_0}$

(d) $\dfrac{\rho B}{B+nP_0}$

2. A ball of radius r and density ρ falls freely under gravity through a distance h before entering water. Velocity of ball does not change even on entering water. If viscosity of water is η the value of h is given by

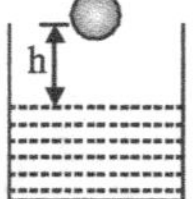

(a) $\dfrac{2}{9}r^2\left(\dfrac{1-\rho}{\eta}\right)g$

(b) $\dfrac{2}{81}r^2\left(\dfrac{\rho-1}{\eta}\right)g$

(c) $\dfrac{2}{81}r^4\left(\dfrac{\rho-1}{\eta}\right)^2 g$

(d) $\dfrac{2}{9}r^4\left(\dfrac{\rho-1}{\eta}\right)^2 g$

3. Two parallel glass plates are dipped partly in the liquid of density 'd' keeping them vertical . If the distance between the plates is 'x', surface tension for liquids is T and angle of contact is θ, then rise of liquid between the plates due to capillary will be

(a) $\dfrac{T\cos\theta}{xd}$

(b) $\dfrac{2T\cos\theta}{xdg}$

(c) $\dfrac{2T}{xdg\cos\theta}$

(d) $\dfrac{T\cos\theta}{xdg}$

4. A liquid is allowed to flow into a tube of truncated cone shape. Identify the correct statement from the following

(a) The speed is high at the wider end and high at the narrow end

(b) The speed is low at the wider end and high at the narrow end

(c) The speed is same at both ends in a streamline flow

(d) The liquid flows with uniform velocity in the tube

5. A wide vessel with a small hole at the bottom is filled with water (density ρ_1, height h_1) and kerosene (density ρ_2, height h_2). Neglecting viscosity effects, the speed with which water flows out is :

(a) $[2g(h_1+h_2)]^{1/2}$

(b) $[2g(h_1\rho_1+h_2\rho_2)]^{1/2}$

(c) $[2g(h_1+h_2(\rho_2/\rho_1))]^{1/2}$

(d) $[2g(h_1+h_2(\rho_1/\rho_2))]^{1/2}$

RESPONSE GRID	1. ⓐⓑⓒⓓ	2. ⓐⓑⓒⓓ	3. ⓐⓑⓒⓓ	4. ⓐⓑⓒⓓ	5. ⓐⓑⓒⓓ

Space for Rough Work

6. A capillary tube of radius r is immersed vertically in a liquid such that liquid rises in it to height h (less than the length of the tube). Mass of liquid in the capillary tube is m. If radius of the capillary tube is increased by 50%, then mass of liquid that will rise in the tube, is

(a) $\dfrac{2}{3}m$ (b) $\dfrac{4}{9}m$ (c) $\dfrac{3}{2}m$ (d) $\dfrac{9}{4}m$

7. A lead shot of 1 mm diameter falls through a long column of glycerine. The variation of its velocity v with distance covered is represented by

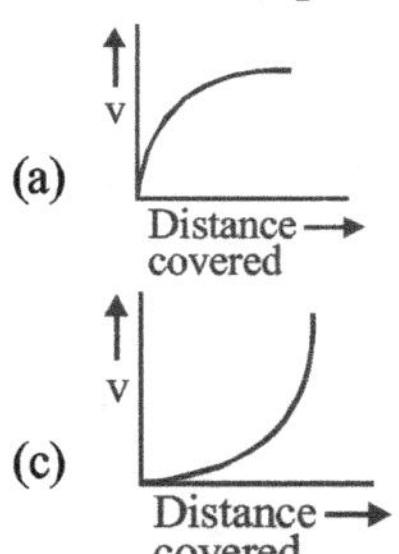

(a) / (b) / (c) / (d)

8. Two mercury drops (each of radius 'r') merge to form bigger drop. The surface energy of the bigger drop, if T is the surface tension, is :

(a) $4\pi r^2 T$ (b) $2\pi r^2 T$
(c) $2^{8/3}\pi r^2 T$ (d) $2^{5/3}\pi r^2 T$

9. Wax is coated on the inner wall of a capillary tube and the tube is then dipped in water. Then, compared to the unwaxed capillary, the angle of contact θ and the height h upto which water rises change. These changes are :
(a) θ increases and h also increases
(b) θ decreases and h also decreases
(c) θ increases and h decreases
(d) θ decreases and h increases

10. A rain drop of radius 0.3 mm has a terminal velocity in air = 1 m/s. The viscosity of air is 8×10^{-5} poise. The viscous force on it is
(a) 45.2×10^{-4} dyne (b) 101.73×10^{-5} dyne
(c) 16.95×10^{-4} dyne (d) 16.95×10^{-5} dyne

11. A water tank of height 10m, completely filled with water is placed on a level ground. It has two holes one at 3 m and the other at 7 m from its base. The water ejecting from
(a) both the holes will fall at the same spot
(b) upper hole will fall farther than that from the lower hole
(c) upper hole will fall closer than that from the lower hole
(d) more information is required

12. Two capillary of length L and 2L and of radius R and 2R are connected in series. The net rate of flow of fluid through them will be (given rate to the flow through single capillary,

$X = \dfrac{\pi PR^4}{8\eta L}$)

(a) $\dfrac{8}{9}X$ (b) $\dfrac{9}{8}X$ (c) $\dfrac{5}{7}X$ (d) $\dfrac{7}{5}X$

13. A candle of diameter d is floating on a liquid in a cylindrical container of diameter D (D >> d) as shown in figure. If it is burning at the rate of 2 cm/hour then the top of the candle will

(a) remain at the same height
(b) fall at the rate of 1 cm/hour
(c) fall at the rate of 2 cm/hour
(d) go up at the rate of 1 cm/hour

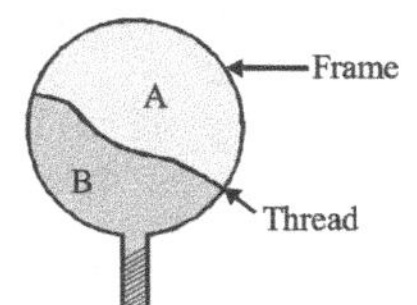

14. An isolated and charged spherical soap bubble has a radius r and the pressure inside is atmospheric. T is the surface tension of soap solution. If charge on drop is $X\,\pi r\sqrt{2rT\varepsilon_0}$ then find the value of X.
(a) 8 (b) 9 (c) 7 (d) 2

15. A thread is tied slightly loose to a wire frame as in figure and the frame is dipped into a soap solution and taken out. The frame is completely covered with the film. When the portion A is punctured with a pin, the thread
(a) becomes concave towards A
(b) becomes convex towards A
(c) remains in the initial position
(d) either (a) or (b) depending on the size of A w.r. t. B

16. Which of the following expressions represents the excess of pressure inside the soap bubble?

(a) $P_i - P_o = \dfrac{s}{r}$ (b) $P_i - P_o = \dfrac{2s}{r}$

(c) $P_i - P_o = \dfrac{2s}{r} + h\rho g$ (d) $P_i - P_o = \dfrac{4s}{r}$

17. A spherical solid ball of volume V is made of a material of density ρ_1. It is falling through a liquid of density ρ_1 ($\rho_2 < \rho_1$). Assume that the liquid applies a viscous force on the ball that is proportional to the square of its speed v, i.e., $F_{viscous} = -kv^2$ ($k > 0$). The terminal speed of the ball is

(a) $\sqrt{\dfrac{Vg(\rho_1 - \rho_2)}{k}}$ (b) $\dfrac{Vg\rho_1}{k}$

(c) $\sqrt{\dfrac{Vg\rho_1}{k}}$ (d) $\dfrac{Vg(\rho_1 - \rho_2)}{k}$

18. Select the correct statements from the following.
(a) Bunsen burner and sprayers work on Bernoulli's principle
(b) Blood flow in arteries is explained by Bernoulli's principle
(c) A siphon works on account of atmospheric pressure.
(d) All are correct

<table>
<tr><td rowspan="3">RESPONSE GRID</td><td>6. ⓐⓑ©ⓓ</td><td>7. ⓐⓑ©ⓓ</td><td>8. ⓐⓑ©ⓓ</td><td>9. ⓐⓑ©ⓓ</td><td>10. ⓐⓑ©ⓓ</td></tr>
<tr><td>11. ⓐⓑ©ⓓ</td><td>12. ⓐⓑ©ⓓ</td><td>13. ⓐⓑ©ⓓ</td><td>14. ⓐⓑ©ⓓ</td><td>15. ⓐⓑ©ⓓ</td></tr>
<tr><td>16. ⓐⓑ©ⓓ</td><td>17. ⓐⓑ©ⓓ</td><td>18. ⓐⓑ©ⓓ</td><td></td><td></td></tr>
</table>

19. The wetability of a surface by a liquid depends primarily on
    (a) surface tension
    (b) density
    (c) angle of contact between the surface and the liquid
    (d) viscosity
20. The relative velocity of two parallel layers of water is 8 cm/sec. If the perpendicular distance between the layers is 0.1 cm, then velocity gradient will be
    (a) 80/sec (b) 60 /sec (c) 50/sec (d) 40/sec
21. Choose the correct statement
    (a) Terminal velocities of rain drops are proportional to square of their radii
    (b) Water proof agents decrease the angle of contact between water and fibres
    (c) Detergents increase the surface tension of water
    (d) Hydraulic machines work on the principle of Torricelli's law
22. When a ball is released from rest in a very long column of viscous liquid, its downward acceleration is 'a' (just after release). Its acceleration when it has acquired two third of the maximum velocity is a/X. Find the value of X.
    (a) 2   (b) 3   (c) 4   (d) 5
23. A ring is cut from a platinum tube 8.5 cm internal and 8.7 cm external diameter. It is supported horizontally from the pan of a balance, so that it comes in contact with the water in a glass vessel. If an extra 3.97. If is required to pull it away from water, the surface tension of water is
    (a) 72 dyne cm^{-1} (b) 70.80 dyne cm^{-1}
    (c) 63.35 dyne cm^{-1} (d) 60 dyne cm^{-1}
24. Which of the following graph represents the variation of surface tension with temperature over small temperature ranges for water?

(a) 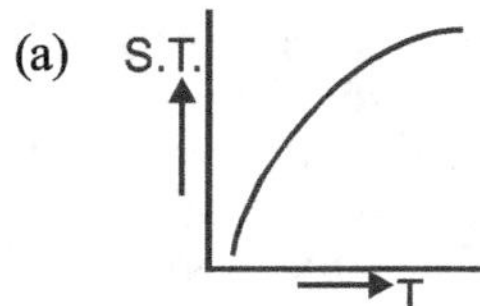
(b) 
(c) 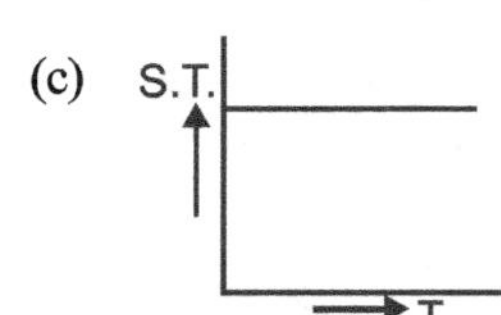
(d) 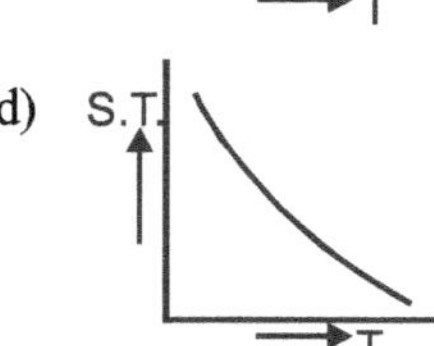

25. When a large air bubble rises from the bottom of a lake to the surface, its radius doubles. If the atmospheric pressure is equal to that of a column of water of height H, then depth of the lake is
    (a) H   (b) 2H   (c) 7H   (d) 8H
26. What is the velocity v of a metallic ball of radius r falling in a tank of liquid at the instant when its acceleration is one -half that of a freely falling body ? (The densities of metal and of liquid are ρ and σ respectively, and the viscosity of the liquid is η).

(a) $\dfrac{r^2 g}{9\eta}(\rho - 2\sigma)$ (b) $\dfrac{r^2 g}{9\eta}(2\rho - \sigma)$

(c) $\dfrac{r^2 g}{9\eta}(\rho - \sigma)$ (d) $\dfrac{2r^2 g}{9\eta}(\rho - \sigma)$

27. Two pieces of metals are suspended from the arms of a balance and are found to be in equilibrium when kept immersed in water. The mass of one piece is 32 g and its density 8 g cm^{-3}. The density of the other is 5 g per cm^3. Then the mass of the other is
    (a) 28 g   (b) 35 g   (c) 21 g   (d) 33.6 g
28. A block of material of specific gravity 0.4 is held submerged at a depth of 1m in a vessel filled with water. The vessel is accelerated upwards with acceleration of $a_o = g/5$. If the block is released at $t = 0$, neglecting viscous effects, it will reach the water surface at t equal to ($g = 10$ m/s^2) :
    (a) 0.60 s   (b) 0.33 s   (c) 3.3 s   (d) 1.2 s
29. Figure shows a capillary rise H. If the air is blown through the horizontal tube in the direction as shown then rise in capillary tube will be
    (a) = H
    (b) > H
    (c) < H
    (d) zero

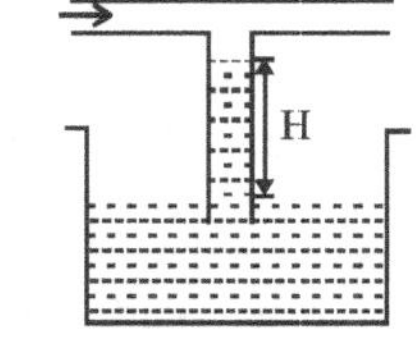

30. A small spherical ball falling through a viscous medium of negligible density has terminal velocity v. Another ball of the same mass but of radius twice that of the earlier falling through the same viscous medium will have terminal velocity
    (a) v   (b) v/4   (c) v/2   (d) 2v
31. Two non-mixing liquids of densities ρ and $n\rho$ (n > 1) are put in a container. The height of each liquid is h. A solid cylinder of length L and density d is put in this container. The cylinder floats with its axis vertical and length pL(p < 1) in the denser liquid. The density d is equal to :
    (a) $\{1 + (n + 1)p\}\rho$ (b) $\{2 + (n + 1)p\}\rho$
    (c) $\{2 + (n - 1)p\}\rho$ (d) $\{1 + (n - 1)p\}\rho$
32. A thin liquid film formed between a U-shaped wire and a light slider supports a weight of 1.5×10^{-2} N (see figure). The length of the slider is 30 cm and its weight negligible. The surface tension of the liquid film is
    (a) 0.0125 Nm^{-1} (b) 0.1 Nm^{-1}
    (c) 0.05 Nm^{-1} (d) 0.025 Nm^{-1}

Space for Rough Work

33. Two liquids of densities d_1 and d_2 are flowing in identical capillary tubes uder the same pressure difference. If t_1 and t_2 are time taken for the flow of equal quantities (mass) of liquids, then the ratio of coefficient of viscosity of liquids must be

(a) $\dfrac{d_1 t_1}{d_2 t_2}$ (b) $\dfrac{t_1}{t_2}$ (c) $\dfrac{d_2}{d_1}\dfrac{t_2}{t_1}$ (d) $\sqrt{\dfrac{d_1 t_1}{d_2 t_2}}$

34. Let T_1 be surface tension between solid and air, T_2 be the surface tension between solid and liquid and T be the surface tension between liquid and air. Then in equilibrium, for a drop of liquid on a clean glass plate, the correct relation is (θ is angle of contact)

(a) $\cos\theta = \dfrac{T}{T_1 + T_2}$ (b) $\cos\theta = \dfrac{T}{T_1 - T_2}$

(c) $\cos\theta = \dfrac{T_1 + T_2}{T}$ (d) $\cos\theta = \dfrac{T_1 - T_2}{T}$

35. A uniform rod of density ρ is placed in a wide tank containing a liquid of density $\rho_0(\rho_0 > \rho)$. The depth of liquid in the tank is half the length of the rod. The rod is in equilibrium, with its lower end resting on the bottom of the tank. In this position the rod makes an angle θ with the horizontal

(a) $\sin\theta = \dfrac{1}{2}\sqrt{\rho_0/\rho}$ (b) $\sin\theta = \dfrac{1}{2}\cdot\dfrac{\rho_0}{\rho}$

(c) $\sin\theta = \sqrt{\rho/\rho_0}$ (d) $\sin\theta = \rho_0/\rho$

36. A spherical ball of iron of radius 2 mm is falling through a column of glycerine. If densities of glycerine and iron are respectively 1.3×10^3 kg/m³ and 8×10^3 kg/m³. η for glycerine $= 0.83$ Nm⁻² sec, then the terminal velocity is

(a) 0.7 m/s (b) 0.07 m/s (c) 0.007 m/s (d) 0.0007 m/s

37. A water film is formed between two straight parallel wires of 10 cm length 0.5 cm apart. If the distance between wires is increased by 1 mm. What will be the work done ? (surface tension of water = 72 dyne/cm)

(a) 36 erg (b) 288 erg (c) 144 erg (d) 72 erg

38. A waterproofing agent changes the angle of contact

(a) from obtuse to acute.

(b) from acute to obtuse.

(c) from obtuse to $\pi/2$.

(d) from acute to $\pi/2$.

39. A thin metal disc of radius r floats on water surface and bends the surface downwards along the perimeter making an angle θ with vertical edge of the disc. If the disc displaces a weight of water W and surface tension of water is T, then the weight of metal disc is:

(a) $2\pi r T + W$ (b) $2\pi r T \cos\theta - W$
(c) $2\pi r T \cos\theta + W$ (d) $W - 2\pi r T \cos\theta$

40. A tank has a small hole at its botom of area of cross-section a. Liquid is being poured in the tank at the rate V m³/s, the maximum level of liquid in the container will be (Area of tank = A)

(a) $\dfrac{V}{gaA}$ (b) $\dfrac{V^2}{2gAa}$ (c) $\dfrac{V^2}{gAa}$ (d) $\dfrac{V}{2gaA}$

41. A jar is filled with two non-mixing liquids 1 and 2 having densities ρ_1 and, ρ_2 respectively. A solid ball, made of a material of density ρ_3, is dropped in the jar. It comes to equilibrium in the position shown in the figure. Which of the following is true for ρ_1, ρ_2 and ρ_3?

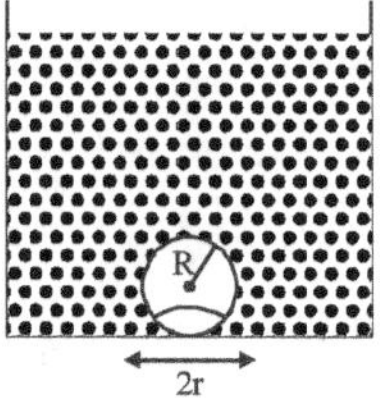

(a) $\rho_3 < \rho_1 < \rho_2$ (b) $\rho_1 > \rho_3 > \rho_2$
(c) $\rho_1 < \rho_2 < \rho_3$ (d) $\rho_1 < \rho_3 < \rho_2$

42. On heating water, bubbles being formed at the bottom of the vessel detach and rise. Take the bubbles to be spheres of radius R and making a circular contact of radius r with the bottom of the vessel. If $r \ll R$ and the surface tension of water is T, value of r just before bubbles detach is: (density of water is ρ_w)

(a) $R^2\sqrt{\dfrac{2\rho_w g}{3T}}$ (b) $R^2\sqrt{\dfrac{\rho_w g}{6T}}$ (c) $R^2\sqrt{\dfrac{\rho_w g}{T}}$ (d) $R^2\sqrt{\dfrac{3\rho_w g}{T}}$

43. The lift of an air plane is based on
(a) Torricelli's theorem
(b) Bernoulli's theorem
(c) Law of gravitation
(d) conservation of linear momentum

44. The cylindrical tube of a spray pump has radius, R, one end of which has n fine holes, each of radius r. If the speed of the liquid in the tube is V, the speed of the ejection of the liquid through the holes is :

(a) $\dfrac{VR^2}{nr^2}$ (b) $\dfrac{VR^2}{n^3 r^2}$ (c) $\dfrac{V^2 R}{nr}$ (d) $\dfrac{VR^2}{n^2 r^2}$

45. Drops of liquid of density ρ are floating half immersed in a liquid of density σ. If the surface tension of liquid is T, the radius of the drop will be

(a) $\sqrt{\dfrac{3T}{g(3\rho - \sigma)}}$ (b) $\sqrt{\dfrac{6T}{g(2\rho - \sigma)}}$ (c) $\sqrt{\dfrac{3T}{g(2\rho - \sigma)}}$ (d) $\sqrt{\dfrac{3T}{g(4\rho - 3\sigma)}}$

RESPONSE GRID					
	33. ⓐⓑⓒⓓ	34. ⓐⓑⓒⓓ	35. ⓐⓑⓒⓓ	36. ⓐⓑⓒⓓ	37. ⓐⓑⓒⓓ
	38. ⓐⓑⓒⓓ	39. ⓐⓑⓒⓓ	40. ⓐⓑⓒⓓ	41. ⓐⓑⓒⓓ	42. ⓐⓑⓒⓓ
	43. ⓐⓑⓒⓓ	44. ⓐⓑⓒⓓ	45. ⓐⓑⓒⓓ		

DAILY PRACTICE PROBLEM DPP CHAPTERWISE CP09 - PHYSICS

Total Questions	45	Total Marks	180
Attempted		Correct	
Incorrect		Net Score	
Cut-off Score	45	Qualifying Score	60
Success Gap = Net Score – Qualifying Score			
Net Score = (Correct × 4) – (Incorrect × 1)			

Date : | **Start Time :** | **End Time :**

PHYSICS CP10

SYLLABUS : Thermal Properties of Matter

Max. Marks : 180   **Marking Scheme :** (+4) for correct & (−1) for incorrect answer   **Time : 60 min.**

INSTRUCTIONS : This Daily Practice Problem Sheet contains 45 MCQs. For each question only one option is correct. Darken the correct circle/ bubble in the Response Grid provided on each page.

1. The total radiant energy per unit area, normal to the direction of incidence, received at a distance R from the centre of a star of radius r, whose outer surface radiates as a black body at a temperature $T\,K$ is given by: (σ is Stefan's constant)

   (a) $\dfrac{\sigma r^2 T^4}{R^2}$

   (b) $\dfrac{\sigma r^2 T^4}{4\pi r^2}$

   (c) $\dfrac{\sigma r^4 T^4}{r^4}$

   (d) $\dfrac{4\pi\sigma r^2 T^4}{R^2}$

2. Three rods of same dimensions are arranged as shown in figure, have thermal conductivities K_1, K_2 and K_3. The points P and Q are maintained at different temeratures for the heat to flow at the same rate along PRQ and PQ. Then which of the following option is correct?

   (a) $K_3 = \dfrac{1}{2}(K_1 + K_2)$

   (b) $K_3 = K_1 + K_2$

   (c) $K_3 = \dfrac{K_1 K_2}{K_1 + K_2}$

   (d) $K_3 = -2(K_1 + K_2)$

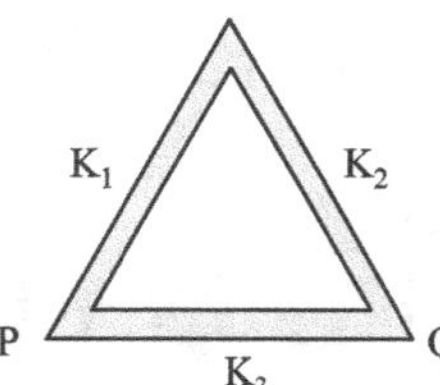

3. The sprinkling of water slightly reduces the temperature of a closed room because
   (a) temperature of water is less than that of the room
   (b) specific heat of water is high
   (c) water has large latent heat of vaporisation
   (d) water is a bad conductor of heat

4. The value of molar heat capacity at constant temperature is
   (a) zero   (b) infinity
   (c) unity   (d) 4.2

5. The specific heat capacity of a metal at low temperature (T) is given as

   $$C_p(kJK^{-1}kg^{-1}) = 32\left(\dfrac{T}{400}\right)^3$$

   A 100 gram vessel of this metal is to be cooled from 20°K to 4°K by a special refrigerator operating at room temperature (27°C). The amount of work required to cool the vessel is
   (a) greater than 0.148 kJ
   (b) between 0.148 kJ and 0.028 kJ
   (c) less than 0.028 kJ
   (d) equal to 0.002 kJ

---

6. The emissive power of a black body at $T = 300K$ is 100 Watt/m^2. Consider a body B of area $A = 10m^2$ coefficient of reflectivity $r = 0.3$ and coefficient of transmission $t = 0.5$. Its temperature is 300K. Then which of the following is incorrect?
(a) The emissive power of B is 20 W/m^2
(b) The emissive power of B is 200 W/m^2
(c) The power emitted by B is 200 Watts
(d) The emissivity of B is 0.2

7. A solid cube and a solid sphere of the same material have equal surface area. Both are at the same temperture $120°C$, then
(a) both the cube and the sphere cool down at the same rate
(b) the cube cools down faster than the sphere
(c) the sphere cools down faster than the cube
(d) whichever is having more mass will cool down faster

8. The density of water at $20°C$ is 998 kg/m^3 and at $40°C$ 992 kg/m^3. The coefficient of volume expansion of water is
(a) $10^{-4}/°C$
(b) $3 \times 10^{-4}/°C$
(c) $2 \times 10^{-4}/°C$
(d) $6 \times 10^{-4}/°C$

9. A metallic rod ℓ cm long, A square cm in cross-section is heated through $t°C$. If Young's modulus of elasticity of the metal is E and the mean coefficient of linear expansion is α per degree celsius, then the compressional force required to prevent the rod from expanding along its length is
(a) $E A \alpha t$
(b) $E A \alpha t/(1 + \alpha t)$
(c) $E A \alpha t/(1 - \alpha t)$
(d) $E \ell \alpha t$

10. If liquefied oxygen at 1 atmospheric pressure is heated from 50 K to 300 K by supplying heat at constant rate. The graph of temperature vs time will be

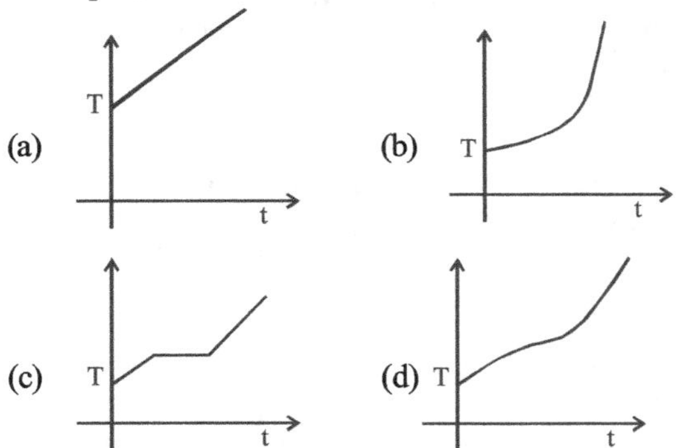

11. If a bar is made of copper whose coefficient of linear expansion is one and a half times that of iron, the ratio of force developed in the copper bar to the iron bar of identical lengths and cross-sections, when heated through the same temperature range (Young's modulus of copper may be taken to be equal to that of iron) is
(a) 3/2
(b) 2/3
(c) 9/4
(d) 4/9

12. A piece of ice falls from a height h so that it melts completely. Only one-quarter of the heat produced is absorbed by the ice and all energy of ice gets converted into heat during its fall. The value of h is :
[Latent heat of ice is 3.4×10^5 J/kg and g = 10 N/kg]
(a) 34 km
(b) 544 km
(c) 136 km
(d) 68 km

13. A body of mass 5 kg falls from a height of 20 metres on the ground and it rebounds to a height of 0.2 m. If the loss in potential energy is used up by the body, then what will be the temperature rise?
(specific heat of material = 0.09 cal gm^{-1} $°C^{-1}$)
(a) 0°C
(b) 4°C
(c) 8°C
(d) None of these

14. Two straight metallic strips each of thickness t and length ℓ are rivetted together. Their coefficients of linear expansions are α_1 and α_2. If they are heated through temperature ΔT, the bimetallic strip will bend to form an arc of radius
(a) $t/\{\alpha_1 + \alpha_2)\Delta T\}$
(b) $t/\{(\alpha_2 - \alpha_1)\Delta T\}$
(c) $t(\alpha_1 - \alpha_2)\Delta T$
(d) $t(\alpha_2 - \alpha_1)\Delta T$

15. The figure shows a system of two concentric spheres of radii r_1 and r_2 are kept at temperatures T_1 and T_2, respectively. The radial rate of flow of heat in a substance between the two concentric spheres is proportional to

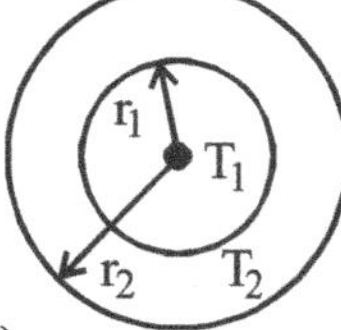

(a) $ln\left(\dfrac{r_2}{r_1}\right)$
(b) $\dfrac{(r_2 - r_1)}{(r_1 r_2)}$
(c) $(r_2 - r_1)$
(d) $\dfrac{r_1 r_2}{(r_2 - r_1)}$

16. A block of steel heated to 100°C is left in a room to cool. Which of the curves shown in fig., represents the correct behaviour?

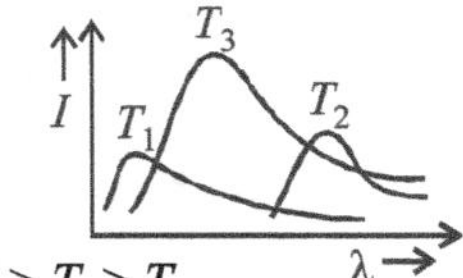

(a) A
(b) B
(c) C
(d) None of these

17. Which of the following will expand the most for same rise in temperature?
(a) Aluminium
(b) Glass
(c) Wood
(d) All will expand same

18. The plots of intensity versus wavelength for three black bodies at temperatures T_1, T_2 and T_3 respectively are as shown. Their temperature are such that
(a) $T_1 > T_2 > T_3$
(b) $T_1 > T_3 > T_2$
(c) $T_2 > T_3 > T_1$
(d) $T_3 > T_2 > T_1$

19. When the temperature of a rod increases from t to t + Δt, its moment of inertia increases from I to I + ΔI. If α be the coefficient of linear expansion of the rod, then the value of $\dfrac{\Delta I}{I}$ is
(a) $2\alpha\Delta t$
(b) $\alpha\Delta T$
(c) $\dfrac{\alpha\Delta t}{2}$
(d) $\dfrac{\Delta t}{\alpha}$

20. Two rods, one of aluminum and the other made of steel, having initial length ℓ_1 and ℓ_2 are connected together to form a single rod of length $\ell_1 + \ell_2$. The coefficients of linear expansion for aluminum and steel are α_a and α_s and respectively. If the length of each rod increases by the same amount when their temperature are raised by t^0C, then find the ratio $\ell_1/(\ell_1 + \ell_2)$
(a) α_s/α_a
(b) α_a/α_s
(c) $\alpha_s/(\alpha_a + \alpha_s)$
(d) $\alpha_a/(\alpha_a + \alpha_s)$

Space for Rough Work

21. A polished metal plate with a rough black spot on it is heated to about 1400 K and quickly taken into a dark room. Which one of the following statements will be true?
(a) The spot will appear brighter than the plate
(b) The spot will appear darker than the plate
(c) The spot and plate will appear equally bright
(d) The spot and the plate will not be visible in the dark room

22. On observing light from three different stars P, Q and R, it was found that intensity of violet colour is maximum in the spectrum of P, the intensity of green colour is maximum in the spectrum of R and the intensity of red colour is maximum in the spectrum of Q. If T_P, T_Q and T_R are the respective absolute temperature of P, Q and R, then it can be concluded from the above observations that
(a) $T_P > T_R > T_Q$ (b) $T_P < T_R < T_Q$
(c) $T_P < T_Q < T_R$ (d) $T_P > T_Q > T_R$

23. A partition wall has two layers of different materials A and B in contact with each other. They have the same thickness but the thermal conductivity of layer A is twice that of layer B. At steady state the temperature difference across the layer B is 50 K, then the corresponding difference across the layer A is
(a) 50 K   (b) 12.5 K   (c) 25 K   (d) 60 K

24. Which of the following statements is/are false about mode of heat transfer?
(a) In radiation, heat is transfered from one medium to another without affecting the intervening medium
(b) Radiation and convection are possible in vaccum while conduction requires material medium.
(c) Conduction is possible in solids while convection occurs in liquids and gases.
(d) All are correct

25. In a vertical U-tube containing a liquid, the two arms are maintained at different temperatures t_1 and t_2. The liquid columns in the two arms have heights l_1 and l_2 respectively. The coefficient of volume expansion of the liquid is equal to

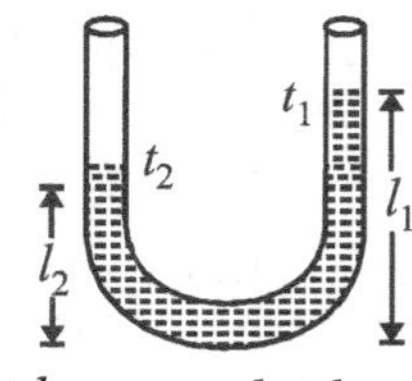

(a) $\dfrac{l_1 - l_2}{l_2 t_1 - l_1 t_2}$ (b) $\dfrac{l_1 - l_2}{l_1 t_1 - l_2 t_2}$ (c) $\dfrac{l_1 + l_2}{l_2 t_1 + l_1 t_2}$ (d) $\dfrac{l_1 + l_2}{l_1 t_1 + l_2 t_2}$

26. The top of an insulated cylindrical container is covered by a disc having emissivity 0.6 and conductivity 0.167 WK^{-1}m^{-1} and thickness 1 cm. The temperature is maintained by circulating oil as shown in figure. Find the radiation loss to the surrounding in Jm^{-2}s^{-1} if temperature of the upper surface of the disc is 27°C and temperature of the surrounding is 27°C.
(a) 595 Jm^{-2}s^{-1} (b) 545 Jm^{-2}s^{-1}
(c) 495 Jm^{-2}s^{-1} (d) None of these

27. Wien's law is concerned with
(a) relation between emissivity and absorptivity of a radiating surface
(b) total radiation, emitted by a hot surface
(c) an expression for spectral distribution of energy of a radiation from any source
(d) a relation between the temperature of a black body and the wavelength at which there is maximum radiant energy per unit wavelength

28. If a piece of metal is heated to temperature θ and then allowed to cool in a room which is at temperature θ_0, the graph between the temperature T of the metal and time t will be closest to

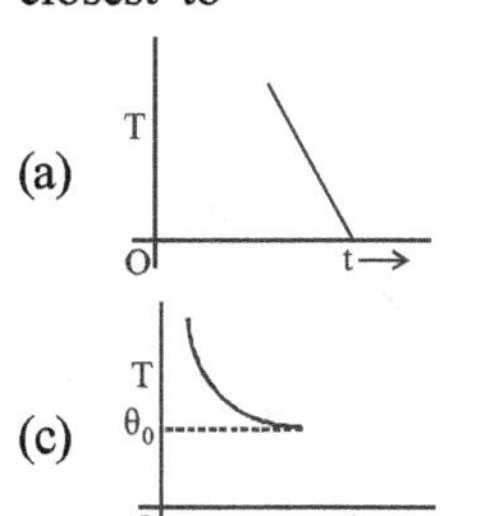
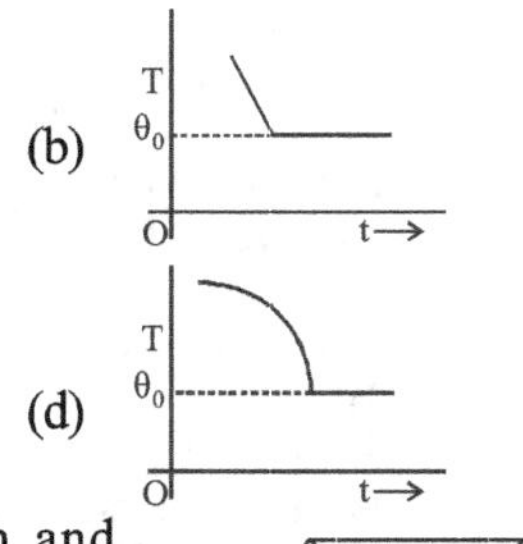

(a)   (b)   (c)   (d)

29. Two rods of same length and transfer a given amount of heat 12 second, when they are joined as shown in figure (i). But when they are joined as shwon in figure (ii), then they will transfer same heat in same conditions in
(a) 24 s   (b) 13 s   (c) 15 s   (d) 48 s

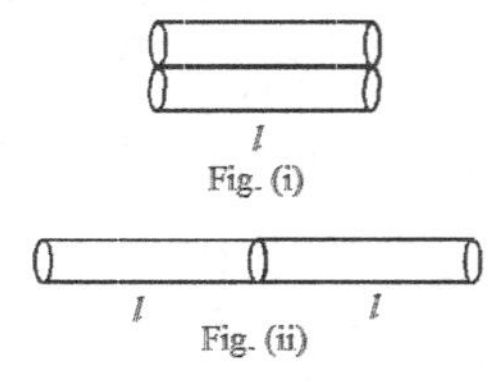

30. Consider a compound slab consisting of two different materials having equal thicknesses and thermal conductivities K and $2K$, respectively. The equivalent thermal conductivity of the slab is
(a) $\dfrac{4}{3}K$ (b) $\dfrac{2}{3}K$ (c) $\sqrt{3}\,K$ (d) $3K$

31. The coefficient of thermal conductivity of copper, mercury and glass are respectively K_c, K_m and K_g such that $K_c > K_m > K_g$. If the same quantity of heat is to flow per sec per unit area of each and corresponding temperature gradients are X_c, X_m and X_g then
(a) $X_c = X_m = X_g$ (b) $X_c > X_m > X_g$
(c) $X_c < X_m < X_g$ (d) $X_m < X_c < X_g$

32. The radiation energy density per unit wavelength at a temperature T has a maximum at a wavelength λ_0. At temperature 2T, it will have a maximum wavelength
(a) $4\lambda_0$ (b) $2\lambda_0$ (c) $\dfrac{\lambda_0}{2}$ (d) $\dfrac{\lambda_0}{4}$

33. Assuming the Sun to be a spherical body of radius R at a temperature of TK, evaluate the total radiant powerd incident of Earth at a distance r from the Sun
(a) $4\pi r_0^2 R^2 \sigma \dfrac{T^4}{r^2}$ (b) $\pi r_0^2 R^2 \sigma \dfrac{T^4}{r^2}$
(c) $r_0^2 R^2 \sigma \dfrac{T^4}{4\pi r^2}$ (d) $R^2 \sigma \dfrac{T^4}{r^2}$

RESPONSE GRID					
21. ⓐⓑⓒⓓ	**22.** ⓐⓑⓒⓓ	**23.** ⓐⓑⓒⓓ	**24.** ⓐⓑⓒⓓ	**25.** ⓐⓑⓒⓓ
26. ⓐⓑⓒⓓ	**27.** ⓐⓑⓒⓓ	**28.** ⓐⓑⓒⓓ	**29.** ⓐⓑⓒⓓ	**30.** ⓐⓑⓒⓓ
31. ⓐⓑⓒⓓ	**32.** ⓐⓑⓒⓓ	**33.** ⓐⓑⓒⓓ		

34. A metal ball immersed in alcohol weighs W_1 at $0°C$ and W_2 at $59°C$. The coefficient of cubical expansion of the metal is less than that of alcohol. Assuming that the density of the metal is large compared to that of alcohol, it can be shown that
(a) $W_1 > W_2$
(b) $W_1 = W_2$
(c) $W_1 < W_2$
(d) $W_1 = (W_2/2)$

35. One end of a thermally insulated rod is kept at a temperature T_1 and the other at T_2. The rod is composed of two sections of length l_1 and l_2 and thermal conductivities K_1 and K_2 respectively. The temperature at the interface of the two sections is

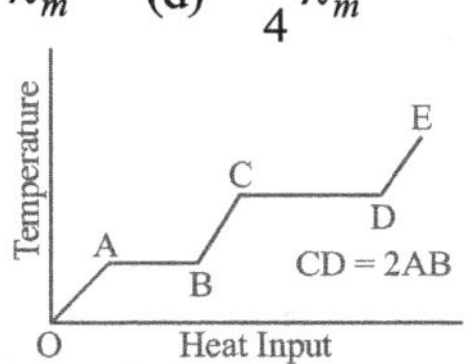

(a) $\dfrac{(K_1l_1T_1 + K_2l_2T_2)}{(K_1l_1 + K_2l_2)}$
(b) $\dfrac{(K_2l_2T_1 + K_1l_1T_2)}{(K_1l_1 + K_2l_2)}$
(c) $\dfrac{(K_2l_1T_1 + K_1l_2T_2)}{(K_2l_1 + K_1l_2)}$
(d) $\dfrac{(K_1l_2T_1 + K_2l_1T_2)}{(K_1l_2 + K_2l_1)}$

36. Two spheres of different materials one with double the radius and one-fourth wall thickness of the other are filled with ice. If the time taken for complete melting of ice in the larger sphere is 25 minute and for smaller one is 16 minute, the ratio of thermal conductivities of the materials of larger spheres to that of smaller sphere is
(a) $4:5$
(b) $5:4$
(c) $25:8$
(d) $8:25$

37. A black body has maximum wavelength λ_m at temperature 2000 K. Its corresponding wavelength at temperature 3000 K will be
(a) $\dfrac{3}{2}\lambda_m$
(b) $\dfrac{2}{3}\lambda_m$
(c) $\dfrac{4}{9}\lambda_m$
(d) $\dfrac{9}{4}\lambda_m$

38. A solid material is supplied with heat at constant rate and the temperature of the material changes as shown. From the graph, the FALSE conclusion drawn is
(a) AB and CD of the graph represent phase changes
(b) AB represents the change of state from solid to liquid
(c) latent heat of fusion is twice the latent heat of vaporization
(d) CD represents change of state from liquid to vapour

39. 10 gm of ice cubes at $0°C$ are released in a tumbler (water equivalent 55 g) at $40°C$. Assuming that negligible heat is taken from the surroundings, the temperature of water in the tumbler becomes nearly $(L = 80 \text{ cal/g})$
(a) $31°C$
(b) $22°C$
(c) $19°C$
(d) $15°C$

40. In a surrounding medium of temperature $10°C$, a body takes 7 min for a fall of temperature from $60°C$ to $40°C$. In what time the temperature of the body will fall from $40°C$ to $28°C$?
(a) $7\,\text{min}$
(b) $11\,\text{min}$
(c) $14\,\text{min}$
(d) $21\,\text{min}$

41. Two rods of same length and area of cross-section A_1 and A_2 have their ends at the same temperature. If K_1 and K_2 are their thermal conductivities, c_1 and c_2 are their specific heats and d_1 and d_2 are their densities, then the rate of flow of heat is the same in both the rods if
(a) $\dfrac{A_1}{A_2} = \dfrac{-k_1}{k_2}$
(b) $\dfrac{A_1}{A_2} = \dfrac{k_1 c_1 d_1}{k_2 c_2 d_2}$
(c) $\dfrac{A_1}{A_2} = \dfrac{k_2 c_1 d_1}{c_2 d_2 k_1}$
(d) $\dfrac{A_1}{A_2} = \dfrac{k_2}{k_1}$

42. A student takes 50gm wax (specific heat $= 0.6 \text{ kcal/kg°C}$) and heats it till it boils. The graph between temperature and time is as follows. Heat supplied to the wax per minute and boiling point are respectively

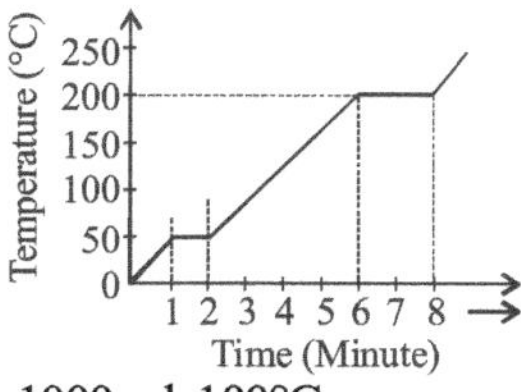

(a) $500\,\text{cal}, 50°C$
(b) $1000\,\text{cal}, 100°C$
(c) $1500\,\text{cal}, 200°C$
(d) $1000\,\text{cal}, 200°C$

43. Consider two identical iron spheres, one which lie on a thermally insulating plate, while the other hangs from an insulatory thread. Equal amount of heat is supplied to the two spheres, then

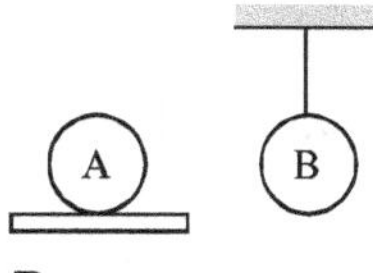

(a) temperature of A will be greater than B
(b) temperature of B will be greater than A
(c) their temperature will be equal
(d) can't be predicted

44. Steam at $100°C$ is passed into 20 g of water at $10°C$. When water acquires a temperature of $80°C$, the mass of water present will be: [Take specific heat of water $= 1\,\text{cal g}^{-1}\,°C^{-1}$ and latent heat of steam $= 540\,\text{cal g}^{-1}$]
(a) $24\,\text{g}$
(b) $31.5\,\text{g}$
(c) $42.5\,\text{g}$
(d) $22.5\,\text{g}$

45. Two solid spheres, of radii R_1 and R_2 are made of the same material and have similar surfaces. The spheres are raised to the same temperature and then allowed to cool under identical conditions. Assuming spheres to be perfect conductors of heat, their initial rates of loss of heat are
(a) R_1^2/R_2^2
(b) R_1/R_2
(c) R_2/R_1
(d) R_2^2/R_1^2

RESPONSE GRID				
34. ⓐⓑⓒⓓ	35. ⓐⓑⓒⓓ	36. ⓐⓑⓒⓓ	37. ⓐⓑⓒⓓ	38. ⓐⓑⓒⓓ
39. ⓐⓑⓒⓓ	40. ⓐⓑⓒⓓ	41. ⓐⓑⓒⓓ	42. ⓐⓑⓒⓓ	43. ⓐⓑⓒⓓ
44. ⓐⓑⓒⓓ	45. ⓐⓑⓒⓓ			

DAILY PRACTICE PROBLEM DPP CHAPTERWISE CP10 - PHYSICS

Total Questions	45	Total Marks	180
Attempted		Correct	
Incorrect		Net Score	
Cut-off Score	45	Qualifying Score	60
Success Gap = Net Score − Qualifying Score			
Net Score = (Correct × 4) − (Incorrect × 1)			

Date :   Start Time :   End Time :

PHYSICS   CP11

SYLLABUS : Thermodynamics

Max. Marks : 180   **Marking Scheme :** (+4) for correct & (–1) for incorrect answer   **Time : 60 min.**

INSTRUCTIONS : This Daily Practice Problem Sheet contains 45 MCQs. For each question only one option is correct. Darken the correct circle/ bubble in the Response Grid provided on each page.

1. The relation between U, P and V for an ideal gas in an adiabatic process is given by relation $U = a + bPV$. Find the value of adiabatic exponent (γ) of this gas

(a) $\dfrac{b+1}{b}$ (b) $\dfrac{b+1}{a}$ (c) $\dfrac{a+1}{b}$ (d) $\dfrac{a}{a+b}$

2. Carbon monoxide is carried around a closed cycle abc in which bc is an isothermal process as shown in the figure. The gas absorbs 7000 J of heat as its temperture increases from 300 K to 1000 K in going from a to b. The quantity of heat rejected by the gas during the process ca is

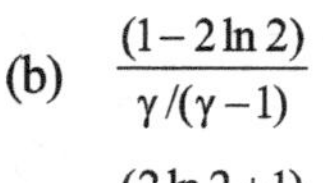

(a) 4200 J   (b) 5000 J   (c) 9000 J   (d) 9800 J

3. A Carnot engine, having an efficiency of $\eta = 1/10$ as heat engine, is used as a refrigerator. If the work done on the system is 10 J, the amount of energy absorbed from the reservoir at lower temperature is

(a) 100 J   (b) 99 J   (c) 90 J   (d) 1 J

4. In a thermodynamic process, fixed mass of a gas is changed in such a manner that the gas release 20 J of heat and 8 J of work was done on the gas. If the initial internal energy of the gas was 30 J. Then the final internal energy will be

(a) 2 joule   (b) 18 joule   (c) 42 joule   (d) 58 joule

5. A closed gas cylinder is divided into two parts by a piston held tight. The pressure and volume of gas in two parts respectively are (P, 5V) and (10P, V). If now the piston is left free and the system undergoes isothermal process, then the volumes of the gas in two parts respectively are

(a) 2V,4V   (b) 3V,3V   (c) 5V,V   (d) $\dfrac{10}{11}$V, $\dfrac{20}{11}$V

6. The efficiency of an ideal gas with adiabatic exponent 'γ' for the shown cyclic process would be

(a) $\dfrac{(2\ln 2 - 1)}{\gamma/(\gamma - 1)}$

(b) $\dfrac{(1 - 2\ln 2)}{\gamma/(\gamma - 1)}$

(c) $\dfrac{(2\ln 2 + 1)}{\gamma/(\gamma - 1)}$

(d) $\dfrac{(2\ln 2 - 1)}{\gamma/(\gamma + 1)}$

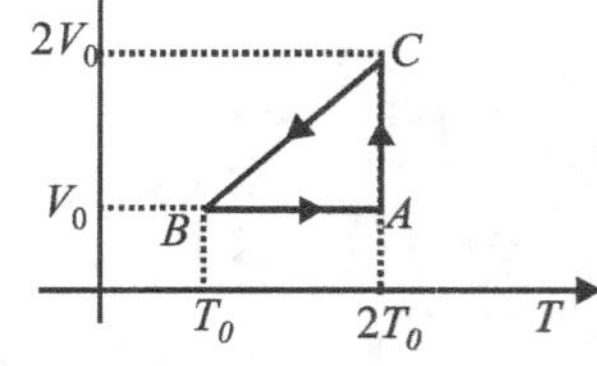

7. A mass of diatomic gas ($\gamma = 1.4$) at a pressure of 2 atmospheres is compressed adiabatically so that its temperature rises from 27°C to 927°C. The pressure of the gas in final state is

(a) 28 atm   (b) 68.7 atm   (c) 256 atm   (d) 8 atm

Space for Rough Work

8. A diatomic ideal gas is used in a Carnot engine as the working substance. If during the adiabatic expansion part of the cycle the volume of the gas increases from V to $32\ V$, the efficiency of the engine is
(a) 0.5   (b) 0.75   (c) 0.99   (d) 0.25

9. The $P\text{-}V$ diagram of a gas system undergoing cyclic process is shown here. The work done during isobaric compression is

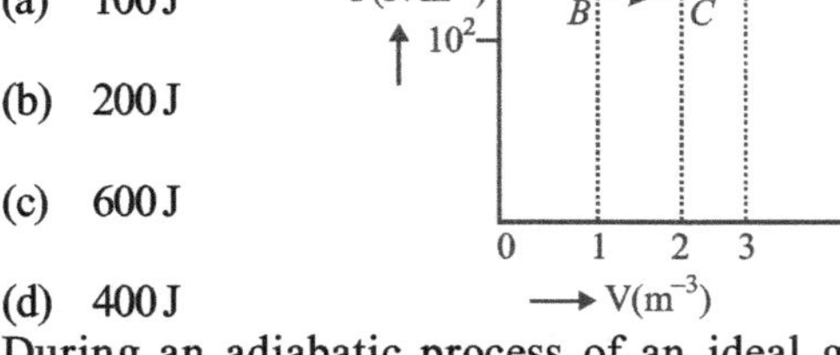

(a) 100 J

(b) 200 J

(c) 600 J

(d) 400 J

10. During an adiabatic process of an ideal gas, if P is proportional to $\dfrac{1}{V^{1.5}}$, then the ratio of specific heat capacities at constant pressure to that at constant volume for the gas is
(a) 1.5   (b) 0.25   (c) 0.75   (d) 0.4

11. The work of 146 kJ is performed in order to compress one kilo mole of gas adiabatically and in this process the temperature of the gas increases by 7°C. The gas is $(R = 8.3\ \text{J mol}^{-1}\text{K}^{-1})$
(a) diatomic
(b) triatomic
(c) a mixture of monoatomic and diatomic
(d) monoatomic

12. Consider a spherical shell of radius R at temperature T. The black body radiation inside it can be considered as an ideal gas of photons with internal energy per unit volume $u = \dfrac{U}{V} \propto T^4$ and pressure $p = \dfrac{1}{3}\left(\dfrac{U}{V}\right)$. If the shell now undergoes an adiabatic expansion the relation between T and R is :
(a) $T \propto \dfrac{1}{R}$ (b) $T \propto \dfrac{1}{R^3}$ (c) $T \propto e^{-R}$ (d) $T \propto e^{-3R}$

13. The specific heat capacity of a metal at low temperature (T) is given as $C(\text{kJK}^{-1}\text{kg}^{-1}) = 32\left(\dfrac{T}{400}\right)^3$. A 100 g vessel of this metal is to be cooled from 20 K to 4 K by a special refrigerator operating at room temperature (27°C). The amount of work required to cool in vessel is
(a) equal to 0.002 kJ
(b) greater than 0.148 kJ
(c) between 0.148 kJ and 0.028 kJ
(d) less than 0.028 kJ

14. 5.6 litre of helium gas at STP is adiabatically compressed to 0.7 litre. Taking the initial temperature to be T_1, the work done in the process is

(a) $\dfrac{9}{8}RT_1$ (b) $\dfrac{3}{2}RT_1$ (c) $\dfrac{15}{8}RT_1$ (d) $\dfrac{9}{2}RT_1$

15. Four curves A, B, C and D are drawn in the figure for a given amount of a gas. The curves which represent adiabatic and isothermal changes are
(a) C and D respectively
(b) D and C respectively
(c) A and B respectively
(d) B and A respectively

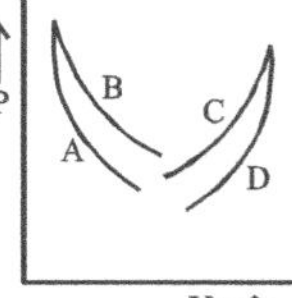

16. In an adiabatic process, the pressure is increased by $\dfrac{2}{3}\%$. If $\gamma = \dfrac{3}{2}$, then the volume decreases by nearly
(a) $\dfrac{4}{9}\%$ (b) $\dfrac{2}{3}\%$ (c) 1%   (d) $\dfrac{9}{4}\%$

17. A reversible engine converts one-sixth of the heat input into work. When the temperature of the sink is reduced by 62°C, the efficiency of the engine is doubled. The temperatures of the source and sink are
(a) 99°C, 37°C   (b) 80°C, 37°C
(c) 95°C, 37°C   (d) 90°C, 37°C

18. A diatomic ideal gas is compressed adiabatically to $\dfrac{1}{32}$ of its initial volume. If the initial temperature of the gas is T_i (in Kelvin) and the final temperature is aT_i, the value of a is
(a) 8   (b) 4   (c) 3   (d) 5

19. When the state of a gas adiabatically changed from an equilibrium state A to another equilibrium state B an amount of work done on the stystem is 35 J. If the gas is taken from state A to B via process in which the net heat absorbed by the system is 12 cal, then the net work done by the system is (1 cal = 4.19 J)
(a) 13.2 J   (b) 15.4 J   (c) 12.6 J   (d) 16.8 J

20. Calculate the work done when 1 mole of a perfect gas is compressed adiabatically. The initial pressure and volume of the gas are 10^5 N/m^2 and 6 litre respectively. The final volume of the gas is 2 litres. Molar specific heat of the gas at constant volume is 3R/2. [Given $(3)^{5/3} = 6.19$]
(a) –957 J   (b) +957 J   (c) – 805 J   (d) + 805 J

21. A Carnot engine whose efficiency is 40%, receives heat at 500K. If the efficiency is to be 50%, the source temperature for the same exhaust temperature is
(a) 900 K   (b) 600 K   (c) 700 K   (d) 800 K

22. 1 gm of water at a pressure of 1.01×10^5 Pa is converted into steam without any change of temperature. The volume of 1 g of steam is 1671 cc and the latent heat of evaporation is 540 cal. The change in internal energy due to evaporation of 1 gm of water is
(a) ≈ 167 cal (b) 500 cal   (c) 540 cal   (d) 581 cal

RESPONSE GRID					
8. ⓐⓑⓒⓓ	**9.** ⓐⓑⓒⓓ	**10.** ⓐⓑⓒⓓ	**11.** ⓐⓑⓒⓓ	**12.** ⓐⓑⓒⓓ
13. ⓐⓑⓒⓓ	**14.** ⓐⓑⓒⓓ	**15.** ⓐⓑⓒⓓ	**16.** ⓐⓑⓒⓓ	**17.** ⓐⓑⓒⓓ
18. ⓐⓑⓒⓓ	**19.** ⓐⓑⓒⓓ	**20.** ⓐⓑⓒⓓ	**21.** ⓐⓑⓒⓓ	**22.** ⓐⓑⓒⓓ

23. One mole of an ideal gas at temperature T was cooled isochorically till the gas pressure fell from P to $\dfrac{P}{n}$. Then, by an isobaric process, the gas was restored to the initial temperature. The net amount of heat absorbed by the gas in the process is

    (a) nRT   (b) $\dfrac{RT}{n}$

    (c) $RT\,(1-n^{-1})$ (d) $RT\,(n-1)$

24. A Carnot engine, having an efficiency of $\eta = \dfrac{1}{10}$ as heat engine, is used as a refrigerator. If the work done on the system is 10 J, the amount of energy absorbed from the reservoir at lower temperature is

    (a) 99 J   (b) 90 J   (c) 1 J   (d) 100 J

25. The volume of an ideal gas is 1 litre and its pressure is equal to 72 cm of mercury column. The volume of gas is made 900 cm^3 by compressing it isothermally. The stress of the gas will be

    (a) 8 cm of Hg   (b) 7 cm of Hg
    (c) 6 cm of Hg   (d) 4 cm of Hg

26. An ideal gas is taken through the cycle $A \to B \to C \to A$, as shown in figure. If the net heat supplied to the gas in the cycle is 5 J, the work done by the gas in the process $C \to A$ is

    (a) -5 J

    (b) -10 J

    (c) -15 J

    (d) -20 J

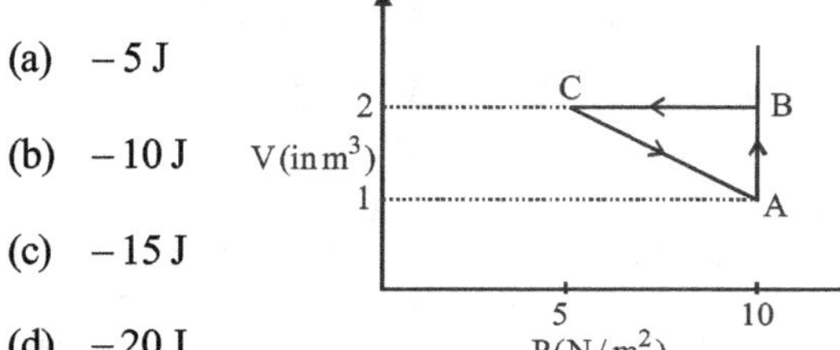

27. An ideal gas undergoing adiabatic change has the following pressure-temperature relationship

    (a) $P^{\gamma-1}T^{\gamma} = $ constant   (b) $P^{\gamma}T^{\gamma-1} = $ constant
    (c) $P^{\gamma}T^{1-\gamma} = $ constant   (d) $P^{1-\gamma}T^{\gamma} = $ constant

28. In a thermodynamic process, fixed mass of a gas is changed in such a manner that the gas release 20 J of heat and 8 J of work was done on the gas. If the initial internal energy of the gas was 30 J, the final internal energy will be

    (a) 2 joule   (b) 18 joule   (c) 42 joule   (d) 58 joule

29. The coefficient of performance of a refrigerator is 5. If the inside temperature of freezer is $-20°$C, then the temperature of the surroundings to which it rejects heat is

    (a) 41°C   (b) 11°C   (c) 21°C   (d) 31°C

30. Monatomic, diatomic and polyatomic ideal gases each undergo slow adiabatic expansions from the same initial volume and same initial pressure to the same final volume. The magnitude of the work done by the environment on the gas is

    (a) the greatest for the polyatomic gas
    (b) the greatest for the monatomic gas
    (c) the greatest for the diatomic gas

    (d) the question is irrelevant, there is no meaning of slow adiabatic expansion

31. The given p-v diagram represents the thermodynamic cycle of an engine, operating with an ideal monatomic gas. The amount of heat, extracted from the source in a single cycle is

    (a) $p_0 v_0$

    (b) $\left(\dfrac{13}{2}\right)p_0 v_0$

    (c) $\left(\dfrac{11}{2}\right)p_0 v_0$

    (d) $4 p_0 v_0$

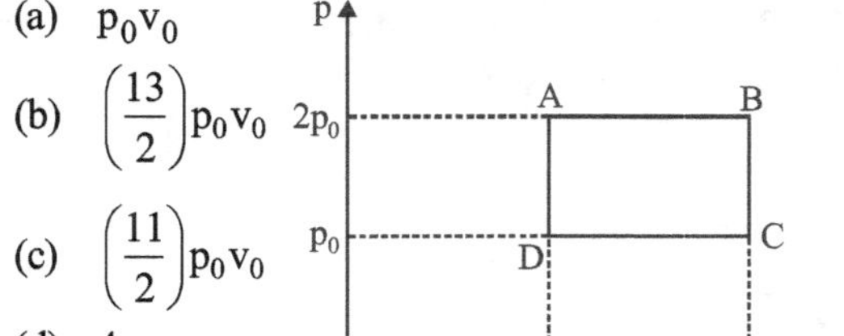

32. For an ideal gas graph is shown for three processes. Process 1, 2 and 3 are respectively.

    (a) Isobaric, adiabatic, isochoric
    (b) Adiabatic, isobaric, isochoric
    (c) Isochoric, adiabatic, isobaric
    (d) Isochoric, isobaric, adiabatic

33. During an adiabatic process an object does 100J of work and its temperature decreases by 5K. During another process it does 25J of work and its temperature decreases by 5K. Its heat capacity for 2nd process is

    (a) 20 J/K   (b) 24 J/K   (c) 15 J/K   (d) 100 J/K

34. A refrigerator works between 4°C and 30°C. It is required to remove 600 calories of heat every second in order to keep the temperature of the refrigerated space constant. The power required is: (Take 1 cal = 4.2 joule)

    (a) 2.365 W   (b) 23.65 W   (c) 236.5 W   (d) 2365 W

35. A perfect gas goes from a state A to another state B by absorbing 8×10^5 J of heat and doing 6.5×10^5 J of external work. It is now transferred between the same two states in another process in which it absorbs 10^5 J of heat. In the second process

    (a) work done by gas is 10^5 J
    (b) work done on gas is 10^5 J
    (c) work done by gas is 0.5×10^5 J
    (d) work done on the gas is 0.5×10^5 J

36. One mole of a diatomic ideal gas undergoes a cyclic process ABC as shown in figure. The process BC is adiabatic. The temperatures at A, B and C are 400 K, 800 K and 600 K respectively. Choose the correct statement:

    (a) The change in internal energy in whole cyclic process is 250 R.
    (b) The change in internal energy in the process CA is 700 R.
    (c) The change in internal energy in the process AB is -350 R.
    (d) The change in internal energy in the process BC is -500 R.

37. Two Carnot engines A and B are operated in series. The engine A receives heat from the source at temperature T_1 and rejects the heat to the sink at temperature T. The second engine B receives the heat at temperature T and rejects to its sink at temperature T_2. For what value of T the efficiencies of the two engines are equal?

(a) $\dfrac{T_1 + T_2}{2}$ (b) $\dfrac{T_1 - T_2}{2}$ (c) $T_1 T_2$ (d) $\sqrt{T_1 T_2}$

38. An ideal gas is initially at P_1, V_1 is expanded to P_2, V_2 and then compressed adiabatically to the same volume V_1 and pressure P_3. If W is the net work done by the gas in complete process which of the following is true ?

(a) $W > 0\,; P_3 > P_1$ (b) $W < 0\,; P_3 > P_1$

(c) $W > 0\,; P_3 < P_1$ (d) $W < 0\,; P_3 < P_1$

39. Which of the following statements is correct for any thermodynamic system ?

(a) The change in entropy can never be zero

(b) Internal energy and entropy are state functions

(c) The internal energy changes in all processes

(d) The work done in an adiabatic process is always zero.

40. One mole of an ideal gas goes from an initial state A to final state B via two processes : It first undergoes isothermal expansion from volume V to 3V and then its volume is reduced from 3V to V at constant pressure. The correct P-V diagram representing the two processes is :

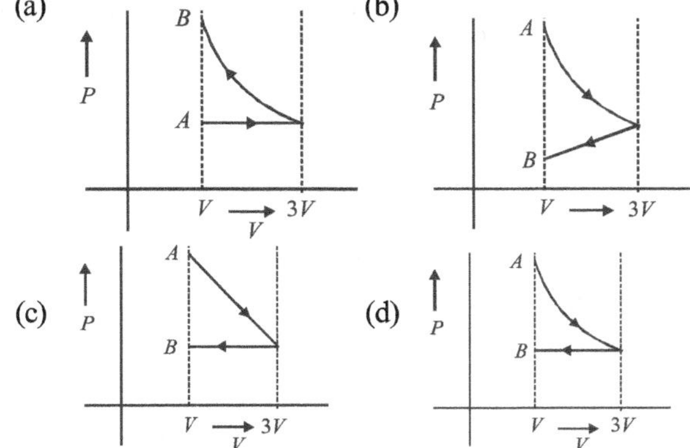

41. What will be the final pressure if an ideal gas in a cylinder is compressed adiabatically to $\dfrac{1}{3}$ rd of its volume?

(a) Final pressure will be three times less than initial pressure.

(b) Final pressure will be three times more than initial pressure.

(c) Change in pressure will be more than three times the initial pressure.

(d) Change in pressure will be less than three times the initial pressure.

42. A gas is compressed isothermally to half its initial volume. The same gas is compressed separately through an adiabatic process until its volume is again reduced to half. Then :

(a) Compressing the gas isothermally will require more work to be done.

(b) Compressing the gas through adiabatic process will require more work to be done.

(c) Compressing the gas isothermally or adiabatically will require the same amount of work.

(d) Which of the case (whether compression through isothermal or through adiabatic process) requires more work will depend upon the atomicity of the gas.

43. An ideal gas goes from state A to state B via three different processes as indicated in the P-V diagram : If Q_1, Q_2, Q_3 indicate the heat a absorbed by the gas along the three processes and $\Delta U_1, \Delta U_2, \Delta U_3$ indicate the change in internal energy along the three processes respectively, then

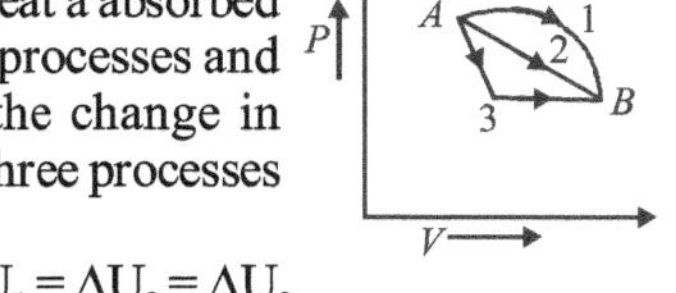

(a) $Q_1 > Q_2 > Q_3$ and $\Delta U_1 = \Delta U_2 = \Delta U_3$

(b) $Q_3 > Q_2 > Q_1$ and $\Delta U_1 = \Delta U_2 = \Delta U_3$

(c) $Q_1 = Q_2 = Q_3$ and $\Delta U_1 > \Delta U_2 > \Delta U_3$

(d) $Q_3 > Q_2 > Q_1$ and $\Delta U_1 > \Delta U_2 > \Delta U_3$

44. In P-V diagram shown in figure ABC is a semicircle. The work done in the process ABC is

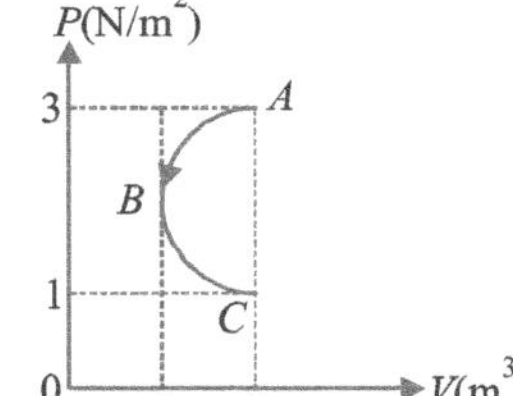

(a) 4 J

(b) $\dfrac{-\pi}{2}$ J

(c) $\dfrac{\pi}{2}$ J

(d) zero

45. For an isothermal expansion of a perfect gas, the value of $\dfrac{\Delta P}{P}$ is equal to

(a) $-\gamma^{1/2}\dfrac{\Delta V}{V}$ (b) $-\dfrac{\Delta V}{V}$ (c) $-\gamma\dfrac{\Delta V}{V}$ (d) $-\gamma^2\dfrac{\Delta V}{V}$

RESPONSE	37. (a)(b)(c)(d)	38. (a)(b)(c)(d)	39. (a)(b)(c)(d)	40. (a)(b)(c)(d)	41. (a)(b)(c)(d)
GRID	42. (a)(b)(c)(d)	43. (a)(b)(c)(d)	44. (a)(b)(c)(d)	45. (a)(b)(c)(d)	

DAILY PRACTICE PROBLEM DPP CHAPTERWISE CP11 - PHYSICS

Total Questions	45	Total Marks	180
Attempted		Correct	
Incorrect		Net Score	
Cut-off Score	45	Qualifying Score	60
Success Gap = Net Score − Qualifying Score			
Net Score = (Correct × 4) − (Incorrect × 1)			

Space for Rough Work

DPP - Daily Practice Problems

Chapter-wise Sheets

Date : ___________   Start Time : ___________   End Time : ___________

PHYSICS $\boxed{\text{CP12}}$

SYLLABUS : Kinetic Theory

Max. Marks : 180   **Marking Scheme :** (+4) for correct & (–1) for incorrect answer   **Time : 60 min.**

INSTRUCTIONS : This Daily Practice Problem Sheet contains 45 MCQs. For each question only one option is correct. Darken the correct circle/ bubble in the Response Grid provided on each page.

1. 4.0 g of a gas occupies 22.4 litres at NTP. The specific heat capacity of the gas at constant volume is $5.0\,JK^{-1}$. If the speed of any quantity x in this gas at NTP is $952\ ms^{-1}$, then the heat capacity at constant pressure is (Take gas constant $R = 8.3\ JK^{-1}\,mol^{-1}$)

   (a) $7.5\ JK^{-1}\,mol^{-1}$ (b) $7.0\ JK^{-1}\,mol^{-1}$

   (c) $8.5\ JK^{-1}\,mol^{-1}$ (d) $8.0\ JK^{-1}\,mol^{-1}$

2. A fixed mass of gas at constant pressure occupies a volume V. The gas undergoes a rise in temperature so that the root mean square velocity of its molecules is doubled. The new volume will be

   (a) V/2   (b) $V/\sqrt{2}$ (c) 2V   (d) 4V

3. A gaseous mixture consists of 16 g of helium and 16 g of oxygen. The ratio $\dfrac{C_p}{C_v}$ of the mixture is

   (a) 1.62   (b) 1.59   (c) 1.54   (d) 1.4

4. Air is pumped into an automobile tube upto a pressure of 200 kPa in the morning when the air temperature is 22°C. During the day, temperature rises to 42°C and the tube expands by 2%. The pressure of the air in the tube at this temperature, will be approximately

   (a) 212 kPa   (b) 209 kPa   (c) 206 kPa   (d) 200 kPa

5. The rms speed of the particles of fume of mass 5×10^{-17} kg executing Brownian motion in air at N.T.P. is ($k = 1.38 \times 10^{-23}$ J/K)

   (a) 1.5 m/s   (b) 3.0 m/s   (c) 1.5 cm/s   (d) 3 cm/s

6. One mole of an ideal monoatomic gas requires 207 J heat to raise the temperature by 10 K when heated at constant pressure. If the same gas is heated at constant volume to raise the temperature by the same 10 K, the heat required is [Given the gas constant R = 8.3 J/ mol. K]

   (a) 198.7 J   (b) 29 J   (c) 215.3 J   (d) 124 J

RESPONSE GRID	1. ⓐⓑⓒⓓ	2. ⓐⓑⓒⓓ	3. ⓐⓑⓒⓓ	4. ⓐⓑⓒⓓ	5. ⓐⓑⓒⓓ
	6. ⓐⓑⓒⓓ				

Space for Rough Work

7. Figure shows the variation in temperature (ΔT) with the amount of heat supplied (Q) in an isobaric process corresponding to a monoatomic (M), diatomic (D) and a polyatomic (P) gas. The initial state of all the gases are the same and the scales for the two axes coincide. Ignoring vibrational degrees of freedom, the lines a, b and c respectively correspond to

(a) P, M and D

(b) M, D and P

(c) P, D and M

(d) D, M and P

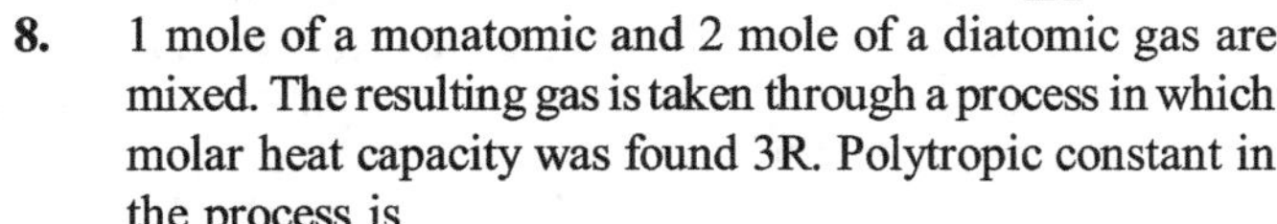

8. 1 mole of a monatomic and 2 mole of a diatomic gas are mixed. The resulting gas is taken through a process in which molar heat capacity was found 3R. Polytropic constant in the process is

(a) –1/5   (b) 1/5   (c) 2/5   (d) –2/5

9. The density of a gas is 6×10^{-2} kg/m³ and the root mean square velocity of the gas molecules is 500 m/s. The pressure exerted by the gas on the walls of the vessel is

(a) 5×10^3 N/m²   (b) 1.2×10^{-4} N/m²
(c) 0.83×10^{-4} N/m²   (d) 30 N/m²

10. The absolute temperature of a gas is increases 3 times. The root mean square velocity of the moelcules will be

(a) 3 times   (b) 9 times
(c) 1/3 times   (d) √3 times

11 Consider an ideal gas confined in an isolated closed chamber. As the gas undergoes an adiabatic expansion, the average time of collision between molecules increases as V^q, where

V is the volume of the gas. The value of q is : $\left(\gamma = \dfrac{C_p}{C_v} \right)$

(a) $\dfrac{\gamma+1}{2}$ (b) $\dfrac{\gamma-1}{2}$ (c) $\dfrac{3\gamma+5}{6}$ (d) $\dfrac{3\gamma-5}{6}$

12. One kg of a diatomic gas is at a pressure of 8×10^4 N/m². The density of the gas is 4 kg/m³. What is the energy of the gas due to its thermal motion?

(a) 5×10^4 J   (b) 6×10^4 J
(c) 7×10^4 J   (d) 3×10^4 J

13. A thermally insulated vessel contains an ideal gas of molecular mass M and ratio of specific heats γ. It is moving with speed v and it suddenly brought to rest. Assuming no heat is lost to the surroundings, its temperature increases by

(a) $\dfrac{(\gamma-1)}{2\gamma R} Mv^2 K$ (b) $\dfrac{\gamma Mv^2}{2R} K$

(c) $\dfrac{(\gamma-1)}{2R} Mv^2 K$ (d) $\dfrac{(\gamma-1)}{2(\gamma+1)R} Mv^2 K$

14. Figure shows a parabolic graph between T and 1/V for a mixture of a gases undergoing an adiabatic process. What is the ratio of V_{rms} of molecules and speed of sound in mixture?

(a) $\sqrt{3/2}$

(b) $\sqrt{2}$

(c) $\sqrt{2/3}$

(d) $\sqrt{3}$

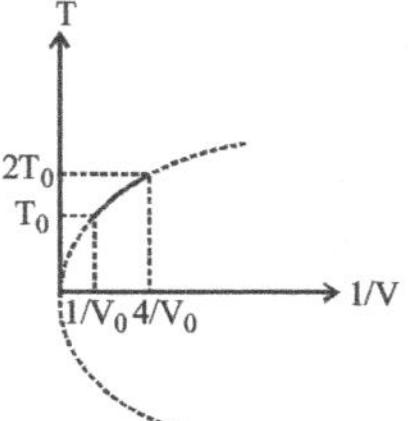

15. The work of 146 kJ is performed in order to compress one kilomole of gas adiabatically and in this process the temperature of the gas increases by 7°C. The gas is ($R = 8.3$ J mol⁻¹ K⁻¹)

(a) diatomic
(b) triatomic
(c) a mixture of monatomic and diatomic
(d) monatomic

16. At what temperature is root mean square velocity of gaseous hydrogen molecules equal to that of oxygen molecules at 47°C?

(a) 40K   (b) 80K   (c) –73K   (d) 3K

17. The kinetic theory of gases states that the average squared velocity of molecules varies linearly with the mean molecular weight of the gas. If the root mean square (rms) velocity of oxygen molecules at a certain temperature is 0.5 km/sec. The rms velocity for hydrogen molecules at the same temperature will be :

(a) 2 km/sec (b) 4 km/sec (c) 8 km/sec (d) 16 km/sec

18. If 2 moles of an ideal monatomic gas at temperature T_0 is mixed with 4 moles of another ideal monatomic gas at temperature $2T_0$, then the temperature of the mixture is

(a) $\dfrac{5}{3} T_0$ (b) $\dfrac{3}{2} T_0$ (c) $\dfrac{4}{3} T_0$ (d) $\dfrac{5}{4} T_0$

19. From the following statements, concerning ideal gas at any given temperature T, select the incorrect one(s)

(a) The coefficient of volume expansion at constant pressure is same for all ideal gas
(b) The average translational kinetic energy per molecule of oxygen gas is $3 KT$ (K being Boltzmann constant)
(c) In a gaseous mixture, the average translational kinetic energy of the molecules of each component is same
(d) The mean free path of molecules increases with decrease in pressure

RESPONSE GRID	7. ⓐⓑⓒⓓ	8. ⓐⓑⓒⓓ	9. ⓐⓑⓒⓓ	10. ⓐⓑⓒⓓ	11. ⓐⓑⓒⓓ
	12. ⓐⓑⓒⓓ	13. ⓐⓑⓒⓓ	14. ⓐⓑⓒⓓ	15. ⓐⓑⓒⓓ	16. ⓐⓑⓒⓓ
	17. ⓐⓑⓒⓓ	18. ⓐⓑⓒⓓ	19. ⓐⓑⓒⓓ		

20. The adjoining figure shows graph of pressure and volume of a gas at two tempertures T_1 and T_2. Which of the following inferences is correct?
    (a) $T_1 > T_2$
    (b) $T_1 = T_2$
    (c) $T_1 < T_2$
    (d) None of these

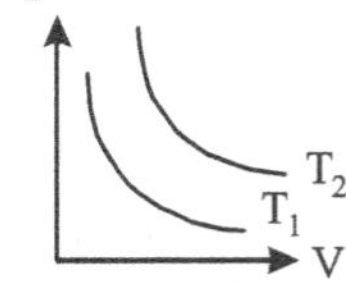

21. The molecules of a given mass of gas have a root mean square velocity of 200m s^{-1} at 27°C and $1.0 \times 10^5 \text{ N m}^{-2}$ pressure. When the temperature is 127°C and the pressure $0.5 \times 10^5 \text{ Nm}^{-2}$, the root mean square velocity in ms^{-1}, is
    (a) $\dfrac{400}{\sqrt{3}}$
    (b) $100\sqrt{2}$
    (c) $\dfrac{100\sqrt{2}}{3}$
    (d) $\dfrac{100}{3}$

22. A graph is plotted with PV/T on y-axis and mass of the gas along x-axis for different gases. The graph is
    (a) a straight line parallel to x-axis for all the gases
    (b) a straight line passing through origin with a slope having a constant value for all the gases
    (c) a straight line passing through origin with a slope having different values for different gases
    (d) a straight line parallel to y-axis for all the gases

23. At identical temperatures, the rms speed of hydrogen molecules is 4 times that for oxygen molecules. In a mixture of these in mass ratio $H_2 : O_2 = 1:8$, the rms speed of all molecules is n times the rms speed for O_2 molecules, where n is
    (a) 3
    (b) 4/3
    (c) $(8/3)^{1/2}$
    (d) $(11)^{1/2}$

24. Work done by a system under isothermal change from a volume V_1 to V_2 for a gases which obeys Vander Waal's equation $(V - \beta n)\left(P + \dfrac{\alpha n^2}{V}\right) = nRT$ is

    (a) $nRT \log_e\left(\dfrac{V_2 - n\beta}{V_1 - n\beta}\right) + \alpha n^2\left(\dfrac{V_1 - V_2}{V_1 V_2}\right)$

    (b) $nRT \log_{10}\left(\dfrac{V_2 - n\beta}{V_1 - n\beta}\right) + \alpha n^2\left(\dfrac{V_1 - V_2}{V_1 V_2}\right)$

    (c) $nRT \log_e\left(\dfrac{V_2 - n\beta}{V_1 - n\beta}\right) + \beta n^2\left(\dfrac{V_1 - V_2}{V_1 V_2}\right)$

    (d) $nRT \log_e\left(\dfrac{V_1 - n\beta}{V_2 - n\beta}\right) + \alpha n^2\left(\dfrac{V_1 V_2}{V_1 - V_2}\right)$

25. Two vessels separately contain two ideal gases A and B at the same temperature. The pressure of A being twice that of B. Under such conditions, the density of A is found to be 1.5 times the density of B. The ratio of molecular weight of A and B is :

26. The temperature of the mixture of one mole of helium and one mole of hydrogen is increased from 0°C to 100°C at constant pressure. The amount of heat delivered will be
    (a) 600 cal (b) 1200 cal (c) 1800 cal (d) 3600 cal

27. If the intermolecular forces vanish away, the volume occupied by the molecules contained in 4.5 g water at standard temperature and pressure will be
    (a) 5.6 litre (b) 4.5 litre (c) 11.2 litre (d) 6.5 litre

28. A gas mixture consists of 2 moles of oxygen and 4 moles of Argon at temperature T. Neglecting all vibrational moles, the total internal energy of the system is
    (a) 4 RT (b) 15 RT (c) 9 RT (d) 11RT

29. A vessel has 6g of hydrogen at pressure P and temperature 500K. A small hole is made in it so that hydrogen leaks out. How much hydrogen leaks out if the final pressure is P/2 and temperature falls to 300 K ?
    (a) 2g (b) 3g (c) 4g (d) 1g

30. For a gas if ratio of specific heats at constant pressure and volume is γ then value of degrees of freedom is
    (a) $\dfrac{3\gamma - 1}{2\gamma - 1}$ (b) $\dfrac{2}{\gamma - 1}$ (c) $\dfrac{9}{2}(\gamma - 1)$ (d) $\dfrac{25}{2}(\gamma - 1)$

31. The given *P-V* curve is predicted by
    (a) Boyle's law
    (b) Charle's law
    (c) Avogadro's law
    (d) Gaylussac's law

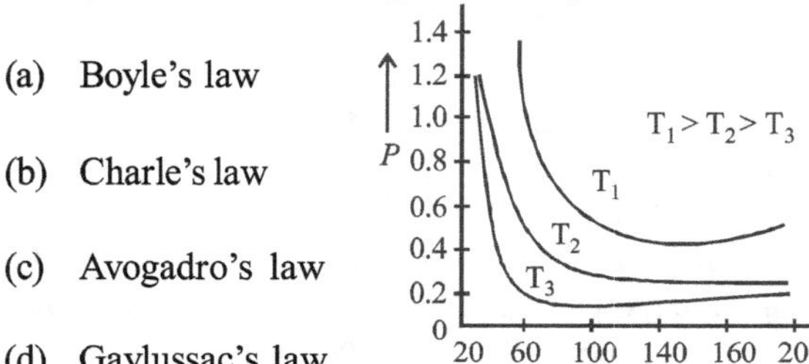

32. Three perfect gases at absolute temperatures T_1, T_2 and T_3 are mixed. The masses of molecules are m_1, m_2 and m_3 and the number of molecules are n_1, n_2 and n_3 respectively. Assuming no loss of energy, the final temperature of the mixture is :

    (a) $\dfrac{n_1 T_1 + n_2 T_2 + n_3 T_3}{n_1 + n_2 + n_3}$

    (b) $\dfrac{n_1 T_1^2 + n_2 T_2^2 + n_3 T_3^2}{n_1 T_1 + n_2 T_2 + n_3 T_3}$

    (c) $\dfrac{n_1^2 T_1^2 + n_2^2 T_2^2 + n_3^2 T_3^2}{n_1 T_1 + n_2 T_2 + n_3 T_3}$

    (d) $\dfrac{(T_1 + T_2 + T_3)}{3}$

33. A gas is enclosed in a cube of side *l*. What will be the change in momentum of the molecule, if it suffers an elastic collision with the plane wall parallel to *yz*-plane and rebounds with the same velocity ?
    $[(V_x, V_y$ & $V_z)$ initial velocities of the gas molecules]
    (a) mv_x (b) zero (c) $- mv_x$ (d) $-2mv_x$

(25.) (a) $\dfrac{3}{4}$ (b) 2 (c) $\dfrac{1}{2}$ (d) $\dfrac{2}{3}$

<table>
<tr><td rowspan="3">**RESPONSE GRID**</td><td>20.ⓐⓑⓒⓓ</td><td>21.ⓐⓑⓒⓓ</td><td>22.ⓐⓑⓒⓓ</td><td>23.ⓐⓑⓒⓓ</td><td>24.ⓐⓑⓒⓓ</td></tr>
<tr><td>25.ⓐⓑⓒⓓ</td><td>26.ⓐⓑⓒⓓ</td><td>27.ⓐⓑⓒⓓ</td><td>28.ⓐⓑⓒⓓ</td><td>29.ⓐⓑⓒⓓ</td></tr>
<tr><td>30.ⓐⓑⓒⓓ</td><td>31.ⓐⓑⓒⓓ</td><td>32.ⓐⓑⓒⓓ</td><td>33.ⓐⓑⓒⓓ</td><td></td></tr>
</table>

34. What will be the ratio of number of molecules of a monoatomic and a diatomic gas in a vessel, if the ratio of their partial pressures is 5 : 3 ?

(a)　5 : 1　　(b)　3 : 1　　(c)　5 : 3　　(d)　3 : 5

35. The average transitional energy and the rms speed of molecules in a sample of oxygen gas at 300 K are 6.21×10^{-21} J and 484 m/s respectively. The corresponding values at 600 K are nearly (assuming ideal gas behaviour)

(a)　12.42×10^{-21} J, 968 m/s　(b)　8.78×10^{-21} J, 684 m/s

(c)　6.21×10^{-21} J, 968 m/s　(d)　12.42×10^{-21} J, 684 m/s

36. At $10°$ C the value of the density of a fixed mass of an ideal gas divided by its pressure is x. At $110°C$ this ratio is:

(a)　x　　(b)　$\dfrac{383}{283}x$　　(c)　$\dfrac{10}{110}x$　　(d)　$\dfrac{283}{383}x$

37. If the potential energy of a gas molecule is $U = M/r^6 - N/r^{12}$, M and N being positive constants. Then the potential energy at equilibrium must be

(a)　zero　　(b)　$M^2/4N$　　(c)　$N^2/4M$　　(d)　$MN^2/4$

38. Consider a gas with density ρ and $\bar{c}$ as the root mean square velocity of its molecules contained in a volume. If the system moves as whole with velocity v, then the pressure exerted by the gas is

(a)　$\dfrac{1}{3}\rho\bar{c}^2$

(b)　$\dfrac{1}{3}\rho(c+v)^2$

(c)　$\dfrac{1}{3}\rho(\bar{c}-v)^2$

(d)　$\dfrac{1}{3}\rho(c^{-2}-v)^2$

39. How is the mean free path (λ) in a gas related to the interatomic distance?

(a)　λ is 10 times the interatomic distance

(b)　λ is 100 times the interatomic distance

(c)　λ is 1000 times the interatomic distance

(d)　λ is $\dfrac{1}{10}$ times of the interatomic distance

40. Four molecules have speeds 2 km/sec, 3 km/sec, 4 km/sec and 5 km/sec. The root mean square speed of these molecules (in km/sec) is

(a)　$\sqrt{54/4}$　(b)　$\sqrt{54/2}$　(c)　3.5　　(d)　$3\sqrt{3}$

41. If R is universal gas constant, the amount of heat needed to raise the temperature of 2 moles of an ideal monoatomic gas from 273 K to 373 K, when no work is done, is

(a)　$100R$　　(b)　$150R$　　(c)　$300R$　　(d)　$500R$

42. N molecules, each of mass m, of gas A and 2 N molecules, each of mass 2 m, of gas B are contained in the same vessel which is maintained at a temperature T. The mean square velocity of molecules of B type is denoted by V_2 and the mean square velocity of A type is denoted by V_1, then $\dfrac{V_1}{V_2}$ is

(a)　2　　　(b)　1　　　(c)　1/3　　(d)　2/3

43. The root mean square value of the speed of the molecules in a fixed mass of an ideal gas is increased by increasing

(a)　the volume while keeping the temperature constant

(b)　the pressure while keeping the volume constant

(c)　the temperature while keeping the pressure constant

(d)　the pressure while keeping the temperature constant

44. The P-V diagram of a diatomic gas is a straight line passing through origin. The molar heat capacity of the gas in the process will be

(a)　4R　　(b)　2.5 R　　(c)　3 R　　(d)　$\dfrac{4R}{3}$

45. For a gas, difference between two specific heats is 5000 J/mole°C. If the ratio of specific heats is 1.6, the two specific heats in J/mole-°C are

(a)　$C_P = 1.33 \times 10^4$, $C_V = 2.66 \times 10^4$

(b)　$C_P = 13.3 \times 10^4$, $C_V = 8.33 \times 10^3$

(c)　$C_P = 1.33 \times 10^4$, $C_V = 8.33 \times 10^3$

(d)　$C_P = 2.6 \times 10^4$, $C_V = 8.33 \times 10^4$

<table>
<tr><td rowspan="3">RESPONSE GRID</td><td>34. ⓐⓑⓒⓓ</td><td>35. ⓐⓑⓒⓓ</td><td>36. ⓐⓑⓒⓓ</td><td>37. ⓐⓑⓒⓓ</td><td>38. ⓐⓑⓒⓓ</td></tr>
<tr><td>39. ⓐⓑⓒⓓ</td><td>40. ⓐⓑⓒⓓ</td><td>41. ⓐⓑⓒⓓ</td><td>42. ⓐⓑⓒⓓ</td><td>43. ⓐⓑⓒⓓ</td></tr>
<tr><td>44. ⓐⓑⓒⓓ</td><td>45. ⓐⓑⓒⓓ</td><td></td><td></td><td></td></tr>
</table>

DAILY PRACTICE PROBLEM DPP CHAPTERWISE CP12 - PHYSICS

Total Questions	45	Total Marks	180
Attempted		Correct	
Incorrect		Net Score	
Cut-off Score	50	Qualifying Score	70
Success Gap = Net Score – Qualifying Score			
Net Score = (Correct × 4) – (Incorrect × 1)			

PHYSICS $\boxed{\text{CP13}}$

SYLLABUS : Oscillations

Max. Marks : 180   **Marking Scheme :** (+4) for correct & (–1) for incorrect answer   **Time : 60 min.**

INSTRUCTIONS : This Daily Practice Problem Sheet contains 45 MCQs. For each question only one option is correct. Darken the correct circle/ bubble in the Response Grid provided on each page.

1. If x, v and a denote the displacement, the velocity and the acceleration of a particle executing simple harmonic motion of time period T, then, which of the following does not change with time?
   (a) aT/x
   (b) $aT + 2\pi v$
   (c) aT/v
   (d) $a^2T^2 + 4\pi^2v^2$

2. A mass is suspended separately by two different springs in successive order, then time periods is t_1 and t_2 respectively. It is connected by both springs as shown in fig. then time period is t_0. The correct relation is
   (a) $t_0^2 = t_1^2 + t_2^2$
   (b) $t_0^{-2} = t_1^{-2} + t_2^{-2}$
   (c) $t_0^{-1} = t_1^{-1} + t_2^{-1}$
   (d) $t_0 = t_1 + t_2$

3. A rod of length ℓ is in motion such that its ends A and B are moving along x-axis and y-axis respectively. It is given that $\dfrac{d\theta}{dt} = 2$ rad/sec always. P is a fixed point on the rod. Let M be the projection of P on x-axis. For the time interval in which θ changes from 0 to $\dfrac{\pi}{2}$, the correct statement is
   (a) The acceleration of M is always directed towards right
   (b) M executes SHM
   (c) M moves with constant speed
   (d) M moves with constant acceleration

4. A particle of mass m executes simple harmonic motion with amplitude a and frequency v. The average kinetic energy during its motion from the position of equilibrium to the end is
   (a) $2\pi^2ma^2v^2$
   (b) $\pi^2ma^2v^2$
   (c) $\dfrac{1}{4}ma^2v^2$
   (d) $4\pi^2ma^2v^2$

5. A mass M attached to a spring oscillates with a period of 2s. If the mass is increased by 2 kg, then the period increases by 2s. Find the initial mass M assuming that Hooke's law is obeyed.
   (a) $\dfrac{2}{3}$kg   (b) $\dfrac{1}{3}$kg   (c) $\dfrac{1}{2}$kg   (d) 1 kg

| **RESPONSE GRID** | 1. ⓐⓑⓒⓓ | 2. ⓐⓑⓒⓓ | 3. ⓐⓑⓒⓓ | 4. ⓐⓑⓒⓓ | 5. ⓐⓑⓒⓓ |

Space for Rough Work

6. The amplitude of a damped oscillator becomes $\left(\dfrac{1}{3}\right)^{rd}$ in 2 seconds. If its amplitude after 6 seconds is $\dfrac{1}{n}$ times the original amplitude, the value of n is

(a) 3^2 (b) 3^3 (c) $\sqrt[3]{3}$ (d) 2^3

7. Assume the earth to be perfect sphere of uniform density. If a body is dropped at one end of a tunnel dug along a diameter of the earth (remember that inside the tunnel the force on the body is – k times the displacement from the centre, k being a constant), it (body) will
(a) reach the earth's centre and stay there
(b) go through the tunnel and comes out at the other end
(c) oscillate simple harmonically in the tunnel
(d) stay somewhere between the earth's centre and one of the ends of tunnel.

8. A particle undergoes simple harmonic motion having time period T. The time taken in 3/8th oscillation is

(a) $\dfrac{3}{8}T$ (b) $\dfrac{5}{8}T$ (c) $\dfrac{5}{12}T$ (d) $\dfrac{7}{12}T$

9. A particle is executing simple harmonic motion with amplitude A. When the ratio of its kinetic energy to the potential energy is $\dfrac{1}{4}$, its displacement from its mean position is

(a) $\dfrac{2}{\sqrt{5}}A$ (b) $\dfrac{\sqrt{3}}{2}A$ (c) $\dfrac{3}{4}A$ (d) $\dfrac{1}{4}A$

10. The length of a simple pendulum executing simple harmonic motion is increased by 21%. The percentage increase in the time period of the pendulum of increased length is
(a) 11%   (b) 21%   (c) 42%   (d) 10%

11. The time period of a mass suspended from a spring is T. If the spring is cut into four equal parts and the same mass is suspended from one of the parts, then the new time period will be

(a) $2T$ (b) $\dfrac{T}{4}$ (c) 2 (d) $\dfrac{T}{2}$

12. Two simple harmonic motions act on a particle. These harmonic motions are $x = A\cos(\omega t + \delta)$, $y = A\cos(\omega t + \alpha)$ when $\delta = \alpha + \dfrac{\pi}{2}$, the resulting motion is
(a) a circle and the actual motion is clockwise
(b) an ellipse and the actual motion is counterclockwise
(c) an elllipse and the actual motion is clockwise
(d) a circle and the actual motion is counter clockwise

13. A point mass oscillates along the x-axis according to the law $x = x_0\cos(\omega t - \pi/4)$. If the acceleration of the particle is written as $a = A\cos(\omega t - \delta)$, then
(a) $A = x_0\omega^2,\ \delta = 3\pi/4$ (b) $A = x_0,\ \delta = -\pi/4$
(c) $A = x_0\omega^2,\ \delta = \pi/4$ (d) $A = x_0\omega^2,\ \delta = -\pi/4$

14. A mass M is suspended from a spring of negligible mass. The spring is pulled a little and then released so that the mass executes SHM of time period T. If the mass is increased by m, the time period becomes $\dfrac{5T}{3}$. Then the ratio of $\dfrac{m}{M}$ is

(a) $\dfrac{3}{5}$ (b) $\dfrac{25}{9}$ (c) $\dfrac{16}{9}$ (d) $\dfrac{5}{3}$

15. A body oscillates with a simple harmonic motion having amplitude 0.05 m. At a certain instant of time, its displacement is 0.01 m and acceleration is 1.0 m/s². The period of oscillation is

(a) 0.1 s   (b) 0.2 s   (c) $\dfrac{\pi}{10}$ s   (d) $\dfrac{\pi}{5}$ s

16. The particle executing simple harmonic motion has a kinetic energy $K_0\cos^2\omega t$. The maximum values of the potential energy and the total energy are respectively
(a) $K_0/2$ and K_0 (b) K_0 and $2K_0$
(c) K_0 and K_0 (d) 0 and $2K_0$

17. A simple pendulum attached to the ceiling of a stationary lift has a time period T. The distance y covered by the lift moving upwards varies with time t as $y = t^2$ where y is in metres and t in seconds. If $g = 10$ m/s², the time period of pendulum will be

(a) $\sqrt{\dfrac{4}{5}}T$ (b) $\sqrt{\dfrac{5}{6}}T$ (c) $\sqrt{\dfrac{5}{4}}T$ (d) $\sqrt{\dfrac{6}{5}}T$

18. A particle moves with simple harmonic motion in a straight line. In first τs, after starting from rest it travels a distance a, and in next τ s it travels 2a, in same direction, then:
(a) amplitude of motion is 3a
(b) time period of oscillations is 8τ
(c) amplitude of motion is 4a
(d) time period of oscillations is 6τ

19. Two simple harmonic motions are represented by the equations $y_1 = 0.1\sin\left(100\pi t + \dfrac{\pi}{3}\right)$ and $y_2 = 0.1\cos\pi t$. The phase difference of the velocity of particle 1 with respect to the velocity of particle 2 is

(a) $\dfrac{\pi}{3}$ (b) $\dfrac{-\pi}{6}$ (c) $\dfrac{\pi}{6}$ (d) $\dfrac{-\pi}{3}$

20. Masses M_A and M_B hanging from the ends of strings of lengths L_A and L_B are executing simple harmonic motions. If their frequencies are $f_A = 2f_B$, then
(a) $L_A = 2L_B$ and $M_A = M_B/2$
(b) $L_A = 4L_B$ regardless of masses
(c) $L_A = L_B/4$ regardless of masses
(d) $L_A = 2L_B$ and $M_A = 2M_B$

RESPONSE GRID					
	6. ⓐⓑⓒⓓ	7. ⓐⓑⓒⓓ	8. ⓐⓑⓒⓓ	9. ⓐⓑⓒⓓ	10. ⓐⓑⓒⓓ
	11. ⓐⓑⓒⓓ	12. ⓐⓑⓒⓓ	13. ⓐⓑⓒⓓ	14. ⓐⓑⓒⓓ	15. ⓐⓑⓒⓓ
	16. ⓐⓑⓒⓓ	17. ⓐⓑⓒⓓ	18. ⓐⓑⓒⓓ	19. ⓐⓑⓒⓓ	20. ⓐⓑⓒⓓ

21. In damped oscillations, the amplitude of oscillations is reduced to one-third of its inital value a_0 at the end of 100 oscillations. When the oscillator completes 200 oscillations, its amplitude must be
(a) $a_0/2$ (b) $a_0/4$ (c) $a_0/6$ (d) $a_0/9$

22. The spring constant from the adjoining combination of springs is
(a) K
(b) 2 K
(c) 4 K
(d) 5 K/2

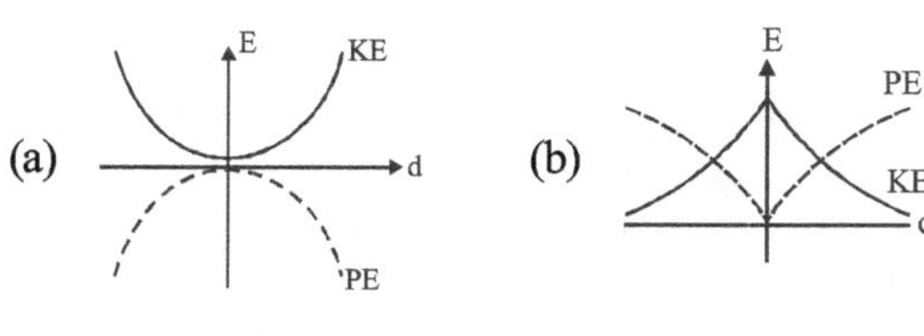

23. A body executes simple harmonic motion. The potential energy (P.E), the kinetic energy (K.E) and total energy (T.E) are measured as a function of displacement x. Which of the following statements is true ?
(a) K.E. is maximum when $x = 0$
(b) T.E is zero when $x = 0$
(c) K.E is maximum when x is maximum
(d) P.E is maximum when $x = 0$

24. A simple harmonic wave having an amplitude a and time period T is represented by the equation $y = 5\sin\pi(t+4)m$. Then the value of amplitude (a) in (m) and time period (T) in second are
(a) $a = 10, T = 2$ (b) $a = 5, T = 1$
(c) $a = 10, T = 1$ (d) $a = 5, T = 2$

25. A particle moves such that its acceleration 'a' is given by a $= -zx$ where x is the displacement from equilibrium position and z is constant. The period of oscillation is
(a) $2\pi/z$ (b) $2\pi/\sqrt{z}$ (c) $\sqrt{2\pi/z}$ (d) $2\sqrt{\pi/z}$

26. The displacement of an object attached to a spring and executing simple harmonic motion is given by $x = 2 \times 10^{-2}\cos\pi t$ metre. The time at which the maximum speed first occurs is
(a) 0.25 s   (b) 0.5 s   (c) 0.75 s   (d) 0.125 s

27. A tunnel has been dug through the centre of the earth and a ball is released in it. It executes S.H.M. with time period
(a) 42 minutes   (b) 1 day
(c) 1 hour   (d) 84.6 minutes

28. The displacement equation of a particle is $x = 3\sin 2t + 4\cos 2t$. The amplitude and maximum velocity will be respectively
(a) 5, 10   (b) 3, 2   (c) 4, 2   (d) 3, 4

29. A body of mass 0.01 kg executes simple harmonic motion about x = 0 under the influence of a force as shown in figure. The time period of SHM is
(a) 1.05 s
(b) 0.52 s
(c) 0.25 s
(d) 0.03 s

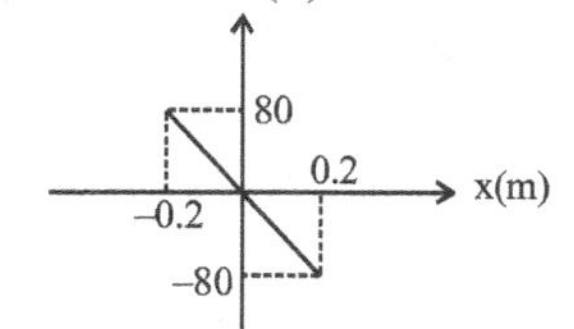

30. Two oscillators are started simultaneously in same phase. After 50 oscillations of one, they get out of phase by π, that is half oscillation. The percentage difference of frequencies of the two oscillators is nearest to
(a) 2%   (b) 1%   (c) 0.5%   (d) 0.25%

31. The length of a second's pendulum at the surface of earth is 1 m. The length of second's pendulum at the surface of moon where g is 1/6th that at earth's surface is
(a) 1/6 m   (b) 6 m   (c) 1/36 m   (d) 36 m

32. A simple spring has length l and force constant K. It is cut into two springs of lengths l_1 and l_2 such that $l_1 = n\, l_2$ (n = an integer). The force constant of spring of length l_1 is
(a) $K(1+n)$ (b) $(K/n)(1+n)$
(c) K (d) $K/(n+1)$

33. The displacement of a particle from its mean position (in metre) is given by $y = 0.2\sin(10\pi t + 1.5\pi)\cos(10\pi t + 1.5\pi)$. The motion of particle is
(a) periodic but not SHM
(b) non-periodic
(c) simple harmonic motion with period 0.1 s
(d) simple harmonic motion with period 0.2s.

34. A point particle of mass 0.1 kg is executing S.H.M. of amplitude 0.1 m. When the particle passes through the mean position, its kinetic energy is 8×10^{-3} joule. Obtain the equation of motion of this particle, if the initial phase of oscillation is 45°.
(a) $y = 0.1\sin\left(\pm 4t + \dfrac{\pi}{4}\right)$ (b) $y = 0.2\sin\left(\pm 4t + \dfrac{\pi}{4}\right)$
(c) $y = 0.1\sin\left(\pm 2t + \dfrac{\pi}{4}\right)$ (d) $y = 0.2\sin\left(\pm 2t + \dfrac{\pi}{4}\right)$

35. For a simple pendulum, a graph is plotted between its kinetic energy (KE) and potential energy (PE) against its displacement d. Which one of the following represents these correctly? (*graphs are schematic and not drawn to scale*)

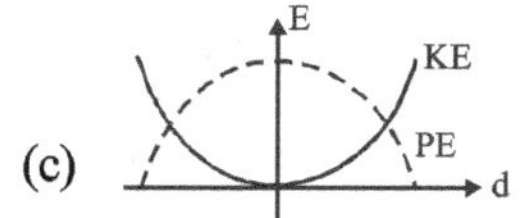

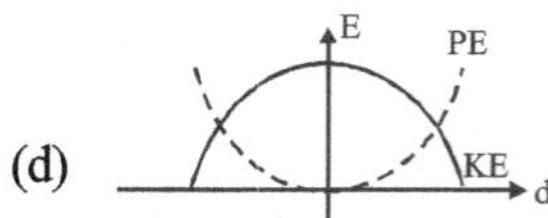

21. (a) (b) (c) (d)	22. (a) (b) (c) (d)

36. The equation of a simple harmonic wave is given by

$$y = 3\sin\frac{\pi}{2}(50t - x)$$

Where x and y are in meters and t is in seconds. The ratio of maximum particle velocity to the wave velocity is

(a) 2π (b) $\frac{3}{2}\pi$ (c) 3π (d) $\frac{2}{3}\pi$

37. If the mass shown in figure is slightly displaced and then let go, then the system shall oscillate with a time period of

(a) $2\pi\sqrt{\dfrac{m}{3k}}$

(b) $2\pi\sqrt{\dfrac{3m}{2k}}$

(c) $2\pi\sqrt{\dfrac{2m}{3k}}$

(d) $2\pi\sqrt{\dfrac{3k}{m}}$

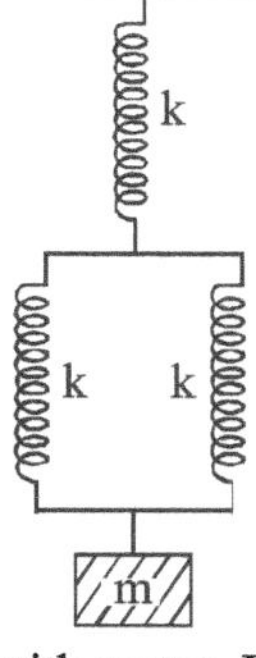

38. A hollow sphere is filled with water. It is hung by a long thread. As the water flows out of a hole at the bottom, the period of oscillation will
(a) first increase and then decrease
(b) first decrease and then increase
(c) go on increasing
(d) go on decreasing

39. The figure shows a position time graph of a particle executing SHM. If the time period of SHM is 2 sec, then the equation of SHM is
(a) $x = 10\cos\pi t$

(b) $x = 5\sin\left(\pi t + \dfrac{\pi}{3}\right)$

(c) $x = 10\sin\left(\pi t + \dfrac{\pi}{3}\right)$

(d) $x = 10\sin\left(\pi t + \dfrac{\pi}{6}\right)$

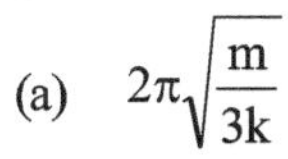

40. A coin is placed on a horizontal platform which undergoes vertical simple harmonic motion of angular frequency ω. The amplitude of oscillation is gradually increased. The coin will leave contact with the platform for the first time
(a) at the mean position of the platform
(b) for an amplitude of $\dfrac{g}{\omega^2}$
(c) for an amplitude of $\dfrac{g^2}{\omega^2}$
(d) at the highest position of the platform

41. The bob of a simple pendulum executes simple harmonic motion in water with a period t, while the period of oscillation of the bob is t_0 in air. Neglecting frictional force of water and given that the density of the bob is $(4/3) \times 1000$ kg/m^3. The relationship between t and t_0 is
(a) $t = 2t_0$ (b) $t = t_0/2$ (c) $t = t_0$ (d) $t = 4t_0$

42. Starting from the origin a body oscillates simple harmonically with a period of 2 s. After what time will its kinetic energy be 75% of the total energy?
(a) $\dfrac{1}{6}$ s   (b) $\dfrac{1}{4}$ s   (c) $\dfrac{1}{3}$ s   (d) $\dfrac{1}{12}$ s

43. A body executes simple harmonic motion under the action of a force F_1 with a time period $\dfrac{4}{5}$ s. If the force is changed to F_2, it executes S.H.M. with time period $\dfrac{3}{5}$ s. If both the forces F_1 and F_2 act simultaneously in the same direction on the body, its time period in second is
(a) $\dfrac{12}{25}$ (b) $\dfrac{7}{5}$ (c) $\dfrac{24}{25}$ (d) $\dfrac{5}{7}$

44. A block connected to a spring oscillates vertically. A damping force F_d, acts on the block by the surrounding medium. Given as $F_d = -bV$, b is a positive constant which depends on :
(a) viscosity of the medium
(b) size of the block
(c) shape of the block
(d) All of these

45. If a simple pendulum of length l has maximum angular displacement θ, then the maximum K.E. of bob of mass m is
(a) $\dfrac{1}{2}ml/g$ (b) $mg/2l$
(c) $mgl(1 - \cos\theta)$ (d) $mgl\sin\theta/2$

| RESPONSE | 36. ⓐⓑⓒⓓ | 37. ⓐⓑⓒⓓ | 38. ⓐⓑⓒⓓ | 39. ⓐⓑⓒⓓ | 40. ⓐⓑⓒⓓ |
| GRID | 41. ⓐⓑⓒⓓ | 42. ⓐⓑⓒⓓ | 43. ⓐⓑⓒⓓ | 44. ⓐⓑⓒⓓ | 45. ⓐⓑⓒⓓ |

DAILY PRACTICE PROBLEM DPP CHAPTERWISE CP13 - PHYSICS

Total Questions	45	Total Marks	180
Attempted		Correct	
Incorrect		Net Score	
Cut-off Score	45	Qualifying Score	60
Success Gap = Net Score − Qualifying Score			
Net Score = (Correct × 4) − (Incorrect × 1)			

Date : | Start Time : | End Time :

PHYSICS $\boxed{\text{CP14}}$

SYLLABUS : Waves

Max. Marks : 180 **Marking Scheme :** (+4) for correct & (–1) for incorrect answer **Time : 60 min.**

INSTRUCTIONS : This Daily Practice Problem Sheet contains 45 MCQs. For each question only one option is correct. Darken the correct circle/ bubble in the Response Grid provided on each page.

---

1. Where should the two bridges be set in a 110cm long wire so that it is divided into three parts and the ratio of the frequencies are 3 : 2 : 1 ?
(a) 20cm from one end and 60cm from other end
(b) 30cm from one end and 70cm from other end
(c) 10cm from one end and 50cm from other end
(d) 50cm from one end and 40cm from other end

2. When a wave travel in a medium, the particle displacement is given by the equation $y = a \sin 2\pi (bt - cx)$ where a, b and c are constants. The maximum particle velocity will be twice the wave velocity if

(a) $c = \dfrac{1}{\pi a}$ (b) $c = \pi a$ (c) $b = ac$ (d) $b = \dfrac{1}{ac}$

3. The wave described by $y = 0.25 \sin (10\pi x - 2\pi t)$,
where x and y are in meters and t in seconds, is a wave travelling along the:
(a) –ve x direction with frequency 1 Hz.
(b) +ve x direction with frequency π Hz and wavelength $\lambda = 0.2$ m.
(c) +ve x direction with frequency 1 Hz and wavelength $\lambda = 0.2$ m
(d) –ve x direction with amplitude 0.25 m and wavelength $\lambda = 0.2$ m

4. The equation of a plane progressive wave is $y = 0.9 \sin 4\pi \left[t - \dfrac{x}{2} \right]$. When it is reflected at a rigid support, its amplitude becomes $\dfrac{2}{3}$ of its previous value. The equation of the reflected wave is

(a) $y = 0.6 \sin 4\pi \left[t + \dfrac{x}{2} \right]$

(b) $y = -0.6 \sin 4\pi \left[t + \dfrac{x}{2} \right]$

(c) $y = -0.9 \sin 8\pi \left[t - \dfrac{x}{2} \right]$

(d) $y = -0.6 \sin 4\pi \left[t + \dfrac{x}{2} \right]$

5. A person carrying a whistle emitting continuously a note of 272 Hz is running towards a reflecting surface with a speed of 18 km h⁻¹. The speed of sound in air is 345 m s⁻¹. The number of beats heard by him is
(a) 4 (b) 6 (c) 8 (d) zero

RESPONSE GRID **1.** ⓐⓑⓒⓓ **2.** ⓐⓑⓒⓓ **3.** ⓐⓑⓒⓓ **4.** ⓐⓑⓒⓓ **5.** ⓐⓑⓒⓓ

Space for Rough Work

6. A closed organ pipe (closed at one end) is excited to support the third overtone. It is found that air in the pipe has
(a) three nodes and three antinodes
(b) three nodes and four antinodes
(c) four nodes and three antinodes
(d) four nodes and four antinodes

7. A wave disturbance in a medium is described by
$$y(x,t) = 0.02\cos\left(50\pi t + \frac{\pi}{2}\right)\cos(10\pi x)$$ where x and y are in metre and t is in second. Which of the following is correct?
(a) A node occurs at $x = 0.15$ m
(b) An antinode occurs at $x = 0.3$ m
(c) The speed wave is 5 ms^{-1}
(d) The wavelength is 0.3 m

8. In a resonance column, first and second resonance are obtained at depths 22.7 cm and 70.2 cm. The third resonance will be obtained at a depth
(a) 117.7 cm   (b) 92.9 cm
(c) 115.5 cm   (d) 113.5 cm

9. An engine approaches a hill with a constant speed. When it is at a distance of 0.9 km, it blows a whistle whose echo is heard by the driver after 5 seconds. If the speed of sound in air is 330 m/s, then the speed of the engine is :
(a) 32 m/s   (b) 27.5 m/s   (c) 60 m/s   (d) 30 m/s

10. Two identical piano wires kept under the same tension T have a fundamental frequency of 600 Hz. The fractional increase in the tension of one of the wires which will lead to occurrence of 6 beats/s when both the wires oscillate together would be
(a) 0.02   (b) 0.03   (c) 0.04   (d) 0.01

11. Two sound sources emitting sound each of wavelength λ are fixed at a given distance apart. A listener moves with a velocity u along the line joining the two sources. The number of beats heard by him per second is
(a) $\dfrac{u}{2\lambda}$ (b) $\dfrac{2u}{\lambda}$ (c) $\dfrac{u}{\lambda}$ (d) $\dfrac{u}{3\lambda}$

12. An observer moves towards a stationary source of sound, with a velocity one-fifth of the velocity of sound. What is the percentage increase in the apparent frequency ?
(a) 0.5%   (b) zero   (c) 20%   (d) 5%

13. Velocity of sound in air is 320 m s^{-1}. A pipe closed at one end has a length of 1 m. Neglecting end correction, the air column in the pipe cannot resonate with sound of frequency
(a) 80 Hz   (b) 240 Hz   (c) 320 Hz   (d) 400 Hz

14. The driver of a car travelling with speed 30 m/sec towards a hill sounds a horn of frequency 600 Hz. If the velocity of sound in air is 330 m/s, the frequency of reflected sound as heard by driver is
(a) 555.5 Hz   (b) 720 Hz   (c) 500 Hz   (d) 550 Hz

15. What will be the frequency of beats formed from the superposition of two harmonic waves shown below?

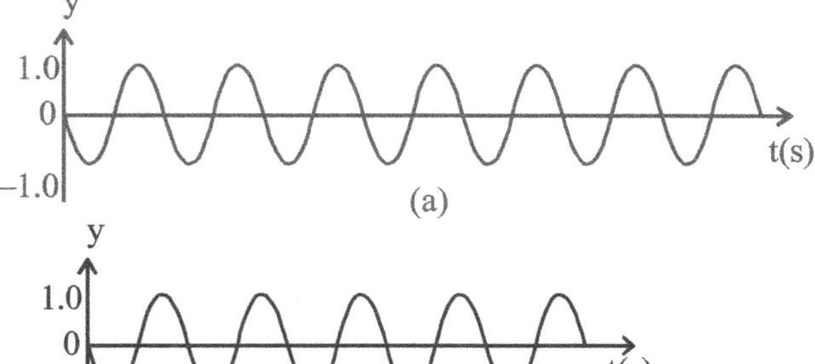

(a) 20 Hz   (b) 11 Hz   (c) 9 Hz   (d) 2 Hz

16. What is the effect of increase in temperature on the frequency of sound produced by an organ pipe?
(a) increases   (b) decreases
(c) no effect   (d) erratic change

17. A cylinderical tube open at both ends, has a fundamental frequency f in air. The tube is dipped vertically in water so that half of it is in water. The fundamental frequency of air column is now
(a) $f/2$ (b) f (c) $3f/4$ (d) $2f$

18. The transverse displacement $y(x, t)$ of a wave on a string is given by $y(x,t) = e^{-\left(ax^2 + bt^2 + 2\sqrt{ab}\,xt\right)}$.
This represents a:
(a) wave moving in $-x$ direction with speed $\sqrt{\dfrac{b}{a}}$
(b) standing wave of frequency $\sqrt{b}$
(c) standing wave of frequency $\dfrac{1}{\sqrt{b}}$
(d) wave moving in $+x$ direction with speed $\sqrt{\dfrac{a}{b}}$

19. A longitudinal wave is represented by
$$x = x_0 \sin 2\pi\left(nt - \frac{x}{\lambda}\right)$$
The maximum particle velocity will be four times the wave velocity if
(a) $\lambda = \dfrac{\pi x_0}{4}$ (b) $\lambda = 2\pi x_0$
(c) $\lambda = \dfrac{\pi x_0}{2}$ (d) $\lambda = 4\pi x_0$

20. Two tones of frequencies n_1 and n_2 are sounded together. The beats can be heard distinctly when
(a) $10 < (n_1 - n_2) < 20$ (b) $5 < (n_1 - n_2) > 20$
(c) $5 < (n_1 - n_2) < 20$ (d) $0 < (n_1 - n_2) < 10$

21. A pipe of length 85 cm is closed from one end. Find the number of possible natural oscillations of air column in the pipe whose frequencies lie below 1250 Hz. The velocity of sound in air is 340 m/s.
  (a) 12   (b) 8   (c) 6   (d) 4

22. A vehicle, with a horn of frequency n is moving with a velocity of 30 m/s in a direction perpendicular to the straight line joining the observer and the vehicle. The observer perceives the sound to have a frequency $n + n_1$. Then (if the sound velocity in air is 300 m/s)
  (a) $n_1 = 10n$ (b) $n_1 = 0$
  (c) $n_1 = 0.1n$ (d) $n_1 = -0.1n$

23. A source of sound gives 5 beats per second, when sounded with another source of frequency 100/sec. The second harmonic of the source, together with a source of frequency 205/sec gives 5 beats per second. What is the frequency of the source?
  (a) 95 sec^{-1} (b) 100 sec^{-1}
  (c) 105 sec^{-1} (d) 205 sec^{-1}

24. If we study the vibration of a pipe open at both ends, then which of the following statements is not true ?
  (a) Odd harmonics of the fundamental frequency will be generated
  (b) All harmonics of the fundamental frequency will be generated
  (c) Pressure change will be maximum at both ends
  (d) Antinode will be at open end

25. 41 forks are so arranged that each produces 5 beats per sec when sounded with its near fork. If the frequency of last fork is double the frequency of first fork, then the frequencies (in Hz) of the first and the last fork are respectively.
  (a) 200, 400   (b) 205, 410
  (c) 195, 390   (d) 100, 200

26. Two points are located at a distance of 10 m and 15 m from the source of oscillation. The period of oscillation is 0.05 sec and the velocity of the wave is 300 m/sec. What is the phase difference between the oscillations of two points?
  (a) $\dfrac{\pi}{3}$ (b) $\dfrac{2\pi}{3}$ (c) π (d) $\dfrac{\pi}{6}$

27. A sound absorber attenuates the sound level by 20 dB. The intensity decreases by a factor of
  (a) 100   (b) 1000   (c) 10000   (d) 10

28. A wave travelling along the x-axis is described by the equation $y(x, t) = 0.005 \cos (\alpha x - \beta t)$. If the wavelength and the time period of the wave are 0.08 m and 2.0s, respectively, then α and β in appropriate units are
  (a) $\alpha = 25.00\,\pi, \beta = \pi$ (b) $\alpha = \dfrac{0.08}{\pi}, \beta = \dfrac{2.0}{\pi}$
  (c) $\alpha = \dfrac{0.04}{\pi}, \beta = \dfrac{1.0}{\pi}$ (d) $\alpha = 12.50\pi, \beta = \dfrac{\pi}{2.0}$

29. The equation $Y = 0.02 \sin (500\pi t) \cos (4.5\,x)$ represents
  (a) progressive wave of frequency 250 Hz along x-axis
  (b) a stationary wave of wavelength 1.4 m
  (c) a transverse progressive wave of amplitude 0.02 m
  (d) progressive wave of speed of about 350 m s^{-1}

30. Which of the following statements is/are incorrect about waves ?
  (a) Waves are patterns of disturbance which move without the actual physical transfer of flow of matter as a whole.
  (b) Waves cannot transport energy.
  (c) The pattern of disturbance in the form of waves carry information that propagate from one point to another.
  (d) All our communications essentially depend on transmission of signals through waves.

31. An organ pipe P_1, closed at one end vibrating in its first harmonic and another pipe P_2, open at both ends vibrating in its third harmonic, are in resonance with a given tuning fork. The ratio of the lengths of P_1 and P_2 is :
  (a) $\dfrac{8}{3}$ (b) $\dfrac{1}{6}$ (c) $\dfrac{1}{2}$ (d) $\dfrac{1}{3}$

32. Two vibrating tuning forks producing waves given by $y_1 = 27 \sin 600\pi t$ and $y_2 = 27 \sin 604\,\pi t$ are held near the ear of a person, how many beats will be heard in three seconds by him ?
  (a) 4   (b) 2   (c) 6   (d) 12

33. A source of sound A emitting waves of frequency 1800 Hz is falling towards ground with a terminal speed v. The observer B on the ground directly beneath the source receives waves of frequency 2150 Hz. The source A receives waves, reflected from ground of frequency nearly: (Speed of sound = 343 m/s)
  (a) 2150 Hz   (b) 2500 Hz   (c) 1800 Hz   (d) 2400 Hz

34. Consider the three waves z_1, z_2 and z_3 as
  $z_1 = A \sin (kx - \omega t)$
  $z_2 = A \sin (kx + \omega t)$
  $z_3 = A \sin (ky - \omega t)$
  Which of the following represents a standing wave?
  (a) $z_1 + z_2$ (b) $z_2 + z_3$
  (c) $z_3 + z_1$ (d) $z_1 + z_2 + z_3$

35. A sonometer wire supports a 4 kg load and vibrates in fundamental mode with a tuning fork of frequency 416 Hz. The length of the wire between the bridges is now doubled. In order to maintain fundamental mode, the load should be changed to
  (a) 1 kg   (b) 2 kg   (c) 4 kg   (d) 16 kg

———————————————————— *Space for Rough Work* ————————————————————

36. The vibrations of a string of length 60 cm fixed at both the ends are represented by the equation $y = 2\sin\left(\dfrac{4\pi x}{15}\right)\cos$ $(96\pi t)$ where x and y are in cm. The maximum number of loops that can be formed in it is
(a) 4   (b) 16   (c) 5   (d) 15

37. If n_1, n_2 and n_3 are the fundamental frequencies of three segments into which a string is divided, then the original fundamental frequency n of the string is given by
(a) $n = n_1 + n_2 + n_3$
(b) $\dfrac{1}{n} = \dfrac{1}{n_1} + \dfrac{1}{n_2} + \dfrac{1}{n_3}$
(c) $\dfrac{1}{\sqrt{n}} = \dfrac{1}{\sqrt{n_1}} + \dfrac{1}{\sqrt{n_2}} + \dfrac{1}{\sqrt{n_3}}$
(d) $\sqrt{n} = \sqrt{n_1} + \sqrt{n_2} + \sqrt{n_3}$

38. An echo repeats two syllables. If the velocity of sound is 330 m/s, then the distance of the reflecting surface is
(a) 66.0 m   (b) 33.0 m   (c) 99.0 m   (d) 16.5 m

39. What is the effect of humidity on sound waves when humidity increases?
(a) Speed of sound waves is more
(b) Speed of sound waves is less
(c) Speed of sound waves remains same
(d) Speed of sound waves becomes zero

40. If the ratio of maximum to minimum intensity in beats is 49, then the ratio of amplitudes of two progressive wave trains is
(a) 7 : 1   (b) 4 : 3   (c) 49 : 1   (d) 16 : 9

41. A whistle of frequency 1000 Hz is sounded on a car travelling towards a cliff with velocity of 18 m s^{-1} normal to the cliff. If velocity of sound (v) = 330 m s^{-1}, then the apparent frequency of the echo as heard by the car driver is nearly
(a) 1115 Hz (b) 115 Hz   (c) 67 Hz   (d) 47.2 Hz

42. The transverse wave represented by the equation
$$y = 4\sin\left(\dfrac{\pi}{6}\right)\sin(3x - 15t) \text{ has}$$
(a) amplitude = 4
(b) wavelength $= 4\dfrac{\pi}{3}$
(c) speed of propagation = 5
(d) period $= \dfrac{\pi}{15}$

43. If the intensities of two interfering waves be I_1 and I_2, the contrast between maximum and minimum intensity is maximum, when
(a) $I_1 >> I_2$ (b) $I_1 << I_2$
(c) $I_1 = I_2$ (d) either I_1 or I_2 is zero

44. The fundamental frequency of a closed organ pipe of length 20 cm is equal to the second overtone of an organ pipe open at both the ends. The length of organ pipe open at both the ends is
(a) 100 cm   (b) 120 cm   (c) 140 cm   (d) 80 cm

45. The equation of a travelling wave is $y = 60\cos(180\,t - 6x)$ where y is in μm, t in second and x in metres. The ratio of maximum particle velocity to velocity of wave propagation is
(a) 3.6×10^{-2} (b) 3.6×10^{-4}
(c) 3.6×10^{-6} (d) 3.6×10^{-11}

RESPONSE GRID	36. ⓐⓑⓒⓓ	37. ⓐⓑⓒⓓ	38. ⓐⓑⓒⓓ	39. ⓐⓑⓒⓓ	40. ⓐⓑⓒⓓ
	41. ⓐⓑⓒⓓ	42. ⓐⓑⓒⓓ	43. ⓐⓑⓒⓓ	44. ⓐⓑⓒⓓ	45. ⓐⓑⓒⓓ

DAILY PRACTICE PROBLEM DPP CHAPTERWISE CP14 - PHYSICS

Total Questions	45	Total Marks	180
Attempted		Correct	
Incorrect		Net Score	
Cut-off Score	50	Qualifying Score	70
Success Gap = Net Score − Qualifying Score			
Net Score = (Correct × 4) − (Incorrect × 1)			

Space for Rough Work

Date :   Start Time :   End Time :

PHYSICS $\boxed{\text{CP15}}$

SYLLABUS : Electric Charges and Fields

Max. Marks : 180 **Marking Scheme :** (+4) for correct & (–1) for incorrect answer **Time : 60 min.**

INSTRUCTIONS : This Daily Practice Problem Sheet contains 45 MCQs. For each question only one option is correct. Darken the correct circle/ bubble in the Response Grid provided on each page.

1. The surface charge density of a thin charged disc of radius R is σ. The value of the electric field at the centre of the disc is $\dfrac{\sigma}{2\epsilon_0}$. With respect to the field at the centre, the electric field along the axis at a distance R from the centre of the disc reduces by
   (a) 70.7% (b) 29.3% (c) 9.7% (d) 14.6%

2. A solid conducting sphere of radius a has a net positive charge 2Q. A conducting spherical shell of inner radius b and outer radius c is concentric with the solid sphere and has a net charge – Q. The surface charge density on the inner and outer surfaces of the spherical shell will be respectively

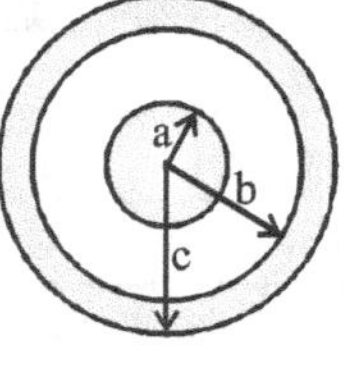

   (a) $-\dfrac{2Q}{4\pi b^2}, \dfrac{Q}{4\pi c^2}$

   (b) $-\dfrac{Q}{4\pi b^2}, \dfrac{Q}{4\pi c^2}$

   (c) $0, \dfrac{Q}{4\pi c^2}$

   (d) $\dfrac{Q}{4\pi c^2}, 0$

3. Two equally charged, identical metal spheres A and B repel each other with a force 'F'. The spheres are kept fixed with a distance 'r' between them. A third identical, but uncharged sphere C is brought in contact with A and then placed at the mid point of the line joining A and B. The magnitude of the net electric force on C is

   (a) F (b) $\dfrac{3F}{4}$ (c) $\dfrac{F}{2}$ (d) $\dfrac{F}{4}$

4. In the figure, the net electric flux through the area A is $\phi = \vec{E} \cdot \vec{A}$ when the system is in air. On immersing the system in water the net electric flux through the area

   (a) becomes zero

   (b) remains same

   (c) increases

   (d) decreases

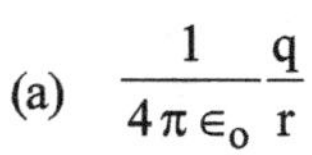

5. ABC is an equilateral triangle. Charges +q are placed at each corner as shown in fig. The electric intensity at centre O will be

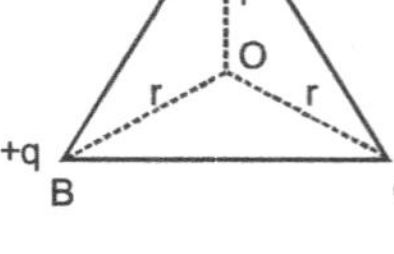

   (a) $\dfrac{1}{4\pi \epsilon_o} \dfrac{q}{r}$

   (b) $\dfrac{1}{4\pi \epsilon_o} \dfrac{q}{r^2}$

   (c) $\dfrac{1}{4\pi \epsilon_o} \dfrac{3q}{r^2}$

   (d) zero

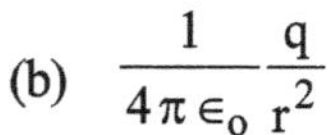

RESPONSE GRID 1. ⓐⓑⓒⓓ 2. ⓐⓑⓒⓓ 3. ⓐⓑⓒⓓ 4. ⓐⓑⓒⓓ 5. ⓐⓑⓒⓓ

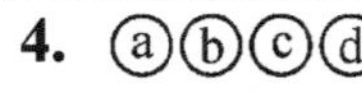
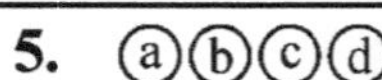

Space for Rough Work

6. An electric dipole is placed in a uniform electric field. The dipole will experience
  (a) a force that will displace it in the direction of the field
  (b) a force that will displace it in a direction opposite to the field.
  (c) a torque which will rotate it without displacement
  (d) a torque which will rotate it and a force that will displace it

7. An uniform electric field E exists along positive x-axis. The work done in moving a charge 0.5 C through a distance 2 m along a direction making an angle $60°$ with x-axis is 10 J. Then the magnitude of electric field is
  (a) $5\,Vm^{-1}$ (b) $2\,Vm^{-1}$ (c) $\sqrt{5}\,Vm^{-1}$ (d) $20\,Vm^{-1}$

8. Which one of the following graphs represents the variation of electric field with distance r from the centre of a charged spherical conductor of radius R?

(a) 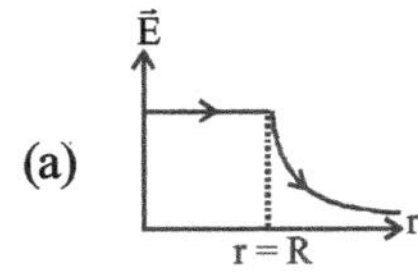 (b) 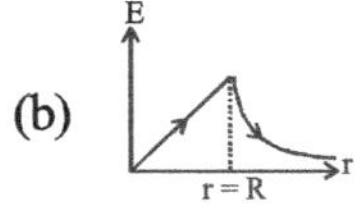

(c) 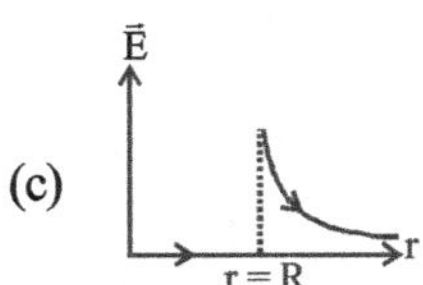 (d) 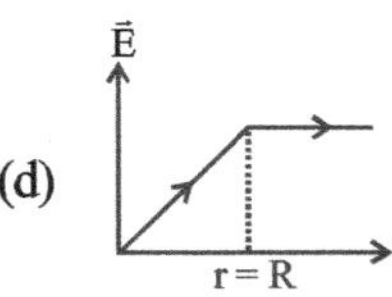

9. A hollow cylinder has a charge q coulomb within it. If ϕ is the electric flux in units of voltmeter associated with the curved surface B, the flux linked with the plane surface A in units of voltmeter will be

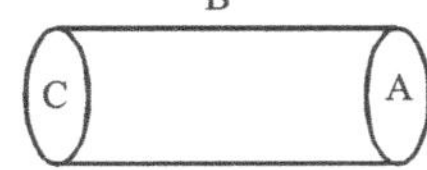

  (a) $\dfrac{q}{2\varepsilon_0}$ (b) $\dfrac{\phi}{3}$
  (c) $\dfrac{q}{\varepsilon_0}-\phi$ (d) $\dfrac{1}{2}\left(\dfrac{q}{\varepsilon_0}-\phi\right)$

10. If E_a be the electric field strength of a short dipole at a point on its axial line and E_e that on the equatorial line at the same distance, then
  (a) $E_e = 2E_a$ (b) $E_a = 2E_e$
  (c) $E_a = E_e$ (d) None of the above

11. Three positive charges of equal value q are placed at vertices of an equilateral triangle. The resulting lines of force should be sketched as in

(a) 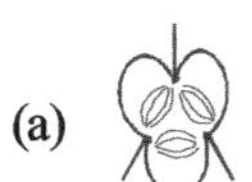 (b)  (c) 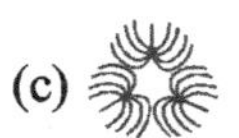 (d)

12. Three point charges Q_1, Q_2, Q_3 in the order are placed equally spaced along a straight line. Q_2 and Q_3 are equal in magnitude but opposite in sign. If the net force on Q_3 is zero. The value of Q_1 is
  (a) $Q_1 = 4(Q_3)$ (b) $Q = 2(Q_3)$
  (c) $Q_1 = \sqrt{2}(Q_3)$ (d) $Q_1 = |\,Q_3\,|$

13. Electric charge is uniformly distributed along a long straight wire of radius 1 mm. The charge per cm length of the wire is Q coulomb. Another cylindrical surface of radius 50 cm and length 1 m symmetrically encloses the wire. The total electric flux passing through the cylindrical surface is
  (a) $\dfrac{Q}{\varepsilon_0}$ (b) $\dfrac{100Q}{\varepsilon_0}$ (c) $\dfrac{10Q}{\pi\varepsilon_0}$ (d) $\dfrac{100Q}{\pi\varepsilon_0}$

14. A small sphere carrying a charge 'q' is hanging in between two parallel plates by a string of length L. Time period of pendulum is T_0. When parallel plates are charged, the time period changes to T. The ratio T/T_0 is equal to

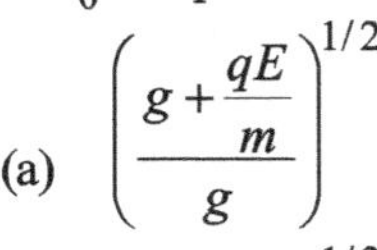 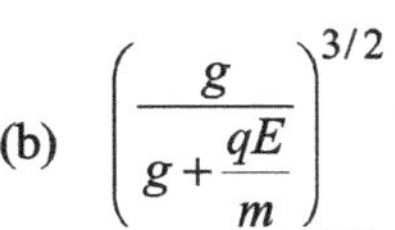

  (a) $\left(\dfrac{g+\dfrac{qE}{m}}{g}\right)^{1/2}$ (b) 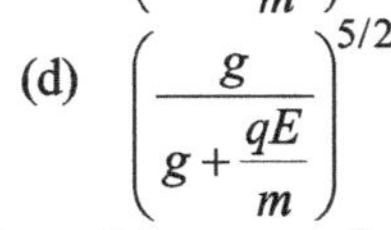 $\left(\dfrac{g}{g+\dfrac{qE}{m}}\right)^{3/2}$
  (c) $\left(\dfrac{g}{g+\dfrac{qE}{m}}\right)^{1/2}$ (d) $\left(\dfrac{g}{g+\dfrac{qE}{m}}\right)^{5/2}$

15. An electric dipole, consisting of two opposite charges of 2×10^{-6} C each separated by a distance 3 cm is placed in an electric field of 2×10^{5} N/C. Torque acting on the dipole is
  (a) $12\times10^{-1}N-m$ (b) $12\times10^{-2}N-m$
  (c) $12\times10^{-3}N-m$ (d) $12\times10^{-4}N-m$

16. The electric field in a certain region is acting radially outward and is given by E = Ar. A charge contained in a sphere of radius 'a' centred at the origin of the field, will be given by
  (a) $A\,\varepsilon_0\,a^2$ (b) $4\pi\varepsilon_0 Aa^3$ (c) $\varepsilon_0 Aa^3$ (d) $4\pi\varepsilon_0 Aa^2$

17. The spatial distribution of electric field due to charges (A, B) is shown in figure. Which one of the following statements is correct?
  (a) A is +ve and B −ve, $|A| > |B|$
  (b) A is −ve and B +ve, $|A| = |B|$
  (c) Both are +ve but A > B
  (d) Both are −ve but A > B

18. Point charges $+4q$, $-q$ and $+4q$ are kept on the X-axis at points $x = 0$, $x = a$ and $x = 2a$ respectively.
  (a) only $-q$ is in stable equilibrium
  (b) none of the charges is in equilibrium
  (c) all the charges are in unstable equilibrium
  (d) all the charges are in stable equilibrium.

19. Figure shows some of the electric field lines corresponding to an electric field. The figure suggests that
  (a) $E_A > E_B > E_C$ (b) $E_A = E_B = E_C$
  (c) $E_A = E_C > E_B$ (d) $E_A = E_C < E_B$

RESPONSE GRID					
	6. ⓐⓑⓒⓓ	7. ⓐⓑⓒⓓ	8. ⓐⓑⓒⓓ	9. ⓐⓑⓒⓓ	10. ⓐⓑⓒⓓ
	11. ⓐⓑⓒⓓ	12. ⓐⓑⓒⓓ	13. ⓐⓑⓒⓓ	14. ⓐⓑⓒⓓ	15. ⓐⓑⓒⓓ
	16. ⓐⓑⓒⓓ	17. ⓐⓑⓒⓓ	18. ⓐⓑⓒⓓ	19. ⓐⓑⓒⓓ	

20. For distance far away from centre of dipole the change in magnitude of electric field with change in distance from the centre of dipole is
(a) zero.
(b) same in equatorial plane as well as axis of dipole.
(c) more in case of equatorial plane of dipole as compared to axis of dipole.
(d) more in case of axis of dipole as compared to equatorial plane of dipole.

21. Two charge q and $-3q$ are placed fixed on x–axis separated by distance d. Where should a third charge $2q$ be placed such that it will not experience any force ?

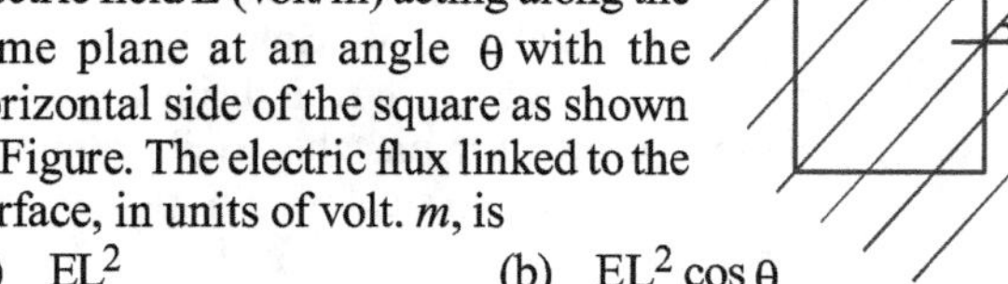

(a) $\dfrac{d-\sqrt{3}\,d}{2}$ (b) $\dfrac{d+\sqrt{3}\,d}{2}$ (c) $\dfrac{d+3d}{2}$ (d) $\dfrac{d-3d}{2}$

22. A charge Q is placed at each of the opposite corners of a square. A charge q is placed at each of the other two corners. If the net electrical force on Q is zero, then Q/q equals:
(a) -1 (b) 1 (c) $-\dfrac{1}{\sqrt{2}}$ (d) $-2\sqrt{2}$

23. Identify the wrong statement in the following. Coulomb's law correctly describes the electric force that
(a) binds the electrons of an atom to its nucleus
(b) binds the protons and neutrons in the nucleus of an atom
(c) binds atoms together to form molecules
(d) binds atoms and molecules together to form solids

24. An oil drop of radius r and density ρ is held stationary in a uniform vertically upwards electric field 'E'. If $\rho_0\ (<\rho)$ is the density of air and e is quanta of charge, then the drop has–
(a) $\dfrac{4\pi r^3\,(\rho-\rho_0)\,g}{3eE}$ excess electrons
(b) $\dfrac{4\pi r^2\,(\rho-\rho_0)\,g}{eE}$ excess electrons
(c) deficiency of $\dfrac{4\pi r^3\,(\rho-\rho_0)\,g}{3eE}$ electrons
(d) deficiency of $\dfrac{4\pi r^2\,(\rho-\rho_0)\,g}{eE}$ electrons

25. A square surface of side L meter in the plane of the paper is placed in a uniform electric field E (volt/m) acting along the same plane at an angle θ with the horizontal side of the square as shown in Figure. The electric flux linked to the surface, in units of volt. m, is
(a) EL^2 (b) $EL^2\cos\theta$
(c) $EL^2\sin\theta$ (d) zero

26. An electric dipole of moment $\vec{p}$ placed in a uniform electric field $\vec{E}$ has minimum potential energy when the angle between $\vec{P}$ and $\vec{E}$ is
(a) zero (b) $\dfrac{\pi}{2}$ (c) π (d) $\dfrac{3\pi}{2}$

27. Which of the following statements is incorrect?
(a) The charge q on a body is always given by $q = $ ne, where n is any integer, positive or negative.
(b) By convention, the charge on an electron is taken to be negative.
(c) The fact that electric charge is always an integral multiple of e is termed as quantisation of charge.
(d) The quatisation of charge was experimentally demonstrated by Newton in 1912.

28. Two positive ions, each carrying a charge q, are separated by a distance d. If F is the force of repulsion between the ions, the number of electrons missing from each ion will be (e being the charge of an electron)
(a) $\dfrac{4\pi\varepsilon_0\,Fd^2}{e^2}$ (b) $\sqrt{\dfrac{4\pi\varepsilon_0\,Fe^2}{d^2}}$
(c) $\sqrt{\dfrac{4\pi\varepsilon_0\,Fd^2}{e^2}}$ (d) $\dfrac{4\pi\varepsilon_0\,Fd^2}{q^2}$

29. Two small similar metal spheres A and B having charges 4q and $-4q$, when placed at a certain distance apart, exert an electric force F on each other. When another identical uncharged sphere C, first touched with A then with B and then removed to infinity, the force of interaction between A and B for the same separation will be
(a) F/2 (b) F/8 (c) F/16 (d) F/32

30. The electric field intensity just sufficient to balance the earth's gravitational attraction on an electron will be: (given mass and charge of an electron respectively are 9.1×10^{-31} kg and 1.6×10^{-19} C.)
(a) $-5.6\times10^{-11}\,\text{N}/\text{C}$ (b) $-4.8\times10^{-15}\,\text{N}/\text{C}$
(c) $-1.6\times10^{-19}\,\text{N}/\text{C}$ (d) $-3.2\times10^{-19}\,\text{N}/\text{C}$

31. An electric dipole is placed at an angle of 30° with an electric field of intensity $2\times10^5\,\text{NC}^{-1}$, It experiences a torque of 4 Nm. Calculate the charge on the dipole if the dipole length is 2 cm.
(a) 8mC (b) 4mC (c) 8mC (d) 2mC

32. A particle of mass m and charge q is placed at rest in a uniform electric field E and then released. The kinetic energy attained by the particle after moving a distance y is
(a) qEy^2 (b) qE^2y (c) qEy (d) q^2Ey

33. There is an electric field E in x-direction. If the work done on moving a charge of 0.2 C through a distance of 2 m along a line making an angle 60° with x-axis is 4 J, then what is the value of E?
(a) 3 N/C (b) 4 N/C (c) 5 N/C (d) 20 N/C

<table>
<tr><td rowspan="3">RESPONSE GRID</td><td>20. (a)(b)(c)(d)</td><td>21. (a)(b)(c)(d)</td><td>22. (a)(b)(c)(d)</td><td>23. (a)(b)(c)(d)</td><td>24. (a)(b)(c)(d)</td></tr>
<tr><td>25. (a)(b)(c)(d)</td><td>26. (a)(b)(c)(d)</td><td>27. (a)(b)(c)(d)</td><td>28. (a)(b)(c)(d)</td><td>29. (a)(b)(c)(d)</td></tr>
<tr><td>30. (a)(b)(c)(d)</td><td>31. (a)(b)(c)(d)</td><td>32. (a)(b)(c)(d)</td><td>33. (a)(b)(c)(d)</td><td></td></tr>
</table>

Space for Rough Work

34. A surface has the area vector $\vec{A} = \left(2\hat{i} + 3\hat{j}\right)m^2$. The flux of an electric field through it if the field is $\vec{E} = 4\hat{i}\,\dfrac{V}{m}$:

(a) 8 V-m　(b) 12 V-m　(c) 20 V-m　(d) zero

35. There exists a non!-uniform electric field along x-axis as shown in the figure below. The field increases at a uniform rate along +ve x-axis. A dipole is placed inside the field as shown. Which one of the following is correct for the dipole?

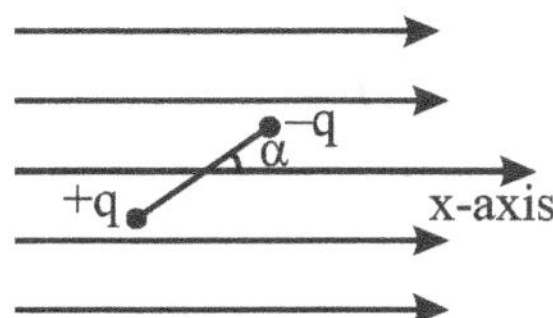

(a) Dipole moves along positive x-axis and undergoes a clockwise rotation
(b) Dipole moves along negative x-axis and undergoes a clockwise rotation
(c) Dipole moves along positive x-axis and undergoes a anticlockwise rotation
(d) Dipole moves along negative x-axis and undergoes a anticlockwise rotation

36. A square surface of side L metres is in the plane of the paper. A uniform electric field $\overrightarrow{E}$ (volt /m), also in the plane of the paper, is limited only to the lower half of the square surface (see figure). The electric flux in SI units associated with the surface is

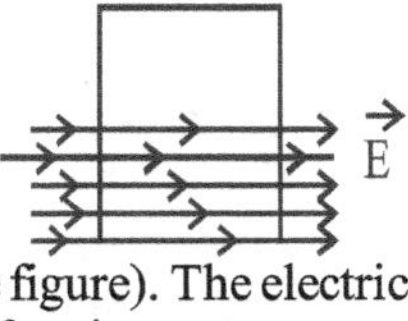

(a) $EL^2/2$　(b) zero　(c) EL^2　(d) $EL^2/(2\varepsilon_0)$

37. Among two discs A and B, first have radius 10 cm and charge 10^{-6} μC and second have radius 30 cm and charge 10^{-5} C. When they are touched, charge on both q_A and q_B respectively will, be

(a) $q_A = 2.75\,\mu C$, $q_B = 3.15\,\mu C$
(b) $q_A = 1.09\,\mu C$, $q_B = 1.53\,\mu C$
(c) $q_A = q_B = 5.5\,\mu C$　(d) None of these

38. The total electric flux emanating from a closed surface enclosing an α-particle (e-electronic charge) is

(a) $\dfrac{2e}{\varepsilon_0}$　(b) $\dfrac{e}{\varepsilon_0}$　(c) $e\varepsilon_0$　(d) $\dfrac{\varepsilon_0 e}{4}$

39. Which of the following is a wrong statement?
(a) The charge of an isolated system is conserved
(b) It is not possible to create or destroy charged particles
(c) It is possible to create or destroy charged particles
(d) It is not possible to create or destroy net charge

40. A charge q is placed at the centre of the open end of a cylindrical vessel. The flux of the electric field through the surface of the vessel is

(a) zero　(b) q/ε_0
(c) $q/2\varepsilon_0$　(d) $2q/\varepsilon_0$

41. If the electric flux entering and leaving a closed surface are 6×10^6 and 9×10^6 S.I. units respectively, then the charge inside the surface of permittivity of free space ε_0 is
(a) $\varepsilon_0 \times 10^6$　(b) $-\varepsilon_0 \times 10^6$
(c) $-2\varepsilon_0 \times 10^6$　(d) $3\varepsilon_0 \times 10^6$

42. Two particle of equal mass m and charge q are placed at a distance of 16 cm. They do not experience any force. The value of $\dfrac{q}{m}$ is

(a) 1　(b) $\sqrt{\dfrac{\pi\varepsilon_0}{G}}$　(c) $\sqrt{\dfrac{G}{4\pi\varepsilon_0}}$　(d) $\sqrt{4\pi\varepsilon_0 G}$

43. A rod of length 2.4 *m* and radius 4.6 *mm* carries a negative charge of 4.2×10^{-7} C spread uniformly over it surface. The electric field near the mid–point of the rod, at a point on its surface is
(a) -8.6×10^5 N C^{-1}　(b) 8.6×10^4 N C^{-1}
(c) -6.7×10^5 N C^{-1}　(d) 6.7×10^4 N C^{-1}

44. A hollow insulated conduction sphere is given a positive charge of 10 μC. What will be the electric field at the centre of the sphere if its radius is 2 m?
(a) Zero　(b) $5\,\mu Cm^{-2}$
(c) $20\,\mu Cm^{-2}$　(d) $8\,\mu Cm^{-2}$

45. A charge Q is enclosed by a Gaussian spherical surface of radius R. If the radius is doubled, then the outward electric flux will
(a) increase four times　(b) be reduced to half
(c) remain the same　(d) be doubled

DAILY PRACTICE PROBLEM DPP CHAPTERWISE CP15 - PHYSICS

Total Questions	45	Total Marks	180
Attempted		Correct	
Incorrect		Net Score	
Cut-off Score	50	Qualifying Score	70
Success Gap = Net Score − Qualifying Score			
Net Score = (Correct × 4) − (Incorrect × 1)			

Space for Rough Work

Date : [ ] Start Time : [ ] End Time : [ ]

PHYSICS $\boxed{\text{CP16}}$

SYLLABUS : Electrostatic Potential & Capacitance

Max. Marks : 180   **Marking Scheme :** (+4) for correct & (–1) for incorrect answer   **Time : 60 min.**

INSTRUCTIONS : This Daily Practice Problem Sheet contains 45 MCQs. For each question only one option is correct. Darken the correct circle/ bubble in the Response Grid provided on each page.

1. If n drops, each charged to a potential V, coalesce to form a single drop. The potential of the big drop will be
   (a) $\dfrac{V}{n^{2/3}}$ (b) $\dfrac{V}{n^{1/3}}$ (c) $Vn^{1/3}$ (d) $Vn^{2/3}$

2. The capacitance of a parallel plate capacitor is C_a (Fig. a). A dielectric of dielectric constant K is inserted as shown in fig. (b) and (c). If C_b and C_c denote the capacitances in fig. (b) and (c), then

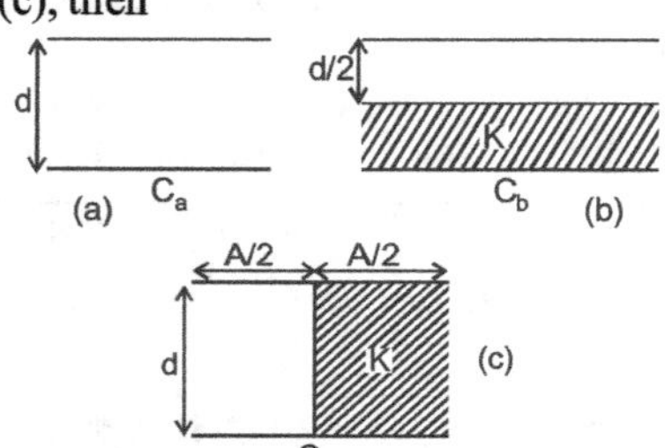

   (a) both $C_b, C_c > C_a$ (b) $C_c > C_a$ while $C_b > C_a$
   (c) both $C_b, C_c < C_a$ (d) $C_a = C_b = C_c$

3. The electric potential $V(x)$ in a region around the origin is given by $V(x) = 4x^2$ volts. The electric charge enclosed in a cube of 1 m side with its centre at the origin is (in coulomb)
   (a) $8\varepsilon_0$ (b) $-4\varepsilon_0$ (c) 0 (d) $-8\varepsilon_0$

4. A parallel plate condenser is immersed in an oil of dielectric constant 2. The field between the plates is
   (a) increased, proportional to 2
   (b) decreased, proportional to $\dfrac{1}{2}$
   (c) increased, proportional to -2
   (d) decreased, proportional to $-\dfrac{1}{2}$

5. What is the effective capacitance between points X and Y?

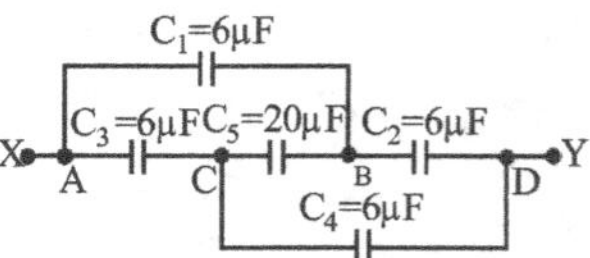

   (a) $24\,\mu F$ (b) $18\,\mu F$ (c) $12\,\mu F$ (d) $6\,\mu F$

6. Two identical particles each of mass m and having charges $-q$ and $+q$ are revolving in a circle of radius r under the influence of electric attraction. Kinetic energy of each particle is $\left(k = \dfrac{1}{4\pi\varepsilon_0} \right)$
   (a) $kq^2/4r$ (b) $kq^2/2r$ (c) $kq^2/8r$ (d) kq^2/r

RESPONSE GRID	1. Ⓐⓑⓒⓓ	2. Ⓐⓑⓒⓓ	3. Ⓐⓑⓒⓓ	4. Ⓐⓑⓒⓓ	5. Ⓐⓑⓒⓓ
	6. Ⓐⓑⓒⓓ				

Space for Rough Work

7. Four metallic plates each with a surface area of one side A, are placed at a distance d from each other. The two outer plates are connected to one point A and the two other inner plates to another point B as shown in the figure. Then the capacitance of the system is

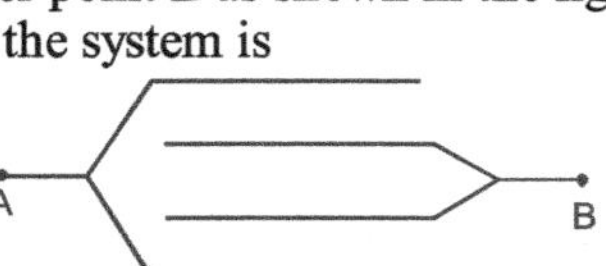

(a) $\dfrac{\varepsilon_0 A}{d}$ (b) $\dfrac{2\varepsilon_0 A}{d}$ (c) $\dfrac{3\varepsilon_0 A}{d}$ (d) $\dfrac{4\varepsilon_0 A}{d}$

8. A parallel plate condenser with a dielectric of dielectric constant K between the plates has a capacity C and is charged to a potential V volt. The dielectric slab is slowly removed from between the plates and then reinserted. The net work done by the system in this process is

(a) zero

(b) $\dfrac{1}{2}(K-1)\,CV^2$

(c) $\dfrac{CV^2(K-1)}{K}$

(d) $(K-1)\,CV^2$

9. If a slab of insulating material 4×10^{-5} m thick is introduced between the plates of a parallel plate capacitor, the distance between the plates has to be increased by 3.5×10^{-5} m to restore the capacity to original value. Then the dielectric constant of the material of slab is

(a) 8   (b) 6   (c) 12   (d) 10

10. A unit charge moves on an equipotential surface from a point A to point B, then

(a) $V_A - V_B = +ve$ (b) $V_A - V_B = 0$

(c) $V_A - V_B = -ve$ (d) it is stationary

11. Identify the false statement.

(a) Inside a charged or neutral conductor, electrostatic field is zero

(b) The electrostatic field at the surface of the charged conductor must be tangential to the surface at any point

(c) There is no net charge at any point inside the conductor

(d) Electrostatic potential is constant throughout the volume of the conductor

12. In a hollow spherical shell, potential (V) changes with respect to distance (s) from centre as

(a) 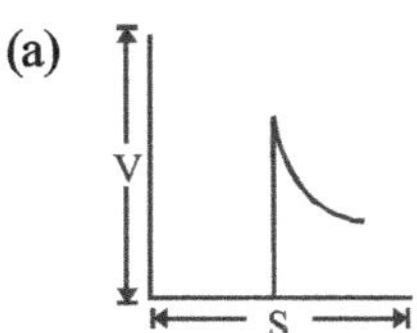   (b)

(c) 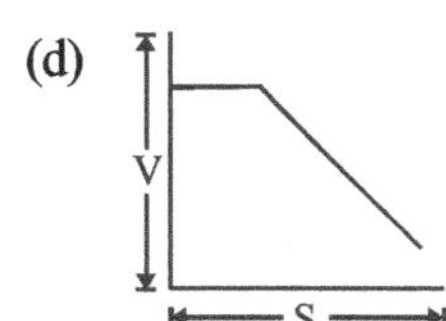   (d)

13. The 1000 small droplets of water each of radius r and charge Q, make a big drop of spherical shape. The potential of big drop is how many times the potential of one small droplet ?

(a) 1   (b) 10   (c) 100   (d) 1000

14. The work done in carrying a charge q once around a circle of radius r with a charge Q placed at the centre will be

(a) $Qq(4\pi\varepsilon_0 r^2)$ (b) $Qq/(4\pi\varepsilon_0 r)$

(c) zero   (d) $Qq^2/(4\pi\varepsilon_0 r)$

15. A parallel plate condenser is filled with two dielectrics as shown. Area of each plate is A m^2 and the separation is t m. The dielectric constants are k_1 and k_2 respectively. Its capacitance in farad will be

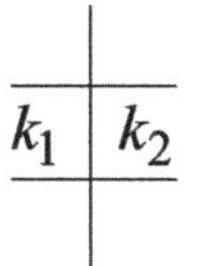

(a) $\dfrac{\varepsilon_o A}{t}\,(k_1 + k_2)$ (b) $\dfrac{\varepsilon_o A}{t}\cdot\dfrac{k_1 + k_2}{2}$

(c) $\dfrac{2\varepsilon_o A}{t}\,(k_1 + k_2)$ (d) $\dfrac{\varepsilon_o A}{t}\cdot\dfrac{k_1 - k_2}{2}$

16. Two metal pieces having a potential difference of 800 V are 0.02 m apart horizontally. A particle of mass 1.96×10^{-15} kg is suspended in equilibrium between the plates. If e is the elementary charge, then charge on the particle is

(a) 8   (b) 6   (c) 0.1   (d) 3

17. A one microfarad capacitor of a TV is subjected to 4000 V potential difference. The energy stored in capacitor is

(a) 8 J   (b) 16 J

(c) 4×10^{-3} J   (d) 2×10^{-3} J

18. An unchanged parallel plate capacitor filled with a dielectric constant K is connected to an air filled identical parallel capacitor charged to potential V_1. If the common potential is V_2, the value of K is

(a) $\dfrac{V_1 - V_2}{V_1}$ (b) $\dfrac{V_1}{V_1 - V_2}$

(c) $\dfrac{V_2}{V_1 - V_2}$ (d) $\dfrac{V_1 - V_2}{V_2}$

19. In the circuit given below, the charge in μC, on the capacitor having 5 μF is

(a) 4.5
(b) 9
(c) 7
(d) 15

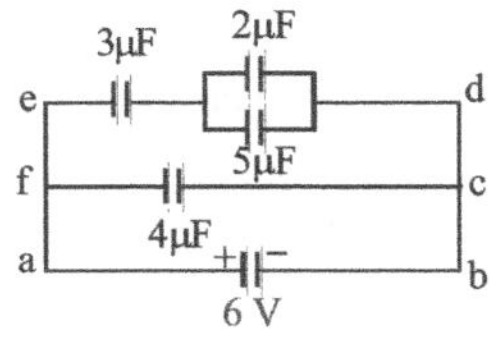

Space for Rough Work

20. Two concentric, thin metallic spheres of radii R_1 and R_2 $(R_1 > R_2)$ bear charges Q_1 and Q_2 respectively. Then the potential at distance r between R_1 and R_2 will be

(a) $k\left(\dfrac{Q_1+Q_2}{r}\right)$

(b) $k\left(\dfrac{Q_1}{r}+\dfrac{Q_2}{R_2}\right)$

(c) $k\left(\dfrac{Q_2}{r}+\dfrac{Q_1}{R_1}\right)$

(d) $k\left(\dfrac{Q_1}{R_1}+\dfrac{Q_2}{R_2}\right)$

21. Charge Q on a capacitor varies with voltage V as shown in the figure, where Q is taken along the X-axis and V along the Y-axis. The area of triangle OAB represents

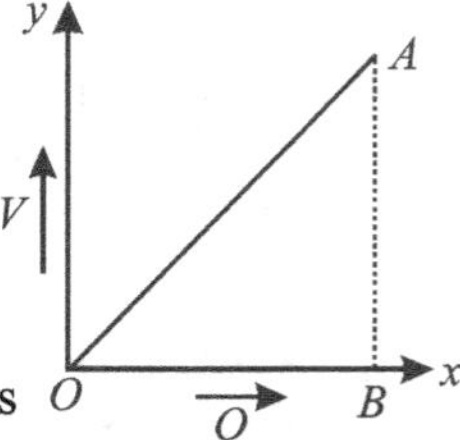

(a) capacitance
(b) capacitive reactance
(c) magnetic field between the plates
(d) energy stored in the capacitor

22. An alpha particle is accelerated through a potential difference of 10^6 volt. Its kinetic energy will be
(a) 1 MeV   (b) 2 MeV   (c) 4 MeV   (d) 8 MeV

23. Four point charges $-Q$, $-q$, $2q$ and $2Q$ are placed, one at each corner of the square. The relation between Q and q for which the potential at the centre of the square is zero is :

(a) $Q=-q$ (b) $Q=-\dfrac{1}{q}$ (c) $Q=q$ (d) $Q=\dfrac{1}{q}$

24. A parallel plate capacitor having a separation between the plates d, plate area A and material with dielectric constant K has capacitance C_0. Now one-third of the material is replaced by another material with dielectric constant 2K, so that effectively there are two capacitors one with area 1/3A, dielectric constant 2K and another with area 2/3A and dielectric constant K. If the capacitance of this new capacitor is C then $\dfrac{C}{C_0}$ is

(a) 1   (b) 4/3   (c) 2/3   (d) 1/3

25. Two condensers, one of capacity C and other of capacity C/2 are connected to a V-volt battery, as shown. The work done in charging fully both the condensers is

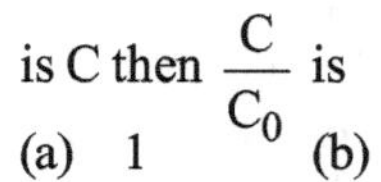

(a) $\dfrac{1}{4}CV^2$ (b) $\dfrac{3}{4}CV^2$ (c) $\dfrac{1}{2}CV^2$ (d) $2CV^2$.

26. A, B and C are three points in a uniform electric field. The electric potential is

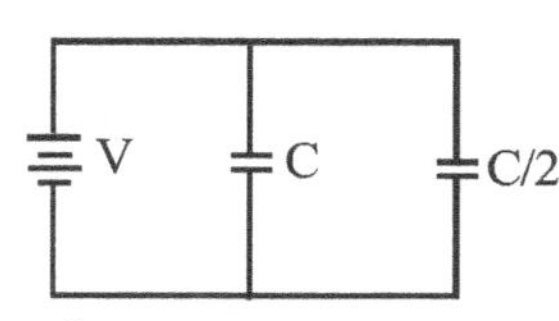

(a) maximum at B
(b) maximum at C
(c) same at all the three points A, B and C
(d) maximum at A

27. Three capacitors are connected in the arms of a triangle ABC as shown in figure 5 V is applied between A and B. The voltage between B and C is

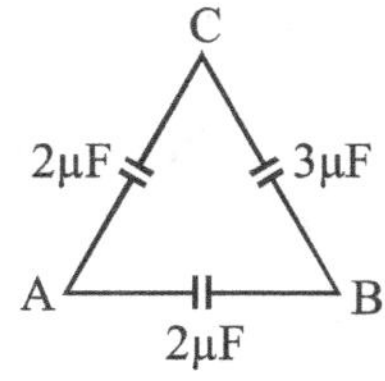

(a) 2V   (b) 1V
(c) 3V   (d) 1.5V

28. Two parallel metal plates having charges + Q and –Q face each other at a certain distance between them. If the plaves are now dipped in kerosene oil tank, the electric field between the plates will
(a) remain same   (b) become zero
(c) increases   (d) decrease

29. An air capacitor C connected to a battery of e.m.f. V acquires a charge q and energy E. The capacitor is disconnected from the battery and a dielectric slab is placed between the plates. Which of the following statements is correct ?
(a) V and q decrease but C and E increase
(b) V remains unchange, but q, E and C increase
(c) q remains unchanged, C increases, V and E decrease
(d) q and C increase but V and E decrease.

30. Choose the wrong statement about equipotential surfaces.
(a) It is a surface over which the potential is constant
(b) The electric field is parallel to the equipotential surface
(c) The electric field is perpendicular to the equipotential surface
(d) The electric field is in the direction of steepest decrease of potential

31. Two spherical conductors A and B of radii a and b (b>a) are placed concentrically in air. The two are connected by a copper wire as shown in figure. Then the equivalent capacitance of the system is

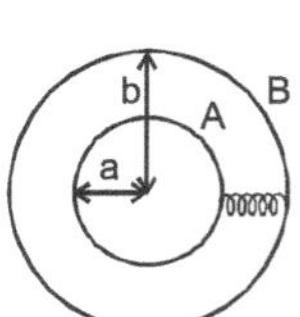

(a) $4\pi\varepsilon_0\dfrac{ab}{b-a}$ (b) $4\pi\varepsilon_0(a+b)$

(c) $4\pi\varepsilon_0 b$ (d) $4\pi\varepsilon_0 a$

32. A capacitor is charged to store an energy U. The charging battery is disconnected. An identical capacitor is now connected to the first capacitor in parallel. The energy in each of the capacitors is
(a) U/2   (b) 3U/2   (c) U   (d) U/4

33. Equipotentials at a great distance from a collection of charges whose total sum is not zero are approximately
(a) spheres   (b) planes
(c) paraboloids   (d) ellipsoids

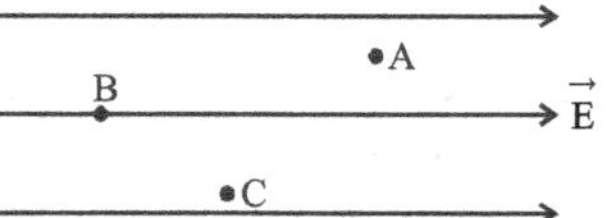

RESPONSE GRID	20. ⓐⓑⓒⓓ	21. ⓐⓑⓒⓓ	22. ⓐⓑⓒⓓ	23. ⓐⓑⓒⓓ	24. ⓐⓑⓒⓓ
	25. ⓐⓑⓒⓓ	26. ⓐⓑⓒⓓ	27. ⓐⓑⓒⓓ	28. ⓐⓑⓒⓓ	29. ⓐⓑⓒⓓ
	30. ⓐⓑⓒⓓ	31. ⓐⓑⓒⓓ	32. ⓐⓑⓒⓓ	33. ⓐⓑⓒⓓ	

34. Which of the following figure shows the correct equipotential surfaces of a system of two positive charges?

(a) 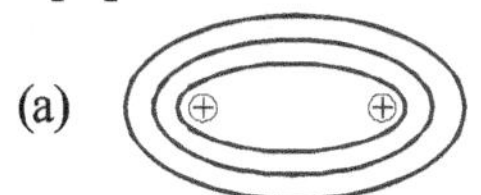

(b) 

(c) 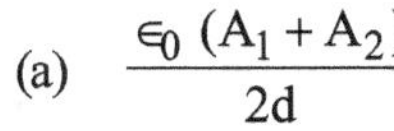

(d) 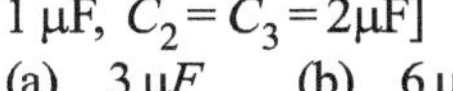

35. Two identical metal plates are given positive charges Q_1 and Q_2 $(< Q_1)$ respectively. If they are now brought close together to form a parallel plate capacitor with capacitance C, the potential difference between them is

(a) $\dfrac{Q_1 + Q_2}{2C}$ (b) $\dfrac{Q_1 + Q_2}{C}$ (c) $\dfrac{Q_1 - Q_2}{C}$ (d) $\dfrac{Q_1 - Q_2}{2C}$

36. The capacitance of the capacitor of plate areas A_1 and A_2 $(A_1 < A_2)$ at a distance d, as shown in figure is

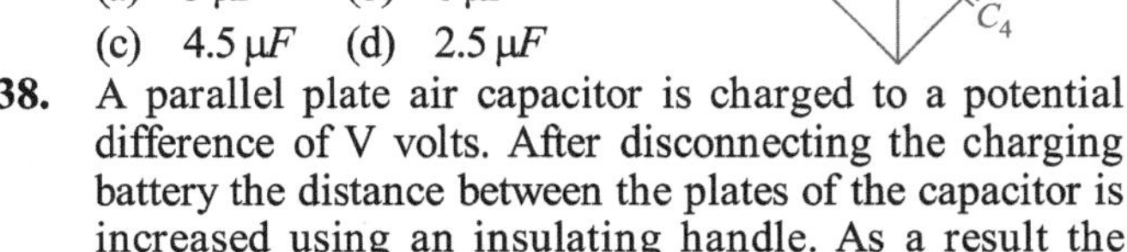

(a) $\dfrac{\epsilon_0 (A_1 + A_2)}{2d}$

(b) $\dfrac{\epsilon_0 A_2}{d}$

(c) $\dfrac{\epsilon_0 \sqrt{A_1 A_2}}{d}$

(d) $\dfrac{\epsilon_0 A_1}{d}$

37. In a given network the equivalent capacitance between A and B is $[C_1 = C_4 = 1\,\mu F, C_2 = C_3 = 2\mu F]$

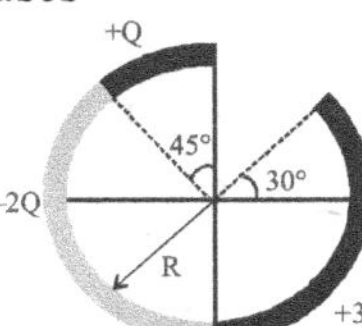

(a) $3\,\mu F$ (b) $6\,\mu F$
(c) $4.5\,\mu F$ (d) $2.5\,\mu F$

38. A parallel plate air capacitor is charged to a potential difference of V volts. After disconnecting the charging battery the distance between the plates of the capacitor is increased using an insulating handle. As a result the potential difference between the plates
(a) does not change (b) becomes zero
(c) increases (d) decreases

39. Figure shows three circular arcs, each of radius R and total charge as indicated. The net electric potential at the centre of curvature is

(a) $\dfrac{Q}{2\pi\varepsilon_0 R}$ (b) $\dfrac{Q}{4\pi\varepsilon_0 R}$

(c) $\dfrac{2Q}{\pi\varepsilon_0 R}$ (d) $\dfrac{Q}{\pi\varepsilon_0 R}$

40. An electric field $\vec{E} = (25\hat{i} + 30\hat{j})NC^{-1}$ exists in a region of space. If the potential at the origin is taken to be zero then the potential at $x = 2\,m$, $y = 2\,m$ is :
(a) $-110\,V$ (b) $-140\,V$ (c) $-120\,V$ (d) $-130\,V$

41. If a unit positive charge is taken from one point to another over an equipotential surface, then
(a) work is done on the charge
(b) work is done by the charge
(c) work done is constant
(d) no work is done

42. Three large plates A, B and C are placed parallel to each other and charges are given as shown. The charge that appears on the left surface of plate B is

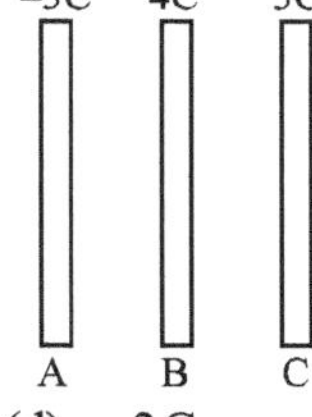

(a) 5C (b) 6C (c) 3C (d) −3C

43. Three charges $2q, -q$ and $-q$ are located at the vertices of an equilateral triangle. At the centre of the triangle
(a) the field is zero but potential is non-zero
(b) the field is non-zero, but potential is zero
(c) both field and potential are zero
(d) both field and potential are non-zero

44. If a charge $-150\,nC$ is given to a concentric spherical shell and a charge $+50\,nC$ is placed at its centre then the charge on inner and outer surface of the shell is
(a) $-50\,nC, -100\,nC$ (b) $+50\,nC, -200\,nC$
(c) $-50\,nC, -200\,nC$ (d) $50\,nC, 100\,nC$

45. Two capacitors of capacitances C_1 and C_2 are connected in parallel across a battery. If Q_1 and Q_2 respectively be the charges on the capacitors, then $\dfrac{Q_1}{Q_2}$ will be equal to

(a) $\dfrac{C_2}{C_1}$ (b) $\dfrac{C_1}{C_2}$ (c) $\dfrac{C_1^2}{C_2^2}$ (d) $\dfrac{C_2^2}{C_1^2}$

DAILY PRACTICE PROBLEM DPP CHAPTERWISE CP16 - PHYSICS

Total Questions	45	Total Marks	180
Attempted		Correct	
Incorrect		Net Score	
Cut-off Score	50	Qualifying Score	70
Success Gap = Net Score − Qualifying Score			
Net Score = (Correct × 4) − (Incorrect × 1)			

Date : Start Time : End Time :

PHYSICS $\boxed{\text{CP17}}$

SYLLABUS : Current Electricity

Max. Marks : 180 **Marking Scheme :** (+4) for correct & (−1) for incorrect answer **Time : 60 min.**

INSTRUCTIONS : This Daily Practice Problem Sheet contains 45 MCQs. For each question only one option is correct. Darken the correct circle/ bubble in the Response Grid provided on each page.

1. When 5V potential difference is applied across a wire of length 0.1 m, the drift speed of electrons is $2.5 \times 10^{-4}\,\text{ms}^{-1}$. If the electron density in the wire is $8 \times 10^{28}\,\text{m}^{-3}$, the resistivity of the material is close to :
   (a) $1.6 \times 10^{-6}\,\Omega\text{m}$
   (b) $1.6 \times 10^{-5}\,\Omega\text{m}$
   (c) $1.6 \times 10^{-8}\,\Omega\text{m}$
   (d) $1.6 \times 10^{-7}\,\Omega\text{m}$

2. Variation of current passing through a conductor as the voltage applied across its ends is varied as shown in the adjoining diagram. If the resistance (R) is determined at the points A, B, C and D, we will find that
   (a) $R_C = R_D$
   (b) $R_B > R_A$
   (c) $R_C > R_B$
   (d) $R_A > R_B$

3. The length of a wire of a potentiometer is 100 cm, and the e. m.f. of its standard cell is E volt. It is employed to measure the e.m.f. of a battery whose internal resistance is $0.5\,\Omega$. If the balance point is obtained at $\ell = 30$ cm from the positive end, the e.m.f. of the battery is
   (a) $\dfrac{30E}{100.5}$
   (b) $\dfrac{30E}{(100-0.5)}$
   (c) $\dfrac{30(E-0.5i)}{100}$
   (d) $\dfrac{30E}{100}$

4. The masses of the three wires of copper are in the ratio of $1:3:5$ and their lengths are in the ratio of $5:3:1$. The ratio of their electrical resistance is
   (a) $1:3:5$
   (b) $5:3:1$
   (c) $1:25:125$
   (d) $125:15:1$

5. n equal resistors are first connected in series and then connected in parallel. What is the ratio of the maximum to the minimum resistance?
   (a) n
   (b) $1/n^2$
   (c) n^2
   (d) $1/n$

6. A battery is charged at a potential of 15V for 8 hours when the current flowing is 10A. The battery on discharge supplies a current of 5A for 15 hours. The mean terminal voltage during discharge is 14V. The "watt-hour" efficiency of the battery is
   (a) 87.5%
   (b) 82.5%
   (c) 80%
   (d) 90%

| RESPONSE GRID | 1. Ⓐ Ⓑ Ⓒ Ⓓ | 2. Ⓐ Ⓑ Ⓒ Ⓓ | 3. Ⓐ Ⓑ Ⓒ Ⓓ | 4. Ⓐ Ⓑ Ⓒ Ⓓ | 5. Ⓐ Ⓑ Ⓒ Ⓓ |
| | 6. Ⓐ Ⓑ Ⓒ Ⓓ | | | | |

Space for Rough Work

7. Shown in the figure below is a meter-bridge set up with null deflection in the galvanometer.

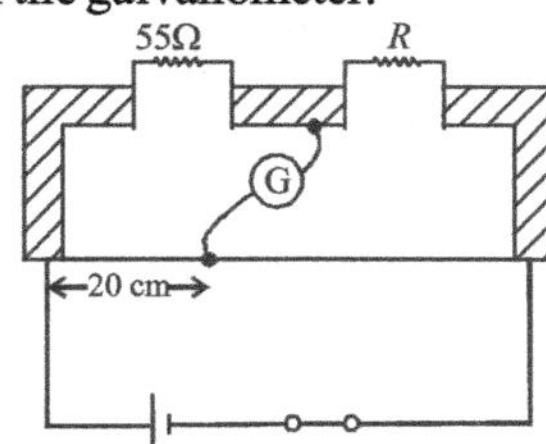

The value of the unknown resistor R is
(a) $13.75\,\Omega$ (b) $220\,\Omega$ (c) $110\,\Omega$ (d) $55\,\Omega$

8. In the equation AB = C, A is the current density, C is the electric field, Then B is
(a) resistivity   (b) conductivity
(c) potential difference   (d) resistance

9. The Kirchhoff's first law ($\Sigma i = 0$) and second law ($\Sigma iR = \Sigma E$), are respectively based on
(a) conservation of charge, conservation of momentum
(b) conservation of energy, conservation of charge
(c) conservation of momentum, conservation of charge
(d) conservation of charge, conservation of energy

10. You are given a resistance coil and a battery. In which of the following cases the largest amount of heat generated ?
(a) When the coil is connected to the battery directly
(b) When the coil is divided into two equal parts and both the parts are connected to the battery in parallel
(c) When the coil is divided into four equal parts and all the four parts are connected to the battery in parallel
(d) When only half the coil is connected to the battery

11. The resistance of the coil of an ammeter is R. The shunt required to increase its range n-fold should have a resistance
(a) $\dfrac{R}{n}$ (b) $\dfrac{R}{n-1}$ (c) $\dfrac{R}{n+1}$ (d) nR

12. On increasing the temperature of a conductor, its resistance increases because the
(a) relaxation time increases
(b) mass of electron increases
(c) electron density decreases
(d) relaxation time decreases

13. An electric current is passed through a circuit containing two wires of the same material, connected in parallel. If the lengths and radii are in the ratio of $\dfrac{4}{3}$ and $\dfrac{2}{3}$, then the ratio of the current passing through the wires will be
(a) 8/9   (b) 1/3   (c) 3   (d) 2

14. In a meter bridge experiment null point is obtained at 20 cm. from one end of the wire when resistance X is balanced against another resistance Y. If $X < Y$, then where will be the new position of the null point from the same end, if one decides to balance a resistance of $4\,X$ against Y
(a) 40 cm   (b) 80 cm   (c) 50 cm   (d) 70 cm

15. In the circuit shown, the current through 8 ohm is same before and after connecting E. The value of E is

(a) 12V
(b) 6V
(c) 4 V
(d) 2V

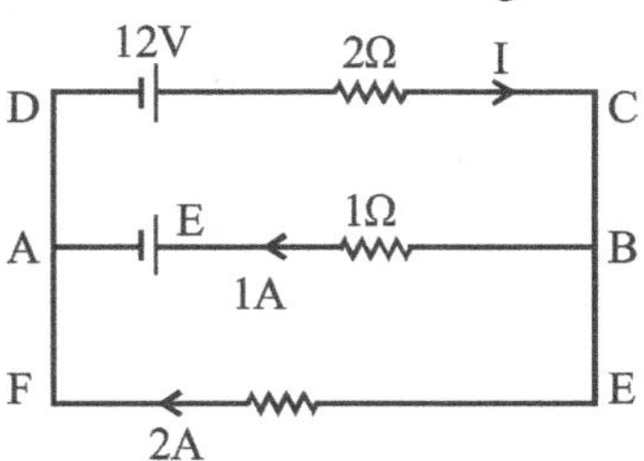

16. Find emf E of the cell as shown in figure.

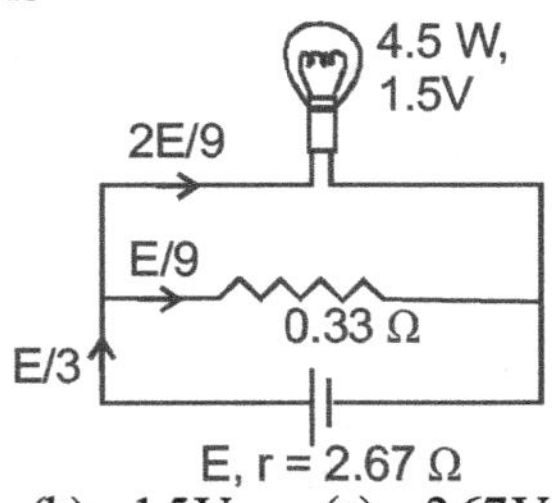

(a) 15V   (b) 10V   (c) 12V   (d) 5V

17. A torch bulb rated as 4.5 W, 1.5 V is connected as shown in fig. The e.m.f. of the cell, needed to make the bulb glow at full intensity is

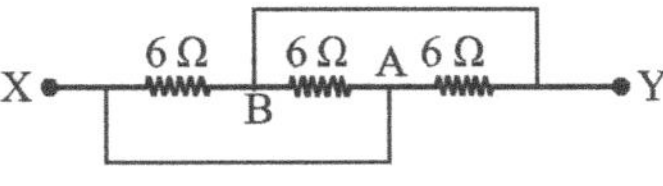

(a) 4.5V   (b) 1.5V   (c) 2.67V   (d) 13.5V

18. In a given network, each resistance has value of $6\,\Omega$. The point X is connected to point A by a copper wire of negligible resistance and point Y is connected to point B by the same wire. The effective resistance between X and Y will be

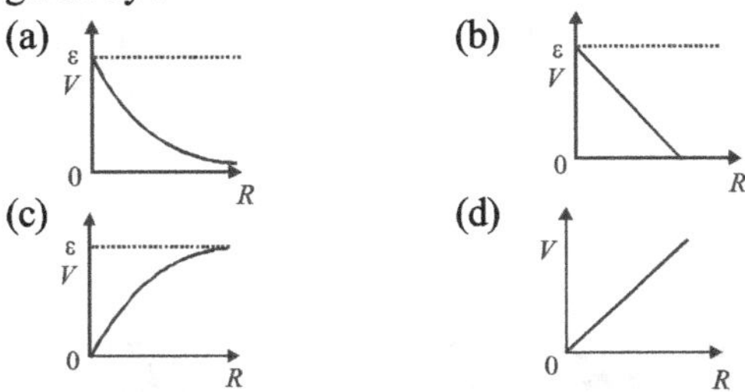

(a) $18\,\Omega$ (b) $6\,\Omega$ (c) $3\,\Omega$ (d) $2\,\Omega$

19. If N, e, τ and m are representing electron density, charge, relaxation time and mass of an electron respectively, then the resistance of wire of length ℓ and cross-sectional area A is given by
(a) $\dfrac{2m\ell}{Ne^2 A\tau}$ (b) $\dfrac{2m\tau A}{Ne^2 \ell}$ (c) $\dfrac{Ne^2 \tau A}{2m\ell}$ (d) $\dfrac{Ne^2 A}{2m\tau\ell}$

20. Cell having an emf ε and internal resistance r is connected across a variable external resistance R. As the resistance R is increased, the plot of potential difference V across R is given by :

(a)	(b)
(c)	(d)

<table>
<tr><td>**Response Grid**</td><td>7. (a)(b)(c)(d)</td><td>8. (a)(b)(c)(d)</td><td>9. (a)(b)(c)(d)</td><td>10. (a)(b)(c)(d)</td><td>11. (a)(b)(c)(d)</td></tr>
<tr><td></td><td>12. (a)(b)(c)(d)</td><td>13. (a)(b)(c)(d)</td><td>14. (a)(b)(c)(d)</td><td>15. (a)(b)(c)(d)</td><td>16. (a)(b)(c)(d)</td></tr>
<tr><td></td><td>17. (a)(b)(c)(d)</td><td>18. (a)(b)(c)(d)</td><td>19. (a)(b)(c)(d)</td><td>20. (a)(b)(c)(d)</td><td></td></tr>
</table>

21. If voltage across a bulb rated 220 Volt-100 Watt drops by 2.5% of its rated value, the percentage of the rated value by which the power would decrease is :
(a) 20% (b) 2.5% (c) 5% (d) 10%

22. If specific resistance of a potentiometer wire is $10^{-7}\ \Omega m$, the current flow through it is 0.1 A and the cross-sectional area of wire is $10^{-6}\ m^2$ then potential gradient will be
(a) 10^{-2} volt/m (b) 10^{-4} volt/m
(c) 10^{-6} volt/m (d) 10^{-8} volt/m

23. Two resistances R_1 and R_2 are made of different materials. The temperature coefficient of the material of R_1 is α and that of material of R_2 is $-\beta$. The resistance of the series combination of R_1 and R_2 will not change with temperature if $\dfrac{R_1}{R_2}$ equal to

(a) $\dfrac{\alpha}{\beta}$ (b) $\dfrac{\alpha+\beta}{\alpha-\beta}$ (c) $\dfrac{\alpha^2+\beta^2}{2\alpha\beta}$ (d) $\dfrac{\beta}{\alpha}$

24. Five cells each of emf E and internal resistance r send the same amount of current through an external resistance R whether the cells are connected in parallel or in series. Then the ratio $\left(\dfrac{R}{r}\right)$ is

(a) 2 (b) $\dfrac{1}{2}$ (c) $\dfrac{1}{5}$ (d) 1

25. The length of a given cylindrical wire is increased by 100%. Due to the consequent decrease in diameter the change in the resistance of the wire will be
(a) 200% (b) 100% (c) 50% (d) 300%

26. Potentiometer wire of length 1 m is connected in series with 490Ω resistance and 2 V battery. If 0.2 mV/cm is the potential gradient, then resistance of the potentiometer wire is
(a) $4.9\ \Omega$ (b) $7.9\ \Omega$ (c) $5.9\ \Omega$ (d) $6.9\ \Omega$

27. See the electric circuit shown in the figure. Which of the following equations is a correct equation for it?
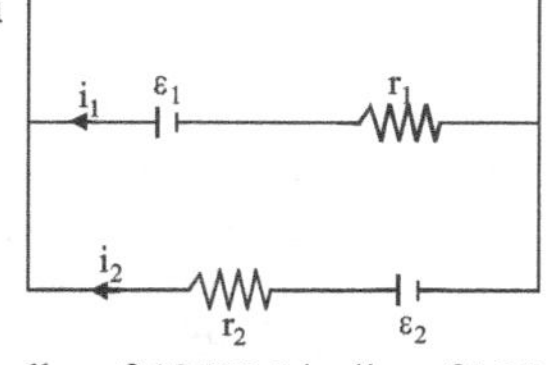
(a) $\varepsilon_2 - i_2\, r_2 - \varepsilon_1 - i_1\, r_1 = 0$
(b) $-\varepsilon_2 - (i_1 + i_2)\,R + i_2\, r_2 = 0$
(c) $\varepsilon_1 - (i_1 + i_2)\,R + i_1\, r_1 = 0$
(d) $\varepsilon_1 - (i_1 + i_2)\,R - i_1\, r_1 = 0$

28. In a large building, there are 15 bulbs of 40 W, 5 bulbs of 100 W, 5 fans of 80 W and 1 heater of 1 kW. The voltage of electric mains is 220 V. The minimum capacity of the main fuse of the building will be:
(a) 8 A (b) 10 A (c) 12 A (d) 14 A

29. Two sources of equal emf are connected to an external resistance R. The internal resistance of the two sources are R_1 and $R_2\ (R_1 > R_1)$. If the potential difference across the source having internal resistance R_2 is zero, then
(a) $R = R_2 - R_1$
(b) $R = R_2 \times (R_1 + R_2)/(R_2 - R_1)$
(c) $R = R_1 R_2/(R_2 - R_1)$
(d) $R = R_1 R_2 /(R_1 - R_2)$

30. The resistance of the series combination of two resistances is S. when they are joined in parallel the total resistance is P. If $S = nP$ then the minimum possible value of n is
(a) 2 (b) 3 (c) 4 (d) 1

31. If an ammeter is to be used in place of a voltmeter, then we must connect with the ammeter a
(a) low resistance in parallel
(b) high resistance in parallel
(c) high resistance in series
(d) low resistance in series.

32. A d.c. main supply of e.m.f. 220 V is connected across a storage battery of e.m.f. 200 V through a resistance of 1Ω. The battery terminals are connected to an external resistance 'R'. The minimum value of 'R', so that a current passes through the battery to charge it is:
(a) $7\ \Omega$ (b) $9\ \Omega$ (c) $11\ \Omega$ (d) Zero

33. In the given circuit diagram when the current reaches steady state in the circuit, the charge on the capacitor of capacitance C will be :
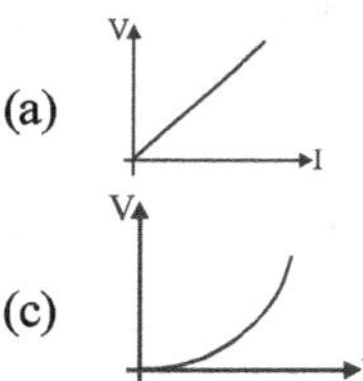
(a) $CE\,\dfrac{r_2}{(r+r_2)}$
(b) $CE\,\dfrac{r_1}{(r_1+r)}$
(c) $CE\,\dfrac{r_2}{(r+r_1)}$
(d) $CE\,\dfrac{r_1}{(r_2+r)}$

34. Suppose the drift velocity v_d in a material varied with the applied electric field E as $v_d \propto \sqrt{E}$. Then $V - I$ graph for a wire made of such a material is best given by :
(a) (b) (c) (d)

35. In a neon gas discharge tube Ne^+ ions moving through a cross-section of the tube each second to the right is 2.9×10^{18}, while 1.2×10^{18} electrons move towards left in the same time; the electronic charge being 1.6×10^{-19} C, the net electric current is
(a) 0.27 A to the right (b) 0.66 A to the right
(c) 0.66 A to the left (d) zero

36. Two rods are joined end to end, as shown. Both have a cross-sectional area of 0.01 cm^2. Each is 1 meter long. One rod is of copper with a resistivity of 1.7×10^{-6} ohm-centimeter, the other is of iron with a resistivity of 10^{-5} ohm-centimeter. How much voltage is required to produce a current of 1 ampere in the rods?
(a) 0.117V
(b) 0.00145 V
(c) 0.0145 V
(d) 1.7×10^{-6} V
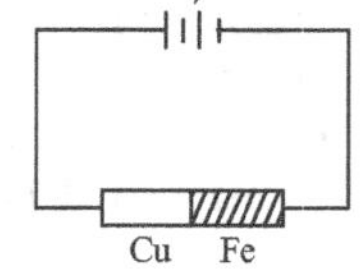

——————————————————————— *Space for Rough Work* ———————————————————————

37. An energy source will supply a constant current into the load if its internal resistance is
    (a) very large as compared to the load resistance
    (b) equal to the resistance of the load
    (c) non-zero but less than the resistance of the load
    (d) zero

38. The resistance of a wire at room temperature 30°C is found to be 10 Ω. Now to increase the resistance by 10%, the temperature of the wire must be [The temperature coefficient of resistance of the material of the wire is 0.002 per °C]
    (a) 36°C (b) 83°C
    (c) 63°C (d) 33°C

39. If current flowing in a conductor changes by 1% then power consumed will change by
    (a) 10% (b) 2% (c) 1% (d) 100%

40. In the circuit shown in figure, the 5Ω resistance develops 20.00 cal/s due to the current flowing through it. The heat developed in 2 Ω resistance (in cal/s) is

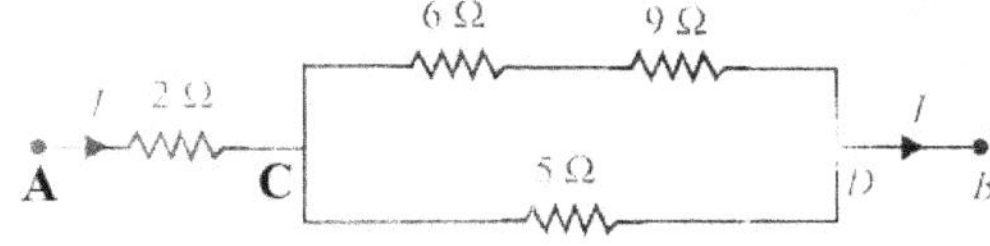

    (a) 23.8 (b) 14.2 (c) 11.9 (d) 7.1

41. In a Wheatstone's bridge, three resistances P, Q and R connected in the three arms and the fourth arm is formed by two resistances S_1 and S_2 connected in parallel. The condition for the bridge to be balanced will be
    (a) $\dfrac{P}{Q} = \dfrac{2R}{S_1 + S_2}$
    (b) $\dfrac{P}{Q} = \dfrac{R(S_1 + S_2)}{S_1 S_2}$
    (c) $\dfrac{P}{Q} = \dfrac{R(S_1 + S_2)}{2S_1 S_2}$
    (d) $\dfrac{P}{Q} = \dfrac{R}{S_1 + S_2}$

42. The electric resistance of a certain wire of iron is R. If its length and radius are both doubled, then
    (a) the resistance and the specific resistance, will both remain unchanged
    (b) the resistance will be doubled and the specific resistance will be halved
    (c) the resistance will be halved and the specific resistance will remain unchanged
    (d) the resistance will be halved and the specific resistance will be doubled

43. A car battery has e.m.f. 12 volt and internal resistance 5×10^{-2} ohm. If it draws 60 amp current, the terminal voltage of the battery will be
    (a) 15 volt (b) 3 volt (c) 5 volt (d) 9 volt

44. A conducting wire of cross-sectional area 1 cm² has 3×10^{23} charge carriers per m³. If wire carries a current of 24 mA, then drift velocity of carriers is
    (a) 5×10^{-2} m/s (b) 0.5 m/s
    (c) 5×10^{-3} m/s (d) 5×10^{-6} m/s

45. In the series combination of n cells each cell having emf ε and internal resistance r. If three cells are wrongly connected, then total emf and internal resistance of this combination will be
    (a) $n\varepsilon, (nr - 3r)$ (b) $(n\varepsilon - 2\varepsilon)\, nr$
    (c) $(n\varepsilon - 4\varepsilon),\, nr$ (d) $(n\varepsilon - 6\varepsilon),\, nr$

RESPONSE	37. ⓐⓑⓒⓓ	38. ⓐⓑⓒⓓ	39. ⓐⓑⓒⓓ	40. ⓐⓑⓒⓓ	41. ⓐⓑⓒⓓ
GRID	42. ⓐⓑⓒⓓ	43. ⓐⓑⓒⓓ	44. ⓐⓑⓒⓓ	45. ⓐⓑⓒⓓ	

DAILY PRACTICE PROBLEM DPP CHAPTERWISE CP17 - PHYSICS

Total Questions	45	Total Marks	180
Attempted		Correct	
Incorrect		Net Score	
Cut-off Score	45	Qualifying Score	60
Success Gap = Net Score – Qualifying Score			
Net Score = (Correct × 4) – (Incorrect × 1)			

Date : [ ]   Start Time : [ ]   End Time : [ ]

PHYSICS $\boxed{\text{CP18}}$

SYLLABUS : Moving Charges and Magnetism

Max. Marks : 180   **Marking Scheme :** (+4) for correct & (–1) for incorrect answer   **Time : 60 min.**

INSTRUCTIONS : This Daily Practice Problem Sheet contains 45 MCQs. For each question only one option is correct. Darken the correct circle/ bubble in the Response Grid provided on each page.

1. An insulating rod of length ℓ carries a charge q distributed uniformly on it. The rod is pivoted at its mid point and is rotated at a frequency f about a fixed axis perpendicular to rod and passing through the pivot. The magnetic moment of the rod system is $\dfrac{1}{2a}\pi q f \ell^2$. Find the value of a.

   (a) 6 (b) 4
   (c) 5 (d) 8

2. A portion of a conductive wire is bent in the form of a semicircle of radius r as shown below in fig. At the centre of semicircle, the magnetic induction will be

   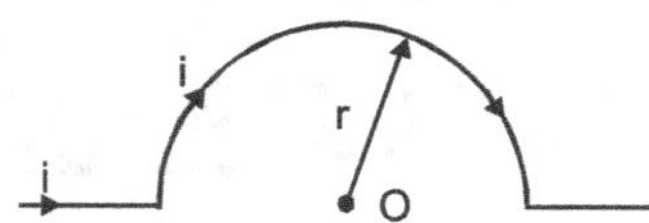

   (a) zero (b) infinite
   (c) $\dfrac{\mu_0}{4\pi}\cdot\dfrac{2\pi i}{r}$ (d) $\dfrac{\mu_0}{4\pi}\cdot\dfrac{\pi i}{r}$

3. A closely wound solenoid of 2000 turns and area of cross-section $1.5 \times 10^{-4}\,m^2$ carries a current of $2.0\,A$. It suspended through its centre and perpendicular to its length, allowing it to turn in a horizontal plane in a uniform magnetic field 5×10^{-2} tesla making an angle of 30° with the axis of the solenoid. The torque on the solenoid will be:

   (a) $3 \times 10^{-2}\,N\text{-}m$ (b) $3 \times 10^{-3}\,N\text{-}m$
   (c) $1.5 \times 10^{-3}\,N\text{-}m$ (d) $1.5 \times 10^{-2}\,N\text{-}m$

4. An alternating electric field, of frequency v, is applied across the dees (radius = R) of a cyclotron that is being used to accelerate protons (mass = m). The operating magnetic field (B) used in the cyclotron and the kinetic energy (K) of the proton beam, produced by it, are given by :

   (a) $B = \dfrac{mv}{e}$ and $K = 2m\pi^2 v^2 R^2$

   (b) $B = \dfrac{2\pi m v}{e}$ and $K = m^2 \pi v R^2$

   (c) $B = \dfrac{2\pi m v}{e}$ and $K = 2m\pi^2 v^2 R^2$

   (d) $B = \dfrac{mv}{e}$ and $K = m^2 \pi v R^2$

5. A galvanometer of 50 ohm resistance has 25 divisions. A current of 4×10^{-4} ampere gives a deflection of one per division. To convert this galvanometer into a voltmeter having a range of 25 volts, it should be connected with a resistance of

   (a) $2450\,\Omega$ in series (b) $2500\,\Omega$ in series.
   (c) $245\,\Omega$ in series. (d) $2550\,\Omega$ in series.

RESPONSE GRID   1. ⓐⓑⓒⓓ   2. ⓐⓑⓒⓓ   3. ⓐⓑⓒⓓ   4. ⓐⓑⓒⓓ   5. ⓐⓑⓒⓓ

Space for Rough Work

6. If we double the radius of a coil keeping the current through it unchanged, then the magnetic field at any point at a large distance from the centre becomes approximately
(a) double
(b) three times
(c) four times
(d) one-fourth

7. A particle of mass m, charge Q and kinetic energy T enters a transverse uniform magnetic field of induction $\vec{B}$. After 3 seconds, the kinetic energy of the particle will be:
(a) 3T
(b) 2T
(c) T
(d) 4T

8. A 10 eV electron is circulating in a plane at right angles to a uniform field at magnetic induction 10^{-4} Wb/m^2 ($= 1.0$ gauss). The orbital radius of the electron is
(a) 12 cm
(b) 16 cm
(c) 11 cm
(d) 18 cm

9. A uniform electric field and a uniform magnetic field exist in a region in the same direction. An electron is projected with velocity pointed in the same direction. The electron will
(a) turn to its right
(b) turn to its left
(c) keep moving in the same direction but its speed will increase
(d) keep moving in the same direction but its speed will decrease

10. Proton, deuteron and alpha particle of same kinetic energy are moving in circular trajectories in a constant magnetic field. The radii of proton, deuteron and alpha particle are respectively r_p, r_d and r_α. Which one of the following relation is correct?
(a) $r_\alpha = r_p = r_d$
(b) $r_\alpha = r_p < r_d$
(c) $r_\alpha > r_d > r_p$
(d) $r_\alpha = r_d > r_p$

11. A moving coil galvanometer has 150 equal divisions. Its current sensitivity is 10-divisions per milliampere and voltage sensitivity is 2 divisions per millivolt. In order that each division reads 1 volt, the resistance in ohms needed to be connected in series with the coil will be
(a) 10^5
(b) 10^3
(c) 9995
(d) 99995

12. A 2 µC charge moving around a circle with a frequency of 6.25×10^{12} Hz produces a magnetic field 6.28 tesla at the centre of the circle. The radius of the circle is
(a) 2.25m
(b) 0.25m
(c) 13.0m
(d) 1.25m

13. A charged particle with charge q enters a region of constant, uniform and mutually orthogonal fields $\vec{E}$ and $\vec{B}$ with a velocity $\vec{v}$ perpendicular to both $\vec{E}$ and $\vec{B}$, and comes out without any change in magnitude or direction of $\vec{v}$. Then
(a) $\vec{v} = \vec{B} \times \vec{E} / E^2$
(b) $\vec{v} = \vec{E} \times \vec{B} / B^2$
(c) $\vec{v} = \vec{B} \times \vec{E} / B^2$
(d) $\vec{v} = \vec{E} \times \vec{B} / E^2$

14. A square current carrying loop is suspended in a uniform magnetic field acting in the plane of the loop. If the force on one arm of the loop is $\vec{F}$, the net force on the remaining three arms of the loop is
(a) $3\vec{F}$
(b) $-\vec{F}$
(c) $-3\vec{F}$
(d) $\vec{F}$

15. A straight section PQ of a circuit lies along the X-axis from $x = -\dfrac{a}{2}$ to $x = \dfrac{a}{2}$ and carries a steady current i. The magnetic field due to the section PQ at a point $X = +a$ will be
(a) proportional to a
(b) proportional to a^2
(c) proportional to $1/a$
(d) zero

16. A and B are two conductors carrying a current i in the same direction. x and y are two electron beams moving in the same direction. Then

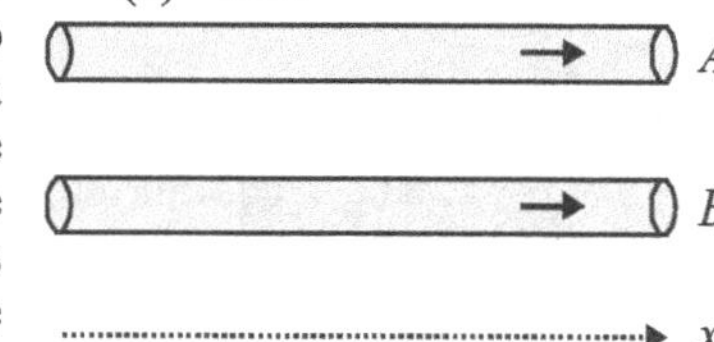

(a) there will be repulsion betwen A and B, attraction between x and y
(b) there will be attraction between A and B, repulsion between x and y
(c) there will be repulsion between A and B and also x and y
(d) there will be attraction between A and B and also x and y

17. A galvanometer of resistance, G is shunted by a resistance S ohm. To keep the main current in the circuit unchanged, the resistance to be put in series with the galvanometer is
(a) $\dfrac{S^2}{(S+G)}$
(b) $\dfrac{SG}{(S+G)}$
(c) $\dfrac{G^2}{(S+G)}$
(d) $\dfrac{G}{(S+G)}$

18. A current I flows in an infinitely long wire with cross section in the form of a semi-circular ring of radius R. The magnitude of the magnetic induction along its axis is:
(a) $\dfrac{\mu_0 I}{2\pi^2 R}$
(b) $\dfrac{\mu_0 I}{2\pi R}$
(c) $\dfrac{\mu_0 I}{4\pi R}$
(d) $\dfrac{\mu_0 I}{\pi^2 R}$

19. Two equal electric currents are flowing perpendicular to each other as shown in the figure. AB and CD are perpendicular to each other and symmetrically placed with respect to the current flow. Where do we expect the resultant magnetic field to be zero?

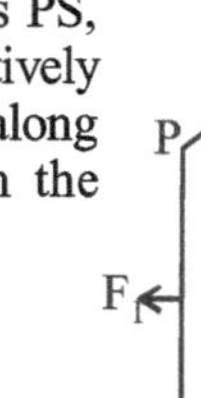

(a) On AB
(b) On CD
(c) On both AB and CD
(d) On both OD and BO

20. A closed loop PQRS carrying a current is placed in a uniform magnetic field.
If the magnetic forces on segments PS, SR, and RQ are F_1, F_2 and F_3 respectively and are in the plane of the paper and along the directions shown, the force on the segment QP is

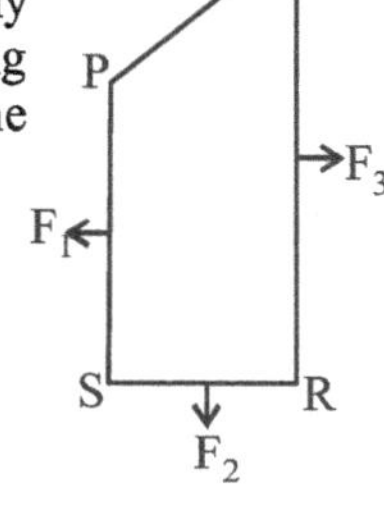

(a) $F_3 - F_1 - F_2$
(b) $\sqrt{(F_3 - F_1)^2 + F_2^2}$
(c) $\sqrt{(F_3 - F_1)^2 + F_2^2}$
(d) $F_3 - F_1 + F_2$

	6. ⓐⓑⓒⓓ	7. ⓐⓑⓒⓓ	8. ⓐⓑⓒⓓ	9. ⓐⓑⓒⓓ	10. ⓐⓑⓒⓓ
RESPONSE	11. ⓐⓑⓒⓓ	12. ⓐⓑⓒⓓ	13. ⓐⓑⓒⓓ	14. ⓐⓑⓒⓓ	15. ⓐⓑⓒⓓ
GRID	16. ⓐⓑⓒⓓ	17. ⓐⓑⓒⓓ	18. ⓐⓑⓒⓓ	19. ⓐⓑⓒⓓ	20. ⓐⓑⓒⓓ

21. A long solenoid carrying a current produces a magnetic field B along its axis. If the current is double and the number of turns per cm is halved, the new value of the magnetic field is
(a) $4B$ (b) $B/2$ (c) B (d) $2B$

22. A particle of charge q and mass m moves in a circular orbit of radius r with angular speed ω. The ratio of the magnitude of its magnetic moment to that of its angular momentum depends on
(a) ω and q (b) ω, q and m
(c) q and m (d) ω and m

23. A current loop in a magnetic field
(a) can be in equilibrium in one orientation
(b) can be in equilibrium in two orientations, both the equilibrium states are unstable
(c) can be in equilibrium in two orientations, one stable while the other is unstable
(d) experiences a torque whether the field is uniform or non-uniform in all orientations

24. Two long parallel wires P and Q are held perpendicular to the plane of paper with distance of 5 m between them. If P and Q carry current of 2.5 amp. and 5 amp. respectively in the same direction, then the magnetic field at a point half-way between the wires is
(a) $\mu_0/17$ (b) $\sqrt{3}\,\mu_0/2\pi$
(c) $\mu_0/2\pi$ (d) $3\mu_0/2\pi$

25. A very long straight wire carries a current I. At the instant when a charge $+Q$ at point P has velocity $\vec{v}$, as shown, the force on the charge is
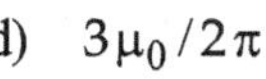
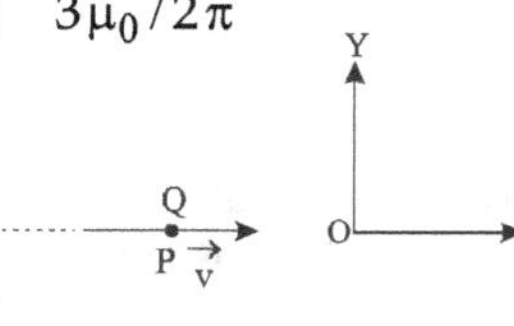
(a) along OY (b) opposite to OY
(c) along OX (d) opposite to OX

26. Two wires with currents 2 A and 1 A are enclosed in a circular loop. Another wire with current 3 A is situated outside the loop as shown. The $\oint \vec{B}.d\vec{l}$ around the loop is
(a) μ_0
(b) $3\mu_0$
(c) $6\mu_0$
(d) $2\mu_0$
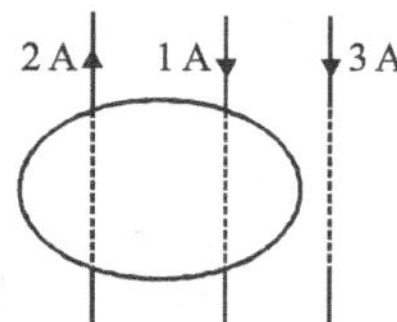

27. If in a circular coil A of radius R, current I is flowing and in another coil B of radius $2R$ a current $2I$ is flowing, then the ratio of the magnetic fields B_A and B_B, produced by them will be
(a) 1 (b) 2 (c) 1/2 (d) 4

28. A charged particle moves through a magnetic field perpendicular to its direction. Then
(a) kinetic energy changes but the momentum is constant
(b) the momentum changes but the kinetic energy is constant
(c) both momentum and kinetic energy of the particle are not constant
(d) both momentum and kinetic energy of the particle are constant

29. The deflection in a galvanometer falls from 50 division to 20 when a 12 ohm shunt is applied. The galvanometer resistance is
(a) 18 ohm (b) 36 ohm (c) 24 ohm (d) 30 ohm

30. When a long wire carrying a steady current is bent into a circular coil of one turn, the magnetic induction at its centre is B. When the same wire carrying the same current is bent to form a circular coil of n turns of a smaller radius, the magnetic induction at the centre will be
(a) B/n (b) nB (c) B/n^2 (d) n^2B

31. The magnetic field due to a current carrying circular loop of radius 3 cm at a point on the axis at a distance of 4 cm from the centre is 54 μT. What will be its value at the centre of loop ?
(a) $125\,\mu T$ (b) $150\,\mu T$
(c) $250\,\mu T$ (d) $75\,\mu T$

32. A charge moving with velocity v in X-direction is subjected to a field of magnetic induction in negative X-direction. As a result, the charge will
(a) remain unaffected
(b) start moving in a circular path Y–Z plane
(c) retard along X-axis
(d) move along a helical path around X-axis

33. An electron travelling with a speed u along the positive x-axis enters into a region of magnetic field where $B = -B_0\,\hat{k}$ $(x>0)$. It comes out of the region with speed v then
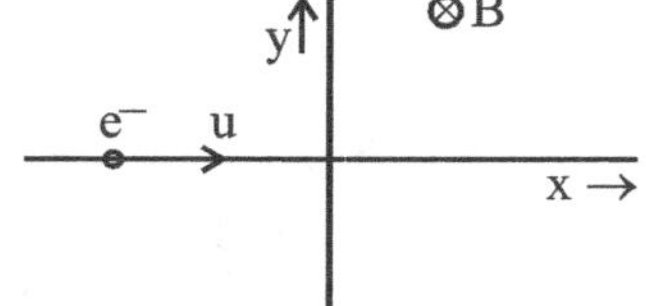
(a) $v = u$ at $y > 0$
(b) $v = u$ at $y < 0$
(c) $v > u$ at $y > 0$
(d) $v > u$ at $y < 0$

34. If an ammeter is to be used in place of a voltmeter, then we must connect with the ammeter a
(a) low resistance in parallel
(b) high resistance in parallel
(c) high resistance in series
(d) low resistance in series

35. An infinite straight conductor carrying current 2 I is split into a loop of radius r as shown in fig. The magnetic field at the centre of the coil is
(a) $\dfrac{\mu_0}{4\pi}\dfrac{2(\pi+1)}{r}$
(b) $\dfrac{\mu_0}{4\pi}\dfrac{2(\pi-1)}{r}$
(c) $\dfrac{\mu_0}{4\pi}\dfrac{(\pi+1)}{r}$
(d) zero
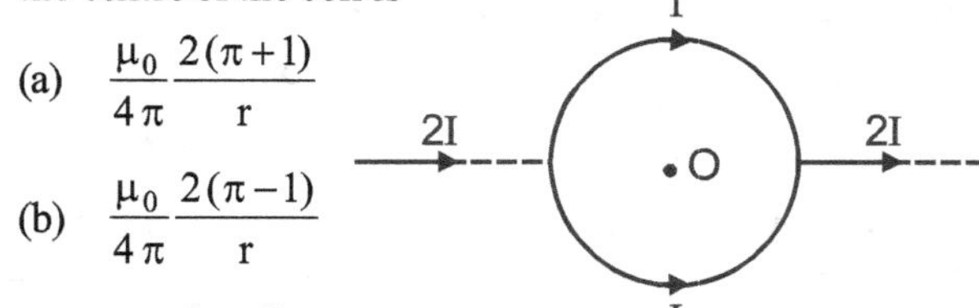

<table>
<tr><td rowspan="3">**RESPONSE GRID**</td><td>21. ⓐⓑⓒⓓ</td><td>22. ⓐⓑⓒⓓ</td><td>23. ⓐⓑⓒⓓ</td><td>24. ⓐⓑⓒⓓ</td><td>25. ⓐⓑⓒⓓ</td></tr>
<tr><td>26. ⓐⓑⓒⓓ</td><td>27. ⓐⓑⓒⓓ</td><td>28. ⓐⓑⓒⓓ</td><td>29. ⓐⓑⓒⓓ</td><td>30. ⓐⓑⓒⓓ</td></tr>
<tr><td>31. ⓐⓑⓒⓓ</td><td>32. ⓐⓑⓒⓓ</td><td>33. ⓐⓑⓒⓓ</td><td>34. ⓐⓑⓒⓓ</td><td>35. ⓐⓑⓒⓓ</td></tr>
</table>

36. A parallel plate capacitor of area 60 cm^2 and separation 3 mm is charged initially to 90 μC. If the medium between the plate gets slightly conducting and the plate loses the charge initially at the rate of 2.5 × 10^{-8} C/s, then what is the magnetic field between the plates ?

(a) 2.5 × 10^{-8} T (b) 2.0 × 10^{-7} T
(c) 1.63 × 10^{-11} T (d) Zero

37. Four wires, each of length 2.0 m, are bent into four loops P, Q, R and S and then suspended in a uniform magnetic field. If the same current is passed in each, then the torque will be maximum on the loop

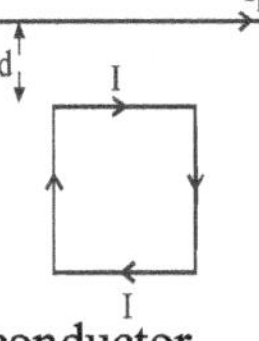

(a) P (b) Q (c) R (d) S

38. A certain region has an electric field $\vec{E} = (2\hat{i} - 3\hat{j})$ N/C and a uniform magnetic field $\vec{B} = (5\hat{i} + 3\hat{j} + 4\hat{k})$ T . The force experienced by a charge 1C moving with velocity $(\hat{i} + 2\hat{j})$ ms^{-1} is

(a) $(10\hat{i} - 7\hat{j} - 7\hat{k})$ (b) $(10\hat{i} + 7\hat{j} + 7\hat{k})$
(c) $(-10\hat{i} + 7\hat{j} + 7\hat{k})$ (d) $(10\hat{i} + 7\hat{j} - 7\hat{k})$

39. A galvanometer of resistance 100 Ω gives a full scale deflection for a current of 10^{-5} A. To convert it into a ammeter capable of measuring upto 1 A, we should connect a resistance of

(a) 1 Ω in parallel (b) 10^{-3} Ω in parallel
(c) 10^{5} Ω in series (d) 100 Ω in series

40. A square loop, carrying a steady current I, is placed in a horizontal plane near a long straight conductor carrying a steady current I_1 at a distance d from the conductor as shown in figure. The loop will experience

(a) a net repulsive force away from the conductor
(b) a net torque acting upward perpendicular to the horizontal plane
(c) a net torque acting downward normal to the horizontal plane
(d) a net attractive force towards the conductor

41. Two coaxial solenoids of different radius carry current I in the same direction. $\vec{F_1}$ be the magnetic force on the inner solenoid due to the outer one and $\vec{F_2}$ be the magnetic force on the outer solenoid due to the inner one. Then :

(a) $\vec{F_1}$ is radially inwards and $\vec{F_2} = 0$
(b) $\vec{F_1}$ is radially outwards and $\vec{F_2} = 0$
(c) $\vec{F_1} = \vec{F_2} = 0$
(d) $\vec{F_1}$ is radially inwards and $\vec{F_2}$ is radially outwards

42. A beam of electrons is moving with constant velocity in a region having simultaneous perpendicular electric and magnetic fields of strength 20 Vm^{-1} and 0.5 T respectively at right angles to the direction of motion of the electrons. Then the velocity of electrons must be

(a) 8 m/s (b) 20 m/s (c) 40 m/s (d) $\dfrac{1}{40}$ m/s

43. The magnetic flux density B at a distance r from a long straight wire carrying a steady current varies with r as

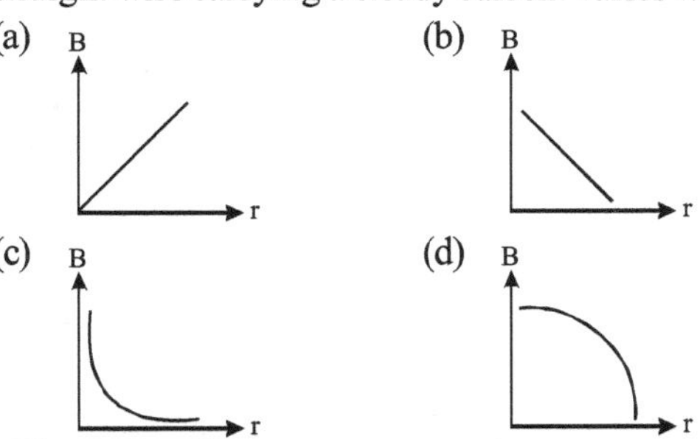

44. The AC voltage across a resistance can be measured using a :

(a) hot wire voltmeter
(b) moving coil galvanometer
(c) potential coil galvanometer
(d) moving magnet galvanometer

45. When a charged particle moving with velocity $\vec{v}$ is subjected to a magnetic field of induction $\vec{B}$, the force on it is non-zero. This implies that

(a) angle between $\vec{v}$ and $\vec{B}$ is necessarily 90°
(b) angle between $\vec{v}$ and $\vec{B}$ can have any value other than 90°
(c) angle between $\vec{v}$ and $\vec{B}$ can have any value other than zero and 180°
(d) angle between $\vec{v}$ and $\vec{B}$ is either zero or 180°

RESPONSE GRID					
	36. ⓐⓑⓒⓓ	37. ⓐⓑⓒⓓ	38. ⓐⓑⓒⓓ	39. ⓐⓑⓒⓓ	40. ⓐⓑⓒⓓ
	41. ⓐⓑⓒⓓ	42. ⓐⓑⓒⓓ	43. ⓐⓑⓒⓓ	44. ⓐⓑⓒⓓ	45. ⓐⓑⓒⓓ

DAILY PRACTICE PROBLEM DPP CHAPTERWISE CP18 - PHYSICS

Total Questions	45	Total Marks	180
Attempted		Correct	
Incorrect		Net Score	
Cut-off Score	45	Qualifying Score	60
Success Gap = Net Score – Qualifying Score			
Net Score = (Correct × 4) – (Incorrect × 1)			

Date :   Start Time :   End Time :

PHYSICS $\boxed{CP19}$

SYLLABUS : Magnetism and Matter

Max. Marks : 180   **Marking Scheme :** (+4) for correct & (–1) for incorrect answer   **Time : 60 min.**

INSTRUCTIONS : This Daily Practice Problem Sheet contains 45 MCQs. For each question only one option is correct. Darken the correct circle/ bubble in the Response Grid provided on each page.

---

1. Two identical magnetic dipoles of magnetic moments 1.0 A-m^2 each, placed at a separation of 2 m with their axis perpendicular to each other. The resultant magnetic field at point midway between the dipole is

  (a) 5×10^{-7} T   (b) $\sqrt{5} \times 10^{-7}$ T

  (c) 10^{-7} T   (d) 2×10^{-7} T

2. Two identical thin bar magnets each of length ℓ and pole strength m are placed at right angles to each other, with north pole of one touching south pole of the other, then the magnetic moment of the system is

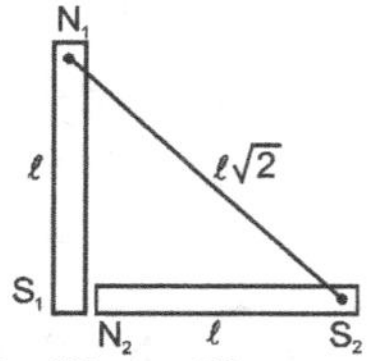

  (a) $1\,m\ell$ (b) $2\,m\ell$ (c) $\sqrt{2}\,m\ell$ (d) $m\ell/2$

3. The magnetic lines of force inside a bar magnet

  (a)   are from north-pole to south-pole of the magnet

  (b)   do not exist

  (c)   depend upon the area of cross-section of the bar magnet

  (d)   are from south-pole to north-pole of the magnet

4. Relative permittivity and permeability of a material ε_r and μ_r, respectively. Which of the following values of these quantities are allowed for a diamagnetic material?

  (a) $\varepsilon_r = 0.5, \mu_r = 1.5$ (b) $\varepsilon_r = 1.5, \mu_r = 0.5$

  (c) $\varepsilon_r = 0.5, \mu_r = 0.5$ (d) $\varepsilon_r = 1.5, \mu_r = 1.5$

5. If the period of oscillation of freely suspended bar magnet in earth's horizontal field H is 4 sec. When another magnet is brought near it, the period of oscillation is reduced to 2s. The magnetic field of second bar magnet is

  (a)   4 H   (b)   3 H   (c)   2 H   (d) $\sqrt{3}$ H

6. Three identical bars A, B and C are made of different magnetic materials. When kept in a uniform magnetic field, the field lines around them look as follows:

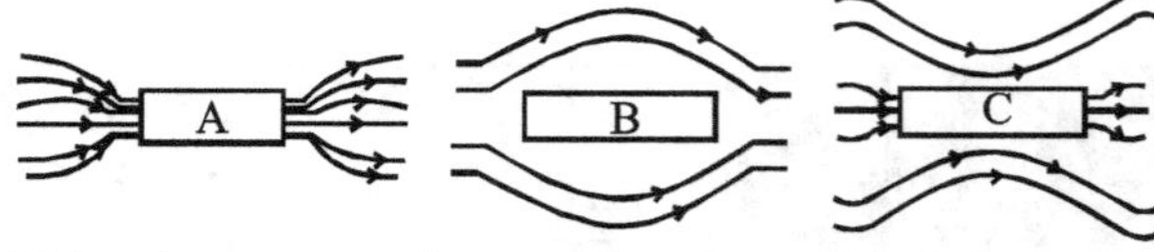

Make the correspondence of these bars with their material being diamagnetic (D), ferromagnetic (F) and paramagnetic (P):

  (a) $A \leftrightarrow D, B \leftrightarrow P, C \leftrightarrow F$

  (b) $A \leftrightarrow F, B \leftrightarrow D, C \leftrightarrow P$

  (c) $A \leftrightarrow P, B \leftrightarrow F, C \leftrightarrow D$

  (d) $A \leftrightarrow F, B \leftrightarrow P, C \leftrightarrow D$

RESPONSE GRID	1. ⓐⓑⓒⓓ	2. ⓐⓑⓒⓓ	3. ⓐⓑⓒⓓ	4. ⓐⓑⓒⓓ	5. ⓐⓑⓒⓓ
	6. ⓐⓑⓒⓓ				

Space for Rough Work

7. Curie temperature is the temperature above which
   (a) a ferromagnetic material becomes paramagnetic
   (b) a paramagnetic material becomes diamagnetic
   (c) a ferromagnetic material becomes diamagnetic
   (d) a paramagnetic material becomes ferromagnetic

8. A watch glass containing some powdered substance is placed between the pole pieces of a magnet. Deep concavity is observed at the centre. The substance in the watch glass is
   (a) iron   (b) chromium   (c) carbon   (d) wood

9. A coil in the shape of an equilateral triangle of side l is suspended between the pole pieces of a permanent magnet such that $\vec{B}$ is in the plane of the coil. If due to a current i in the triangle a torque τ acts on it, the side l of the triangle is

   (a) $\dfrac{2}{\sqrt{3}}\left(\dfrac{\tau}{\text{B.i}}\right)^{\frac{1}{2}}$ (b) $2\left(\dfrac{\tau}{\sqrt{3}\text{B.i}}\right)^{\frac{1}{2}}$

   (c) $\dfrac{2}{\sqrt{3}}\left(\dfrac{\tau}{\text{B.i}}\right)$ (d) $\dfrac{1}{\sqrt{3}}\dfrac{\tau}{\text{B.i}}$

10. A compass needle whose magnetic moment is 60 Am^2, is directed towards geographical north at any place experiencing moment of force of 1.2×10^{-3} Nm. At that place the horizontal component of earth field is 40 micro W/m^2. What is the value of dip angle at that place?
    (a) 30°   (b) 60°   (c) 45°   (d) 15°

11. The materials suitable for making electromagnets should have
    (a) high retentivity and low coercivity
    (b) low retentivity and low coercivity
    (c) high retentivity and high coercivity
    (d) low retentivity and high coercivity

12. The length of a magnet is large compared to its width and breadth. The time period of its oscillation in a vibration magnetometer is 2s. The magnet is cut along its length into three equal parts and these parts are then placed on each other with their like poles together. The time period of this combination will be

    (a) $2\sqrt{3}$ s   (b) $\dfrac{2}{3}$ s   (c) 2 s   (d) $\dfrac{2}{\sqrt{3}}$ s

13. Hysteresis loops for two magnetic materials A and B are given below :

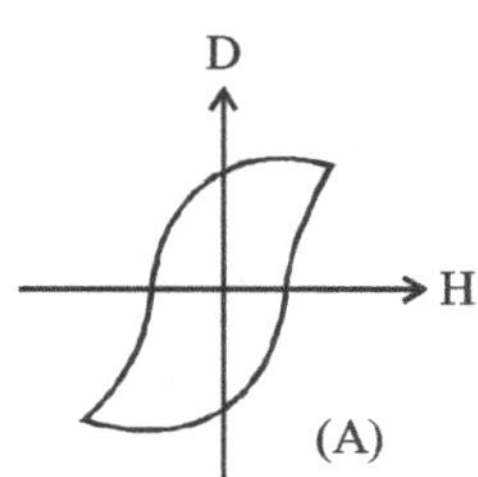

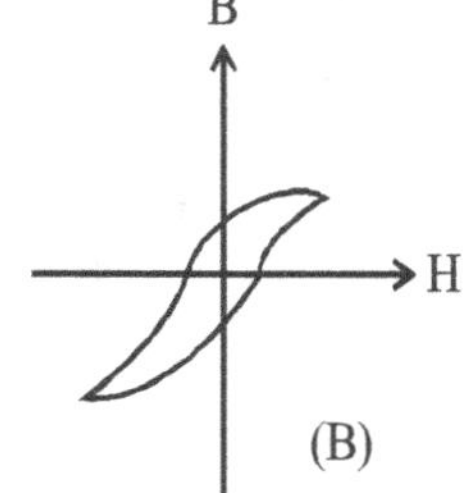

These materials are used to make magnets for elecric generators, transformer core and electromagnet core. Then it is proper to use :
    (a) A for transformers and B for electric generators.
    (b) B for electromagnets and transformers.
    (c) A for electric generators and trasformers.
    (d) A for electromagnets and B for electric generators.

14. Which of the following is responsible for the earth's magnetic field?
    (a) Convective currents in earth's core.
    (b) Diversive current in earth's core.
    (c) Rotational motion of earth.
    (d) Translational motion of earth.

15. In a vibration megnetometer, the time period of a bar magnet oscillating in horizontal component of earth's magnetic field is 2 sec. When a magnet is brought near and parallel to it, the time period reduces to 1 sec. The ratio H/F of the horizontal component H and the field F due to magnet will be
    (a) 3   (b) 1/3   (c) $\sqrt{3}$ (d) $1/\sqrt{3}$

16. Let V and H be the vertical and horizontal components of earth's magnetic field at any point on earth. Near the north pole
    (a) $V \gg H$ (b) $V \ll H$ (c) $V = H$ (d) $V = H = 0$

17. A thin circular wire carrying a current I has a magnetic moment M. The shape of the wire is changed to a square and it carries the same current. It will have a magnetic moment

    (a) M (b) $\dfrac{4}{\pi^2}M$ (c) $\dfrac{4}{\pi}M$ (d) $\dfrac{\pi}{4}M$

18. A bar magnet of magnetic moment M is placed at right angles to a magnetic induction B. If a force F is experienced by each pole of the magnet, the length of the magnet will be
    (a) F/MB (b) MB/F (c) BF/M (d) MF/B

19. If the susceptibility of dia, para and ferro magnetic materials are χ_d, χ_p, χ_f respectively, then
    (a) $\chi_d < \chi_p < \chi_f$ (b) $\chi_d < \chi_f < \chi_p$
    (c) $\chi_f < \chi_d < \chi_p$ (d) $\chi_f < \chi_p < \chi_d$

20. The basic magnetization curve for a ferromagnetic material is shown in figure. Then, the value of relative permeability is highest for the point

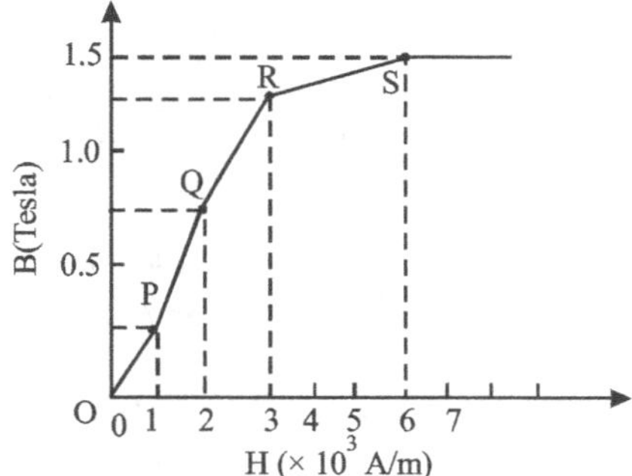

    (a) P   (b) Q   (c) R   (d) S

21. A magnetic needle suspended by a silk thread is vibrating in the earth's magnetic field. if the temperature of the needle is increased by 700°C, then
(a) time period decreases
(b) time period increases
(c) time period remains unchanged
(d) the needle stops vibrating

22. Torques τ_1 and τ_2 are required for a magnetic needle to remain perpendicular to the magnetic fields at two different places. The magnetic fields at those places are B_1 and B_2 respectively; then ratio $\dfrac{B_1}{B_2}$ is
(a) $\dfrac{\tau_2}{\tau_1}$
(b) $\dfrac{\tau_1}{\tau_2}$
(c) $\dfrac{\tau_1 + \tau_2}{\tau_1 - \tau_2}$
(d) $\dfrac{\tau_1 - \tau_2}{\tau_1 + \tau_2}$

23. A bar magnet has a length 8 cm. The magnetic field at a point at a distance 3 cm from the centre in the broad side-on position is found to be $4\times10^{-6}\ T$. The pole strength of the magnet is.
(a) 6×10^{-5} Am
(b) 5×10^{-5} Am
(c) 2×10^{-4} Am
(d) 3×10^{-4} Am

24. A vibration magnetometer consists of two identical bar magnets placed one over the other such that they are perpendicular and bisect each other. The time period of oscillation in a horizontal magnetic field is $2^{5/4}$ seconds. One of the magnets is removed and if the other magnet oscillates in the same field, then the time period in seconds is
(a) $2^{1/4}$
(b) $2^{1/2}$
(c) 2
(d) $2^{3/4}$

25. A magnetic needle is kept in a non-uniform magnetic field. It experiences
(a) neither a force nor a torque
(b) a torque but not a force
(c) a force but not a torque
(d) a force and a torque

26. The angle of dip at a place is 37° and the vertical component of the earth's magnetic field is 6×10^{-5}T. The earth's magnetic field at this place is (tan 37° = 3/4)
(a) 7×10^{-5} T
(b) 6×10^{-5} T
(c) 5×10^{-5} T
(d) 10^{-4} T

27. Needles N_1, N_2 and N_3 are made of a ferromagnetic, a paramagnetic and a diamagnetic substance respectively. A magnet when brought close to them will
(a) attract N_1 and N_2 strongly but repel N_3
(b) attract N_1 strongly, N_2 weakly and repel N_3 weakly
(c) attract N_1 strongly, but repel N_2 and N_3 weakly
(d) attract all three of them

28. The figure shows the various positions (labelled by subscripts) of small magnetised needles P and Q. The arrows show the direction of their magnetic moment. Which configuration corresponds to the lowest potential energy among all the configurations shown ?
(a) PQ_3
(b) PQ_4
(c) PQ_5
(d) PQ_6

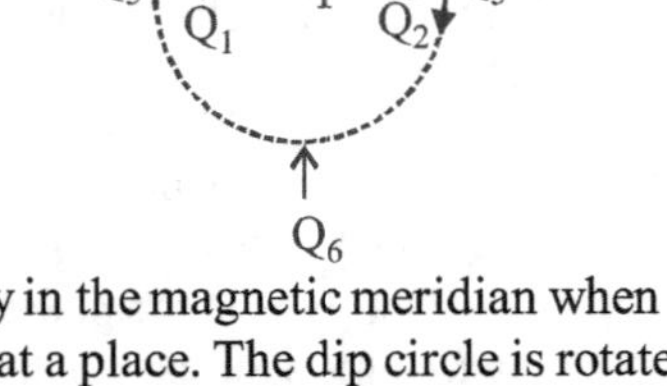

29. A dip needle lies initially in the magnetic meridian when it shows an angle of dip θ at a place. The dip circle is rotated through an angle x in the horizontal plane and then it shows an angle of dip θ′.
Then $\dfrac{\tan \theta'}{\tan \theta}$ is
(a) $\dfrac{1}{\cos x}$
(b) $\dfrac{1}{\sin x}$
(c) $\dfrac{1}{\tan x}$
(d) $\cos x$

30. Two tangent galvanometers having coils of the same radius are connected in series. A current flowing in them produces deflections of 60° and 45° respectively. The ratio of the number of turns in the coils is
(a) $4/3$
(b) $\dfrac{\sqrt{3}+1}{1}$
(c) $\dfrac{\sqrt{3}+1}{\sqrt{3}-1}$
(d) $\dfrac{\sqrt{3}}{1}$

31. Following figures show the arrangement of bar magnets in different configurations. Each magnet has magnet ic dipole moment $\bar{m}$. Which configuration has highest net magnetic dipole moment?

(a) 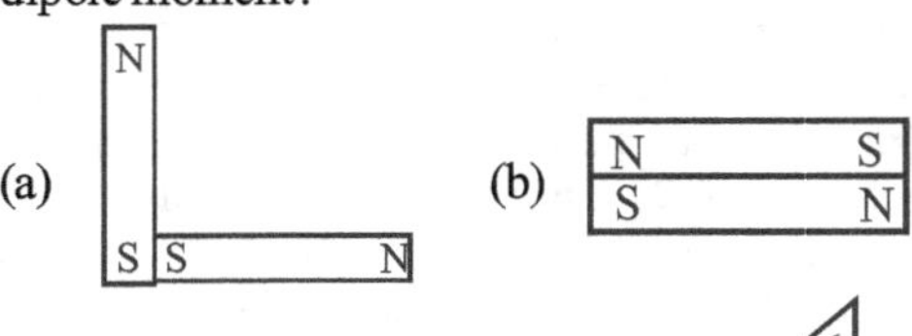
(b)
(c) 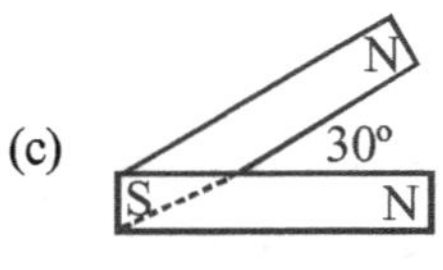
(d) 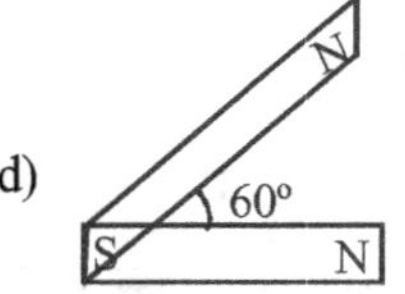

32. A compass needle which is allowed to move in a horizontal plane is taken to a geomagnetic pole. It :
(a) will become rigid showing no movement
(b) will stay in any position
(c) will stay in north-south direction only
(d) will stay in east-west direction only

33. If a magnetic dipole of moment M situated in the direction of a magnetic field B is rotated by 180°, then the amount of work done is
(a) MB
(b) $2MB$
(c) $\dfrac{MB}{\sqrt{2}}$
(d) 0

34. A bar magnet is oscillating in the earth's magnetic field with a period T. What happens to its period of motion, if its mass is quadrupled
(a) motion remains simple harmonic with new period = T/2
(b) motion remains simple harmonic with new period = 2 T
(c) motion remains simple harmonic with new period = 4T
(d) motion remains simple harmonic and the period stays nearly constant

35. The magnetic field of earth at the equator is approximately 4×10^{-5} T. The radius of earth is 6.4×10^6 m. Then the dipole moment of the earth will be nearly of the order of:
(a) $10^{23}\,\mathrm{A\,m^2}$　(b) $10^{20}\,\mathrm{A\,m^2}$　(c) $10^{16}\,\mathrm{A\,m^2}$　(d) $10^{10}\,\mathrm{A\,m^2}$

36. The relative permeability of a medium is 0.075. What is its magnetic susceptibility?
(a) 0.925　(b) -0.925　(c) 1.075　(d) -1.075

37. A dip circle is so set that its needle moves freely in the magnetic meridian. In this position, the angle of dip is 40°. Now the dip circle is rotated so that the plane in which the needle moves makes an angle of 30° with the magnetic meridian. In this position, the needle will dip by an angle
(a) 40°　(b) 30°　(c) more than 40°　(d) less than 40°

38. The mid points of two small magnetic dipoles of length d in end-on positions, are separated by a distance x, (x > > d). The force between them is proportional to x^{-n} where n is:

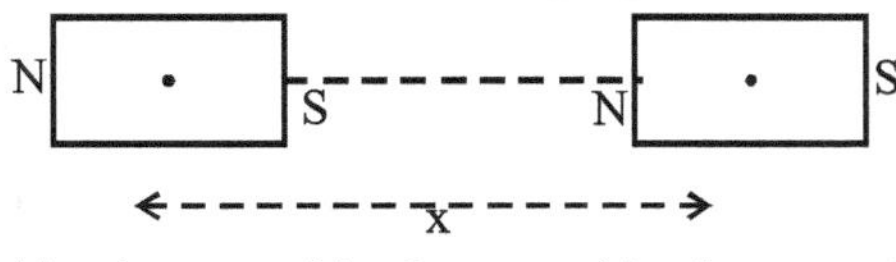

(a) 1　　(b) 2　　(c) 3　　(d) 4

39. At a temperatur of 30°C, the susceptibility of a ferromagnetic material is found to be χ. Its susceptibility at 333°C is
(a) χ　(b) 0.5χ　(c) 2χ　(d) 11.1χ

40. The susceptibility of annealed iron at saturation is 5500. Find the permeability of annealed iron at saturation.
(a) 6.9×10^{-3}　(b) 5.1×10^{-2}　(c) 5×10^2　(d) 3.2×10^{-5}

41. A short magnet oscillates in an oscillation magnetometer with a time period of 0.10s where the earth's horizontal magnetic field is 24 μT. A downward current of 18 A is established in a vertical wire placed 20 cm east of the magnet. Find the new time period.
(a) 0.076 s　(b) 0.5 s　(c) 0.1 s　(d) 0.2 s

42. A permanent magnet in the shape of a thin cylinder of length 10 cm has magnetisation $(M) = 10^6$ A m^{-1}. Its magnetization current I_M is
(a) 10^5 A　(b) 10^6 A　(c) 10^7 A　(d) 10^8 A

43. The earth's magnetic field lines resemble that of a dipole at the centre of the earth. If the magnetic moment of this dipole is close to 8×10^{22} Am^2, the value of earth's magnetic field near the equator is close to (radius of the earth = 6.4×10^6 m)
(a) 0.6 Gauss　　　　　(b) 1.2 Gauss
(c) 1.8 Gauss　　　　　(d) 0.32 Gauss

44. The coercivity of a small magnet where the ferromagnet gets demagnetized is 3×10^3 Am^{-1}. The current required to be passed in a solenoid of length 10 cm and number of turns 100, so that the magnet gets demagnetized when inside the solenoid, is:
(a) 30 mA　(b) 60 mA　(c) 3 A　(d) 6 A

45. A thin bar magnet of length 2 ℓ and breadth 2 b pole strength m and magnetic moment M is divided into four equal parts with length and breadth of each part being half of original magnet.
Then, the magnetic moment of each part is
(a) M/4　(b) M　(c) M/2　(d) 2 M

RESPONSE GRID					
	34. (a)(b)(c)(d)	35. (a)(b)(c)(d)	36. (a)(b)(c)(d)	37. (a)(b)(c)(d)	38. (a)(b)(c)(d)
	39. (a)(b)(c)(d)	40. (a)(b)(c)(d)	41. (a)(b)(c)(d)	42. (a)(b)(c)(d)	43. (a)(b)(c)(d)
	44. (a)(b)(c)(d)	45. (a)(b)(c)(d)			

DAILY PRACTICE PROBLEM DPP CHAPTERWISE CP19 - PHYSICS

Total Questions	45	Total Marks	180
Attempted		Correct	
Incorrect		Net Score	
Cut-off Score	50	Qualifying Score	70
Success Gap = Net Score − Qualifying Score			
Net Score = (Correct × 4) − (Incorrect × 1)			

Date :   Start Time :   End Time :

PHYSICS   CP20

SYLLABUS : Electromagnetic Induction

Max. Marks : 180   **Marking Scheme :** (+4) for correct & (–1) for incorrect answer   **Time : 60 min.**

INSTRUCTIONS : This Daily Practice Problem Sheet contains 45 MCQs. For each question only one option is correct. Darken the correct circle/ bubble in the Response Grid provided on each page.

1. A metal disc of radius 100 cm is rotated at a constant angular speed of 60 rad/s in a plane at right angles to an external field of magnetic induction 0.05 Wb/m^2. The emf induced between the centre and a point on the rim will be
   (a) 3 V   (b) 1.5 V   (c) 6 V   (d) 9 V

2. In a coil of resistance $100\,\Omega$, a current is induced by changing the magnetic flux through it as shown in the figure. The magnitude of change in flux through the coil is
   (a) 250 Wb
   (b) 275 Wb
   (c) 200 Wb
   (d) 225 Wb

   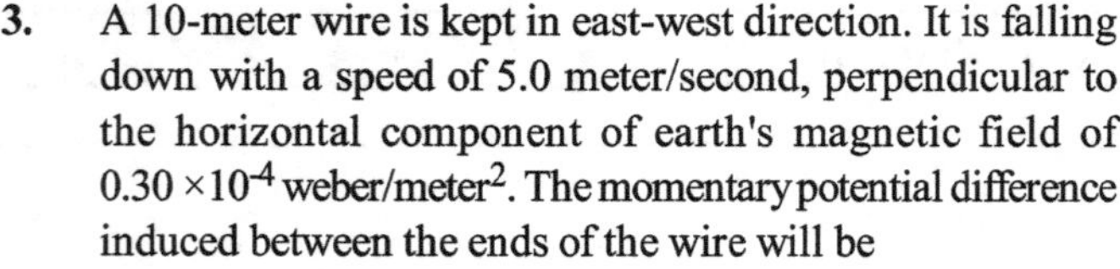

3. A 10-meter wire is kept in east-west direction. It is falling down with a speed of 5.0 meter/second, perpendicular to the horizontal component of earth's magnetic field of 0.30×10^{-4} weber/meter^2. The momentary potential difference induced between the ends of the wire will be
   (a) 0.0015 V   (b) 0.015 V
   (c) 0.15 V   (d) 1.5 V

4. The figure shows certain wire segments joined together to form a coplanar loop. The loop is placed in a perpendicular magnetic field in the direction going into the plane of the figure. 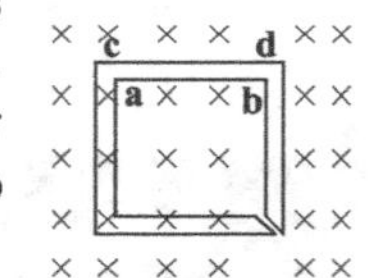 The magnitude of the field increases with time. I_1 and I_2 are the currents in the segments ab and cd. Then,
   (a) $I_1 > I_2$ (b) $I_1 < I_2$
   (c) I_1 is in the direction ba and I_2 is in the direction cd
   (d) I_1 is in the direction ab and I_2 is in the direction dc

5. Two solenoids of equal number of turns have their lengths and the radii in the same ratio 1 : 2. The ratio of their self inductances will be
   (a) 1 : 2   (b) 2 : 1   (c) 1 : 1   (d) 1 : 4

6. A metal conductor of length 1 m rotates vertically about one of its ends at angular velocity 5 radians per second. If the horizontal component of earth's magnetic field is 0.2×10^{-4}T, then the e.m.f. developed between the two ends of the conductor is
   (a) 5 mV   (b) 50 μV   (c) 5 μV   (d) 50 mV

7. Eddy currents do not produce
   (a) heat   (b) a loss of energy
   (c) spark   (d) damping of motion

Space for Rough Work

8. A conducting square frame of side 'a' and a long staight wire carrying current I are located in the same plane as shown in the figure. The frame moves to the right with a constant velocity 'V'. The emf induced in the frame will be proportional to

(a) $\dfrac{1}{(2x-a)^2}$

(b) $\dfrac{1}{(2x+a)^2}$

(c) $\dfrac{1}{(2x-a)(2x+a)}$

(d) $\dfrac{1}{x^2}$

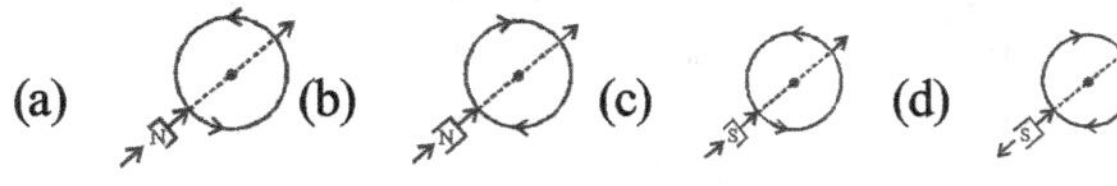

9. Which of the following figure correctly depicts the Lenz's law. The arrows show the movement of the labelled pole of a bar magnet into a closed circular loop and the arrows on the circle show the direction of the induced current

(a) 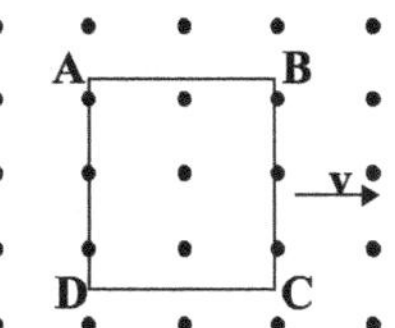 (b) (c) (d)

10. The magnetic flux (in weber) linked with a coil of resistance $10\,\Omega$ is varying with respect to time t as $\phi = 4t^2 + 2t + 1$. Then the current in the coil at time $t = 1$ second is

(a) 0.5 A   (b) 2 A   (c) 1.5 A   (d) 1 A

11. Two coaxial solenoids are made by winding thin insulated wire over a pipe of cross-sectional area $A = 10\ cm^2$ and length = 20 cm. If one of the solenoid has 300 turns and the other 400 turns, their mutual inductance is ($\mu_0 = 4\pi \times 10^{-7}\,Tm\,A^{-1}$)

(a) $2.4\pi \times 10^{-5}\,H$ (b) $4.8\pi \times 10^{-4}\,H$

(c) $4.8\pi \times 10^{-5}\,H$ (d) $2.4\pi \times 10^{-4}\,H$

12. When the current changes from +2 A to –2A in 0.05 second, an e.m.f. of 8 V is induced in a coil. The coefficient of self - induction of the coil is

(a) 0.2 H   (b) 0.4 H   (c) 0.8 H   (d) 0.1 H

13. A long solenoid has 500 turns. When a current of 2 ampere is passed through it, the resulting magnetic flux linked with each turn of the solenoid is 4×10^{-3} Wb. The self- inductance of the solenoid is

(a) 2.5 henry   (b) 2.0 henry

(c) 1.0 henry   (d) 40 henry

14. A metallic square loop ABCD is moving in its own plane with velocity v in a uniform magnetic field perpendicular to its plane as shown in the figure. An electric field is induced

15. In an AC generator, a coil with N turns, all of the same area A and total resistance R, rotates with frequency ω in a magnetic field B. The maximum value of emf generated in the coil is

(a) N.A.B.R.ω (b) N.A.B.

(c) N.A.B.R.   (d) N.A.B.ω

16. In an inductor of self-inductance $L = 2$ mH, current changes with time according to relation $i = t^2 e^{-t}$. At what time emf is zero?

(a) 4s   (b) 3s   (c) 2s   (d) 1s

17. Choke coil works on the principle of

(a) transient current   (b) self induction

(c) mutual induction   (d) wattless current

18. A coil having n turns and resistance $R\,\Omega$ is connected with a galvanometer of resistance $4R\ \Omega$. This combination is moved in time t seconds from a magnetic field W_1 weber to W_2 weber. The induced current in the circuit is

(a) $-\dfrac{(W_1 - W_2)}{Rnt}$ (b) $-\dfrac{n(W_2 - W_1)}{5\,Rt}$

(c) $-\dfrac{(W_2 - W_1)}{5\,Rnt}$ (d) $-\dfrac{n(W_2 - W_1)}{Rt}$

19. A thin circular ring of area A is held perpendicular to a uniform magnetic field of induction B. A small cut is made in the ring and a galvanometer is connected across the ends such that the total resistance of the circuit is R. When the ring is suddenly squeezed to zero area, the charge flowing through the galvanometer is

(a) $\dfrac{BR}{A}$ (b) $\dfrac{AB}{R}$ (c) ABR   (d) $\dfrac{B^2A}{R^2}$

20. A boat is moving due east in a region where the earth's magnetic field is $5.0 \times 10^{-5}\,NA^{-1}\,m^{-1}$ due north and horizontal. The boat carries a vertical aerial 2 m long. If the speed of the boat is $1.50\ ms^{-1}$, the magnitude of the induced emf in the wire of aerial is:

(a) 0.75 mV (b) 0.50 mV (c) 0.15 mV (d) 1 mV

21. In a coil of area 10 cm^2 and 10 turns with magnetic field directed perpendicular to the plane and is changing at the rate of 10^8 Gauss/second. The resistance of the coil is 20Ω. The current in the coil will be

(a) 0.5 A   (b) 5 A   (c) 50 A   (d) 5×10^8 A

22. A horizontal straight wire 20 m long extending from east to west falling with a speed of 5.0 m/s, at right angles to the horizontal component of the earth's magnetic field 0.30×10^{-4} Wb/m^2. The instantaneous value of the e.m.f. induced in the wire will be

(a) 3mV   (b) 4.5mV   (c) 1.5mV   (d) 6.0mV

Questions (following 8):

(a) in AD, but not in BC   (b) in BC, but not in AD

(c) neither in AD nor in BC   (d) in both AD and BC

RESPONSE GRID	8. ⓐⓑ©ⓓ 9. ⓐⓑ©ⓓ 10. ⓐⓑ©ⓓ 11. ⓐⓑ©ⓓ 12. ⓐⓑ©ⓓ
	13. ⓐⓑ©ⓓ 14. ⓐⓑ©ⓓ 15. ⓐⓑ©ⓓ 16. ⓐⓑ©ⓓ 17. ⓐⓑ©ⓓ
	18. ⓐⓑ©ⓓ 19. ⓐⓑ©ⓓ 20. ⓐⓑ©ⓓ 21. ⓐⓑ©ⓓ 22. ⓐⓑ©ⓓ

23. The self inductance of a long solenoid cannot be increased by
(a)   increasing its area of cross section
(b)   increasing its length
(c)   changing the medium with greater permeability
(d)   increasing the current through it

24. A metallic rod of length 'ℓ' is tied to a string of length 2ℓ and made to rotate with angular speed ω on a horizontal table with one end of the string fixed. If there is a vertical magnetic field 'B' in the region, the e.m.f. induced across the ends of the rod is

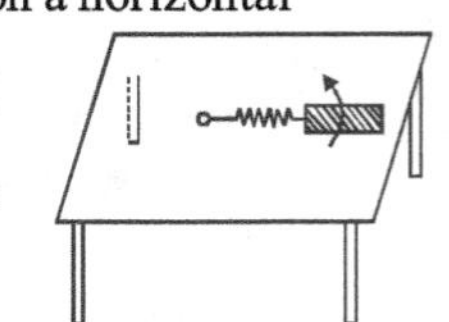

(a) $\dfrac{2B\omega\ell^2}{2}$ (b) $\dfrac{3B\omega\ell^2}{2}$ (c) $\dfrac{4B\omega\ell^2}{2}$ (d) $\dfrac{5B\omega\ell^2}{2}$

25. Lenz's law gives
(a)   the magnitude of the induced e.m.f.
(b)   the direction of the induced current
(c)   both the magnitude and direction of the induced current
(d)   the magnitude of the induced current

26. A metal ring is held horizontally and bar magnet is dropped through the ring with its length along the axis of the ring. The acceleration of the falling magnet
(a)   is equal to g
(b)   is less than g
(c)   is more than g
(d)   depends on the diameter of ring and length of magnet

27. The pointer of a dead-beat galvanometer gives a steady deflection because
(a)   eddy currents are produced in the conducting frame over which the coil is wound.
(b)   its magnet is very strong.
(c)   its pointer is very light.
(d)   its frame is made of ebonite.

28. A metal rod of length l cuts across a uniform magnetic field B with a velocity v. If the resistance of the circuit of which the rod forms a part is r, then the force required to move the rod is
(a) $\dfrac{B^2 l^2 v}{r}$ (b) $\dfrac{Blv}{r}$ (c) $\dfrac{B^2 lv}{r}$ (d) $\dfrac{B^2 l^2 v^2}{r}$

29. In an A.C. generator, when the plane of the armature is perpendicular to the magnetic field
(a)   both magnetic flux and emf are maximum
(b)   both magnetic flux and emf are zero
(c)   both magnetic flux and emf are half of their respective maximum values
(d)   magnetic flux is maximum and emf is zero

30. A copper disc of radius 0.1 m rotated about its centre with 10 revolutions per second in a uniform magnetic field of 0.1 tesla with its plane perpendicular to the field. The e.m.f. induced across the radius of disc is
(a) $\dfrac{\pi}{10}$ volt (b) $\dfrac{2\pi}{10}$ volt
(c) $\pi \times 10^{-2}$ volt (d) $2\pi \times 10^{-2}$ volt

31. The mutual inductance of a pair of coils, each of N turns, is M henry. If a current of I ampere in one of the coils is brought to zero in t second, the emf induced per turn in the other coil, in volt, will be
(a) $\dfrac{MI}{t}$ (b) $\dfrac{NMI}{t}$ (c) $\dfrac{MN}{It}$ (d) $\dfrac{MI}{Nt}$

32. Consider the situation shown in figure. If the switch is closed and after some time it is opened again, the closed loop will show
(a)   a clockwise current
(b)   an anticlockwise current
(c)   an anticlockwise current and then clockwise
(d)   a clockwise current and then an anticlock wise current.

33. A magnet is moved towards a coil (i) quickly (ii) slowly, then the induced e.m.f. is
(a)   larger in case (i)
(b)   smaller in case (i)
(c)   equal to both the cases
(d)   larger or smaller depending upon the radius of the coil

34. A circular wire of radius r rotates about its own axis with angular speed ω in a magnetic field B perpendicular to its plane, then the induced e.m.f. is
(a) $\dfrac{1}{2}Br\omega^2$ (b) $Br\omega^2$ (c) $2Br\omega^2$ (d) zero

35. A conducting ring of radius 1 m kept in a uniform magnetic field B of 0.01 T, rotates uniformly with an angular velocity 100 rad s^{-1} with its axis of rotation perpendicular to B. The maximum induced emf in it is
(a) $1.5\pi V$ (b) πV (c) $2\pi V$ (d) $0.5\pi V$

36. A magnetic field of 2×10^{-2} T acts at right angles to a coil of area 100 cm^2, with 50 turns. The average e.m.f. induced in the coil is 0.1 V, when it is removed from the field in t sec. The value of t is
(a) 10 s (b) 0.1 s (c) 0.01 s (d) 1 s

37. The magnetic flux through a circuit of resistance R changes by an amount $\Delta\phi$ in a time Δt. Then the total quantity of electric charge Q that passes any point in the circuit during the time Δt is represented by
(a) $Q = R.\dfrac{\Delta\phi}{\Delta t}$ (b) $Q = \dfrac{1}{R}.\dfrac{\Delta\phi}{\Delta t}$
(c) $Q = \dfrac{\Delta\phi}{R}$ (d) $Q = \dfrac{\Delta\phi}{\Delta t}$

RESPONSE GRID	23. ⓐⓑⓒⓓ	24. ⓐⓑⓒⓓ	25. ⓐⓑⓒⓓ	26. ⓐⓑⓒⓓ	27. ⓐⓑⓒⓓ
	28. ⓐⓑⓒⓓ	29. ⓐⓑⓒⓓ	30. ⓐⓑⓒⓓ	31. ⓐⓑⓒⓓ	32. ⓐⓑⓒⓓ
	33. ⓐⓑⓒⓓ	34. ⓐⓑⓒⓓ	35. ⓐⓑⓒⓓ	36. ⓐⓑⓒⓓ	37. ⓐⓑⓒⓓ

38. Fig shown below represents an area $A = 0.5$ m^2 situated in a uniform magnetic field $B = 2.0$ weber/m^2 and making an angle of $60°$ with respect to magnetic field.

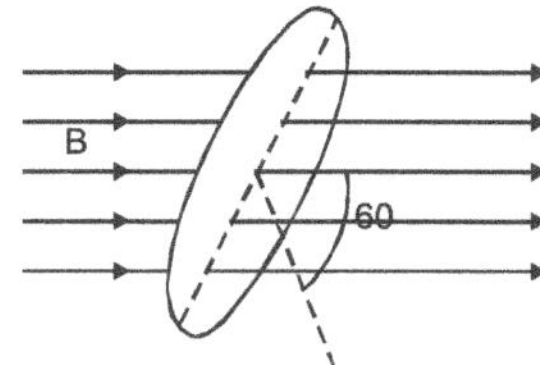

The value of the magnetic flux through the area would be equal to

(a) 2.0 weber (b) $\sqrt{3}$ weber

(c) $\sqrt{3}/2$ weber (d) 0.5 weber

39. As a result of change in the magnetic flux linked to the closed loop shown in the fig, an e.m.f. V volt is induced in the loop. The work done (joule) in taking a charge Q coulomb once along the loop is

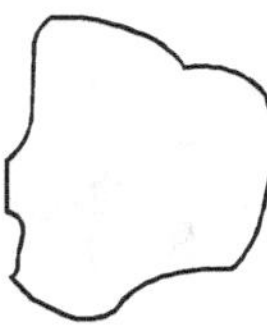

(a) QV (b) 2QV (c) QV/2 (d) Zero

40. Two coils are placed close to each other. The mutual inductance of the pair of coils depends upon
(a) the rates at which currents are changing in the two coils
(b) relative position and orientation of the two coils
(c) the materials of the wires of the coils
(d) the currents in the two coils

41. When current i passes through an inductor of self inductance L, energy stored in it is $\frac{1}{2}L i^2$. This is stored in the

(a) current (b) voltage
(c) magnetic field (d) electric field

42. A conducting wire frame is placed in a magnetic field which is directed into the paper. The magnetic field is increasing at a constant rate. The directions of induced current in wires AB and CD are

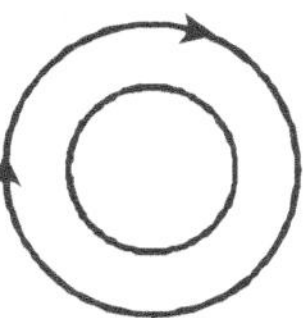

(a) B to A and D to C
(b) A to B and C to D
(c) A to B and D to C
(d) B to A and C to D

43. Two different wire loops are concentric and lie in the same plane. The current in the outer loop (I) is clockwise and I increases with time. The induced current in the inner loop
(a) is clockwise
(b) is zero
(c) is counter clockwise
(d) has a direction that depends on the ratio of the loop radii.

44. When current in a coil changes from 5 A to 2 A in 0.1 s, average voltage of 50 V is produced. The self - inductance of the coil is :
(a) 6 H (b) 0.67 H (c) 3 H (d) 1.67 H

45. Two conducting circular loops of radii R_1 and R_2 are placed in the same plane with their centres coinciding. If $R_1 >> R_2$, the mutual inductance M between them will be directly proportional to

(a) R_1/R_2 (b) R_2/R_1 (c) R_1^2/R_2 (d) R_2^2/R_1

RESPONSE GRID	38. ⓐⓑⓒⓓ	39. ⓐⓑⓒⓓ	40. ⓐⓑⓒⓓ	41. ⓐⓑⓒⓓ	42. ⓐⓑⓒⓓ
	43. ⓐⓑⓒⓓ	44. ⓐⓑⓒⓓ	45. ⓐⓑⓒⓓ		

DAILY PRACTICE PROBLEM DPP CHAPTERWISE CP20 - PHYSICS

Total Questions	45	Total Marks	180
Attempted		Correct	
Incorrect		Net Score	
Cut-off Score	50	Qualifying Score	70
Success Gap = Net Score – Qualifying Score			
Net Score = (Correct × 4) – (Incorrect × 1)			

Space for Rough Work

PHYSICS $\boxed{\text{CP21}}$

SYLLABUS : Alternating Current

Max. Marks : 180   **Marking Scheme :** (+4) for correct & (–1) for incorrect answer   **Time : 60 min.**

INSTRUCTIONS : This Daily Practice Problem Sheet contains 45 MCQs. For each question only one option is correct. Darken the correct circle/ bubble in the Response Grid provided on each page.

1. In a series resonant LCR circuit, the voltage across R is 100 volts and $R = 1\,k\Omega$ with $C = 2\,\mu F$. The resonant frequency ω is 200 rad/s. At resonance, the voltage across L is
   (a) $2.5 \times 10^{-2}\,V$ (b) $40\,V$
   (c) $250\,V$ (d) $4 \times 10^{-3}\,V$

2. An alternating voltage $V = V_0 \sin \omega t$ is applied across a circuit. As a result, a current $I = I_0 \sin (\omega t - \pi/2)$ flows in it. The power consumed per cycle is
   (a) zero   (b) $0.5\,V_0 I_0$
   (c) $0.707\,V_0 I_0$ (d) $1.414\,V_0 I_0$

3. For the circuit shown in the fig., the current through the inductor is 0.9 A while the current through the condenser is 0.4 A. Then
   (a) current drawn from generator $I = 1.13\,A$
   (b) $\omega = 1/(1.5\,LC)$
   (c) $I = 0.5\,A$
   (d) $I = 0.6\,A$

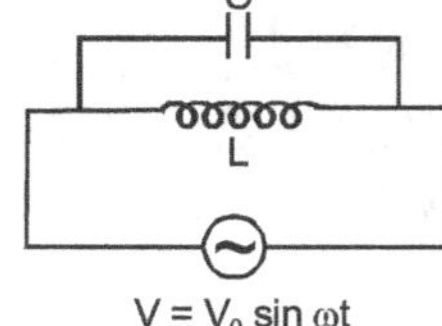

4. A capacitor has capacity C and reactance X. If capacitance and frequency become double, then reactance will be
   (a) 4X   (b) X/2   (c) X/4   (d) 2X

5. A coil of inductance 300 mH and resistance 2Ω is connected to a source of voltage 2V. The current reaches half of its steady state value in
   (a) $0.1\,s$ (b) $0.05\,s$ (c) $0.3\,s$ (d) $0.15\,s$

6. In an A.C. circuit, a resistance of R ohm is connected in series with an inductance L. If phase angle between voltage and current be 45°, the value of inductive reactance will be
   (a) R/4   (b) R/2   (c) R   (d) R/5

7. A bulb is rated at 100 V, 100 W, it can be treated as a resistor. Find out the inductance of an inductor (called choke coil) that should be connected in series with the bulb to operate the bulb at its rated power with the help of an ac source of 200 V and 50 Hz.
   (a) $\dfrac{\pi}{\sqrt{3}}H$ (b) $100\,H$ (c) $\dfrac{\sqrt{2}}{\pi}H$ (d) $\dfrac{\sqrt{3}}{\pi}H$

8. An ac source of angular frequency ω is fed across a resistor r and a capacitor C in series. The current registered is I. If now the frequency of source is changed to $\omega/3$ (but maintaining the same voltage), the current in the circuit is found to be halved. The ratio of reactance to resistance at the original frequency ω is
   (a) $\sqrt{\dfrac{3}{5}}$ (b) $\sqrt{\dfrac{2}{5}}$ (c) $\sqrt{\dfrac{1}{5}}$ (d) $\sqrt{\dfrac{4}{5}}$

RESPONSE GRID				
1. ⓐⓑⓒⓓ	2. ⓐⓑⓒⓓ	3. ⓐⓑⓒⓓ	4. ⓐⓑⓒⓓ	5. ⓐⓑⓒⓓ
6. ⓐⓑⓒⓓ	7. ⓐⓑⓒⓓ	8. ⓐⓑⓒⓓ		

Space for Rough Work

9. Large transformers, when used for some time, become hot and are cooled by circulating oil. The heating of transformer is due to
(a) heating effect of current alone
(b) hysteresis loss alone
(c) both the hysteresis loss and heating effect of current
(d) none of the above

10. An inductor of inductance $L = 400$ mH and resistors of resistance $R_1 = 2\Omega$ and $R_2 = 2\Omega$ are connected to a battery of emf 12 V as shown in the figure. The internal resistance of the battery is negligible. The switch S is closed at $t = 0$. The potential drop across L as a function of time is

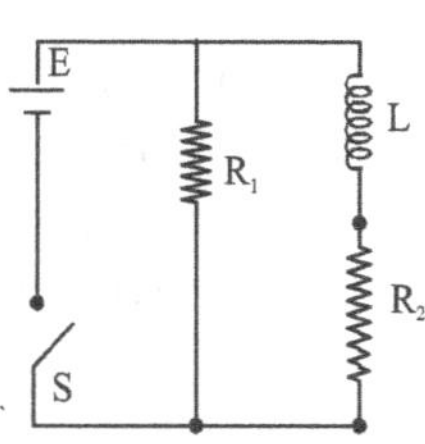

(a) $\dfrac{12}{t}e^{-3t}$ V
(b) $6(1 - e^{-t/0.2})$V
(c) $12e^{-5t}$ V
(d) $6e^{-5t}$ V

11. An ideal coil of 10H is connected in series with a resistance of 5Ω and a battery of 5V. 2second after the connection is made, the current flowing in ampere in the circuit is
(a) $(1 - e^{-1})$ (b) $(1 - e)$ (c) e (d) e^{-1}

12. In an A.C. circuit, the current flowing in inductance is $I = 5\sin(100\,t - \pi/2)$ amperes and the potential difference is $V = 200\sin(100\,t)$ volts. The power consumption is equal to
(a) 1000 watt
(b) 40 watt
(c) 20 watt
(d) Zero

13. In an oscillating LC circuit the maximum charge on the capacitor is Q. The charge on the capacitor when the energy is stored equally between the electric and magnetic field is
(a) $\dfrac{Q}{2}$
(b) $\dfrac{Q}{\sqrt{3}}$
(c) $\dfrac{Q}{\sqrt{2}}$
(d) Q

14. A fully charged capacitor C with initial charge q_0 is connected to a coil of self inductance L at $t = 0$. The time at which the energy is stored equally between the electric and the magnetic fields is:
(a) $\dfrac{\pi}{4}\sqrt{LC}$ (b) $2\pi\sqrt{LC}$ (c) $\sqrt{LC}$ (d) $\pi\sqrt{LC}$

15. For an LCR series circuit with an A.C. source of angular frequency ω
(a) circuit will be capacitive if $\omega > \dfrac{1}{\sqrt{LC}}$
(b) circuit will be inductive if $\omega = \dfrac{1}{\sqrt{LC}}$
(c) power factor of circuit will be unity if capacitive reactance equals inductive reactance
(d) current will be leading voltage if $\omega > \dfrac{1}{\sqrt{LC}}$

16. The r.m.s. value of potential difference V shown in the figure is

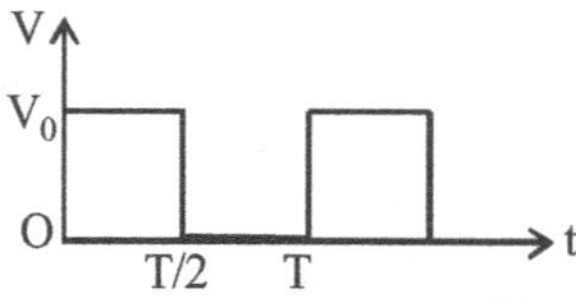

(a) V_0 (b) $V_0/\sqrt{2}$ (c) $V_0/2$ (d) $V_0/\sqrt{3}$

17. Which of the following statements is/are incorrect?
(a) If the resonance is less sharp, not only is the maximum current less, the circuit is close to resonance for a larger range $\Delta\omega$ of frequencies and the tuning of the circuit will not be good.
(b) Less sharp the resonance less is the selectivity of the circuit or *vice–versa*.
(c) If quality factor is large, i.e., R is low or L is large, the circuit is more selective.
(d) Below resonance, voltage leads the current while above it, current leads the voltage.

18. A lamp consumes only 50% of peak power in an a.c. circuit. What is the phase difference between the applied voltage and the circuit current?
(a) $\dfrac{\pi}{6}$ (b) $\dfrac{\pi}{3}$ (c) $\dfrac{\pi}{4}$ (d) $\dfrac{\pi}{2}$

19. A step down transformer reduces 220 V to 110 V. The primary draws 5 ampere of current and secondary supplies 9 ampere. The efficiency of transformer is
(a) 20%   (b) 44%   (c) 90%   (d) 100%

20. The voltage time (V-t) graph for triangular wave having peak value V_0 is as shown in figure. The rms value of V in time interval from $t = 0$ to T/4 is $\dfrac{V_0}{\sqrt{x}}$ then find the value of x.

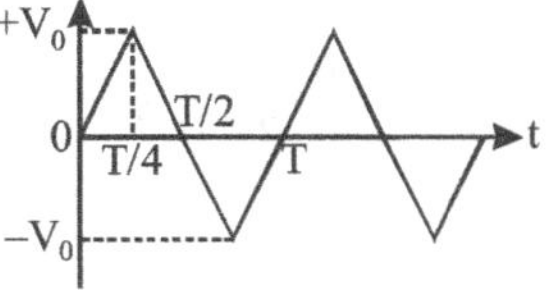

(a) 5   (b) 4   (c) 7   (d) 3

21. The tuning circuit of a radio receiver has a resistance of $50\,\Omega$, an inductor of 10 mH and a variable capacitor. A 1 MHz radio wave produces a potential difference of 0.1 mV. The values of the capacitor to produce resonance is (Take $\pi^2 = 10$)
(a) 2.5 pF   (b) 5.0 pF   (c) 25 pF   (d) 50 pF

22. In an alternating current circuit in which an inductance and capacitance are joined in series, current is found to be maximum when the value of inductance is 0.5 henry and the value of capacitance is $8\,\mu$F. The angular frequency of applied alternating voltage will be
(a) 5000 rad/sec   (b) 4000 rad/sec
(c) 2×10^5 rad/sec   (d) 500 rad/sec

23. A coil has resistance 30 ohm and inductive reactance 20 ohm at 50 Hz frequency. If an ac source, of 200 volt, 100 Hz, is connected across the coil, the current in the coil will be
(a) 4.0A   (b) 8.0A   (c) $\dfrac{20}{\sqrt{13}}$A   (d) 2.0A

RESPONSE GRID	9. (a)(b)(c)(d)	10. (a)(b)(c)(d)	11. (a)(b)(c)(d)	12. (a)(b)(c)(d)	13. (a)(b)(c)(d)
	14. (a)(b)(c)(d)	15. (a)(b)(c)(d)	16. (a)(b)(c)(d)	17. (a)(b)(c)(d)	18. (a)(b)(c)(d)
	19. (a)(b)(c)(d)	20. (a)(b)(c)(d)	21. (a)(b)(c)(d)	22. (a)(b)(c)(d)	23. (a)(b)(c)(d)

24. In the figure shown, three AC voltmeters are connected. At resonance 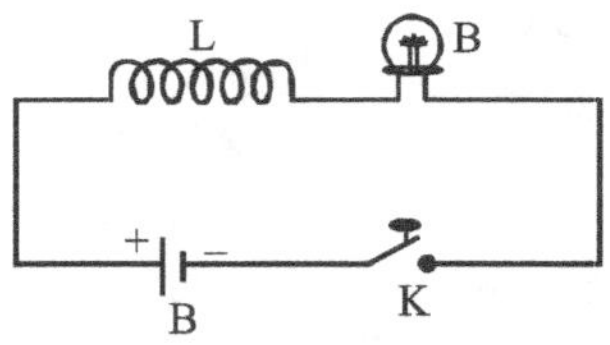

(a) $V_2 = 0$ (b) $V_1 = 0$
(c) $V_3 = 0$ (d) $V_1 = V_2 \neq 0$

25. A.C. power is transmitted from a power house at a high voltage as

(a) the rate of transmission is faster at high voltages

(b) it is more economical due to less power loss

(c) power cannot be transmitted at low voltages

(d) a precaution against theft of transmission lines

26. A transformer has an efficiency of 80%. It works at 4 kW and 100 V. If secondary voltage is 240 V, the current in primary coil is

(a) 0.4 A   (b) 4 A   (c) 10 A   (d) 40 A

27. A 12 Ω resistor and a 0.21 henry inductor are connected in series to an a.c. source operating at 20 volt, 50 cycle. The phase angle between the current and source voltage is

(a) 30°   (b) 40°   (c) 80°   (d) 90°

28. In LCR series circuit fed by a DC source, how does the amplitude of charge oscillations vary with time during discharge ?

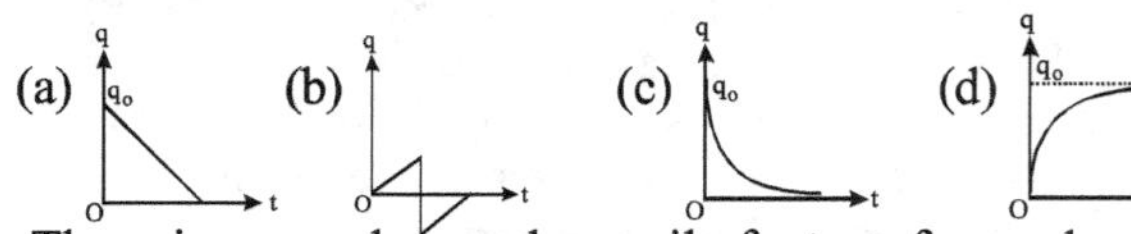

29. The primary and secondary coil of a transformer have 50 and 1500 turns respectively. If the magnetic flux ϕ linked with the primary coil is given by $\phi = \phi_0 + 4t$, where ϕ is in webers, t is time in seconds and ϕ_0 is a constant, the output voltage across the secondary coil is

(a) 120 volts   (b) 220 volts
(c) 30 volts   (d) 90 volts

30. The primary winding of a transformer has 100 turns and its secondary winding has 200 turns. The primary is connected to an A.C. supply of 120 V and the current flowing in it is 10 A. The voltage and the current in the secondary are

(a) 240 V, 5 A   (b) 240 V, 10 A
(c) 60 V, 20 A   (d) 120 V, 20 A

31. The resistance in the following circuit is increased at a particular instant. At this instant the value of resistance is 10Ω. The current in the circuit will be now 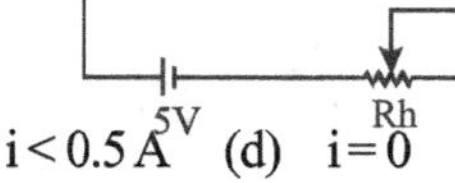

(a) $i = 0.5$ A (b) $i > 0.5$ A (c) $i < 0.5$ A (d) $i = 0$

32. The current in a LR circuit builds up to $\frac{3}{4}th$ of its steady state value in 4s. The time constant of this circuit is

(a) $\dfrac{1}{\ell n\,2}s$ (b) $\dfrac{2}{\ell n\,2}s$ (c) $\dfrac{3}{\ell n\,2}s$ (d) $\dfrac{4}{\ell n\,2}s$

33. An LCR series circuit is connected to a source of alternating current. At resonance, the applied voltage and the current flowing through the circuit will have a phase difference of

(a) π (b) $\dfrac{\pi}{2}$ (c) $\dfrac{\pi}{4}$ (d) 0

34. What is the value of inductance L for which the current is maximum in a series LCR circuit with $C = 10\ \mu F$ and $\omega = 1000 s^{-1}$?

(a) 1 mH

(b) cannot be calculated unless R is known

(c) 10 mH

(d) 100 mH

35. In the circuit of Fig, the bulb will become suddenly bright if

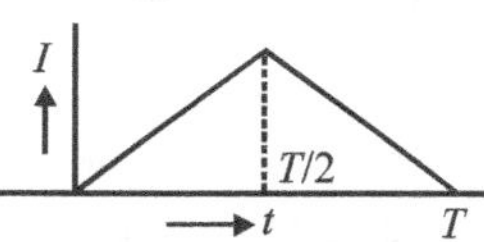

(a) contact is made or broken

(b) contact is made

(c) contact is broken

(d) won't become bright at all

36. The voltage of an ac source varies with time according to the equation $V = 100 \sin 100\,\pi t \cos 100\,\pi t$ where t is in seconds and V is in volt. Then

(a) the peak voltage of the source is 100 volt

(b) the peak voltage of the source is 50 volt

(c) the peak voltage of the source is $100/\sqrt{2}$ volt

(d) the frequency of the source is 50 Hz

37. The current (I) in the inductance is varying with time according to the plot shown in figure.

Which one of the following is the correct variation of voltage with time in the coil?

(a) 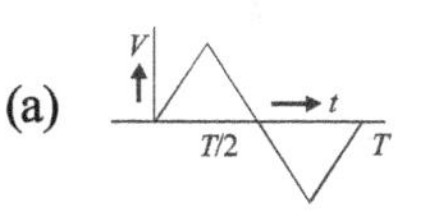   (b) 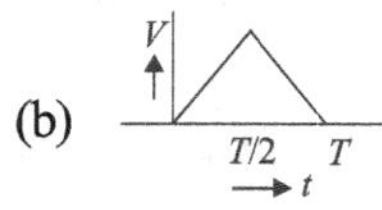

(c) 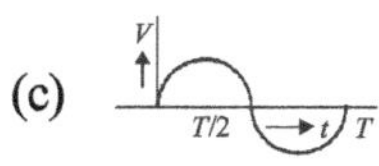   (d) 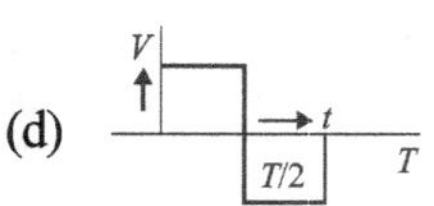

38. Using an A.C. voltmeter the potential difference in the electrical line in a house is read to be 234 volt. If the line frequency is known to be 50 cycles/second, the equation for the line voltage is

(a) $V = 165 \sin(100\,\pi t)$ (b) $V = 331 \sin(100\,\pi t)$

(c) $V = 220 \sin(100\,\pi t)$ (d) $V = 440 \sin(100\,\pi t)$

39. In the circuit shown, when the switch is closed, the capacitor charges with a time constant

(a) RC

(b) 2RC

(c) $\dfrac{1}{2}RC$

(d) $RC \ln 2$

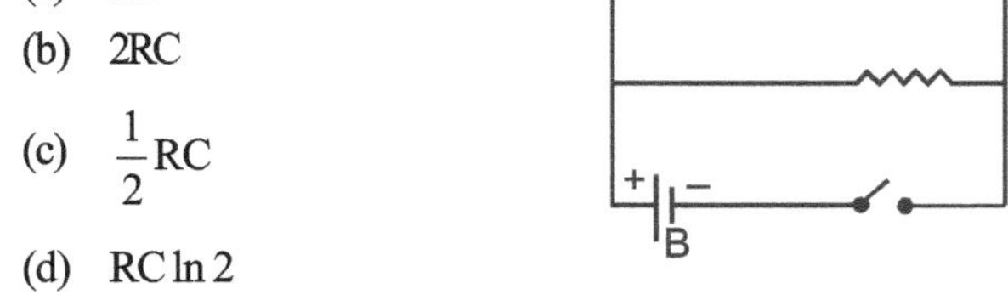

40. A 100 μF capacitor in series with a 40Ω resistance is connected to a 110 V, 60 Hz supply.

What is the maximum current in the circuit?

(a) 3.24 A   (b) 4.25 A   (c) 2.25 A   (d) 5.20 A

41. The core of any transformer is laminated so as to

(a) reduce the energy loss due to eddy currents

(b) make it light weight

(c) make it robust and strong

(d) increase the secondary voltage

42. An AC generator of 220 V having internal resistance $r = 10\Omega$ and external resistance $R = 100\Omega$. What is the power developed in the external circuit?

(a) 484 W   (b) 400 W   (c) 441 W   (d) 369 W

43. What is increased in step-down transformer?

(a) Voltage   (b) Current

(c) Power   (d) Current density

44. In the circuit shown below, the key K is closed at $t = 0$. The current through the battery is

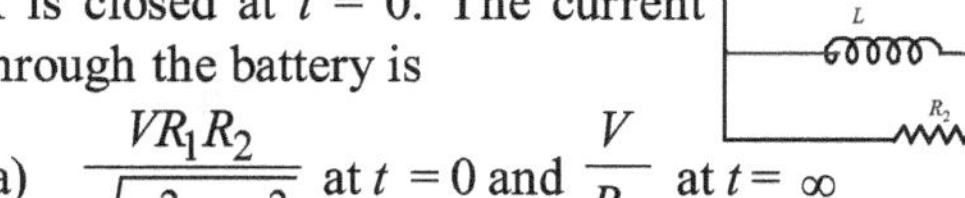

(a) $\dfrac{VR_1R_2}{\sqrt{R_1^2 + R_2^2}}$ at $t = 0$ and $\dfrac{V}{R_2}$ at $t = \infty$

(b) $\dfrac{V}{R_2}$ at $t = 0$ and $\dfrac{V(R_1 + R_2)}{R_1R_2}$ at $t = \infty$

(c) $\dfrac{V}{R_2}$ at $t = 0$ and $\dfrac{VR_1R_2}{\sqrt{R_1^2 + R_2^2}}$ at $t = \infty$

(d) $\dfrac{V(R_1 + R_2)}{R_1R_2}$ at $t = 0$ and $\dfrac{V}{R_2}$ at $t = \infty$

45. The inductance between A and D is

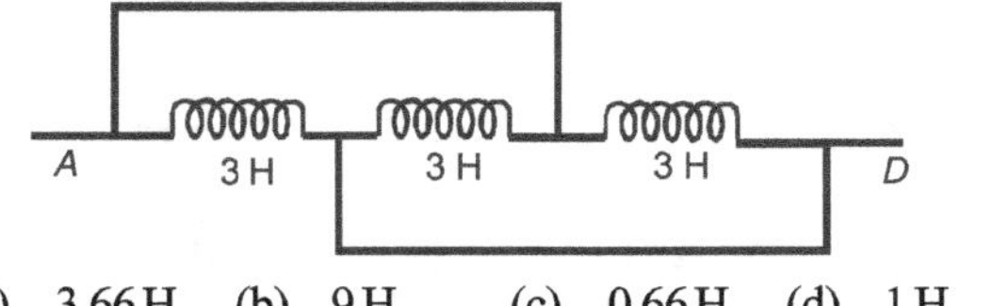

(a) 3.66 H   (b) 9 H   (c) 0.66 H   (d) 1 H

<table>
<tr><td rowspan="2">RESPONSE GRID</td><td>38. ⓐⓑⓒⓓ</td><td>39. ⓐⓑⓒⓓ</td><td>40. ⓐⓑⓒⓓ</td><td>41. ⓐⓑⓒⓓ</td><td>42. ⓐⓑⓒⓓ</td></tr>
<tr><td>43. ⓐⓑⓒⓓ</td><td>44. ⓐⓑⓒⓓ</td><td>45. ⓐⓑⓒⓓ</td><td></td><td></td></tr>
</table>

DAILY PRACTICE PROBLEM DPP CHAPTERWISE CP21 - PHYSICS

Total Questions	45	Total Marks	180
Attempted		Correct	
Incorrect		Net Score	
Cut-off Score	50	Qualifying Score	70
Success Gap = Net Score − Qualifying Score			
Net Score = (Correct × 4) − (Incorrect × 1)			

Date : [ ]   **Start Time :** [ ]   **End Time :** [ ]

PHYSICS $\boxed{CP22}$

SYLLABUS : Electromagnetic Waves

Max. Marks : 180   **Marking Scheme :** (+4) for correct & (–1) for incorrect answer   **Time : 60 min.**

INSTRUCTIONS : This Daily Practice Problem Sheet contains 45 MCQs. For each question only one option is correct. Darken the correct circle/ bubble in the Response Grid provided on each page.

1. An electromagnetic wave in vacuum has the electric and magnetic field $\vec{E}$ and $\vec{B}$, which are always perpendicular to each other. The direction of polarization is given by $\vec{X}$ and that of wave propagation by $\vec{k}$. Then

   (a) $\vec{X} \parallel \vec{B}$ and $\vec{k} \parallel \vec{B} \times \vec{E}$ (b) $\vec{X} \parallel \vec{E}$ and $\vec{k} \parallel \vec{E} \times \vec{B}$

   (c) $\vec{X} \parallel \vec{B}$ and $\vec{k} \parallel \vec{E} \times \vec{B}$ (d) $\vec{X} \parallel \vec{E}$ and $\vec{k} \parallel \vec{B} \times \vec{E}$

2. The rms value of the electric field of the light coming from the Sun is 720 N/C. The average total energy density of the electromagnetic wave is
   (a) 4.58×10^{-6} J/m^3 (b) 6.37×10^{-9} J/m^3
   (c) 81.35×10^{-12} J/m^3 (d) 3.3×10^{-3} J/m^3

3. In order to establish an instantaneous displacemet current of 1 mA in the space between the plates of 2μF parallel plate capacitor, the potential difference need to apply is
   (a) $100\,\text{Vs}^{-1}$ (b) $200\,\text{Vs}^{-1}$ (c) $300\,\text{Vs}^{-1}$ (d) $500\,\text{Vs}^{-1}$

4. During the propagation of electromagnetic waves in a medium:

   (a) Electric energy density is double of the magnetic energy density.

   (b) Electric energy density is half of the magnetic energy density.

   (c) Electric energy density is equal to the magnetic energy density.

   (d) Both electric and magnetic energy densities are zero.

5. An electromagnetic wave with frequency ω and wavelength λ travels in the $+y$ direction. Its magnetic field is along $+x$-axis. The vector equation for the associated electric field (of amplitude E_0) is

   (a) $\vec{E} = -E_0 \cos\left(\omega t + \dfrac{2\pi}{\lambda} y\right) \hat{x}$

   (b) $\vec{E} = E_0 \cos\left(\omega t - \dfrac{2\pi}{\lambda} y\right) \hat{x}$

   (c) $\vec{E} = E_0 \cos\left(\omega t - \dfrac{2\pi}{\lambda} y\right) \hat{z}$

   (d) $\vec{E} = -E_0 \cos\left(\omega t + \dfrac{2\pi}{\lambda} y\right) \hat{z}$

RESPONSE GRID   1. ⓐⓑⓒⓓ   2. ⓐⓑⓒⓓ   3. ⓐⓑⓒⓓ   4. ⓐⓑⓒⓓ   5. ⓐⓑⓒⓓ

Space for Rough Work

6. An electromagnetic wave of frequency $\nu = 3.0$ MHz passes from vacuum into a dielectric medium with permittivity $\in = 4.0$. Then
(a) wavelength is halved and frequency remains unchanged
(b) wavelength is doubled and frequency becomes half
(c) wavelength is doubled and the frequency remains unchanged
(d) wavelength and frequency both remain unchanged.

7. The average electric field of electromagnetic waves in certain region of free space is 9×10^{-4} NC^{-1}. Then the average magnetic field in the same region is of the order of
(a) 27×10^{-4} T
(b) 3×10^{-12} T
(c) $\left(\dfrac{1}{3}\right) \times 10^{-12}$ T
(d) 3×10^{12} T

8. The electric field of an electromagnetic wave travelling through vaccum is given by the equation $E = E_0 \sin (kx - \omega t)$. The quantity that is independent of wavelength is
(a) $k\omega$
(b) $\dfrac{k}{\omega}$
(c) $k^2\omega$
(d) ω

9. The electric and the magnetic field associated with an E.M. wave, propagating along the +z-axis, can be represented by
(a) $\left[\vec{E} = E_0\hat{i}, \vec{B} = B_0\hat{j}\right]$
(b) $\left[\vec{E} = E_0\vec{k}, \vec{B} = B_0\hat{i}\right]$
(c) $\left[\vec{E} = E_0\hat{j}, \vec{B} = B_0\hat{i}\right]$
(d) $\left[\vec{E} = E_0\hat{j}, \vec{B} = B_0\hat{k}\right]$

10. The energy of electromagnetic wave in vacuum is given by the relation
(a) $\dfrac{E^2}{2\varepsilon_0} + \dfrac{B^2}{2\mu_0}$
(b) $\dfrac{1}{2}\varepsilon_0 E^2 + \dfrac{1}{2}\mu_0 B^2$
(c) $\dfrac{E^2 + B^2}{c}$
(d) $\dfrac{1}{2}\varepsilon_0 E^2 + \dfrac{B^2}{2\mu_0}$

11. A plane electromagnetic wave is incident on a plane surface of area A, normally and is perfectly reflected. If energy E strikes the surface in time t then average pressure exerted on the surface is (c = speed of light)
(a) zero
(b) E/Atc
(c) 2E/Atc
(d) E/c

12. An electromagnetic wave travels along z-axis. Which of the following pairs of space and time varying fields would generate such a wave ?
(a) E_x, B_y
(b) E_y, B_x
(c) E_z, B_x
(d) E_y, B_z

13. The magnetic field in a travelling electromagnetic wave has a peak value of 20 nT. The peak value of electric field strength is :

14. Microwave oven acts on the principle of :
(a) giving rotational energy to water molecules
(b) giving translational energy to water molecules
(c) giving vibrational energy to water molecules
(d) transferring electrons from lower to higher energy levels in water molecule

15. Displacement current is
(a) continuous when electric field is changing in the circuit
(b) continuous when magnetic field is changing in the circuit
(c) continuous in both types of fields
(d) continuous through wires and resistance only

16. The electric field associated with an e.m. wave in vacuum is given by $\vec{E} = \hat{i}\, 40 \cos (kz - 6 \times 10^8 t)$, where E, z and t are in volt/m, meter and seconds respectively. The value of wave vector k is
(a) 2 m^{-1}
(b) 0.5 m^{-1}
(c) 6 m^{-1}
(d) 3 m^{-1}

17. The charge on a parallel plate capacitor varies as $q = q_0 \cos 2\pi\nu t$. The plates are very large and close together (area = A, separation = d). The displacement current through the capacitor is
(a) $q_0\, 2\pi\nu \sin\pi\nu t$
(b) $-q_0\, 2\pi\nu \sin 2\pi\nu t$
(c) $q_0\, 2\pi \sin\pi\nu t$
(d) $q_0\, \pi\nu \sin 2\pi\nu t$

18. A radiation of energy 'E' falls normally on a perfectly reflecting surface. The momentum transferred to the surface is (C = Velocity of light)
(a) $\dfrac{2E}{C}$
(b) $\dfrac{2E}{C^2}$
(c) $\dfrac{E}{C^2}$
(d) $\dfrac{E}{C}$

19. Match List - I (Electromagnetic wave type) with List - II (Its association/application) and select the correct option from the choices given below the lists:

	List 1		List 2
1.	Infrared waves	(i)	To treat muscular strain
2.	Radio waves	(ii)	For broadcasting
3.	X-rays	(iii)	To detect fracture of bones
4.	Ultraviolet rays	(iv)	Absorbed by the ozone layer of the atmosphere

	1	2	3	4
(a)	(iv)	(iii)	(ii)	(i)
(b)	(i)	(ii)	(iv)	(iii)
(c)	(iii)	(ii)	(i)	(iv)
(d)	(i)	(ii)	(iii)	(iv)

20. A plane electromagnetic wave travels in free space along X-direction. If the value of $\vec{B}$ (in tesla) at a particular point in space and time is $1.2 \times 10^{-8}\ \hat{k}$. The value of $\vec{E}$ (in Vm^{-1}) at that point is
(a) $1.2\, \hat{j}$
(b) $3.6\, \hat{k}$
(c) $1.2\, \hat{k}$
(d) $3.6\, \hat{j}$

(a) 3 V/m (b) 6 V/m (c) 9 V/m (d) 12 V/m

<table>
<tr><td rowspan="3">RESPONSE GRID</td><td>6. (a)(b)(c)(d)</td><td>7. (a)(b)(c)(d)</td><td>8. (a)(b)(c)(d)</td><td>9. (a)(b)(c)(d)</td><td>10. (a)(b)(c)(d)</td></tr>
<tr><td>11. (a)(b)(c)(d)</td><td>12. (a)(b)(c)(d)</td><td>13. (a)(b)(c)(d)</td><td>14. (a)(b)(c)(d)</td><td>15. (a)(b)(c)(d)</td></tr>
<tr><td>16. (a)(b)(c)(d)</td><td>17. (a)(b)(c)(d)</td><td>18. (a)(b)(c)(d)</td><td>19. (a)(b)(c)(d)</td><td>20. (a)(b)(c)(d)</td></tr>
</table>

21. If v_s, v_x and v_m are the speed of soft gamma rays, X-rays and microwaves respectively in vacuum, then
(a) $v_s > v_x > v_m$ (b) $v_s < v_x < v_m$
(c) $v_s > v_x < v_m$ (d) $v_s = v_x = v_m$

22. Photons of an electromagnetic radiation has an energy 11 keV each. To which region of electromagnetic spectrum does it belong ?
(a) X-ray region   (b) Ultra violet region
(c) Infrared region   (d) Visible region

23. A plane electromagnetic wave travels in free space along x-axis. At a particular point in space, the electric field along y-axis is 9.3 V m^{-1}. The magnetic induction (B) along z-axis is
(a) $3.1 \times 10^{-8} \text{ T}$ (b) $3 \times 10^{-5} \text{ T}$
(c) $3 \times 10^{-6} \text{ T}$ (d) $9.3 \times 10^{-6} \text{ T}$

24. The ratio of amplitude of magnetic field to the amplitude of electric field for an electromagnetic wave propagating in vacuum is equal to :
(a) the speed of light in vacuum
(b) reciprocal of speed of light in vacuum
(c) the ratio of magnetic permeability to the electric susceptibility of vacuum
(d) unity

25. A plane electromagnetic wave is incident on a material surface. If the wave delivers momentum p and energy E, then
(a) $p = 0, E = 0$ (b) $p \neq 0, E \neq 0$
(c) $p \neq 0, E = 0$ (d) $p = 0, E \neq 0$

26. Intensity of electromagnetic wave will be
(a) $I = c\mu_0 B_0^2 / 2$ (b) $I = c\varepsilon_0 B_0^2 / 2$
(c) $I = B_0^2 / c\mu_0$ (d) $I = E_0^2 / 2c\varepsilon_0$

27. The decreasing order of wavelength of infrared, microwave, ultraviolet and gamma rays is
(a) microwave, infrared, ultraviolet, gamma rays
(b) gamma rays, ultraviolet, infrared, micro-waves
(c) microwaves, gamma rays, infrared, ultraviolet
(d) infrared, microwave, ultraviolet, gamma rays

28. Which radiation in sunlight, causes heating effect ?
(a) Ultraviolet   (b) Infrared
(c) Visible light   (d) All of these

29. The speed of electromagnetic wave in vacuum depends upon the source of radiation. It
(a) increases as we move from γ-rays to radio waves
(b) decreases as we move from γ-rays to radio waves
(c) is same for all of them
(d) None of these

30. When an electromagnetic waves enter the ionised layer of ionosphere, the motion of electron cloud produces a space current and the electric field has its own capacitative displacement current, then
(a) the space current is in phase of displacement current
(b) the space current lags behind the displacement current by a phase 180°.
(c) the space current lags behind the displacement current by a phase 90°.
(d) the space current leads the displacement current by a phase 90°.

31. The displacement current is
(a) $\varepsilon_0 \, d\phi_E / dt$ (b) $\dfrac{\varepsilon_0}{R} d\phi_E / dt$
(c) $\varepsilon_0 E / R$ (d) $\varepsilon_0 q \, C / R$

32. Electromagnetic radiation of highest frequency is
(a) infrared radiations   (b) visible radiation
(c) radio waves   (d) γ-rays

33. A point source of electromagnetic radiation has an average power output of 1500 W. The maximum value of electric field at a distance of 3m from this sources in Vm^{-1} is
(a) 500   (b) 100   (c) $\dfrac{500}{3}$ (d) $\dfrac{250}{3}$

34. Frequency of a wave is 6×10^{15} Hz. The wave is
(a) radiowave   (b) microwave
(c) x-ray   (d) ultraviolet

35. The electromagnetic waves do not transport
(a) energy   (b) charge
(c) momentum   (d) information

36. Which of the following statement is false for the properties of electromagnetic waves?
(a) Both electric and magnetic field vectors attain the maxima and minima at the same place and same time.
(b) The energy in electromagnetic wave is divided equally between electric and magnetic vectors
(c) Both electric and magnetic field vectors are parallel to each other and perpendicular to the direction of propagation of wave
(d) These waves do not require any material medium for propagation.

<table>
<tr><td rowspan="3">RESPONSE
GRID</td><td>21. ⓐ ⓑ ⓒ ⓓ</td><td>22. ⓐ ⓑ ⓒ ⓓ</td><td>23. ⓐ ⓑ ⓒ ⓓ</td><td>24. ⓐ ⓑ ⓒ ⓓ</td><td>25. ⓐ ⓑ ⓒ ⓓ</td></tr>
<tr><td>26. ⓐ ⓑ ⓒ ⓓ</td><td>27. ⓐ ⓑ ⓒ ⓓ</td><td>28. ⓐ ⓑ ⓒ ⓓ</td><td>29. ⓐ ⓑ ⓒ ⓓ</td><td>30. ⓐ ⓑ ⓒ ⓓ</td></tr>
<tr><td>31. ⓐ ⓑ ⓒ ⓓ</td><td>32. ⓐ ⓑ ⓒ ⓓ</td><td>33. ⓐ ⓑ ⓒ ⓓ</td><td>34. ⓐ ⓑ ⓒ ⓓ</td><td>35. ⓐ ⓑ ⓒ ⓓ</td></tr>
</table>

36. ⓐ ⓑ ⓒ ⓓ

37. Which of the following electromagnetic waves has minimum frequency ?
    (a) Microwaves (b) Audible waves
    (c) Ultrasonic wave (d) Radiowaves

38. The wave impendance of free space is
    (a) zero (b) $376.6\,\Omega$ (c) $33.66\,\Omega$ (d) $3.76\,\Omega$

39. A plane electromagnetic wave in a non-magnetic dielectric medium is given by $\vec{E} = \vec{E}_0 (4 \times 10^{-7} x - 50t)$ with distance being in meter and time in seconds. The dielectric constant of the medium is :
    (a) 2.4 (b) 5.8 (c) 8.2 (d) 4.8

40. We consider the radiation emitted by the human body. Which of the following statements is true?
    (a) the radiation emitted lies in the ultraviolet region and hence is not visible.
    (b) the radiation emitted is in the infra-red region.
    (c) the radiation is emitted only during the day.
    (d) the radiation is emitted during the summers and absorbed during the winters.

41. In a plane electromagnetic wave propagating in space has an electric field of amplitude 9×10^3 V/m, then the amplitude of the magnetic field is
    (a) 2.7×10^{12} T (b) 9.0×10^{-3} T
    (c) 3.0×10^{-4} T (d) 3.0×10^{-5} T

42. Out of the following options which one can be used to produce a propagating electromagnetic wave ?
    (a) A charge moving at constant velocity
    (b) A stationary charge
    (c) A chargeless particle
    (d) An accelerating charge

43. Radio waves of constant amplitude can be generated with
    (a) rectifier (b) filter
    (c) F.E.T. (d) oscillator

44. In an electromagnetic wave
    (a) power is transmitted along the magnetic field
    (b) power is transmitted along the electric field
    (c) power is equally transferred along the electric and magnetic fields
    (d) power is transmitted in a direction perpendicular to both the fields

45. If c is the speed of electromagnetic waves in vacuum, its speed in a medium of dielectric constant K and relative permeability μ_r is
    (a) $v = \dfrac{1}{\sqrt{\mu_r K}}$ (b) $v = c\sqrt{\mu_r K}$
    (c) $v = \dfrac{c}{\sqrt{\mu_r K}}$ (d) $v = \dfrac{K}{\sqrt{\mu_r C}}$

RESPONSE GRID					
	37. ⓐⓑⓒⓓ	38. ⓐⓑⓒⓓ	39. ⓐⓑⓒⓓ	40. ⓐⓑⓒⓓ	41. ⓐⓑⓒⓓ
	42. ⓐⓑⓒⓓ	43. ⓐⓑⓒⓓ	44. ⓐⓑⓒⓓ	45. ⓐⓑⓒⓓ	

DAILY PRACTICE PROBLEM DPP CHAPTERWISE CP22 - PHYSICS

Total Questions	45	Total Marks	180
Attempted		Correct	
Incorrect		Net Score	
Cut-off Score	50	Qualifying Score	70
Success Gap = Net Score – Qualifying Score			
Net Score = (Correct × 4) – (Incorrect × 1)			

Space for Rough Work

Date : ____________   Start Time : ____________   End Time : ____________

PHYSICS $\boxed{CP23}$

SYLLABUS : Ray Optics and Optical Instruments

Max. Marks : 180   **Marking Scheme :** (+4) for correct & (–1) for incorrect answer   **Time : 60 min.**

INSTRUCTIONS : This Daily Practice Problem Sheet contains 45 MCQs. For each question only one option is correct. Darken the correct circle/ bubble in the Response Grid provided on each page.

1. A double convex lens is made of glass which has its refractive index 1.45 for violet rays and 1.50 for red rays. If the focal length for violet ray is 20cm, the focal length for red ray will be
   (a) 9 cm   (b) 18 cm   (c) 20 cm   (d) 22 cm

2. If the refractive index of the material of a prism is $\cot\dfrac{A}{2}$ and the angle of prism is A, then angle of minimum deviation is
   (a) $\pi - 2A$ (b) $\pi - A$ (c) $\dfrac{\pi}{2} - 2A$ (d) $\dfrac{\pi}{2} - A$

3. If two + 5 diopter lenses are mounted at some distance apart, the equivalent power will always be negative if the distance is
   (a) greater than 40 cm   (b) equal to 40 cm
   (c) equal to 10 cm   (d) less than 10 cm

4. Refraction of light from air to glass and from air to water are shown in figure (i) and figure (ii) below. The value of the angle θ in the case of refraction as shown in figure (iii) will be
   (a) 30°   (b) 35°   (c) 60°   (d) 41°

5. A fish looking up through the water sees the outside world contained in a circular horizon. If the refractive index of water is $\dfrac{4}{3}$ and the fish is 12 cm below the surface, the radius of this circle in cm is
   (a) $36\sqrt{5}$ (b) $4\sqrt{5}$ (c) $36\sqrt{7}$ (d) $36/\sqrt{7}$

6. If f_V and f_R are the focal lengths of a convex lens for violet and red light respectively and F_V and F_R are the focal lengths of concave lens for violet and red light respectively, then we have
   (a) $f_V < f_R$ and $F_V > F_R$ (b) $f_V < f_R$ and $F_V < F_R$
   (c) $f_V > f_R$ and $F_V > F_R$ (d) $f_V > f_R$ and $F_V < F_R$

Space for Rough Work

7. Spherical aberration in a lens :
(a) is minimum when most of the deviation is at first surface
(b) is minimum when most of the deviation is at the second surface
(c) is minimum when the total deviation is equally distributed over the two surfaces
(d) does not depend on the above considerations

8. A rod of length 10 cm lies along the principal axis of a concave mirror of focal length 10 cm in such a way that its end closer to the pole is 20 cm away from the mirror. The length of the image is :
(a) 10 cm   (b) 15 cm   (c) 2.5 cm   (d) 5 cm

9. A telescope consists of two thin lenses of focal lengths, 0.3 m and 3 cm respectively. It is focused on moon which subtends an angle of 0.5° at the objective. Then the angle subtended at the eye by the final image will be
(a) 5°   (b) 0.25°   (c) 0.5°   (d) 0.35°

10. The layered lens as shown is made of two types of transparent materials—one indicated by horizontal lines and the other by vertical lines. The number of images formed of an object will be
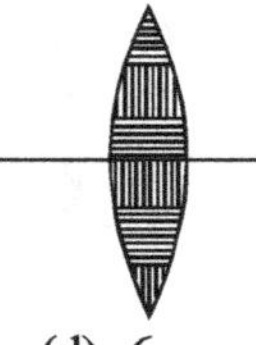
(a) 1   (b) 2   (c) 3   (d) 6

11. A man's near point is 0.5 m and far point is 3 m. Power of spectacle lenses required for (i) reading purposes, (ii) seeing distant objects, respectively, are
(a) –2 D and + 3 D   (b) +2 D and –3 D
(c) +2 D and –0.33 D   (d) –2 D and + 0.33 D

12. A ray of light falls on a transparent glass slab of refractive index 1.62. If the reflected ray and the refracted ray are mutually perpendicular, the angle of incidence is
(a) $\tan^{-1}(1.62)$
(b) $\tan^{-1}\left(\dfrac{1}{1.62}\right)$
(c) $\tan^{-1}(1.33)$
(d) $\tan^{-1}\left(\dfrac{1}{1.33}\right)$

13. A telescope has an objective of focal length 100 cm and an eyepiece of focal length 5 cm. What is the magnifying power of the telescope when the final image is formed at the least distance of distinct vision ?
(a) 20   (b) 24   (c) 28   (d) 32

14. Which light rays undergoes two internal reflection inside a raindrop, which of the rainbow is formed?
(a) Primary rainbow   (b) Secondary rainbow
(c) Both (a) and (b)   (d) Can't say

15. When a plane mirror is placed horizontally on a level ground at a distance of 60 m from the foot of a tower, the top of the tower and its image in the mirror subtend an angle of 90° at the eye. The height of the tower will be

(a) 30 m   (b) 60 m   (c) 90 m   (d) 120 m

16. A parallel beam of light is incident on the surface of a transparent hemisphere of radius R and refractive index 2.0 as shown in figure. The position of the image formed by refraction at the first surface is :
(a) $R/2$
(b) R
(c) $2R$
(d) $3R$

17. A lens made of glass whose index of refraction is 1.60 has a focal length of + 20 cm in air. Its focal length in water, whose refractive index is 1.33, will be
(a) three times longer than in air
(b) two times longer than in air
(c) same as in air
(d) None of these

18. A compound microscope has an eye piece of focal length 10 cm and an objective of focal length 4 cm. Calculate the magnification, if an object is kept at a distance of 5 cm from the objective so that final image is formed at the least distance vision (20 cm) :
(a) 12   (b) 11   (c) 10   (d) 13

19. For a prism kept in air it is found that for an angle of incidence 60°, the angle of Prism A, angle of deviation δ and angle of emergence 'e' become equal. Then the refractive index of the prism is
(a) 1.73   (b) 1.15   (c) 1.5   (d) 1.33

20. A person can see clearly only upto a distance of 30 cm. He wants to read a book placed at a distance of 50 cm from his eyes. What is the power of the lens of his spectacles ?
(a) –1.0 D   (b) –1.33 D   (c) –1.67 D   (d) –2.0 D

21. An object is placed at a distance of 40 cm in front of a concave mirror of focal length 20 cm. The image produced is
(a) real, inverted and smaller in size
(b) real, inverted and of same size
(c) real and erect
(d) virtual and inverted

22. A vessel of depth x is half filled with oil of refractive index μ_1 and the other half is filled with water of refractive index μ_2. The apparent depth of the vessel when viewed from above is
(a) $\dfrac{x(\mu_1+\mu_2)}{2\mu_1\mu_2}$
(b) $\dfrac{x\mu_1\mu_2}{2(\mu_1+\mu_2)}$
(c) $\dfrac{x\mu_1\mu_2}{(\mu_1+\mu_2)}$
(d) $\dfrac{2x(\mu_1+\mu_2)}{\mu_1\mu_2}$

RESPONSE GRID					
7. ⓐⓑⓒⓓ	8. ⓐⓑⓒⓓ	9. ⓐⓑⓒⓓ	10. ⓐⓑⓒⓓ	11. ⓐⓑⓒⓓ
12. ⓐⓑⓒⓓ	13. ⓐⓑⓒⓓ	14. ⓐⓑⓒⓓ	15. ⓐⓑⓒⓓ	16. ⓐⓑⓒⓓ
17. ⓐⓑⓒⓓ	18. ⓐⓑⓒⓓ	19. ⓐⓑⓒⓓ	20. ⓐⓑⓒⓓ	21. ⓐⓑⓒⓓ
22. ⓐⓑⓒⓓ				

23. The following figure shows refraction of light at the interface of three media Correct the order of optical density (d) of the media is

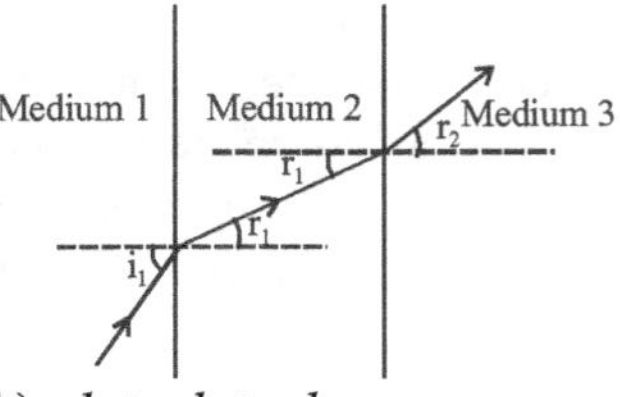

   (a) $d_1 > d_2 > d_3$ (b) $d_2 > d_1 > d_3$
   (c) $d_3 > d_3 > d_2$ (d) $d_2 > d_3 > d_1$

24. Light travels in two media A and B with speeds 1.8×10^8 m s^{-1} and 2.4×10^8 m s^{-1} respectively. Then the critical angle between them is

   (a) $\sin^{-1}\left(\dfrac{2}{3}\right)$ (b) $\tan^{-1}\left(\dfrac{3}{4}\right)$

   (c) $\tan^{-1}\left(\dfrac{2}{3}\right)$ (d) $\sin^{-1}\left(\dfrac{3}{4}\right)$

25. The refractive index of a glass is 1.520 for red light and 1.525 for blue light. Let D_1 and D_2 be angles of minimum deviation for red and blue light respectively in a prism of this glass. Then,
   (a) $D_1 < D_2$ (b) $D_1 = D_2$
   (c) D_1 can be less than or greater than D_2 depending upon the angle of prism
   (d) $D_1 > D_2$

26. Which of the following is not due to total internal reflection?
   (a)   Working of optical fibre
   (b)   Difference between apparent and real depth of pond
   (c)   Mirage on hot summer days
   (d)   Brilliance of diamond

27. A body is located on a wall. Its image of equal size is to be obtained on a parallel wall with the help of a convex lens. The lens is placed at a distance 'd' ahead of second wall, then the required focal length will be

   (a)   only $\dfrac{d}{4}$

   (b)   only $\dfrac{d}{2}$

   (c)   more than $\dfrac{d}{4}$ but less than $\dfrac{d}{2}$

   (d)   less than $\dfrac{d}{4}$

28. A concave mirror forms the image of an object on a screen. If the lower half of the mirror is covered with an opaque card, the effect would be to make the
   (a)   image less bright.
   (b)   lower half of the image disappear.
   (c)   upper half of the image disappear.
   (d)   image blurred.

29. A ray of light passes through an equilateral prism such that the angle of incidence is equal to the angle of emergence and the latter is equal to $\dfrac{3}{4}$ th of angle of prism. The angle of deviation is
   (a)   25°   (b)   30°   (c)   45°   (d)   35°

30. The power of a biconvex lens is 10 dioptre and the radius of curvature of each surface is 10 cm. Then the refractive index of the material of the lens is

   (a) $\dfrac{3}{2}$ (b) $\dfrac{4}{3}$ (c) $\dfrac{9}{8}$ (d) $\dfrac{5}{3}$

31. A microscope is focussed on a mark on a piece of paper and then a slab of glass of thickness 3 cm and refractive index 1.5 is placed over the mark. How should the microscope be moved to get the mark in focus again ?
   (a)   4.5 cm downward   (b)   1 cm downward
   (c)   2 cm upward   (d)   1 cm upward

32. What causes chromatic aberration?
   (a)   Marginal rays
   (b)   Central rays
   (c)   Difference in radii of curvature of its surfaces
   (d)   Variation of focal length of lens with colour

33. The graph between angle of deviation (δ) and angle of incidence (i) for a triangular prism is represented by

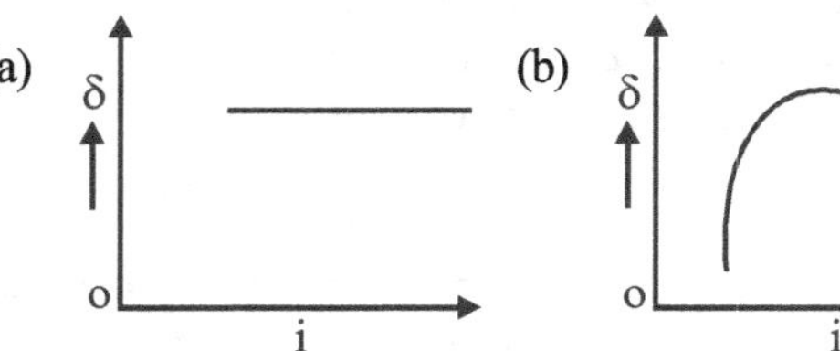

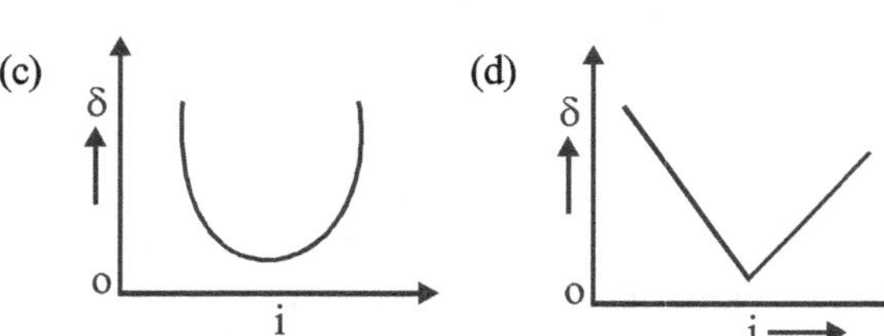

34. The ratio of thickness of plates of two transparent medium A and B is 6 : 4. If light takes equal time in passing through them, then refractive index of A with respect to B will be
   (a)   1.33   (b)   1.75   (c)   1.4   (d)   1.5

35. A rectangular block of glass is placed on a mark made on the surface of the table and it is viewed from the vertical position of eye. If refractive index of glass be μ and its thickness d, then the mark will appear to be raised up by

   (a) $\dfrac{(\mu+1)d}{\mu}$ (b) $\dfrac{(\mu-1)d}{\mu}$ (c) $\dfrac{(\mu+1)}{\mu d}$ (d) $\dfrac{(\mu-1)\mu}{d}$

36. If a glass prism is dipped in water, its dispersive power
  (a) increases
  (b) decreases
  (c) does not change
  (d) may increase or decrease depending on whether the angle of the prism is less than or greater than 60°

37. A planoconcave lens is placed on a paper on which a flower is drawn. How far above its actual position does the flower appear to be?

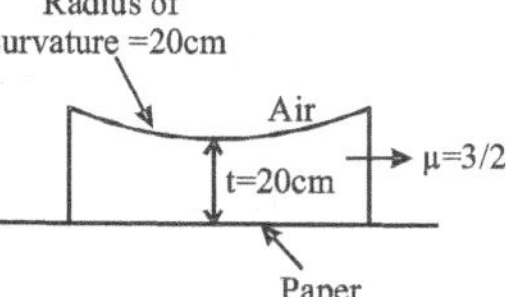

  (a) 10 cm   (b) 15 cm
  (c) 50 cm   (d) None of these

38. To get three images of a single object, one should have two plane mirrors at an angle of
  (a) 60°   (b) 90°   (c) 120°   (d) 30°

39. Light propagates with speed of $2.2 \times 10^8\, m/s$ and $2.4 \times 10^8\, m/s$ in the media P and Q respectively. The critical angle of incidence for light undergoing reflection from P and Q is

  (a) $\sin^{-1}\left(\dfrac{1}{11}\right)$
  (b) $\sin^{-1}\left(\dfrac{11}{12}\right)$

  (c) $\sin^{-1}\left(\dfrac{5}{12}\right)$
  (d) $\sin^{-1}\left(\dfrac{5}{11}\right)$

40. A thin convergent glass lens ($\mu_g = 1.5$) has a power of $+ 5.0$ D. When this lens is immersed in a liquid of refractive index μ, it acts as a divergent lens of focal length 100 cm. The value of μ must be
  (a) 4/3   (b) 5/3   (c) 5/4   (d) 6/5

41. A ray of light travelling inside a rectangular glass block of refractive index $\sqrt{2}$ is incident on the glass-air surface at an angle of incidence of 45°. The refractive index of air is one. Under these conditions the ray will
  (a) emerge into the air without any deviation
  (b) be reflected back into the glass
  (c) be absorbed
  (d) emerge into the air with an angle of refraction equal to 90°

42. A small coin is resting on the bottom of a beaker filled with liquid. A ray of light from the coin travels upto the surface of the liquid and moves along its surface. How fast is the light travelling in the liquid?

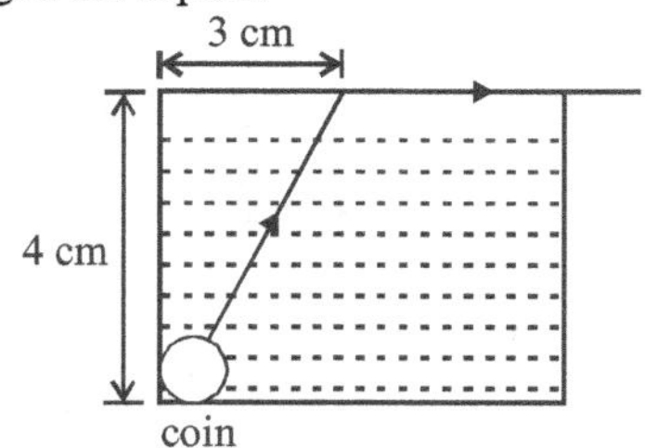

  (a) 2.4×10^8 m/s
  (b) 3.0×10^8 m/s
  (c) 1.2×10^8 m/s
  (d) 1.8×10^8 m/s

43. A ray PQ incident on the refracting face BA is refracted in the prism BAC as shown in the figure and emerges from the other refracting face AC as RS such that AQ = AR. If the angle of prism A = 60° and the refractive index of the material of prism is $\sqrt{3}$, then the angle of deviation of the ray is

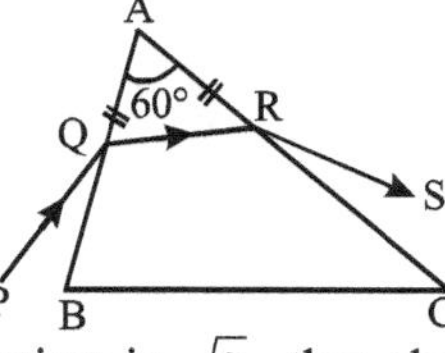

  (a) 60°
  (b) 45°
  (c) 30°
  (d) None of these

44. When a biconvex lens of glass having refractive index 1.47 is dipped in a liquid, it acts as a plane sheet of glass. This implies that the liquid must have refractive index.
  (a) equal to that of glass
  (b) less then one
  (c) greater than that of glass
  (d) less then that of glass

45. If a thin prism of glass is dipped in water then minimum deviation (with respect to air) of light produced by prism will be $\left({}_w\mu_g = \dfrac{3}{2},\ {}_a\mu_w = \dfrac{4}{3}\right)$

  (a) $\dfrac{1}{5}$
  (b) $\dfrac{1}{4}$
  (c) $\dfrac{1}{2}$
  (d) $\dfrac{1}{3}$

RESPONSE	36. (a)(b)(c)(d)	37. (a)(b)(c)(d)	38. (a)(b)(c)(d)	39. (a)(b)(c)(d)	40. (a)(b)(c)(d)
GRID	41. (a)(b)(c)(d)	42. (a)(b)(c)(d)	43. (a)(b)(c)(d)	44. (a)(b)(c)(d)	45. (a)(b)(c)(d)

DAILY PRACTICE PROBLEM DPP CHAPTERWISE CP23 - PHYSICS

Total Questions	45	Total Marks	180
Attempted		Correct	
Incorrect		Net Score	
Cut-off Score	45	Qualifying Score	60
Success Gap = Net Score − Qualifying Score			
Net Score = (Correct × 4) − (Incorrect × 1)			

Date :   Start Time :   End Time :

PHYSICS $\boxed{\text{CP24}}$

SYLLABUS : Wave Optics

Max. Marks : 180   **Marking Scheme :** (+4) for correct & (–1) for incorrect answer   **Time : 60 min.**

INSTRUCTIONS : This Daily Practice Problem Sheet contains 45 MCQs. For each question only one option is correct. Darken the correct circle/ bubble in the Response Grid provided on each page.

1. In young's double-slit experiment, the intensity of light at a point on the screen where the path difference is λ is I, λ being the wavelength of light used. The intensity at a point where the path difference is $\dfrac{\lambda}{4}$ will be

   (a) $\dfrac{I}{4}$ (b) $\dfrac{I}{2}$ (c) I   (d) zero

2. A beam of light is incident on a glass slab ($\mu = 1.54$) in a direction as shown in the figure. The reflected light is analysed by a polaroid prism. On rotating the polaroid, ($\tan 57° = 1.54$)

   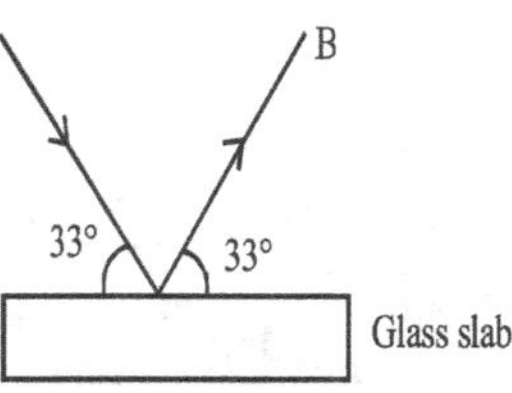

   (a) the intensity remains unchanged
   (b) the intensity is reduced to zero and remains at zero
   (c) the intensity gradually reduces to zero and then again increase
   (d) the intensity increases continuously

3. Two sources of light of wavelengths 2500 Å and 3500 Å are used in Young's double slit expt. simultaneously. Which orders of fringes of two wavelength patterns coincide?
   (a) 3rd order of 1st source and 5th of the 2nd
   (b) 7th order of 1st and 5th order of 2nd

   (c) 5th order of 1st and 3rd order of 2nd
   (d) 5th order of 1st and 7th order of 2nd

4. Figure shows behavior of a wavefront when it passes through a prism.

   Which of the following statements is/are correct ?
   (a) Lower portion of wavefront (B') is delayed resulting in a tilt.
   (b) Time taken by light to reach A' is equal to the time taken to reach B' from B.
   (c) Speed of wavefront is same everywhere.
   (d) A particle on wavefront A' B' is in phase with a particle on wavefront AB.

5. When the angle of incidence is 60° on the surface of a glass slab, it is found that the reflected ray is completely polarised. The velocity of light in glass is

   (a) $\sqrt{2} \times 10^8\,\text{ms}^{-1}$ (b) $\sqrt{3} \times 10^8\,\text{ms}^{-1}$

   (c) $2 \times 10^8\,\text{ms}^{-1}$ (d) $3 \times 10^8\,\text{ms}^{-1}$

RESPONSE GRID   1. ⓐⓑⓒⓓ   2. ⓐⓑⓒⓓ   3. ⓐⓑⓒⓓ   4. ⓐⓑⓒⓓ   5. ⓐⓑⓒⓓ

Space for Rough Work

6. Figure shows two coherent sources S_1 and S_2 vibrating in same phase. AB is an irregular wire lying at a far distance from the sources S_1 and S_2. Let $\dfrac{\lambda}{d} = 10^{-3}$ and $\angle BOA = 0.12°$.
How many bright spots will be seen on the wire, including points A and B?
(a) 5
(b) 4
(c) 2
(d) 7

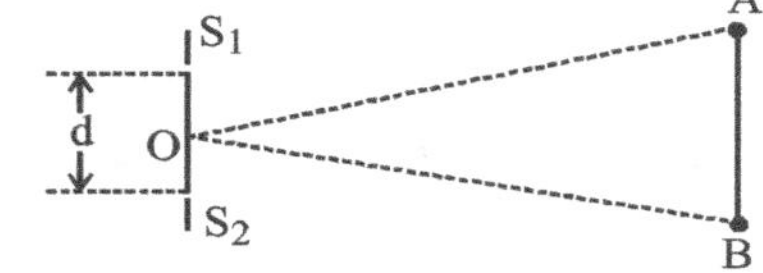

7. Two identical light waves, propagating in the same direction, have a phase difference δ. After they superpose, the intensity of the resulting wave will be proportional to
(a) $\cos \delta$ (b) $\cos (\delta/2)$
(c) $\cos^2 (\delta/2)$ (d) $\cos^2 \delta$

8. In YSDE, both slits are covered by transparent slab. Upper slit is covered by slab of R.I. 1.5 and thickness t and lower is covered by R.I. $\dfrac{4}{3}$ and thickness 2t, then central maxima

(a) shifts in +ve y-axis direction
(b) shifts in –ve y-axis direction
(c) remains at same position
(d) may shift in upward or downward depending upon wavelength of light

9. A beam of light of $\lambda = 600$ nm from a distant source falls on a single slit 1 mm wide and the resulting diffraction pattern is observed on a screen 2 m away. The distance between first dark fringes on either side of the central bright fringe is
(a) 1.2 cm   (b) 1.2 mm
(c) 2.4 cm   (d) 2.4 mm

10. A parallel beam of light of wavelength λ is incident normally on a narrow slit. A diffraction pattern is formed on a screen placed perpendicular to the direction of the incident beam. At the second minimum of the diffraction pattern, the phase difference between the rays coming from the two edges of slit is
(a) $\pi\lambda$ (b) 2π
(c) 3π (d) 4π

11. The diffraction effects in a microscopic specimen become important when the separation between two points is
(a) much greater than the wavelength of light used.
(b) much less than the wavelength of light used.
(c) comparable to the wavelength of light used.
(d) independent of the wavelength of light used.

12. On a rainy day, if there is an oil drop on tar road coloured rings are seen around this drop. This is due to
(a) total internal reflection of light
(b) polarisation
(c) diffraction pattern
(d) interference pattern produced due to oil film

13. In a Young's double slit experiment, the intensity at a point where the path difference $\dfrac{\lambda}{6}$ (λ – is wavelength of the light) is I. If I_0 denotes the maximum intensity, then $\dfrac{I}{I_0}$ is equal to
(a) $\dfrac{1}{2}$ (b) $\dfrac{\sqrt{3}}{2}$ (c) $\dfrac{1}{\sqrt{2}}$ (d) $\dfrac{3}{4}$

14. According to Huygens, medium through which light waves travel is
(a) vacuum only   (b) luminiferous ether
(c) liquid only   (d) solid only

15. If we observe the single slit Fraunhofer diffraction with wavelength λ and slit width b, the width of the central maxima is 2θ. On decreasing the slit width for the same λ
(a) θ increases
(b) θ remains unchanged
(c) θ decreases
(d) θ increases or decreases depending on the intensity of light

16. Aperture of the human eye is 2 mm. Assuming the mean wavelength of light to be 5000 Å, the angular resolution limit of the eye is nearly
(a) 2 minute   (b) 1 minute
(c) 0.5 minute   (d) 1.5 minute

17. Unpolarised light is incident on a dielectric of refractive index $\sqrt{3}$. What is the angle of incidence if the reflected beam is completely polarised?
(a) 30°   (b) 45°
(c) 60°   (d) 75°

18. The figure shows the interference pattern obtained in a double-slit experiment using light of wavelength 600nm. 1, 2, 3, 4 and 5 are marked on five fringes.
The third order bright fringe is
(a) 2   (b) 3   (c) 4   (d) 5

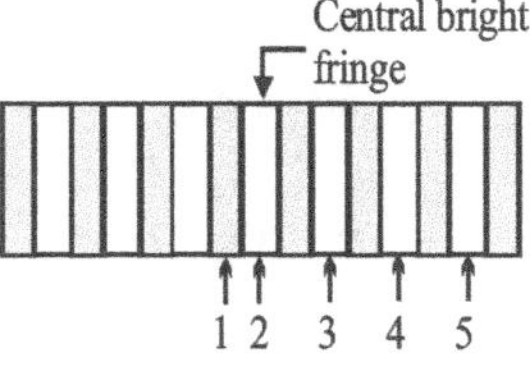

19. Which of the following diagrams represent the variation of electric field vector with time for a circularly polarised light ?

(a) (b) (c) (d)
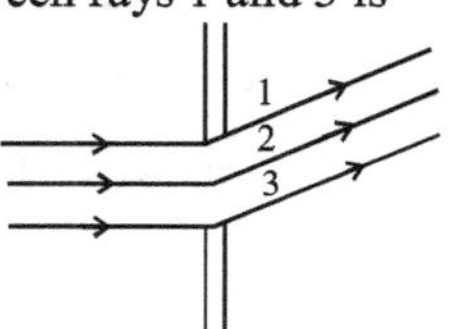

20. With a monochromatic light, the fringe-width obtained in a Young's double slit experiment is 0.133 cm. The whole set-up is immersed in water of refractive index 1.33, then the new fringe-width is
(a) 0.133 cm (b) 0.1 cm
(c) 1.33 cm (d) 0.2 cm

21. The condition for obtaining secondary maxima in the diffraction pattern due to single slit is

(a) $a \sin\theta = n\lambda$ (b) $a \sin\theta = \left(2n-1\dfrac{\lambda}{2}\right)$

(c) $a \sin\theta = (2n-1)\lambda$ (d) $a \sin\theta = \dfrac{n\lambda}{2}$

22. In double slit experiment, the angular width of the fringes is $0.20°$ for the sodium light $(\lambda = 5890 \text{Å})$. In order to increase the angular width of the fringes by 10%, the necessary change in wavelength is
(a) zero (b) increased by 6479 Å
(c) decreased by 589 Å (d) increased by 589 Å

23. In Young's double slit experiment with sodium vapour lamp of wavelength 589 nm and the slits 0.589 mm apart, the half angular width of the central maximum is
(a) $\sin^{-1}(0.01)$ (b) $\sin^{-1}(0.0001)$
(c) $\sin^{-1}(0.001)$ (d) $\sin^{-1}(0.1)$

24. The adjacent figure shows Fraunhoffer's diffraction due to a single slit. If first minimum is obtained in the direction shown, then the path difference between rays 1 and 3 is
(a) 0
(b) $\lambda/4$
(c) $\lambda/2$
(d) λ

25. A YDSE is conducted in water (μ_1) as shown in figure. A glass plate of thickness t and refractive index μ_2 is placed in the path of S_2. The optical path difference at O is
(a) $(\mu_2-1)t$
(b) $(\mu_1-1)t$

(c) $\left(\dfrac{\mu_2}{\mu_1}-1\right)t$

(d) $(\mu_2-\mu_1)t$

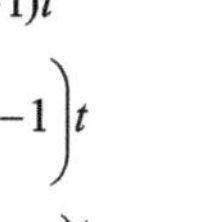
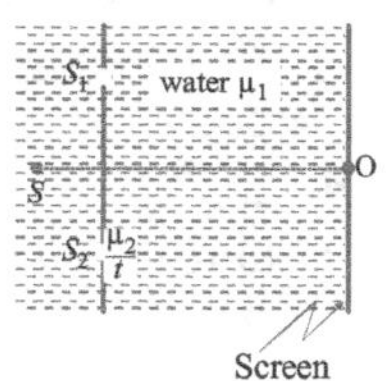

26. In a Fresnel biprism experiment, the two positions of lens give separation between the slits as 16 cm and 9 cm respectively. What is the actual distance of separation?
(a) 12.5 cm (b) 12 cm (c) 13 cm (d) 14 cm

27. If two waves represented by $y_1 = 4 \sin \omega t$ and $y_2 = \left(\omega t + \dfrac{\pi}{3}\right)$ interfere at a point, then the amplitude of the resulting wave will be about
(a) 7 (b) 6 (c) 5 (d) 3.5

28. In Young's double slit experiment, the separation between the slits is halved and the distance between the slits and screen is doubled. The fringe width will
(a) be halved (b) be doubled
(c) be quadrupled (d) remain unchanged

29. At the first minimum adjacent to the central maximum of a single-slit diffraction pattern, the phase difference between the Huygen's wavelet from the edge of the slit and the wavelet from the midpoint of the slit is :

(a) $\dfrac{\pi}{2}$ radian (b) π radian

(c) $\dfrac{\pi}{8}$ radian (d) $\dfrac{\pi}{4}$ radian

30. The central fringe of the interference pattern produced by light of wavelength 6000Å is found to shift to the position of 4th bright fringe after a glass plate of refractive index 1.5 is introduced in front of one of slits in Young's experiment. The thickness of the glass plate will be
(a) 4.8 μm (b) 8.23 μm
(c) 14.98 μm (d) 3.78 μm

31. Sodium light $(\lambda = 6 \times 10^{-7}\text{m})$ is used to produce interference pattern. The observed fringe width is 0.12 mm. The angle between two interfering wave trains, is
(a) 1×10^{-3} rad (b) 1×10^{-2} rad
(c) 5×10^{-3} rad (d) 5×10^{-2} rad

32. The Young's double slit experiment is performed with blue and with green light of wavelengths 4360Å and 5460Å respectively. If x is the distance of 4th maxima from the central one, then
(a) x (blue) = x (green) (b) x (blue) > x (green)
(c) x (blue) < x (green) (d) $\dfrac{x(\text{blue})}{x(\text{green})} = \dfrac{5460}{4360}$

33. If yellow light emitted by sodium lamp in Young's double slit experiment is replaced by a monochromatic blue light of the same intensity
(a) fringe width will decrease
(b) finge width will increase
(c) fringe width will remain unchanged
(d) fringes will become less intense

RESPONSE GRID	19. ⓐⓑⓒⓓ	20. ⓐⓑⓒⓓ	21. ⓐⓑⓒⓓ	22. ⓐⓑⓒⓓ	23. ⓐⓑⓒⓓ
	24. ⓐⓑⓒⓓ	25. ⓐⓑⓒⓓ	26. ⓐⓑⓒⓓ	27. ⓐⓑⓒⓓ	28. ⓐⓑⓒⓓ
	29. ⓐⓑⓒⓓ	30. ⓐⓑⓒⓓ	31. ⓐⓑⓒⓓ	32. ⓐⓑⓒⓓ	33. ⓐⓑⓒⓓ

Space for Rough Work

34. When unpolarised light is incident on a plane glass plate at Brewster's angle, then which of the following statements is correct?
    (a) Reflected and refracted rays are completely polarised with their planes of polarization parallel to each other
    (b) Reflected and refracted rays are completely polarised with their planes of polarization perpendicular to each other
    (c) Reflected light is plane polarised but transmitted light is partially polarised
    (d) Reflected light is partially polarised but refracted light is plane polarised

35. The maximum number of possible interference maxima for slit- separation equal to twice the wavelength in Young's double-slit experiment is
    (a) infinite (b) five (c) three (d) zero

36. In the figure shown if a parallel beam of white light is incident on the plane of the slits then the distance of the nearest white spot on the screen from O is d/A. Find the value of A. (assume $d \ll D$, $\lambda \ll d$]
    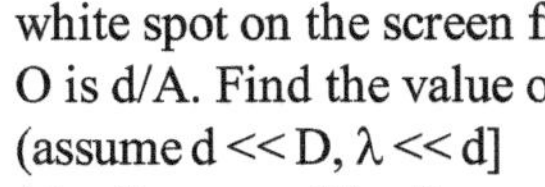
    (a) 3 (b) 5 (c) 6 (d) 4

37. Two light waves superimposing at the mid-point of the screen are coming from coherent sources of light with phase difference 3π rad. Their amplitudes are 1 cm each. The resultant amplitude at the given point will be.
    (a) 5 cm (b) 3 cm (c) 2 cm (d) zero

38. Spherical wavefronts, emanating from a point source, strike a plane reflecting surface. What will happen to these wave fronts, immediately after reflection?
    (a) They will remain spherical with the same curvature, both in magnitude and sign.
    (b) They will become plane wave fronts.
    (c) They will remain spherical, with the same curvature, but sign of curvature reversed.
    (d) They will remain spherical, but with different curvature, both in magnitude and sign.

39. Two coherent point sources S_1 and S_2 are separated by a small distance d as shown. The fringes obtained on the vertical screen will be :
    (a) points
    (b) straight bands
    (c) concentric circles
    (d) semicircles

40. In the phenomena of diffraction of light, when blue light is used in the experiment in spite of red light, then
    (a) fringes will become narrower
    (b) fringes will become broader
    (c) no change in fringe width
    (d) None of these

41. On a hot summer night, the refractive index of air is smallest near the ground and increases with height from the ground. When a light beam is directed horizontally, the Huygens' principle leads us to conclude that as it travels, the light beam :
    (a) bends downwards
    (b) bends upwards
    (c) becomes narrower
    (d) goes horizontally without any deflection

42. If I_0 is the intensity of the principal maximum in the single slit diffraction pattern, then what will be its intensity when the slit width is doubled?
    (a) $4I_0$ (b) $2I_0$ (c) $\dfrac{I_0}{2}$ (d) I_0

43. Conditions of diffraction is
    (a) $\dfrac{a}{\lambda} = 1$ (b) $\dfrac{a}{\lambda} \gg 1$ (c) $\dfrac{a}{\lambda} \ll 1$
    (d) None of these

44. In Fresnel's biprism expt., a mica sheet of refractive index 1.5 and thickness 6×10^{-6} m is placed in the path of one of interfering beams as a result of which the central fringe gets shifted through 5 fringe widths. The wavelength of light used is
    (a) 6000 Å (b) 8000 Å (c) 4000 Å (d) 2000 Å

45. Two nicols are oriented with their principal planes making an angle of 60°. Then the percentage of incident unpolarised light which passes through the system is
    (a) 100 (b) 50 (c) 12.5 (d) 37.5

DAILY PRACTICE PROBLEM DPP CHAPTERWISE CP24 - PHYSICS

Total Questions	45	Total Marks	180
Attempted		Correct	
Incorrect		Net Score	
Cut-off Score	45	Qualifying Score	60
Success Gap = Net Score – Qualifying Score			
Net Score = (Correct × 4) – (Incorrect × 1)			

Date : Start Time : End Time :

PHYSICS $\boxed{\text{CP25}}$

SYLLABUS : Dual Nature of Radiation and Matter

Max. Marks : 180   **Marking Scheme :** (+4) for correct & (–1) for incorrect answer   **Time : 60 min.**

INSTRUCTIONS : This Daily Practice Problem Sheet contains 45 MCQs. For each question only one option is correct. Darken the correct circle/ bubble in the Response Grid provided on each page.

1. A particle of mass 1 mg has the same wavelength as an electron moving with a velocity of 3×10^6 ms^{-1}. The velocity of the particle is:
   (a) 2.7×10^{-18} ms^{-1} (b) 9×10^{-2} ms^{-1}
   (c) 3×10^{-31} ms^{-1} (d) 2.7×10^{-21} ms^{-1}

2. An electron of mass m and a photon have same energy E. The ratio of de-Broglie wavelengths associated with them is :

   (a) $\dfrac{1}{c}\left(\dfrac{E}{2m}\right)^{\frac{1}{2}}$ (b) $\left(\dfrac{E}{2m}\right)^{\frac{1}{2}}$

   (c) $c(2mE)^{\frac{1}{2}}$ (d) $\dfrac{1}{c}\left(\dfrac{2m}{E}\right)^{\frac{1}{2}}$

3. All electrons ejected from a surface by incident light of wavelength 200nm can be stopped before travelling 1m in the direction of uniform electric field of 4N/C. The work function of the surface is
   (a) 4 eV   (b) 6.2 eV   (c) 2 eV   (d) 2.2 eV

4. The maximum kinetic energy of the electrons hitting a target so as to produce X-ray of wavelength 1 Å is
   (a) 1.24 keV   (b) 12.4 keV
   (c) 124 keV   (d) None of these

5. An X-ray tube is operated at 15 kV. Calculate the upper limit of the speed of the electrons striking the target.
   (a) 7.26×10^7 m/s   (b) 7.62×10^9 m/s
   (c) 7.62×10^7 cm/s   (d) 7.26×10^9 m/s

6. A and B are two metals with threshold frequencies 1.8×10^{14} Hz and 2.2×10^{14} Hz. Two identical photons of energy 0.825 eV each are incident on them. Then photoelectrons are emitted in (Take h = 6.6×10^{-34} Js)
   (a) B alone   (b) A alone
   (c) neither A nor B   (d) both A and B.

7. If E_1, E_2, E_3 are the respective kinetic energies of an electron, an alpha-particle and a proton, each having the same de-Broglie wavelength, then
   (a) $E_1 > E_3 > E_2$ (b) $E_2 > E_3 > E_1$
   (c) $E_1 > E_2 > E_3$ (d) $E_1 = E_2 = E_3$

| RESPONSE GRID | 1. ⓐⓑⓒⓓ | 2. ⓐⓑⓒⓓ | 3. ⓐⓑⓒⓓ | 4. ⓐⓑⓒⓓ | 5. ⓐⓑⓒⓓ |
| | 6. ⓐⓑⓒⓓ | 7. ⓐⓑⓒⓓ | | | |

Space for Rough Work

8. Which of the following when falls on a metal will emit photoelectrons ?
(a) UV radiations   (b) Infrared radiation
(c) Radio waves   (d) Microwaves

9. The stopping potential (V_0) versus frequency (v) plot of a substance is shown in figure, the threshold wavelength is
(a) 5×10^{14} m
(b) 6000 Å
(c) 5000 Å
(d) Cannot be estimated from given data

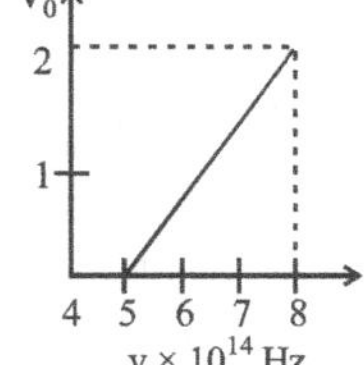

10. A material particle with a rest mass m_0 is moving with speed of light c. The de-Broglie wavelength associated is given by
(a) $\dfrac{h}{m_0 c}$ (b) $\dfrac{m_0 c}{h}$ (c) zero   (d) ∞

11. A 200 W sodium street lamp emits yellow light of wavelength 0.6 μm. Assuming it to be 25% efficient in converting electrical energy to light, the number of photons of yellow light it emits per second is
(a) 1.5×10^{20} (b) 6×10^{18}
(c) 62×10^{20} (d) 3×10^{19}

12. A proton has kinetic energy E = 100 keV which is equal to that of a photon. The wavelength of photon is λ_2 and that of proton is λ_1. The ratio of λ_2/λ_1 is proportional to
(a) E^2 (b) $E^{1/2}$ (c) E^{-1} (d) $E^{-1/2}$

13. In photoelectric effect the work function of a metal is 3.5 eV. The emitted electrons can be stopped by applying a potential of –1.2 V. Then
(a) the energy of the incident photon is 4.7 eV
(b) the energy of the incident photon is 2.3 eV
(c) if higher frequency photon be used, the photoelectric current will rise
(d) when the energy of photon is 3.5 eV, the photoelectric current will be maximum

14. The threshold frequency for a metallic surface corresponds to an energy of 6.2 eV and the stopping potential for a radiation incident on this surface is 5 V. The incident radiation lies in
(a) ultra-violet region   (b) infra-red region
(c) visible region   (d) X-ray region

15. When photons of energy hv fall on an aluminium plate (of work function E_0), photoelectrons of maximum kinetic energy K are ejected. If the frequency of the radiation is doubled, the maximum kinetic energy of the ejected photoelectrons will be
(a) 2K   (b) K   (c) $K + hv$ (d) $K + E_0$

16. Which metal will be suitable for a photoelectric cell using light of wavelength 4000Å. The work functions of sodium and copper are respectively 2.0 eV and 4.0 eV.
(a) Sodium   (b) Copper
(c) Both   (d) None of these

17. The maximum velocity of an electron emitted by light of wavelength λ incident on the surface of a metal of work-function φ is
(a) $\sqrt{\dfrac{2(hc + \lambda\phi)}{m\lambda}}$ (b) $\dfrac{2(hc + \lambda\phi)}{m\lambda}$
(c) $\sqrt{\dfrac{2(hc - \lambda\phi)}{m\lambda}}$ (d) $\sqrt{\dfrac{2(h\lambda - \phi)}{m}}$

18. If the kinetic energy of a free electron doubles, it's deBroglie wavelength changes by the factor
(a) 2   (b) $\dfrac{1}{2}$ (c) $\sqrt{2}$ (d) $\dfrac{1}{\sqrt{2}}$

19. Radiations of two photon's energy, twice and ten times the work function of metal are incident on the metal surface successsively. The ratio of maximum velocities of photoelectrons emitted in two cases is
(a) 1 : 2   (b) 1 : 3   (c) 1 : 4   (d) 1 : 1

20. The cathode of a photoelectric cell is changed such that the work function changes from W_1 to W_2 $(W_2 > W_1)$. If the current before and after changes are I_1 and I_2, all other conditions remaining unchanged, then (assuming $hv > W_2$)
(a) $I_1 = I_2$ (b) $I_1 < I_2$
(c) $I_1 > I_2$ (d) $I_1 < I_2 < 2I_1$

21. Monochromatic radiation emitted when electron on hydrogen atom jumps from first excited to the ground state irradiates a photosensitive material. The stopping potential is measured to be 3.57 V. The threshold frequency of the materials is :
(a) 4×10^{15} Hz   (b) 5×10^{15} Hz
(c) 1.6×10^{15} Hz   (d) 2.5×10^{15} Hz

22. Photoelectric work function of a metal is 1eV. Light of wavelength $\lambda = 3000$ Å falls on it. The photo electrons come out with velocity
(a) 10 metres/sec   (b) 10^2 metres/sec
(c) 10^4 metres/sec   (d) 10^6 metres/sec

23. When the energy of the incident radiation is incredased by 20%, the kinetic energy of the photoelectrons emitted from a metal surface increased from 0.5 eV to 0.8 eV. The work function of the metal is :
(a) 0.65 eV   (b) 1.0 eV   (c) 1.3 eV   (d) 1.5 eV

24. The maximum distance between interatomic lattice planes is 15 Å. The maximum wavelength of X-rays which are diffracted by this crystal will be
(a) 15 Å   (b) 20 Å   (c) 30 Å   (d) 45 Å

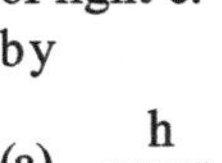

RESPONSE GRID	**8.** ⓐⓑⓒⓓ	**9.** ⓐⓑⓒⓓ	**10.** ⓐⓑⓒⓓ	**11.** ⓐⓑⓒⓓ	**12.** ⓐⓑⓒⓓ
	13. ⓐⓑⓒⓓ	**14.** ⓐⓑⓒⓓ	**15.** ⓐⓑⓒⓓ	**16.** ⓐⓑⓒⓓ	**17.** ⓐⓑⓒⓓ
	18. ⓐⓑⓒⓓ	**19.** ⓐⓑⓒⓓ	**20.** ⓐⓑⓒⓓ	**21.** ⓐⓑⓒⓓ	**22.** ⓐⓑⓒⓓ
	23. ⓐⓑⓒⓓ	**24.** ⓐⓑⓒⓓ			

25. In photoelectric effect, stopping potential for a light of frequency n_1 is V_1. If light is replaced by another having a frequency n_2 then its stopping potential will be

(a) $V_1 - \dfrac{h}{e}(n_2 - n_1)$ (b) $V_1 + \dfrac{h}{e}(n_2 + n_1)$

(c) $V_1 + \dfrac{h}{e}(n_2 - 2n_1)$ (d) $V_1 + \dfrac{h}{e}(n_2 - n_1)$

26. The maximum kinetic energy of the photoelectrons ejected from a photocathode when it is irradiated with light of wavelength 440nm is 1eV. If the threshold energy of the surface is 1.9eV, then which of the following statement is/are incorrect?
   (a) The threshold frequency for photo sensitive metal is 4.6×10^{14}Hz
   (b) The minimum wavelength of incident light required for photoemission is 6513 Å.
   (c) The maximum wavelength of incident light required for photoemission is 6513 Å.
   (d) The energy of incident photon is 2.9 eV.

27. The work functions of metals A and B are in the raio 1 : 2. If light of frequencies f and 2f are incident on the surfaces of A and B respectively, the ratio of the maximum kinetic energies of photoelectrons emitted is (f is greater than threshold frequency of A, 2f is greater than threshold frequency of B)
   (a) 1 : 1   (b) 1 : 2   (c) 1 : 3   (d) 1 : 4

28. Which one of the following graphs represents the variation of maximum kinetic energy (E_K) of the emitted electrons with frequency υ in photoelectric effect correctly ?

(a) 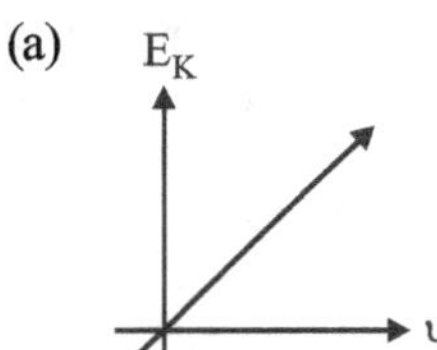   (b) 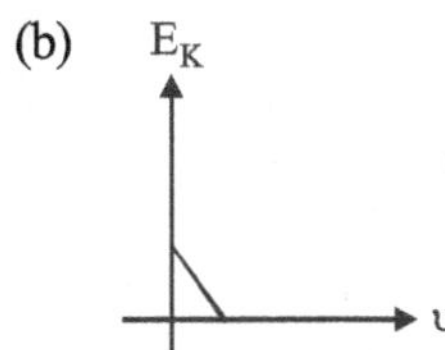

(c) 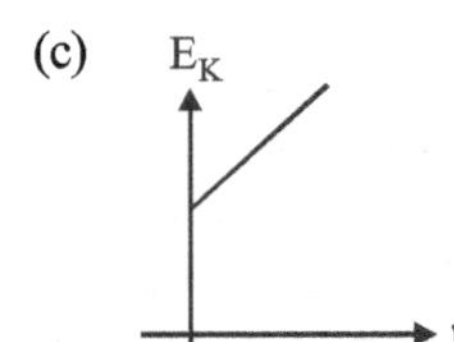   (d) 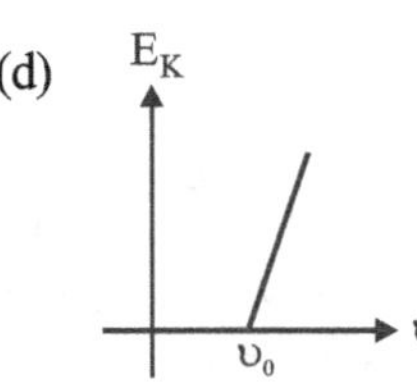

29. The potential difference that must be applied to stop the fastest photoelectrons emitted by a nickel surface, having work function 5.01 eV, when ultraviolet light of 200 nm falls on it, must be:
   (a) 2.4 V   (b) -1.2 V   (c) -2.4 V   (d) 1.2 V

30. X-rays are produced in X-ray tube operating at a given accelerating voltage. The wavelength of the continuous X-rays has values from
   (a) 0 to ∞
   (b) λ_{min} to ∞, where $\lambda_{min} > 0$
   (c) 0 to λ_{max}, where $\lambda_{max} < \infty$
   (d) λ_{min} to λ_{max}, where $0 < \lambda_{min} < \lambda_{max} < \infty$

31. Electrons used in an electron microscope are accelerated by a voltage of 25 kV. If the voltage is increased to 100kV then the de–Broglie wavelength associated with the electrons would
   (a) increase by 2 times   (b) decrease by 2 times
   (c) decrease by 4 times   (d) increase by 4 times

32. In the Davisson and Germer experiment, the velocity of electrons emitted from the electron gun can be increased by
   (a) increasing the potential difference between the anode and filament
   (b) increasing the filament current
   (c) decreasing the filament current
   (d) decreasing the potential difference between the anode and filament

33. Two radiations of photons energies 1 eV and 2.5 eV, successively illuminate a photosensitive metallic surface of work function 0.5 eV. The ratio of the maximum speeds of the emitted electrons is :
   (a) 1 : 4   (b) 1 : 2   (c) 1 : 1   (d) 1 : 5

34. Photoelectric emission is observed from a metallic surface for frequencies v_1 and v_2 of the incident light rays ($v_1 > v_2$). If the maximum values of kinetic energy of the photoelectrons emitted in the two cases are in the ratio of 1 : k, then the threshold frequency of the metallic surface is

(a) $\dfrac{v_1 - v_2}{k - 1}$ (b) $\dfrac{kv_1 - v_2}{k - 1}$

(c) $\dfrac{kv_2 - v_1}{k - 1}$ (d) $\dfrac{v_2 - v_1}{k}$

35. Which of the following is/are false regarding cathode rays?
   (a) They produce heating effect
   (b) They don't deflect in electric field
   (c) They cast shadow
   (d) They produce fluorescence

36. The ratio of the respective de Broglie wavelengths associated with electrons accelerated from rest with the voltages 100 V, 200 V and 300 V is

(a) 1 : 2 : 3   (b) 1 : 4 : 9   (c) $1 : \dfrac{1}{\sqrt{2}} : \dfrac{1}{\sqrt{3}}$ (d) $1 : \dfrac{1}{2} : \dfrac{1}{3}$

Response Grid	25.ⓐⓑⓒⓓ	26.ⓐⓑⓒⓓ	27.ⓐⓑⓒⓓ	28.ⓐⓑⓒⓓ	29.ⓐⓑⓒⓓ
	30.ⓐⓑⓒⓓ	31.ⓐⓑⓒⓓ	32.ⓐⓑⓒⓓ	33.ⓐⓑⓒⓓ	34.ⓐⓑⓒⓓ
	35.ⓐⓑⓒⓓ	36.ⓐⓑⓒⓓ			

37. A 5 watt source emits monochromatic light of wavelength 5000 Å. When placed 0.5 m away, it liberates photoelectrons from a photosensitive metallic surface. When the source is moved to a distance of 1.0 m, the number of photoelectrons liberated will be reduced by a factor of
(a) 8   (b) 16   (c) 2   (d) 4

38. In the photoeletric effect, electrons are emitted
(a) at a rate that is proportional to the amplitude of the incident radiation
(b) with a maximum velocity proportional to the frequency of the incident radiation
(c) at a rate that is independent of the emitter
(d) only if the frequency of the incident radiations is above a certain threshold value

39. The threshold frequency for a photosensitive metal is 3.3×10^{14} Hz. If light of frequency 8.2×10^{14} Hz is incident on this metal, the cut-off voltage for the photoelectric emission is nearly
(a) 2V   (b) 3V   (c) 5V   (d) 1V

40. In an experiment on photoelectric effect, a student plots stopping potential V_0 against reciprocal of the wavelength λ of the incident light for two different metals A and B. These are shown in the figure.

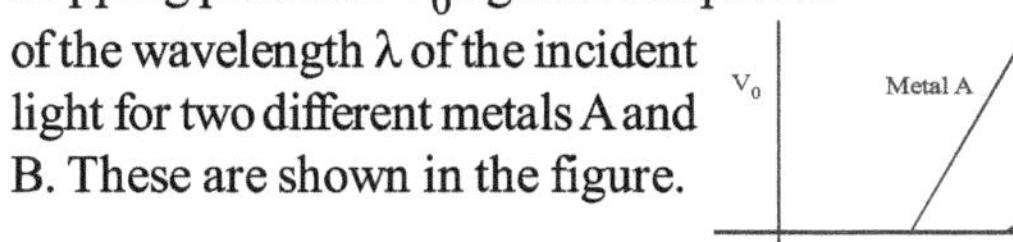

Looking at the graphs, you can most appropriately say that:
(a) Work function of metal B is greater than that of metal A
(b) For light of certain wavelength falling on both metal, maximum kinetic energy of electrons emitted from A will be greater than those emitted from B.

(c) Work function of metal A is greater than that of metal B
(d) Students data is not correct

41. White X-rays are called white due to the fact that
(a) they are electromagnetic radiations having nature same as that of white light.
(b) they are produced most abundantly in X ray tubes.
(c) they have a continuous wavelength range.
(d) they can be converted to visible light using coated screens and photographic plates are affected by them just like light.

42. The wavelength associated with an electron, accelerated through a potential difference of 100 V, is of the order of
(a) 1000 Å   (b) 100 Å   (c) 10.5 Å   (d) 1.2 Å

43. Monochromatic light of frequency 6.0×10^{14} Hz is produced by a laser. The power emitted is 2×10^{-3} w. The number of photons emitted, on the average, by the sources per second is
(a) 5×10^{16} (b) 5×10^{17} (c) 5×10^{14} (d) 5×10^{15}

44. The de-Broglie wavelength of neutron in thermal equilibrium at temperature T is
(a) $\dfrac{30.8}{\sqrt{T}}$ Å   (b) $\dfrac{3.08}{\sqrt{T}}$ Å   (c) $\dfrac{0.308}{\sqrt{T}}$ Å   (d) $\dfrac{0.0308}{\sqrt{T}}$ Å

45. Which of the following cannot be explained on the basis of photoelectric theory?
(a) Instantaneous emission of photoelectrons
(b) Existence of threshold frequency
(c) Sufficiently intense beam of radiation can emit photoelectrons
(d) Existence of stopping potential

RESPONSE GRID					
37.（a）（b）（c）（d）	38.（a）（b）（c）（d）	39.（a）（b）（c）（d）	40.（a）（b）（c）（d）	41.（a）（b）（c）（d）	
42.（a）（b）（c）（d）	43.（a）（b）（c）（d）	44.（a）（b）（c）（d）	45.（a）（b）（c）（d）		

DAILY PRACTICE PROBLEM DPP CHAPTERWISE CP25 - PHYSICS

Total Questions	45	Total Marks	180
Attempted		Correct	
Incorrect		Net Score	
Cut-off Score	45	Qualifying Score	60
Success Gap = Net Score – Qualifying Score			
Net Score = (Correct × 4) – (Incorrect × 1)			

Date :   **Start Time :**   **End Time :**

PHYSICS   CP26

SYLLABUS : Atoms

Max. Marks : 180   **Marking Scheme :** (+4) for correct & (–1) for incorrect answer   **Time : 60 min.**

INSTRUCTIONS : This Daily Practice Problem Sheet contains 45 MCQs. For each question only one option is correct. Darken the correct circle/ bubble in the Response Grid provided on each page.

1. The potential energy associated with an electron in the orbit
   (a) increases with the increases in radii of the orbit
   (b) decreases with the increase in the radii of the orbit
   (c) remains the same with the change in the radii of the orbit
   (d) None of these

2. The diagram shows the energy levels for an electron in a certain atom. Which transition shown represents the emission of a photon with the most energy?

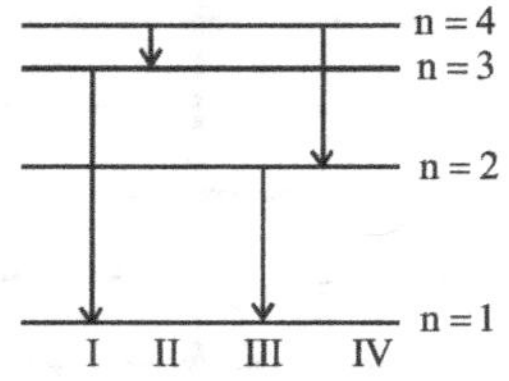

   (a) IV   (b) III   (c) II   (d) I

3. Electrons in a certain energy level $n = n_1$, can emit 3 spectral lines. When they are in another energy level, $n = n_2$. They can emit 6 spectral lines. The orbital speed of the electrons in the two orbits are in the ratio of

   (a) 4 : 3   (b) 3 : 4   (c) 2 : 1   (d) 1 : 2

4. In Rutherford scattering experiment, the number of α-particles scattered at $60°$ is 5×10^6. The number of α-particles scattered at $120°$ will be

   (a) 15×10^6 (b) $\dfrac{3}{5} \times 10^6$

   (c) $\dfrac{5}{9} \times 10^6$ (d) None of these

5. In the Bohr model an electron moves in a circular orbit around the proton. Considering the orbiting electron to be a circular current loop, the magnetic moment of the hydrogen atom, when the electron is in n^{th} excited state, is :

   (a) $\left(\dfrac{e}{2m} \dfrac{n^2 h}{2\pi} \right)$ (b) $\left(\dfrac{e}{m} \right)\dfrac{nh}{2\pi}$

   (c) $\left(\dfrac{e}{2m} \right)\dfrac{nh}{2\pi}$ (d) $\left(\dfrac{e}{m} \right)\dfrac{n^2 h}{2\pi}$

RESPONSE GRID	1. ⓐⓑⓒⓓ	2. ⓐⓑⓒⓓ	3. ⓐⓑⓒⓓ	4. ⓐⓑⓒⓓ	5. ⓐⓑⓒⓓ

Space for Rough Work

6. A 12.5 eV electron beam is used to bombard gaseous hydrogen at room temperature. It will emit :
(a) 2 lines in the Lyman series and 1 line in the Balmar series
(b) 3 lines in the Lyman series
(c) 1 line in the Lyman series and 2 lines in the Balmar series
(d) 3 lines in the Balmer series

7. A Hydrogen atom and a Li^{++} ion are both in the second excited state. If ℓ_H and ℓ_{Li} are their respective electronic angular momenta, and E_H and E_{Li} their respective energies, then
(a) $\ell_H > \ell_{Li}$ and $|E_H| > |E_{Li}|$
(b) $\ell_H = \ell_{Li}$ and $|E_H| < |E_{Li}|$
(c) $\ell_H = \ell_{Li}$ and $|E_H| > |E_{Li}|$
(d) $\ell_H < \ell_{Li}$ and $|E_H| < |E_{Li}|$

8. The radius of hydrogen atom in its ground state is 5.3×10^{-11} m. After collision with an electron it is found to have a radius of 21.2×10^{-11} m. What is the principal quantum number n of the final state of the atom
(a) $n = 4$ (b) $n = 2$ (c) $n = 16$ (d) $n = 3$

9. When hydrogen atom is in its first excited level, its radius is
(a) four times its ground state radius
(b) twice
(c) same
(d) half

10. Consider 3rd orbit of He^+ (Helium), using non-relativistic approach, the speed of electron in this orbit will be [given K $= 9 \times 10^9$ constant, Z = 2 and h (Plank's Constant) $= 6.6 \times 10^{-34}$ J s]
(a) 1.46×10^6 m/s   (b) 0.73×10^6 m/s
(c) 3.0×10^8 m/s   (d) 2.92×10^6 m/s

11. An electron in the hydrogen atom jumps from excited state n to the ground state. The wavelength so emitted illuminates a photosensitive material having work function 2.75 eV. If the stopping potential of the photoelectron is 10 V, the value of n is
(a) 3   (b) 4   (c) 5   (d) 2

12. The electron in a hydrogen atom makes a transition from an excited state to the ground state. Which of the following statements is true?
(a) Its kinetic energy increases and its potential energy decreases.
(b) Its kinetic energy decreases, potential energy increases.
(c) Its kinetic and its potential energy increases.
(d) Its kinetic, potential energy decrease.

13. An energy of 24.6 eV is required to remove one of the electrons from a neutral helium atom. The energy in (eV) required to remove both the electrons from a neutral helium atom is
(a) 38.2   (b) 49.2   (c) 51.8   (d) 79.0

14. One of the lines in the emission spectrum of Li^{2+} has the same wavelength as that of the 2nd line of Balmer series in hydrogen spectrum. The electronic transition corresponding to this line is n = 12 → n = x. Find the value of x.
(a) 8   (b) 6   (c) 7   (c) 5

15. If the atom $_{100}Fm^{257}$ follows the Bohr model and the radius of $_{100}Fm^{257}$ is n times the Bohr radius, then find n.
(a) 100   (b) 200   (c) 4   (d) 1/4

16. The energy of He^+ in the ground state is -54.4 eV, then the energy of Li^{++} in the first excited state will be
(a) -30.6 eV   (b) 27.2 eV
(c) -13.6 eV   (d) -27.2 eV

17. If the angular momentum of an electron in an orbit is J then the K.E. of the electron in that orbit is
(a) $\dfrac{J^2}{2mr^2}$ (b) $\dfrac{Jv}{r}$ (c) $\dfrac{J^2}{2m}$ (d) $\dfrac{J^2}{2\pi}$

18. Suppose an electron is attracted towards the origin by a force $\dfrac{k}{r}$ where 'k' is a constant and 'r' is the distance of the electron from the origin. By applying Bohr model to this system, the radius of the nth orbital of the electron is found to be 'r_n' and the kinetic energy of the electron to be 'T_n'. Then which of the following is true?
(a) $T_n \propto \dfrac{1}{n^2}, r_n \propto n^2$ (b) T_n independent of n, $r_n \propto n$
(c) $T_n \propto \dfrac{1}{n}, r_n \propto n$ (d) $T_n \propto \dfrac{1}{n}, r_n \propto n^2$

19. In Hydrogen spectrum, the wavelength of H_α line is 656 nm, whereas in the spectrum of a distant galaxy, H_α line wavelength is 706 nm. Estimated speed of the galaxy with respect to earth is
(a) 2×10^8 m/s   (b) 2×10^7 m/s
(c) 2×10^6 m/s   (d) 2×10^5 m/s

20. In the hydrogen atom, an electron makes a transition from n = 2 to n = 1. The magnetic field produced by the circulating electron at the nucleus
(a) decreases 16 times   (b) increases 4 times
(c) decreases 4 times   (d) increases 32 times

21. What is the radius of iodine atom (At. no. 53, mass no. 126)
(a) 2.5×10^{-11} m   (b) 2.5×10^{-9} m
(c) 7×10^{-9} m   (d) 7×10^{-6} m

22. When an α-particle of mass 'm' moving with velocity 'v' bombards on a heavy nucleus of charge 'Ze', its distance of closest approach from the nucleus depends on m as :
(a) $\dfrac{1}{m}$ (b) $\dfrac{1}{\sqrt{m}}$ (c) $\dfrac{1}{m^2}$ (d) m

23. The ionization energy of the electron in the hydrogen atom in its ground state is 13.6 eV. The atoms are excited to higher energy levels to emit radiations of 6 wavelengths. Maximum wavelength of emitted radiation corresponds to the transition between
    (a) $n = 3$ to $n = 1$ states (b) $n = 2$ to $n = 1$ states
    (c) $n = 4$ to $n = 3$ states (d) $n = 3$ to $n = 2$ states

24. The wavelengths involved in the spectrum of deuterium $\left(\begin{smallmatrix}2\\1\end{smallmatrix}D\right)$ are slightly different from that of hydrogen spectrum, because
    (a) the size of the two nuclei are different
    (b) the nuclear forces are different in the two cases
    (c) the masses of the two nuclei are different
    (d) the attraction between the electron and the nucleus is differernt in the two cases

25. An electron in hydrogen atom makes a transition $n_1 \rightarrow n_2$ where n_1 and n_2 are principal quantum numbers of the two states. Assuming Bohr's model to be valid the time period of the electron in the initial state is eight times that in the final state. The possible values of n_1 and n_2 are
    (a) $n_1 = 4$ and $n_2 = 2$ (b) $n_1 = 6$ and $n_2 = 2$
    (c) $n_1 = 8$ and $n_2 = 1$ (d) $n_1 = 8$ and $n_2 = 2$

26. Ina hydrogen like atom electronmake transition from an energy level with quantum number n to another with quantum number $(n-1)$. If $n \gg 1$, the frequency of radiation emitted is proportional to :
    (a) $\dfrac{1}{n}$ (b) $\dfrac{1}{n^2}$ (c) $\dfrac{1}{n^{3/2}}$ (d) $\dfrac{1}{n^3}$

27. The spectrum obtained from a sodium vapour lamp is an example of
    (a) band spectrum
    (b) continuous spectrum
    (c) emission spectrum
    (d) absorption spectrum

28. Ionization potential of hydrogen atom is 13.6eV. Hydrogen atoms in the ground state are excited by monochromatic radiation of photon energy 12.1 eV. According to Bohr's theory, the spectral lines emitted by hydrogen will be
    (a) three (b) four (c) one (d) two

29. The Bohr model of atoms
    (a) predicts the same emission spectra for all types of atoms
    (b) assumes that the angular momentum of electrons is quantised
    (c) uses Einstein's photoelectric equation
    (d) predicts continuous emission spectra for atoms

30. The largest wavelength in the ultraviolet region of the hydrogen spectrum is 122 nm. The smallest wavelength in the infrared region of the hydrogen spectrum (to the nearest integer) is
    (a) 802 nm (b) 823 nm (c) 1882 nm (d) 1648 nm

31. A doubly ionised Li atom is excited from its ground state($n = 1$) to $n = 3$ state. The wavelengths of the spectral lines are given by λ_{32}, λ_{31} and λ_{21}. The ratio $\lambda_{32}/\lambda_{31}$ and $\lambda_{21}/\lambda_{31}$ are, respectively
    (a) 8.1, 0.67 (b) 8.1, 1.2
    (c) 6.4, 1.2   (d) 6.4, 0.67

32. In Rutherford scattering experiment, what will be the correct angle for α-scattering for an impact parameter, $b = 0$?
    (a) 90° (b) 270° (c) 0° (d) 180°

33. Consider 3rd orbit of He^+ (Helium), using non-relativistic approach, the speed of electron in this orbit will be [given $K = 9 \times 10^9$ constant, $Z = 2$ and h (Plank's Constant) $= 6.6 \times 10^{-34}$ J s]
    (a) 1.46×10^6 m/s   (b) 0.73×10^6 m/s
    (c) 3.0×10^8 m/s   (d) 2.92×10^6 m/s

34. The ionization energy of hydrogen atom is 13.6 eV. Following Bohr's theory, the energy corresponding to a transition between 3rd and 4th orbit is
    (a) 3.40 eV (b) 1.51 eV (c) 0.85 eV (d) 0.66 eV

35. The transition from the state $n = 3$ to $n = 1$ in a hydrogen like atom results in ultraviolet radiation. Infrared radiation will be obtained in the transition from :
    (a) $2 \rightarrow 1$ (b) $3 \rightarrow 2$ (c) $4 \rightarrow 2$ (d) $4 \rightarrow 3$

36. Given the value of Rydberg constant is 10^7m^{-1}, the wave number of the last line of the Balmer series in hydrogen spectrum will be :
    (a) $0.025 \times 10^4 \text{m}^{-1}$ (b) $0.5 \times 10^7 \text{m}^{-1}$
    (c) $0.25 \times 10^7 \text{m}^{-1}$ (d) $2.5 \times 10^7 \text{m}^{-1}$

37. Which of the plots shown in the figure represents speed (v_n) of the electron in a hydrogen atom as a function of the principal quantum number (n)?

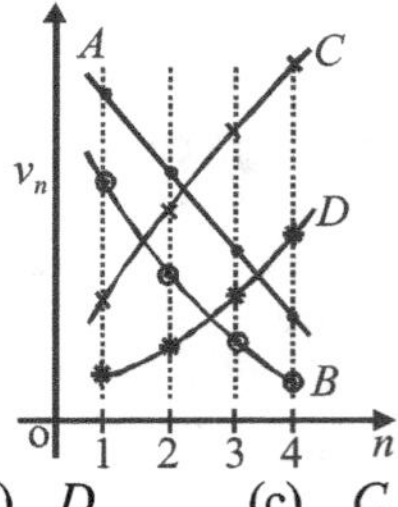

    (a) B (b) D (c) C (d) A

RESPONSE GRID	23. (a)(b)(c)(d)	24. (a)(b)(c)(d)	25. (a)(b)(c)(d)	26. (a)(b)(c)(d)	27. (a)(b)(c)(d)
	28. (a)(b)(c)(d)	29. (a)(b)(c)(d)	30. (a)(b)(c)(d)	31. (a)(b)(c)(d)	32. (a)(b)(c)(d)
	33. (a)(b)(c)(d)	34. (a)(b)(c)(d)	35. (a)(b)(c)(d)	36. (a)(b)(c)(d)	37. (a)(b)(c)(d)

38. The ionisation potential of H-atom is 13.6 V. When it is excited from ground state by monochromatic radiations of 970.6 Å, the number of emission lines will be (according to Bohr's theory)
(a) 10   (b) 8   (c) 6   (d) 4

39. The energy of hydrogen atom in nth orbit is E_n, then the energy in nth orbit of single ionised helium atom will be
(a) $4E_n$ (b) $E_n/4$ (c) $2E_n$ (d) $E_n/2$

40. In the Rutherford experiment, α-particles are scattered from a nucleus as shown. Out of the four paths, which path is not possible?

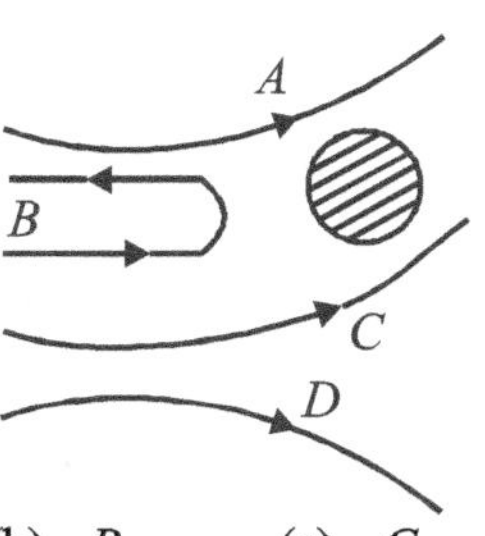

(a) D (b) B (c) C (d) A

41. An electron changes its position from orbit $n = 2$ to the orbit $n = 4$ of an atom. The wavelength of the emitted radiations is (R = Rydberg's constant)
(a) $\dfrac{16}{R}$ (b) $\dfrac{16}{3R}$ (c) $\dfrac{16}{5R}$ (d) $\dfrac{16}{7R}$

42. In a Rutherford scattering experiment when a projectile of charge Z_1 and mass M_1 approaches a target nucleus of charge Z_2 and mass M_2, the distance of closest approach is r_0. The energy of the projectile is
(a) directly proportional to $Z_1 Z_2$
(b) inversely proportional to Z_1
(c) directly proportional to mass M_1
(d) directly proportional to $M_1 \times M_2$

43. The wavelength of the first spectral line in the Balmer series of hydrogen atom is 6561 A°. The wavelength of the second spectral line in the Balmer series of singly-ionized helium atom is
(a) 1215 Å   (b) 1640 Å   (c) 2430 Å   (d) 4687 Å

44. If υ_1 is the frequency of the series limit of Lyman series, υ_2 is the frequency of the first line of Lyman series and υ_3 is the frequency of the series limit of the Balmer series then
(a) $\upsilon_1 - \upsilon_2 = \upsilon_3$ (b) $\upsilon_1 = \upsilon_2 - \upsilon_3$
(c) $\dfrac{1}{\upsilon_2} = \dfrac{1}{\upsilon_1} + \dfrac{1}{\upsilon_3}$ (d) $\dfrac{1}{\upsilon_1} = \dfrac{1}{\upsilon_2} + \dfrac{1}{\upsilon_3}$

45. In a hypothetical Bohr hydrogen atom, the mass of the electron is doubled. The energy E'_0 and radius r'_0 of the first orbit will be (r_0 is the Bohr radius)
(a) -11.2 eV   (b) -6.8 eV   (c) -13.6 eV   (d) -27.2 eV

RESPONSE GRID					
	38. ⓐⓑⓒⓓ	39. ⓐⓑⓒⓓ	40. ⓐⓑⓒⓓ	41. ⓐⓑⓒⓓ	42. ⓐⓑⓒⓓ
	43. ⓐⓑⓒⓓ	44. ⓐⓑⓒⓓ	45. ⓐⓑⓒⓓ		

DAILY PRACTICE PROBLEM DPP CHAPTERWISE CP26 - PHYSICS

Total Questions	45	Total Marks	180
Attempted		Correct	
Incorrect		Net Score	
Cut-off Score	50	Qualifying Score	70
Success Gap = Net Score − Qualifying Score			
Net Score = (Correct × 4) − (Incorrect × 1)			

Date :   Start Time :   End Time :

PHYSICS $\boxed{\text{CP27}}$

SYLLABUS : Nuclei

Max. Marks : 180   **Marking Scheme :** (+4) for correct & (–1) for incorrect answer   **Time : 60 min.**

INSTRUCTIONS : This Daily Practice Problem Sheet contains 45 MCQs. For each question only one option is correct. Darken the correct circle/ bubble in the Response Grid provided on each page.

1. The mass of a $^{7}_{3}Li$ nucleus is 0.042 u less than the sum of the masses of all its nucleons. The binding energy per nucleon of $^{7}_{3}Li$ nucleus is nearly
   - (a) 46 MeV
   - (b) 5.6 MeV
   - (c) 3.9 MeV
   - (d) 23 MeV

2. In the nuclear decay given below:
   $$^{A}_{Z}X \longrightarrow {}^{A}_{Z+1}Y \longrightarrow {}^{A-4}_{Z-1}B^{*} \longrightarrow {}^{A-4}_{Z-1}B,$$
   the particles emitted in the sequence are
   - (a) γ, β, α
   - (b) β, γ, α
   - (c) α, β, γ
   - (d) β, α, γ

3. If the nuclear radius of ^{27}Al is 3.6 Fermi, the approximate nuclear radius of ^{64}Cu in Fermi is :
   - (a) 2.4
   - (b) 1.2
   - (c) 4.8
   - (d) 3.6

4. Which of the following statements is true for nuclear forces?
   - (a) they obey the inverse square law of distance
   - (b) they obey the inverse third power law of distance
   - (c) they are short range forces
   - (d) they are equal in strength to electromagnetic forces.

5. A radioactive sample at any instant has its disintegration rate 5000 disintegrations per minute. After 5 minutes, the rate is 1250 disintegrations per minute. Then, the decay constant (per minute) is
   - (a) $0.4 \ln 2$
   - (b) $0.2 \ln 2$
   - (c) $0.1 \ln 2$
   - (d) $0.8 \ln 2$

6. The radioactivity of a sample is R_1 at a time T_1 and R_2 at a time T_2. If the half-life of the specimen is T, the number of atoms that have disintegrated in the time $(T_1 - T_2)$ is proportional to
   - (a) $(R_1 T_1 - R_2 T_2)$
   - (b) $(R_1 - R_2)$
   - (c) $(R_1 - R_2)/T$
   - (d) $(R_1 - R_2)\,T$

7. In the reaction, $^{2}_{1}H + {}^{3}_{1}H \longrightarrow {}^{4}_{2}He + {}^{1}_{0}n$, if the binding energies of $^{2}_{1}H$, $^{3}_{1}H$ and $^{4}_{2}He$ are respectively, a, b and c (in MeV), then the energy (in MeV) released in this reaction is
   - (a) $a+b+c$
   - (b) $a+b-c$
   - (c) $c-a-b$
   - (d) $c+a-b$

8. If M (A; Z), M_p and M_n denote the masses of the nucleus $^{A}_{Z}X$, proton and neutron respectively in units of u ($1u = 931.5$ MeV/c^2) and BE represents its bonding energy in MeV, then
   - (a) $M(A, Z) = ZM_p + (A - Z)M_n - BE/c^2$
   - (b) $M(A, Z) = ZM_p + (A-Z)M_n + BE$
   - (c) $M(A, Z) = ZM_p + (A - Z)M_n - BE$
   - (d) $M(A, Z) = ZM_p + (A - Z)M_n + BE/c^2$

RESPONSE GRID					
	1. ⓐⓑ©ⓓ	2. ⓐⓑ©ⓓ	3. ⓐⓑ©ⓓ	4. ⓐⓑ©ⓓ	5. ⓐⓑ©ⓓ
	6. ⓐⓑ©ⓓ	7. ⓐⓑ©ⓓ	8. ⓐⓑ©ⓓ		

Space for Rough Work

9. How does the binding energy per nucleon vary with the increase in the number of nucleons?
   (a) Increases continuously with mass number
   (b) Decreases continuously with mass number
   (c) First decreases and then increases with increase in mass number
   (d) First increases and then decreases with increase in mass number

10. The energy spectrum of β-particles [Number N(E) as a function of β-energy E] emitted from a radioactive source is

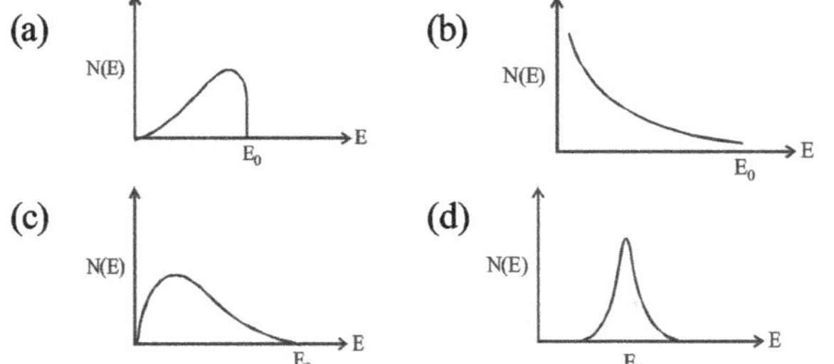

11. A radioactive nucleus undergoes a series of decay according to the scheme

$$A \xrightarrow{a} A_1 \xrightarrow{\beta} A_2 \xrightarrow{\alpha} A_3 \xrightarrow{\gamma} A_4$$

If the mass number and atomic number of 'A' are 180 and 72 respectively, then what are these numbers for A_4
   (a) 172 and 69   (b) 174 and 70
   (c) 176 and 69   (d) 176 and 70

12. The activity of a radioactive sample is measured as 9750 counts per minute at $t = 0$ and as 975 counts per minute at $t = 5$ minutes. The decay constant is approximately
   (a) 0.922 per minute   (b) 0.691 per minute
   (c) 0.461 per minute   (d) 0.230 per minute

13. Actinium 231, $^{231}AC_{89}$, emit in succession two β particles, four α-particles, one β and one α plus several γ rays. What is the resultant isotope?
   (a) $^{221}Au_{79}$ (b) $^{211}Au_{79}$
   (c) $^{221}Pb_{82}$ (d) $^{211}Pb_{82}$

14. Fusion reactions take place at high temperature because
   (a) atoms are ionised at high temperature
   (b) molecules break up at high temperature
   (c) nuclei break up at high temperature
   (d) kinetic energy is high enough to overcome repulsion between nuclei

15. If M_O is the mass of an oxygen isotope $_8O^{17}$, M_P and M_N are the masses of a proton and a neutron respectively, the nuclear binding energy of the isotope is
   (a) $(M_O - 17M_N)c^2$ (b) $(M_O - 8M_P)c^2$
   (c) $(M_O - 8M_P - 9M_N)c^2$ (d) $M_O c^2$

16. Which of the following nuclear reactions is not possible?
   (a) $^{12}_{6}C + ^{12}_{6}C \longrightarrow ^{20}_{10}Ne + ^{4}_{2}He$
   (b) $^{9}_{4}Be + ^{1}_{1}H \longrightarrow ^{6}_{3}Li + ^{4}_{2}He$
   (c) $^{11}_{5}Be + ^{1}_{1}H \longrightarrow ^{9}_{4}Be + ^{4}_{2}He$
   (d) $^{7}_{3}Li + ^{4}_{2}He \longrightarrow ^{1}_{1}H + ^{10}_{4}B$

17. The ratio of half-life times of two elements A and B is $\dfrac{T_A}{T_B}$. The ratio of respective decay constant $\dfrac{\lambda_A}{\lambda_B}$, is
   (a) T_B / T_A (b) T_A / T_B
   (c) $\dfrac{T_A + T_B}{T_A}$ (d) $\dfrac{T_A - T_B}{T_A}$

18. Two radioactive materials X_1 and X_2 have decay constants 10λ and λ respectively. If initially they have the same number of nuclei, then the ratio of the number of nuclei of X_1 to that of X_2 will be 1/e after a time
   (a) $1/10\lambda$ (b) $1/11\lambda$
   (c) $11/10\lambda$ (d) $1/9\lambda$

19. In a radioactive material the activity at time t_1 is R_1 and at a later time t_2, it is R_2. If the decay constant of the material is λ, then
   (a) $R_1 = R_2 e^{\lambda(t_1 - t_2)}$ (b) $R_1 = R_2 e^{(t_2 / t_1)}$
   (c) $R_1 = R_2$ (d) $R_1 = R_2 e^{-\lambda(t_1 - t_2)}$

20. The correct relation between t_{av} = average life and $t_{1/2}$ = half life for a radioactive nuclei.
   (a) $t_{av} = t_{1/2}$ (b) $t_{av} = \dfrac{1}{2} t_{1/2}$
   (c) $0.693\, t_{av} = t_{1/2}$ (d) $t_{av} = 0.693\, t_{1/2}$

21. If the nuclear force between two protons, two neutrons and between proton and neutron is denoted by F_{pp}, F_{nn} and F_{pn} respectively, then
   (a) $F_{pp} \approx F_{nn} \approx F_{pn}$ (b) $F_{pp} \neq F_{nn}$ and $F_{pp} = F_{nn}$
   (c) $F_{pp} = F_{nn} = F_{pn}$ (d) $F_{pp} \neq F_{nn} \neq F_{pn}$

22. Which one is correct about fission?
   (a) Approx. 0.1% mass converts into energy
   (b) Most of energy of fission is in the form of heat
   (c) In a fission of U^{235} about 200 eV energy is released
   (d) On an average, one neutron is released per fission of U^{235}

Space for Rough Work

23. If 200 MeV energy is released in the fission of a single U^{235} nucleus, the number of fissions required per second to produce 1 kilowatt power shall be (Given $1\,eV = 1.6 \times 10^{-19}$ J)
  (a) 3.125×10^{13} (b) 3.125×10^{14}
  (c) 3.125×10^{15} (d) 3.125×10^{16}

24. In any fission process, the ratio of

$$\frac{\text{mass of fission products}}{\text{mass of parent nucleus}}\ \text{is}$$

  (a) equal to 1
  (b) greater than 1
  (c) less than 1
  (d) depends on the mass of the parent nucleus

25. In an α-decay the kinetic energy of α-particle is 48 MeV and Q-value of the reaction is 50 MeV. The mass number of the mother nucleus is X. Find value of X/25.
  (Assume that daughter nucleus is in ground state)
  (a) 2   (b) 4   (c) 6   (d) 8

26. A sample of radioactive element has a mass of 10gm at an instant $t=0$. The approximate mass of this element in the sample after two mean lives is
  (a) 6.30 gm   (b) 1.35 gm
  (c) 2.50 gm   (d) 3.70 gm

27. Consider a radioactive material of half-life 1.0 minute. If one of the nuclei decays now, the next one will decay
  (a) after 1 minute
  (b) after $\dfrac{1}{\log_e 2}$ minute
  (c) after $\dfrac{1}{N}$ minute, where N is the number of nuclei present at that moment
  (d) after any time

28. The mass of α-particle is
  (a) less than the sum of masses of two protons and two neutrons
  (b) equal to mass of four protons
  (c) equal to mass of four neutrons
  (d) equal to sum of masses of two protons and two neutron

29. The decay constants of a radioactive substance for α and β emission are λ_α and λ_β respectively. If the substance emits α and β simultaneously, then the average half life of the material will be
  (a) $\dfrac{2T_\alpha T_\beta}{T_\alpha + T_\beta}$ (b) $T_\alpha + T_\beta$
  (c) $\dfrac{T_\alpha T_\beta}{T_\alpha + T_\beta}$ (d) $\dfrac{1}{2}\left(T_\alpha + T_\beta\right)$

30. If the end A of a wire is irradiated with α-rays and the other end B is irradiated with β-rays. Then
  (a) a current will flow from A to B
  (b) a current will flow from B to A
  (c) there will be no current in the wire
  (d) a current will flow from each end to the mid-point of the wire

31. A radioactive nucleus of mass M emits a photon of frequency ν and the nucleus recoils. The recoil energy will be
  (a) $Mc^2 - h\nu$ (b) $h^2\nu^2 / 2Mc^2$
  (c) zero   (d) $h\nu$

32. Radioactive element decays to form a stable nuclide. The rate of decay of reactant is correctly depicted by

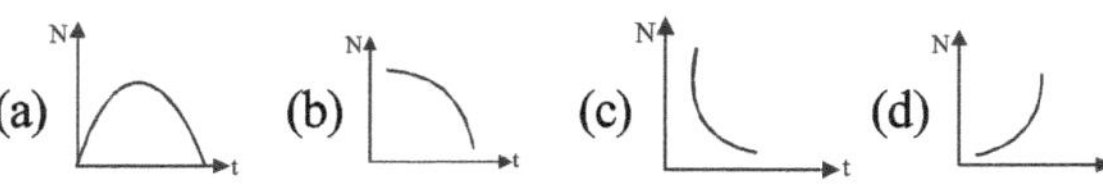

33. A nucleus of mass $M + \Delta m$ is at rest and decays into two daughter nuclei of equal mass $\dfrac{M}{2}$ each. Speed of light is c. The speed of daughter nuclei is
  (a) $c\,\dfrac{\Delta m}{M + \Delta m}$ (b) $c\sqrt{\dfrac{2\Delta m}{M}}$ (c) $c\sqrt{\dfrac{\Delta m}{M}}$ (d) $c\sqrt{\dfrac{\Delta m}{M + \Delta m}}$

34. Atomic weight of Boron is 10.81 and it has two isotopes $_5B^{10}$ and $_5B^{11}$. Then the ratio $_5B^{10} :_5 B^{11}$ in nature would be
  (a) $19:81$ (b) $10:11$ (c) $15:16$ (d) $81:19$

35. A nucleus ruptures into two nuclear parts, which have their velocity ratio equal to 2:1. What will be the ratio of their nuclear size (nuclear radius)?
  (a) $2^{1/3}:1$ (b) $1:2^{1/3}$ (c) $3^{1/2}:1$ (d) $1:3^{1/2}$

36. A nucleus of uranium decays at rest into nuclei of thorium and helium. Then :
  (a) the helium nucleus has less momentum than the thorium nucleus.
  (b) the helium nucleus has more momentum than the thorium nucleus.
  (c) the helium nucleus has less kinetic energy than the thorium nucleus.
  (d) the helium nucleus has more kinetic energy than the thorium nucleus.

37. If radius of the $_{12}^{27}$Al nucleus is taken to be R_{Al}, then the radius of $_{53}^{125}$Te nucleus is nearly:
  (a) $\dfrac{5}{3}R_{Al}$ (b) $\dfrac{3}{5}R_{Al}$ (c) $\left(\dfrac{13}{53}\right)^{1/3}R_{Al}$ (d) $\left(\dfrac{53}{13}\right)^{1/3}R_{Al}$

RESPONSE GRID	23. ⓐⓑⓒⓓ	24. ⓐⓑⓒⓓ	25. ⓐⓑⓒⓓ	26. ⓐⓑⓒⓓ	27. ⓐⓑⓒⓓ
	28. ⓐⓑⓒⓓ	28. ⓐⓑⓒⓓ	29. ⓐⓑⓒⓓ	30. ⓐⓑⓒⓓ	31. ⓐⓑⓒⓓ
	32. ⓐⓑⓒⓓ	33. ⓐⓑⓒⓓ	34. ⓐⓑⓒⓓ	35. ⓐⓑⓒⓓ	36. ⓐⓑⓒⓓ
	37. ⓐⓑⓒⓓ				

38. M_n and M_p represent mass of neutron and proton respectively. If an element having atomic mass M has N-neutron and Z-proton, then the correct relation will be
(a) $M < [NM_n + ZM_p]$
(b) $M > [NM_n + ZM_p]$
(c) $M = [NM_n + ZM_p]$
(d) $M = N[M_n + M_p]$

39. After 300 days, the activity of a radioactive sample is 5000 dps (disintegrations per sec). The activity becomes 2500 dps after another 150 days. The initial activity of the sample in dps is
(a) 20,000
(b) 10,000
(c) 7,000
(d) 25,000

40. Order of magnitude of density of uranium nucleus is ($m_p = 1.67 \times 10^{-27}$ kg)
(a) 10^{20} kg $/$ m^3
(b) 10^{17} kg $/$ m^3
(c) 10^{14} kg $/$ m^3
(d) 10^{11} kg $/$ m^3

41. The electrons cannot exist inside the nucleus because
(a) de-Broglie wavelength associated with electron in β-decay is much less than the size of nucleus
(b) de-Broglie wavelength associated with electron in β-decay is much greater than the size of nucleus
(c) de-Broglie wavelength associated with electron in β-decay is equal to the size of nucleus
(d) negative charge cannot exist in the nucleus

42. If the total binding energies of $^{2}_{1}$H, $^{4}_{2}$He, $^{56}_{26}$Fe & $^{235}_{92}$U nuclei are 2.22, 28.3, 492 and 1786 MeV respectively, identify the most stable nucleus of the following.
(a) $^{56}_{26}$Fe
(b) $^{2}_{1}$H
(c) $^{235}_{92}$U
(d) $^{4}_{2}$He

43. At a specific instant emission of radioactive compound is deflected in a magnetic field. The compound cannot emit
(a) electrons
(b) protons
(c) He^{2+}
(d) neutrons

44. A nuclear reaction is given by
$$_{Z}X^{A} \rightarrow \,_{Z+1}Y^{A} + _{-1}e^{0} + \bar{\nu}, \text{ represents}$$
(a) fission
(b) β-decay
(c) $\propto$-decay
(d) fusion

45. Radioactive material 'A' has decay constant '8 λ' and material 'B' has decay constant 'λ'. Initially they have same number of nuclei. After what time, the ratio of number of nuclei of material 'B' to that 'A' will be $\dfrac{1}{e}$?
(a) $\dfrac{1}{7\lambda}$
(b) $\dfrac{1}{8\lambda}$
(c) $\dfrac{1}{9\lambda}$
(d) $\dfrac{1}{\lambda}$

RESPONSE GRID					
	38. (a)(b)(c)(d)	39. (a)(b)(c)(d)	40. (a)(b)(c)(d)	41. (a)(b)(c)(d)	42. (a)(b)(c)(d)
	43. (a)(b)(c)(d)	44. (a)(b)(c)(d)	45. (a)(b)(c)(d)		

DAILY PRACTICE PROBLEM DPP CHAPTERWISE CP27 - PHYSICS

Total Questions	45	Total Marks	180
Attempted		Correct	
Incorrect		Net Score	
Cut-off Score	50	Qualifying Score	70
Success Gap = Net Score – Qualifying Score			
Net Score = (Correct × 4) – (Incorrect × 1)			

Space for Rough Work

Date : | Start Time : | End Time :

PHYSICS $\boxed{\text{CP28}}$

SYLLABUS : Semiconductor Electronics: Materials, Devices and Simple Circuits

Max. Marks : 180   **Marking Scheme :** (+4) for correct & (–1) for incorrect answer   **Time : 60 min.**

INSTRUCTIONS : This Daily Practice Problem Sheet contains 45 MCQs. For each question only one option is correct. Darken the correct circle/ bubble in the Response Grid provided on each page.

1. A change of 8.0 mA in the emitter current bring a change of 7.9 mA in the collector current. The values of parameters α and β are respectively
   (a) 0.99, 90 (b) 0.96, 79 (c) 0.97, 99 (d) 0.99, 79

2. A pure semiconductor has equal electron and hole concentration of 10^{16} m^{-3}. Doping by indium increases number of hole concentration n_h to 5×10^{22} m^{-3}. Then, the value of number of electron concentration n_e in the doped semiconductor is
   (a) $10^6/m^3$ (b) $10^{22}/m^3$
   (c) $2 \times 10^6/m^3$ (d) $2 \times 10^9/m^3$

3. For LED's to emit light in visible region of electromagnetic light, it should have energy band gap in the range of:
   (a) 0.1 eV to 0.4 eV (b) 0.5 eV to 0.8 eV
   (c) 0.9 eV to 1.6 eV (d) 1.7 eV to 3.0 eV

4. A common emitter amplifier has a voltage gain of 50, an input impedance of 100Ω and an output impedance of 200Ω. The power gain of the amplifier is
   (a) 1000 (b) 1250 (c) 100 (d) 500

5. Which logic gate with inputs A and B performs the same operation as that performed by the following circuit?

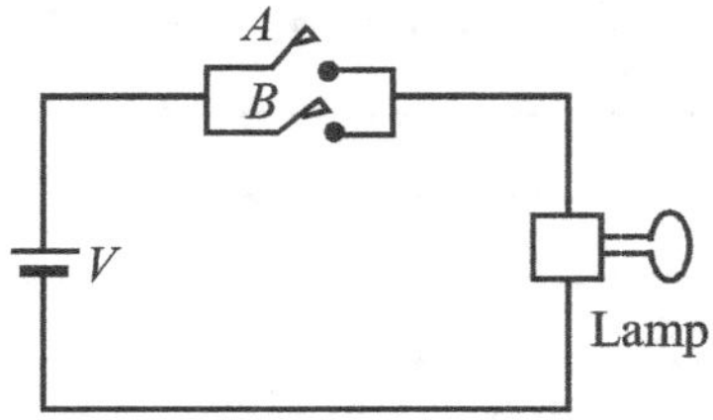

   (a) NAND gate (b) OR gate
   (c) NOR gate (d) AND gate

6. In an unbiased p-n junction, holes diffuse from the p-region to n-region because of
   (a) the potential difference across the p-n junction
   (b) the attraction of free electrons of n-region
   (c) the higher hole concentration in p-region than that in n-region
   (d) the higher concentration of electrons in the n-region than that in the p-region

7. A silicon diode has a threshold voltage of 0.7 V. If an input voltage given by $2 \sin(\pi t)$ is supplied to a half wave rectifier circuit using this diode, the rectified output has a peak value of
   (a) 2V (b) 1.4V (c) 1.3V (d) 0.7V

RESPONSE GRID

1. (a)(b)(c)(d) 2. (a)(b)(c)(d) 3. (a)(b)(c)(d) 4. (a)(b)(c)(d) 5. (a)(b)(c)(d)
6. (a)(b)(c)(d) 7. (a)(b)(c)(d)

Space for Rough Work

8. The current gain for a transistor working as common-base amplifier is 0.96. If the emitter current is 7.2 mA, then the base current is
(a) 0.29 mA (b) 0.35 mA (c) 0.39 mA (d) 0.43 mA

9. In a npn transistor 10^{10} electrons enter the emitter in 10^{-6} s. 4% of the electrons are lost in the base. The current transfer ratio will be
(a) 0.98 (b) 0.97 (c) 0.96 (d) 0.94

10. Assuming that the silicon diode having resistance of 20 Ω, the current through the diode is (knee voltage 0.7 V)

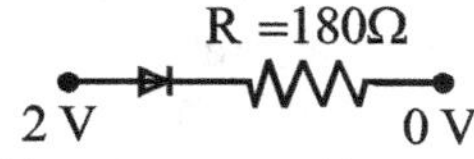

(a) 0 mA (b) 10 mA (c) 6.5 mA (d) 13.5 mA

11. Transfer characteristics [output voltage (V_0) vs input voltage (V_i)] for a base biased transistor in CE configuration is as shown in the figure. For using transistor as a switch, it is used 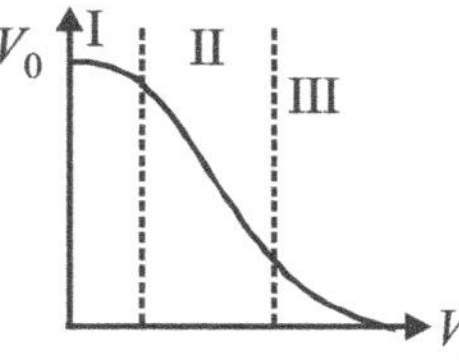
(a) in region III
(b) both in region (I) and (III)
(c) in region II
(d) in region (I)

12. A half-wave rectifier is being used to rectify an alternating voltage of frequency 50 Hz. The number of pulses of rectified current obtained in one second is
(a) 50 (b) 25 (c) 100 (d) 2000

13. A diode having potential difference 0.5 V across its junction which does not depend on current, is connected in series with resistance of 20Ω across source. If 0.1 A current passes through resistance then what is the voltage of the source?
(a) 1.5 V (b) 2.0 V (c) 2.5 V (d) 5 V

14. In common emitter amplifier, the current gain is 62. The collector resistance and input resistance are 5 kΩ an 500Ω respectively. If the input voltage is 0.01V, the output voltage is
(a) 0.62 V (b) 6.2 V (c) 62 V (d) 620 V

15. On doping germanium with donor atoms of density 10^{17} cm^{-3} its conductivity in mho/cm will be
[Given : $\mu_e = 3800$ cm^2/V–s and $n_i = 2.5 \times 10^{13}$ cm^{-13}]
(a) 30.4 (b) 60.8 (c) 91.2 (d) 121.6

16. The voltage gain of an amplifier with 9% negative feedback is 10. The voltage gain without feedback will be
(a) 90 (b) 10 (c) 1.25 (d) 100

17. A system of four gates is set up as shown. The 'truth table' corresponding to this system is :

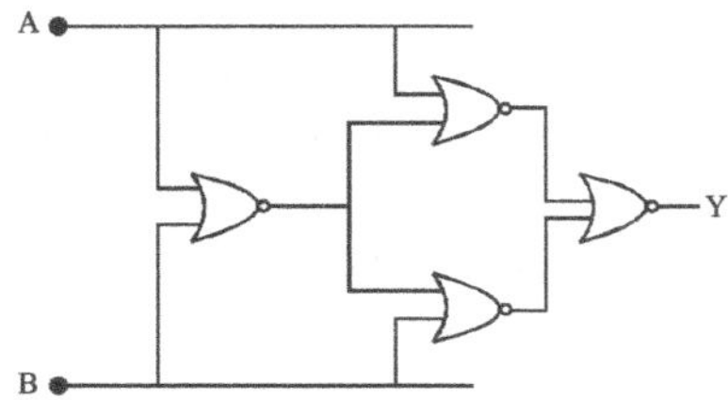

(a)

A	B	Y
0	0	1
0	1	0
1	0	0
1	1	1

(b)

A	B	Y
0	0	0
0	1	0
1	0	1
1	1	0

(c)

A	B	Y
0	0	1
0	1	0
1	0	1
1	1	0

(d)

A	B	Y
0	0	1
0	1	1
1	0	0
1	1	0

18. The intrinsic conductivity of germanium at 27° is 2.13 mho m^{-1} and mobilities of electrons and holes are 0.38 and 0.18 m^{2}V^{-1}s^{-1} respectively. The density of charge carriers is
(a) 2.37×10^{19} m^{-3} (b) 3.28×10^{19} m^{-3}
(c) 7.83×10^{19} m^{-3} (d) 8.47×10^{19} m^{-3}

19. The logic circuit shown below has the input waveforms 'A' and 'B' as shown. Pick out the correct output waveform

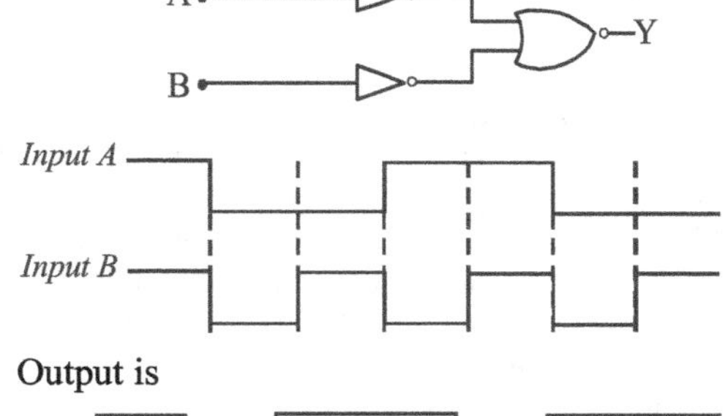

Output is

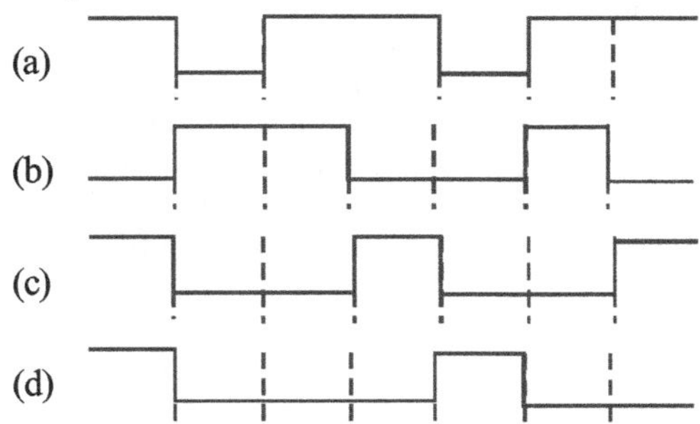

20. Pure Si at 500K has equal number of electron (n_e) and hole (n_h) concentrations of 1.5×10^{16} m^{-3}. Doping by indium increases n_h to 4.5×10^{22} m^{-3}. The doped semiconductor is of
(a) n–type with electron concentration $n_e = 5 \times 10^{22}$ m^{-3}
(b) p–type with electron concentration $n_e = 2.5 \times 10^{10}$ m^{-3}
(c) n–type with electron concentration $n_e = 2.5 \times 10^{23}$ m^{-3}
(d) p–type having electron concentration $n_e = 5 \times 10^9$ m^{-3}

21. Which of the following statements is incorrect?
(a) The resistance of intrinsic semiconductors decrease with increase of temperature
(b) Doping pure Si with trivalent impurities give p-type semiconductors
(c) The majority carriers in n-type semiconductors are holes
(d) A p-n junction can act as a semiconductor diode

22. The relation between number of free electrons (n) in a semiconductor and temperature (T) is given by

  (a) $n \propto T$ (b) $n \propto T^2$ (c) $n \propto \sqrt{T}$ (d) $n \propto T^{3/2}$

23. If a PN junction diode of depletion layer width W and barrier height V_0 is forward biased, then
  (a) W increases, V_0 decreases
  (b) W decreases, V_0 increases
  (c) both W and V_0 increase
  (d) both W and V_0 decrease

24. The circuit has two oppositively connected ideal diodes in parallel. The current flowing in the circuit is

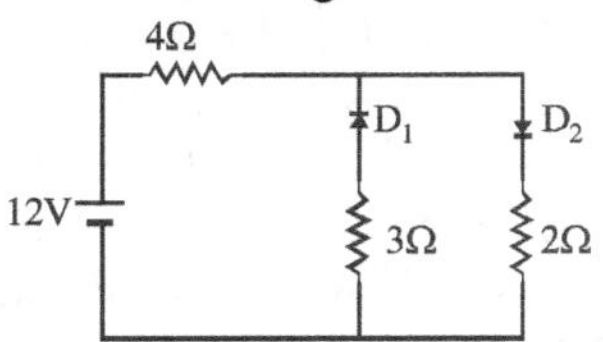

  (a) 1.71 A   (b) 2.00 A   (c) 2.31 A   (d) 1.33 A

25. For a transistor amplifier in common emitter configuration for load impedance of 1kΩ ($h_{fe} = 50$ and $h_{0e} = 25$) the current gain is
  (a) -24.8 (b) -15.7 (c) -5.2 (d) -48.78

26. A PN-junction has a thickness of the order of
  (a) 1 cm   (b) 1 mm   (c) 10^{-6} m   (d) 10^{-12} cm

27. A working transistor with its three legs marked P, Q and R is tested using a multimeter. No conduction is found between P and Q. By connecting the common (negative) terminal of the multimeter to R and the other (positive) terminal to P or Q, some resistance is seen on the multimeter. Which of the following is true for the transistor?
  (a) It is an npn transistor with R as base
  (b) It is a pnp transistor with R as base
  (c) It is a pnp transistor with R as emitter
  (d) It is an npn transistor with R as collector

28. If in a p-n junction, a square input signal of 10 V is applied as shown, then the output across R_L will be

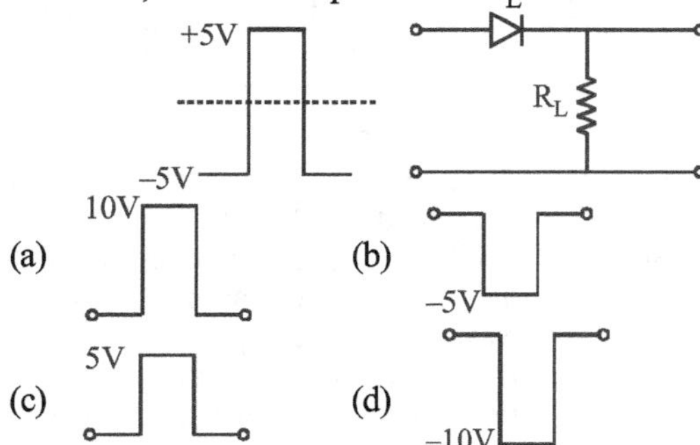

29. When n-type semiconductor is heated
  (a) number of electrons increases while that of holes decreases
  (b) number of holes increases while that of electrons decreases

  (c) number of electrons and holes remain same
  (d) number of electrons and holes increases equally.

30. The ratio of electron and hole currents in a semiconductor is 7/4 and the ratio of drift velocities of electrons and holes is 5/4, then the ratio of concentrations of electrons and holes will be
  (a) 5/7   (b) 7/5   (c) 25/49   (d) 49/25

31. C and Si both have same lattice structure, having 4 bonding electrons in each. However, C is insulator whereas Si is intrinsic semiconductor. This is because :
  (a) In case of C the valence band is not completely filled at absolute zero temperature.
  (b) In case of C the conduction band is partly filled even at absolute zero temperature.
  (c) The four bonding electrons in the case of C lie in the second orbit, whereas in the case of Si they lie in the third.
  (d) The four bonding electrons in the case of C lie in the third orbit, whereas for Si they lie in the fourth orbit.

32. Which one of the following represents forward bias diode ?
  (a) $-4V$ ▷ R ∿∿ $-3V$
  (b) $-2V$ ▷ R ∿∿ $+2V$
  (c) $3V$ ▷ R ∿∿ $5V$
  (d) $0V$ ▷ R ∿∿ $-2V$

33. An oscillator is nothing but an amplifer with
  (a) positive feedback   (b) negative feedback
  (c) large gain   (d) no feedback

34. The current gain in the common emitter mode of a transistor is 10. The input impedance is 20kΩ and load of resistance is 100kΩ. The power gain is
  (a) 300   (b) 500   (c) 200   (d) 100

35. The input signal given to a CE amplifier having a voltage gain of 150 is $V_i = 2 \cos\left(15t + \dfrac{\pi}{3}\right)$. The corresponding output signal will be :
  (a) $75 \cos\left(15t + \dfrac{2\pi}{3}\right)$ (b) $2 \cos\left(15t + \dfrac{5\pi}{6}\right)$
  (c) $300 \cos\left(15t + \dfrac{4\pi}{3}\right)$ (d) $300 \cos\left(15t + \dfrac{\pi}{3}\right)$

36. To use a transistor as an amplifier
  (a) the emitter base junction is forward biased and the base collector junction is reverse biased
  (b) no bias voltage is required
  (c) both junctions are forward biased
  (d) both junctions are reverse biased.

RESPONSE GRID	22. ⓐⓑⓒⓓ	23. ⓐⓑⓒⓓ	24. ⓐⓑⓒⓓ	25. ⓐⓑⓒⓓ	26. ⓐⓑⓒⓓ
	27. ⓐⓑⓒⓓ	28. ⓐⓑⓒⓓ	29. ⓐⓑⓒⓓ	30. ⓐⓑⓒⓓ	31. ⓐⓑⓒⓓ
	32. ⓐⓑⓒⓓ	33. ⓐⓑⓒⓓ	34. ⓐⓑⓒⓓ	35. ⓐⓑⓒⓓ	36. ⓐⓑⓒⓓ

Space for Rough Work

37. A piece of copper and another of germanium are cooled from room temperature to 77K. The resistance of
  (a) copper increases and germanium decreases
  (b) each of them decreases
  (c) each of them increases
  (d) copper decreases and germanium increases

38. A d.c. battery of V volt is connected to a series combination of a resistor R and an ideal diode D as shown in the figure below. The potential difference across R will be

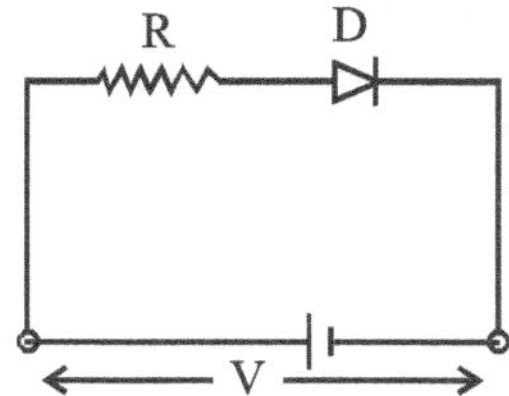

  (a) 2V when diode is forward biased
  (b) Zero when diode is forward biased
  (c) 5V when diode is reverse biased
  (d) 6V when diode is forward biased

39. The current gain for a transistor working as common-base amplifier is 0.96. If the emitter current is 7.2 mA, then the base current is
  (a) 0.29 mA (b) 0.35 mA (c) 0.39 mA (d) 0.43 mA

40. In the circuit given below, A and B represent two inputs and C represents the output.

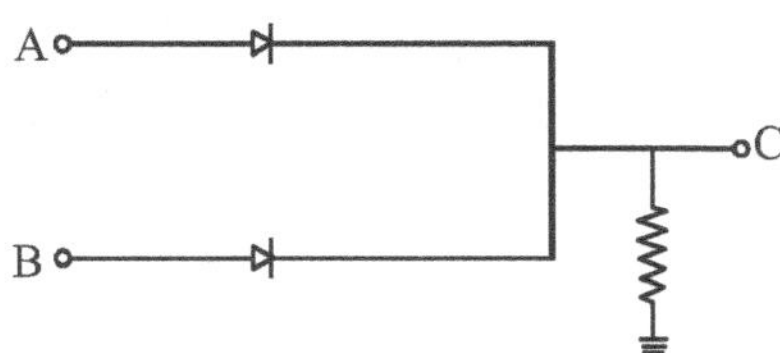

The circuit represents
  (a) NOR gate   (b) AND gate
  (c) NAND gate   (d) OR gate

41. The I-V characteristic of a P-N junction diode is shown below. The approximate dynamic resistance of the p-n junction when a forward bias voltage of 2 volt is applied is

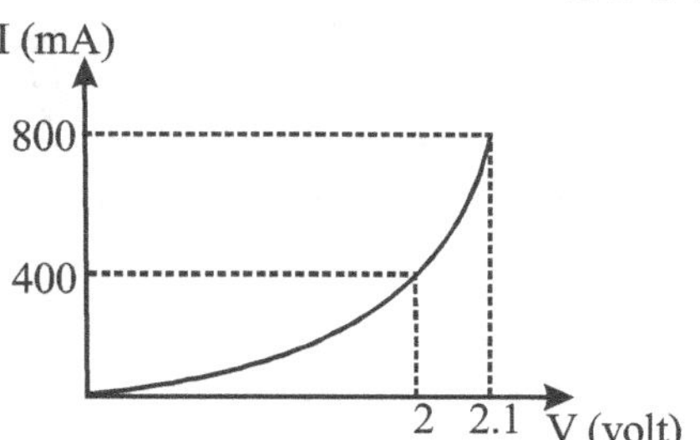

  (a) $1\,\Omega$ (b) $0.25\,\Omega$ (c) $0.5\,\Omega$ (d) $5\,\Omega$

42. The circuit diagram shows a logic combination with the states of outputs X, Y and Z given for inputs P, Q, R and S all at state 1. When inputs P and R change to state 0 with inputs Q and S still at 1, the states of outputs X, Y and Z change to

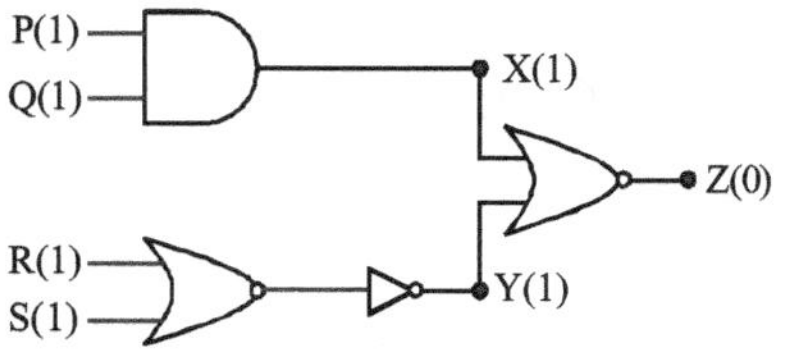

  (a) 1, 0, 0   (b) 1, 1, 1   (c) 0, 1, 0   (d) 0, 0, 1

43. The following configuration of gate is equivalent to

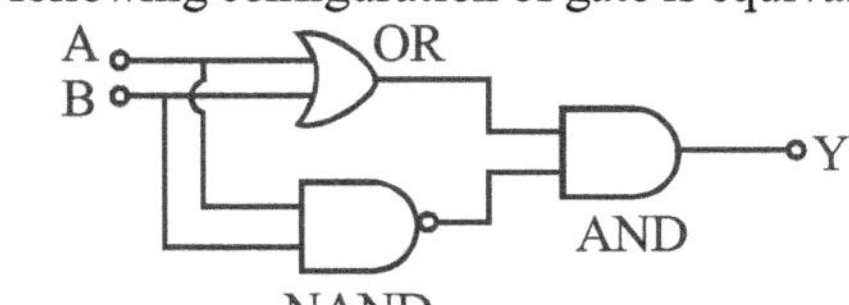

  (a) NAND gate   (b) XOR gate
  (c) OR gate   (d) NOR gate

44. A p-n photodiode is made of a material with a band gap of 2.0 eV. The minimum frequency of the radiation that can be absorbed by the material is nearly
  (a) $10 \times 10^{14}\,Hz$ (b) $5 \times 10^{14}\,Hz$
  (c) $1 \times 10^{14}\,Hz$ (d) $20 \times 10^{14}\,Hz$

45. The average value of output direct current in a full wave rectifier is
  (a) I_0/π (b) $I_0/2$ (c) $\pi I_0/2$ (d) $2I_0/\pi$

RESPONSE GRID					
	37. (a)(b)(c)(d)	38. (a)(b)(c)(d)	39. (a)(b)(c)(d)	40. (a)(b)(c)(d)	41. (a)(b)(c)(d)
	42. (a)(b)(c)(d)	43. (a)(b)(c)(d)	44. (a)(b)(c)(d)	45. (a)(b)(c)(d)	

DAILY PRACTICE PROBLEM DPP CHAPTERWISE CP28 - PHYSICS

Total Questions	45	Total Marks	180
Attempted		Correct	
Incorrect		Net Score	
Cut-off Score	50	Qualifying Score	70
Success Gap = Net Score − Qualifying Score			
Net Score = (Correct × 4) − (Incorrect × 1)			

1. **(b)** In CGS system,

$$d = 4\frac{g}{cm^3}$$

The unit of mass is 100g and unit of length is 10 cm, so

$$density = \frac{4\left(\frac{100g}{100}\right)}{\left(\frac{10}{10}cm\right)^3}$$

$$= \frac{\left(\frac{4}{100}\right)}{\left(\frac{1}{10}\right)^3}\frac{(100g)}{(10cm)^3}$$

$$= \frac{4}{100} \times (10)^3 \cdot \frac{100g}{(10cm)^3}$$

$$= 40 \text{ unit}$$

2. **(a)** $T = P^a D^b S^c$

$M^0 L^0 T^1 = (ML^{-1}T^{-2})^a (ML^{-3})^b (MT^{-2})^c$

$= M^{a+b+c} L^{-a-3b} T^{-2a-2c}$

Applying principle of homogeneity

$a+b+c = 0; \ -a-3b = 0; \ -2a-2c = 1$

on solving, we get $a = -3/2, b = 1/2, c = 1$

3. **(a)** Number of significant figures in $23.023 = 5$
Number of significant figures in $0.0003 = 1$
Number of significant figures in $2.1 \times 10^{-3} = 2$

4. **(a)** $Y = \dfrac{Stress}{Strain} = \dfrac{Force/Area}{Dimensionless} \Rightarrow Y = Pressure.$

5. **(d)** For angular momentum, the dimensional formula is $[ML^2T^{-1}]$. For other three, it is $[ML^2T^{-2}]$.

6. **(c)** $\dfrac{\Delta P}{P} \times 100 = \dfrac{\Delta F}{F} \times 100 + 2\dfrac{\Delta \ell}{\ell} \times 100 = 4\% + 2 \times 2\%$

$$= 8\%$$

7. **(d)** Conductance,

$$G = \frac{1}{resistance} = mho(\Omega^{-1}) \text{ or siemen (S)}$$

8. **(d)** $F \propto v \Rightarrow F = kv \Rightarrow [k] = \left[\dfrac{F}{v}\right] = \left[\dfrac{MLT^{-2}}{LT^{-1}}\right] = [ML^0T^{-1}]$

9. **(c)** $\dfrac{0.2}{25} \times 100 = 0.8\%$

10. **(c)** Weber is the unit of magnetic flux in S.I. system.
$1 \text{ Wb(S.I unit)} = 10^8 \text{ maxwell}$

11. **(b)** Solar constant = energy/area/time

$$= \frac{ML^2 T^{-2}}{L^2 T} = [M^1 T^{-3}].$$

12. **(b)** $b = \lambda_m T = LK = [M^0 L^1 T^0 K^1]$

13. **(d)** Let unit 'u' related with e, a_0, h and c as follows.

$$[u] = [e]^a [a_0]^b [h]^c [C]^d$$

Using dimensional method,

$[M^{-1}L^{-2}T^{+4}A^{+2}] = [A^1 T^1]^a [L]^b [ML2T^{-1}]^c [LT^{-1}]^d$

$[M^{-1}L^{-2}T^{+4}A^{+2}] = [M^c L^{b+2c+d} T^{a-c-d} A^a]$

$a = 2, b = 1, c = -1, d = -1$

$$\therefore \quad u = \frac{e^2 a_0}{hc}$$

14. **(c)** From $F = \dfrac{1}{4\pi\varepsilon_o}\dfrac{e^2}{r^2}$

$$\therefore \quad \frac{e^2}{\varepsilon_o} = 4\pi F r^2 \text{ (dimensionally)}$$

$$\frac{e^2}{\varepsilon_o hc} = \frac{4\pi F r^2}{hc} = \frac{(MLT^{-2})L^2}{ML^2T^{-1}[LT^{-1}]} = [M^0 L^0 T^0 A^0],$$

$\dfrac{e^2}{\varepsilon_o hc}$ is called fine structure constant & has value

$$\frac{1}{137}.$$

15. **(d)** $Density = \dfrac{Mass}{Volume}$

$$\rho = \frac{M}{L^3} \qquad \therefore \quad \frac{\Delta\rho}{\rho} = \frac{\Delta M}{M} + 3\frac{\Delta L}{L}$$

% error in density = % error in Mass
$$+ 3 \text{ (% error in length]}$$
$$= 4 + 3(3) = 13\%$$

16. **(d)** Poisson's ratio is a unitless quantity.

17. **(d)** Dimensionally $\varepsilon_0 L = $ Capacitance (c)

$$\therefore \quad \varepsilon_0 L \frac{\Delta V}{\Delta t} = \frac{C\Delta V}{\Delta t} = \frac{q}{\Delta t} = I$$

18. **(c)** $\dfrac{\Delta V}{V} = 3\dfrac{\Delta r}{r}$ or $6\% = 3\dfrac{\Delta r}{r}$ or $\dfrac{\Delta r}{r} = 2\%$

Now surface area $s = 4\pi r^2$ or $\log s = \log 4\pi + 2\log r$

$$\therefore \quad \frac{\Delta s}{s} = 2\frac{\Delta r}{r} = 2 \times 2\% = 4\%.$$

19. **(d)** Let $(M) = V^a F^b E^c$
Putting the dimensions of V, F and E, we have
$(M) = (LT^{-1})^a \times (MLT^{-2})^b \times (ML^2T^{-2})^c$
or $M^1 = M^{b+c} L^{a+b+2c} T^{-a-2b-2c}$
Equating the powers of dimensions, we have

$b + c = 1$

$a + b + 2c = 0$; $-a - 2b - 2c = 0$

which give $a = -2$, $b = 0$ and $c = 1$.

Therefore $(M) = (V^{-2} F^0 E)$.

20. **(d)** Number of significant figures in multiplication is three, corresponding to the minimum number

$107.88 \times 0.610 = 65.8068 = 65.8$

21. **(d)** A quantity which has dimensions and a constant value is called dimensional constant. Therefore, gravitational constant (G) is a dimensional constant.

22. **(a)** $\dfrac{[ML^2T^{-2}][ML^2T^{-1}]^2}{[M^5][M^{-1}L^3T^{-2}]^2} = [M^0L^0T^0]$ = angle.

23. **(a)** The mean value of refractive index,

$$\mu = \frac{1.34 + 1.38 + 1.32 + 1.36}{4} = 1.35$$

and

$$\Delta\mu = \frac{|(1.35 - 1.34)| + |(1.35 - 1.38)| + |(1.35 - 1.32)| + |(1.35 - 1.36)|}{4}$$

$$= 0.02$$

Thus $\dfrac{\Delta\mu}{\mu} \times 100 = \dfrac{0.02}{1.35} \times 100 = 1.48$

24. **(c)** $\dfrac{eV}{T} = \dfrac{W}{T} = \dfrac{PV}{T} = R$

and $\dfrac{R}{N} = $ Boltzmann constant.

25. **(b)** Mobility $\mu = \dfrac{\text{drift velocity}}{\text{electric field}} \dfrac{V_d}{E} = \dfrac{(ms^{-1})}{(Vm^{-1})} = \dfrac{m^2 s^{-3}}{V}$

$$\left(\because \text{Volt} = V = \frac{\text{joule}(J)}{\text{coulomb}(C)} \right)$$

$$= \frac{m^2 s^{-1}C}{J} = \frac{m^2 s^{-1} As}{kg\, m^2 s^{-2}} \text{[Coulomb, } c = As]$$

$$= kg^{-1} s^2 A = M^{-1} T^2 A$$

26. **(a)**

27. **(b)** $v = k \lambda^a \rho^b g^c$

$[M^0 LT^{-1}] = L^a (ML^{-3})^b (LT^{-2})^c$

$\qquad = M^b L^{a-3b+c} T^{-2c}$

$\therefore$ $b = 0$; $a - 3b + c = 1$

$-2c = -1 \Rightarrow c = 1/2$ $\qquad \therefore$ $a = \dfrac{1}{2}$

$v \propto \lambda^{1/2} \rho^0 g^{1/2}$ or $v^2 \propto \lambda g$

28. **(b)** $[\text{momentum}] = [M][L][T^{-1}] = [MLT^{-1}]$

Planck's constant $= \dfrac{E}{\nu} = \dfrac{[M][LT^{-1}]^2}{T^{-1}} = ML^2T^{-1}$

29. **(d)** Let dimensions of length is related as,

$$L = [c]^x [G]^y \left[\frac{e^2}{4\pi\varepsilon_0} \right]^z$$

$$\frac{e^2}{4\pi\varepsilon_0} = ML^3T^{-2}$$

$L = [LT^{-1}]^x [M^{-1}L^3T^{-2}]^y [ML^3T^{-2}]^z$

$[L] = [L^{x+3y+3z} M^{-y+z} T^{-x-2y-2z}]$

Comparing both sides

$-y + z = 0 \Rightarrow y = z$ $\qquad$ ...(i)

$x + 3y + 3z = 1$ $\qquad$ ...(ii)

$-x - 4z = 0$ $\quad (\because y = z)$ $\qquad$ ...(iii)

From (i), (ii) & (iii)

$z = y = \dfrac{1}{2}$, $x = -2$

Hence, $L = c^{-2} \left[G \cdot \dfrac{e^2}{4\pi\varepsilon_0} \right]^{1/2}$

30. **(c)** Impulse = change in momentum

31. **(c)** We know that $\dfrac{Q^2}{2C}$ is energy of capacitor so it represent the dimension of energy $= [ML^2T^{-2}]$.

32. **(b)** Let $M = p^n v^m$

$ML^{-2} T^{-1} = (ML^{-1} T^{-2})^n (LT^{-1})^m$

$\qquad = M^n L^{-n+m} T^{-2n-m}$

$\therefore$ $n = 1$; $-n + m = -2$

$\therefore$ $m = -2 + n = -2 + 1 = -1$ $\qquad \therefore$ $m = -n$

33. **(c)** $I = AT^2 e^{-B/kT}$

Dimensions of $A = I/T^2$; $\qquad$ Dimensions of $B = kT$

($\because$ power of exponential is dimensionless)

$$AB^2 = \frac{I}{T^2}(kT)^2 = I k^2$$

34. **(a)** $\eta = \dfrac{p(r^2 - x^2)}{4vl} = \dfrac{[ML^{-1}T^{-2}][L^2]}{[LT^{-1}][L]} = [ML^{-1}T^{-1}]$

35. **(a)** The unit of λ, x and A are the same

36. **(c)** $L + B = 2.331 + 2.1 \cong 4.4$ cm

Since minimum significant figure is 2.

37. **(c)** Given, $x = \cos(\omega t + kx)$

$(\omega t + kx)$ is an angle and hence it is a dimension less quantity.

$[(\omega t + kx)] = [M^0L^0T^0]$

or $\quad [\omega t] = [M^0L^0T^0]$

$$[\omega] = \frac{[M^0L^0T^0]}{[T]} = [M^0L^0T^{-1}]$$

38. **(c)** $10\, VD = 9\, MD$, $1\, VD = \dfrac{9}{10} MD$

Vernier constant $= 1\, MD - 1\, VD$

$= \left(1 - \dfrac{9}{10}\right) MD = \dfrac{1}{10} MD = \dfrac{1}{10} \times \dfrac{1}{2} = 0.05$ mm

39. **(c)** $[\text{Energy density}] = \dfrac{[\text{Work done}]}{[\text{Volume}]}$

$$= \dfrac{ML^2T^{-2}}{L^3} = ML^{-1}T^{-2}$$

$[\text{Young's Modulus}] = \left[\dfrac{F}{A} \times \dfrac{l}{\Delta l}\right]$

$$= \dfrac{MLT^{-2}}{L^2} \cdot \dfrac{L}{L} = [ML^{-1}T^{-2}]$$

40. **(b)** As $\dfrac{a}{V^2} = P$

$$\therefore \ a = PV^2 = \dfrac{\text{dyne}}{\text{cm}^2}(\text{cm}^3)^2 = \text{dyne cm}^4$$

41. **(a)** Reyonld's constant is a pure number, hence it has no dimensions.

42. **(d)** $\omega k = \dfrac{1}{T} \times \dfrac{1}{L} = [L^{-1}\,T^{-1}]$

The dimensions of the quantities in a, b, c are of velocity $[LT^{-1}]$

43. **(a)** M = Pole strength × length
$= \text{amp} - \text{metre} \times \text{metre} = \text{amp} - \text{metre}^2$

44. **(b)** According to the question.

$$t = (90 \pm 1) \text{ or, } \dfrac{\Delta t}{t} = \dfrac{1}{90}$$

$l = (20 \pm 0.1)$ or, $\dfrac{\Delta l}{l} = \dfrac{0.1}{20}$

$\dfrac{\Delta g}{g}\% = ?$

As we know,

$$t = 2\pi\sqrt{\dfrac{l}{g}}$$

$$\Rightarrow \quad g = \dfrac{4\pi^2 l}{t^2}$$

or, $\quad \dfrac{\Delta g}{g} = \pm\left(\dfrac{\Delta l}{l} + 2\dfrac{\Delta t}{t}\right)$

$$= \left(\dfrac{0.1}{20} + 2 \times \dfrac{1}{90}\right)$$

$$= 0.027$$

$$\therefore \quad \dfrac{\Delta g}{g}\% = 2.7\%$$

45. **(a)** Dimension of magnetic flux
= Dimension of voltage × Dimension of time
$= [ML^2T^{-3}A^{-1}]\ [T] = [ML^2T^{-2}A^{-1}]$

$\because \text{Voltage} = \dfrac{\text{work}}{\text{charge}}$

1. **(a)** Acceleration of the particle $a = 2t - 1$

The particle retards when acceleration is opposite to velocity.

$\Rightarrow a \cdot v < 0 \Rightarrow (2t-1)(t^2-t) < 0 \Rightarrow t(2t-1)(t-1) < 0$

Now t is always positive

$\therefore (2t-1)(t-1) < 0$

or $2t - 1 < 0$ and $t - 1 > 0 \Rightarrow t < \dfrac{1}{2}$ and $t > 1$.

This is not possible

or $2t - 1 > 0$ & $t - 1 < 0 \Rightarrow 1/2 < t < 1$

2. **(b)** $x = \alpha t^3$ and $y = \beta t^3$

$v_x = \dfrac{dx}{dt} = 3\alpha t^2$ and $v_y = \dfrac{dy}{dt} = 3\beta t^2$

$\therefore v = \sqrt{v_x^2 + v_y^2} = \sqrt{9\alpha^2 t^4 + 9\beta^2 t^4}$

$= 3t^2 \sqrt{\alpha^2 + \beta^2}$

3. **(d)** $\text{Average speed} = \dfrac{\text{Total distance travelled}}{\text{Total time taken}}$

$= \dfrac{x}{\dfrac{2x/5}{v_1} + \dfrac{3x/5}{v_2}} = \dfrac{5v_1 v_2}{3v_1 + 2v_2}$

4. **(a)** Instantaneous speed is the distance being covered by the particle per unit time at the given instant. It is equal to the magnitude of the instantaneous velocity at the given instant.

5. **(a)** $v = \alpha \sqrt{x}$, $\dfrac{dx}{dt} = \alpha \sqrt{x} \Rightarrow \dfrac{dx}{\sqrt{x}} = \alpha\, dt$

$\displaystyle\int_0^x \dfrac{dx}{\sqrt{x}} = \alpha \int_0^t dt$

$\left[\dfrac{2\sqrt{x}}{1}\right]_0^x = \alpha [t]_0^t$

$\Rightarrow 2\sqrt{x} = \alpha t \Rightarrow x = \dfrac{\alpha^2}{4} t^2$

6. **(c)** $\dfrac{1}{2}(1+4) \times 4 - \dfrac{1}{2} \times 1 \times 2 - \dfrac{1}{2} \times 3 \times 4 = 3\,\text{m}$

7. **(b)** The distance travel in n^{th} second is

$S_n = u + \frac{1}{2}(2n-1)a$ ....(1)

so distance travel in t^{th} & $(t+1)^{\text{th}}$ second are

$S_t = u + \frac{1}{2}(2t-1)a$ ....(2)

$S_{t+1} = u + \frac{1}{2}(2t+1)a$ ....(3)

As per question,

$S_t + S_{t+1} = 100 = 2(u+at)$ ....(4)

Now from first equation of motion the velocity, of particle after time t, if it moves with an accleration a is

$v = u + a t$ ....(5)

where u is initial velocity

So from eq(4) and (5), we get $v = 50$ cm/sec.

8. **(d)** Relative speed of police with respect to thief

$= 10 - 9 = 1$ m/s

Instantaneous separation = 100 m

$\text{Time} = \dfrac{\text{Distance}}{\text{Velocity}} = \dfrac{100}{1} = 100\,\text{sec}.$

9. **(d)** $x = \dfrac{a}{b}(1 - e^{-b \times \frac{1}{b}}) = \dfrac{a}{b}(1 - e^{-1}) = \dfrac{a}{b}(1 - \dfrac{1}{e})$

$= \dfrac{a}{b} \dfrac{(e-1)}{e} = \dfrac{a}{b} \dfrac{(2.718-1)}{2.718} = \dfrac{a}{b} \dfrac{(1.718)}{2.718} = 0.637 \dfrac{a}{b} \simeq \dfrac{2}{3} a/b$

velocity $v = \dfrac{dx}{dt} = ae^{-bt}$, $v_0 = a$

accleration $a = \dfrac{dv}{dt} = -abe^{-bt}$ & $a_0 = -ab$

At $t = 0$, $x = \dfrac{a}{b}(1-1) = 0$ and

At $t = \dfrac{1}{b}$, $x = \dfrac{a}{b}(1 - e^{-1}) = \dfrac{a}{b}(1 - \dfrac{1}{e}) = \dfrac{2}{3} a/b$

At $t = \infty$, $x = \dfrac{a}{b}$

It cannot go beyond this, so point $x > \dfrac{a}{b}$ is not reached by the particle.

At $t = 0$, $x = 0$, at $t = \infty$, $x = \dfrac{a}{b}$, therefore the particle does not come back to its starting point at $t = \infty$.

10. **(d)** Ist part: $u = 0$, $t = 5$s, $v = 108$ km/hr $= 30$ m/s

$v = u + at \Rightarrow 30 = 0 + a \times 5 \Rightarrow a = 6$ m/s^2

$s = ut + \dfrac{1}{2}at^2 = 0 \times 5 + \dfrac{1}{2} \times 6 \times 5^2 = 75$ m

IIIrd part: $s = 45$m, $u = 30$m/s, $v = 0$

$a = \dfrac{v^2 - u^2}{2s} = \dfrac{-30 \times 30}{2 \times 45} = -10\,\text{m}/s^2$

$v = u + at \Rightarrow 0 = 30 - 10 \times t \Rightarrow t = 3$s

IInd part :

$s = s_1 + s_2 + s_3$

$395 = 75 + s_2 + 45 \Rightarrow s_2 = 275$ m

$t = \dfrac{275}{30} = 9.16 = 9.2$s.

Total time taken $= (5 + 9.2 + 3)\,\text{sec} = 17.2$ sec

11. **(a)** $\dfrac{dv}{dt} = -kv^3$ or $\dfrac{dv}{v^3} = -k\,dt$

Integrating we get, $-\dfrac{1}{2v^2} = -kt + c$ ...(1)

At $t = 0$, $v = v_0$ $\therefore -\dfrac{1}{2v_0^2} = c$

Putting in (1)

$$-\frac{1}{2v^2} = -kt - \frac{1}{2v_0{}^2} \text{ or } \frac{1}{2v_0^2} - \frac{1}{2v^2} = -kt$$

$$\text{or } \left[\frac{1}{2v_0^2} + kt\right] = \frac{1}{2v^2} \text{ or } \left[1 + 2v_0^2 \, kt\right] = \frac{v_0^2}{v^2}$$

$$\text{or } v^2 = \frac{v_0^2}{1 + 2v_0^2 \, kt} \quad \text{or } v = \frac{v_0}{\sqrt{1 + 2v_0^2 \, kt}}$$

12. (c) We know that, $v = \dfrac{dx}{dt} \Rightarrow dx = v\,dt$

Integrating, $\displaystyle\int_0^x dx = \int_0^t v\,dt$

$$\text{or } x = \int_0^t (v_0 + gt + ft^2)\,dt$$

$$= \left[v_0 t + \frac{gt^2}{2} + \frac{ft^3}{3}\right]_0^t$$

$$\text{or, } x = v_0 t + \frac{gt^2}{2} + \frac{ft^3}{3}$$

At $t = 1$, $x = v_0 + \dfrac{g}{2} + \dfrac{f}{3}$.

13. (c) Let man will catch the bus after 't' sec. So he will cover distance ut.

Similarly, distance travelled by the bus will be $\dfrac{1}{2}at^2$

For the given condition

$$ut = 45 + \frac{1}{2}at^2 = 45 + 1.25t^2 \quad [\text{As } a = 2.5 \text{ m/s}^2]$$

$$\Rightarrow u = \frac{45}{t} + 1.25t$$

To find the minimum value of u $\dfrac{du}{dt} = 0$
so we get t = 6 sec then,

$$u = \frac{45}{6} + 1.25 \times 6 = 7.5 + 7.5 = 15\,\text{m/s}$$

14. (b) For the body starting from rest

$$x_1 = 0 + \frac{1}{2}at^2$$

$$\Rightarrow x_1 = \frac{1}{2}at^2$$

For the body moving with constant speed

$$x_2 = vt$$

$$\therefore \; x_1 - x_2 = \frac{1}{2}at^2 - vt$$

at $t = 0$, $x_1 - x_2 = 0$

For $t < \dfrac{v}{a}$; the slope is negative

For $t = \dfrac{v}{a}$; the slope is zero

For $t > \dfrac{v}{a}$; the slope is positive

These characteristics are represented by graph (b).

15. (d) The stone reaches its maximum height after time t_1 given by

$$t_1 = \frac{u}{g} \quad (\because v = u - gt)$$

$$= \frac{10}{10} = 1 \text{ sec}$$

Again it reaches to its initial position in 1 sec and falls with same initial speed of 10 m/s.

Let t_2 be the time taken to reach the ground, then

$$v_{ground} = u + gt_2$$

But $v_{ground}^2 = u^2 + 2gh$

$$= (10)^2 + 2 \times 10 \times 40 = 900$$

$$\Rightarrow v_{ground} = \sqrt{900} = 30\,\text{m/s}$$

$$\therefore \; t_2 = \frac{v_{ground} - u}{g} = \frac{30 - 10}{10} = 2 \text{ sec.}$$

$\therefore$ Total required time $= (1 + 1 + 2)\sec = 4 \sec$

16. (b)
$$L = \frac{1}{2}gt^2 - \frac{1}{2}g(t - T)^2$$

$$\Rightarrow t = \frac{T}{2} + \frac{L}{gt}.$$

17. (b) $S = AB = \dfrac{1}{2}g\,t_1{}^2 \Rightarrow 2S = AC = \dfrac{1}{2}g\,(t_1 + t_2)^2$

and $3S = AD = \dfrac{1}{2}g\,(t_1 + t_2 + t_3)^2$

$$t_1 = \sqrt{\frac{2S}{g}}$$

$$t_1 + t_2 = \sqrt{\frac{4S}{g}}, \; t_2 = \sqrt{\frac{4S}{g}} - \sqrt{\frac{2S}{g}}$$

$$t_1 + t_2 + t_3 = \sqrt{\frac{6S}{g}}$$

$$t_3 = \sqrt{\frac{6S}{g}} - \sqrt{\frac{4S}{g}}$$

$$t_1 : t_2 : t_3 :: 1 : (\sqrt{2} - 1) : (\sqrt{3} - \sqrt{2})$$

18. (c) Height of tap = 5m and (g) = 10 m/sec². For the first drop,

$$5 = ut + \frac{1}{2}gt^2 = (0 \times t) + \frac{1}{2} \times 10t^2 = 5t^2 \text{ or } t^2 = 1 \text{ or } t = 1.$$

It means that the third drop leaves after one second of the first drop. Or, each drop leaves after every 0.5 sec. Distance covered by the second drop in 0.5 sec

$$= \mathrm{ut} + \frac{1}{2}\mathrm{gt}^2 = (0 \times 0.5) + \frac{1}{2} \times 10 = (0.5)^2 = 1.25\,\mathrm{m}.$$

Therefore, distance of the second drop above the ground $= 5 - 1.25 = 3.75$ m.

19. (c) $\because t = \sqrt{x} + 3$

$\Rightarrow \sqrt{x} = t - 3 \Rightarrow x = (t-3)^2$

$v = \dfrac{dx}{dt} = 2(t-3) = 0$

$\Rightarrow t = 3$

$\therefore x = (3-3)^2$

$\Rightarrow x = 0.$

20. (c) We have, $S_n = u + \dfrac{a}{2}(2n-1)$

or $65 = u + \dfrac{a}{2}(2 \times 5 - 1)$

or $65 = u + \dfrac{9}{2}a$ ..... (1)

Also, $105 = u + \dfrac{a}{2}(2 \times 9 - 1)$

or $105 = u + \dfrac{17}{2}a$ ..... (2)

Equation $(2) - (1)$ gives,

$40 = \dfrac{17}{2}a - \dfrac{9}{2}a = 4a$ or $a = 10\,\mathrm{m/s}^2.$

Substitute this value in (1) we get,

$u = 65 - \dfrac{9}{2} \times 10 = 65 - 45 = 20\,\mathrm{m/s}$

$\therefore$ The distance travelled by the body in 20 s is,

$s = \mathrm{ut} + \dfrac{1}{2}at^2 = 20 \times 20 + \dfrac{1}{2} \times 10 \times (20)^2$

$= 400 + 2000 = 2400\,\mathrm{m}.$

21. (d) Speed, $u = 60 \times \dfrac{5}{18}\,\mathrm{m/s} = \dfrac{50}{3}\,\mathrm{m/s}$

$d = 20\mathrm{m},\ u' = 120 \times \dfrac{5}{18} = \dfrac{100}{3}\,\mathrm{m/s}$

Let declaration be a then $(0)^2 - u^2 = -2ad$

or $u^2 = 2ad$ ...(1)

and $(0)^2 - u'^2 = -2ad'$

or $u'^2 = 2ad'$ ...(2)

(2) divided by (1) gives,

$4 = \dfrac{d'}{d} \Rightarrow d' = 4 \times 20 = 80\mathrm{m}$

22. (b) $8 = a\,t_1$ and $0 = 8 - a(4 - t_1)$

or $t_1 = \dfrac{8}{a}$ $\therefore$ $8 = a\left(4 - \dfrac{8}{a}\right)$

$8 = 4\,a - 8$ or $a = 4$ and $t_1 = 8/4 = 2$ sec

Now, $s_1 = 0 \times 2 + \dfrac{1}{2} \times 4\,(2)^2$ or $s_1 = 8\,\mathrm{m}$

$s_2 = 8 \times 2 - \dfrac{1}{2} \times 4 \times (2)^2$ or $s_2 = 8\,\mathrm{m}$

$\therefore$ $s_1 + s_2 = 16$ m

23. (d)

24. (a) $x = \dfrac{1}{t+5}$

$\therefore$ $v = \dfrac{dx}{dt} = \dfrac{-1}{(t+5)^2}$

$\therefore$ $a = \dfrac{d^2 x}{dt^2} = \dfrac{2}{(t+5)^3} = 2x^3$

Now $\dfrac{1}{(t+5)} \propto v^{\frac{1}{2}}$

$\therefore$ $\dfrac{1}{(t+5)^3} \propto v^{\frac{3}{2}} \propto a$

25. (d)

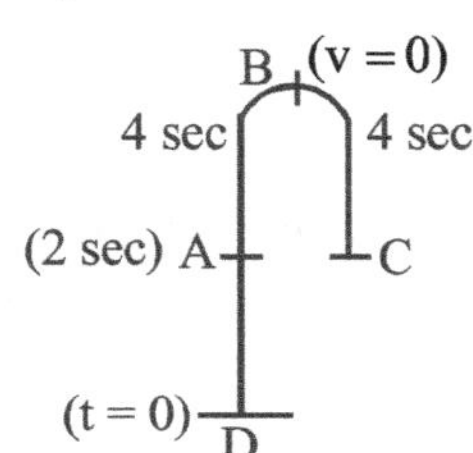

As the time taken from D to A = 2 sec. and D → A → B → C = 10 sec (given). As ball goes from B → C (u = 0, t = 4 sec) $v_c = 0 + 4g.$

As it moves from C to D, $s = \mathrm{ut} + \dfrac{1}{2}\mathrm{gt}^2$

$s = 4g \times 2 + \dfrac{1}{2}g \times 4 = 10\,g.$

26. (d) $y = \dfrac{1}{2}g(n+1)^2 - \dfrac{1}{2}gn^2$

$= \dfrac{g}{2}[(n+1)^2 - n^2] = \dfrac{g}{2}(2n+1)$ ......(i)

Also, $h = \dfrac{g}{2}(2n-1)$ ......(ii)

From (i) and (ii)

$y = h + g$

27. (b) The stone rises up till its vertical velocity is zero and again reached the top of the tower with a speed u (downward). The speed of the stone at the base is 3u.

Hence $(3\mathrm{u})^2 = (-\mathrm{u})^2 + 2gh$ or $h = \dfrac{4u^2}{g}$

28. (b) $x = 40 + 12\,t - t^3$

$$v = \frac{dx}{dt} = 12 - 3t^2$$

For $v = 0;\ t = \sqrt{\dfrac{12}{3}} = 2\ \text{sec}$

So, after 2 seconds velocity becomes zero.
Value of x in 2 secs $= 40 + 12 \times 2 - 2^3$
$$= 40 + 24 - 8 = 56\ \text{m}$$

29. (b) The slope of v-t graph is constant and velocity decreasing for first half. It is positive and constant over next half.

30. (c) Here, $f = f_0\left(1 - \dfrac{t}{T}\right)$ or, $\dfrac{dv}{dt} = f_0\left(1 - \dfrac{t}{T}\right)$

or, $dv = f_0\left(1 - \dfrac{t}{T}\right)dt$

$$\therefore v = \int dv = \int\left[f_0\left(1 - \frac{t}{T}\right)\right]dt$$

or, $v = f_0\left(t - \dfrac{t^2}{2T}\right) + C$

where C is the constant of integration.
At $t = 0,\ v = 0$.

$$\therefore 0 = f_0\left(0 - \frac{0}{2T}\right) + C \Rightarrow C = 0$$

$$\therefore v = f_0\left(t - \frac{t^2}{2T}\right)$$

If $f = 0$, then

$$0 = f_0\left(1 - \frac{t}{T}\right) \Rightarrow t = T$$

Hence, particle's velocity in the time interval $t = 0$ and $t = T$ is given by

$$v_x = \int_{t=0}^{t=T} dv = \int_{t=0}^{T}\left[f_0\left(1 - \frac{t}{T}\right)\right]dt$$

$$= f_0\left[\left(t - \frac{t^2}{2T}\right)\right]_0^{T}$$

$$= f_0\left(T - \frac{T^2}{2T}\right) = f_0\left(T - \frac{T}{2}\right)$$

$$= \frac{1}{2}f_0 T.$$

31. (a) Using $v^2 = u^2 - 2gh$ i.e., $h = \dfrac{u^2 - v^2}{2g}$,

$$AB = \frac{\left(\frac{u}{2}\right)^2 - \left(\frac{u}{3}\right)^2}{2g}$$

and $BC = \dfrac{\left(\frac{u}{3}\right)^2 - \left(\frac{u}{4}\right)^2}{2g}$

$$\therefore \frac{AB}{BC} = \frac{\left(\frac{u}{2}\right)^2 - \left(\frac{u}{3}\right)^2}{\left(\frac{u}{3}\right)^2 - \left(\frac{u}{4}\right)^2} = \frac{\left(\frac{1}{2}\right)^2 - \left(\frac{1}{3}\right)^2}{\left(\frac{1}{3}\right)^2 - \left(\frac{1}{4}\right)^2} = \frac{20}{7}$$

32. (a) Velocity of boat $= \dfrac{8+8}{2} = 8\ \text{km h}^{-1}$

Velocity of water $= 4\ \text{km h}^{-1}$

$$t = \frac{8}{8-4} + \frac{8}{8+4} = \frac{8}{3}\text{h} = 160\ \text{minutes}$$

33. (b) $v_{av} = \dfrac{x + 2x + 3x}{t_1 + t_2 + t_3}$

$$t_1 = \frac{2x}{v_{max}},\ t_2 = \frac{2x}{v_{max}},\ t_3 = \frac{6x}{v_{max}}$$

$$v_{av} = \frac{6x\ v_{max}}{10x}$$

$$\frac{v_{av}}{v_{max}} = \frac{3}{5}$$

34. (b) No external force is acting, therefore,
$$50\,u + 0.5 \times 2 = 0$$
where u is the velocity of man.

$$u = -\frac{1}{50}\,\text{ms}^{-1}$$

Negative sign of u shows that man moves upward.
Time taken by the stone to reach the ground

$$= \frac{10}{2} = 5\text{S}$$

Distance moved by the man

$$= 5 \times \frac{1}{50} = 0.1\,\text{m}$$

$\therefore$ when the stone reaches the floor, the distance of the man above floor $= 10.1\ m$

35. (a) Use $\vec{v}_{AB} = \vec{v}_A - \vec{v}_B$.

36. (c) Downward motion
$$v^2 - 0^2 = 2 \times 9.8 \times 5$$

$\Rightarrow \quad v = \sqrt{98} = 9.9$

Also for upward motion

$0^2 - u^2 = 2 \times (-9.8) \times 1.8$

$\Rightarrow \quad u = \sqrt{3528} = 5.94$

Fractional loss $= \dfrac{9.9 - 5.94}{9.9} = 0.4$

37. (c) Distance travelled by the stone in the last second is

$\dfrac{9h}{25} = \dfrac{g}{2}(2t-1) \quad (\because \ u=0) \qquad \ldots(i)$

Distance travelled by the stone in t s is

$h = \dfrac{1}{2} gt^2 \quad (\text{using } s = ut + \dfrac{1}{2} at^2) \qquad \ldots(ii)$

Divide (i) by (ii), we get

$\dfrac{9}{25} = \dfrac{(2t-1)}{t^2}$

$9t^2 = 50t - 25, \ 9t^2 - 50t + 25 = 0$

Solving, we get

$t = 5s \ \text{ or } \ t = \dfrac{5}{9} s$

Substituting t = 5s in (ii), we get

$h = \dfrac{1}{2} \times 9.8 \times (5)^2 = 122.5 \text{ m}$

38. (b) $y \propto t^2; v \propto t'; a \propto t^\circ$

39. (b) Average velocity for the second half of the distance is

$= \dfrac{v_1 + v_2}{2} = \dfrac{4+8}{2} = 6\,\text{m s}^{-1}$

Given that first half distance is covered with a velocity of $6\,\text{m s}^{-1}$. Therefore, the average velocity for the whole time of motion is $6\,\text{m s}^{-1}$

40. (b) Bullet will take $\dfrac{100}{1000} = 0.1$ sec to reach target.

During this period vertical distance (downward) travelled by the bullet

$= \dfrac{1}{2} gt^2 = \dfrac{1}{2} \times 10 \times (0.1)^2 = 0.05\,\text{m} = 5\text{cm}$

So the gun should be aimed 5 cm above the target.

41. (c) The distance covered in n^{th} second is

$S_n = u + \dfrac{1}{2}(2n-1)a$

where u is initial velocity & a is acceleration

then $26 = u + \dfrac{19a}{2} \qquad \ldots(1)$

$28 = u + \dfrac{21a}{2} \qquad \ldots(2)$

$30 = u + \dfrac{23a}{2} \qquad \ldots(3)$

$32 = u + \dfrac{25a}{2} \qquad \ldots(4)$

From eqs. (1) and (2) we get u = 7m/sec, a=2m/sec^2

$\therefore$ The body starts with initial velocity u =7m/sec and moves with uniform acceleration a = 2m/sec^2

42. (a) $8 = \dfrac{x}{t_1}, \ 12 = \dfrac{x}{t_2}$

$\overline{v} = \dfrac{2x}{t_1 + t_2} = \dfrac{2x}{\dfrac{x}{8} + \dfrac{x}{12}} = \dfrac{2 \times 8 \times 12}{12 + 8} = 9.6 \text{ ms}^{-1}$

43. (b) Distance = Area under $v - t$ graph $= A_1 + A_2 + A_3 + A_4$

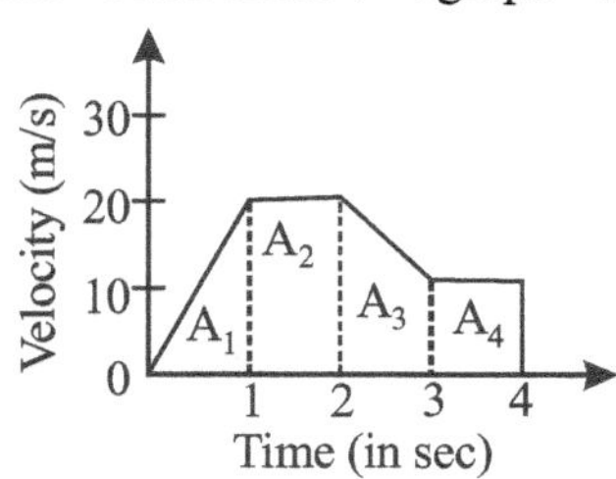

$= \dfrac{1}{2} \times 1 \times 20 + (20 \times 1) + \dfrac{1}{2}(20 + 10) \times 1 + (10 \times 1)$

$= 10 + 20 + 15 + 10 = 55\,\text{m}$

44. (a) $\because \ h = \dfrac{1}{2} gt^2$

$\therefore \ h_1 = \dfrac{1}{2} g(5)^2 = 125$

$h_1 + h_2 = \dfrac{1}{2} g(10)^2 = 500$

$\Rightarrow h_2 = 375$

$h_1 + h_2 + h_3 = \dfrac{1}{2} g(15)^2 = 1125$

$\Rightarrow h_3 = 625$

$h_2 = 3h_1, \ h_3 = 5h_1$

or $h_1 = \dfrac{h_2}{3} = \dfrac{h_3}{5}$

45. (d) Distance from A to $B = S = \dfrac{1}{2} ft_1^2$

Distance from B to $C = (ft_1)t$

Distance from C to $D = \dfrac{u^2}{2a} = \dfrac{(ft_1)^2}{2(f/2)} = ft_1^2 = 2S$

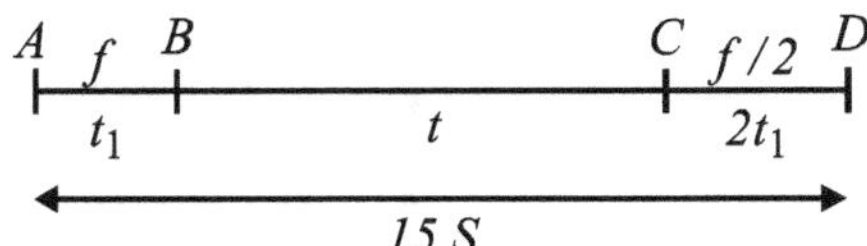

$\Rightarrow \ S + f t_1 t + 2S = 15S$

$\Rightarrow \ f t_1 t = 12S \qquad \ldots(i)$

$\dfrac{1}{2} f t_1^2 = S \qquad \ldots(ii)$

Dividing (i) by (ii), we get $t_1 = \dfrac{t}{6}$

$\Rightarrow \ S = \dfrac{1}{2} f \left(\dfrac{t}{6}\right)^2 = \dfrac{f t^2}{72}$

1. **(b)** $\vec{u} = \hat{i} + 2\hat{j} = u_x\hat{i} + u_y\hat{j} \Rightarrow u\cos\theta = 1,\ u\sin\theta = 2$

$$y = x\tan\theta - \frac{1}{2}\frac{gx^2}{u_x^2}$$

$$\therefore\ y = 2x - \frac{1}{2}gx^2 = 2x - 5x^2$$

2. **(c)** $500\cos\theta = 250 \Rightarrow \cos\theta = \frac{1}{2}$

or $\theta = 60°$.

3. **(c)** As time periods are equal therefore ratio of angular

speeds will be $1:1$. $\left(\omega = \frac{2\pi}{T}\right)$.

4. **(d)**

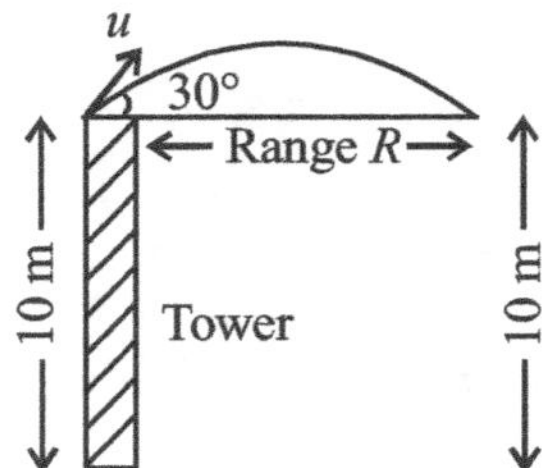

From the figure it is clear that range is required

$$R = \frac{u^2\sin 2\theta}{g} = \frac{(10)^2\sin(2\times 30°)}{10} = 5\sqrt{3} = 8.66\text{ m}$$

5. **(a)** Horizontal component of velocity $v_x = 500$ m/s and vertical component of velocity while striking the ground.

$u_v = 0 + 10 \times 10 = 100$ m/s

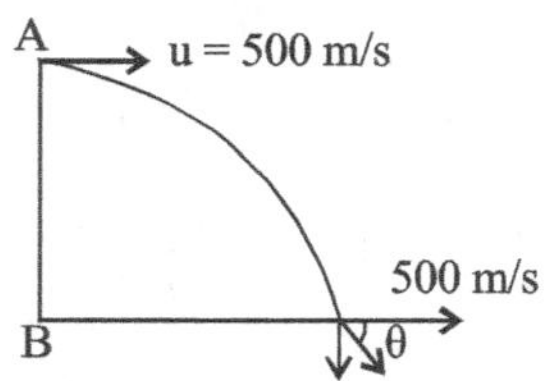

$\therefore$ Angle with which it strikes the ground

$$\theta = \tan^{-1}\left(\frac{u_v}{u_x}\right) = \tan^{-1}\left(\frac{100}{500}\right) = \tan^{-1}\left(\frac{1}{5}\right)$$

6. **(b)**

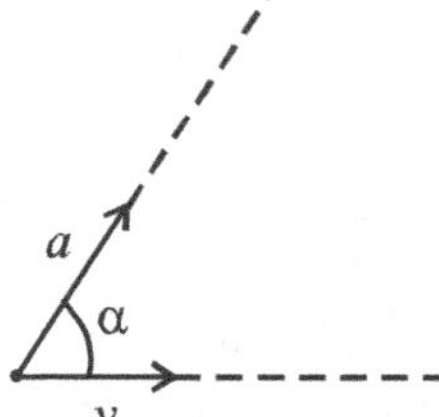

The velocity of first particle, $v_1 = v$
The velocity of second particle, $v_2 = at$
Relative velocity, $\vec{v}_{12} = \vec{v}_1 - \vec{v}_2$

or $v_{12}^2 = v^2 + (at)^2 - 2v\cdot at\cos\alpha$

For least value of relative velocity, $\dfrac{dv_{12}}{dt} = 0$

or $\dfrac{d}{dt}\left[v^2 + a^2t^2 - 2vat\cos\alpha\right] = 0$

or $0 + a^2 \times 2t - 2va\cos\alpha = 0$

or $t = \dfrac{v\cos\alpha}{a}$

7. **(d)** $t = \dfrac{2u\sin 30°}{g\cos 30°} = \dfrac{2(10)\,(1/2)}{10\,(\sqrt{3}/2)} = \dfrac{2}{\sqrt{3}}\sec$

$R = 10\cos 30°\,t - \dfrac{1}{2}g\sin 30°\,t^2$

$$= \frac{10\sqrt{3}}{2}\left(\frac{2}{\sqrt{3}}\right) - \frac{1}{2}(10)\left(\frac{1}{2}\right)\frac{4}{3} = 10 - \frac{10}{3} = \frac{20}{3}\text{ m}$$

8. **(b)** $\overrightarrow{AB} = (4\hat{i} + 5\hat{j} + 6\hat{k}) - (3\hat{i} + 4\hat{j} + 5\hat{k}) = \hat{i} + \hat{j} + \hat{k}$

$\overrightarrow{CD} = (4\hat{i} + 6\hat{j}) - (7\hat{i} + 9\hat{j} + 3\hat{k}) = 3\hat{i} - 3\hat{j} + 3\hat{k}$

$\overrightarrow{AB}$ and $\overrightarrow{CD}$ are parallel, because its cross-product is 0.

9. **(c)** Here $v = 0.5$ m/sec. $u = ?$

so $\sin\theta = \dfrac{u}{v} \Rightarrow \dfrac{u}{.5} = \dfrac{1}{2}$ or $u = 0.25$ ms^{-1}

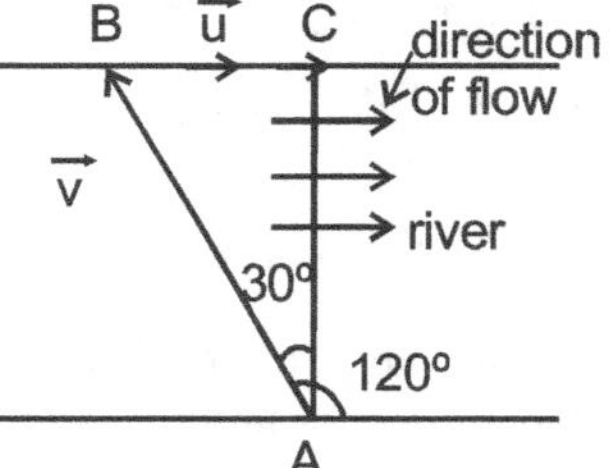

10. **(d)** Max. height $= H = \dfrac{v^2\sin^2(90-\theta)}{2g}$ .....(i)

Time of flight, $T = \dfrac{2v\sin(90-\theta)}{g}$ ...(ii)

From (i), $\dfrac{v\cos\theta}{g} = \sqrt{\dfrac{2H}{g}}$

From (ii), $T = 2\sqrt{\dfrac{2H}{g}} = \sqrt{\dfrac{8H}{g}}$

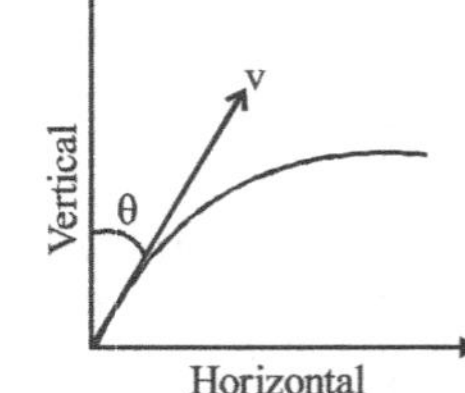

11. **(c)** Yes, the person can catch the ball when horizontal velocity is equal to the horizontal component of ball's velocity, the motion of ball will be only in vertical direction with respect to person for that,

$$\frac{v_o}{2} = v_o \cos\theta \text{ or } \theta = 60°$$

12. **(b)** Two vectors are

$$\vec{A} = \cos\omega t\,\hat{i} + \sin\omega t\,\hat{j}$$

$$\vec{B} = \cos\frac{\omega t}{2}\hat{i} + \sin\frac{\omega t}{2}\hat{j}$$

For two vectors $\vec{A}$ and $\vec{B}$ to be orthogonal $A.B = 0$

$$\vec{A}.\vec{B} = 0 = \cos\omega t.\cos\frac{\omega t}{2} + \sin\omega t.\sin\frac{\omega t}{2}$$

$$= \cos\left(\omega t - \frac{\omega t}{2}\right) = \cos\left(\frac{\omega t}{2}\right)$$

So, $\dfrac{\omega t}{2} = \dfrac{\pi}{2}$ $\therefore t = \dfrac{\pi}{\omega}$

13. **(a)** $\vec{v_1} = 50\,\text{km h}^{-1}$ due North;

$\vec{v_2} = 50\,\text{km h}^{-1}$ due West. Angle between $\vec{v_1}$ and $\vec{v_2} = 90°$

$-\vec{v_1} = 50\,\text{km h}^{-1}$ due South

$\therefore$ Change in velocity

$$= |\vec{v_2} - \vec{v_1}| = |\vec{v_2} + (-\vec{v_1})|$$

$$= \sqrt{v_2^2 + v_1^2} = \sqrt{50^2 + 50^2} = 70.7 \text{ km/h}$$

The direction of this change in velocity is in South-West.

14. **(b)** $\vec{v} = 6\hat{i} + 8\hat{j}$

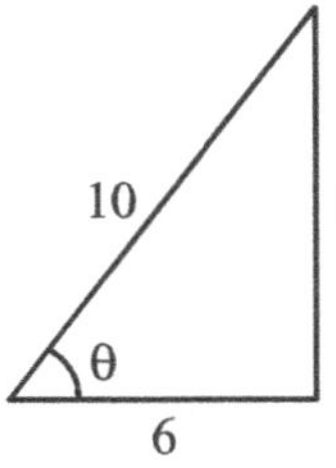

Comparing with $\vec{v} = v_x\hat{i} + v_y\hat{j}$, we get

$v_x = 6\,\text{ms}^{-1}$ and $v_y = 8\,\text{ms}^{-1}$

Also, $v^2 = v_x^2 + v_y^2 = 36 + 64 = 100$

or $v = 10 \text{ ms}^{-1}$

$$\sin\theta = \frac{8}{10} \text{ and } \cos\theta = \frac{6}{10}$$

$$R = \frac{v^2 \sin 2\theta}{g} = \frac{2v^2 \sin\theta\cos\theta}{g}$$

$$R = 2 \times 10 \times 10 \times \frac{8}{10} \times \frac{6}{10} \times \frac{1}{10} = 9.6\,\text{m}$$

15. **(d)** $s = t^3 + 5$

$$\Rightarrow \text{ velocity, } v = \frac{ds}{dt} = 3t^2$$

Tangential acceleration $a_t = \dfrac{dv}{dt} = 6t$

Radial acceleration $a_c = \dfrac{v^2}{R} = \dfrac{9t^4}{R}$

At $t = 2s$, $a_t = 6 \times 2 = 12 \text{ m/s}^2$

$$a_c = \frac{9 \times 16}{20} = 7.2 \text{ m/s}^2$$

$\therefore$ Resultant acceleration

$$= \sqrt{a_t^2 + a_c^2} = \sqrt{(12)^2 + (7.2)^2} = \sqrt{144 + 51.84}$$

$$= \sqrt{195.84} = 14 \text{ m/s}^2$$

16. **(b)** $$\frac{B}{2} = \sqrt{A^2 + B^2 + 2AB\cos\theta} \quad ...... \text{(i)}$$

$$\therefore \quad \tan 90° = \frac{B\sin\theta}{A + B\cos\theta} \Rightarrow A + B\cos\theta = 0$$

$$\therefore \quad \cos\theta = -\frac{A}{B}$$

Hence, from (i) $\dfrac{B^2}{A} = A^2 + B^2 - 2A^2 \Rightarrow A = \sqrt{3}\,\dfrac{B}{2}$

$$\Rightarrow \cos\theta = -\frac{A}{B} = -\frac{\sqrt{3}}{2} \quad \therefore \theta = 150°$$

17. **(b)** Suppose velocity of rain

$$\vec{v}_R = v_x\hat{i} - v_y\hat{j}$$

and the velocity of the man

$$\vec{v}_m = u\,\hat{i}$$

$\therefore$ Velocity of rain relative to man

$$\vec{v}_{Rm} = \vec{v}_R - \vec{v}_m = (v_x - u)\hat{i} - v_y\hat{j}$$

According to given condition that rain appears to fall vertically, so $(v_x - u)$ must be zero.

$\therefore \quad\quad v_x - u = 0 \text{ or } v_x = u$

When he doubles his speed,

$$\vec{v'}_m = 2u\,\hat{i}$$

Now $\vec{v}_{Rm} = \vec{v}_R - \vec{v'}_m$

$$= (v_x\hat{i} - v_y\hat{j}) - (2u\hat{i})$$

$$= (v_x - 2u)\hat{i} - v_y\hat{j}$$

The $\vec{v}_{Rm}$ makes an angle θ with the vertical

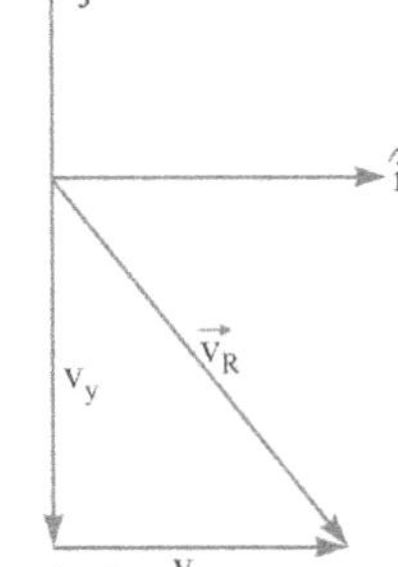

$$\tan\theta = \frac{x - \text{componend of } \vec{v}_{Rm}}{y - \text{componend of } \vec{v}_{Rm}}$$

$$= \frac{(v_x - 2u)}{-v_y}$$

$$= \frac{u - 2u}{-v_y}$$

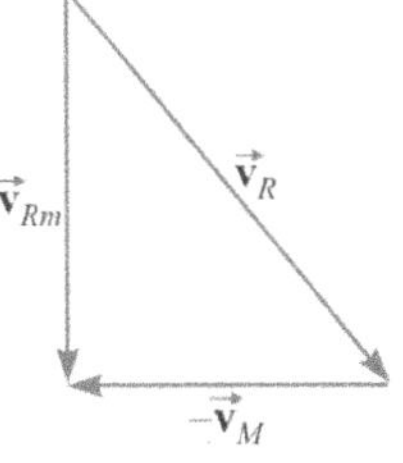

which gives

$$v_y = \frac{u}{\tan\theta}$$

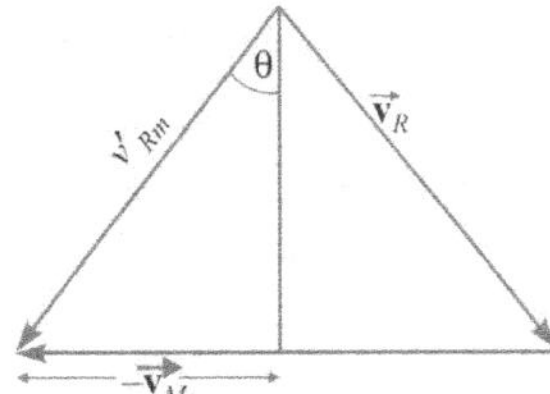

Thus the velocity of rain

$$\vec{v}_R = v_x \hat{\mathbf{i}} - v_y \hat{\mathbf{i}}$$

$$= u\,\hat{\mathbf{i}} - \frac{u}{\tan\theta}\,\hat{\mathbf{j}}.$$

18. (c) For projectile A

Maximum height, $H_A = \dfrac{u_A^2 \sin^2 45^\circ}{2g}$

For projectile B

Maximum height, $H_B = \dfrac{u_B^2 \sin^2 \theta}{2g}$

As we know, $H_A = H_B$

$$\frac{u_A^2 \sin^2 45^\circ}{2g} = \frac{u_B^2 \sin^2 \theta}{2g}$$

$$\frac{\sin^2 \theta}{\sin^2 45^\circ} = \frac{u_A^2}{u_B^2}$$

$$\sin^2 \theta = \left(\frac{u_A}{u_B}\right)^2 \sin^2 45^\circ$$

$$\sin^2 \theta = \left(\frac{1}{\sqrt{2}}\right)^2 \left(\frac{1}{\sqrt{2}}\right)^2 = \frac{1}{4}$$

$$\sin \theta = \frac{1}{2} \Rightarrow \theta = \sin^{-1}\left(\frac{1}{2}\right) = 30^\circ$$

19. (a) The angle for which the ranges are same is complementary.

Let one angle be θ, then other is $90^\circ - \theta$

$$T_1 = \frac{2u\sin\theta}{g}, \quad T_2 = \frac{2u\cos\theta}{g}$$

$$T_1 T_2 = \frac{4u^2 \sin\theta \cos\theta}{g} = 2R \quad \left(\because R = \frac{u^2 \sin^2\theta}{g}\right)$$

Hence it is proportional to R.

20. (c) When particle thrown in vertically downward direction with velocity u then final velocity at the ground level

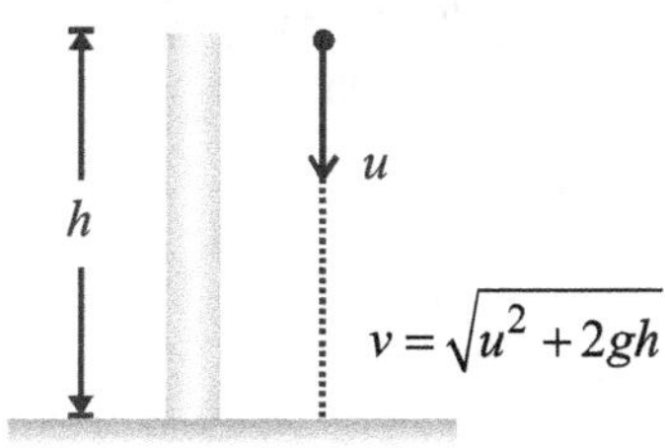

$$v = \sqrt{u^2 + 2gh}$$

Another particle is thrown horizontally with same velocity then velocity of particle at the surface of earth.

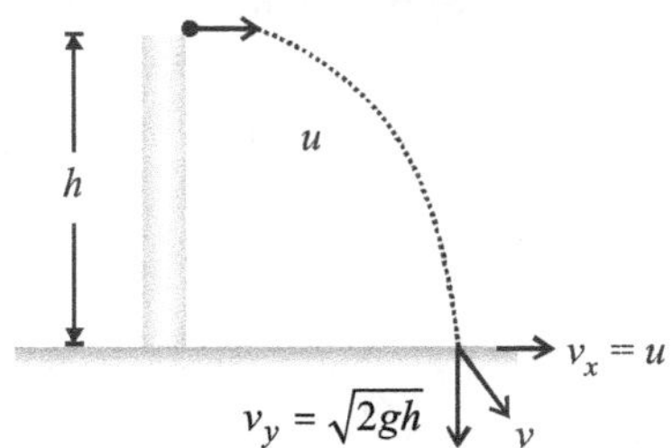

Horizontal component of velocity $v_x = u$

$\therefore$ Resultant velocity, $v = \sqrt{u^2 + 2gh}$

For both the particles, final velocities when they reach the earth's surface are equal.

21. (b) $\hat{r} = 0.5\hat{i} + 0.8\hat{j} + c\hat{k}$

$$|\hat{r}| = 1 = \sqrt{(0.5)^2 + (0.8)^2 + c^2}$$

$$(0.5)^2 + (0.8)^2 + c^2 = 1$$

$$c^2 = 0.11 \Rightarrow c = \sqrt{0.11}$$

22. (c) The pilot will see the ball falling in straight line because the reference frame is moving with the same horizontal velocity but the observer at rest will see the ball falling in parabolic path.

23. (a) $R = 2H$ (given)

We know, $R = 4H \cot\theta \Rightarrow \cot\theta = \dfrac{1}{2}$

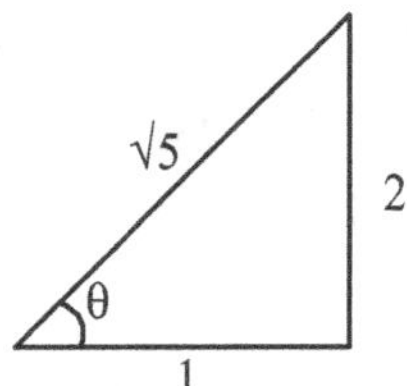

From triangle we can say that $\sin\theta = \dfrac{2}{\sqrt{5}}$, $\cos\theta = \dfrac{1}{\sqrt{5}}$

$\therefore$ Range of projectile $R = \dfrac{2v^2 \sin\theta \cos\theta}{g}$

$$= \frac{2v^2}{g} \times \frac{2}{\sqrt{5}} \times \frac{1}{\sqrt{5}} = \frac{4v^2}{5g}$$

24. (a) Note that the given angles of projection add upto 90°. For complementary angles of projection $(45^\circ + \alpha)$ and $(45^\circ - \alpha)$ with same initial velocity u, range R is same.

$$\theta_1 + \theta_2 = (45^\circ + \alpha) + (45^\circ - \alpha) = 90^\circ$$

So, the ratio of horizontal ranges is $1 : 1$.

25. (a) The components of 1 N and 2N forces along $+ x$ axis $= 1 \cos 60^\circ + 2 \sin 30^\circ$

$$= 1 \times \frac{1}{2} + 2 \times \frac{1}{2} = \frac{1}{2} + 1 = \frac{3}{2} = 1.5\,N$$

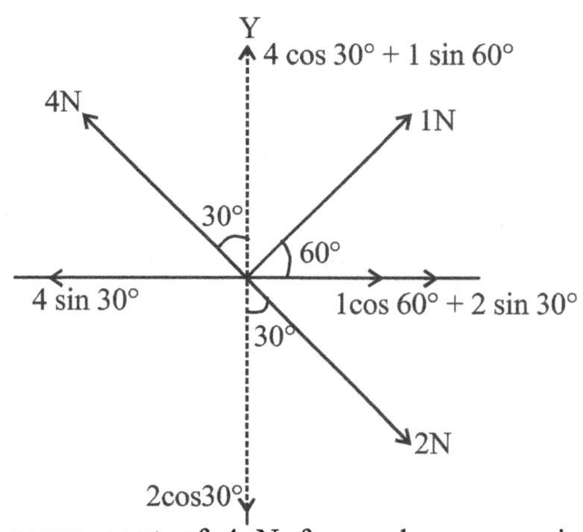

The component of 4 N force along –x-axis

$$= 4\sin 30° = 4 \times \frac{1}{2} = 2N.$$

Therefore, if a force of 0.5N is applied along + x-axis, the resultant force along x-axis will become zero and the resultant force will be obtained only along y-axis.

26. (d) $F_x = \dfrac{dp_x}{dt} = -2\sin\theta.$

Similarly, $F_y = \dfrac{dp_y}{dx} = 2\cos\theta.$

Angle θ between two vectors

$$\cos\theta = \frac{F_x p_x + F_y p_y}{|\vec{F}|\,|\vec{p}|}$$

$$= \frac{(-2\sin\theta)(2\cos\theta) + (2\cos\theta)(2\sin\theta)}{|\vec{F}|\,|\vec{p}|}$$

$$\Rightarrow \cos\theta = 0 \Rightarrow \theta = 90°$$

27. (a) The motion of the train will affect only the horizontal component of the velocity of the ball. Since, vertical component is same for both observers, the y_m will be same, but R will be different.

28. (d) As body covers equal angle in equal time intervals. Its angular velocity and hence magnitude of linear velocity is constant.

29. (a) For A: It goes up with velocity u will it reaches its maximum height (i.e. velocity becomes zero) and comes back to O and attains velocity u.

Using $v^2 = u^2 + 2as \Rightarrow v_A = \sqrt{u^2 + 2gh}$

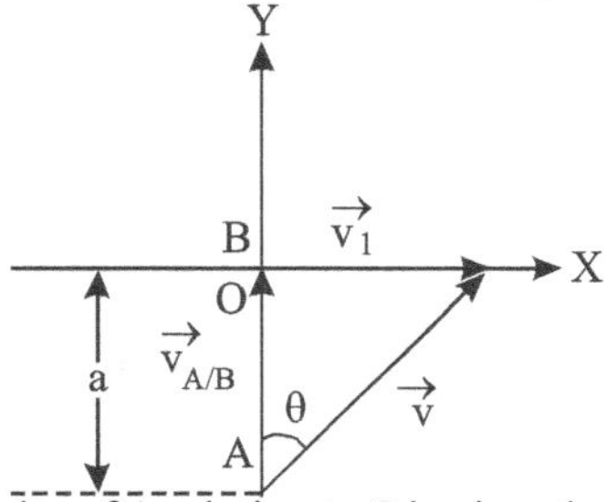

For B, going down with velocity u

$$\Rightarrow v_B = \sqrt{u^2 + 2gh}$$

For C, horizontal velocity remains same, i.e. u. Vertical velocity $= \sqrt{0 + 2gh} = \sqrt{2gh}$

The resultant $v_C = \sqrt{v_x^2 + v_y^2} = \sqrt{u^2 + 2gh}$.

Hence $v_A = v_B = v_C$

30. (d) $\vec{v}_{av} = \dfrac{\Delta\vec{r}\ (\text{displacement})}{\Delta t\ (\text{time taken})}$

$$= \frac{(13-2)\hat{i} + (14-3)\hat{j}}{5-0} = \frac{11}{5}(\hat{i} + \hat{j})$$

31. (c) Position vector

$\vec{r} = \cos wt\ \hat{x} + \sin\omega t\ \hat{y}$

$\therefore$ Velocity, $\vec{v} = -\omega\sin\omega t\ \hat{x} + \omega\cos\omega t\ \hat{y}$

and acceleration,

$\vec{a} = -\omega^2\cos\omega t\ \hat{x} + \omega\sin\omega t\ \hat{y} = -\omega 2\ \vec{r}$

$\vec{r} \cdot \vec{v} = 0$ hence $\vec{r} \perp \vec{v}$ and

$\vec{a}$ is directed towards the origin.

32. (d)

Velocity of A relative to B is given by

$$\vec{v}_{A/B} = \vec{v}_A - \vec{v}_B = \vec{v} - \vec{v}_1 \qquad ....(1)$$

By taking x-components of equation (1), we get

$$0 = v\sin\theta - v_1 \Rightarrow \sin\theta = \frac{v_1}{v} \qquad ....(2)$$

By taking Y-components of equation (1), we get

$$v_y = v\cos\theta \qquad .....(3)$$

Time taken by boy at A to catch the boy at B is given by

$$t = \frac{\text{Relative displacement along Y - axis}}{\text{Relative velocity along Y - axis}}$$

$$= \frac{a}{v\cos\theta} = \frac{a}{v.\sqrt{1-\sin^2\theta}} = \frac{a}{v.\sqrt{1-\left(\dfrac{v_1}{v}\right)^2}}$$

$$[\text{From equation (1)}]$$

$$= \frac{a}{v.\sqrt{\dfrac{v^2 - v_1^2}{v^2}}} = \frac{a}{\sqrt{v^2 - v_1^2}} = \sqrt{\frac{a^2}{v^2 - v_1^2}}$$

33. (b) $H = \dfrac{u^2\sin^2 45°}{2g} = \dfrac{u^2}{4g} \qquad ...(1)$

$$R = \frac{u^2 \sin 90°}{g} = \frac{u^2}{g}$$

$$\therefore \frac{R}{2} = \frac{u^2}{2g} \qquad \qquad ...(2)$$

$$\therefore \tan\alpha = \frac{H}{R/2}$$

$$= \frac{\dfrac{u^2}{4g}}{\dfrac{u^2}{2g}} = \frac{1}{2} \qquad \therefore \alpha = \tan^{-1}\left(\frac{1}{2}\right)$$

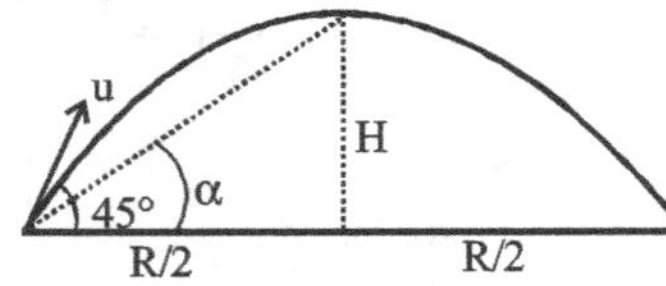

34. (b) Here, $x = 4\sin(2\pi t)$ ...(*i*)

$\qquad\qquad\quad y = 4\cos(2\pi t)$ ...(*ii*)

Squaring and adding equation (*i*) and (*ii*)

$x^2 + y^2 = 4^2 \Rightarrow R = 4$

Motion of the particle is circular motion, acceleration

vector is along $-\vec{R}$ and its magnitude $= \dfrac{v^2}{R}$

Velocity of particle, $v = \omega R = (2\pi)(4) = 8\pi$

35. (d) $|\vec{A}+\vec{B}|^2 = |\vec{A}-\vec{B}|^2$

$|\vec{A}+\vec{B}|^2 = |\vec{A}|^2 + |\vec{B}|^2 + 2\vec{A}.\vec{B} = A^2 + B^2 + 2AB\cos\theta$

$|\vec{A}-\vec{B}|^2 = |\vec{A}|^2 + |\vec{B}|^2 - 2\vec{A}.\vec{B}$

$= A^2 + B^2 - 2AB\cos\theta$

So, $A^2 + B^2 + 2AB\cos\theta$

$= A^2 + B^2 - 2AB\cos\theta$

$4AB\cos\theta = 0 \Rightarrow \cos\theta = 0$

$\therefore \theta = 90°$

So, angle between A & B is 90°.

36. (b) $\vec{v} = 6\hat{i} + 8\hat{j}$

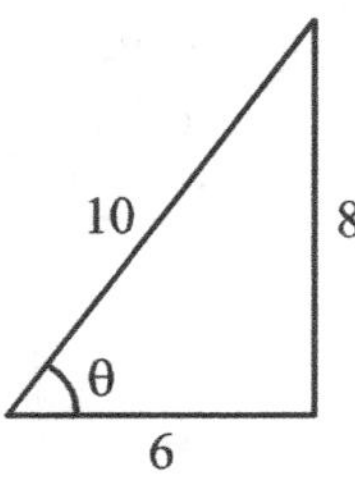

Comparing with $\vec{v} = v_x\hat{i} + v_y\hat{j}$, we get

$v_x = 6\,\text{ms}^{-1}$ and $v_y = 8\,\text{ms}^{-1}$

Also, $v^2 = v_x^2 + v_y^2 = 36 + 64 = 100$

or $v = 10\,\text{ms}^{-1}$

$\sin\theta = \dfrac{8}{10}$ and $\cos\theta = \dfrac{6}{10}$

$$R = \frac{v^2 \sin 2\theta}{g} = \frac{2v^2 \sin\theta\cos\theta}{g}$$

$$R = 2 \times 10 \times 10 \times \frac{8}{10} \times \frac{6}{10} \times \frac{1}{10} = 9.6\,\text{m}$$

37. (a) Range of a projectile is maximum when it is projected at an angle of 45° and is given by

$$R_{max} = \frac{u^2}{g}, \quad \text{where u is the velocity of projection}$$

$$\Rightarrow R = \frac{u^2}{g} \qquad \therefore u^2 = Rg \quad ...(i)$$

Now, to hit a target at a distance (R/2) from the gun, we must have

$$\frac{R}{2} = \frac{u^2 \sin 2\theta}{g}, \quad \text{where } \theta \text{ is the angle of projection.}$$

$$\Rightarrow \frac{R}{2} = \frac{Rg \sin 2\theta}{g}; \text{ from (i)}$$

$$\Rightarrow \sin 2\theta = \frac{1}{2} \Rightarrow \sin 2\theta = \sin 30°$$

$$\Rightarrow 2\theta = 30° \quad \therefore \theta = 15°$$

38. (a) Distance covered in one circular loop $= 2\pi r$

$= 2 \times 3.14 \times 100 = 628\,\text{m}$

$$\text{Speed} = \frac{628}{62.8} = 10\,\text{m/sec}$$

Displacement in one circular loop $= 0$

$$\text{Velocity} = \frac{0}{\text{time}} = 0$$

39. (a) $\overrightarrow{PQ} + \overrightarrow{QR} = \overrightarrow{PR}$

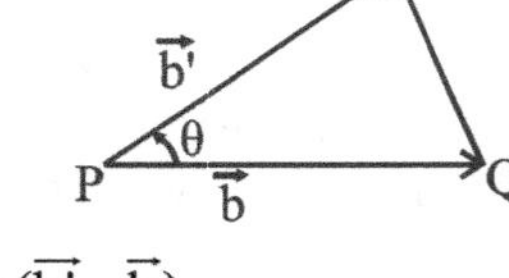

$\therefore \overrightarrow{QR} = \vec{b'} - \vec{b}$

Now $|\vec{b'} - \vec{b}|^2 = (\vec{b'} - \vec{b}).(\vec{b'} - \vec{b})$

$\qquad\qquad = b'^2 - 2bb'\cos\theta + b^2$

$\qquad\qquad = 2b^2(1 - \cos\theta) \qquad [\because b' = b]$

$\vec{b'} - \vec{b} = \sqrt{2}b\sqrt{1 - \cos\theta}$

$\qquad\qquad = \sqrt{2}b\left(\sqrt{2}\sin\frac{\theta}{2}\right) = 2b\sin\frac{\theta}{2}$

40. (a) $H_1 = \dfrac{u^2 \sin^2\theta}{2g}$

and $H_2 = \dfrac{u^2 \sin^2(90° - \theta)}{2g} = \dfrac{u^2 \cos^2\theta}{2g}$

$H_1 H_2 = \dfrac{u^2 \sin^2\theta}{2g} \times \dfrac{u^2 \cos^2\theta}{2g} = \dfrac{(u^2 \sin 2\theta)^2}{16g^2} = \dfrac{R^2}{16}$

$\therefore R = 4\sqrt{H_1 H_2}$

41. (c) $\vec{P} = \text{vector sum} = \vec{A} + \vec{B}$

$\vec{Q} = \text{vector differences} = \vec{A} - \vec{B}$

Since $\vec{P}$ and $\vec{Q}$ are perpendicular

$\therefore \vec{P}.\vec{Q}=0$

$\Rightarrow (\vec{A}+\vec{B}).(\vec{A}-\vec{B})=0 \Rightarrow A^2=B^2 \Rightarrow |A|=|B|$

42. **(b)** $y=bx^2$

Differentiating w.r.t to t an both sides, we get

$$\frac{dy}{dx}=b2x\frac{dx}{dt}$$

$v_y = 2bxv_x$

Again differentiating w.r.t to t on both sides we get

$$\frac{dv_y}{dt}=2bv_x\frac{dx}{dt}+2bx\frac{dv_x}{dt}=2bv_x^2+0$$

$[\dfrac{dv_x}{dt} = 0$, because the particle has constant acceleration along y-direction]

Now, $\dfrac{dv_y}{dt}=a=2bv_x^2$;

$$v_x^2=\frac{a}{2b}$$

$$v_x=\sqrt{\frac{a}{2b}}$$

43. **(a)** Arc length $=$ radius $\times$ angle

So, $|\vec{B}-\vec{A}|=|\vec{A}|\,\Delta\theta$

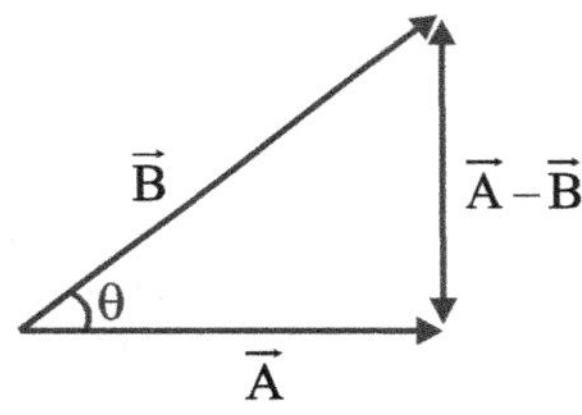

44. **(c)** Speed, V = constant (from question)

Centripetal acceleration,

$$a=\frac{V^2}{r}$$

ra = constant

Hence graph (c) correctly describes relation between acceleration and radius.

45. **(c)** From question,

Horizontal velocity (initial),

$$u_x=\frac{40}{2}=20\,\text{m/s}$$

Vertical velocity (initial), $50=u_y t+\dfrac{1}{2}gt^2$

$\Rightarrow \quad u_y\times 2+\dfrac{1}{2}(-10)\times 4$

or, $\quad 50=2u_y-20$

or, $\quad u_y=\dfrac{70}{2}=35\,\text{m/s}$

$\therefore \quad \tan\theta=\dfrac{u_y}{u_x}=\dfrac{35}{20}=\dfrac{7}{4}$

$\Rightarrow \quad$ Angle $\theta=\tan^{-1}\dfrac{7}{4}$

1. **(d)** Here $m = 0.5\,kg$; $u = -10\,m/s$;
$t = 1/50\,s$; $v = +15\,ms^{-1}$
Force $= m(v-u)/t = 0.5(10+15) \times 50 = 625\,N$

2. **(b)**

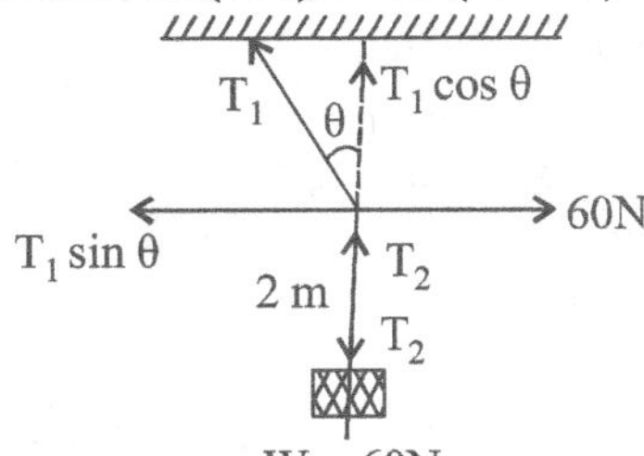

In eqbm $T_1 \cos\theta = T_2 = 60N$.   ...(1)
$T_1 \sin\theta = 60\,N$ ...(2)
$\therefore$ $\tan\theta = 1$
$\theta = 45°$.

3. **(d)** Mass of rocket $(m) = 5000\,Kg$
Exhaust speed $(v) = 800\,m/s$
Acceleration of rocket $(a) = 20\,m/s^2$
Gravitational acceleration $(g) = 10\,m/s^2$
We know that upward force
$F = m(g+a) = 5000(10+20)$
$= 5000 \times 30 = 150000\,N$.
We also know that amount of gas ejected

$$\left(\frac{dm}{dt}\right) = \frac{F}{v} = \frac{150000}{800} = 187.5\,kg/s$$

4. **(b)** (i) If a body is moved up an inclined plane, then the work done against friction will be zero as there is no friction. But work must be done against gravity. So this statement is incorrect.

(ii) This statement is correct, because moving vehicles are stopped by air friction only.

(iii) The normal reaction acting on a body on an inclined plane is given by,
$R = mg\cos\theta$
Where θ is the angle of inclination.
As θ increases, $\cos\theta$ decreases and hence R decreases. So this statement is incorrect.

(iv) The applied force needed to rub the duster upward,

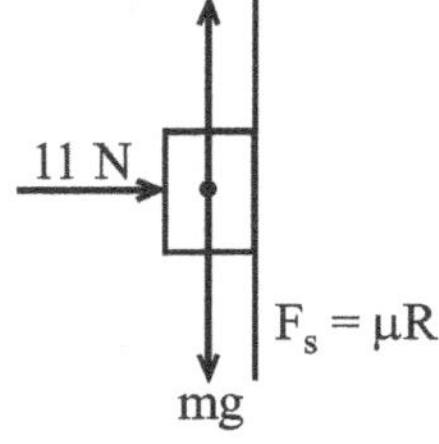

$F_{applied} = mg + \mu R = 0.5 \times 10 + 0.5 \times 11$
$= 5 + 5.5 = 10.5\,N$
$\therefore$ The work done in rubbing it upward through a distance of 10 cm,

$W = F_{applied} \times d = 10.5 \times 0.10 = 1.05\,J$
Hence this statement is incorrect.

5. **(b)** Momentum $P = mv = m\sqrt{2gh}$
($\because v^2 = u^2 + 2gh$; Here $u = 0$)
When stone hits the ground momentum
$$P = m\sqrt{2gh}$$
when same stone dropped from $2h$ (100% of initial) then momentum
$$P' = m\sqrt{2g(2h)} = \sqrt{2}P$$
Which is changed by 41% of initial.

6. **(c)** Change in momentum along the wall
$= mv\cos 60° - mv\cos 60° = 0$
Change in momentum perpendicular to the wall
$= mv\sin 60° - (-mv\sin 60°) = 2mv\sin 60°$

$\therefore$ Applied force $= \dfrac{\text{Change in momentum}}{\text{Time}}$

$= \dfrac{2\,mv\sin 60°}{0.20}$

$= \dfrac{2 \times 3 \times 10 \times \sqrt{3}}{2 \times 20} = 50 \times 3\sqrt{3}$

$= 150\sqrt{3}$ newton

7. **(b)**

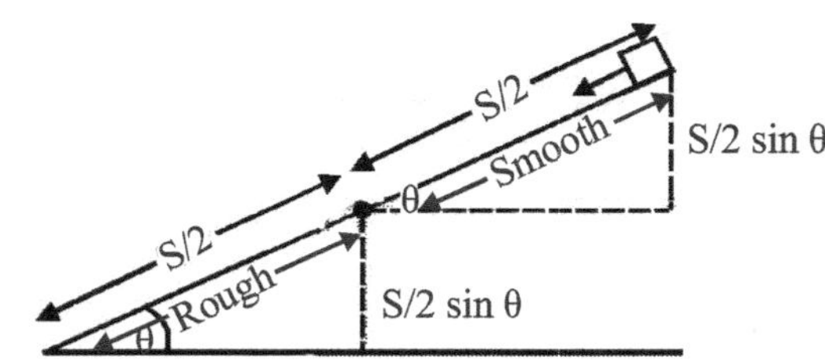

For upper half of inclined plane
$v^2 = u^2 + 2a\,S/2 = 2(g\sin\theta)\,S/2 = gS\sin\theta$
For lower half of inclined plane
$0 = u^2 + 2g(\sin\theta - \mu\cos\theta)\,S/2$
$\Rightarrow -gS\sin\theta = gS(\sin\theta - \mu\cos\theta)$
$\Rightarrow 2\sin\theta = \mu\cos\theta$

$\Rightarrow \mu = \dfrac{2\sin\theta}{\cos\theta} = 2\tan\theta$

8. **(c)** Forces acting on the block are as shown in the fig. Normal reaction N is provided by the force $m\alpha$ due to acceleration α

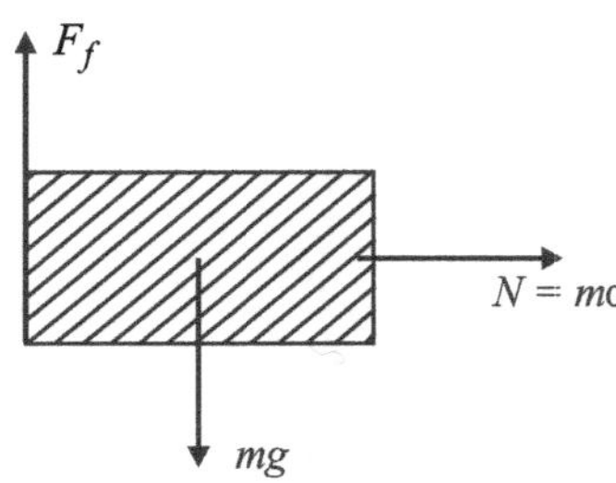

$\therefore \quad N = m\,\alpha$

For the block not to fall, frictional force, $F_f \geq mg$

$\Rightarrow \quad \mu N \geq mg$

$\Rightarrow \quad \mu m \alpha \geq mg$

$\Rightarrow \quad \alpha \geq g/\mu$

9. (b) $v = \sqrt{gr} = \sqrt{10 \times 40} = 20 \text{ m s}^{-1}$

10. (a)

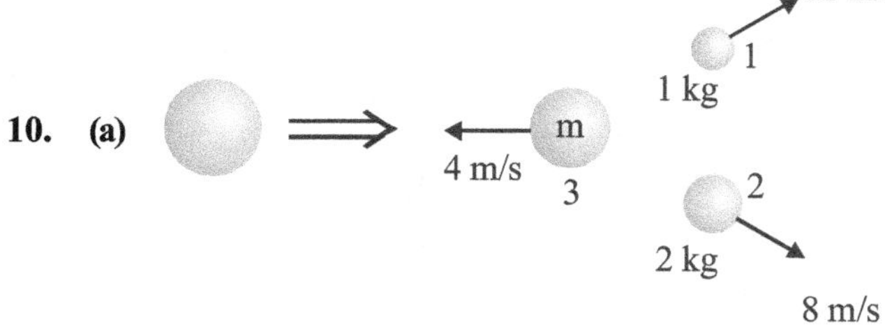

According to conservation of linear momentum

$$P_3 = \sqrt{p_1^2 + p_2^2}$$

$$\Rightarrow m \times 4 = \sqrt{(1 \times 12)^2 + (2 \times 8)^2} = 20 \Rightarrow m = 5 \text{ kg.}$$

11. (c) Let T be the tension in the branch of a tree when monkey is descending with acceleration a. Then $mg - T = ma$; and $T = 75\%$ of weight of monkey

$$= \left(\frac{75}{100}\right) mg = \left(\frac{1}{4}\right) mg \text{ or } a = \frac{g}{4}.$$

12. (d) $v = u - at \Rightarrow t = \dfrac{u}{a}$ [As $v = 0$]

$$t = \frac{u \times m}{F} = \frac{30 \times 1000}{5000} = 6 \sec$$

13. (c) Applying law of conservation of linear momentum

$$m_1 v_1 + m_2 v_2 = 0, \quad \frac{m_1}{m_2} = -\frac{v_2}{v_1} \text{ or } \frac{v_1}{v_2} = -\frac{m_2}{m_1}$$

14. (a) The frictional force acting on M is μmg

$$\therefore \text{ Acceleration} = \frac{\mu mg}{M}$$

15. (c) $\dfrac{dM}{dt} = 0.1 \text{ kg/s}, \; v_{gas} = 50 \text{ m/s}$,

Mass of the rocket = 2 kg. Mv = constant

$$-v\frac{dM}{dt} + M\frac{dv}{dt} = 0 \; . \; \therefore \; \frac{dv}{dt} = \frac{1}{M} v \frac{dM}{dt}$$

$$\Rightarrow \text{Acceleration} = \frac{1}{2} \times 50 \times 0.1 = 2.5 \text{ m/s}^2$$

16. (a) Coefficient of static friction,

$$\mu_s = \tan 30° = \frac{1}{\sqrt{3}} = 0.577 \cong 0.6$$

$$S = ut + \frac{1}{2} at^2$$

$$4 = \frac{1}{2} a(4)^2 \Rightarrow a = \frac{1}{2} = 0.5$$

$$[\because \; s = 4m \text{ and } t = 4s \text{ given}]$$

$$a = g \sin\theta - \mu_k (g) \cos\theta$$

$$\Rightarrow \mu_k = \frac{0.9}{\sqrt{3}} = 0.5$$

17. (c) All blocks will move with the same aceleration Let it be a . Then

$$F = 4Ma \Rightarrow a = \frac{F}{4M}$$

From the figures it is clear that

$T_1 = 3\,Ma$, $T_2 = 2\,Ma$ and $T_3 = Ma$

Putting the value of a, we get

$$T_1 = \frac{3}{4}F \; , \; T_2 = \frac{F}{2} \text{ and } T_3 = \frac{F}{4}$$

18. (c) Maximum force by surface when friction works

$$F = \sqrt{f^2 + R^2} = \sqrt{(\mu R)^2 + R^2} = R\sqrt{\mu^2 + 1}$$

Minimum force = R when there is no friction

Hence ranging from R to $R\sqrt{\mu^2 + 1}$ [where, R = mg]

19. (c) Motion with constant momentum along a straight line. According to Newton's second law rate of change of momentum is directly proportional to force applied.

20. (b) For the motion of both the blocks

$$m_1 a = T - \mu_k m_1 g$$
$$m_2 g - T = m_2 a$$

$$a = \frac{m_2 g - \mu_k\, m_1 g}{m_1 + m_2}$$

$$m_2 g - T = (m_2)\left(\frac{m_2 g - \mu_k\, m_1 g}{m_1 + m_2}\right)$$

solving we get tension in the string

$$T = \frac{m_1 m_2\,(1 + \mu_k)\,g}{m_1 + m_2}$$

21. (d) Acceleration of block while sliding down upper half = $g \sin \phi$;

retardation of block while sliding down lower half = $-(g \sin \phi - \mu g \cos \phi)$

For the block to come to rest at the bottom, acceleration in I half = retardation in II half.

$$g \sin \phi = -(g \sin \phi - \mu g \cos \phi)$$

$$\Rightarrow \mu = 2 \tan \phi$$

22. **(d)** The particle is moving in circular path

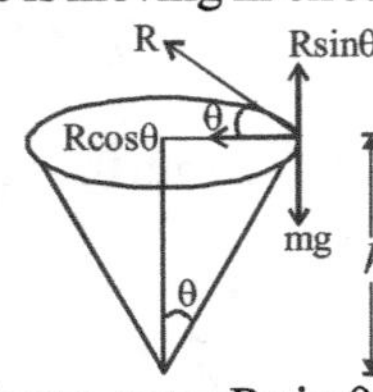

From the figure, $mg = R \sin \theta$ ... (i)

$$\frac{mv^2}{r} = R \cos \theta \qquad \text{... (ii)}$$

From equations (i) and (ii) we get

$$\tan \theta = \frac{rg}{v^2} \text{ but } \tan \theta = \frac{r}{h}$$

$$\therefore h = \frac{v^2}{g} = \frac{(0.5)^2}{10} = 0.025 \text{m} = 2.5 \text{cm}$$

23. **(b)** By spitting or sneezing we get a momentum in opposite direction which will help us in getting off the plane. In all other cases we will slip on ice as there is no friction.

24. **(a)** Force required to just move a body
$(F) =$ force due to static friction $= \mu_s \, mg$
When body moves with a constant acceleration (a) then
$F - f_k = ma$, where f_k is the force of kinetic friction $= \mu_k \, mg$

$$\therefore a = \frac{F - f_k}{m} = \frac{F - f_k}{m} = \frac{\mu_s mg - \mu_k mg}{m}$$

$$= (\mu_s - \mu_k)\, g = (0.75 - 0.5)\, g = \frac{g}{4}.$$

25. **(c)** Considering the two masses and the rope a system, then

Initial net force $= [25 - (15 + 5)]g = 5g$

Final net force $= [(25 + 5) - 15]g = 15\,g$

$\Rightarrow$ (acceleration)$_{\text{final}} = 3$ (acceleration)$_{\text{initial}}$

26. **(c)**

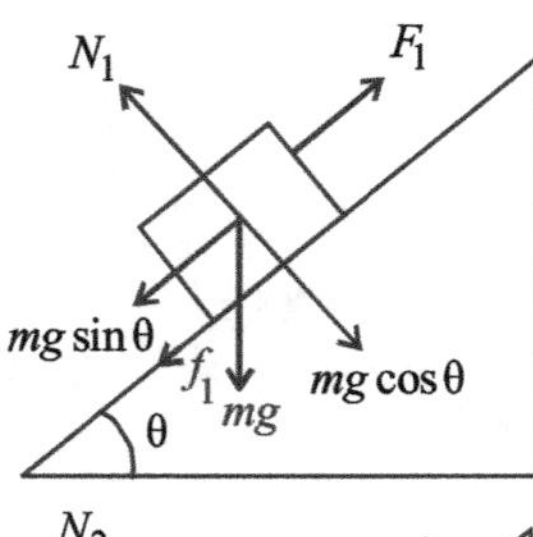

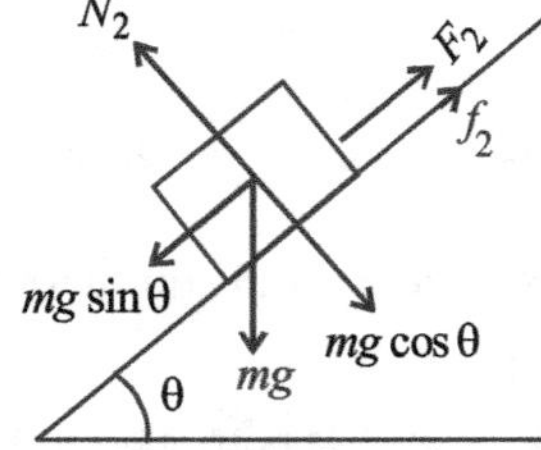

For the upward motion of the body
$mg \sin \theta + f_1 = F_1$
or, $F_1 = mg \sin \theta + \mu mg \cos \theta$

For the downward motion of the body,
$mg \sin \theta - f_2 = F_2$
or $F_2 = mg \sin \theta - \mu mg \cos \theta$

$$\therefore \frac{F_1}{F_2} = \frac{\sin \theta + \mu \cos \theta}{\sin \theta - \mu \cos \theta}$$

$$\Rightarrow \frac{\tan \theta + \mu}{\tan \theta - \mu} = \frac{2\mu + \mu}{2\mu - \mu} = \frac{3\mu}{\mu} = 3$$

27. **(b)** Considering the equilibrium of B
$-m_B g + T = m_B a$
Since the block A slides down with constant speed.
$a = 0$.
Therefore $T = m_B g$
Considering the equilibrium of A, we get
$10a = 10g \sin 30° - T - \mu N$
where $N = 10g \cos 30°$

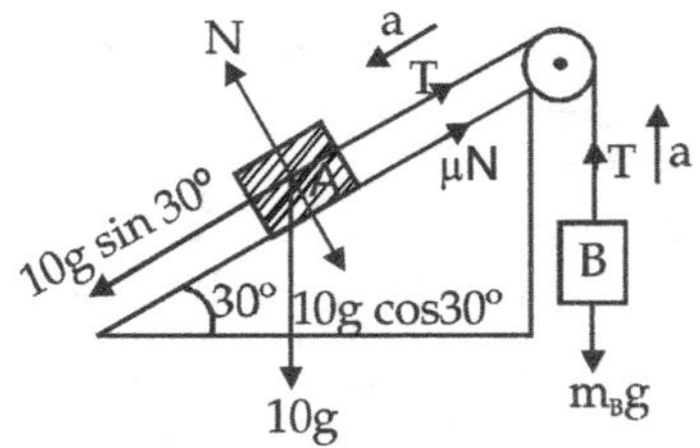

$$\therefore 10a = \frac{10}{2} g - T - \mu \times 10g \cos 30°$$

but $a = 0$, $T = m_B g$

$$0 = 5g - m_B g - \frac{0.2\sqrt{3}}{2} \times 10 \times g$$

$$\Rightarrow m_B = 3.268 \approx 3.3 \text{ kg}$$

28. **(a)** When tension in the cable is equal to the weight of cable, the system is in equilibrium. It means the system is at rest or moving with uniform velocity.

29. **(c)** Tension at the highest point

$$T_{\text{top}} = \frac{mv^2}{r} - mg = 2mg \quad (\because v_{\text{top}} = \sqrt{3gr})$$

Tension at the lowest point
$T_{\text{bottom}} = 2mg + 6mg = 8mg$

$$\therefore \frac{T_{\text{top}}}{T_{\text{bottom}}} = \frac{2mg}{8mg} = \frac{1}{4}.$$

30. **(d)** When brakes are on, the wheels of the cycle will slide on the road instead of rolling there. It means the sliding friction will come into play instead of rolling friction. The value of sliding friction is more than that of rolling friction.

31. **(a)** When car moves towards right with acceleration a then due to pseudo force the plumb line will tilt in backward direction making an angle θ with vertical

From the figure

$\tan \theta = a / g$

$\therefore \theta = \tan^{-1}(a / g)$

32. **(b)** See fig.

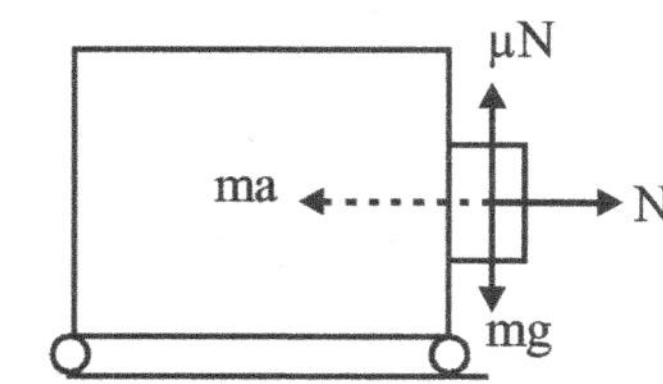

If a = acceleration of the cart, then N = ma

∴ μN = mg or μ ma = mg or a = g/μ

33. **(a)**

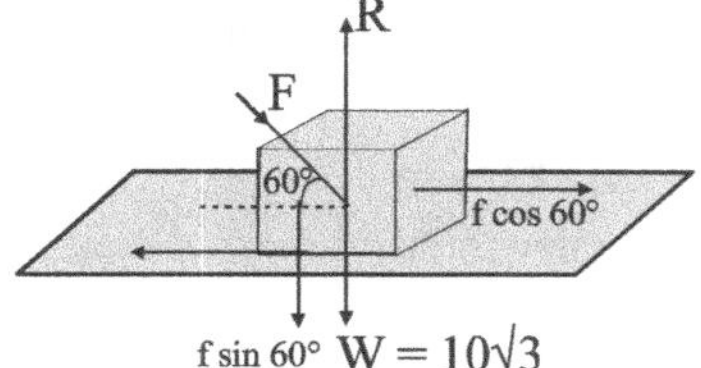

f = μR

$F \cos 60° = \mu(W + F \sin 60°)$

Substituing $\mu = \dfrac{1}{2\sqrt{3}}$ and $W = 10\sqrt{3}$ we get F = 20 N

34. **(d)** When the block slides down the plane with a constant speed, then the inclination of the plane is equal to angle of repose (θ).

Coeff. of friction = tan of the angle of repose = tan θ.

35. **(d)** Writing free body-diagrams for *m* & *M*,

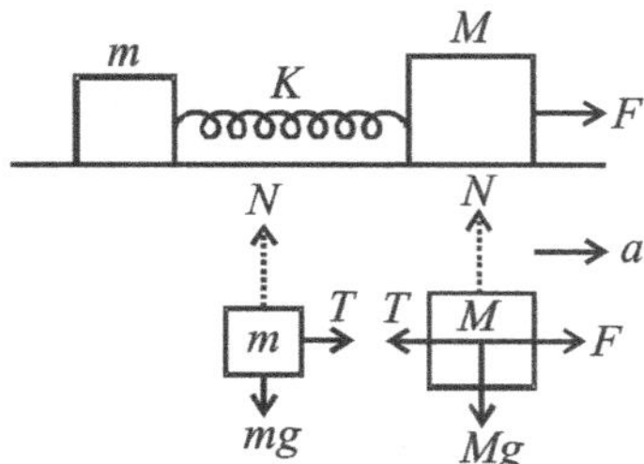

we get $T = ma$ and $F - T = Ma$

where *T* is force due to spring

$\Rightarrow F - ma = Ma$ or, $F = Ma + ma$

∴ $a = \dfrac{F}{M+m}$.

Now, force acting on the block of mass m is

$ma = m\left(\dfrac{F}{M+m}\right) = \dfrac{mF}{m+M}$.

36. **(a)** At limiting equilibrium, $\mu = \tan \theta$

$\tan\theta = \mu = \dfrac{dy}{dx} = \dfrac{x^2}{2}$ (from question)

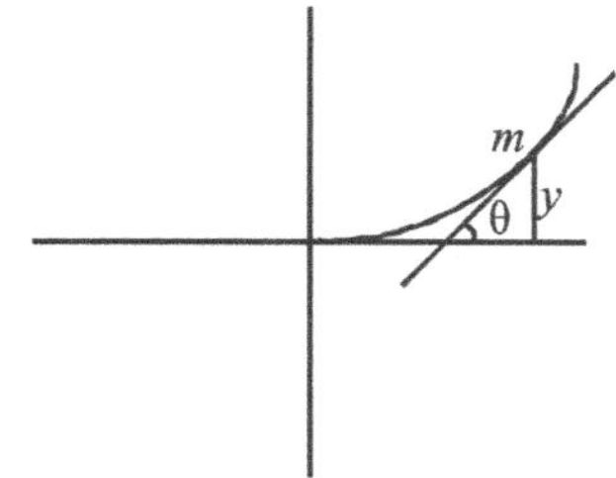

∵ Coefficient of friction μ = 0.5

∴ $0.5 = \dfrac{x^2}{2}$

$\Rightarrow x = \pm 1$

Now, $y = \dfrac{x^3}{6} = \dfrac{1}{6} m$

37. **(a)** As the ball, m = 10 g = 0.01 kg rebounds after striking the wall

∴ Change in momentum $= mv - (-mv) = 2\,mv$

Inpulse = Change in momentum = $2mv$

∴ $v = \dfrac{\text{Impulse}}{2m} = \dfrac{0.54 \text{ N s}}{2 \times 0.01 \text{ kg}} = 27 \text{ m s}^{-1}$

38. **(b)** From the F.B.D.

N = mg cos θ

F = ma = mg sin θ − μN

$\Rightarrow$ a = g(sin θ − μ cos θ)

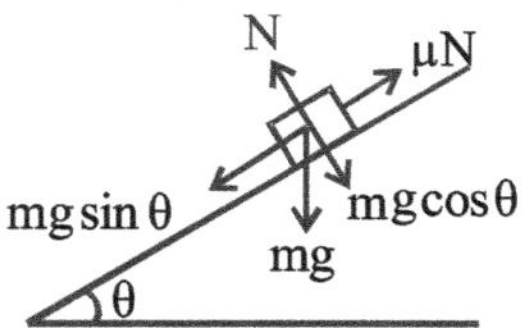

Now using, $v^2 - u^2 = 2as$

or, $v^2 = 2 \times g(\sin\theta - \mu\cos\theta)\ell$

(ℓ = length of incline)

or, $v = \sqrt{2g\ell(\sin\theta - \mu\cos\theta)}$

39. **(a)** During collision of ball with the wall horizontal momentum changes (vertical momentum remains constant)

∴ $F = \dfrac{\text{Change in horizontal momentum}}{\text{Time of contact}}$

$= \dfrac{2P\cos\theta}{0.1} = \dfrac{2mv\cos\theta}{0.1}$

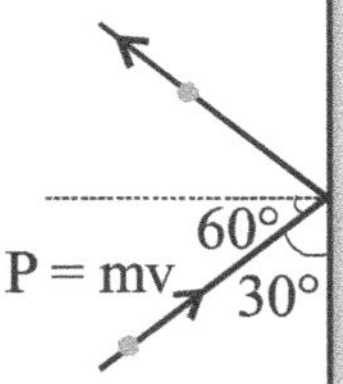

$= \dfrac{2 \times 0.1 \times 10 \times \cos 60°}{0.1} = 10\text{N}$

40. **(d)** Given $F = 600 - (2 \times 10^5 t)$

The force is zero at time t, given by

$0 = 600 - 2 \times 10^5 t$

$\Rightarrow t = \dfrac{600}{2 \times 10^5} = 3 \times 10^{-3}$ seconds

∴ Impulse $= \int_0^t F\,dt = \int_0^{3\times10^{-3}} (600 - 2 \times 10^5 t)\,dt$

$$= \left[600t - \frac{2 \times 10^5 t^2}{2} \right]_0^{3 \times 10^{-3}}$$

$$= 600 \times 3 \times 10^{-3} - 10^5 (3 \times 10^{-3})^2$$

$$= 1.8 - 0.9 = 0.9\,\text{Ns}$$

41. **(d)** According to question, two stones experience same centripetal force

i.e. $F_{C_1} = F_{C_2}$

or, $\dfrac{mv_1^2}{r} = \dfrac{2mv_2^2}{(r/2)}$ or, $V_1^2 = 4V_2^2$

So, $V_1 = 2V_2$ i.e., $n = 2$

42. **(b)** $T_1 = m(g + a) = 0.1(10 + 5) = 1.5\text{N}$

$T_2 = m(g - a) = 0.1(10 - 5) = 0.5\text{N}$

$\Rightarrow T_1 - T_2 = (1.5 - 0.5)\text{N} = 1\text{N}$

43. **(d)** As shown in the figure, the three forces are represented by the sides of a triangle taken in the same order. Therefore the resultant force is zero. $\vec{F}_{net} = m\vec{a}$. Therefore acceleration is also zero i.e., velocity remains unchanged.

44. **(b)** Rate of flow of water will depend on the net acceleration due to gravity.

When the lift is moving upward with acceleration a ,

$g'_u = g + a$

When the lift is moving downward with acceleration on a, $g'_d = g - a$

$\therefore\quad g'_u > g > g'_d \quad \therefore R_u > R_0 > R_d$

45. **(d)** According to law of conservation of momentum the third piece has momentum

$= 1 \times -(3\hat{i} + 4\hat{j})\ \text{kg ms}^{-1}$

Impulse = Average force × time

$\Rightarrow$ Average force $= \dfrac{\text{Impulse}}{\text{time}}$

$= \dfrac{\text{Change in momentum}}{\text{time}} = \dfrac{-(3\hat{i} + 4\hat{j})\text{kg ms}^{-1}}{10^{-4}\,\text{s}}$

1. **(b)** $k = 5 \times 10^3 \,\text{N/m}$

$$W = \frac{1}{2}k\left(x_2^2 - x_1^2\right) = \frac{1}{2} \times 5 \times 10^3 \left[(0.1)^2 - (0.05)^2\right]$$

$$= \frac{5000}{2} \times 0.15 \times 0.05 = 18.75 \,\text{Nm}$$

2. **(a)** Given: Mass of particle, $M = 10\text{g} = \dfrac{10}{1000}\,\text{kg}$

radius of circle $R = 6.4$ cm

Kinetic energy E of particle $= 8 \times 10^{-4}$ J

acceleration $a_t = ?$

$$\frac{1}{2}mv^2 = E$$

$$\Rightarrow \quad \frac{1}{2}\left(\frac{10}{1000}\right)v^2 = 8 \times 10^{-4}$$

$$\Rightarrow \quad v^2 = 16 \times 10^{-2}$$

$$\Rightarrow \quad v = 4 \times 10^{-1} = 0.4 \,\text{m/s}$$

Now, using

$$v^2 = u^2 + 2a_t s \qquad\qquad (s = 4\pi R)$$

$$(0.4)^2 = 0^2 + 2a_t\left(4 \times \frac{22}{7} \times \frac{6.4}{100}\right)$$

$$\Rightarrow \quad a_t = (0.4)^2 \times \frac{7 \times 100}{8 \times 22 \times 6.4} = 0.1 \,\text{m/s}^2$$

3. **(b)** We know that $F \times v = $ Power

$\therefore F \times v = c$ where c = constant

$$m\frac{dv}{dt} \times v = c \qquad \left(\because F = ma = \frac{mdv}{dt}\right)$$

$$m\int_0^v v\,dv = c\int_0^t dt \qquad \Rightarrow \frac{1}{2}mv^2 = ct$$

$$v = \sqrt{\frac{2c}{m}} \times t^{1/2}$$

$$\frac{dx}{dt} = \sqrt{\frac{2c}{m}} \times t^{1/2} \qquad \text{where } v = \frac{dx}{dt}$$

$$\int_0^x dx = \sqrt{\frac{2c}{m}} \times \int_0^t t^{1/2}\,dt$$

$$x = \sqrt{\frac{2c}{m}} \times \frac{2t^{3/2}}{3} \quad \Rightarrow \quad x \propto t^{3/2}$$

4. **(a)** When ball collides with the ground it loses its 50% of energy

$$\therefore \frac{KE_f}{KE_i} = \frac{1}{2} \Rightarrow \frac{\frac{1}{2}mV_f^2}{\frac{1}{2}mV_i^2} = \frac{1}{2}$$

or $\dfrac{V_f}{V_i} = \dfrac{1}{\sqrt{2}}$

or, $\dfrac{\sqrt{2gh}}{\sqrt{v_0^2 + 2gh}} = \dfrac{1}{\sqrt{2}}$

or, $4gh = v_0^2 + 2gh$

$\therefore v_0 = 20\,\text{ms}^{-1}$

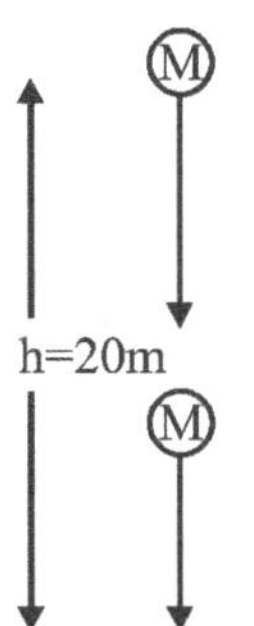

5. **(c)** As the cord is trying to hold the motion of the block, work done by the cord is negative.

$$W = -M(g-a)\,d = -M\left(g - \frac{g}{4}\right)d = \frac{-3Mgd}{4}$$

6. **(b)** According to principle of conservation of energy

Loss in potential energy = Gain in kinetic energy

$$\Rightarrow mgh = \frac{1}{2}mv^2 \Rightarrow v = \sqrt{2gh}$$

If h_1 and h_2 are initial and final heights, then

$$v_1 = \sqrt{2gh_1}, v_2 = \sqrt{2gh_2}$$

Loss in velocity

$$\Delta v = v_1 - v_2 = \sqrt{2gh_1} - \sqrt{2gh_2}$$

$\therefore$ Fractional loss in velocity

$$= \frac{\Delta v}{v_1} = \frac{\sqrt{2gh_1} - \sqrt{2gh_2}}{\sqrt{2gh_1}} = 1 - \sqrt{\frac{h_2}{h_1}}$$

$$= 1 - \sqrt{\frac{1.8}{5}} = 1 - \sqrt{0.36} = 1 - 0.6 = 0.4 = \frac{2}{5}$$

7. **(a)** As $u_2 = 0$ and $m_1 = m_2$, therefore from

$m_1 u_1 + m_2 u_2 = m_1 v_1 + m_2 v_2$ we get $u_1 = v_1 + v_2$

Also, $e = \dfrac{v_2 - v_1}{u_1} = \dfrac{v_2 - v_1}{v_2 + v_1} = \dfrac{1 - v_1/v_2}{1 + v_1/v_2}$,

which gives $\dfrac{v_1}{v_2} = \dfrac{1-e}{1+e}$

8. **(d)** As we know power $P = \dfrac{dw}{dt}$

$\Rightarrow \quad w = Pt = \dfrac{1}{2}mv^2$

So, $v = \sqrt{\dfrac{2Pt}{m}}$

Hence, acceleration $a = \dfrac{dv}{dt} = \sqrt{\dfrac{2P}{m}} \cdot \dfrac{1}{2\sqrt{t}}$

Therefore, force on the particle at time 't'

$= ma = \sqrt{\dfrac{2Km^2}{m}} \cdot \dfrac{1}{2\sqrt{t}} = \sqrt{\dfrac{Km}{2t}} = \sqrt{\dfrac{mK}{2}}\, t^{-1/2}$

9. **(b)** $x = \dfrac{t^3}{3} \Rightarrow \dfrac{dx}{dt} = \dfrac{3t^2}{3} = t^2 \Rightarrow v = t^2$

when, $t = 2$ sec, $v = t^2 = (2)^2 = 4$ m/s

Work done = K.E. acquired $= \dfrac{1}{2}mv^2$

$= \dfrac{1}{2} \times (2) \times (4)^2 = 16\,\text{J}$

10. **(b)** For elastic collision in one dimension

$v_1 = \dfrac{2m_2 u_2}{m_1 + m_2} + \dfrac{(m_1 - m_2)u_1}{(m_1 + m_2)}$

As mass 2m, is at rest, So $u_2 = 0$

$\Rightarrow \quad v_1 = \dfrac{(8m - 2m)u}{8m + 2m} = \dfrac{3}{5}u$

Final energy of sphere $= (K.E.)_f$

$= \dfrac{1}{2}(8m)\left(\dfrac{3u}{5}\right)^2 = \dfrac{1}{2}(8m)u^2 \times \left(\dfrac{3}{5}\right)^2$

$= \dfrac{9}{25}E = 0.36\,E$

11. **(b)** As we know work done in stretching spring

$w = \dfrac{1}{2}kx^2$

where k = spring constant
x = extension
Case (a) If extension (x) is same,

$W = \dfrac{1}{2}K\,x^2$

So, $W_P > W_Q \qquad (\because K_P > K_Q)$

Case (b) If spring force (F) is same $W = \dfrac{F^2}{2K}$

So, $W_Q > W_P$

12. **(b)** If the particle is released at the origin, it will try to go in the direction of force. Here $\dfrac{dU}{dx}$ is positive and hence force is negative, as a result it will move towards $-$ve x-axis.

13. **(c)** The potential energy of a spring is given by,

$U = \dfrac{1}{2}kx^2 \Rightarrow 10\,\text{J} = \dfrac{1}{2}ks^2 \qquad ....\,(i)$

The potential energy stored when stretched

through$(2s) = \dfrac{1}{2}k(2s^2) = \dfrac{1}{2}ks^2 \times 4$

Substituting from (i)
P.E. $= 40\,\text{J}$.
But to increase 's' to '2s', the work done
$= 40 - 10 = 30\,\text{J}$.

14. **(b)** Power $= \dfrac{\text{Work done}}{\text{Time}} = \dfrac{\dfrac{1}{2}m\left(v^2 - u^2\right)}{t}$

$P = \dfrac{1}{2} \times \dfrac{2.05 \times 10^6 \times \left[(25)^2 - \left(5^2\right)\right]}{5 \times 60}$

$P = 2.05 \times 10^6\,\text{W} = 2.05\,\text{MW}$

15. **(b)** Work done = Area under F-x graph
= area of rectangle ABCD + area of rectangle LCFE
+ area of rectangle GFIH + area of triangle IJK

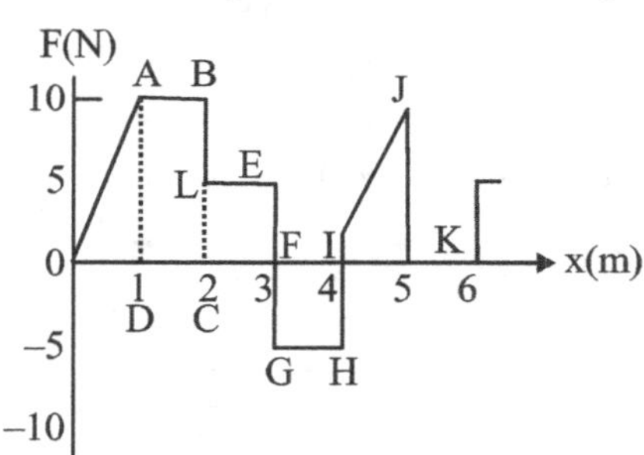

$= (2-1) \times (10-0) + (3-2)(5-0)\ (4-3)(-5-0)$

$+ \dfrac{1}{2}(5-4)(10-0) = 15\,J$

16. **(c)**

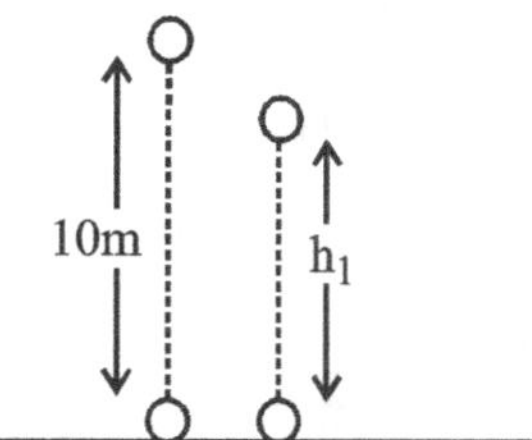

Just before impact, energy
$E = mgh = 10\,mg \qquad ....\,(1)$
Just after impact

$E_1 = mgh - \dfrac{25}{100}mgh = 0.75\,mgh$

Hence, $mgh_1 = E_1 \qquad$ (from given figure)

$$mgh_1 = 0.75\, mg\,(10)$$
$$h_1 = 7.5\,m$$

17. (d) When C strikes A

$$\frac{1}{2}mv_0^2 = \frac{1}{2}mv'^2 + \frac{1}{2}kx_0^2 \quad (v' = \text{velocity of A})$$

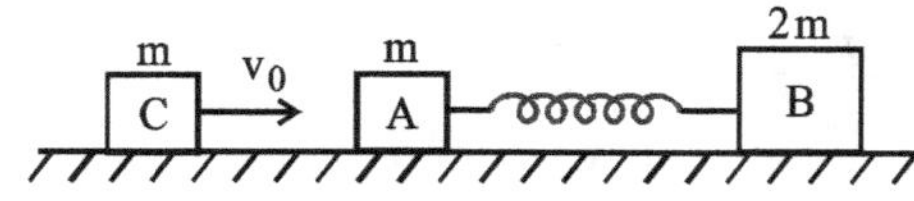

$$kx_0^2 = m(v_0^2 - v'^2) \qquad \text{.... (i)}$$

$$\frac{1}{2}2mv'^2 = \frac{1}{2}kx_0^2$$

(When A and B Block attains K.E.)

$$\therefore \quad \frac{1}{2}kx_0^2 = mv'^2 \qquad \text{.... (ii)}$$

From (i) and (ii),

$$kx_0^2 = mv_0^2 - mv'^2 = mv_0^2 - \frac{k}{2}x_0^2$$

$$\Rightarrow \quad kx_0^2 + \frac{k}{2}x_0^2 = mv_0^2$$

$$\frac{3}{2}kx_0^2 = mv_0^2 \quad \therefore \quad k = \frac{2}{3}m\frac{v_0^2}{x_0^2}$$

18. (a) Given : $k_A = 300\,N/m,\ k_B = 400\,N/m$

Let the combination of springs is compressed by force F. Spring A is compressed by x. Therefore compression in spring B

$$x_B = (8.75 - x)\ cm$$

$$F = 300 \times x = 400(8.75 - x)$$

Solving we get, $x = 5\ cm$

$$x_B = 8.75 - 5 = 3.75\ cm$$

$$\frac{E_A}{E_B} = \frac{\frac{1}{2}k_A(x_A)^2}{\frac{1}{2}k_B(x_B)^2} = \frac{300 \times (5)^2}{400 \times (3.75)^2} = \frac{4}{3}$$

19. (d) Given force $\vec{F} = 2t\hat{i} + 3t^2\hat{j}$

According to Newton's second law of motion,

$$m\frac{d\vec{v}}{dt} = 2t\hat{i} + 3t^2\hat{j} \quad (m = 1\,kg)$$

$$\Rightarrow \quad \int_0^{\bar{v}} d\vec{v} = \int_0^t \left(2t\hat{i} + 3t^2\hat{j}\ dt\ \right)$$

$$\Rightarrow \quad \vec{v} = t^2\hat{i} + t^3\hat{j}$$

Power $P = \vec{F}\cdot\vec{v} = (2t\hat{i} + 3t^2\hat{j})\cdot(t^2\hat{i} + t^3\hat{j})$
$$= (2t^3 + 3t^5)W$$

20. (a) According to conservation of linear momentum,
$$M_b V_b = M_{bl} V_{bl} + M_b V_b^1 \qquad \text{....(i)}$$

where v_b is velocity of bullet before collision v_b^1 velocity of bullet after collision and v_{bl} is the velocity of block.

K.E. of block = P.E. of block

$$\frac{1}{2}M_{bl}V_{bl}^2 = M_{bl}\,gh\ (h = 0.2m)$$

Solving we get $V_{bl} = 2ms^{-1}$
Now from eq (i)

$$20 \times 10^{-3} \times 600 = 4 \times 2 + 20 \times 10^{-3}\ V_b^1$$

Solving we get $\quad V_b^1 = 200\ m/s$

21. (d) $\sin\theta = \dfrac{1}{x}$

From free body diagram of the body

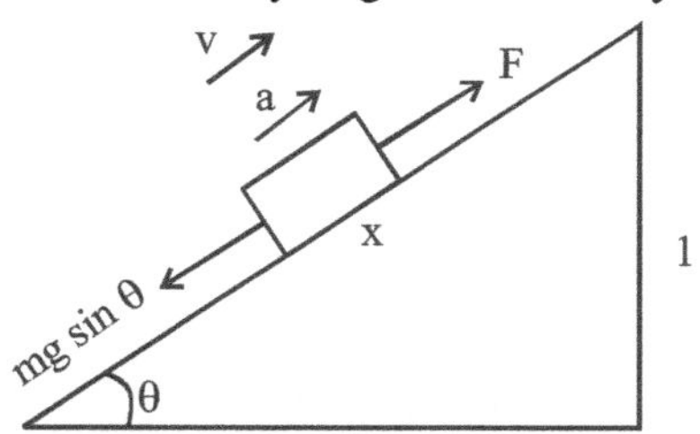

$$F - mg\sin\theta = ma$$

$$F = m\,(g\sin\theta + a) = m\left(\frac{g}{x} + a\right) \qquad \text{.......(1)}$$

Displacement of the body till its velocity reaches v

$$v^2 = 0 + 2as \quad \Rightarrow \quad s = \frac{v^2}{2a}$$

Now, work done $= F\,s\cos 0° = \dfrac{m}{x}(g + ax) \times \dfrac{v^2}{2a}$

$$= \frac{mv^2}{2ax}(g + ax)$$

22. (c) $t_{AB} = \sqrt{\dfrac{2h}{g}}$

$$t_{BC} + t_{CB} = 2\sqrt{\frac{2h_1}{g}}$$

$$= 2\sqrt{\frac{2e^2 h}{g}} = 2e\sqrt{\frac{2h}{g}}$$

$$t_{BD} + t_{DB} = 2e^2\sqrt{\frac{2h}{g}}$$

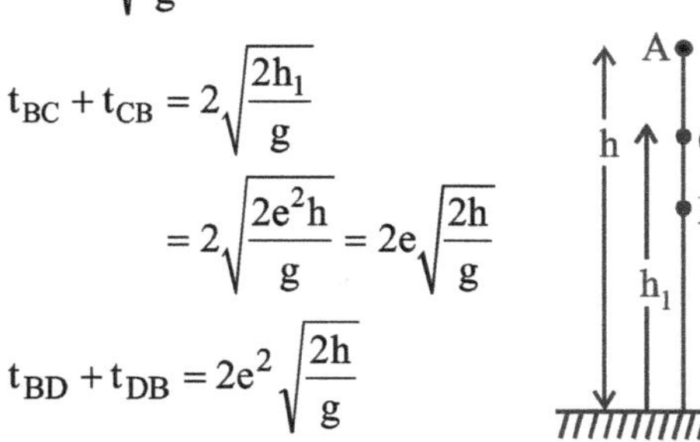

$\therefore$ Total time taken by the body in coming to rest

$$= \sqrt{\frac{2h}{g}} + 2e\sqrt{\frac{2h}{g}} + 2e^2\sqrt{\frac{2h}{g}} + ...$$

$$= \sqrt{\frac{2h}{g}} + 2e\sqrt{\frac{2h}{g}}\,[1 + e + e^2 + ...]$$

$$= \sqrt{\frac{2h}{g}} + 2e\sqrt{\frac{2h}{g}} \times \frac{1}{1-e} = \sqrt{\frac{2h}{g}} \left[\frac{1+e}{1-e}\right] = t\left(\frac{1+e}{1-e}\right)$$

23. (a) Velocity is maximum when K.E. is maximum
For minimum. P.E.,

$$\frac{dV}{dx} = 0 \Rightarrow x^3 - x = 0 \Rightarrow x = \pm 1$$

$$\Rightarrow \text{Min. P.E.} = \frac{1}{4} - \frac{1}{2} = -\frac{1}{4} \text{ J}$$

$$\text{K.E.}_{(max.)} + \text{P.E.}_{(min.)} = 2 \text{ (Given)}$$

$$\therefore \text{K.E.}_{(max.)} = 2 + \frac{1}{4} = \frac{9}{4}$$

$$\text{K.E.}_{max.} = \frac{1}{2}mv^2_{max.}$$

$$\Rightarrow \frac{1}{2} \times 1 \times v^2_{max.} = \frac{9}{4} \Rightarrow v_{max.} = \frac{3}{\sqrt{2}}$$

24. (a) Given, $h = 60m$, $g = 10 \text{ ms}^{-2}$,
Rate of flow of water $= 15$ kg/s
$\therefore$ Power of the falling water
$= 15 \text{ kgs}^{-1} \times 10 \text{ ms}^{-2} \times 60 \text{ m} = 900$ watt.
Loss in energy due to friction

$$= 9000 \times \frac{10}{100} = 900 \text{ watt.}$$

$\therefore$ Power generated by the turbine
$= (9000 - 900)$ watt $= 8100$ watt $= 8.1$ kW

24. (b) Let initial velocity of the bullet be v.
By linear momentum conservation

$$\frac{m}{2}v = \left(\frac{m}{2} + m\right)v_1$$

(v_1 = combined velocity)

$$v_1 = \frac{v}{3} \qquad \qquad \text{.... (1)}$$

retardation $= \mu g$

$$0 = \left(\frac{v}{3}\right)^2 - 2\mu gd \Rightarrow v = 3\sqrt{2\mu gd}$$

25. (c) Force constant of a spring

$$k = \frac{F}{x} = \frac{mg}{x} = \frac{1 \times 10}{2 \times 10^{-2}} \Rightarrow k = 500 N/m$$

Increment in the length $= 60 - 50 = 10$ cm

$$U = \frac{1}{2}kx^2 = \frac{1}{2}500\left(10 \times 10^{-2}\right)^2 = 2.5 J$$

26. (b) Constant power of car $P_0 = F.v = ma.v$

$$P_0 = m\frac{dv}{dt}.v$$

$$P_0 dt = mvdv \text{ Integrating}$$

$$P_0 t = \frac{mv^2}{2}$$

$$v = \sqrt{\frac{2P_0 t}{m}}$$

$\because P_0$, m and 2 are constant

$$\therefore \qquad v \propto \sqrt{t}$$

27. (a) $x = 3t - 4t^2 + t^3$

$$\frac{dx}{dt} = 3 - 8t + 3t^2$$

$$\text{Acceleration} = \frac{d^2x}{dt^2} = -8 + 6t$$

Acceleration after 4 sec
$= -8 + 6 \times 4 = 16 \text{ ms}^{-2}$
Displacement in 4 sec
$= 3 \times 4 - 4 \times 4^2 + 4^3 = 12$ m
$\therefore$ Work $=$ Force $\times$ displacement
$=$ Mass $\times$ acc. $\times$ disp.
$= 3 \times 10^{-3} \times 16 \times 12 = 576$ mJ

28. (c) $K_i = \frac{1}{2}m_1 u_1^2$,

$$K_f = \frac{1}{2}m_1 v_1^2, v_1 = \frac{m_1 - m_2}{m_1 + m_2}u_1$$

Fractional loss

$$\frac{K_i - K_f}{K_i} = \frac{\frac{1}{2}m_1 u_1^2 - \frac{1}{2}m_1 v_1^2}{\frac{1}{2}m_1 u_1^2}$$

$$= 1 - \frac{v_1^2}{u_1^2} = 1 - \frac{(m_1 - m_2)^2}{(m_1 + m_2)^2} = \frac{4m_1 m_2}{(m_1 + m_2)^2}$$

$$(m_2 = m; \ m_1 = nm); \qquad = \frac{4n}{(1+n^2)}$$

Energy transfer is maximum when $K_f = 0$

$$\frac{4n}{(1+n^2)} = 1 \Rightarrow 4n = 1 + n^2 + 2n \Rightarrow n^2 + 1 - 2n = 0$$

$$(n-1)^2 = 0 \qquad n = 1 \text{ ie. } m_2 = m, \ m_1 = m$$

Transfer will be maximum when both masses are equal and one is at rest.

29. (a) For inelastic collision, linear momentum is conserved

$$\Rightarrow mv_1 = 2mv_2 \Rightarrow v_2 = \frac{v_1}{2}$$

Loss in K.E. $=$ Gain in P.E.

$$= \frac{1}{2}mv_1^2 - \frac{1}{2}(2m)v_2^2 = 2mgh$$

$$\Rightarrow 4 mgh = mv_1^2 - \frac{mv_1^2}{2} = \frac{mv_1^2}{2} = \frac{mv^2}{2}$$

$$\Rightarrow h = \frac{v^2}{8g}$$

30. (c) Volume of water to raise $= 22380\, l = 22380 \times 10^{-3}\,\text{m}^3$

$$P = \frac{mgh}{t} = \frac{V\rho gh}{t} \Rightarrow t = \frac{V\rho gh}{P}$$

$$t = \frac{22380 \times 10^{-3} \times 10^3 \times 10 \times 10}{10 \times 746} = 15\ \text{min}$$

31. (b) $E = \dfrac{p^2}{2m}$

or, $E_1 = \dfrac{p_1^2}{2m_1}, E_2 = \dfrac{p_2^2}{2m_2}$

or, $m_1 = \dfrac{p_1^2}{2E_1}, m_2 = \dfrac{p_2^2}{2E_2}$

$m_1 > m_2 \Rightarrow \dfrac{m_1}{m_2} > 1$

$\therefore \dfrac{p_1^2 E_2}{E_1 p_2^2} > 1 \Rightarrow \dfrac{E_2}{E_1} > 1 \quad [\because p_1 = p_2]$

or, $E_2 > E_1$

32. (d) From, $F = ma$

$$a = \frac{F}{m} = \frac{0.1x}{10} = 0.01x = V\frac{dV}{dx}$$

So, $\displaystyle\int_{V_1}^{V_2} V dV = \int_{20}^{30} \frac{x}{100} dx$

$$-\frac{V^2}{2}\Bigg|_{V_1}^{V_2} = \frac{x^2}{200}\Bigg|_{20}^{30} = \frac{30 \times 30}{200} - \frac{20 \times 20}{200}$$

$$= 4.5 - 2 = 2.5$$

$$= \frac{1}{2}m\left(V_2^2 - V_1^2\right) = 10 \times 2.5\ \text{J} = -25\text{J}$$

Final K.E.

$$= \frac{1}{2}mV_2^2 = \frac{1}{2}mV_1^2 - 25 = \frac{1}{2} \times 10 \times 10 \times 10 - 25$$

$$= 500 - 25 = 475\ \text{J}$$

33. (c) Friction is a non-conservative force. Work done by a non-conservative force over a closed path is not zero.

34. (b) $F = \dfrac{12}{100} \times 1000 \times 10\ \text{N} = 1200\ \text{N}$

$P = Fv = 1200\ \text{N} \times 15\ \text{ms}^{-1} = 18\ \text{kW}.$

35. (c) When the ball is released from the top of tower then ratio of distances covered by the ball in first, second and third second

$h_I : h_{II} : h_{III} = 1 : 3 : 5 : [\text{Because } h_n \propto (2n-1)]$

$\therefore$ Ratio of work done $mgh_I : mgh_{II} : mgh_{III} = 1 : 3 : 5$

36. (c) $m_2 \qquad m_1$

$\textcircled{B} \rightarrow v \quad \textcircled{A}$

$\qquad u = 0$

conservation of linear momentum along x-direction

$$m_2v = m_1v_x \Rightarrow \frac{m_2v}{m_1} = v_x$$

along y-direction

$$m_2 \times \frac{v}{2} = m_1v_y \Rightarrow v_y = \frac{m_2v}{2m_1}$$

Note: Let A moves in the direction, which makes an angle θ with initial direction i.e.

$$\tan\theta = \frac{v_y}{v_x} = \frac{m_2v}{2m_1} \Bigg/ \frac{m_2v}{m_1}$$

$$\tan\theta = \frac{1}{2}$$

$$\Rightarrow \quad \theta = \tan^{-1}\left(\frac{1}{2}\right) \text{ to the } x\text{-axis.}$$

37. (b) Let the block compress the spring by x before stopping. Kinetic energy of the block = (P.E of compressed spring) + work done against friction.

$$\frac{1}{2} \times 2 \times (4)^2 = \frac{1}{2} \times 10{,}000 \times x^2 + 15 \times x$$
$$10{,}000\, x^2 + 30x - 32 = 0$$

$$\Rightarrow 5000x^2 + 15x - 16 = 0$$

$$\therefore \quad x = \frac{-15 \pm \sqrt{(15)^2 - 4 \times (5000)(-16)}}{2 \times 5000}$$

$$= 0.055\text{m} = 5.5\text{cm}.$$

38. (a) Amount of water flowing per second from the pipe

$$= \frac{m}{time} = \frac{m}{\ell} \cdot \frac{\ell}{t} = \left(\frac{m}{\ell}\right)v$$

Power = K.E. of water flowing per second

$$= \frac{1}{2}\left(\frac{m}{\ell}\right)v \cdot v^2$$

$$= \frac{1}{2}\left(\frac{m}{\ell}\right)v^3$$

$$= \frac{1}{2} \times 100 \times 8 = 400\ W$$

39. (b) Mass of over hanging chain $m' = \dfrac{4}{2} \times (0.6)\text{kg}$

Let at the surface PE $= 0$
C.M. of hanging part $= 0.3$ m below the table

$$U_i = -m'gx = -\frac{4}{2} \times 0.6 \times 10 \times 0.30$$

$\Delta U = m'gx = 3.6\text{J} = $ Work done in putting the entire chain on the table.

40. **(d)**

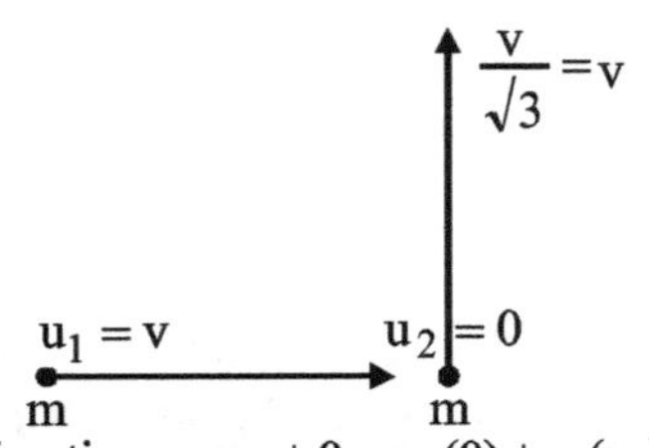

In x-direction : $mv + 0 = m(0) + m(v_2)_x$

In y-direction : $0 + 0 = m\left(\dfrac{v}{\sqrt{3}}\right) + m(v_2)_y$ is

$\Rightarrow (v_2)_y = \dfrac{v}{\sqrt{3}}$ and $(v_2)_x = v$

$\therefore \ v_2 = \sqrt{\left(\dfrac{v}{\sqrt{3}}\right)^2 + v^2}$

$\Rightarrow v_2 = \sqrt{\dfrac{v^2}{3} + v^2} = v\sqrt{\dfrac{4}{3}} = \dfrac{2v}{\sqrt{3}}$

Alternative method : In x-direction,
$mv = mv_1 \cos\theta$ ...(1)
where v_1 is the velocity of second mass
In y-direction,

$0 = \dfrac{mv}{\sqrt{3}} - mv_1 \sin\theta$

or $m_1 v_1 \sin\theta = \dfrac{mv}{\sqrt{3}}$ ...(2)

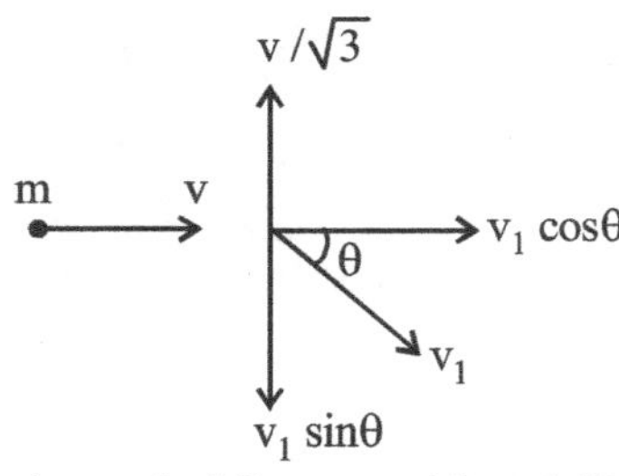

Squaring and adding eqns. (1) and (2)

$v_1{}^2 = v^2 + \dfrac{v^2}{\sqrt{3}} \Rightarrow v_1 = \dfrac{2}{\sqrt{3}} v$

41. **(b)**

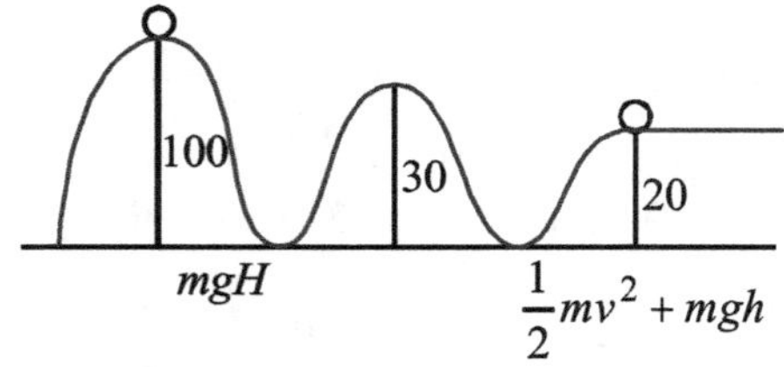

Using conservation of energy,

$m(10 \times 100) = m\left(\dfrac{1}{2}v^2 + 10 \times 20\right)$

or $\dfrac{1}{2}v^2 = 800$ or $v = \sqrt{1600} = 40\,\text{m/s}$

42. **(b)**

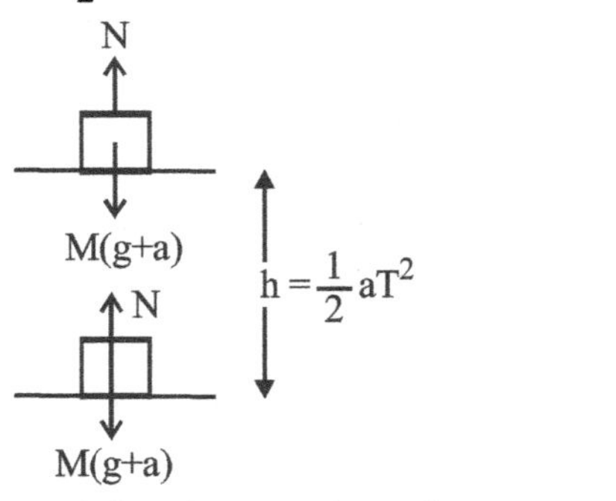

Work done by normal reaction

$= Nh = M(g+a)\dfrac{1}{2}aT^2 = \dfrac{1}{2}M(g+a)aT^2$

43. **(c)** Applying W-E theorem on the block for any compression x :

$W_{ext} + W_g + W_{spring} = \Delta KE$

$\Rightarrow Fx + 0 - \dfrac{1}{2}Kx^2 = \dfrac{1}{2}mv^2$

$\Rightarrow$ KE vs x is inverted parabola.

44. **(d)** $\text{K.E.} = \dfrac{1}{2}mv^2$

Further, $v^2 = u^2 + 2as = 0 + 2ad = 2ad$
$= 2(F/m)d$

Hence, $\text{K.E.} = \dfrac{1}{2}m \times 2(F/m)d = Fd$

or, K.E. acquired = Work done
$= F \times d = \text{constant}.$
i.e., it is independent of mass m.

45. **(a)** Gravitational potential energy of ball gets converted into elastic potential energy of the spring.

$mg(h+d) = \dfrac{1}{2}kd^2$

Net work done $= mg(h+d) - \dfrac{1}{2}kd^2 = 0$

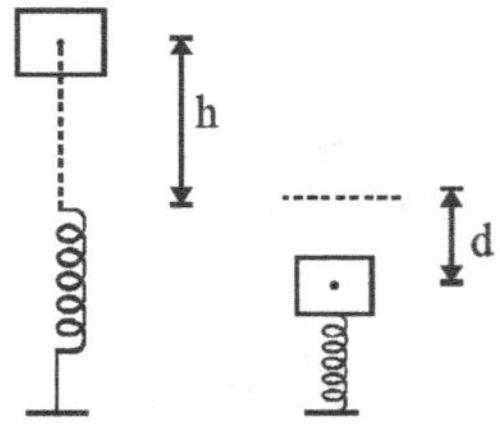

1. (a) Here $a = \dfrac{2}{\sqrt{3}}R$

Now, $\dfrac{M}{M'} = \dfrac{\dfrac{4}{3}\pi R^3}{a^3}$

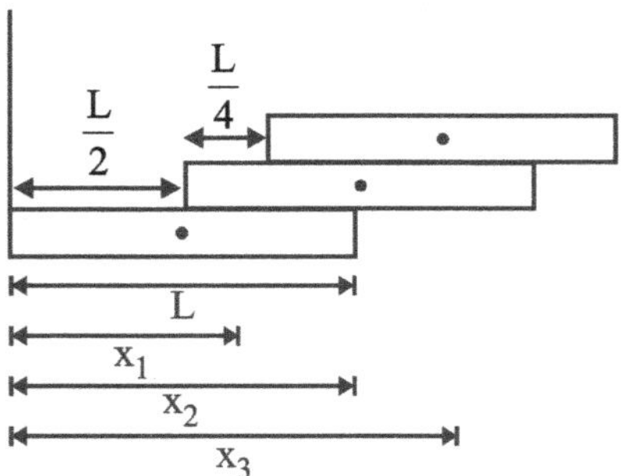

$= \dfrac{\dfrac{4}{3}\pi R^3}{\left(\dfrac{2}{\sqrt{3}}R\right)^3} = \dfrac{\sqrt{3}}{2}\pi.$ $M' = \dfrac{2M}{\sqrt{3}\pi}$

Moment of inertia of the cube about the given axis,

$I = \dfrac{M'a^2}{6} = \dfrac{\dfrac{2M}{\sqrt{3}\pi}\times\left(\dfrac{2}{\sqrt{3}}R\right)^2}{6} = \dfrac{4MR^2}{9\sqrt{3}\pi}$

2. (d) Initially centre of mass is at the centre. When sand is poured it will fall and again after a limit, centre of mass will rise.

3. (a) Does not shift as no external force acts. The centre of mass of the system continues its original path. It is only the internal forces which comes into play while breaking.

4. (d) Let the mass of loop P (radius $= r$) $= m$

So, the mass of loop Q (radius $= nr$) $= nm$

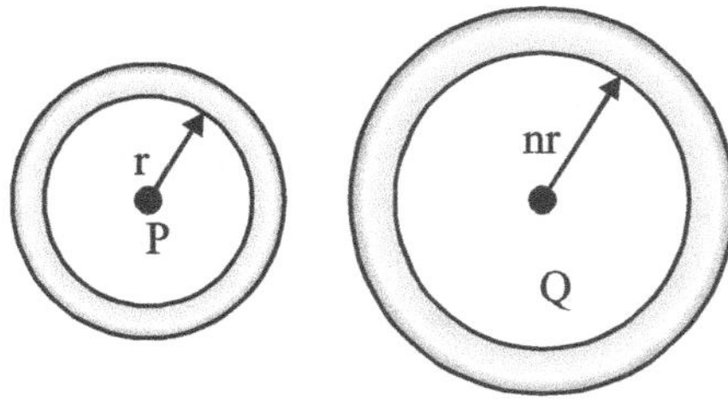

Moment of inertia of loop P, $I_P = mr^2$
Moment of inertia of loop Q, $I_Q = nm(nr)^2 = n^3 mr^2$

$\therefore \dfrac{I_Q}{I_P} = n^3 = 8 \Rightarrow n = 2$

5. (d) When the ball is hit by a cue, the linear impulse imparted to the ball = change in momentum = mv_0

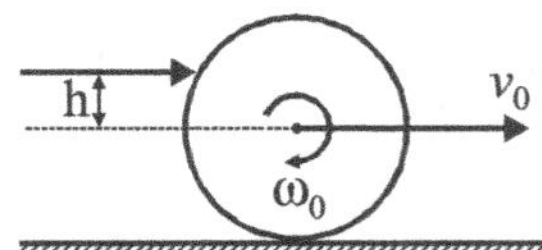

Angular momentum = Moment of momentum

$I\omega_0 = (mv_0)h$

$\dfrac{2}{5}mr^2\omega_0 = mv_0 h$ or $\omega_0 = \dfrac{5v_0 h}{2r^2}$

6. (d)

$x_1 = \dfrac{L}{2}, \ x_2 = L, \ x_3 = \dfrac{5L}{4}$

$\therefore X_{CM} = \dfrac{m_1 x_1 + m_2 x_2 + m_3 x_3}{m_1 + m_2 + m_3}$

$= \dfrac{M\times\dfrac{L}{2} + M\times L + M\times\dfrac{5L}{4}}{M + M + M}$

$= \dfrac{\dfrac{11}{4}ML}{3M} = \dfrac{11L}{12}$

7. (c)

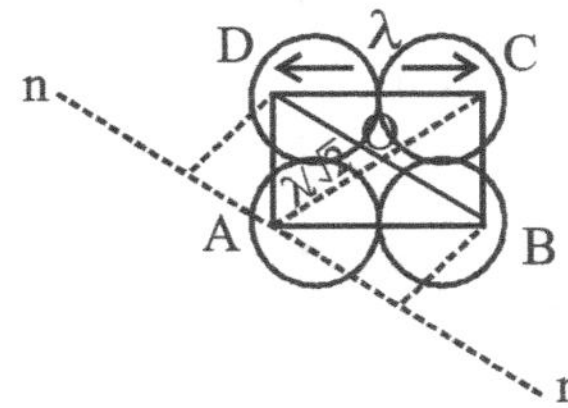

$I_{nn'}$ = M.I due to the point mass at B +
$\phantom{I_{nn'} = }$ M.I due to the point mass at D +
$\phantom{I_{nn'} = }$ M.I due to the point mass at C.

$I_{nn'} = 2\times m\left(\dfrac{\ell}{\sqrt{2}}\right)^2 + m(\sqrt{2}\ell)^2$

$= m\ell^2 + 2m\ell^2 = 3m\ell^2$

8. (c)

From conservation of angular momentum about any fix point on the surface,

$mr^2\omega_0 = 2mr^2\omega$

$\Rightarrow \omega = \omega_0/2 \Rightarrow v = \dfrac{\omega_0 r}{2}$ $[\because v = r\omega]$

9. (d) Initial position of cm $= \dfrac{m_2\ell}{m_1 + m_2}$

Also $x_{cm} = \dfrac{m_1 \Delta x_1 + m_2 \Delta x_2}{m_1 + m_2} = \dfrac{m_1 v_0 t + 0}{m_1 + m_2}$

$\therefore$ final position $= \dfrac{m_2 \ell}{m_1 + m_2} + \dfrac{m_1 v_0 t}{m_1 + m_2}$

10. (a) Here, $L = 1.8\ \text{kg m}^2\ \text{s}^{-1}$, $M = 1.5\ \text{kg}$,
$\omega = 0.3\ \text{rad s}^{-1}$
Angular momentum, $L = I\omega$
$L = k^2 M\omega \qquad (\because I = MK^2)$
or $1.8 = k^2 \times 1.5 \times (0.3)$

$\Rightarrow k^2 = \dfrac{1.8}{1.5 \times 0.3} = 4$

$\Rightarrow k = 2\ \text{m}.$

11. (b) $\vec{\tau} = \vec{r} \times \vec{F} \Rightarrow \vec{r} . \vec{\tau} = 0 \qquad \vec{F} . \vec{\tau} = 0$

Since, $\vec{\tau}$ is perpendicular to the plane of $\vec{r}$ and $\vec{F}$, hence the dot product of $\vec{\tau}$ with $\vec{r}$ and $\vec{F}$ is zero.

12. (c)

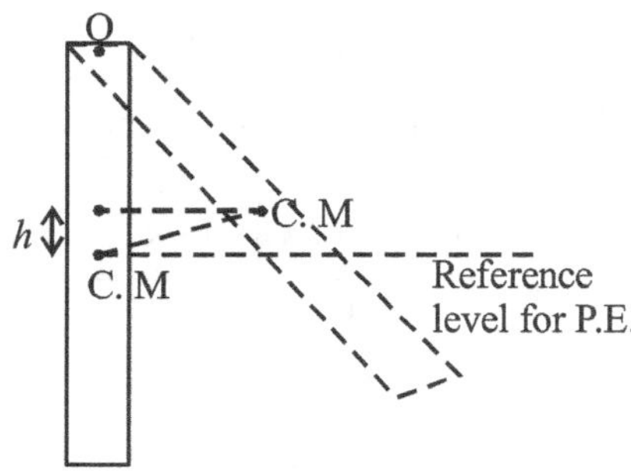

The moment of inertia of the rod about O is $\dfrac{1}{3} m\ell^2$.

The maximum angular speed of the rod is when the rod is instantaneously vertical. The energy of the rod in this condition is $\dfrac{1}{2} I\omega^2$ where I is the moment of inertia of the rod about O. When the rod is in its extreme portion, its angular velocity is zero momentarily. In this case, the energy of the rod is mgh where h is the maximum height to which the centre of mass (C.M) rises

$\therefore mgh = \dfrac{1}{2} I\omega^2 = \dfrac{1}{2}\left(\dfrac{1}{3} ml^2\right)\omega^2$

$\Rightarrow h = \dfrac{\ell^2 \omega^2}{6g}$

13. (b)

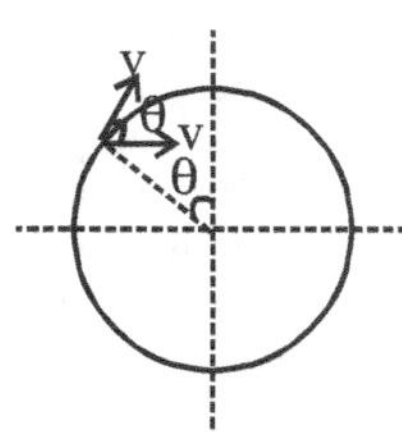

$v_R = \sqrt{v^2 + v^2 + 2v^2 \cos\theta} = \sqrt{2v^2(1 + \cos\theta)}$

$= 2v \cos\dfrac{\theta}{2}$

14. (b) $K.E_{\text{rotational}} = \dfrac{1}{2} I\omega^2$

$= \dfrac{1}{2}\dfrac{2}{5}\omega r^2 d^2 \left(\because I_{\text{Solid sphere}} = \dfrac{2}{5} mr^2\right)$

$K.E_{\text{translational}} = \dfrac{1}{2} mv^2$

$\therefore \dfrac{K.E_{\text{rotational}}}{K.E_{\text{translational}}} = \dfrac{2}{5}$

Hence option (b) is correct

15. (c) Kinetic energy $_{(\text{rotational})}$ $K_R = \dfrac{1}{2} I\omega^2$

Kinetic energy $_{(\text{translational})}$ $K_T = \dfrac{1}{2} Mv^2$

$(v = R\omega)$

M.I.$_{(\text{initial})}$ $I_{\text{ring}} = MR^2$; $\omega_{\text{initial}} = \omega$
M.I.$_{(\text{new})}$ $I'_{(\text{system})} = MR^2 + 2mR^2$

$\omega'_{(\text{system})} = \dfrac{M\omega}{M + 2m}$

Solving we get loss in K.E.

$= \dfrac{Mm}{(M + 2m)}\omega^2 R^2$

16. (b) For no angular acceleration $\tau_{\text{net}} = 0$
$\Rightarrow F_1 \times 5 = F_2 \times 30$ (given $F_2 = 4N$) $\Rightarrow F_1 = 24N$

17. (c) For toppling $Mg\dfrac{L}{2} = F_1 \times h$

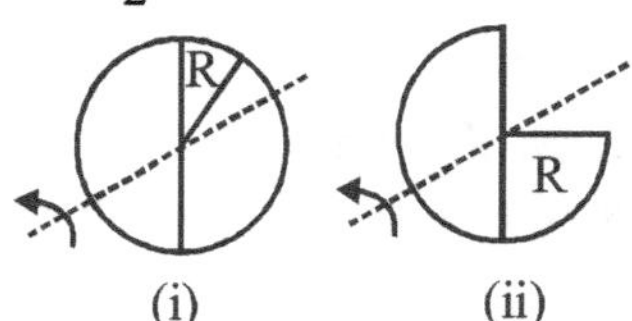

For sliding
$\mu Mg = F_2$
For sliding to occur first
$F_1 > F_2$

or $\dfrac{mgL}{2} > \mu Mg$ or $L > 2\mu h$

18. (a)

Moment of inertia of a ring about a given axis is
$I = MR^2$

Mass of the remaining portion of the ring $= \dfrac{3M}{4}$

Moment of inertia of the remaining portion of the ring about a given axis is

$I' = \dfrac{3}{4} MR^2$

Given $I' = kMR^2$

$\therefore \quad k = 3/4.$

19. **(b)** Applying angular momentum conservation

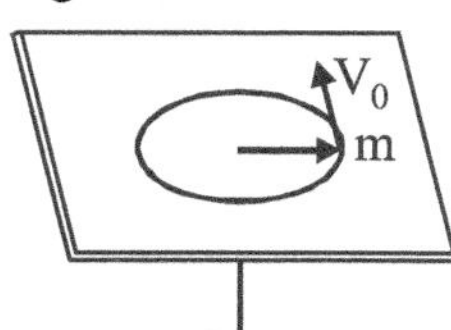

$$mV_0R_0 = (m)(V^1)\left(\frac{R_0}{2}\right)$$

$$\therefore \quad v^1 = 2V_0$$

Therefore, new $KE = \frac{1}{2}m(2V_0)^2 = 2mv_0^2$

20. **(c)** If rotation axis is passing through its middle point & is $\perp$ to its plane, then moment of inertia about YY' is

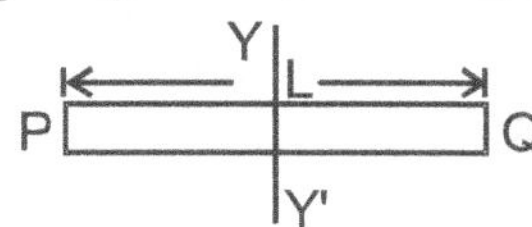

$$I = \frac{ML^2}{12} \quad \text{where } M = \text{volume} \times \text{density} = (L \times A) \times \rho$$

$$\text{so } I = \frac{L^3 A\rho}{12}$$

so rotational $K.E = \frac{1}{2}I\omega^2 = \frac{L^3 A\rho\omega^2}{24}$

21. **(c)** If a body rolls on a horizontal surface, it possesses both translational and rotational kinetic energies. The net kinetic energy is given by

$$K_{net} = \frac{1}{2}mv^2\left(1 + \frac{K^2}{R^2}\right),$$

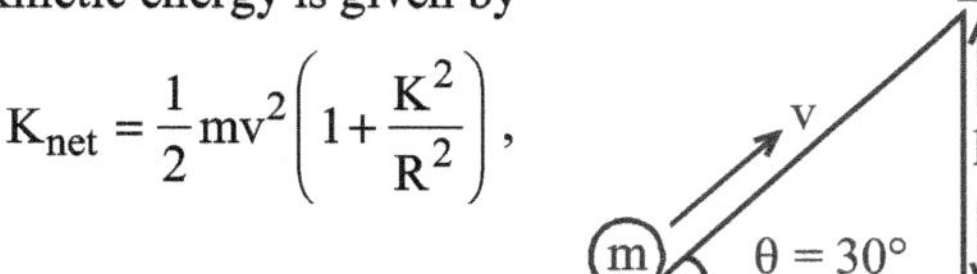

where K is the radius of gyration.
So from law of conservation of energy,

$$\frac{1}{2}mv^2\left(1 + \frac{K^2}{R^2}\right) = mgh ,$$

where h is the height attained by the sphere.

i.e., $\frac{1}{2} \times 2 \times (10)^2\left(1 + \frac{2}{5}\right) = 2 \times 9.8 \times h.$

i.e., $\frac{1}{2} \times 100 \times \left(\frac{7}{5}\right) = 9.8h$

or $\quad h = \frac{700}{98} = 7.1\,m$

22. **(c)** After collision velocity of COM of A becomes zero and that of B becomes equal to initial velocity of COM of A. But angular velocity of A remains unchanged as the two spheres are smooth.

23. **(b)** M.I. of disc $= \frac{1}{2}MR^2 = \frac{1}{2}M\left(\frac{M}{\pi t\rho}\right) = \frac{1}{2}\frac{M^2}{\pi t\rho}$

$$\left(As \, \rho = \frac{M}{\pi R^2 t} \text{ Therefore } R^2 = \frac{M}{\pi t\rho}\right)$$

If mass and thickness are same then, $I \propto \frac{1}{\rho}$

$$\therefore \frac{I_1}{I_2} = \frac{\rho_2}{\rho_1} = \frac{3}{1}$$

24. **(c)** When the system is released, heavier mass move downward and the lighter one upward. Thus, centre of mass will move towards the heavier mass with acceleration

$$a = \left(\frac{3m - m}{3m + m}\right)g = \frac{g}{2}$$

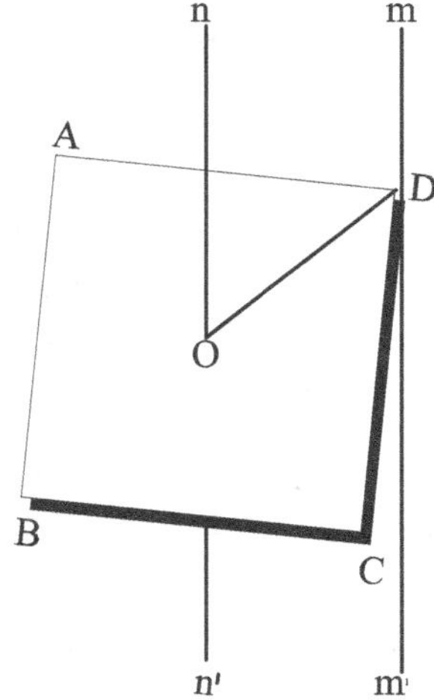

25. **(c)** $K = K_{ring} + K_{particles}$

$$= \left[\frac{1}{2}mv_0^2 + \frac{1}{2}I\omega^2\right] + \left[\frac{1}{2}m(\sqrt{2}v_0)^2 + \frac{1}{2}m(2v_0)^2 + \frac{1}{2}m(\sqrt{2}v_0)^2 + 0\right]$$

Also $\omega = \frac{v_0}{R}$, $I = mR^2$

$$\therefore \quad K = 5mv_0^2$$

26. **(d)** $I_{nn'} = \frac{1}{12}M(a^2 + a^2) = \frac{Ma^2}{6}$

Also, $DO = \frac{DB}{2} = \frac{\sqrt{2}a}{2} = \frac{a}{\sqrt{2}}$

According to parallel axis theorem

$$I_{mm'} = I_{nn'} + M\left(\frac{a}{\sqrt{2}}\right)^2 = \frac{Ma^2}{6} + \frac{Ma^2}{2}$$

$$= \frac{Ma^2 + 3Ma^2}{6} = \frac{2}{3}Ma^2$$

27. **(a)** From law of conservation of angular momentum,

$$I\omega = I'\omega'$$

Given $I' = I/n$

$$\therefore \quad \omega' = n\omega \quad \text{or} \quad \omega' \propto n$$

28. **(b)**

29. **(d)** Melting of ice produces water which will spread over larger distance away from the axis of rotation. This increases the moment of inertia so angular velocity decreases

30. **(c)**
$$I_p = \frac{mr^2}{2} + 2\left[\frac{mr^2}{2} + m(2r)^2\right] + \left[\frac{mr^2}{2} + m(2r)^2\right]$$

$$+ \left[\frac{mr^2}{2} + (2r)^2\right] + 2\left[\frac{mr^2}{2} + m(2\sqrt{3}r)^2\right]$$

$$= \frac{111}{2}mr^2$$

31. **(d)**
$$0 = \frac{m_1(-x_1) + m_2 x_2}{m_1 + m_2}$$

$$\therefore \quad m_1 x_1 = m_2 x_2$$

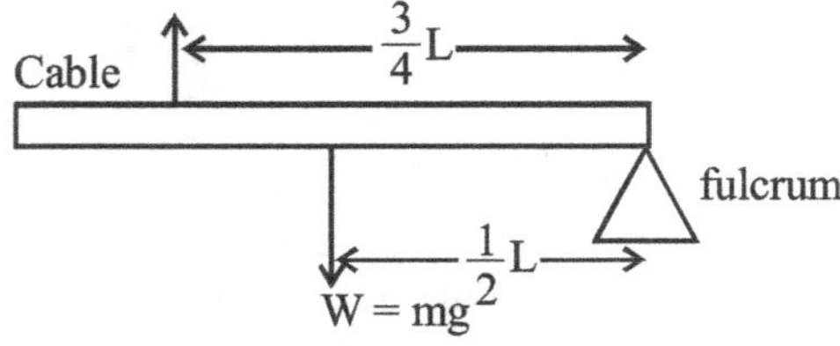

Now, $0 = \dfrac{-m_1(x_1 - d) + m_2(x_2 - d)}{m_1 + m_2}$

$0 = m_1(d - x_1) + m_2(x_2 - d')$

$\Rightarrow 0 = m_1 d - m_1 x_1 + m_2 x_2 - m_2 d'$

$$\therefore \quad d' = \frac{m_1}{m_2}d$$

32. **(c)** This is a torque problem. While the fulcrum can be placed anywhere, placing it at the far right end of the bar eliminated cable B from the calculation. There are now only two forces acting on the bar ; the weight that produces a counterclockwise rotation and the tension in cable A that produces a clockwise rotation. Since the bar is in equilibrium, these two torques must sum to zero.

$$\Sigma\tau = T_A(3/4L) - Mg(1/2L) = 0$$

Therefore

$$T_A = (MgL/2)/(3L/4) = (MgL/2)(4/3L) = 2Mg/3$$

33. **(b)** Couple produces purely rotational motion.

34. **(a)**

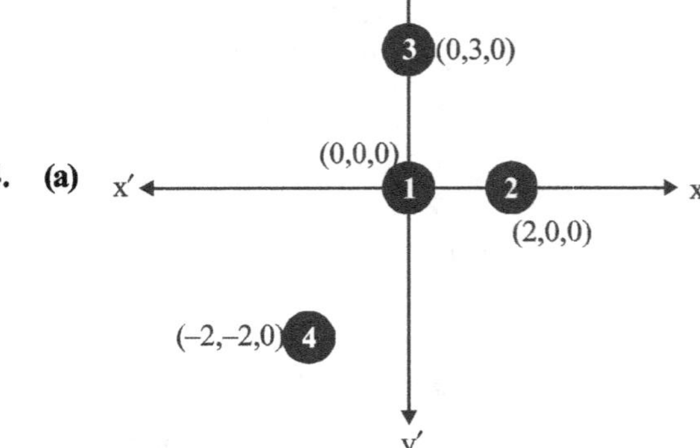

$I_1 = I_2 = 0$, because these particles are placed on x-axis
The M.I. of system about x-axis, $= I_1 + I_2 + I_3 + I_4$
$= 0 + 0 + 3 \times (3)^2 + 4 \times (-2)^2 = 27 + 16 = 43\ kg-m^2$

35. **(b)**

36. **(b)** $I = 1.2\ kg\,m^2$, $E_r = 1500\ J$,
$\alpha = 25\ rad/sec^2$, $\omega_1 = 0$, $t = ?$

As $E_r = \dfrac{1}{2}I\omega^2$, $\omega = \sqrt{\dfrac{2E_r}{I}} = \sqrt{\dfrac{2 \times 1500}{1.2}} = 50\ rad/sec$

From $\omega_2 = \omega_1 + \alpha t$
$50 = 0 + 25\,t$, $\quad \therefore \quad t = 2\ seconds$

37. **(b)** Since no external torque act on gymnast, so angular momentum ($L = I\omega$) is conserved. After pulling her arms & legs, the angular velocity increases but moment of inertia of gymnast, decreases in such a way that angular momentum remains constant.

38. **(b)** The *M.I.* about the axis of rotation is not constant as the perpendicular distance of the bead with the axis of rotation increases.
Also since no external torque is acting.

$$\therefore \tau_{ext} = \frac{dL}{dt} \Rightarrow L = constant \Rightarrow I\omega = constant$$

Since, I increases, ω decreases.

39. **(c)**

Moment of inertia about z-axis, $I_z = mr^2$
(about centre of mass)
Applying parallel axes theorem,

$$I_z = I_{cm} + mk^2$$

$$I_{cm} = I_z - m\left(\frac{2}{\pi}r\right)^2 = mr^2 - \frac{m4r^2}{\pi^2} = mr^2\left(1 - \frac{4}{\pi^2}\right)$$

i.e., $k = 4$

40. **(c)** When two small spheres of mass m are attached gently, the external torque, about the axis of rotation, is zero and therefore the angular momentum about the axis of rotation is constant.

$$\therefore\ I_1\omega_1 = I_2\omega_2 \ \Rightarrow\ \omega_2 = \frac{I_1}{I_2}\omega_1$$

Here $I_1 = \dfrac{1}{2}MR^2$

and $I_2 = \dfrac{1}{2}MR^2 + 2mR^2$

$$\therefore\ \omega_2 = \frac{\dfrac{1}{2}MR^2}{\dfrac{1}{2}MR^2 + 2mR^2}\times\omega_1 = \frac{M}{M+4m}\omega_1$$

41. **(b)** $\quad Tr = \dfrac{mr^2}{2}\alpha_1 \qquad\qquad .... (1)$

$Tr = \dfrac{mr^2}{2}\alpha \qquad\qquad .... (2)$

$\alpha_1 = \alpha \qquad\qquad\qquad\qquad .... (3)$

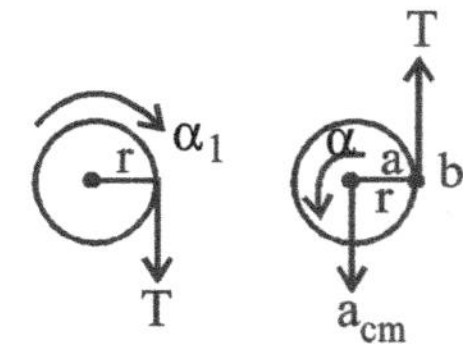

Acceleration of point b = acceleration of point a

$r\alpha_1 = a_{cm} - r\alpha \qquad\qquad .... (4)$

Hence, $2r\alpha = a_{cm}$

42. **(c)** $\quad X_{C.M.} = \dfrac{1\times 0 + 2\times 2 + 3\times 0 + 4\times 2 + 5\times 1}{1+2+3+4+5}$

$\qquad = \dfrac{4+8+5}{15} = \dfrac{17}{15} = 1.1$

$Y_{C.M} = \dfrac{1\times 0 + 2\times 0 + 3\times 2 + 4\times 2 + 5\times 1}{1+2+3+4+5}$

$\qquad = \dfrac{6+8+5}{15} = 1.3$

43. **(d)** $\quad I_{AX} = m(AB)^2 + m(OC)^2 = m\ell^2 + m\,(\ell\cos 60°)^2$

$\qquad = m\ell^2 + m\ell^2/4 = 5/4\ m\ell^2$

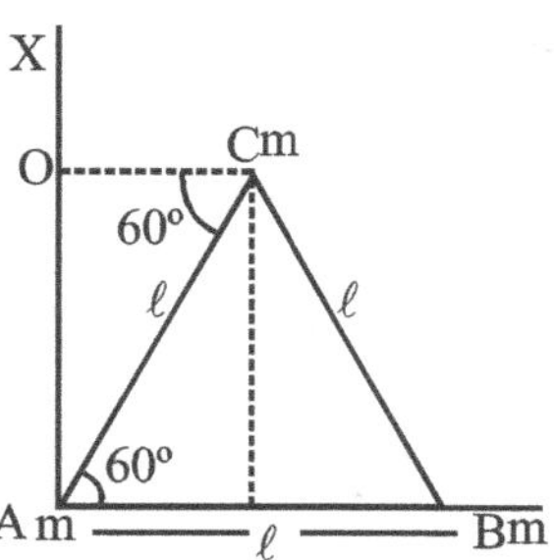

44. **(c)** Angle turned in three seconds, $\theta_{3s} = 2\pi\times 10 = 20\pi\,\text{rad}$.

From $\theta = \omega_0 t + \dfrac{1}{2}\alpha t^2 \Rightarrow 20\pi = 0 + \dfrac{1}{2}\alpha\times(3)^2$

$\Rightarrow \alpha = \dfrac{40\pi}{9}\,\text{rad/s}^2$

Now angle turned in 6 sec from the starting

$\theta_{6s} = \omega_0 t + \dfrac{1}{2}\alpha t^2 = 0 + \dfrac{1}{2}\times\left(\dfrac{40\pi}{9}\right)\times(6)^2 = 80\pi\,\text{rad}$

$\therefore$ Angle turned between $t = 3s$ to $t = 6s$

$\theta_{\text{last 3s}} = \theta_{6s} - \theta_{3s} = 80\pi - 20\pi = 60\pi$

Number of revolutions $= \dfrac{60\pi}{2\pi} = 30$.

45. **(c)** $\quad a = \dfrac{f}{m} = \mu g$

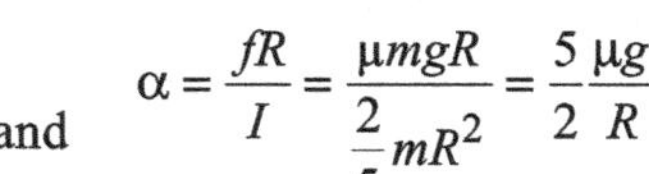
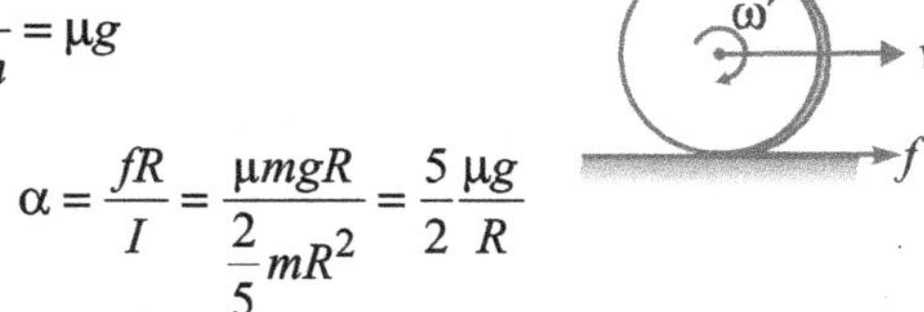

and $\quad \alpha = \dfrac{fR}{I} = \dfrac{\mu mgR}{\dfrac{2}{5}mR^2} = \dfrac{5}{2}\dfrac{\mu g}{R}$

Now $v = 0 + at$

and $\omega' = \omega - \alpha t$

Also $\omega' = \dfrac{v}{R}$

After solving above equations, we get $\quad \omega' = \dfrac{2\omega}{7}$

1. **(a)** The escape velocity on the earth is defined as

$$v_e = \sqrt{2g_e R_e}$$

Where R_e & g_e are the radius & acceleration due to gravity of earth.

Now for planet $g_P = 2g_e$, $R_P = R_e/4$

So $v_P = \sqrt{2g_P R_P} = \sqrt{2 \times 2g_e \times R_e/4} = \dfrac{v_e}{\sqrt{2}}$

2. **(c)** Applying conservation of energy principle, we get

$$\frac{1}{2}mk^2 v_e^2 - \frac{GMm}{R} = -\frac{GMm}{r}$$

$$\Rightarrow \frac{1}{2}mk^2 \frac{2GM}{R} - \frac{GMm}{R} = -\frac{GMm}{r}$$

$$\Rightarrow \frac{k^2}{R} - \frac{1}{R} = -\frac{1}{r} \Rightarrow \frac{1}{r} = \frac{1}{R} - \frac{k^2}{R}$$

$$\Rightarrow \frac{1}{r} = \frac{1}{R}(1-k^2) \Rightarrow r = \frac{R}{1-k^2}$$

3. **(d)** The gravitational force due to the whole sphere at A point is

$$F_1 = \frac{GM_e m_0}{(2R)^2}, \text{ where } m_0 \text{ is the assumed rest mass at point A.}$$

In the second case, when we made a cavity of radius $(R/2)$, then gravitational force at point A is

$$F_2 = \frac{GM_e m_0}{(R + R/2)^2} \qquad \therefore F_2/F_1 = 1/9$$

4. **(c)** According to Kepler's law of period $T^2 \propto R^3$

$$\frac{T_1^2}{T_2^2} = \frac{R_1^3}{R_2^3} = \frac{(6R)^3}{(3R)^3} = 8$$

$$\frac{24 \times 24}{T_2^2} = 8$$

$$T_2^2 = \frac{24 \times 24}{8} = 72 = 36 \times 2$$

$$T_2 = 6\sqrt{2}$$

5. **(d)** Total energy $= -KE = \dfrac{PE}{2}$

$$K.E = \frac{1}{2}mv^2$$

$$\therefore \text{ Total energy} = -\frac{1}{2}mv^2$$

6. **(a)** The force of attraction between sphere and shaded

$$\text{position } dF = GM \frac{\left(\dfrac{m}{l}dx\right)}{x^2}$$

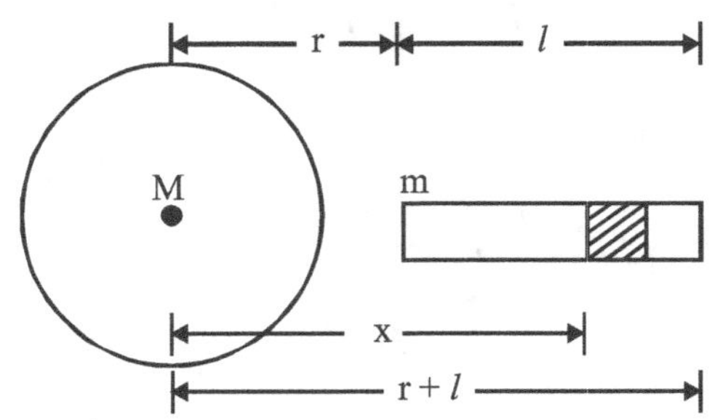

$$F = \int_r^{r+l} \frac{GMm}{lx^2}dx = \frac{GMm}{l}\int_r^{r+l}\frac{1}{x^2}dx$$

$$= \frac{GMm}{l}\int_r^{r+l}x^{-2}dx = \frac{GMm}{l}\left[\frac{x^{-2+1}}{-2+1}\right]_r^{r+l}$$

$$= -\frac{GMm}{l}\left[x^{-1}\right]_r^{r+l} = -\frac{GMm}{l}\left[\frac{1}{x}\right]_r^{r+l} = \frac{GMm}{r(r+l)}$$

7. **(b)** $F = \dfrac{k}{R} = \dfrac{Mv^2}{R}$. Hence $v \propto R^0$

8. **(d)** $\dfrac{mv^2}{(R+x)} = \dfrac{GmM}{(R+x)^2}$ also $g = \dfrac{GM}{R^2}$

$$\therefore \frac{mv^2}{(R+x)} = m\left(\frac{GM}{R^2}\right)\frac{R^2}{(R+x)^2}$$

$$\therefore \frac{mv^2}{(R+x)} = mg\frac{R^2}{(R+x)^2}$$

$$\therefore v^2 = \frac{gR^2}{R+x} \Rightarrow v = \left(\frac{gR^2}{R+x}\right)^{1/2}$$

9. **(b)** $v = \dfrac{3}{4}v_e$

$$\text{K.E.} = \frac{1}{2}mv^2 = \frac{1}{2}m\left(\frac{3}{4}v_e\right)^2 = \frac{9}{32}mv_e^2$$

$$= \frac{9}{32}m\left(\frac{2GM}{R}\right)$$

$$\text{K.E.} = \frac{9}{16}\frac{GMm}{R} \; ; \; \text{P.E.} = -\frac{GMm}{R}$$

$$\text{Total energy} = \text{K.E.} + \text{P.E.} = -\frac{7}{16}\frac{GMm}{R}$$

Let the height above the surface of earth be h, then

$$\text{P.E.} = -\frac{GMm}{h}$$

$$-\frac{7}{16}\frac{GMm}{R} = -\frac{GMm}{h} \quad \therefore h = \frac{16R}{7}$$

10. **(a)** When closer to the sun, velocity of planet will be greater. So time taken in covering a given area will be less.

11. **(c)** Applying conservation of total mechanical energy principle

$$\frac{1}{2}mv^2 = mg_A h_A = mg_B h_B$$

$$\Rightarrow g_A h_A = g_B h_B$$

$$\Rightarrow h_B = \left(\frac{g_A}{g_B}\right) h_A = 9 \times 2 = 18 \, m$$

12. **(b)** Due to inertia of motion it will move tangentially to the original orbit with same velocity.

13. **(a)** $F \propto xM \times (1-x)M = xM^2(1-x)$

For maximum force, $\dfrac{dF}{dx} = 0$

$$\Rightarrow \frac{dF}{dx} = M^2 - 2xM^2 = 0 \Rightarrow x = 1/2$$

14. **(c)** Mass of the satellite = m and height of satellite from earth (h) $= 6.4 \times 10^6$ m.

We know that gravitational potential energy of the satellite at height

$$h = -\frac{GM_e m}{R_e + h} = -\frac{gR_e^2 m}{2R_e} = -\frac{gR_e m}{2} = -0.5\, mgR_e$$

(where, $GM_e = gR_e^2$ and $h = R_e$)

15. **(d)** Acceleration due to gravity on earth's surface

$$g = G\frac{M}{R^2}$$

This implies that as radius decreases, the acceleration due to gravity increases.

$$\frac{\Delta g}{g} = -2\frac{\Delta R}{R} \quad \text{But } \frac{\Delta R}{R} = -1\%$$

('–' sign is due to shrinking of earth)

$$\therefore \quad \frac{\Delta g}{g} = -2 \times (-1\%) = 2\%$$

16. **(a)** According to kepler's law of area

$$\frac{dA}{dt} = \frac{L}{2m}$$

For central forces, torque = 0

$$\therefore \ L = \text{constant}$$

$$\therefore \quad \frac{dA}{dt} = \text{constant}$$

17. **(b)** Potential energy of particle at the centre of square

$$= -4\left(\frac{GMm}{\dfrac{a}{\sqrt{2}}}\right)$$

$$\therefore \ -4\left(\frac{GMm}{\dfrac{a}{\sqrt{2}}}\right) + \frac{1}{2}mv^2 = 0 \ \Rightarrow v^2 = \frac{8\sqrt{2}\,GM}{a}$$

18. **(c)** The potential energy for a conservative force is defined as

$$F = \frac{-dU}{dr} \quad \text{or} \quad U = -\int_{\infty}^{r}\vec{F}.\vec{dr} \qquad \text{......(i)}$$

$$\text{or } U_r = \int_{\infty}^{r}\frac{GM_1 M_2}{r^2}\,dr = \frac{-GM_1 M_2}{r} \qquad \text{......(ii)}$$

$(\because U_\infty = 0)$

If we bring the mass from the infinity to the centre of earth, then we obtain work, 'so it has negative (gravitational force do work on the object) sign & potential energy decreases. But if we bring the mass from the surface of earth to infinite, then we must do work against gravitational force & potential energy of the mass increases.

Now in equation (i) if $F = \dfrac{GM_1 M_2}{r^{5/2}}$ instead of

$F = \dfrac{GM_1 M_2}{r^2}$ then

$$U_r = \int_{\infty}^{r}\frac{GM_1 M_2}{r^{5/2}}\,dr = \frac{-2}{3}\frac{GM_1 M_2}{r^{3/2}}$$

$$\Rightarrow U_r \propto \frac{1}{r^{+3/2}}$$

19. **(b)** As we know, the minimum speed with which a body is projected so that it does not return back is called escape speed.

$$V_e = \sqrt{\frac{2GM}{r}} = \sqrt{\frac{2GM}{R+h}} = \sqrt{\frac{2GM}{4R}}$$

$$= \left(\frac{GM}{2R}\right)^{\frac{1}{2}} \quad (\because h = 3R)$$

20. **(a)** Acceleration due to gravity at a height h above the earth's surface is

$$g_h = g\left(1 - \frac{2h}{R}\right)$$

Acceleration due to gravity at a depth d below the earth's surface is

$$g_d = g\left(1 - \frac{d}{R}\right)$$

Now, $\dfrac{g_h}{g_d} = \dfrac{\left(1 - \dfrac{2h}{R}\right)}{\left(1 - \dfrac{d}{R}\right)} = \dfrac{(R - 2h)}{(R - d)}$

As h = 1 km, d = 1 km

$$\therefore \quad \frac{g_h}{g_d} = \frac{R - 2}{R - 1}$$

21. **(a)** At the surface of earth, the value of g = 9.8m/sec^2. If we go towards the centre of earth or we go above the surface of earth, then in both the cases the value of g decreases.

Hence $W_1 = mg_{mine}$, $W_2 = mg_{sea\ level}$, $W_3 = mg_{moun}$

So $W_1 < W_2 > W_3$ (g at the sea level = g at the suface of earth)

22. **(d)** Time period does not depend upon the mass of satellite

23. **(a)** $T = \dfrac{2\pi r}{v_0} = \dfrac{2\pi r}{(gR^2/r)^{1/2}} = \dfrac{2\pi r^{3/2}}{\sqrt{gR^2}} = \dfrac{2\pi}{\omega}$

Hence, $r^{3/2} = \dfrac{\sqrt{gR^2}}{\omega}$ or $r^3 = \dfrac{gR^2}{\omega^2}$

or, $r = (gR^2/\omega^2)^{1/3}$

24. **(b)** $g' = g - \omega^2 R \cos^2 \lambda$

To make effective acceleration due to gravity zero at equator $\lambda = 0$ and $g' = 0$

$\therefore 0 = g - \omega^2 R \Rightarrow \omega = \sqrt{\dfrac{g}{R}} = \dfrac{1}{800}\ \dfrac{rad}{s}$

25. **(a)** $mg = 72$ N   (body weight on the surface)

$g = \dfrac{GM}{R^2}$

At a height $H = \dfrac{R}{2}$,

$g' = \dfrac{GM}{\left(R+\dfrac{R}{2}\right)^2} = \dfrac{4\ GM}{9\ R^2}$

Body weight at height $H = \dfrac{R}{2}$,

$mg' = m \times \dfrac{4\ GM}{9\ R^2}$

$= m \times \dfrac{4}{9} \times g = \dfrac{4}{9}mg$

$= \dfrac{4}{9} \times 72 = 32$ N

26. **(c)** At a height h,

$g' = g\dfrac{R^2}{(R+h)^2} \Rightarrow mg' = mg\left(\dfrac{R}{R+h}\right)^2$

$\Rightarrow W' = W\left(\dfrac{R}{R+h}\right)^2$

Here, $h = R/2$

$\therefore\ W' = \dfrac{4}{9}W$

27. **(c)** Gravitational P.E. = m × gravitational potential
$U = mV$, so the graph of U will be same as that of V for a spherical shell.

28. **(c)** Applying the properties of ellipse, we have

$\dfrac{2}{R} = \dfrac{1}{r_1} + \dfrac{1}{r_2} = \dfrac{r_1 + r_2}{r_1 r_2}$

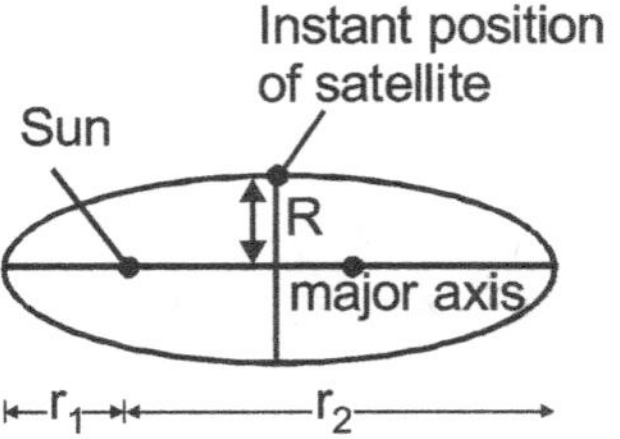

$R = \dfrac{2 r_1 r_2}{r_1 + r_2}$

29. **(c)** In a circular or elliptical orbital motion, torque is always acting parallel to displacement or velocity. So, angular momentum is conserved. In attractive field, potential energy is negative. Kinetic energy changes as velocity increase when distance is less. So, option (c) is correct.

30. **(a)** Here, $v = \sqrt{\dfrac{2GM}{R}}$ and $kv = \sqrt{\dfrac{2GM}{R+R}}$.

Solving $k = \dfrac{1}{\sqrt{2}}$

31. **(a)** $g = \dfrac{G\,(2M)}{(2R)^2} = \dfrac{GM}{2R^2}$

From $h = \dfrac{1}{2}gt^2$ $[\because U = 0]$

$t = \sqrt{\dfrac{2h}{g}} = 2\sqrt{\dfrac{hR^2}{GM}}$

32. **(b)** $P.E. = \int_{R_0}^{R} \dfrac{GMm}{r^2}\,dr = -GMm\left[\dfrac{1}{R} - \dfrac{1}{R_0}\right]$

The K.E. acquired by the body at the surface $= \dfrac{1}{2}m\,v^2$

$\therefore\ \dfrac{1}{2}mv^2 = -GMm\left[\dfrac{1}{R} - \dfrac{1}{R_0}\right]$

$v = \sqrt{2GM\left(\dfrac{1}{R_0} - \dfrac{1}{R}\right)}$

33. **(b)** $\dfrac{mv^2}{R} = \dfrac{k}{R^2}$ or $mv^2 = \dfrac{k}{R}$

Kinetic energy $= \dfrac{1}{2}mv^2 = \dfrac{k}{2R}$

In case of satellites $P.E = -2\,K.E$

and $T.E = P.E + K.E$

Total energy $= \dfrac{k}{2R} - \dfrac{k}{R} = -\dfrac{k}{2R}$

34. **(d)** Variation of g with altitude is,

$g_h = g\left[1 - \dfrac{2h}{R}\right]$;

variation of g with depth is,

$$g_d = g\left[1 - \frac{d}{R}\right]$$

Equating g_h and g_d, we get $d = 2h$

35. (a) The total momentum will be zero and hence velocity will be zero just after collisiion. The pull of earth will make it fall down.

36. (b) Loss in potential energy = Gain in kinetic energy

$$-\frac{GMm}{R} - \left(-\frac{3}{2}\frac{GMm}{R}\right) = \frac{1}{2}mv^2$$

$$\Rightarrow \frac{GMm}{2R} = \frac{1}{2}mv^2 \Rightarrow v = \sqrt{\frac{GM}{R}} = \sqrt{gR}$$

37. (d)

38. (b) $g \propto \dfrac{1}{R^2}$

R decreasing g increase hence, curve b represents correct variation.

39. (d) Angular momentum, $L = I\omega$; moment of inertia of sphere along the axis passing through centre of mass,

$$I = \frac{2}{5}MR^2 \text{ and } \omega = \frac{2\pi}{T}.$$

Putting these values, $L = \dfrac{4\pi\,MR^2}{5T}$

40. (c) $T = 2\pi\sqrt{\dfrac{(R+h)^3}{GM}}$

$$T_1 = 2\pi\sqrt{\frac{R^3}{GM}}, \quad T_2 = 2\pi\sqrt{\frac{(1.01R)^3}{GM}}$$

$$\frac{T_2 - T_1}{T_1} \times 100 = 1.5\%$$

41. (a) The gravitational potential at the centre of uniform spherical shell is equal to the gravitational potential at the surface of shell i.e.,

$$V = \frac{-GM}{a}, \text{ where a is radius of spherical shell}$$

Now, if the shell shrinks then its radius decrease then density increases, but mass is constant. so from above expression if a decreases, then V increases.

42. (b) $g' = g\left(1 - \dfrac{d}{R}\right) \Rightarrow \dfrac{g}{n} = g\left(1 - \dfrac{d}{R}\right)$

$$\Rightarrow d = \left(\frac{n-1}{n}\right)R$$

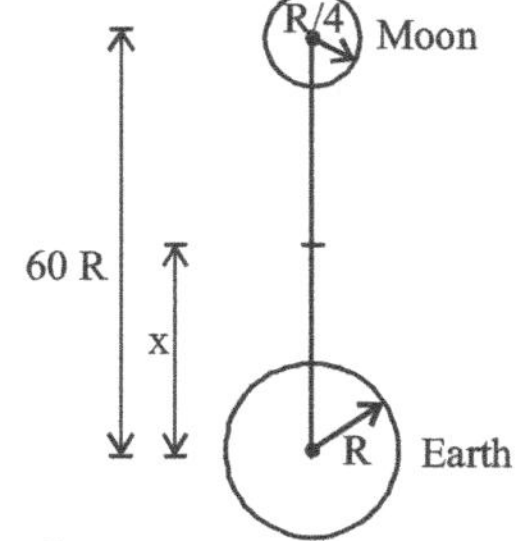

43. (d) $E_{earth} = E_{moon}$

$$\Rightarrow \frac{GM}{x^2} = \frac{GM/81}{(60R - x)^2}$$

$$\Rightarrow \frac{1}{x} = \frac{1}{9(60R - x)}$$

$\Rightarrow x = 54$ R from centre of earth.

44. (b) Acceleration due to gravity at lattitude 'λ' is given by

$$g_\lambda = g_e - R_e\omega^2\cos^2\lambda$$

At equator, $\lambda = 90° \Rightarrow \cos\lambda = \cos 90° = 0$

or $g_\lambda = g_e = g$ (as given in question)

At 30°, $g_{30} = g - R\omega^2\cos^2 30 = g - \dfrac{3}{4}R\omega^2$

or, $g - g_{30} = \dfrac{3}{4}R\omega^2$

45. (a) As we know,

$$\text{Gravitational potential energy} = \frac{-GMm}{r}$$

and orbital velocity, $v_0 = \sqrt{GM/R + h}$

$$E_f = \frac{1}{2}mv_0^2 - \frac{GMm}{3R} = \frac{1}{2}m\frac{GM}{3R} - \frac{GMm}{3R}$$

$$= \frac{GMm}{3R}\left(\frac{1}{2} - 1\right) = \frac{-GMm}{6R}$$

$$E_i = \frac{-GMm}{R} + K$$

$$E_i = E_f$$

Therefore minimum required energy, $K = \dfrac{5GMm}{6R}$

1. **(c)** We know that Young's modulus

$$Y = \frac{F}{\pi r^2} \times \frac{L}{\ell}$$

Since Y, F are same for both the wires, we have,

$$\frac{1}{r_1^2} \frac{L_1}{\ell_1} = \frac{1}{r_2^2} \frac{L_2}{\ell_2}$$

or, $\dfrac{\ell_1}{\ell_2} = \dfrac{r_2^2 \times L_1}{r_1^2 \times L_2} = \dfrac{(D_2/2)^2 \times L_1}{(D_1/2)^2 \times L_2}$

or, $\dfrac{\ell_1}{\ell_2} = \dfrac{D_2^2 \times L_1}{D_1^2 \times L_2} = \dfrac{D_2^2}{(2D_2)^2} \times \dfrac{L_2}{2L_2} = \dfrac{1}{8}$

So, $\ell_1 : \ell_2 = 1 : 8$

2. **(a)** From the graph, it is clear that for the same value of load, elongation is maximum for wire OA. Hence OA is the thinnest wire among the four wires.

3. **(b)** Small amount of work done in extending the spring by dx is

$dW = k \, x \, dx$

$\therefore W = k \displaystyle\int_{0.05}^{0.15} x \, dx$

$= \dfrac{800}{2}\left[(0.15)^2 - (0.05)^2 \right]$

$= 400\,[(0.15+0.05)(0.15-0.05)]$

$= 400 \times 0.2 \times 0.1 = 8\,\text{J}$

4. **(c)** Using the usual expression for the Young's modulus, the force constant for the wire can be written as

$k = \dfrac{F}{\Delta l} = \dfrac{YA}{L}$ where the symbols have their usual meanings. Now the two wires together will have an effective force constant $\left[\dfrac{k_1 k_2}{k_1 + k_2} \right]$. Substituting the corresponding lengths and the Young's moduli we get the answer.

5. **(b)** Compressibility of water,
$K = 45.4 \times 10^{-11}\,\text{Pa}^{-1}$
density of water $P = 10^3\,\text{kg/m}^3$
depth of ocean, $h = 2700\,\text{m}$

We have to find $\dfrac{\Delta V}{V} = ?$

As we know, compressibility,

$K = \dfrac{1}{B} = \dfrac{(\Delta V / V)}{P}\ (P = \rho g h)$

So, $(\Delta V/V) = K\rho g h$
$= 45.4 \times 10^{-11} \times 10^3 \times 10 \times 2700$
$= 1.2258 \times 10^{-2}$

6. **(a)** Young's modulus $Y = \dfrac{W}{A} \cdot \dfrac{l}{\Delta l}$

$$\frac{W_1}{Y_1} = \frac{W_2}{Y_2}$$

$[\because A, l, \Delta l$ same for both brass and steel$]$

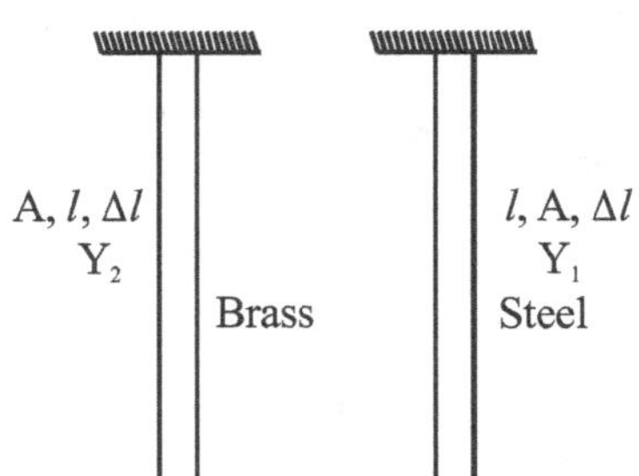

$\dfrac{W_1}{W_2} = \dfrac{Y_1}{Y_2} = 2$ $[Y_{\text{steel}}/Y_{\text{brass}} = 2$ given$]$

7. **(b)** Solids are least compressible whereas gases are highly compressible.

8. **(d)** $Y_c \times (\Delta L_c / L_c) = Y_s \times (\Delta L_s / L_s)$

$\Rightarrow 1 \times 10^{11} \times \left(\dfrac{1 \times 10^{-3}}{1} \right) = 2 \times 10^{11} \times \left(\dfrac{\Delta L_s}{0.5} \right)$

$\therefore \Delta L_s = \dfrac{0.5 \times 10^{-3}}{2} = 0.25\,\text{mm}$

Therefore, total extension of the composite wire =
$\Delta L_c + \Delta L_s$
$= 1\,\text{mm} + 0.25\,\text{mm} = 1.25\,\text{mm}$

9. **(b)** Bulk modulus $B = \dfrac{-P}{(\Delta V / V)} = \dfrac{-PV}{\Delta V}$ ....(1)

and $\Delta V = \gamma V \Delta T = 3\alpha.V.T$ or $\dfrac{-V}{\Delta V} = \dfrac{1}{3\alpha.T.}$ ...(2)

From eqs. (1) and (2), $B = P/(3\alpha.T)$ or $T = \dfrac{P}{3\alpha B}$

10. **(a)** When same stress is applied at two different temperatures, the increase in length is more at higher temperature. Thus $T_1 > T_2$.

11. **(c)** According to questions,

$\dfrac{\ell_s}{\ell_b} = a,\ \dfrac{r_s}{r_b} = b,\ \dfrac{y_s}{y_b} = c,\ \dfrac{\Delta \ell s}{\Delta \ell_b} = ?$

As, $y = \dfrac{F\ell}{A\Delta \ell} \Rightarrow \Delta \ell = \dfrac{F\ell}{Ay}$

$\Delta \ell_s = \dfrac{3mg\ell_s}{\pi r_s^2 \cdot y_s}$ $[\because F_s = (M+2M)g]$

$$\Delta\ell_b = \frac{2Mg\ell_b}{\pi r_b^2 \cdot y_b} \quad [\because F_b = 2Mg]$$

$$\therefore \frac{\Delta\ell_s}{\Delta\ell_b} = \frac{\dfrac{3Mg\ell_s}{\pi r_s^2 \cdot y_s}}{\dfrac{2Mg.\ell_b}{\pi r_b^2 \cdot y_b}} = \frac{3a}{2b^2 c}$$

12. (b) We know that $Y = F L/\pi r^2 \ell$ or $r^2 = F L/(Y \pi \ell)$

$$\therefore \quad R_B^2 = FL/(Y_B \pi \ell) \text{ and } R_S^2 = FL/(Y_S \pi \ell)$$

$$\text{or } \frac{R_B^2}{R_S^2} = \frac{Y_S}{Y_B} = \frac{2\times 10^{10}}{10^{10}} = 2$$

$$\text{or } R_B^2 = 2R_S^2 \text{ or } R_B = \sqrt{2}\, R_S$$

$$\therefore R_S = R_B/\sqrt{2}$$

13. (c)

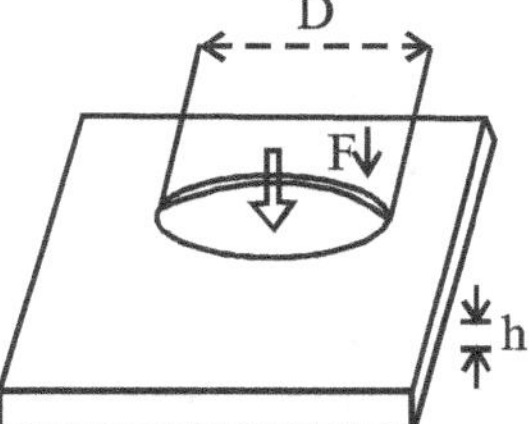

Shearing strain is created along the side surface of the punched disk. Note that the forces exerted on the disk are exerted along the circumference of the disk, and the total force exerted on its center only.
Let us assume that the shearing stress along the side surface of the disk is uniform, then

$$F = \int_{\text{surface}} dF_{\max} = \int_{\text{surface}} \sigma_{\max} dA = \sigma_{\max} \int_{\text{surface}} dA$$

$$= \int \sigma_{\max} . A = \sigma_{\max} . 2\pi\left(\frac{D}{2}\right)h$$

$$= 3.5\times 10^8 \times \left(\frac{1}{2}\times 10^{-2}\right)\times 0.3\times 10^{-2}\times 2\pi$$

$$= 3.297\times 10^4 \simeq 3.3\times 10^4\,\text{N}$$

14. (d) Bulk modulus is given by, $k = \dfrac{F/A}{\Delta V/V}$

$$= \frac{mg}{A\left(\dfrac{\Delta V}{V}\right)} = \frac{h\rho g}{\left(\dfrac{\Delta V}{V}\right)}, \quad \left(\because \rho = \frac{m}{V}, V = A\times h\right)$$

Given, $h = 400\,\text{m}, \dfrac{\Delta V}{V} = \dfrac{0.2}{100}$

and $\rho = 1\times 10^3\,\text{kg/m}^3$

$$\therefore k = \frac{400\times 10^3 \times 9.8}{0.2/100} = 196\times 10^7\,\text{N m}^{-2}$$

$$k = 1.96\times 10^9\,\text{N m}^{-2}.$$

15. (a) $C_1 = \dfrac{\pi\eta(r_2^4 - r_1^4)}{2\ell}$, $C_2 = \dfrac{\pi\eta r^4}{2\ell}$

Initial volume = Final volume

$$\therefore \pi[r_2^2 - r_1^2]\ell\rho = \pi r^2 \ell\rho$$

$$\Rightarrow r^2 = r_2^2 - r_1^2 \Rightarrow r^2 = (r_2 + r_1)(r_2 - r_1)$$

$$\Rightarrow r^2 = (8.02 + 7.98)(8.02 - 7.98)$$
$$\Rightarrow r^2 = 16\times 0.04 = 0.64\,\text{cm} \Rightarrow r = 0.8\,\text{cm}$$

$$\therefore \frac{C_1}{C_2} = \frac{r_2^4 - r_1^4}{r^4} = \frac{[8.02]^4 - [7.98]^4}{[0.8]^4}$$

16. (c)

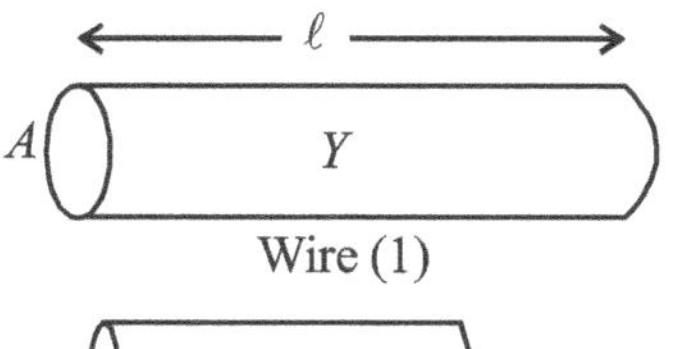

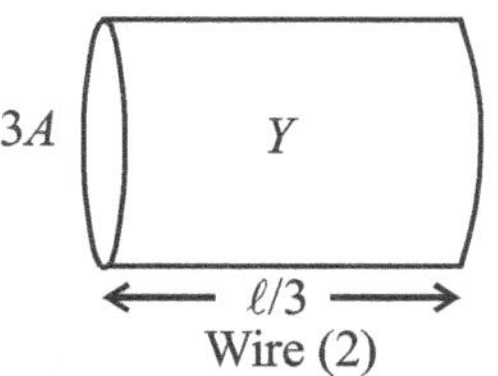

As shown in the figure, the wires will have the same Young's modulus (same material) and the length of the wire of area of cross-section $3A$ will be $\ell/3$ (same volume as wire 1).
For wire 1,

$$Y = \frac{F/A}{\Delta x/\ell} \qquad \text{...(i)}$$

For wire 2,

$$Y = \frac{F'/3A}{\Delta x/(\ell/3)} \qquad \text{...(ii)}$$

From (i) and (ii), $\dfrac{F}{A}\times\dfrac{\ell}{\Delta x} = \dfrac{F'}{3A}\times\dfrac{\ell}{3\Delta x} \Rightarrow F' = 9F$

17. (c) Poisson's ratio, $\sigma = \dfrac{\text{lateral strain }(\beta)}{\text{longitudinal strain }(\alpha)}$

For material like copper, $\sigma = 0.33$
And, $y = 3k(1 - 2\sigma)$

Also, $\dfrac{9}{y} = \dfrac{1}{k} + \dfrac{3}{n}$

$y = 2n(1 + \sigma)$
Hence, $n < y < k$

18. (b) Stress $= 1\ kg\ wt/mm^2 = 9.8\ N/mm^2$
$\qquad = 9.8 \times 10^6\ N/m^2$.

$Y = 1 \times 10^{11}\ N/m^2, \qquad \dfrac{\Delta\ell}{\ell} \times 100 = ?$

$Y = \dfrac{Stress}{Strain} = \dfrac{Stress}{\Delta\ell/\ell}$

$\therefore\ \dfrac{\Delta\ell}{\ell} = \dfrac{Stress}{Y} = \dfrac{9.8 \times 10^6}{1 \times 10^{11}}$

$\dfrac{\Delta\ell}{\ell} \times 100 = 9.8 \times 10^{-11} \times 100 \times 10^6$

$\qquad = 9.8 \times 10^{-3} = 0.0098\ \%$

19. (d)
$$W_1 = \frac{1}{2} kx^2$$
and
$$W_2 = \frac{1}{2} k(x+y)^2$$
$\therefore$
$$W = W_2 - W_1 = \frac{1}{2} k(x+y)^2 - \frac{1}{2} kx^2$$
$$= \frac{1}{2} ky(2x+y)$$

20. (c) Here, $k_Q = \dfrac{k_p}{2}$

According to Hooke's law
$\therefore\ F_p = -k_p\, x_p$

$F_Q = -k_Q x_Q \Rightarrow \dfrac{F_p}{F_Q} = \dfrac{k_p\, x_p}{k_Q\, x_Q}$

$F_p = F_Q$ [Given]

$\therefore\ \dfrac{x_p}{x_Q} = \dfrac{k_Q}{k_p}$ ...(i)

Energy stored in a spring is $U = \dfrac{1}{2} kx^2$

$\therefore\ \dfrac{U_p}{U_Q} = \dfrac{k_p x_p^2}{k_Q x_Q^2} = \dfrac{k_p}{k_Q} \times \dfrac{k_Q^2}{k_p^2} = \dfrac{1}{2} \qquad \left[\because k_Q = \dfrac{k_p}{2}\right]$

$\Rightarrow\ U_p = \dfrac{U_Q}{2} = \dfrac{E}{2} \qquad\qquad [\because U_Q = E]$

21. (a) Young's modulus $Y = \dfrac{stress}{strain}$

$stress = Y \times strain$
Stress in steel wire = Applied pressure
Pressure = stress = $Y \times$ strain

Strain $= \dfrac{\Delta L}{L} = \alpha \Delta T$ (As length is constant)

$= 2 \times 10^{11} \times 1.1 \times 10^{-5} \times 100 = 2.2 \times 10^8\ Pa$

22. (b) Let T be the tension in the ring, then

$Y = \dfrac{T.2\pi r}{A.2\pi(R-r)} = \dfrac{Tr}{A(R-r)} \quad \therefore\ T = \dfrac{YA(R-r)}{r}$

23. (a) Ratio of radii $r_1 : r_2 = 1 : 2$

Ratio of area, $A_1 : A_2 = \pi r_1^2 : \pi r_2^2$

$A_1 : A_2 = 1 : 4$
Now, $Stress_1 : Stress_2 = 4 : 1$
So, $Strain_1 : Strain_2 = 4 : 1$

$\therefore\ \dfrac{l_1}{l_2} = \dfrac{4}{1} \Rightarrow 4l_2 = l_1 = 8$

$\therefore\ l_2 = 2\ mm$
Increase in length of B is 2 mm.

24. (b) $\dfrac{dV}{V} = (1 + 2\sigma)\dfrac{dL}{L}$

$\dfrac{dV}{V} = 2 \times 2 \times 10^{-3} = 4 \times 10^{-3}$

$\left[\because \sigma = 0.5 = \dfrac{1}{2}\right]$

$\therefore$ Percentage change in volume $= 4 \times 10^{-1} = 0.4\%$

25. (b) $r\theta = \ell\phi \Rightarrow \phi = \dfrac{r\theta}{\ell} = \dfrac{6mm \times 30°}{1m} = 0.18°$

26. (d) Bulk modulus $B = \dfrac{|-dp|}{\left|\left(\dfrac{dV}{V}\right)\right|}$

$\therefore$ Pressure, $dp = B\left(\dfrac{\Delta V}{V}\right)$

27. (a) Given: $F = 100\ kN = 10^5\ N$
$Y = 2 \times 10^{11}\ Nm^{-2}$
$\ell_0 = 1.0\ m$
radius $r = 10\ mm = 10^{-2}\ m$

From formula, $Y = \dfrac{Stress}{Strain}$

$\Rightarrow$ Strain $= \dfrac{Stress}{Y} = \dfrac{F}{AY}$

$= \dfrac{10^5}{\pi r^2 Y} = \dfrac{10^5}{3.14 \times 10^{-4} \times 2 \times 10^{11}}$

$= \dfrac{1}{628}$

Therefore % strain $= \dfrac{1}{628} \times 100 = 0.16\%$

28. (c)

For a beam, the depression at the centre is given by,

$\delta = \left(\dfrac{f\,L}{4Ybd^3}\right)$

[f, L, b, d are constants for a particular beam]

i.e. $\delta \propto \dfrac{1}{Y}$

29. (b) $K = \dfrac{F}{x} = \dfrac{4 \times 9.8}{2 \times 10^{-2}} = 19.6 \times 10^2$

Work done $= \dfrac{1}{2} \times 19.6 \times 10^2 \times (0.05)^2 = 2.45\,J$

30. (c) If ℓ is the original length of wire, then change in length of first wire, $\Delta\ell_1 = (\ell_1 - \ell)$

change in length of second wire, $\Delta\ell_2 = (\ell_2 - \ell)$

Now, $Y = \dfrac{T_1}{A} \times \dfrac{\ell}{\Delta\ell_1} = \dfrac{T_2}{A} \times \dfrac{\ell}{\Delta\ell_2}$

or $\dfrac{T_1}{\Delta\ell_1} = \dfrac{T_2}{\Delta\ell_2}$ or $\dfrac{T_1}{\ell_1 - \ell} = \dfrac{T_2}{\ell_2 - \ell}$

or $T_1\ell_2 - T_1\ell = T_2\ell_1 - \ell T_2$ or $\ell = \dfrac{T_2\ell_1 - T_1\ell_2}{T_2 - T_1}$

31. (a) $\delta = \dfrac{W\ell^3}{3\,YI}$, where W = load, ℓ = length of beam and I is geometrical moment of inertia for rectangular beam,

$I = \dfrac{bd^3}{12}$ where b = breadth and d = depth

For square beam b = d

$\therefore I_1 = \dfrac{b^4}{12}$

For a beam of circular cross-section, $I_2 = \left(\dfrac{\pi r^4}{4}\right)$

$\therefore \delta_1 = \dfrac{W\ell^3 \times 12}{3Yb^4} = \dfrac{4W\ell^3}{Yb^4}$ (for sq. cross section)

and $\delta_2 = \dfrac{W\ell^3}{3Y(\pi r^4/4)} = \dfrac{4W\ell^3}{3Y(\pi r^4)}$

(for circular cross-section)

Now $\dfrac{\delta_1}{\delta_2} = \dfrac{3\pi r^4}{b^4} = \dfrac{3\pi r^4}{(\pi r^2)^2} = \dfrac{3}{\pi}$

($\because b^2 = \pi r^2$ i.e., they have same cross-sectional area)

32. (a) Compressibility $= \dfrac{1}{\text{Bulk modulus}}$

As bulk modulus is least for ethanol (0.9) and maximum for mercury (25) among ehtanol, mercury and water.

Hence compression in volume $\dfrac{\Delta V}{V}$

Ethanol > Water > Mercury

33. (c) The given graph does not obey Hooke's law. and there is no well defined plastic region. So the graph represents elastomers.

34. (a) $U/\text{volume} = \dfrac{1}{2} Y \times \text{strain}^2 = 3600\ \text{J m}^{-3}$

[Strain = 0.06×10^{-2}]

35. (d) Potential energy per unit volume of the wire is given by :

$u = \dfrac{1}{2} \dfrac{(\text{Stress})^2}{\text{Young's modulus}} = \dfrac{1}{2} \dfrac{S^2}{Y}$

As stress, $S = \dfrac{\text{Force}}{\text{Area}}$

$\therefore \dfrac{S_1}{S_2} = \left(\dfrac{F_1}{F_2}\right)\left(\dfrac{A_2}{A_1}\right)$

As $F_1 = F_2$ (Given)

$\therefore \dfrac{S_1}{S_2} = \left(\dfrac{F_1}{F_2}\right)\left(\dfrac{A_2}{A_1}\right) = \left(\dfrac{A_2}{A_1}\right)$ ..(i)

The two wires are of the same material, therefore their Young's moduli will be same i.e., $Y_1 = Y_2$

$\therefore \dfrac{u_1}{u_2} = \left(\dfrac{S_1}{S_2}\right)^2 = \left(\dfrac{A_2}{A_1}\right)^2$

$= \left[\dfrac{\pi\left(\dfrac{d_2}{2}\right)^2}{\pi\left(\dfrac{d_1}{2}\right)^2}\right]^2 = \left[\left(\dfrac{d_2}{d_1}\right)^2\right]^2$

$= \left(\dfrac{d_2}{d_1}\right)^4 = \left(\dfrac{2}{1}\right)^4 = \dfrac{16}{1}$ $\left(\because \dfrac{d_1}{d_2} = \dfrac{1}{2}\,(\text{Given})\right)$

36. (b) Using Hooke's law, $F = kx$ we can write

$\qquad 4 = k(a - \ell_0)$ ...(i)

and $\qquad 5 = k(b - \ell_0)$ ...(ii)

If ℓ be the length under tension 9N, then

$\qquad 9 = k(\ell - \ell_0)$ ...(iii)

After solving above equations, we get

$\qquad \ell = (5b - 4a)$.

37. (b) $F = Y \times A \times \dfrac{l}{L} \Rightarrow F \propto r^2$ (Y, l and and L are constant)

If diameter is made four times then force required will be 16 times, i.e., $16 \times 10^3\,N$

38. (c) Young's modulus of elasticity is

$Y = \dfrac{F/A}{\Delta L/L}$

$\therefore \Delta L = \dfrac{FL}{AY}$

So, $\Delta L \propto \dfrac{L}{A}$

$\therefore \dfrac{\Delta L_2}{\Delta L_1} = \dfrac{L_2}{L_1} \times \dfrac{A_1}{A_2} = \dfrac{2}{1} \times \dfrac{2}{1} = 4$

$\Delta L_2 = 4 \times \Delta L_1 = 4 \times 1 = 4\ \text{cm}$

39. (a) $y = \dfrac{F/A}{\Delta l/l} = \dfrac{F}{A} \cdot \dfrac{l}{\Delta l}$

$= \dfrac{20 \times 1}{10^{-6} \times 10^{-4}} = 2 \times 10^{11}\,\mathrm{Nm^{-2}}$

40. (d) $K = \dfrac{\Delta P}{\Delta V/V} = \dfrac{h\rho g}{\Delta V/V} = \dfrac{200 \times 10^3 \times 10}{0.1/100} = 2 \times 10^9$

41. (d) Bulk Modulus $= \dfrac{dp}{\dfrac{dv}{v}}$

$dp = h\rho g = 200 \times 10^3 \times 9.8$

$\dfrac{dv}{v} = \dfrac{0.1}{100}$

Bulk modulus $= \dfrac{200 \times 10^3 \times 9.8}{0.1/100} = 19.6 \times 10^8\,\mathrm{N/m^2}$

42. (c)

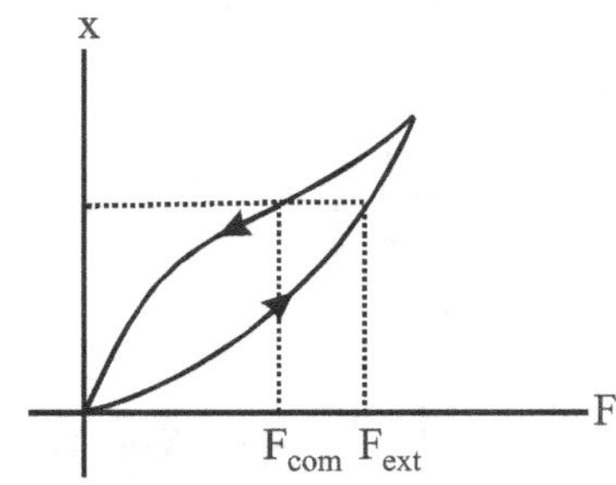

From the figure, it is clear that
$F_{com} < F_{ext}$.

43. (d) $\dfrac{\Delta r/r}{\Delta l/l} = 0.5 = \dfrac{1}{2},\ \dfrac{\Delta r}{r} = \dfrac{1}{2}\dfrac{\Delta l}{l}$

44. (b) As $Y = \dfrac{\dfrac{F}{A}}{\dfrac{\Delta l}{l}} \Rightarrow \Delta l = \dfrac{Fl}{AY}$

But $V = Al$ so $A = \dfrac{V}{l}$

Therefore $\Delta l = \dfrac{Fl^2}{VY} \propto l^2$

Hence graph of Δl versus l^2 will give a straight line.

45. (b) $K = \dfrac{F}{x} = \dfrac{4 \times 9.8}{2 \times 10^{-2}} = 19.6 \times 10^2$

Work done $= \dfrac{1}{2} \times 19.6 \times 10^2 \times (0.05)^2 = 2.45\,J$

1. **(a)** Bulk modulus,

$$B = -\frac{\Delta P}{\left(\dfrac{\Delta V}{V_0}\right)} \;\Rightarrow\; \Delta V = -V_0\frac{\Delta P}{B}$$

or $V - V_0 = -V_0\dfrac{\Delta P}{B}$ (Here V_0 = volume at the surface

and V = volume at the depth)

or $V = V_0 - V_0\dfrac{\Delta P}{B} \;\Rightarrow\; V = V_0\left(1 - \dfrac{\Delta P}{B}\right)$

$\therefore$ Density, $\rho' = \dfrac{m}{V} = \dfrac{m}{V_0\left(1 - \dfrac{\Delta P}{B}\right)}$

$$= \frac{m}{\dfrac{m}{\rho}\left(1 - \dfrac{nP_0 - P_0}{B}\right)} \quad (\because \Delta P = nP_0 - P_0)$$

$$\rho' = \frac{\rho B}{B - (n-1)P_0}$$

2. **(c)** Velocity of ball when it strikes the water surface

$v = \sqrt{2gh}$ ...(i)

Terminal velocity of ball inside the water

$v = \dfrac{2}{9}r^2 g\dfrac{(\rho - 1)}{\eta}$ ...(ii)

Equation (i) and (ii) we get $\sqrt{2gh} = \dfrac{2}{9}\dfrac{r^2 g}{\eta}(\rho - 1)$

$\Rightarrow h = \dfrac{2}{81}r^4\left(\dfrac{\rho - 1}{\eta}\right)^2 g$

3. **(b)**

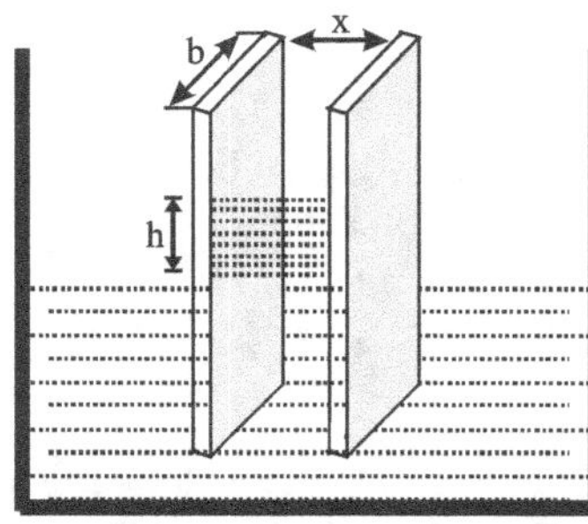

Let the width of each plate is b and due to surface tension liquid will rise upto height h then upward force due to surface tension.

$= 2Tb\cos\theta$ ...(i)

Weight of the liquid rises in between the plates

$= Vdg = (bxh)dg$ ...(ii)

Equating (i) and (ii) we get, $2T\cos\theta = xhdg$

$\therefore\; h = \dfrac{2T\cos\theta}{xdg}$

4. **(b)** The theorem of continuity is valid.

$\therefore A_1 v_1 \rho = A_2 v_2 \rho$ as the density of the liquid can be taken as uniform.

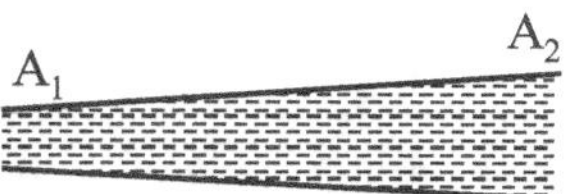

$\therefore A_1 v_1 = A_2 v_2$

$\Rightarrow$ Smaller the area, greater the velocity.

5. **(c)** $P_a + \dfrac{1}{2}\rho_1 v_1^2 + 0 = P_a + \dfrac{1}{2}\rho_2 v_2^2 + (\rho_1 g h_1 + \rho_2 g h_2)$

As $v_2 \ll v_1, \therefore v_1 = \sqrt{2g(h_1 + h_2)\left(\dfrac{\rho_2}{\rho_1}\right)}$.

6. **(c)** $h = \dfrac{2T\cos\theta}{r\rho g} \Rightarrow h \propto \dfrac{1}{r} \Rightarrow \dfrac{h_2}{h_1} = \dfrac{r_1}{r_2} = \dfrac{2}{3}$

$$\left(\because r_1 = r,\; r_2 = r + 50\% \text{ of } r = \dfrac{3}{2}r\right)$$

New mass $m_2 = \pi r_2^2 h_2 \rho = \pi\left(\dfrac{3}{2}r_1\right)^2\left(\dfrac{2}{3}h_1\right)\rho$

$$= \frac{3}{2}\left(\pi r_1^2 h_1\right)\rho = \frac{3}{2}m$$

7. **(a)** When a body falls through a viscous liquid, its velocity increases due to gravity but after some time its velocity becomes uniform because of viscous force becoming equal to the gravitational force. Viscous force itself is a variable force which increases as velocity increases, so curve (a) represents the correct alternative.

8. **(c)** Sum of volumes of 2 smaller drops

= Volume of the bigger drop

$2.\dfrac{4}{3}\pi r^3 = \dfrac{4}{3}\pi R^3 \;\Rightarrow\; R = 2^{1/3}\, r$

Surface energy $= T.4\pi R^2$

$= T4\pi 2^{2/3} r^2 = T.2^{8/3}\,\pi r^2$.

9. **(c)** Angle of contact θ

$$\cos\theta = \frac{T_{SA} - T_{SL}}{T_{LA}}$$

when water is on a waxy or oily surface

$T_{SA} < T_{SL}$ $\cos\theta$ is negative i.e., $90° < \theta < 180°$

i.e., angle of contact θ increases

And for $\theta > 90°$ liquid level in capillary tube fall. i.e., h decreases

10. **(a)** $F = 6\pi\eta r v$

$= 6 \times 3.14 \times (8 \times 10^{-5}) \times 0.03 \times 100$

$= 4.52 \times 10^{-3}$ dyne

11. **(a)** Velocity of water from hole $= v_1 = \sqrt{2gh}$

Velocity of water from hole B

$$v_2 = \sqrt{2g(H_0 - h)}$$

Time of reaching the ground from hole B

$$t_1 = \sqrt{2(H_0 - h)/g}$$

Time of reaching the ground from hole A

$$t_2 = \sqrt{2h/g}$$

12. (a) Fluid resistance is given by $R = \dfrac{8\eta L}{\pi r^4}$

When two capillary tubes of same size are joined in parallel, then equivalent fluid resistance is

$$R_S = R_1 + R_2 = \frac{8\eta L}{\pi R^4} + \frac{8\eta \times 2L}{\pi (2R)^4} = \left(\frac{8\eta L}{\pi R^4}\right) \times \frac{9}{8}$$

Rate of flow $= \dfrac{P}{R_S} = \dfrac{\pi P R^4}{8\eta L} \times \dfrac{8}{9} = \dfrac{8}{9} X \left[\text{as } X = \dfrac{\pi P R^4}{8\eta L} \right]$

13. (b) The candle floats on the water with half its length above and below water level. Let its length be 10 cm with 5 cm below the surface and 5 cm above it. If its length is reduced to 8 cm, it will have 4 cm above water surface. So we see tip going down by 1 cm.
∴ rate of fall of tip = 1 cm/hour.

14. (a) Inside pressure must be $\dfrac{4T}{r}$ greater than outside pressure in bubble.

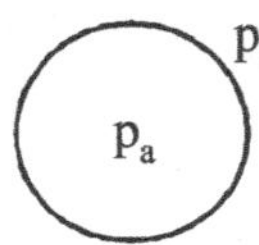

This excess pressure is provided by charge on bubble.

$$\frac{4T}{r} = \frac{\sigma^2}{2\varepsilon_0}; \quad \frac{4T}{r} = \frac{Q^2}{16\pi^2 r^4 \times 2\varepsilon_0} \left[\sigma = \frac{Q}{4\pi r^2} \right]$$

$$Q = 8\pi r \sqrt{2rT\varepsilon_0}$$

15. (a) Because film tries to cover minimum surface area.

16. (d)

17. (a) The condition for terminal speed (v_t) is
Weight = Buoyant force + Viscous force

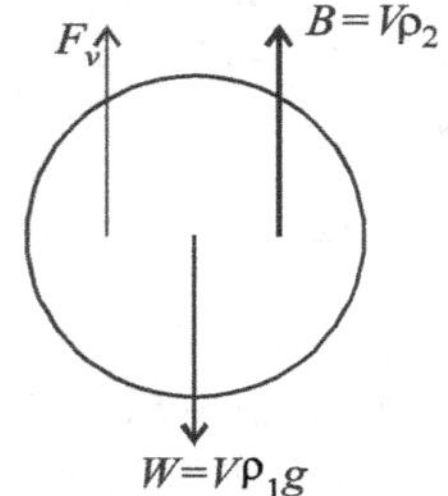

$$\therefore V\rho_1 g = V\rho_2 g + k v_t^2 \qquad \therefore v_t = \sqrt{\frac{Vg(\rho_1 - \rho_2)}{k}}$$

18. (d) According to Bernoulli's theorem, when velocity of liquid flow increases, the pressure decreases.

19. (c) Wetability of a surface by a liquid primarily depends on angle of contact between the surface and liquid.
If angle of contact is acute liquids wet the solid and vice-versa.

20. (a) $dv = 8$ cm/s and $dx = 0.1$ cm

Velocity gradient $= \dfrac{dv}{dx} = \dfrac{8}{0.1} = 80/s.$

21. (a) Terminal velocities of rain drops are proportional to square of their radii.
Terminal velocity of a body is given by

$$v_T = \frac{2R^2}{9\eta}(d - \sigma)g. \text{ or, } V \propto R^2$$

22. (b)

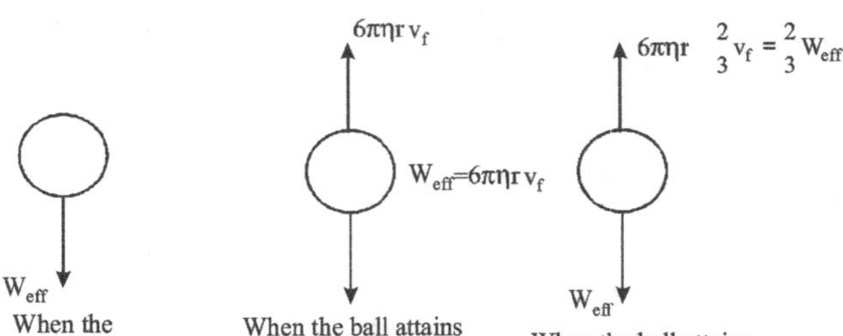

When the ball is just released, the net force on ball is
$W_{eff} (= mg -$ buoyant force)
The terminal velocity v_f of the ball is attained when net force on the ball is zero.
∴ Viscous force $6\pi\eta r\, v_f = W_{eff}$

When the ball acquires $\dfrac{2}{3}$rd of its maximum velocity v_f the viscous force is $= \dfrac{2}{3}W_{eff}$

Hence net force is $W_{eff} - \dfrac{2}{3}W_{eff} = \dfrac{1}{3}W_{eff}$
∴ required acceleration is a/3

23. (a) $(2\pi r_1 + 2\pi r_2)\sigma = mg$

$$\left[2\pi \times \frac{8.7}{2} + 2\pi \times \frac{8.5}{2} \right]\sigma = 3.97 \times 980$$

$$\Rightarrow \sigma = 72 \text{ dyne cm}^{-1}$$

24. (b) Over a small temperature ranges, S.T. of water decreases linearly with rise of temperature.

25. (c) Volume of air bubble $V = \dfrac{4}{3}\pi r^3$

We get, $V \propto r^3$
If r is 2 times, V becomes 8 times at the surface of lake.
Pressure at the surface of lake is given by
$P_1 = 1$ atmosphere, $V_1 = 8V$
$\Rightarrow P_1 = Hdg \qquad$ where, d = density of water
Pressure at the bottom of lake,
$P_2 =$ Pressure of atmosphere + Pressure of water
$P_2 = Hdg + hdg = (H + h)dg \quad$ where, h = depth of lake
Let final volume, $V_2 = V$.
Because temperature is constant, hence from Boyle's law
$P_1 V_1 = P_2 V_2 \Rightarrow Hdg \times 8V = (H + h)dg \times V \Rightarrow h = 7H.$

26. (c)

27. **(b)** Volume of first piece of metal $= \dfrac{32}{8} = 4\,\mathrm{cm}^3$

Upthrust $= 4$ gf

Effective weight $= (32 - 4)$ gf $= 28$ gf

If m be the mass of second body, volume of second body is $\dfrac{m}{5}$

Now, $28 = m - \dfrac{m}{5} \Rightarrow m = 35$ g

28. **(b)** $g_{\text{eff.}} = 12\ \mathrm{m/s}^2,\ = \dfrac{\rho_m}{\rho_w} = \dfrac{4}{10}$

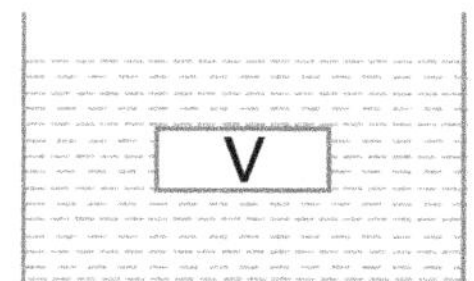

$$a = \dfrac{V\rho_w \times 12 - V\rho_m \times 12}{V\rho_m} = 18\,\mathrm{m/s}^2$$

$$1 = \dfrac{1}{2} \times 18\,t^2,\ t = \dfrac{1}{3}\,\mathrm{s}.$$

29. **(b)** Due to increase in velocity, pressure will be low above the surface of water.

30. **(c)** If ρ is the density of the ball and ρ' that of the another ball, m for the balls are the same, but $r' = 2r$

$\therefore\ mg = 6\pi r\eta v$ (by Stoke's law)

or, $6\pi r\eta v = 6\pi 2r\eta v'$ So, $v' = \dfrac{v}{2}$

31. **(d)** As we know,

Pressure $P = Vdg$

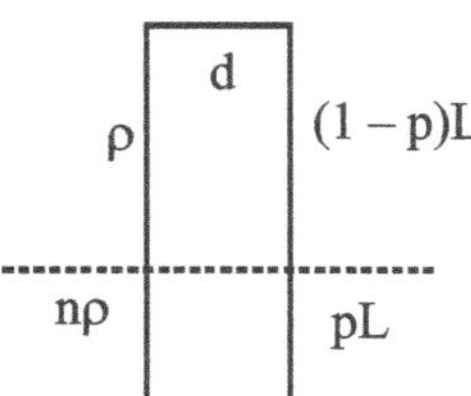

Here, $\mathrm{LA}\,d\,g = (pL)A\,(n\rho)g + (1-p)LA\rho\,g$

$\Rightarrow\ d = (1-p)\rho + pn\,\rho = [1 + (n-1)p]\rho$

32. **(d)** At equilibrium, weight of the given block is balanced by force due to surface tension, i.e.,

$2L.\,S = W$

or $S = \dfrac{W}{2L} = \dfrac{1.5 \times 10^{-2}\,N}{2 \times 0.3\,m} = 0.025\,Nm^{-1}$

33. **(a)**

34. **(d)** $T_1 + T\cos(\pi - \theta) = T_2$

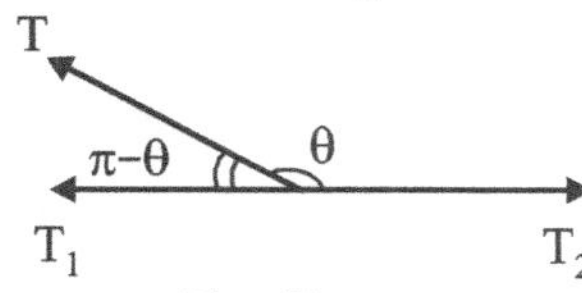

$\therefore\ \cos(\pi - \theta) = \dfrac{T_2 - T_1}{T}$

$\therefore\ -\cos\theta = \dfrac{T_2 - T_1}{T}$

$\therefore\ \cos\theta = \dfrac{T_1 - T_2}{T}$

35. **(a)** Let $L = PQ =$ length of rod

$\therefore\ SP = SQ = \dfrac{L}{2}$

Weight of rod, $W = A l \rho g.$
Acting at point S

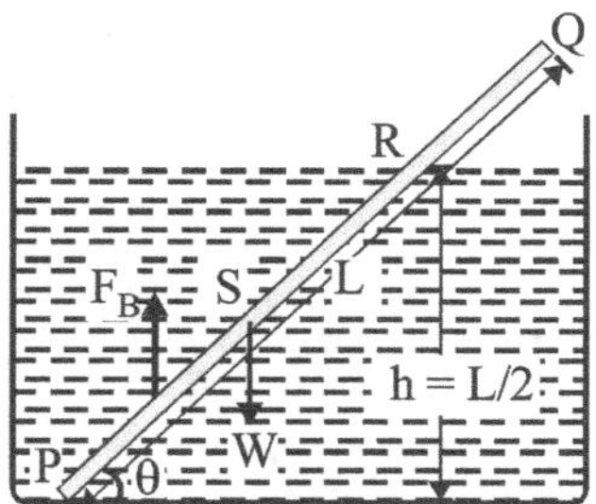

And force of buoyancy,

$F_B = Al\rho_0 g$. $[l = PR]$

Which acts at mid-point of PR.

For rotational equilibrium.

$$Al\rho_0 g \times \dfrac{\ell}{2}\cos\theta = AL\rho g \times \dfrac{L}{2}\cos\theta$$

$$\Rightarrow \dfrac{l^2}{L^2} = \dfrac{\rho}{\rho_0} \Rightarrow \dfrac{l}{L} = \sqrt{\dfrac{\rho}{\rho_0}}$$

From figure, $\sin\theta = \dfrac{h}{l} = \dfrac{L}{2l} = \dfrac{1}{2}\sqrt{\dfrac{\rho_0}{\rho}}$

36. **(b)** Terminal velocity, $v_0 = \dfrac{2\,r^2(\rho - \rho_0)g}{9\eta}$

$$= \dfrac{2 \times (2 \times 10^{-3})^2 \times (8 - 1.3) \times 10^3 \times 9.8}{9 \times 0.83} = 0.07\,\mathrm{ms}^{-1}$$

37. **(c)** Work done = Surface tension × increase in area of the film

$W = S \times \Delta A$

Increase in area = Final area − initial area

$\qquad\qquad = 10 \times (0.5 + 0.1) - 10 \times 0.5 = 1\ \mathrm{cm}^2$

$\therefore\ W = 72 \times 2 \times 1 = 144$ erg

[$\because$ There are 2 free surfaces; $\therefore\ \Delta A = 2 \times 1$].

38. **(b)** Waterproofing agents are used so that the material does not get wet. This means angle of contact is obtuse.

39. **(c)**

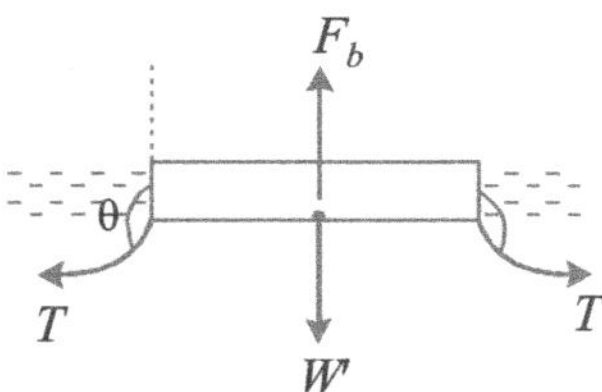

For floating disc, $F_{\text{net}} = 0$

or $\qquad F_b + 2\pi r T \cos\theta = W'$

or $\qquad W + 2\pi r T \cos\theta = W'$

40. **(b)**

41. **(d)** From the figure it is clear that liquid 1 floats on liquid 2. The lighter liquid floats over heavier liquid. Therefore we can conclude that $\rho_1 < \rho_2$

Also $\rho_3 < \rho_2$ otherwise the ball would have sink to the bottom of the jar.

Also $\rho_3 > \rho_1$ otherwise the ball would have floated in liquid 1. From the above discussion we conclude that
$$\rho_1 < \rho_3 < \rho_2.$$

42. **(a)** When the bubble gets detached,

Buoyant force = force due to surface tension

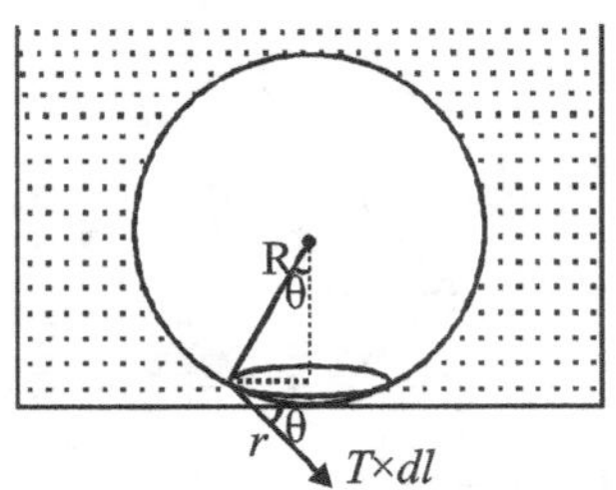

Force due to excess pressure = upthrust

Access pressure in air bubble = $\dfrac{2T}{R}$

$$\frac{2T}{R}(\pi r^2) = \frac{4\pi R^3}{3}\rho_w g$$

$$\Rightarrow \quad r^2 = \frac{2R^4\rho_w g}{3T} \Rightarrow r = R^2\sqrt{\frac{2\rho_w g}{3T}}$$

43. **(b)** Bernoulli's theorem.

44. **(a)** Inflow rate of volume of the liquid = Outflow rate of volume of the liquid

$$\pi R^2 V = n\pi r^2(v) \Rightarrow v = \frac{\pi R^2 V}{n\pi r^2} = \frac{VR^2}{nr^2}$$

45. **(c)** $\qquad T \times 2\pi r + mg = F_b$

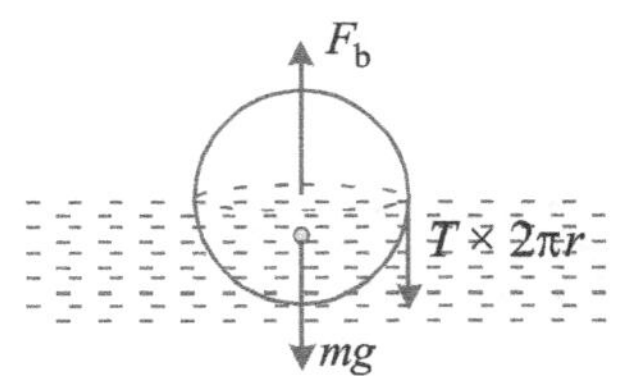

or $\qquad T \times 2\pi r + \rho\dfrac{4}{3}\pi r^3 g = \left[\dfrac{\dfrac{4}{3}\pi r^3}{2}\right]\sigma g$

$\therefore \qquad r = \sqrt{\dfrac{3T}{g(2\rho - \sigma)}}$

1. **(a)** $E = \dfrac{S}{S_0}\sigma T^4 = \dfrac{4\pi r^2}{4\pi R^2}\sigma T^4$

$= \sigma\dfrac{r^2}{R^2}T^4$

2. **(c)**

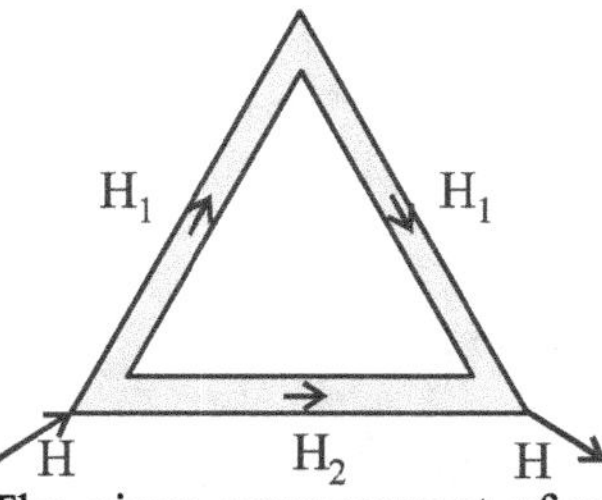

The given arrangement of rods can be redrawn as follows

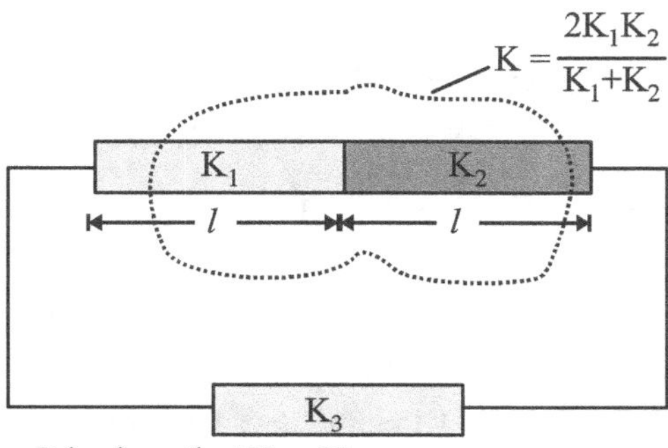

It is given that $H_1 = H_2$

$\Rightarrow \dfrac{KA(\theta_1 - \theta_2)}{2l} = \dfrac{K_3 A(\theta_1 - \theta_2)}{l} \Rightarrow K_3 = \dfrac{K}{2} = \dfrac{K_1 K_2}{K_1 + K_2}$

3. **(c)** $Q = mc\Delta T$

$Q = mc\,(T - T_0)$ ......(i)

$Q = Kt$ whereas K is heating rate

∴ from 50 to boiling temperature, T increases linearly.

At vaporization, equation is $Q = mL$

so, temperature remains constant till vaporisation is complete

After that, again Eqn (i) is followed and temperature increases linearly

4. **(b)** At constant temperature molar heat capacity

$C_T = \dfrac{\Delta Q}{n\Delta T}$

T is const. $\Rightarrow \Delta T = 0$

∴ $C_T = \dfrac{\Delta Q}{0} = \infty$

5. **(d)** Required work = energy released

Here, $Q = \int mc\,dT$

$= \int_{20}^{4} 0.1 \times 32 \times \left(\dfrac{T^3}{400^3}\right) dT \approx 0.002\,\text{kJ}.$

Therefore, required work $= 0.002\,\text{kJ}$

6. **(b)** Since, $e = a = 0.2$

Since $a = (1 - r - t) = 0.2$ for the body B

Thus emissive power of B is given by,

$E = a\,E_b = (100)\,(0.2) = 20\,\text{W/m}^2$

7. **(b)** Rate of cooling of a body $R = \dfrac{\Delta\theta}{t} = \dfrac{A\varepsilon\sigma(T^4 - T_0^4)}{mc}$

$\Rightarrow R \propto \dfrac{A}{m} \propto \dfrac{\text{Area}}{\text{Volume}}\quad [m = \rho \times V]$

$\Rightarrow$ For the same surface area. $R \propto \dfrac{1}{\text{Volume}}$

∵ Volume of cube < Volume of sphere

$\Rightarrow R_{\text{cube}} > R_{\text{Sphere}}$ i.e., cube, cools down with faster rate.

8. **(b)** From question,

$\Delta\rho = (998 - 992)\,\text{kg/m}^3 = 6\,\text{kg/m}^3$

$\rho = \dfrac{998 + 992}{2}\,\text{kg/m}^3 = 995\,\text{kg/m}^3$

$\rho = \dfrac{m}{V}$

$\Rightarrow \dfrac{\Delta\rho}{\rho} = -\dfrac{\Delta V}{V} \Rightarrow \left|\dfrac{\Delta\rho}{\rho}\right| = \left|\dfrac{\Delta V}{V}\right|$

∴ Coefficient of volume expansion of water,

$\dfrac{1}{V}\dfrac{\Delta V}{\Delta t} = \dfrac{1}{\rho}\dfrac{\Delta\rho}{\Delta t} = \dfrac{6}{995 \times 20} \approx 3 \times 10^{-4}\,/\,^\circ\text{C}$

9. **(a)** $E = \dfrac{F/A}{\Delta l/l} = \dfrac{\text{stress}}{\text{strain}}$ where $\Delta\ell = (\ell' - \ell) = \ell\alpha t$ so $F = EA\alpha t$

10. **(c)**

11. **(a)** $F = Y\alpha t A$ or $F \propto \alpha$

($\because$ Y t A is same for both copper and iron)

or $F_C \propto \alpha_C$ and $F_I \propto \alpha_I$

∴ $\dfrac{F_C}{F_I} = \dfrac{3/2}{1} = \dfrac{3}{2}$

12. **(c)** According to question only one-quarter of the heat produced by falling piece of ice is absorbed in the melting of ice.

i.e., $\dfrac{mgh}{4} = mL$

$\Rightarrow h = \dfrac{4L}{g} = \dfrac{4 \times 3.4 \times 10^5}{10} = 136\,\text{km}.$

13. **(d)** $W = W_1 - W_2 = mgh - mgh' = mg\,(h - h')$

$= 5 \times 10\,(20 - 0.2) = 5 \times 10 \times 19.8$

$= 5 \times 198 = 990$ joule

This energy is converted into heat when the ball strikes the earth. Heat produced is

$$Q = \frac{990}{4.2} \text{ calorie}$$

$$\Delta T = \frac{Q}{mc} = \frac{99 \times 100}{42 \times 5000 \times 0.09} = \frac{11}{32} \, ^\circ C$$

14. (b) Let the angle subtended by the arc formed be θ. Then

$$\theta = \frac{\ell}{r} \text{ or } \theta = \frac{\Delta\ell}{\Delta r} = \frac{\ell_2 - \ell_1}{r_1 - r_2}$$

$$\therefore \quad \theta = \frac{\ell(\alpha_2 - \alpha_1)\Delta T}{t} \text{ or } \frac{\ell}{r} = \frac{\ell(\alpha_2 - \alpha_1)\Delta T}{t}$$

So, $\quad r = \dfrac{t}{(\alpha_2 - \alpha_1)\Delta T}$

15. (d)

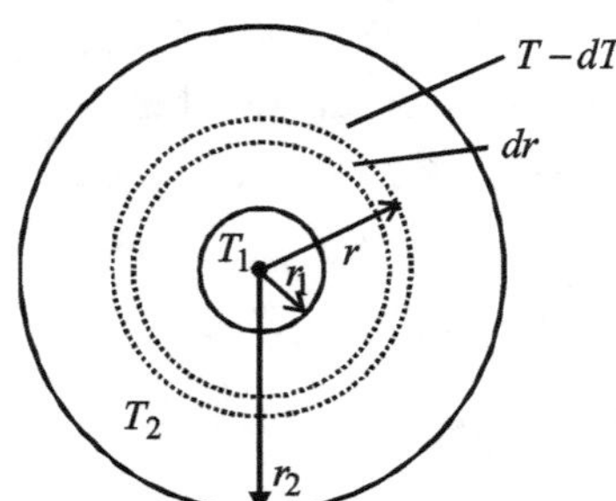

Consider a shell of thickness (dr) and of radius (r) and let the temperature of inner and outer surfaces of this shell be T and $(T - dT)$ respectively.

$\dfrac{dQ}{dt}$ = rate of flow of heat through it

$$= \frac{KA[(T - dT) - T]}{dr} = \frac{-KA\, dT}{dr}$$

$$= -4\pi K r^2 \frac{dT}{dr} \qquad (\because A = 4\pi r^2)$$

To measure the radial rate of heat flow, integration technique is used, since the area of the surface through which heat will flow is not constant.

Then, $\left(\dfrac{dQ}{dt}\right) \displaystyle\int_{r_1}^{r_2} \frac{1}{r^2}\, dr = -4\pi K \int_{T_1}^{T_2} dT$

$$\frac{dQ}{dt}\left[\frac{1}{r_1} - \frac{1}{r_2}\right] = -4\pi K \left[T_2 - T_1\right]$$

or $\dfrac{dQ}{dt} = \dfrac{-4\pi K r_1 r_2 (T_2 - T_1)}{(r_2 - r_1)}$

$\therefore \quad \dfrac{dQ}{dt} \propto \dfrac{r_1 r_2}{(r_2 - r_1)}$

16. (a) According to Newton's law of cooling if temperature difference between body & surrounding is large, then rate of cooling is also fast hence curve A shows correct behaviour.

17. (a) Among glass, wood and metals, metals expand more for same rise in temperature.

18. (b) According to Wein's law $\lambda_m \propto \dfrac{1}{T}$ and from the figure

$(\lambda_m)_1 < (\lambda_m)_3 < (\lambda_m)_2$ therefore $T_1 > T_3 > T_2$.

19. (a) Moment of inertia of a rod,

$$I = \frac{1}{12} ML^2$$

Differentiating w.r.t. to ΔL, we get

$$\frac{\Delta I}{\Delta L} = \frac{1}{12} \times 2ML$$

$$\Delta I = \frac{1}{12} 2ML\Delta L \qquad \therefore \frac{\Delta I}{I} = 2\frac{\Delta L}{L}$$

As we know, $\Delta L = L\alpha \Delta t$ or $\dfrac{\Delta L}{L} = \alpha \Delta t$

Substituting the value $\dfrac{\Delta L}{L}$, we get

$$\frac{\Delta I}{I} = 2\alpha\Delta t$$

20. (c) The lengths of each rod increases by the same amount

$$\therefore \quad \Delta\ell_a = \Delta\ell_s \Rightarrow \ell_1 \alpha_a t = \ell_2 \alpha_s t$$

$$\Rightarrow \frac{\ell_2}{\ell_1} = \frac{\alpha_a}{\alpha_s} \Rightarrow \frac{\ell_2}{\ell_1} + 1 = \frac{\alpha_a}{\alpha_s} + 1$$

$$\Rightarrow \frac{\ell_2 + \ell_1}{\ell_1} = \frac{\alpha_a + \alpha_s}{\alpha_s} \Rightarrow \frac{\ell_1}{\ell_1 + \ell_2} = \frac{\alpha_s}{\alpha_a + \alpha_s}$$

21. (a) According to Kirchhoff law, good absorbers are good emitters. Since black spot is good absorber so it is also a good emitter & will be brighter than plate.

22. (a) From Wein's displacement law

$\lambda_m \times T$ = constant

P – max. intensity is at violet

$\Rightarrow \lambda_m$ is minimum $\Rightarrow$ temp maximum

R – max. intensity is at green

$\Rightarrow \lambda_m$ is moderate $\Rightarrow$ temp moderate

Q – max. intensity is at red $\Rightarrow \lambda_m$ is maximum $\Rightarrow$ temp. minimum   i.e., $T_p > T_R > T_Q$

23. (c)

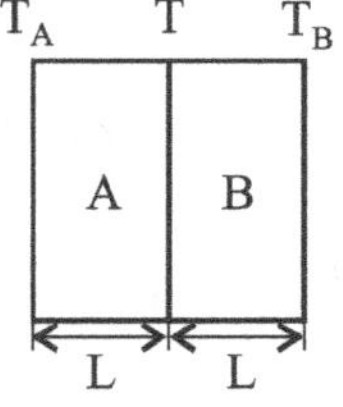

Let T be temperature of the junction

Here, $K_A = 2K_B$, $T - T_B = 50K$

At the steady state,

$$H_A = H_B$$

$$\therefore \quad \frac{K_A A(T_A - T)}{L} = \frac{K_B A(T - T_B)}{L}$$

$$2K_B(T_A - T) = K_B(T - T_B)$$

$$T_A - T = \frac{T - T_B}{2}$$

$$= \frac{50K}{2} = 25K$$

24. (b)

25. (a) Suppose, height of liquid in each arm before rising the temperature is l.

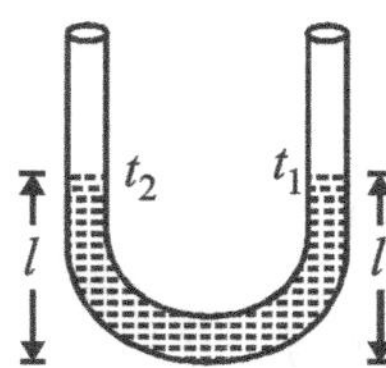 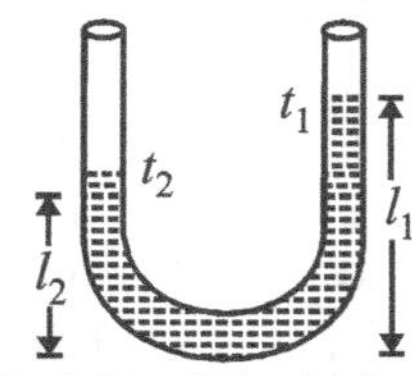

With temperature rise height of liquid in each arm increases *i.e.* $l_1 > l$ and $l_2 > l$

Also $l = \dfrac{l_1}{1+\gamma\, t_1} = \dfrac{l_2}{1+\gamma\, t_2}$

$\Rightarrow l_1 + \gamma\, l_1 t_2 = l_2 + \gamma\, l_2 t_1 \Rightarrow \gamma = \dfrac{l_1 - l_2}{l_2 t_1 - l_1 t_2}.$

26. (a) The rate of heat loss per unit area due to radiation
$$= \epsilon\sigma\,(T^4 - T_0^4)$$
$$= 0.6 \times 5.67 \times 10^{-8}\,[(400)^4 - (300)^4] = 595\ \text{Jm}^{-2}\text{s}^{-1}.$$

27. (d) According to Wein's displacement law, product of wavelength belonging to maximum intensity and temperature is constant i.e., $\lambda_m T = $ constant.

28. (c) According to Newton's law of cooling, the temperature goes on decreasing with time non-linearly.

29. (d) $\quad t \propto \dfrac{\ell}{A}, \quad t' \propto \dfrac{2\ell}{A/2}$

$$\frac{t'}{t} = 4\frac{\ell/A}{\ell/A}$$
$$t' = 4 \times t$$
$$3/t' = 48s$$

30. (a) In series, equivalent thermal conductivity

$$K_{eq} = \frac{2K_1 K_2}{K_1 + K_2}$$

or, $K_{eq} = \dfrac{2 \times K \times 2K}{K + 2K} = \dfrac{4}{3}K$

31. (c) $\quad Q = -KA\left(\dfrac{d\theta}{dx}\right) \times t$

32. (c) Using Wein's law, $\lambda_m T = $ constant
$$\lambda_1 T_1 = \lambda_2 T_2$$

$$\lambda_2 = \lambda_1 \frac{T_1}{T_2}$$

$$\lambda_2 = \frac{\lambda_0 T}{2T} = \frac{\lambda_0}{2}$$

33. (b) Total power radiated by Sun $= \sigma T^4 \times 4\pi R^2$
The intensity of power at earth's surface

$$= \frac{\sigma T^4 \times 4\pi R^2}{4\pi r^2}$$

Total power received by Earth

$$= \frac{\sigma T^4 R^2}{r^2}(\pi r_0^2)$$

34. (c) The upthrust is given by $\dfrac{4}{3}\pi R_t^{\,3}\rho\,g$

Here $R_t^{\,3} = R_0^{\,3}(1 + \gamma_m t)$ and $\rho_t = \rho_0\,/(1 + \gamma_a t)$

So, the upthrust at t°C is given by

$$= \frac{4}{3}\pi R_0^{\,3}\,(1 + \gamma_m t) \times \{\rho_0\,/(1 + \gamma_a t)\}\,g$$

As $\gamma_m < \gamma_a$, hence upthrust at t°C < upthrust at 0°C

So, the upthrust is decreased. Hence weight in liquid gets increased.

35. (d) Let T be the temperature of the interface. As the two sections are in series, the rate of flow of heat in them will be equal.

T_1	ℓ_1		ℓ_2	T_2
	K_1		K_2	

$\therefore \dfrac{K_1 A(T_1 - T)}{\ell_1} = \dfrac{K_2 A(T - T_2)}{\ell_2},$

where A is the area of cross-section.

or, $\quad K_1 A(T_1 - T)\ell_2 = K_2 A(T - T_2)\ell_1$

or, $\quad K_1 T_1 \ell_2 - K_1 T\ell_2 = K_2 T\ell_1 - K_2 T_2\ell_1$

or, $\quad (K_2\ell_1 + K_1\ell_2)T = K_1 T_1\ell_2 + K_2 T_2\ell_1$

$\therefore\ T = \dfrac{K_1 T_1\ell_2 + K_2 T_2\ell_1}{K_2\ell_1 + K_1\ell_2} = \dfrac{K_1\ell_2 T_1 + K_2\ell_1 T_2}{K_1\ell_2 + K_2\ell_1}.$

36. (d) Radius of small sphere = r
Thickness of small sphere = t
Radius of bigger sphere = 2r
Thickness of bigger sphere = t/4
Mass of ice melted = (volume of sphere) × (density of ice)
Let K_1 and K_2 be the thermal conductivities of larger and smaller sphere.
For bigger sphere,

$$\frac{K_1 4\pi\,(2r)^2 \times 100}{t/4} = \frac{\dfrac{4}{3}\pi(2r)^3\rho L}{25 \times 60}$$

For smaller sphere,

$$\frac{K_2 \times 4\pi r^2 \times 100}{t} = \frac{\dfrac{4}{3}\pi r^3\rho L}{16 \times 60}$$

$$\therefore\ \frac{K_1}{K_2} = \frac{8}{25}$$

37. (b) According to Wein's displacement law,
$\lambda_m T = 2.88 \times 10^{-3}$
When $T = 2000$ K,
$\lambda_m (2000) = 2.88 \times 10^{-3}$ ....(1)
When $T = 3000$ K,
$\lambda'_m (3000) = 2.88 \times 10^{-3}$ ....(2)
Dividing (1) by (2),

$$\frac{2}{3}\frac{\lambda_m}{\lambda'_m} = 1 \Rightarrow \frac{\lambda_m}{\lambda'_m} = \frac{3}{2} \Rightarrow \lambda'_m = \frac{2}{3}\lambda_m$$

38. (c) AB represents latent heat of fusion
$Q_1 = mL_F$
Here, $L_F \propto$ length of line AB
CD represents latent heat of vaporization $Q_2 = mL_V$
Here, $L_V \propto$ length of line CD
$\therefore Q_2 = 2Q_1$ $[\because$ As CD $= 2$AB]

39. (b) Let the final temperature be T

Heat gained by ice $= mL + m \times s \times (T - 0)$

$= 10 \times 80 + 10 \times 1 \times T$

Heat lost by water $= 55 \times 1 \times (40 - T)$

By using law of calorimetery,

$800 + 10\,T = 55 \times (40 - T)$

$\Rightarrow T = 21.54°C = 22°C$

40. (a) According to Newton's law of cooling,

$$\frac{\theta_1 - \theta_2}{t} = K\left[\frac{\theta_1 + \theta_2}{2} - \theta_0\right]$$

where θ_0 is the surrounding temperature.

$$\therefore \quad \frac{60 - 40}{7} = K\left(\frac{60 + 40}{2} - 10\right)$$

$$\Rightarrow \frac{20}{7} = 40K \Rightarrow K = \frac{1}{14}$$

$$\therefore \quad \frac{40 - 28}{t} = K\left[\frac{40 + 28}{2} - 10\right] \Rightarrow \frac{12}{t} = 24K$$

$$\text{or} \quad t = \frac{12}{24K} = \frac{12 \times 14}{24} = 7\,\text{min}$$

41. (d) $\dfrac{Q}{t} = K_1 A_1 \dfrac{d\theta}{dx} = K_2 A_2 \dfrac{d\theta}{dx}$

42. (c) Since specific heat $= 0.6\ kcal/g \times °C = 0.6\ cal/g \times °C$
From graph it is clear that in a minute, the temperature is raised from $0°C$ to $50°C$.
$\Rightarrow$ Heat required for a minute $= 50 \times 0.6 \times 50 = 1500\ cal$.
Also from graph, Boiling point of wax is $200°C$.

43. (b) Temperature of B will be higher because, due to expansion centre of mass B will come down same heat is supplied but in B, potential energy is decreased therefore internal energy gain will be more.

44. (d) According to the principle of calorimetry.
Heat lost = Heat gained
$mL_v + ms_w\Delta\theta = m_w s_w \Delta\theta$
$\Rightarrow m \times 540 + m \times 1 \times (100 - 80)$
$= 20 \times 1 \times (80 - 10)$
$\Rightarrow m = 2.5$ g
Therefore total mass of water at $80°C$
$= (20 + 2.5)$ g $= 22.5$ g

45. (a) Initial rate of loss of heat $= \dfrac{\sigma T^4 \times A_1 \times e}{\sigma T^4 \times A_2 \times e} = \dfrac{R_1^2}{R_2^2}$

1. **(a)** $U = a + bPV$ ......(1)

In adiabatic change,

$$dU = -dW = \frac{nR}{\gamma - 1}(T_2 - T_1) = \frac{nR}{\gamma - 1}(dT)$$

$$\Rightarrow U = \int dU = \frac{nR}{\gamma - 1}\int dT$$

or $\quad U = \left(\frac{nR}{\gamma - 1}\right)T + a = \frac{PV}{\gamma - 1} + a$ ......(2)

where a is the constant of integration.

Comparing (1) and (2), we get

$$b = \frac{1}{\gamma - 1} \Rightarrow \gamma = \frac{b+1}{b}.$$

2. **(d)** For path ab : $(\Delta U)_{ab} = 7000\,J$

By using $\Delta U = \mu C_V \Delta T$

$$7000 = \mu \times \frac{5}{2} R \times 700 \Rightarrow \mu = 0.48$$

For path ca :

$$(\Delta Q)_{ca} = (\Delta U)_{ca} + (\Delta W)_{ca} \quad ...(i)$$

$\because (\Delta U)_{ab} + (\Delta U)_{bc} + (\Delta U)_{ca} = 0$

$\because 7000 + 0 + (\Delta U)_{ca} = 0 \Rightarrow (\Delta U)_{ca} = -7000\,J$ ...(ii)

Also $(\Delta W)_{ca} = P_1(V_1 - V_2) = \mu R(T_1 - T_2)$
$= 0.48 \times 8.31 \times (300 - 1000) = -2792.16 J$ ...(iii)

On solving equations (i), (ii) and (iii)

$$(\Delta Q)_{ca} = -7000 - 2792.16 = -9792.16\,J \approx -9800\,J$$

3. **(c)** The efficiency (η) of a Carnot engine and the coefficient of performance (β) of a refrigerator are related as

$$\beta = \frac{1-\eta}{\eta} \qquad \text{Here, } \eta = \frac{1}{10}$$

$$\therefore \beta = \frac{1 - \dfrac{1}{10}}{\left(\dfrac{1}{10}\right)} = 9.$$

Also, Coefficient of performance (β) is given by $\beta = \dfrac{Q_2}{W}$,

where Q_2 is the energy absorbed from the reservoir.

or, $9 = \dfrac{Q_2}{10} \qquad \therefore Q_2 = 90\,J.$

4. **(b)** According to first law of thermodynamics,

$\Delta Q = \Delta U + \Delta W$

ΔQ = heat absorbed by gas

ΔW = work done by gas.

$-20J = \Delta U - 8J$

$\Delta U = -12J = U_{Final} - U_{initial}$

$U_{initial} = 30J$.

$U_{Final} = 30 - 12 = 18\,J$.

5. **(a)** The volume on both sides will be so adjusted that the original pressure × volume is kept constant as the piston moves slowly (isothermal change)

$P5V = P'V'$ ....(1)

$10PV = P'V''$ ....(2)

From (1) and (2), $V'' = 2V'$
and from $V' + V'' = 6V$

$\qquad V' = 2V, \; V'' = 4V$

6. **(a)** $W_{AB} = 0$, $\qquad W_{BC} = P\Delta V = nR\Delta T = -nRT_0$

$$W_{CA} = nRT \ln \frac{V_f}{V_i} = nR(2T_0)\ln 2$$

$$Q_{BC} = nC_p\Delta T = \left(\frac{nR\gamma}{\gamma - 1}\right)T_0$$

Efficiency, $\qquad \eta = \dfrac{W}{Q} = \left[\dfrac{2\ln 2 - 1}{\gamma/(\gamma - 1)}\right]$

7. **(c)** $T_1 = 273 + 27 = 300\,K$
$T_2 = 273 + 927 = 1200\,K$
For adiabatic process,
$P^{1-\gamma} T^{\gamma} = $ constant
$\Rightarrow P_1^{1-\gamma} T_1^{\gamma} = P_2^{1-\gamma} T_2^{\gamma}$

$$\Rightarrow \left(\frac{P_2}{P_1}\right)^{1-\gamma} = \left(\frac{T_1}{T_2}\right)^{\gamma} \quad \Rightarrow \left(\frac{P_1}{P_2}\right)^{1-\gamma} = \left(\frac{T_2}{T_1}\right)^{\gamma}$$

$$\left(\frac{P_1}{P_2}\right)^{1-1.4} = \left(\frac{1200}{300}\right)^{1.4} \quad \Rightarrow \left(\frac{P_1}{P_2}\right)^{-0.4} = (4)^{1.4}$$

$$\left(\frac{P_2}{P_1}\right)^{0.4} = 4^{1.4}$$

$$P_2 = P_1\, 4^{\left(\frac{1.4}{0.4}\right)} = P_1\, 4^{\left(\frac{7}{2}\right)}$$
$$= P_1(2^7) = 2 \times 128 = 256\ \text{atm}$$

8. **(b)**

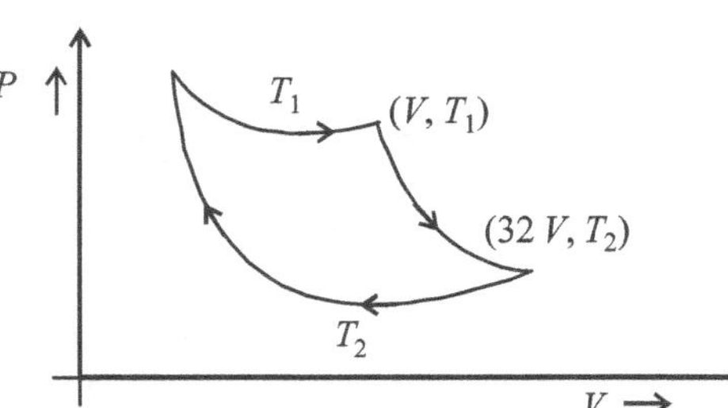

We have, $TV^{\gamma - 1} = $ constant

$\Rightarrow T_1 V^{\gamma - 1} = T_2 (32V)^{\gamma - 1}$

$\Rightarrow T_1 = (32)^{\gamma - 1} . T_2$

For diatomic gas, $\gamma = \dfrac{7}{5}$

$\therefore \gamma - 1 = \dfrac{2}{5}$

$\therefore T_1 = (32)^{\frac{2}{5}} T_2 \Rightarrow T_1 = 4T_2$

Now, efficiency $= 1 - \dfrac{T_2}{T_1}$

$= 1 - \dfrac{T_2}{4T_2} = 1 - \dfrac{1}{4} = \dfrac{3}{4} = 0.75$.

9. **(d)** Isobaric compression is represented by curve AO
Work done = area under AD
$= 2 \times 10^2 \times (3 - 1)$
$= 4 \times 10^2 = 400$ J.

10. **(a)** As $P \propto \dfrac{1}{V^{1.5}}$, So $PV^{1.5} = $ constant

$\therefore \gamma = 1.5 \; (\because \text{Process is adiabatic})$

As we know, $\dfrac{C_p}{C_v} = \gamma$ $\qquad \therefore \dfrac{C_p}{C_v} = 1.5$

11. **(a)** $W = \dfrac{nR\Delta T}{1 - \gamma} \Rightarrow -146000 = \dfrac{1000 \times 8.3 \times 7}{1 - \gamma}$

or $1 - \gamma = -\dfrac{58.1}{146} \Rightarrow \gamma = 1 + \dfrac{58.1}{146} = 1.4$

Hence the gas is diatomic.

12. **(a)** As, $P = \dfrac{1}{3}\left(\dfrac{U}{V}\right)$

But $\dfrac{U}{V} = KT^4$

So, $P = \dfrac{1}{3}KT^4$

or $\dfrac{uRT}{V} = \dfrac{1}{3}KT^4$ [As $PV = u\,RT$]

$\dfrac{4}{3}\pi R^3 T^3 = $ constant

Therefore, $T \propto \dfrac{1}{R}$

13. **(c)** Heat required to change the temperature of vessel by a small amount dT
$$-dQ = mCdT$$
Total heat required

$-Q = m \int_{20}^{4} 32\left(\dfrac{T}{400}\right)^3 dT = \dfrac{100 \times 10^{-3} \times 32}{(400)^3}\left[\dfrac{T^4}{4}\right]_{20}^{4}$

$\Rightarrow Q = 0.001996$ kJ
Work done required to maintain the temperature of sink to T_2

$W = Q_1 - Q_2 = \dfrac{Q_1 - Q_2}{Q_2}Q_2 = \left(\dfrac{T_1}{T_2} - 1\right)Q_2$

$\Rightarrow W = \left(\dfrac{T_1 - T_2}{T_2}\right)Q_2$

For $T_2 = 20$ K

$W_1 = \dfrac{300 - 20}{20} \times 0.001996 = 0.028$ kJ

For $T_2 = 4$ K

$W_2 = \dfrac{300 - 4}{4} \times 0.001996 = 0.148$ kJ

As temperature is changing from 20k to 4 k, work done required will be more than W_1 but less than W_2.

14. **(a)** Initially
$V_1 = 5.6\ell$, $T_1 = 273$K, $P_1 = 1$ atm,

$\gamma = \dfrac{5}{3}$ (For monatomic gas)

The number of moles of gas is

$n = \dfrac{5.6\ell}{22.4\ell} = \dfrac{1}{4}$

Finally (after adiabatic compression)
$V_2 = 0.7\ell$
For adiabatic compression

$T_1 V_1^{\gamma - 1} = T_2 V_2^{\gamma - 1}$

$\therefore T_2 = T_1\left(\dfrac{V_1}{V_2}\right)^{\gamma - 1} = T_1\left(\dfrac{5.6}{0.7}\right)^{\frac{5}{3} - 1}$

$= T_1(8)^{2/3} = 4T_1$

We know that work done in adiabatic process is

$W = \dfrac{nR\Delta T}{\gamma - 1} = \dfrac{9}{8}RT_1$

15. **(c)** Curve A, B shows expansion. For expansion of a gas,
$W_{\text{isothermal}} > W_{\text{adiabatic}}$
$P_{\text{isothermal}} > P_{\text{adiabatic}}$
$T_{\text{isothermal}} > T_{\text{adiabatic}}$
$\Rightarrow$ Slope of curve for isothermal change < slope of curve for adiabatic change.
So, curve B shows isothermal change and curve A shows adiabatic change.

16. **(a)** $PV^{3/2} = K$, $\qquad \log P + \dfrac{3}{2}\log V = \log K$

$\dfrac{\Delta P}{P} + \dfrac{3}{2}\dfrac{\Delta V}{V} = 0$

$\dfrac{\Delta V}{V} = -\dfrac{2}{3}\dfrac{\Delta P}{P}$ or $\dfrac{\Delta V}{V} = \left(-\dfrac{2}{3}\right)\left(\dfrac{2}{3}\right) = -\dfrac{4}{9}$

17. **(a)** Initially the efficiency of the engine was $\dfrac{1}{6}$ which

increases to $\dfrac{1}{3}$ when the sink temperature reduces by 62° C.

$$\eta = \frac{1}{6} = 1 - \frac{T_2}{T_1}, \quad \text{when } T_2 = \text{sink temperature}$$

T_1 = source temperature

$$\Rightarrow T_2 = \frac{5}{6} T_1$$

Secondly,

$$\frac{1}{3} = 1 - \frac{T_2 - 62}{T_1} = 1 - \frac{T_2}{T_1} + \frac{62}{T_1} = 1 - \frac{5}{6} + \frac{62}{T_1}$$

or, $T_1 = 62 \times 6 = 372K = 372 - 273 = 99°C$

$$\& \ T_2 = \frac{5}{6} \times 372 = 310 K = 310 - 273 = 37°C$$

18. (b) For an adiabatic process, the temperature-volume relationship is

$$T_1 V_1^{\gamma - 1} = T_2 V_2^{\gamma - 1} \Rightarrow T_1 = T_2 \left(\frac{V_2}{V_1}\right)^{\gamma - 1}$$

Here $\gamma = 1.4$ (for diatomic gas). $V_2 = \dfrac{V_1}{32}, T_1 = T_i, T_2 = aT_i$

$$\therefore T_i = aT_i \left[\frac{1}{32}\right]^{1.4 - 1} \quad \therefore T_i = aT_i \left[\frac{1}{2^5}\right]^{0.4} = \frac{aT_i}{4}$$

$$\therefore \ a = 4$$

19. (b) In the first-case adiabatic change,
$\Delta Q = 0, \Delta W = -35 \, J$
From 1st law of thermodynamics,
$\Delta Q = \Delta U + \Delta W,$
or $\quad 0 = \Delta U - 35$
$\therefore \Delta U = 35 \, J$
In the second case
$\Delta Q = 12 \, cal = 12 \times 4.2 \, J = 50.4 \, J$
$\Delta W = \Delta Q - \Delta U = 50.4 - 35 = 15.4 \, J$

20. (a) For an adiabatic change PV^γ = constant
$$P_1 V_1^\gamma = P_2 V_2^\gamma$$
As molar specific heat of gas at constant volume

$$C_v = \frac{3}{2} R$$

$$C_P = C_V + R = \frac{3}{2} R + R = \frac{5}{2} R ;$$

$$\gamma = \frac{C_P}{C_V} = \frac{(5/2) R}{(3/2) R} = \frac{5}{3}$$

$\therefore$ From eqn. (1)

$$P_2 = \left(\frac{V_1}{V_2}\right)^\gamma P_1 = \left(\frac{6}{2}\right)^{5/3} \times 10^5 \, N/m^2$$

$$= (3)^{5/3} \times 10^5 = 6.19 \times 10^5 \, N/m^2$$

Work done

$$= \frac{1}{1 - (5/3)} [6.19 \times 10^5 \times 2 \times 10^{-3} - 10^{-5} \times 6 \times 10^{-3}]$$

$$= -\left[\frac{2 \times 10^2 \times 3}{2} (6.19 - 3)\right]$$

$$= -3 \times 10^2 \times 3.19 = -957 \text{ joules}$$

[−ve sign shows external work done on the gas]

21. (b) Efficiency of Carnot engine, $\eta = 1 - \dfrac{T_2}{T_1}$

where T_1 and T_2 be the temperature of source and sink respectively.

$$\therefore \quad \frac{T_2}{T_1} = 1 - \eta = 1 - \frac{40}{100} = \frac{60}{100} = \frac{3}{5} \quad (\because \eta = 40\%)$$

$$T_2 = \frac{3}{5} T_1 = \frac{3}{5} \times 500 \, K = 300 \, K \quad ...(i)$$

$$(\because T_1 = 500 \, K)$$

Let T_1' be the temperature of the source for the same sink temperature when efficiency $\eta' = 50\%$

$$\therefore \frac{T_2}{T_1'} = 1 - \eta' = 1 - \frac{50}{100} = \frac{1}{2}$$

$$T_1' = 2T_2 = 2 \times 300 \, K = 600 \, K \quad \text{(Using eq. (i))}$$

22. (b) $dW = P \Delta V = 1.01 \times 10^5 [1671 - 1] \times 10^{-6} \text{ Joule}$

$$= \frac{1.01 \times 167}{4.2} \text{ cal.}$$

$$= 40 \text{ cal. nearly}$$

$\Delta Q = mL = 1 \times 540,$

$\Delta Q = \Delta W + \Delta U$

or $\quad \Delta U = 540 - 40 = 500 \text{ cal.}$

23. (c) The temperature remains unchanged therefore

$$U_f = U_i.$$

Also, $\Delta Q = \Delta W.$

In the first step which is isochoric, $\Delta W = 0.$

In second step, pressure $= \dfrac{P}{n}$. Volume V is increased from V to nV.

$$\therefore \quad W = \frac{P}{n}(nV - V)$$

$$= PV\left(\frac{n-1}{n}\right)$$

$$= RT(1 - n^{-1})$$

24. (b) Efficiency of carnot engine

$$n = 1 - \frac{T_2}{T_1} \text{ i.e., } \frac{1}{10} = 1 - \frac{T_2}{T_1}$$

$$\Rightarrow \frac{T_2}{T_1} = 1 - \frac{1}{10} = \frac{9}{10} \Rightarrow \frac{T_1}{T_2} = \frac{10}{9}$$

$$\therefore \quad w = Q_2\left(\frac{T_1}{T_2} - 1\right)$$

$$\text{i.e., } 10 = Q_2\left(\frac{10}{9} - 1\right) \ 10 = Q_2\left(\frac{1}{9}\right)$$

$$\Rightarrow Q_2 = 90J$$

So, 90 J heat is absorbed at lower temperature.

25. **(a)** $V_1 = 1\ell = 1000 \text{ cm}^3$, $P_1 = 72$ cm of Hg.
$V_2 = 900 \text{ cm}^3$, $P_2 = ?$
$\because$ The process is isothermal
$\therefore$ $P_1 V_1 = P_2 V_2$
$72 \times 1000 = P_2 \times 900$
$P_2 = 80$ cm of Hg
$\therefore$ Stress $= P_2 - P_1 = 80 - 72 = 8$ cm of Hg.

26. **(a)** Process A $\to$ B occurs at constant pressure Hence work done in this process is

$$W_{AB} = PdV = P(V_2 - V_1)$$
$$= 10 \times (2-1) = 10 \text{ J}$$

Process B $\to$ C, occurs at constant volume.

Hence, $W_{BC} = 0$

Given : $Q = 5$ J therefore, total work done is $W_1 = 5$ J

($\because \Delta U = 0$ in a cyclic process)

Therefore, we have

$$W_1 = W_{AB} + W_{BC} + W_{CA}$$

or $5 \text{ J} = 10 \text{ J} + 0 + W_{CA}$

$\therefore$ $W_{CA} = -5$ joule

27. **(d)** We know that in adiabatic process,
$PV^\gamma = $ constant ....(1)
From ideal gas equation, we know that
$PV = nRT$

$$V = \frac{nRT}{P}$$ ....(2)

Puttingt the value from equation (2) in equation (1),

$$P\left(\frac{nRT}{P}\right)^\gamma = \text{constant}$$

$P^{(1-\gamma)} T^\gamma = $ constant

28. **(b)** According to first law of thermodynamics,

$\Delta Q = \Delta U + \Delta W$
$\Delta Q = $ heat absorbed by gas
$\Delta W = $ work done by gas.
$-20 \text{J} = \Delta U - 8 \text{J}$
$\Delta U = -12 \text{J} = U_{Final} - U_{initial}$
$U_{initial} = 30 \text{J}.$
$U_{Final} = 30 - 12 = 18 \text{J}.$

29. **(d)** Coefficient of performance,

$$\text{Cop} = \frac{T_2}{T_1 - T_2}$$

$$5 = \frac{273 - 20}{T_1 - (273 - 20)} = \frac{253}{T_1 - 253}$$

$5T_1 - (5 \times 253) = 253$
$5T_1 = 253 + (5 \times 253) = 1518$

$$\therefore T_1 = \frac{1518}{5} = 303.6$$

or, $T_1 = 303.6 - 273 = 30.6 \cong 31°C$

30. **(a)** $W = \dfrac{nRdT}{\gamma - 1}$ γ is minimum for a polyatomic gas

Hence, W is greatest for polyatomic gas

31. **(b)** Heat is extracted from the source in path DA and AB is

$$\Delta Q = \frac{3}{2} R\left(\frac{P_0 V_0}{R}\right) + \frac{5}{2} R\left(\frac{2P_0 V_0}{R}\right)$$

$$\Rightarrow \frac{3}{2} P_0 V_0 + \frac{5}{2} 2P_0 V_0 = \left(\frac{13}{2}\right) P_0 V_0$$

32. **(d)** Isochoric proceess $dV = 0$

$W = 0$ proceess 1

Isobaric : $W = P \Delta V = nR\Delta T$

Adiabatic $|W| = \dfrac{nR\Delta T}{\gamma - 1}$ $0 < \gamma - 1 < 1$

As workdone in case of adiabatic process is more so process 3 is adiabatic and process 2 is isobaric

33. **(c)** For adiabatic process, $dU = -100$ J
which remains same for other processes also.
Let C be the heat capacity of 2nd process then
$-(C) 5 = dU + dW$
$= -100 + 25 = -75$
$\therefore C = 15$ J/K

34. **(c)** Coefficient of performance of a refrigerator,

$$\beta = \frac{Q_2}{W} = \frac{T_2}{T_1 - T_2}$$ (Where Q_2 is heat removed)

Given: $T_2 = 4°C = 4 + 273 = 277$ k
$T_1 = 30°C = 30 + 273 = 303$ k

$$\therefore \quad \beta = \frac{600 \times 4.2}{W} = \frac{277}{303 - 277}$$

$\Rightarrow$ $W = 236.5$ joule

Power $P = \dfrac{W}{t} = \dfrac{236.5 \text{ joule}}{1 \sec} = 236.5$ watt.

35. **(d)** $dU = dQ - dW = (8 \times 10^5 - 6.5 \times 10^5) = 1.5 \times 10^5$ J

$dW = dQ - dU = 10^5 - 1.5 \times 10^5 = -0.5 \times 10^5$ J

$-$ ve sign indicates that work done on the gas is 0.5×10^5 J .

36. **(d)** In cyclic process, change in total internal energy is zero.
$\Delta U_{cyclic} = 0$

$$\Delta U_{BC} = nC_v\Delta T = 1 \times \frac{5R}{2}\Delta T$$

Where, C_v = molar specific heat at constant volume.

For BC, $\Delta T = -200$ K

$\therefore \quad \Delta U_{BC} = -500R$

37. **(d)** Efficiency of engine A, $\eta_1 = 1 - \dfrac{T}{T_1}$,

Efficiency of engine B, $\eta_2 = 1 - \dfrac{T_2}{T}$

Here, $\eta_1 = \eta_2$

$\therefore \quad \dfrac{T}{T_1} = \dfrac{T_2}{T} \Rightarrow T = \sqrt{T_1 T_2}$

38. **(b)** In the first process W is + ve as ΔV is positive, in the second process W is – ve as ΔV is – ve and area under the curve of second process is more

$\therefore \quad$ Net Work < 0 and also $P_3 > P_1$.

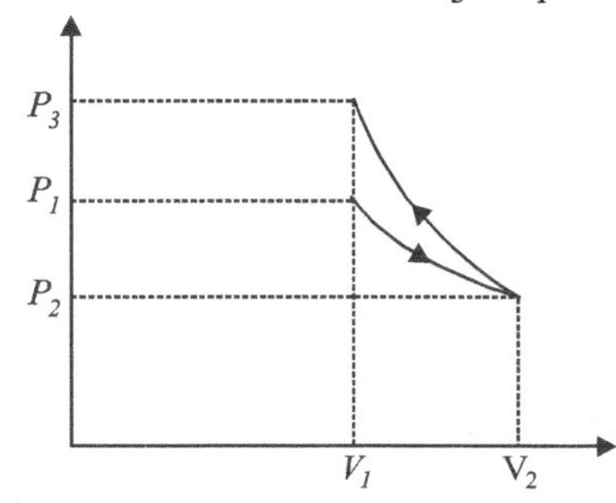

39. **(b)** Internal energy and entropy are state function, they do not depend upon path but on the state.

40. **(d)** 1st process is isothermal expansion which is only correct shown in option (d)

2nd process is isobaric compression which is correctly shown in option (d)

41. **(c)** $P_1 V_1^{\gamma} = P_2 V_2^{\gamma}$ (Adiabatic change)

$$P_2 = P_1 \left(\dfrac{V_1}{V_2}\right)^{\gamma} = P_1 \left(\dfrac{V_1}{V_1/3}\right)^{\gamma} = P_2 (3)^{\gamma}$$

42. **(b)** W_{ext} = negative of area with volume-axis

W(adiabatic) > W(isothermal)

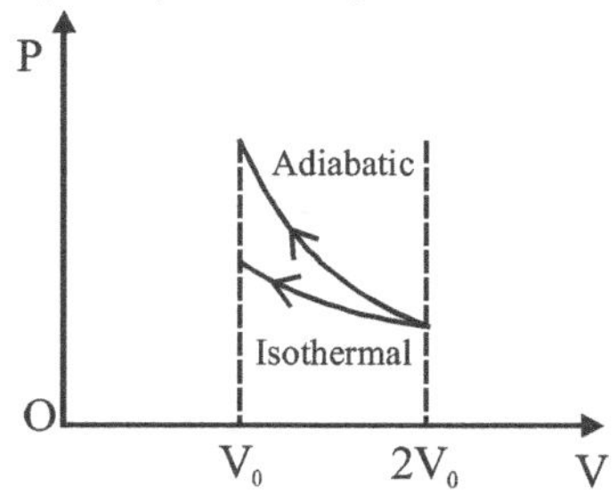

43. **(a)** Initial and final condition is same for all process

$\Delta U_1 = \Delta U_2 = \Delta U_3$

from first law of thermodynamics

$\Delta Q = \Delta U + \Delta W$

Work done

$\Delta W_1 > \Delta W_2 > \Delta W_3$ (Area of P.V. graph)

So $\Delta Q_1 > \Delta Q_2 > \Delta Q_3$

44. **(c)** $W = \dfrac{\pi r_1 r_2}{2} = \dfrac{\pi \times 1 \times 1}{2}$

$= \pi/2$ J

45. **(b)** Differentiate PV = constant w.r.t V

$\Rightarrow P\Delta V + V \Delta P = 0 \Rightarrow \dfrac{\Delta P}{P} = -\dfrac{\Delta V}{V}$

1. **(d)** Molar mass of the gas = 4g/mol

Speed of any quantity x

$$V = \sqrt{\frac{\gamma RT}{m}} \Rightarrow 952 = \sqrt{\frac{\gamma \times 3.3 \times 273}{4 \times 10^{-3}}}$$

$$\Rightarrow \gamma = 1.6 = \frac{16}{10} = \frac{8}{5}$$

Also, $\gamma = \dfrac{C_P}{C_V} = \dfrac{8}{5}$

So, $C_P = \dfrac{8 \times 5}{5} = 8 JK^{-1}mol^{-1}$

2. **(d)** Since v_{rms} is doubled by increasing the temp. so by

$v_{rms} = \sqrt{\dfrac{3KT}{m}}$, the temp. increase by four times.

Now for constant pressure $\dfrac{V_1}{T_1} = \dfrac{V_2}{T_2}$

$V_1 = V, T_1 = T°K, T_2 = 4T°K, V_2 = ?$

$V_2 = 4V$

3. **(a)** For mixture of gas, $C_v = \dfrac{n_1 C_{v_1} + n_2 C_{v_2}}{n_1 + n_2}$

$$= \frac{4 \times \frac{3}{2}R + \frac{1}{2} \times \frac{5}{2}R}{\left(4 + \frac{1}{2}\right)} = \frac{6R + \frac{5}{4}R}{\frac{9}{2}} = \frac{29R \times 2}{9 \times 4} = \frac{29R}{18}$$

and $C_p = \dfrac{n_1 C_{p_1} + n_2 C_{p_2}}{(n_1 + n_2)} = \dfrac{4 \times \frac{5R}{2} + \frac{1}{2} \times \frac{7R}{2}}{\left(4 + \frac{1}{2}\right)}$

$$= \frac{10R + \frac{7}{4}R}{\frac{9}{2}} = \frac{47R}{18}$$

$\therefore \dfrac{C_p}{C_v} = \dfrac{47R}{18} \times \dfrac{18}{29R} = 1.62$

4. **(b)** $\dfrac{P_1 V_1}{T_1} = \dfrac{P_2 V_2}{T_2}$ Here, $P_1 = 200 kPa$

$T_1 = 22°C = 295 K, \qquad T_2 = 42°C = 315 K$

$V_2 = V_1 + \dfrac{2}{100} V_1 = 1.02 V_1$

$\therefore P_2 = \dfrac{200 \times 315 V_1}{295 \times 1.02 V_1} = 209.37 kPa$

5. **(c)** By kinetic theory of gases,
rms (root mean square) velocity of gas

$$V_{rms} = \sqrt{\frac{3RT}{M}} = \sqrt{\frac{3KT}{m}}$$

Where M and m are mol. wt and mass of gas respectively

$$V_{rms} = \sqrt{\frac{3 \times 1.38 \times 10^{-23} \times 273}{5 \times 10^{-17}}}$$

$$= 1.5 \times 10^{-2} m/s = 1.5 cm/s$$

6. **(d)** $C_p = \dfrac{5}{2}R$ and $C_v = \dfrac{3}{2}R$

We know that $Q_v = nC_v \Delta T$ and $Q_p = nC_p \Delta T$

$$\Rightarrow \frac{Q_v}{Q_p} = \frac{3}{5}.$$

Given $Q_p = 207 J \Rightarrow Q_v \cong 124 J$

7. **(c)** On giving same amount of heat at constant pressure, there is change in temperature for mono, dia and polyatomic gas.

$$(\Delta Q)_P = \mu C_p \Delta T \left(\mu = \frac{\text{No. of molecules}}{\text{Avogadro's no.}} \right)$$

or $\quad \Delta T \propto \dfrac{1}{\text{no. of molecules}}$

8. **(a)** $C = C_{v\,mix} + \dfrac{R}{1-n}$ .....(1)

Now, $C_{vmix} = \dfrac{n_1 C_{v1} + n_2 C_{v2}}{n_1 + n_2}$

$$= \frac{1 \times \frac{3R}{2} + 2 \times \frac{5R}{2}}{1 + 2} = \frac{13R}{6}$$

From (1), $3R = \dfrac{13R}{6} + \dfrac{R}{1-n} \Rightarrow n = -\dfrac{1}{5}$

9. **(a)** $P = \dfrac{1}{3}\rho \bar{v}^2 = \dfrac{1}{3} \times (6 \times 10^{-2}) \times (500)^2$

$$= 5 \times 10^3 N/m^2$$

10. **(d)** $v_{rms} = \sqrt{\dfrac{3kT}{m}}$ ....(1)

$v'_{rms} = \sqrt{\dfrac{3k \times 3T}{m}}$ ....(2)

Equ. (2) is dividing by equ. (1)

$$\frac{v'_{rms}}{v_{rms}} = \sqrt{\frac{3k.3T.m}{m.3kT}} = \sqrt{3}$$

$$v'_{rms} = \sqrt{3}\,v_{rms}$$

11. (a) $\tau = \dfrac{1}{\sqrt{2}\pi d^2 \left(\dfrac{N}{V}\right)\sqrt{\dfrac{3RT}{M}}}$

$$\tau \propto \frac{V}{\sqrt{T}}$$

As, $TV^{\gamma-1} = K$

So, $\tau \propto V^{\gamma + 1/2}$

Therefore, $q = \dfrac{\gamma+1}{2}$

12. (a) Volume $= \dfrac{mass}{density} = \dfrac{1}{4}\,m^3$

$$K.E = \frac{5}{2}PV = \frac{5}{2} \times 8 \times 10^4 \times \frac{1}{4} = 5 \times 10^4 J$$

13. (c) As no heat is lost,

Loss of kinetic energy = gain of internal energy of gas

$$\frac{1}{2}mv^2 = nC_V \Delta T \Rightarrow \frac{1}{2}mv^2 = \frac{m}{M} \cdot \frac{R}{\gamma - 1}\Delta T$$

$$\Rightarrow \Delta T = \frac{Mv^2(\gamma - 1)}{2R}K$$

14. (b) From graph, $T^2 V = $ const. .....(1)

As we know that $TV^{\gamma-1} = $ const

$$\Rightarrow VT^{\frac{1}{\gamma-1}} = \text{const.} \qquad ....(2)$$

On comparing (1) and (2), we get

$$\Rightarrow \gamma = 3/2$$

Also $v_{rms} = \sqrt{\dfrac{3P}{\rho}}$ and $v_{sound} = \sqrt{\dfrac{P\gamma}{\rho}}$

$$\Rightarrow \frac{v_{rms}}{v_{sound}} = \sqrt{\frac{3}{\gamma}} = \sqrt{2}$$

15. (a) $W = \dfrac{nR\Delta T}{1-\gamma} \Rightarrow -146000 = \dfrac{1000 \times 8.3 \times 7}{1-\gamma}$

or $1 - \gamma = -\dfrac{58.1}{146} \Rightarrow \gamma = 1 + \dfrac{58.1}{146} = 1.4$

Hence the gas is diatomic.

16. (a) $C_{rms} = \sqrt{\dfrac{3RT}{M}}$

M is molecular wt.

$$= \sqrt{\frac{3R(273+47)}{16}} = \sqrt{\frac{3RT}{2}}$$

$$\Rightarrow T = 40\,K.$$

17. (a) When temperature is same according to kinetic theory of gases, kinetic energy of molecules will be same.

$$K.E. = \frac{1}{2} \times 32 \times \left(\frac{1}{2}\right)^2 = \frac{1}{2} \times 2 \times v^2$$

RMS velocity of hydrogen molecules = 2 km/sec.

18. (a) Let T be the temperature of the mixture, then

$$U = U_1 + U_2$$

$$\Rightarrow \frac{f}{2}(n_1 + n_2)\,RT$$

$$= \frac{f}{2}(n_1)\,(R)\,(T_0) + \frac{f}{2}(n_2)\,(R)\,(2T_0)$$

$$\Rightarrow (2+4)T = 2T_0 + 8T_0 \;(\because\; n_1 = 2, n_2 = 4)$$

$$\therefore\; T = \frac{5}{3}T_0$$

19. (b) Coefficient of volume expansion at constant pressure is $\dfrac{1}{273}$ for all gases. The average transnational K.E. is same for molecules of all gases and for each molecules it is $\dfrac{3}{2}kT$

Mean free path $\lambda = \dfrac{kT}{\sqrt{2}\,\pi d^2 P}$ (as P decreases, λ increases)

20. (c) For a given pressure, volume will be more if temperature is more (Charle's law)

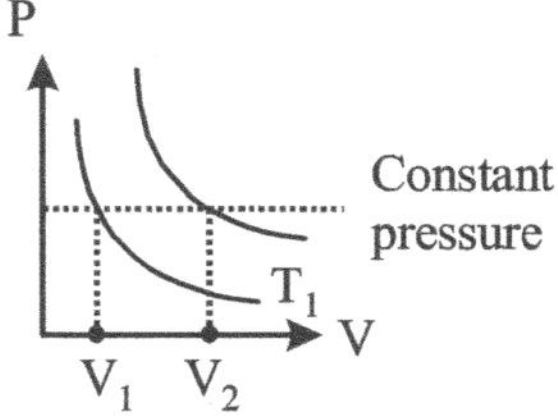

From the graph it is clear that $V_2 > V_1 \Rightarrow T_2 > T_1$

21. (a) $\dfrac{c_2}{c_1} = \sqrt{\dfrac{400}{300}} = \dfrac{2}{\sqrt{3}} \Rightarrow c_2 = \dfrac{2}{\sqrt{3}} \times 200 = \dfrac{400}{\sqrt{3}}\,ms^{-1}$

22. (c) $\dfrac{PV}{T} = nR = \left(\dfrac{m}{M}\right)R$ or $\dfrac{PV}{T} = \left(\dfrac{R}{M}\right)m$

i.e., $\dfrac{PV}{T}$ versus m graph is straight line passing through origin with slope R/M, i.e. the slope depends on molecular mass of the gas M and is different for different gases.

23. (d) Molecule number ratio is $H_2 : O_2 = \dfrac{2}{3} : \dfrac{1}{3}$.

That gives $(c_{rms})^2 = 16\left(\dfrac{2}{3}\right) + 1\left(\dfrac{1}{3}\right)$ times the value for O_2.

24. (a) According to Vander Waal's equation

$$P = \frac{nRT}{V - n\beta} - \frac{\alpha n^2}{V^2}$$

Work done,

$$W = \int_{V_1}^{V_2} PdV = nRT \int_{V_1}^{V_2} \frac{dV}{V - n\beta} - \alpha n^2 \int_{V_1}^{V_2} \frac{dV}{V^2}$$

$$= nRT \left[\log_e (V - n\beta)\right]_{V_1}^{V_2} + \alpha n^2 \left[\frac{1}{V}\right]_{V_1}^{V_2}$$

$$= nRT \log_e \left(\frac{V_2 - n\beta}{V_1 - n\beta}\right) + \alpha n^2 \left[\frac{V_1 - V_2}{V_1 V_2}\right]$$

25. (a) From $PV = nRT$

$$P_A = \frac{\rho_A M_A}{RT} \text{ and } P_B = \frac{\rho_B M_B}{RT}$$

From question,

$$\frac{P_A}{P_B} = \frac{\rho_A}{\rho_B} \frac{M_A}{M_B} = 2\frac{M_A}{M_B} = \frac{3}{2}$$

So, $\dfrac{M_A}{M_B} = \dfrac{3}{4}$

26. (b) $(C_p)_{mix} = \dfrac{\mu_1 C_{p_1} + \mu_2 C_{p_2}}{\mu_1 + \mu_2}$

$$\left(C_{p_1}(He) = \frac{5}{2}R \text{ and } C_{p_2}(H_2) = \frac{7}{2}R\right)$$

$$(C_p)_{mix} = = \frac{1 \times \frac{5}{2}R + 1 \times \frac{7}{2}R}{1 + 1} \quad 3R = 3 \times 2 = 6 \text{ cal/mol.}°C$$

∴ Amount of heat needed to raise the temperature from $0°C$ to $100°C$

$$(\Delta Q)_p = \mu C_p \Delta T = 2 \times 6 \times 100 = 1200 \, cal$$

27. (a) 1 mole = 22.4 L at S.T.P.

$$\frac{4.5g}{18g} = 22.4 \times \frac{4.5}{18} = 5.6 \text{ L}$$

28. (d) Internal energy of 2 moles of oxygen

$$U_{O_2} = \mu \left(\frac{5}{2}RT\right) = 2.\frac{5}{2}RT = 5RT$$

Internal energy of 4 moles of Argon.

$$U_{Ar} = \mu \left(\frac{3}{2}RT\right) = 4.\frac{3}{2}RT = 6RT$$

∴ Total internal energy

$$U = U_{O_2} + U_{Ar} = 11RT$$

29. (d) $PV = \dfrac{m}{M}RT$

Initially, $PV = \dfrac{6}{M}R \times 500$

Finally, $\dfrac{P}{2}V = \dfrac{(6-x)}{M}R \times 300$ (if x g gas leaks out)

Hence, $2 = \dfrac{6}{6-x} \times \dfrac{5}{3}$ ∴ x = 1 gram

30. (b) $\gamma = 1 + \dfrac{2}{f}, \Rightarrow \gamma - 1 = \dfrac{2}{f} \Rightarrow \dfrac{f}{2} = \dfrac{1}{\gamma - 1} \Rightarrow f = \dfrac{2}{\gamma - 1}$

31. (a)

32. (a) Number of moles of first gas $= \dfrac{n_1}{N_A}$

Number of moles of second gas $= \dfrac{n_2}{N_A}$

Number of moles of third gas $= \dfrac{n_3}{N_A}$

If there is no loss of energy then

$$P_1V_1 + P_2V_2 + P_3V_3 = PV$$

$$\frac{n_1}{N_A}RT_1 + \frac{n_2}{N_A}RT_2 + \frac{n_3}{N_A}RT_3 = \frac{n_1 + n_2 + n_3}{N_A}RT_{mix}$$

$$\Rightarrow T_{mix} = \frac{n_1T_1 + n_2T_2 + n_3T_3}{n_1 + n_2 + n_3}$$

33. (d) Since it hits the plane wall parallel to $y\,z$ – plane and it rebounds with same velocity, its y and z components of velocity do not change, but the x-component reverses the sign.

∴ Velocity after collision is $(-v_x, v_y \text{ and } v_z)$. The change in momentum is

$$- mv_x - mv_x = - 2mv_x$$

34. (c) V and T will be same for both gases.

$$P_1V = \mu_1 RT \text{ and } P_2V = \mu_2 RT$$

$$(P_1/P_2) = \frac{5}{3} \qquad \therefore \left(\frac{\mu_1}{\mu_2}\right) = \frac{5}{3}$$

By definition, $\mu_1 = \dfrac{N_1}{N_A}$ and $\mu_2 = \dfrac{N_2}{N_A}$

$$\therefore \frac{N_1}{N_2} = \frac{\mu_1}{\mu_2} = \frac{5}{3}$$

35. (d) $E = \dfrac{3}{2} \times 300$; $E' = \dfrac{3}{2}R(600) = 2E = 2 \times 6.21 \times 10^{-21}$

$$= 12.42 \times 10^{-21} \text{ J.}$$

$$v_{rms} = \sqrt{\frac{3R \times 300}{M}} \; ; \; v'_{rms} = \sqrt{\frac{3R \times 600}{M}} = \sqrt{2} \, v_{rms}$$

$$= 684.44 \text{ m/s}$$

36. (d) Let the mass of the gas be m.

At a fixed temperature and pressure, volume is fixed.

Density of the gas, $\rho = \dfrac{m}{V}$

Now $\dfrac{\rho}{P} = \dfrac{m}{PV} = \dfrac{m}{nRT}$

$$\Rightarrow \frac{m}{nRT} = x \text{ (By question)}$$

$$\Rightarrow xT = \text{constant} \Rightarrow x_1T_1 = x_2T_2$$

$$\Rightarrow x_2 \Rightarrow \frac{x_1 T_1}{T_2} = \frac{283}{383}x \begin{bmatrix} \because \\ T_1 = 283K \\ T_2 = 383K \end{bmatrix}$$

37. (b) $F = \dfrac{dU}{dr} = -\dfrac{d}{dr}\left[\dfrac{M}{r^3} - \dfrac{N}{R^{12}}\right] = -\left[\dfrac{-6M}{r^2} + \dfrac{12N}{r^{13}}\right]$

In equilibrium position, $F = 0$

$$\therefore \quad \frac{6M}{r^2} - \frac{12N}{r^{13}} = 0 \quad \text{or,} \quad r^6 = \frac{2N}{M}$$

$\therefore$ Potential energy at equilibrium position

$$U = \frac{M}{(2N/M)} - \frac{N}{(2N/M)^2} = \frac{M^2}{2N} - \frac{M^2}{4N} = \frac{M^2}{4N}$$

38. (a) Pressure of the gas will not be affected by motion of the system, hence by

$$v_{rms} = \sqrt{\frac{3P}{\rho}} \Rightarrow \bar{c}^2 = \frac{3P}{\rho} \Rightarrow P = \frac{1}{3}\rho\bar{c}^2$$

39. (b) Mean free path in a gas is 100 times the interatomic distance.

40. (a) $v_{rms} = \left[\dfrac{(2)^2 + (3)^2 + (4)^2 + (5)^2}{4}\right]^{1/2} = \sqrt{\dfrac{54}{4}}$

41. (c) If a gas is heated at constant volume then no work is done. The heat supplied is given by

$$dQ = nC_v dT$$

But $C_v = \dfrac{f}{2}R$ where f is the degree of freedom of the gas

$$\therefore \quad dQ = \frac{nfRdT}{2}$$

$$= \frac{2 \times 3 \times R \times (373 - 273)}{2} = 300\,R$$

42. (b) For 1 molecule of a gas, $V_{rms} = \sqrt{\dfrac{3KT}{m}}$

where m is the mass of one molecule

For N molecule of a gas, $V_1 = \sqrt{\dfrac{3KT \times N}{m}}$

For 2N molecule of a gas $V_2 = \sqrt{\dfrac{3KT \times 2N}{(2m)}}$

$$\therefore \quad \frac{V_1}{V_2} = 1$$

43. (c)

44. (c) P-V diagram of the gas is a straight line passing through origin. Hence $P \propto V$ or $PV^{-1} = $ constant
Molar heat capacity in the process $PV^x = $ constant

$$C = \frac{R}{\gamma - 1} + \frac{R}{1 - x}; \ \text{ Here } \gamma = 1.4 \ \text{(For diatomic gas)}$$

$$\Rightarrow C = \frac{R}{1.4 - 1} + \frac{R}{1 + 1} \Rightarrow C = 3R$$

45. (c) Given

$$C_P - C_V = 5000 \ \text{J/mole}\,^\circ\text{C} \ \text{.......(i)}$$

$$\frac{C_P}{C_V} = 1.6 \qquad\qquad \text{.......(ii)}$$

From Equation (i) & (ii),

$$\Rightarrow \frac{C_P}{C_V} - \frac{C_V}{C_V} = \frac{5000}{C_V}$$

$$\Rightarrow 1.6 - 1 = \frac{5000}{C_V}$$

$$\Rightarrow C_V = \frac{5000}{0.6} = 8.33 \times 10^3$$

Hence $C_P = 1.6\,C_V = 1.6 \times 8.33 \times 10^3$

$C_P = 1.33 \times 10^4$

1. (a) For an SHM, the acceleration $a = -\omega^2 x$ where ω^2 is a constant. Therefore, $\dfrac{a}{x}$ is a constant. The time period T is also constant. Therefore, $\dfrac{aT}{x}$ is a constant.

2. (b) $t_1 = 2\pi \sqrt{\dfrac{m}{k_1}}$ or $t_1^2 = \dfrac{4\pi^2 m}{k_1}$ or $k_1 = \dfrac{4\pi^2 m}{t_1^2}$

Similarly, $k_2 = \dfrac{4\pi^2 m}{t_2^2}$ and $(k_1 + k_2) = \dfrac{4\pi^2 m}{t_0^2}$

$\therefore \dfrac{4\pi^2 m}{t_0^2} = \dfrac{4\pi^2 m}{t_1^2} + \dfrac{4\pi^2 m}{t_2^2}$ or $\dfrac{1}{t_0^2} = \dfrac{1}{t_1^2} + \dfrac{1}{t_2^2}$

3. (b)

$\dfrac{d\theta}{dt} = 2 \quad \therefore \quad \theta = 2t$

Let $BP = a$, $\therefore x = OM = a \sin\theta = a \sin(2t)$

Hence M executes SHM within the given time period and its acceleration is opposite to x that means towards left.

4. (b) The kinetic energy of a particle executing S.H.M. is given by

$K = \dfrac{1}{2} ma^2 \omega^2 \sin^2 \omega t$

where, m = mass of particle
a = amplitude
ω = angular frequency
t = time

Now, average K.E. $= <K> = <\dfrac{1}{2} m\omega^2 a^2 \sin^2 \omega t>$

$= \dfrac{1}{2} m\omega^2 a^2 <\sin^2 \omega t>$

$= \dfrac{1}{2} m\omega^2 a^2 \left(\dfrac{1}{2}\right) \quad \left(\because <\sin^2\theta> = \dfrac{1}{2}\right)$

$= \dfrac{1}{4} m\omega^2 a^2 = \dfrac{1}{4} ma^2 (2\pi v)^2 \quad (\because \omega = 2\pi v)$

or, $<K> = \pi^2 ma^2 v^2$

5. (a) We know that $T = 2\pi \sqrt{\dfrac{M}{k}}$

From first case, $2 = 2\pi \sqrt{\dfrac{M}{k}} \qquad ....(1)$

In second case, $4 = 2\pi \sqrt{\dfrac{M+2}{k}} \qquad ....(2)$

From eq. (1) and eq. (2)

$\dfrac{4}{2} = \sqrt{\dfrac{M+2}{M}} \Rightarrow 4 = 1 + \dfrac{2}{M}$

$\dfrac{2}{M} = 3 \Rightarrow M = \dfrac{2}{3} \text{ kg}$

6. (b) Amplitude of a damped oscillator at any instant t is given by
$A = A_0 e^{-bt/2m}$
where A_0 is the original amplitude
From question,

When $t = 2$ s, $A = \dfrac{A_0}{3}$

$\therefore \dfrac{A_0}{3} = A_0 e^{-2b/2m}$

or, $\dfrac{1}{3} = e^{-b/m} \qquad \qquad \ldots(i)$

When $t = 6$ s, $A = \dfrac{A_0}{n}$

$\therefore \dfrac{A_0}{n} = A_0 e^{-6b/2m}$

or, $\dfrac{1}{n} = e^{-3b/m} = (e^{-b/m})^3$

or, $\dfrac{1}{n} = \left(\dfrac{1}{3}\right)^3 \qquad$ (Using eq. (i))

$\therefore n = 3^3$

7. (c) Acceleration due to gravity at a depth 'd' is given by,

$g' = g\left(1 - \dfrac{d}{R}\right) = g\left(\dfrac{R-d}{R}\right) = \dfrac{g}{R} y$

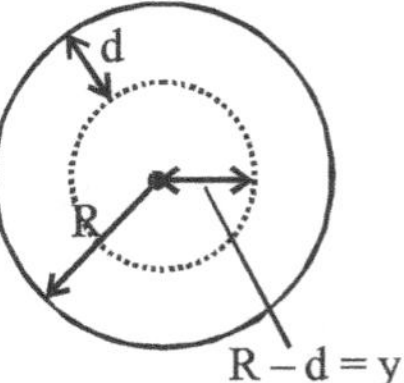

or acceleration $\propto$ displacement
which is the condition for SHM. So, body will oscillate simple harmonically in tunnel.

8. **(c)** Time to complete 1/4th oscillation is $\dfrac{T}{4}$ s. Time to complete $\dfrac{1}{8}$ th vibration from extreme position is obtained from

$$y = \frac{a}{2} = a \cos \omega t = a \cos \frac{2\pi}{T} t \text{ or } t = \frac{T}{6} s$$

So time to complete 3/8th oscillation

$$= \frac{T}{4} + \frac{T}{6} = \frac{5T}{12}$$

9. **(a)** As we know, kinetic energy $= \dfrac{1}{2} m\omega^2 (A^2 - x^2)$

Potential energy $= \dfrac{1}{2} m\omega^2 x^2$

$$\therefore \frac{\dfrac{1}{2} m\omega^2 (A^2 - x^2)}{\dfrac{1}{2} m\omega^2 x^2} = \frac{1}{4} \Rightarrow \frac{A^2 - x^2}{x^2} = \frac{1}{4}$$

$$4A^2 - 4x^2 = x^2 \Rightarrow x^2 = \frac{4}{5} A^2 \quad \therefore x = \frac{2}{\sqrt{5}} A.$$

10. **(d)** $T = 2\pi \sqrt{\dfrac{\ell}{g}}$ and $T' = 2\pi \sqrt{\dfrac{1.21\ell}{g}}$

$$(\because \ell' = \ell + 21\% \text{ of } \ell)$$

$$\% \text{ increase} = \frac{T' - T}{T} \times 100$$

$$= \frac{\sqrt{1.21\ell} - \sqrt{\ell}}{\sqrt{\ell}} \times 100 = \left(\sqrt{1.21} - \sqrt{1} \times 100 \right)$$

$$= (1.1 - 1) \times 100 = 10\%$$

11. **(d)** $T = 2\pi \sqrt{\dfrac{m}{k}}$

When a spring is cut into n parts
Spring constant for each part $= nk$
Here, $n = 4$

$$T_1 = 2\pi \sqrt{\frac{m}{4k}} = \frac{T}{2}$$

12. **(d)** $x = A \cos(\omega t + \delta)$

$$y = A \cos(\omega t + \alpha) \qquad ....(1)$$

When $\delta = \alpha + \dfrac{\pi}{2}$

$$x = A \cos\left(\frac{\pi}{2} + \omega t + \alpha \right)$$

$$x = -A \sin(\omega t + \alpha) \qquad ....(2)$$

Squaring (1) and (2) and then adding
$x^2 + y^2 = A^2 [\cos^2(\omega t + \alpha) + \sin^2(\omega t + \alpha)]$
or $x^2 + y^2 = A^2$, which is the equation of a circle. The present motion is anticlockwise.

13. **(a)** Here,

$$x = x_0 \cos(\omega t - \pi/4)$$

$$\therefore \text{ Velocity, } v = \frac{dx}{dt} = -x_0 \omega \sin\left(\omega t - \frac{\pi}{4} \right)$$

Acceleration,

$$a = \frac{dv}{dt} = -x_0 \omega^2 \cos\left(\omega t - \frac{\pi}{4} \right)$$

$$= x_0 \omega^2 \cos\left[\pi + \left(\omega t - \frac{\pi}{4} \right) \right]$$

$$= x_0 \omega^2 \cos\left(\omega t + \frac{3\pi}{4} \right) \qquad ...(1)$$

Acceleration, $a = A \cos(\omega t + \delta)$ ...(2)
Comparing the two equations, we get

$$A = x_0 \omega^2 \text{ and } \delta = \frac{3\pi}{4}.$$

14. **(c)** $T = 2\pi \sqrt{\dfrac{M}{k}}$

$$T' = 2\pi \sqrt{\frac{M+m}{k}} = \frac{5T}{3}$$

$$\therefore 2\pi \sqrt{\frac{M+m}{k}} = \frac{5}{3} \times 2\pi \sqrt{\frac{M}{k}}$$

$$M + m = \frac{25}{9} \times M$$

$$1 + \frac{m}{M} = \frac{25}{9} \Rightarrow \frac{m}{M} = \frac{25}{9} - 1 = \frac{16}{9}$$

15. **(d)** $A = 0.05 \text{ m}, y = 0.01 \text{ m}$
Acceleration, $a = 1.0 \text{ m/s}^2$
We have, $a = -\omega^2 y$ or $|a| = \omega^2 y$

$$\Rightarrow 1.0 = \omega^2 \times 0.01$$

$$\therefore \omega^2 = \frac{1.0}{0.01} = 100 \Rightarrow \omega = 10$$

Now, time period, $T = \dfrac{2\pi}{\omega} = \dfrac{2\pi}{10} = \dfrac{\pi}{5}$ sec.

16. **(c)** We have, $U + K = E$
where, U = potential energy, K = Kinetic energy, E = Total energy.
Also, we know that, in S.H.M., when potential energy is maximum, K.E. is zero and vice-versa.

$$\therefore U_{\max} + 0 = E \Rightarrow U_{\max} = E$$

Further,

$$K.E. = \frac{1}{2} m\omega^2 a^2 \cos^2 \omega t$$

But by question, $K.E. = K_0 \cos^2 \omega t$

$$\therefore K_0 = \frac{1}{2} m\omega^2 a^2$$

Hence, total energy, $E = \dfrac{1}{2} m\omega^2 a^2 = K_0$

$$\therefore U_{\max} = K_0 \ \& \ E = K_0.$$

17. **(b)** Distance covered by lift is given by
$y = t^2$

∴ Acceleration of lift upwards

$$= \frac{d^2 y}{dt^2} = \frac{d}{dt}(2t) = 2 \text{ m/s}^2 = \frac{g}{5}$$

Now, $T = 2\pi \sqrt{\dfrac{\ell}{g}}$

$$T' = 2\pi \sqrt{\frac{\ell}{g + \dfrac{g}{5}}} = 2\pi \sqrt{\frac{\ell}{\dfrac{6}{5}g}} = \sqrt{\frac{5}{6}}T.$$

18. **(d)** In simple harmonic motion, starting from rest,
At $t = 0$, $x = A$
$x = A\cos\omega t$ ..... (i)
When $t = \tau$, $x = A - a$
When $t = 2\tau$, $x = A - 3a$
From equation (i)
$A - a = A\cos\omega\tau$ ......(ii)
$A - 3a = A\cos 2\omega\tau$ ....(iii)
As $\cos 2\omega\tau = 2\cos^2\omega\tau - 1$ ...(iv)
From equation (ii), (iii) and (iv)

$$\frac{A - 3a}{A} = 2\left(\frac{A-a}{A}\right)^2 - 1$$

$$\Rightarrow \quad \frac{A-3a}{A} = \frac{2A^2 + 2a^2 - 4Aa - A^2}{A^2}$$

$$\Rightarrow \quad A^2 - 3aA = A^2 + 2a^2 - 4Aa$$
$$\Rightarrow \quad 2a^2 = aA$$
$$\Rightarrow \quad A = 2a$$

$$\Rightarrow \quad \frac{a}{A} = \frac{1}{2}$$

Now, $A - a = A\cos\omega\tau$

$$\Rightarrow \quad \cos\omega\tau = \frac{A-a}{A}$$

$$\Rightarrow \quad \cos\omega\tau = \frac{1}{2} \quad \text{or} \quad \frac{2\pi}{T}\tau = \frac{\pi}{3}$$

$$\Rightarrow \quad T = 6\tau$$

19. **(b)** $v_1 = \dfrac{dy_1}{dt} = 0.1 \times 100\pi \cos\left(100\pi t + \dfrac{\pi}{3}\right)$

$$v_2 = \frac{dy_2}{dt} = -0.1\pi \sin \pi t = 0.1\pi \cos\left(\pi t + \frac{\pi}{2}\right)$$

∴ Phase diff. $= \phi_1 - \phi_2 = \dfrac{\pi}{3} - \dfrac{\pi}{2} = \dfrac{2\pi - 3\pi}{6} = -\dfrac{\pi}{6}$

20. **(c)** $f_A = \dfrac{1}{2\pi}\sqrt{\dfrac{g}{L_A}}$ and $f_B = \dfrac{f_A}{2} = \dfrac{1}{2\pi}\sqrt{\dfrac{g}{L_B}}$

∴ $\dfrac{f_A}{f_{A/2}} = \dfrac{1}{2\pi}\sqrt{\dfrac{g}{L_A}} \times 2\pi\sqrt{\dfrac{L_B}{g}} \Rightarrow 2 = \sqrt{\dfrac{L_B}{L_A}} \Rightarrow 4 = \dfrac{L_B}{L_A}$,

regardless of mass

21. **(d)**

22. **(c)** Here all the three springs are connected in parallel to
mass m. Hence equivalent spring constant
$k = K + K + 2K = 4K$.

23. **(a)** K.E. $= \dfrac{1}{2}m\omega^2(a^2 - x^2)$

When $x = 0$, K.E is maximum and is equal to $\dfrac{1}{2}m\omega^2 a^2$.

24. **(d)** $y = 5\sin(\pi t + 4\pi)$, comparing it with standard equation

$$y = a\sin(\omega t + \phi) = a\sin\left(\frac{2\pi t}{T} + \phi\right)$$

$a = 5m$ and $\dfrac{2\pi t}{T} = \pi t \Rightarrow T = 2\sec$.

25. **(b)** $T = 2\pi\sqrt{\dfrac{\text{displacement}}{\text{acceleration}}} = 2\pi\sqrt{\dfrac{x}{zx}} = 2\pi/\sqrt{z}$

26. **(b)** Here, $x = 2 \times 10^{-2}\cos\pi t$
Speed is given by

$$v = \frac{dx}{dt} = 2 \times 10^{-2}\,\pi\sin\pi t$$

For the first time, the speed to be maximum,

$$\sin\pi t = 1 \quad \text{or,} \quad \sin\pi t = \sin\frac{\pi}{2}$$

$$\Rightarrow \quad \pi t = \frac{\pi}{2} \quad \text{or,} \quad t = \frac{1}{2} = 0.5\,\text{sec.}$$

27. **(d)** $T = 2\pi\sqrt{\dfrac{R}{g}} = 2\pi\sqrt{\dfrac{64 \times 10^6}{9.8}} = 2 \times \dfrac{22}{7} \times \dfrac{8 \times 10^3}{7 \times \sqrt{2}}$

$$= \frac{\sqrt{2} \times 22 \times 8 \times 1000}{49 \times 60}\,\text{min} = 84.6\,\text{min}$$

28. **(a)** $x = 3\sin 2t + 4\cos 2t$. From given equation

$$a_1 = 3,\ a_2 = 4,\ \text{and}\ \phi = \frac{\pi}{2}$$

$$\therefore a = \sqrt{a_1^2 + a_2^2} = \sqrt{3^2 + 4^2} = 5$$

$$\Rightarrow v_{\max} = a\omega = 5 \times 2 = 10$$

29. **(d)** Slope of F - x curve $= -k = -\dfrac{80}{0.2} \Rightarrow k = 400\,\text{N/m}$,

Time period, $T = 2\pi\sqrt{\dfrac{m}{k}} = 0.0314\,\text{sec.}$

30. **(b)** Phase change π in 50 oscillations.
Phase change 2π in 100 oscillations.
So frequency different $\sim$ 1 in 100.

31. **(a)** $T = 2\pi\sqrt{\dfrac{\ell}{g}}$; $2 = 2\pi\sqrt{\dfrac{\ell}{g}} = 2\pi\sqrt{\dfrac{\ell'}{(g/6)}}$

Time period will remain constant if on moon,
$\ell' = \ell/6 = 1/6\,\text{m}$

32. **(b)** Let k be the force constant of spring of length l_2. Since
$l_1 = n\,l_2$, where n is an integer, so the spring is made of
$(n + 1)$ equal parts in length each of length l_2.

$\therefore \quad \dfrac{1}{K} = \dfrac{(n+1)}{k}$ or $k = (n+1)\,K$

The spring of length $l_1\,(= n\,l_2)$ will be equivalent to n springs connected in series where spring constant

$k' = \dfrac{k}{n} = (n+1)\,K/n$ & spring constant of length ℓ_2 is $K(n+1)$.

33. (c) Given

$y = 0.2\sin(10\pi t + 1.5\pi)\cos(10\pi t + 1.5\pi)$

We know that $2\sin A\cos A = \sin 2A$, we get

$y = 0.1\sin 2(10\pi t + 1.5\pi) = 0.1\sin(20\pi t + 3\pi)$

On comparing with wave equation

$y = a\sin(\omega t + \phi)$ we get

$\omega = 20\pi$

$T = \dfrac{2\pi}{\omega} = \dfrac{2\pi}{20\pi} = \dfrac{1}{10}\,\sec. = 0.1\sec.$

34. (a) The displacement of a particle in S.H.M. is given by

$y = a\sin(\omega t + \phi)$

$\text{velocity} = \dfrac{dy}{dt} = \omega a\cos(\omega t + \phi)$

The velocity is maximum when the particle passes through the mean position i.e.,

$\left(\dfrac{dy}{dt}\right)_{max} = \omega a$

The kinetic energy at this instant is given by

$\dfrac{1}{2}m\left(\dfrac{dy}{dt}\right)^2_{max} = \dfrac{1}{2}m\omega^2 a^2 = 8 \times 10^{-3}\,\text{joule}$

or $\quad \dfrac{1}{2} \times (0.1)\,\omega^2 \times (0.1)^2 = 8 \times 10^{-3}$

Solving we get $\quad \omega = \pm 4$

Substituting the values of a, ω and ϕ in the equation of S.H.M., we get

$y = 0.1\sin(\pm 4t + \pi/4)$ metre.

35. (d) $\text{K.E} = \dfrac{1}{2}k(A^2 - d^2)$

and $\text{P.E.} = \dfrac{1}{2}kd^2$

At mean position $d = 0$. At extrement positions $d = A$

36. (b) $y = 3\sin\dfrac{\pi}{2}(50t - x)$

$y = 3\sin\left(25\pi t - \dfrac{\pi}{2}x\right)$ on comparing with the standard wave equation

$y = a\sin(\omega t - kx)$

Wave velocity $v = \dfrac{\omega}{k} = \dfrac{25\pi}{\pi/2} = 50\,\text{m/sec.}$

The velocity of particle

$v_p = \dfrac{\partial y}{\partial t} = 75\pi\cos\left(25\pi t - \dfrac{\pi}{2}x\right)$

$v_{p\,max} = 75\pi$

then $\dfrac{v_{p\,max}}{v} = \dfrac{75\pi}{50} = \dfrac{3\pi}{2}$

37. (b) The equivalent situation is a series combination of two springs of spring constants k and 2k. If k' is the equivalent spring constant, then

$k' = \dfrac{(k)(2k)}{3k} = \dfrac{2k}{3}$

$\Rightarrow T = 2\pi\sqrt{\dfrac{3m}{2k}}$

38. (a) Time period of simple pendulum $T = 2\pi\sqrt{\left(\dfrac{l}{g}\right)} \propto \sqrt{l}$

where l is effective length.

[i.e distance between centre of suspension and centre of gravity of bob]

Initially, centre of gravity is at the centre of sphere. When water leaks the centre of gravity goes down until it is half filled; then it begins to go up and finally it again goes at the centre. That is effective length first increases and then decreases. As $T \propto \sqrt{l}$, so time period first increases and then decreases.

39. (d) At $t = 0$, $x = 5 = \dfrac{A}{2}$

$\Rightarrow$ Initial phase, $\phi = 30° = \dfrac{\pi}{6}$

$\Rightarrow x = A\sin(\omega t + \phi)$

$= 10\sin\left(\dfrac{2\pi}{T}t + \dfrac{\pi}{6}\right) = 10\sin\left(\pi t + \dfrac{\pi}{6}\right)$

40. (b) For block A to move in S.H.M.

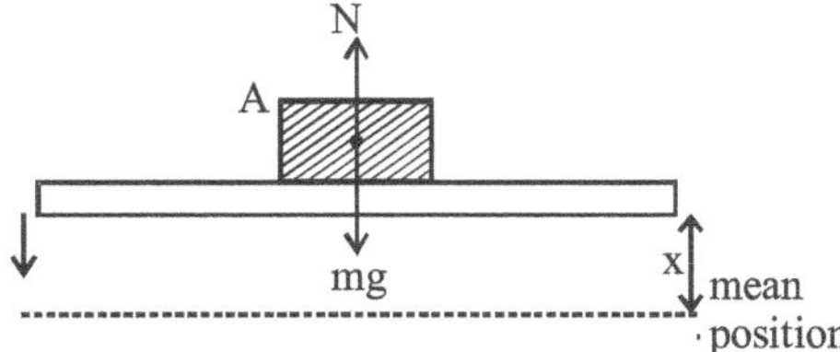

$mg - N = m\omega^2 x$

where x is the distance from mean position

For block to leave contact $N = 0$

$\Rightarrow mg = m\omega^2 x \Rightarrow x = \dfrac{g}{\omega^2}$

41. (a) $t = 2\pi\sqrt{\dfrac{\ell}{g_{\text{eff}}}}$; $t_0 = 2\pi\sqrt{\dfrac{\ell}{g}}$

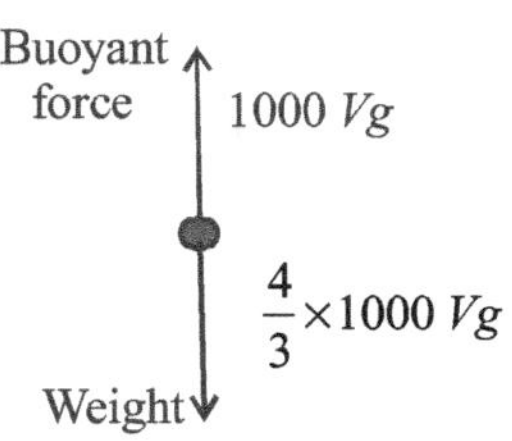

Net force $= \left(\dfrac{4}{3} - 1\right) \times 1000 \, Vg = \dfrac{1000}{3} Vg$

$g_{eff} = \dfrac{1000 \, Vg}{3 \times \dfrac{4}{3} \times 1000 V} = \dfrac{g}{4}$

$\therefore t = 2\pi \sqrt{\dfrac{\ell}{g/4}}$

$t = 2t_0$

42. (a) K.E. of a body undergoing SHM is given by,

$$K.E. = \dfrac{1}{2} ma^2 \omega^2 \cos^2 \omega t$$

$$T.E. = \dfrac{1}{2} ma^2 \omega^2$$

Given K.E. = 0.75 T.E.

$$\Rightarrow 0.75 = \cos^2 \omega t \Rightarrow \omega t = \dfrac{\pi}{6}$$

$$\Rightarrow t = \dfrac{\pi}{6 \times \omega} \Rightarrow t = \dfrac{\pi \times 2}{6 \times 2\pi} \Rightarrow t = \dfrac{1}{6} \, s$$

43. (a) Under the action of first force, $F_1 = m\omega_1^2 y$

Under the action of second force,

$F_2 = m\omega_2^2 y$

Under the action of resultant force,

$F_1 + F_2 = m\omega^2 y$

$$\Rightarrow m\omega^2 y = m\omega_1^2 y + m\omega_2^2 y$$

$$\Rightarrow \omega^2 = \omega_1^2 + \omega_2^2$$

$$\Rightarrow \left(\dfrac{2\pi}{T}\right)^2 = \left(\dfrac{2\pi}{T_1}\right)^2 + \left(\dfrac{2\pi}{T_2}\right)^2$$

$$\Rightarrow T = \sqrt{\dfrac{T_1^2 T_2^2}{T_1^2 + T_2^2}} = \sqrt{\dfrac{\left(\dfrac{4}{5}\right)^2 \cdot \left(\dfrac{3}{5}\right)^2}{\left(\dfrac{4}{5}\right)^2 + \left(\dfrac{3}{5}\right)^2}} = \dfrac{12}{25}.$$

44. (d) $F = -bV$, b depends on all the three i.e, shape and size of he block and viscosity of the medium.

45. (c) When the bob moves from maximum angular displacement θ to mean position, then the loss of gravitational potential energy is mgh where $h = l(1 - \cos \theta)$

1. **(a)**

$$n_1 : n_2 : n_3 = 3 : 2 : 1$$

$$n \propto \frac{1}{\ell}$$

$$\ell_1 : \ell_2 : \ell_3 = \frac{1}{3} : \frac{1}{2} : \frac{1}{1} = 2 : 3 : 6$$

$$\ell_1 + \ell_2 + \ell_3 = 110$$

$$\Rightarrow 2x + 3x + 6x = 110 \Rightarrow x = 10$$

∴ The two bridges should be set at $2x$ i.e, 20 cm from one end and $6x$ i.e, 60 cm from the other end.

2. **(a)** Equation of the harmonic progressive wave given by :
$y = a \sin 2\pi (bt - cx)$.
Here $\upsilon = b$

$$k = \frac{2\pi}{\lambda} = 2\pi c \text{ take, } \frac{1}{\lambda} = c$$

∴ Velocity of the wave $= \upsilon\lambda = b\dfrac{1}{c} = \dfrac{b}{c}$

$$\frac{dy}{dt} = a\, 2\pi b \cos 2\pi (bt - cx) = a\omega \cos (\omega t - kx)$$

Maximum particle velocity $= a\omega = a2\pi b = 2\pi\, ab$

given this is $2 \times \dfrac{b}{c}$ i.e. $2\pi a = \dfrac{2}{c}$ or $c = \dfrac{1}{\pi a}$

3. **(c)** $y = 0.25 \sin (10\pi x - 2\pi t)$
Comparing this equation with the standard wave equation
$y = a \sin (kx - \omega t)$
We get, $k = 10\pi$

$$\Rightarrow \frac{2\pi}{\lambda} = 10\pi \Rightarrow \lambda = 0.2 \text{ m}$$

And $\omega = 2\pi$ or, $2\pi v = 2\pi \Rightarrow v = 1$ Hz.
The sign inside the bracket is negative, hence the wave travels in $+$ ve x- direction.

4. **(b)** Amplitude of reflected wave $= \dfrac{2}{3} \times 0.9 = 0.6$

It would travel along negative direction of x-axis, and on reflection at a rigid support, there occurs a phase change of π.

5. **(c)** Velocity of source $= 18 \text{ km h}^{-1} = 5 \text{ m s}^{-1}$
(i) S moves towards listener (v_S)
(ii) listener moves towards source (v_L)

$$v' = \frac{v + v_L}{v - v_S} v = 280 \text{ Hz , Beats} = v' - v = 8.$$

6. **(d)** Third overtone has a frequency $7\,n$, which means

$$L = \frac{7\lambda}{4} = \text{three full loops} + \text{one half loop, which would}$$

make four nodes and four antinodes.

7. **(c)** Comparing it with $y(x, t) = A \cos(\omega t + \pi/2) \cos kx$.
If $kx = \pi/2$, a node occurs ; ∴ $10\,\pi x = \pi/2 \Rightarrow x = 0.05$ m
If $kx = \pi$, an antinode occurs $\Rightarrow 10\pi x = \pi$
$\Rightarrow x = 0.1$ m

Also speed of wave $\omega/k = \dfrac{50\pi}{10\pi} = 5 \text{m/s}$ and

$$\lambda = 2\pi/k = 2\pi/10\pi = 0.2 \text{ m}$$

8. **(a)** $\ell_1 + x = \dfrac{\lambda}{4} = 22.7$ equation (1)

$$\ell_2 + x = \frac{3\lambda}{4} = 70.2 \qquad \text{equation (2)}$$

$$l_3 + x = \frac{5\lambda}{4} \qquad \text{equation (3)}$$

From equation (1) and (2)

$$x = \frac{\ell_2 - 3\ell_1}{2} = \frac{70.2 - 68.1}{2} = \frac{2.1}{2} = 1.05 \text{ cm}$$

From equation (2) and (3) $\dfrac{\ell_3 + x}{\ell_1 + x} = 5$

$$\ell_3 = 5\ell_1 + 4x = 5 \times 22.7 + 4 \times 1.05 = 117.7 \text{ cm}$$

9. **(d)**

Let after 5 sec engine at point C

$$t = \frac{AB}{330} + \frac{BC}{330}$$

$$5 = \frac{0.9 \times 1000}{330} + \frac{BC}{330}$$

∴ BC $= 750$ m
Distance travelled by engine in 5 sec
$= 900 \text{ m} - 750 \text{ m} = 150 \text{ m}$
Therefore velocity of engine

$$= \frac{150 \text{ m}}{5 \text{ sec}} = 30 \text{ m/s}$$

10. **(a)** For fundamental mode,

$$f = \frac{1}{2\ell} \sqrt{\frac{T}{\mu}}$$

Taking logarithm on both sides, we get

$$\log f = \log\left(\frac{1}{2\ell}\right) + \log\left(\sqrt{\frac{T}{\mu}}\right)$$

$$= \log\left(\frac{1}{2\ell}\right) + \frac{1}{2}\log\left(\frac{T}{\mu}\right)$$

or $\log f = \log\left(\frac{1}{2\ell}\right) + \frac{1}{2}[\log T - \log \mu]$

Differentiating both sides, we get

$$\frac{df}{f} = \frac{1}{2}\frac{dT}{T} \quad \text{(as } \ell \text{ and } \mu \text{ are constants)}$$

$$\Rightarrow \frac{dT}{T} = 2 \times \frac{df}{f}$$

Here $df = 6$

$f = 600$ Hz

$$\therefore \frac{dT}{T} = \frac{2 \times 6}{600} = 0.02$$

11. (b) Frequency received by listener from the rear source,

$$n' = \frac{v-u}{v} \times n = \frac{v-u}{v} \times \frac{v}{\lambda} = \frac{v-u}{\lambda}$$

Frequency received by listener from the front source,

$$n'' = \frac{v+u}{v} \times \frac{v}{\lambda} = \frac{v+u}{\lambda}$$

No. of beats $= n'' - n'$

$$= \frac{v+u}{\lambda} - \frac{v-u}{\lambda} = \frac{v+u-v+u}{\lambda} = \frac{2u}{\lambda}$$

12. (c) $n' = n\left[\dfrac{v+v_0}{v}\right] = n\left[\dfrac{v+\dfrac{v}{5}}{v}\right] = n\left[\dfrac{6}{5}\right]$

$$\frac{n'}{n} = \frac{6}{5}; \quad \frac{n'-n}{n} = \frac{6-5}{5} \times 100 = 20\%$$

13. (c) In a closed organ pipe the fundamental frequency is

$$\upsilon = \frac{\upsilon}{4L}$$

$$\upsilon = \frac{320 \text{ ms}^{-1}}{4 \times 1\text{ m}} = 80 \text{ Hz}$$

In a closed organ pipe only odd harmonics are present.
So, it can resonate with 80 Hz, 240 Hz, 400 Hz, 560 Hz.

14. (b)

$$f \overset{\bullet}{\underset{S}{\bigcirc}} \xrightarrow[30 \text{ ms}^{-1}]{} \dashrightarrow \big|\, f' \quad f'' \overset{\bullet}{\underset{O}{\bigcirc}} \xrightarrow[30 \text{ ms}^{-1}]{} \leftarrow \big|\, f'$$

f' is the apparent frequency received by an observer at
the hill. f'' is the frequency of the reflected sound as
heard by driver.

$$f' = \frac{v}{v-30} f,$$

$$f'' = \frac{v+30}{v} f' = \frac{v+30}{v-30} f = \frac{360}{300} \times 600$$

$$= 720 \text{ Hz}$$

15. (d) Figure(a) represents a harmonic wave of frequency
7.0 Hz, figure (b) represents a harmonic wave of
frequency 5.0 Hz. Therefore beat frequency
$v_s = 7 - 5 = 2.0$ Hz.

16. (a) $\upsilon \propto \sqrt{T}$

17. (b) In fundamental mode,

$$\frac{\lambda}{2} = l \Rightarrow \lambda = 2l$$

$$\therefore f = \frac{v}{\lambda} = \frac{v}{2l} \qquad \text{.......(1)}$$

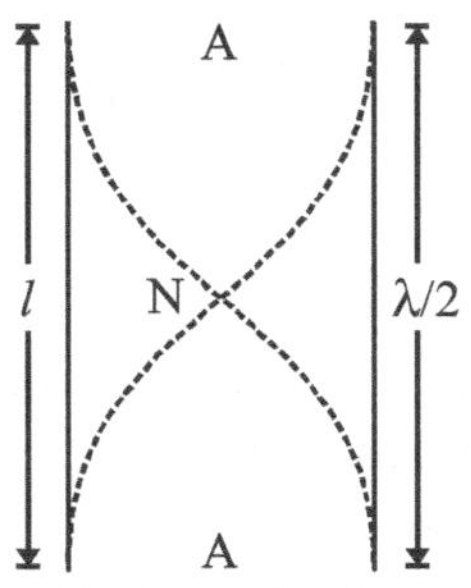

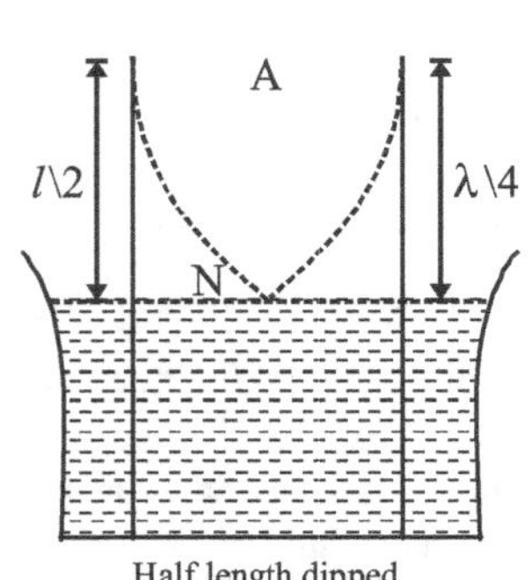

In half length dipped in water mode,

$$\frac{l}{2} = \frac{\lambda}{4} \Rightarrow \lambda = 2l$$

$$\therefore f' = \frac{v}{\lambda} = \frac{v}{2l} = f$$

18. (a) Given wave equation is $y(x,t)$

$$= e^{\left(-ax^2 + bt^2 + 2\sqrt{ab}\,xt\right)}$$

$$= e^{-[(\sqrt{ax})^2 + (\sqrt{b}t)^2 + 2\sqrt{a}x.\sqrt{b}t]}$$

$$= e^{-(\sqrt{a}x + \sqrt{b}t)^2}$$

$$= e^{-\left(x + \sqrt{\frac{b}{a}}t\right)^2}$$

It is a function of type $y = f(x + vt)$

$$\Rightarrow \text{Speed of wave} = \sqrt{\frac{b}{a}}$$

19. (c) Particle velocity

$$v = \frac{d}{dt}\left[x_0 \sin 2\pi\left(nt - \frac{x}{\lambda}\right)\right]$$

$$= 2\pi n x_0 \cos 2\pi\left(nt - \frac{x}{\lambda}\right)$$

$$\therefore \text{Maximum particle velocity} = 2\pi n x_0$$

$$\text{Wave velocity} = \frac{\lambda}{T} = n\lambda$$

Given, $2\pi n x_0 = 4n\lambda \Rightarrow \lambda = \frac{2\pi n x_0}{4n} = \frac{\pi x_0}{2}$

20. (d) As number of beats/sec = diff. in frequencies has to be
less than 10, therefore $0 < (n_1 - n_2) < 10$

21. **(c)** Length of pipe $= 85$ cm $= 0.85$m
Frequency of oscillations of air column in closed organ pipe is given by,

$$f = \frac{(2n-1)v}{4L}$$

$$f = \frac{(2n-1)v}{4L} \le 1250$$

$$\Rightarrow \quad \frac{(2n-1)\times 340}{0.85 \times 4} \le 1250$$

$$\Rightarrow \quad 2n-1 \le 12.5 \approx 6$$

22. **(b)** As the source is not moving towards or away from the observer in a straight line, so the Doppler's effect will not be observed by the observer.

23. **(c)** Frequency of first source with 5 beats/ sec = 100 Hz and frequency of second source with 5 beats/sec = 205 Hz. The frequency of the first source = $100 \pm 5 = 105$ or 95 Hz. Therefore, frequency of second harmonic of source = 210 Hz or 190 Hz. As the second harmonic gives 5 beats/ second with the sound of frequency 205 Hz, therefore, frequency of second harmonic source should be 210 Hz or frequency of source = 105 Hz.

24. **(c)** Pressure change will be minimum at both ends. In fact, pressure variation is maximum at $\ell/2$ because the displacement node is pressure antinode.

25. **(a)** $n_{Last} = n_{First} + (N-1)x$
$2n = n + (41-1) \times 5$
$\Rightarrow n_{First} = 200$ Hz and $n_{Last} = 400$ Hz

26. **(b)** Here, $T = 0.05$ sec, $v = 300$ ms^{-1}.

Now $\lambda = \dfrac{v}{v} = vT = (300 \times 0.05)$m

or, $\lambda = 15$ m
Phase of the point at 10 m from the source

$$= \frac{2\pi}{\lambda} \times x = \frac{2\pi}{15} \times 10 = \frac{4\pi}{3} \text{ rad}$$

Phase of the point at 15 m from the source

$$\frac{2\pi}{\lambda} \times x = \frac{2\pi}{15} \times 15 = 2\pi \text{ rad}$$

$\therefore$ The phase difference between the points

$$= 2\pi - \frac{4\pi}{3} = \frac{2\pi}{3} \text{ rad}$$

27. **(a)** We have, $L_1 = 10\log\left(\dfrac{I_1}{I_0}\right)$; $L_2 = 10\log\left(\dfrac{I_2}{I_0}\right)$

$$\therefore \; L_1 - L_2 = 10\log\left(\frac{I_1}{I_0}\right) - 10\log\left(\frac{I_2}{I_0}\right)$$

or, $\Delta L = 10\log\left(\dfrac{I_1}{I_0} \times \dfrac{I_0}{I_2}\right)$ or, $\Delta L = 10\log\left(\dfrac{I_1}{I_2}\right)$

or, $20 = 10\log\left(\dfrac{I_1}{I_2}\right)$ or, $2 = \log\left(\dfrac{I_1}{I_2}\right)$

or, $\dfrac{I_1}{I_2} = 10^2$ or, $I_2 = \dfrac{I_1}{100}$.
$\Rightarrow$ Intensity decreases by a factor 100.

28. **(a)** $y(x, t) = 0.005 \cos(\alpha x - \beta t)$ (Given)
Comparing it with the standard equation of wave
$y(x, t) = a \cos(kx - \omega t)$ we get
$k = \alpha$ and $\omega = \beta$

But $k = \dfrac{2\pi}{\lambda}$ and $\omega = \dfrac{2\pi}{T}$

$$\Rightarrow \frac{2\pi}{\lambda} = \alpha \text{ and } \frac{2\pi}{T} = \beta$$

Given that $\lambda = 0.08$ m and $T = 2.0$s

$$\therefore \; \alpha = \frac{2\pi}{0.08} = 25\pi \quad \text{and} \quad \beta = \frac{2\pi}{2} = \pi$$

29. **(b)** Equation is of stationary wave. Comparing with the standard equation

$$y = 2A \sin\left(\frac{2\pi}{T}\right) t \; \cos\left(\frac{2\pi}{\lambda}\right) x$$

$$\frac{2\pi}{\lambda} = 4.5 \text{ or } \lambda = \frac{2\pi}{4.5} = 1.4 \text{m}$$

30. **(b)** Waves are kind of disturbances which moves from one place to another without the actual physical transfer of matter of the medium as a whole. The particles of the medium only oscillate but do not travel from one place to another.
Waves transport energy and the pattern of disturbance has information that propagate from one point to another. Here, wave pattern propagates.
All our communication essentially depend on transmission of signals through the waves.

31. **(b)** $\dfrac{v}{4\ell_1} = \dfrac{3v}{2\ell_2},$ $\therefore \; \dfrac{\ell_1}{\ell_2} = \dfrac{1}{6}$

32. **(c)** $\omega_1 = 600\pi, \omega_2 = 604\pi,$
$f_1 = 300$ Hz, $f_2 = 302$ Hz
Beat frequency, $f_2 - f_1 = 2$ Hz
$\Rightarrow$ number of beats in three seconds = 6

33. **(b)** Given $f_A = 1800$Hz
$v_t = v$
$f_B = 2150$ Hz
Reflected wave frequency received by A, $f_A{}' = ?$
Applying doppler's effect of sound,

$$f' = \frac{v_s f}{v_s - v_t}$$

here, $v_t = v_s\left(1 - \dfrac{f_A}{f_B}\right)$

$$= 343\left(1 - \frac{1800}{2150}\right)$$

$v_t = 55.8372$ m/s

Now, for the reflected wave,

$$\therefore \quad f_A' = \left(\frac{v_s + v_t}{v_s - v_t}\right) f_A$$

$$= \left(\frac{343 + 55.83}{343 - 55.83}\right) \times 1800$$

$$= 2499.44 \approx 2500 \text{Hz}$$

34. (a) Standing waves are produced when two waves propagate in opposite direction

As z_1 & z_2 are propagating in +ve x-axis & −ve x-axis

so, $z_1 + z_2$ will represent a standing wave.

35. (d) Load supported by sonometer wire = 4 kg
Tension in sonometer wire = 4 g
If μ = mass per unit length

then frequency $\upsilon = \dfrac{1}{2l}\sqrt{\dfrac{T}{\mu}}$

$$\Rightarrow \quad 416 = \frac{1}{2l}\sqrt{\frac{4g}{\mu}}$$

When length is doubled, i.e., $l' = 2l$
Let new load = L
As, $\upsilon' = \upsilon$

$$\therefore \quad \frac{1}{2l'}\sqrt{\frac{Lg}{\mu}} = \frac{1}{2l}\sqrt{\frac{4g}{\mu}}$$

$$\Rightarrow \quad \frac{1}{4l}\sqrt{\frac{Lg}{\mu}} = \frac{1}{2l}\sqrt{\frac{4g}{\mu}}$$

$$\Rightarrow \quad \sqrt{L} = 2 \times 2 \quad \Rightarrow \quad L = 16\,\text{kg}$$

36. (b) Let the string vibrates in p loops, wavelength of the pth mode of vibration is given by

$$\lambda_p = \frac{2l}{p}$$

Given, $y = 2\sin\left(\dfrac{4\pi x}{15}\right)\cos(96\pi t)$

or $y = 2\left[\sin\left(\dfrac{4\pi x}{15} + 96\pi t\right) + \sin\left(\dfrac{4\pi x}{15} - 96\pi t\right)\right]$

Comparing it with standard equation, we get

$$\upsilon = \frac{96\pi}{2\pi} = 48 \text{ Hz and } k = \frac{4\pi}{15}$$

$$\frac{1}{48} = \frac{2 \times 60}{p} \times \frac{4\pi}{15 \times 96\pi}$$

$$\Rightarrow p = 16.$$

37. (b)

$$n = \frac{1}{2l}\sqrt{\frac{T}{m}}$$

or, $n \propto \dfrac{1}{l}$ or nl = constant, K

$$\therefore \quad n_1 l_1 = K,$$

$$n_2 l_2 = K, \ n_3 l_3 = K$$

Also, $l = l_1 + l_2 + l_3$

or, $\dfrac{K}{n} = \dfrac{K}{n_1} + \dfrac{K}{n_2} + \dfrac{K}{n_3}$

or, $\dfrac{1}{n} = \dfrac{1}{n_1} + \dfrac{1}{n_2} + \dfrac{1}{n_3}$

38. (a) Time taken for two syllables $t = \dfrac{2}{5}$ sec.

$$x + x = v \times t = 330 \times \frac{2}{5} \quad \therefore \ x = 66\,\text{m}$$

39. (a) Velocity of sound $= \sqrt{\dfrac{\gamma RT}{M}}$

When water vapour are represent in air average molecular weight of air decreases and hence velocity increases.

40. (b) $\dfrac{I_{max}}{I_{min}} = \dfrac{(a+b)^2}{(a-b)^2} = 49 \qquad \therefore \ \dfrac{a+b}{a-b} = 7$

$7a - 7b = a + b$ or $6a = 8b$ or $\dfrac{a}{b} = \dfrac{8}{6} = \dfrac{4}{3}$

41. (a) By the concept of accoustic, the observer and source are moving towards each other, each with a velocity of 18 m s^{-1}.

$$\therefore v' = \frac{330 + 18}{330 - 18} \times 1000 \quad \approx 1115 \text{ Hz}$$

42. (c) Compare the given equation with standard form

$$y = r\sin\left[\frac{2\pi x}{\lambda} - \frac{2\pi t}{T}\right]$$

$$\frac{2\pi}{\lambda} = 3, \lambda = \frac{2\pi}{3} \text{ and } \frac{2\pi}{T} = 15$$

$$T = \frac{2\pi}{15}$$

Speed of propagation, $v = \dfrac{\lambda}{T} = \dfrac{2\pi/3}{2\pi/15} = 5$

43. (c) The contrast will be maximum, when $I_1 = I_2$ i.e.

$a = b$. In that event, $I_{min} = (a-b)^2 = 0$, where a and b are the amplitudes of interfering waves.

44. (b) Fundamental frequency of closed organ pipe

$$V_c = \frac{V}{4l_c}$$

Fundamental frequency of open organ pipe

$$V_0 = \frac{V}{2l_0}$$

Second overtone frequency of open organ pipe $= \dfrac{3V}{2l_0}$

From question,

$$\dfrac{V}{4l_c} = \dfrac{3V}{2l_0}$$

$$\Rightarrow \quad l_0 = 6l_c = 6 \times 20 = 120 \text{ cm}$$

45. **(b)** $y = 60 \cos(180t - 6x)$ ....(1)

$$\omega = 180, k = 6 \Rightarrow \dfrac{2\pi}{\lambda} = 6$$

$$v = \dfrac{\omega}{k} = \dfrac{2\pi}{T} \times \dfrac{\lambda}{2\pi} = \dfrac{180}{6} = 30 \text{ m}/\text{s}$$

Differentiating (1) w.r.t. t,

$$v = \dfrac{dy}{dt} = -60 \times 180 \, \sin(180t - 6x)$$

$$v_{max} = 60 \times 180 \, \mu\text{m/s}$$
$$= 10800 \, \mu\text{m/s} = 0.0108 \text{ m/s}$$

$$\dfrac{v_{max}}{v} = \dfrac{0.0108}{30} = 3.6 \times 10^{-4}$$

1. **(a)** Electric field intensity at the centre of the disc.

$$E = \frac{\sigma}{2\,\epsilon_0} \quad \text{(given)}$$

Electric field along the axis at any distance x from the centre of the disc

$$E' = \frac{\sigma}{2\,\epsilon_0}\left(1 - \frac{x}{\sqrt{x^2 + R^2}}\right)$$

From question, x = R (radius of disc)

$$\therefore E' = \frac{\sigma}{2\,\epsilon_0}\left(1 - \frac{R}{\sqrt{R^2 + R^2}}\right)$$

$$= \frac{\sigma}{2\,\epsilon_0}\left(\frac{\sqrt{2}R - R}{\sqrt{2}R}\right)$$

$$= \frac{4}{14}E$$

$\therefore$ % reduction in the value of electric field

$$= \frac{\left(E - \frac{4}{14}E\right) \times 100}{E} = \frac{1000}{14}\% \approx 70.7\%$$

2. **(a)** Surface charge density $(\sigma) = \dfrac{\text{Charge}}{\text{Surface area}}$

So $\sigma_{\text{inner}} = \dfrac{-2Q}{4\pi b^2}$

and $\sigma_{\text{Outer}} = \dfrac{Q}{4\pi c^2}$

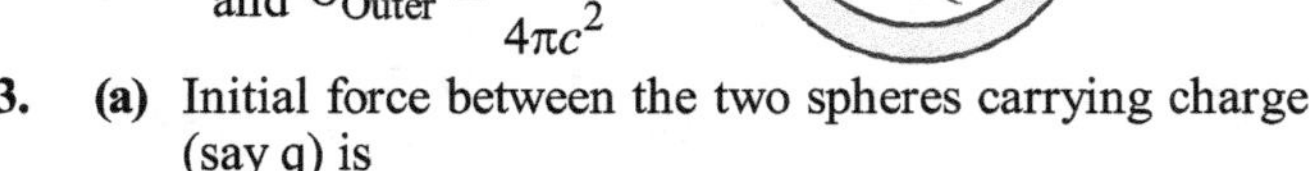

3. **(a)** Initial force between the two spheres carrying charge (say q) is

$$F = \frac{1}{4\pi\varepsilon_0}\frac{q^2}{r^2} \quad \text{(r is the distance between them)}$$

Further when an uncharged sphere is kept in touch with the sphere of charge q, the net charge on both become $\dfrac{q+0}{2} = \dfrac{q}{2}$. Force on the 3rd charge, when placed in center of the 1st two

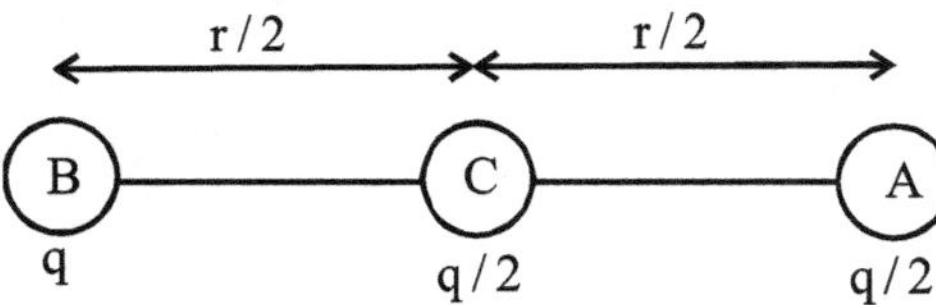

$$F_3 = \frac{1}{4\pi\varepsilon_0}\frac{q\left(\frac{q}{2}\right)}{\left(\frac{r}{2}\right)^2} - \frac{1}{4\pi\varepsilon_0}\frac{\left(\frac{q}{2}\right)^2}{\left(\frac{r}{2}\right)^2}$$

$$= \frac{1}{4\pi\varepsilon_0}\frac{q^2}{r^2}[2 - 1] = F$$

4. **(d)** Since electric field $\vec{E}$ decreases inside water, therefore flux $\phi = \vec{E}.\vec{A}$ also decreases.

5. **(d)** Unit positive charge at O will be repelled equally by three charges at the three corners of triangle. By symmetry, resultant $\vec{E}$ at O would be zero.

6. **(c)** When a dipole is placed in a uniform electric field, two equal and opposite forces act on it. Therefore, a torque acts which rotates the dipole.

7. **(d)** Force acting on the charged particle due to electric field $= q\vec{E}$

work done in moving through distance S,

$$W = q\vec{E}.\vec{S} = (qE) \times S \times \cos\theta$$

$\therefore 10\,\text{J} = (0.5\,\text{C}) \times E \times 2\cos 60°$

$E = 10 \times 2 = 20\,\text{NC}^{-1} = 20\,\text{Vm}^{-1}$

8. **(c)** The charged sphere is a conductor. Therefore the field inside is zero and outside it is proportional to $1/r^2$

9. **(d)** Since $\phi_{\text{total}} = \phi_A + \phi_B + \phi_C = \dfrac{q}{\varepsilon_0}$,

where q is the total charge.

As shown in the figure, flux associated with the curved surface B is $\phi = \phi_B$

Let us assume flux linked with the plane surfaces A and C be

$\phi_A = \phi_C = \phi'$

Therefore,

$$\frac{q}{\varepsilon_0} = 2\phi' + \phi_B = 2\phi' + \phi$$

$$\Rightarrow \phi' = \frac{1}{2}\left(\frac{q}{\varepsilon_0} - \phi\right)$$

10. **(b)** We have $E_a = \dfrac{2kp}{r^3}$ and $E_e = \dfrac{kp}{r^3}$; $\therefore E_a = 2E_e$

11. **(c)** Electric lines of force due to a positive charge is spherically symmetric.

All the charges are positive and equal in magnitude. So repulsion takes place. Due to which no lines of force are present inside the equilateral triangle and the resulting lines of force obtained as shown:

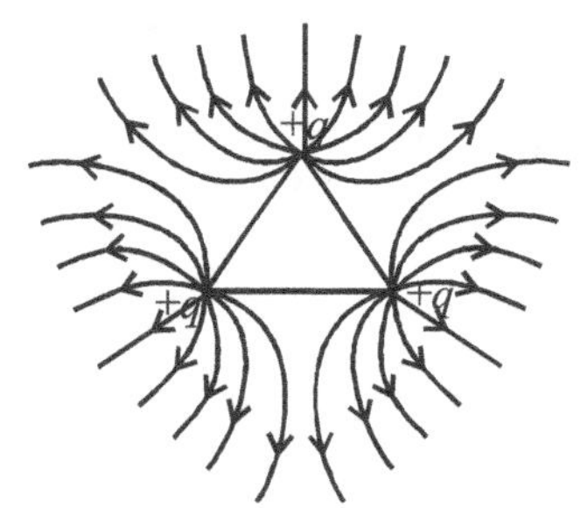

12. (a)

$Q_1 \quad Q_2 \quad Q_3$

with spacing a between Q_1–Q_2 and Q_2–Q_3.

$Q_2 = -Q_3 = Q$

Force on Q_3 due to Q_2 + Force on Q_3 due to $Q_1 = 0$.

$$\frac{1}{4\pi \in_0}\left(\frac{-Q^2}{a^2}\right)+\frac{1}{4\pi \in_0}\frac{Q_1 Q}{4a^2}=0 \Rightarrow Q_1 = 4Q_3$$

13. (b) Charge per cm length of the wire = qC

∴ Charge per metre of the wire = 100q C

According to Gauss's law,

Total electric flux passing through the cylindrical surface

$$\phi = \frac{q_{enclosed}}{\varepsilon_0} = \frac{100q}{\varepsilon_0}$$

14. (c) $T_0 = 2\pi\sqrt{\dfrac{L}{g}}$

When the plates are charged, the net acceleration is,

$g' = g + a$

$g' = g + \dfrac{qE}{m} \qquad \left(a = \dfrac{qE}{m}\right)$

∴ $T = 2\pi\sqrt{\dfrac{L}{g+\dfrac{qE}{m}}}$

∴ $\dfrac{T}{T_0} = \left(\dfrac{g}{g+\dfrac{qE}{m}}\right)^{1/2}$

15. (c) Charges (q) $= 2 \times 10^{-6}$ C, Distance (d) $= 3$ cm $= 3 \times 10^{-2}$ m and electric field (E) $= 2 \times 10^5$ N/C. Torque $(\tau) = q.d.$

$E =(2 \times 10^{-6}) \times (3 \times 10^{-2}) \times (2 \times 10^5)$

$= 12 \times 10^{-3}$ N–m.

16. (b) Net flux emmited from a spherical surface of radius a according to Gauss's theorem

$\phi_{net} = \dfrac{q_{in}}{\varepsilon_0}$

or, $(Aa)(4\pi a^2) = \dfrac{q_{in}}{\varepsilon_0}$

So, $q_{in} = 4\pi\varepsilon_0 A\, a^3$

17. (a) Since lines of force starts from A and ends at B, so A is +ve and B is –ve. Lines of forces are more crowded near A, so A > B.

18. (c) Net force on each of the charge due to the other charges is zero. However, disturbance in any direction other than along the line on which the charges lie, will not make the charges return.

19. (c)

20. (d) For distances far away from centre of dipole

$$E_{axis} = E_a = \frac{1}{4\pi\varepsilon_0}\frac{2p}{r^3}$$

$$E_{equa} = E_e = \frac{1}{4\pi\varepsilon_0}\frac{p}{r^3}$$

$$\frac{d}{dr}(E_a) = \frac{1}{4\pi\varepsilon_0}2p\frac{d}{dr}(r^{-3})$$

$$= -6\cdot\frac{1}{4\pi\varepsilon_0}\frac{p}{r^4} \qquad \ldots(i)$$

$$\frac{d}{dr}(E_e) = \frac{1}{4\pi\varepsilon_0}p\frac{d}{dr}(r^{-3})$$

$$= -3\frac{1}{4\pi\varepsilon_0}\frac{p}{r^4} \qquad \ldots(ii)$$

From equation (i) and (ii) the magnitude of change in electric field w.r.t. distance is more in case of axis of dipole as compared to equatorial plane.

21. (b)

$2q \quad\quad\quad q \quad -3q$
$P \quad\quad\quad A \quad B$
with P–$A = \ell$ and A–$B = d$.

Let a charge $2q$ be placed at P, at a distance I from A where charge q is placed, as shown in figure.

The charge $2q$ will not experience any force, when force of repulsion on it due to q is balanced by force of attraction on it due to $-3q$ at B where $AB = d$

$$\frac{(2q)(q)}{4\pi\varepsilon_0\ell^2} = \frac{(2q)(-3q)}{4\pi\varepsilon_0(\ell+d)^2}$$

or $(\ell + d)^2 = 3\ell^2$

or $2\ell^2 - 2\ell d - d^2 = 0$

∴ $\ell = \dfrac{2d \pm \sqrt{4d^2 + 2d^2}}{4} = \dfrac{d}{2} \pm \dfrac{\sqrt{3}d}{2}$

$\ell = \dfrac{d + \sqrt{3}d}{2}$

22. **(d)** Let F be the force between Q and Q. The force between q and Q should be attractive for net force on Q to be zero. Let F' be the force between Q and q. The resultant of F' and F' is R. For equilibrium

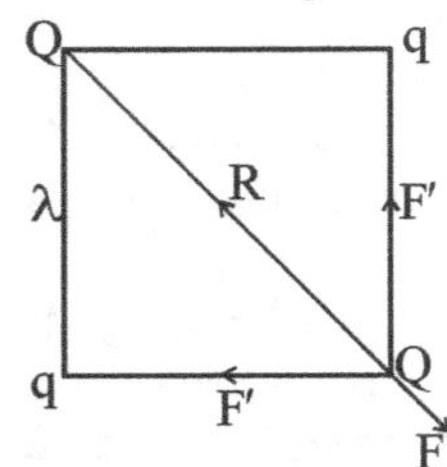

$$\vec{R}+\vec{F}=0 \qquad\qquad \sqrt{2}\,F'=-F$$

$$\sqrt{2}\times k\frac{Qq}{\ell^2}=-k\frac{Q^2}{(\sqrt{2}\,\ell)^2} \;\Rightarrow\; \frac{Q}{q}=-2\sqrt{2}$$

23. **(b)** Nuclear force binds the protons and neutrons in the nucleus of an atom.

24. **(c)** Net downward force on the drop $=\dfrac{4}{3}\pi r^3(\rho-\rho_0)\,g$

For equilibrium, electric force must be upwards i.e. charge on the drop is positive.

$$neE=\frac{4}{3}\pi r^3(\rho-\rho_0)\,g \quad\text{i.e.}\quad n=\frac{4\pi r^3(\rho-\rho_0)\,g}{3eE}$$

25. **(d)** Electric flux, $\phi=EA\cos\theta$,

where θ = angle between E and normal to the surface.

Here $\theta=\dfrac{\pi}{2}$

$\Rightarrow\quad \phi=0$

26. **(a)** Potential energy of an electric dipole in an electric field

is, $U=-\vec{p}.\vec{E}$ i.e. $U=-pE\cos\theta$

For minimum U, $\theta=0°$

$\Rightarrow U_{min}=-pE\cos 0=-pE$

27. **(c)** Milikan demonstrated the quantisation of charge experimentally. Charge on electron $=-e=-1.6\times10^{-19}$ C. Addition of charge can occur in integral multiples of e.

28. **(c)** Let n be the number of electrons missing.

$$F=\frac{1}{4\pi\varepsilon_0}\cdot\frac{q^2}{d^2}$$

$$\Rightarrow\quad q=\sqrt{4\pi\varepsilon_0 d^2 F}=ne$$

$$\therefore\quad n=\sqrt{\frac{4\pi\varepsilon_0 F d^2}{e^2}}$$

29. **(b)** $F=\dfrac{1}{4\pi\varepsilon_0}\dfrac{(4q)\,(-4q)}{r^2}$

when C is touched with A, then charge on A & C each = $2q$ after that C is touched with B, charge on

$$B=\frac{2q+(-4q)}{2}=-q$$

Now, force $F'=\dfrac{1}{4\pi\varepsilon_0}\dfrac{(2q)\,(-q)}{r^2}\Rightarrow F'=\dfrac{F}{8}$

30. **(a)** $-eE=mg$

$$\vec{E}=-\frac{9.1\times10^{-31}\times10}{1.6\times10^{-19}}=-5.6\times10^{-11}\,\text{N/C}$$

31. **(d)** Torque, $\vec{\tau}=\vec{p}\times\vec{E}=pE\sin\theta$

$$4=p\times 2\times10^5\times\sin 30°$$

$$\text{or, } p=\frac{4}{2\times10^5\times\sin 30°}=4\times10^{-5}\,\text{Cm}$$

Dipole moment, $p=q\times l$

$$q=\frac{p}{l}=\frac{4\times10^{-5}}{0.02}=2\times10^{-3}\,\text{C}=2\text{mC}$$

32. **(c)** K.E. $=$ Force $\times$ distance $=qE.y$

33. **(d)** Charge (q) $=0.2$ C; Distance (d) $=2$ m; Angle $\theta=60°$ and Work done (W) $=4$J.

Work done in moving the charge (W)

$=$ F.d $\cos\theta=qEd\cos\theta$

$$\text{or, } E=\frac{W}{qd\cos\theta}=\frac{4}{0.2\times2\times\cos 60°}=\frac{4}{0.4\times0.5}=20\,\text{N/C}.$$

34. **(a)** $\phi=\vec{E}.\vec{A}=4\hat{i}.(2\hat{i}+3\hat{j})=8$ V-m

35. **(d)** The dipole is placed in a non-uniform field, therefore a force as well as a couple acts on it. The force on the negative charge is more ($F\propto E$) and is directed along negative x-axis. Thus the dipole moves along negative x-axis and rotates in an anticlockwise direction.

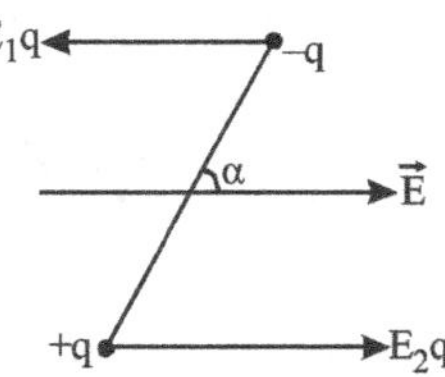

36. **(b)** Flux $=\vec{E}.\vec{A}$.

$\vec{E}$ is electric field vector & $\vec{A}$ is area vector.

Here, angle between $\vec{E}$ & $\vec{A}$ is 90°.

So, $\vec{E}.\vec{A}=0$; Flux $=0$

37. **(c)** The charge on disc A is 10^{-6} μC. The charge on disc B is 10×10^{-6} μC. The total charge on both $=11$ μC. When touched, this charge will be distributed equally i.e. 5.5 μC on each disc.

38. **(a)** According to Gauss's law total electric flux through a closed surface is $\dfrac{1}{\varepsilon_0}$ times the total charge inside that surface.

Electric flux, $\phi_E=\dfrac{q}{\varepsilon_0}$

Charge on α-particle $= 2e$

$$\phi_E = \frac{2e}{\varepsilon_0}$$

39. **(b)** It is possible to create or destroy charged particles but it is not possible to create or destroy net charge. The charge of an isolated system is conserved.

40. **(a)** The flux is zero according to Gauss' Law because it is a open surface which enclosed a charge q.

41. **(d)** By Gauss law, we know that

$$\phi = \frac{q}{\varepsilon_0} \text{ Here, Net electric flux, } \phi = \phi_2 - \phi_1$$

$$= 9 \times 10^6 - 6 \times 10^6 = \frac{q}{\varepsilon_0} \Rightarrow q = 3 \times 10^6 \times \varepsilon_0.$$

42. **(d)** They will not experience any force if $|\vec{F}_G| = |\vec{F}_e|$

$$\Rightarrow G\frac{m^2}{(16 \times 10^{-2})^2} = \frac{1}{4\pi\varepsilon_0} \cdot \frac{q^2}{(16 \times 10^{-2})^2} \Rightarrow \frac{q}{m} = \sqrt{4\pi\varepsilon_0 G}$$

43. **(c)** Here, $\ell = 2.4\ m$, $r = 4.6\ mm = 4.6 \times 10^{-3}\ m$

$q = -4.2 \times 10^{-7}\ C$

Linear charge density, $\lambda = \frac{q}{\ell}$

$$= \frac{-4.2 \times 10^{-7}}{2.4} = -1.75 \times 10^{-7}\ C\ m^{-1}$$

Electric field, $E = \dfrac{\lambda}{2\pi\varepsilon_0 r}$

$$= \frac{-1.75 \times 10^{-7}}{2 \times 3.14 \times 8.854 \times 10^{-12} \times 4.6 \times 10^{-3}}$$

$$= -6.7 \times 10^5\ N\ C^{-1}$$

44. **(a)** Charge resides on the outer surface of a conducting hollow sphere of radius R. We consider a spherical surface of radius r < R.

By Gauss theorem

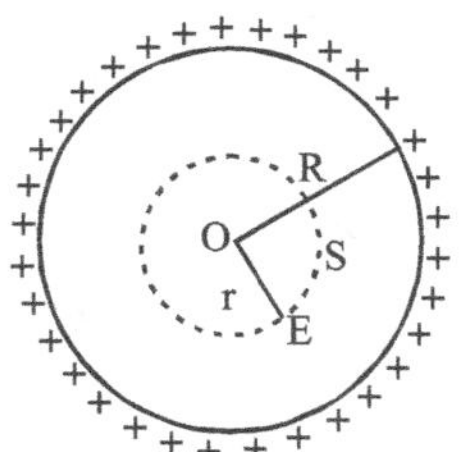

$$\int_s \vec{E}.\vec{ds} = \frac{1}{\varepsilon_0} \times \text{charge enclosed or } E \times 4\pi r^2 = \frac{1}{\varepsilon_0} \times 0$$

$$\Rightarrow E = 0$$

i.e electric field inside a hollow sphere is zero.

45. **(c)** By Gauss's theorem, $\phi = \dfrac{Q_{in}}{\epsilon_0}$

Thus, the net flux depends only on the charge enclosed by the surface. Hence, there will be no effect on the net flux if the radius of the surface is doubled.

1. **(d)** As volume remains constant, therefore,

$$\frac{4}{3}\pi R^3 = n \times \frac{4}{3}\pi r^3 \qquad \therefore \ R = n^{1/3} r.$$

New potential $= V' = \dfrac{nq}{4\pi\varepsilon_0 R} = \dfrac{nq}{4\pi\varepsilon_0 (n^{1/3} r)}$

$$= n^{2/3}\frac{q}{4\pi\varepsilon_0 r} = n^{2/3}\,V.$$

2. **(a)** $C_a = \dfrac{\epsilon_0 A}{d}$ and $C_b = \dfrac{\epsilon_0 A}{\dfrac{d}{2} + \dfrac{d}{2K}} = \dfrac{2\,\epsilon_0 A(1+K)}{d}$

and $C_c = \dfrac{\epsilon_0 \dfrac{A}{2}}{d} + \dfrac{\epsilon_0 \dfrac{A}{2}K}{d} = \dfrac{\epsilon_0 A}{2d}(1+K)$

or $C_b = \dfrac{\epsilon_0 A}{d}2(1+K) > C_a$

or $C_c = \dfrac{\epsilon_0 A}{d}\dfrac{1+K}{2} > C_a \quad \therefore C_b$ and $C_c > C_a$

3. **(c)** Charges reside only on the outer surface of a conductor with cavity.

4. **(b)** In oil, C becomes twice, V becomes half. Therefore, $E = V/d$ becomes half.

5. **(d)**

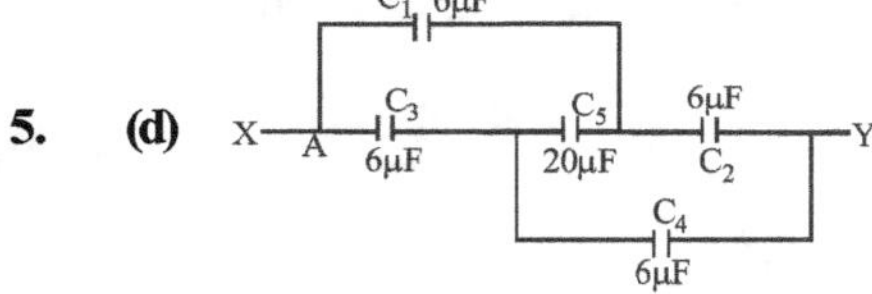

Equivalent circuit

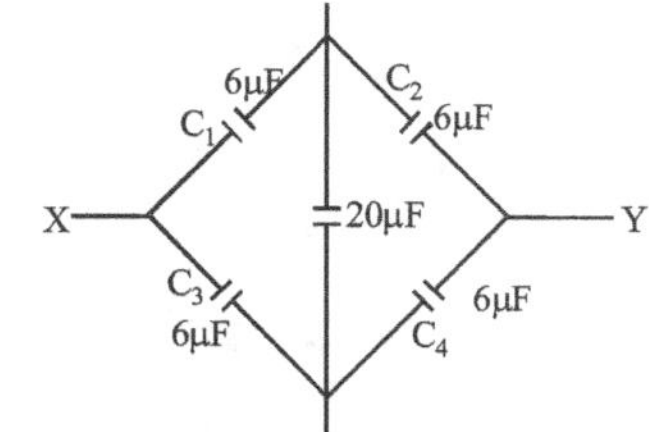

Here, $\dfrac{C_1}{C_3} = \dfrac{C_2}{C_4}$

Hence, no charge will flow through 20μF

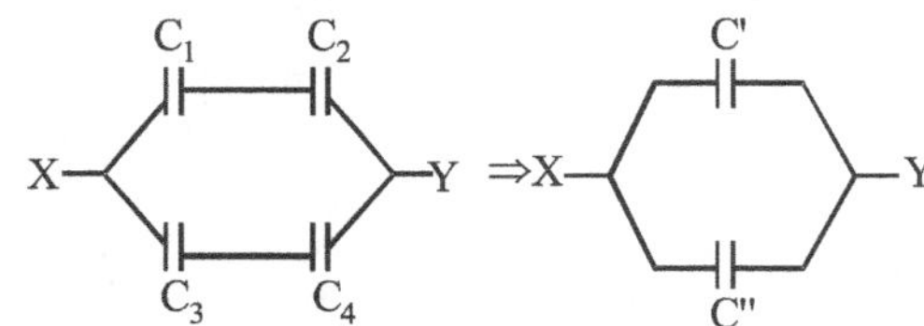

C_1 and C_2 are in series, also C_3 and C_4 are in series.
Hence, $C' = 3\ \mu F$, $C'' = 3\ \mu F$
C' and C'' are in parallel.
Hence net capacitance $= C' + C'' = 3 + 3 = 6\ \mu F$

6. **(c)**

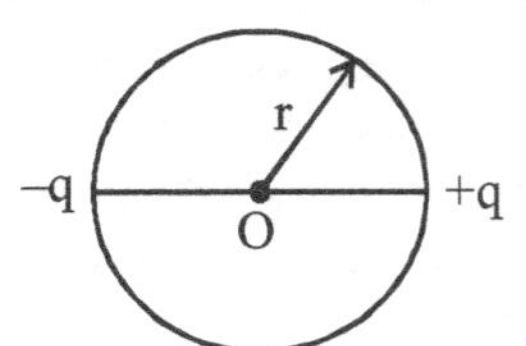

$$\frac{mv^2}{r} = \frac{kq^2}{(2r)^2} \ ; \ mv^2 = \frac{kq^2}{4r}$$

Kinetic energy of each particle

$$= \frac{1}{2}mv^2 = \frac{kq^2}{8r}$$

7. **(b)** It consists of two capacitors in parallel, therefore, the total capacitance is $= \dfrac{2\,\epsilon_0 A}{d}$

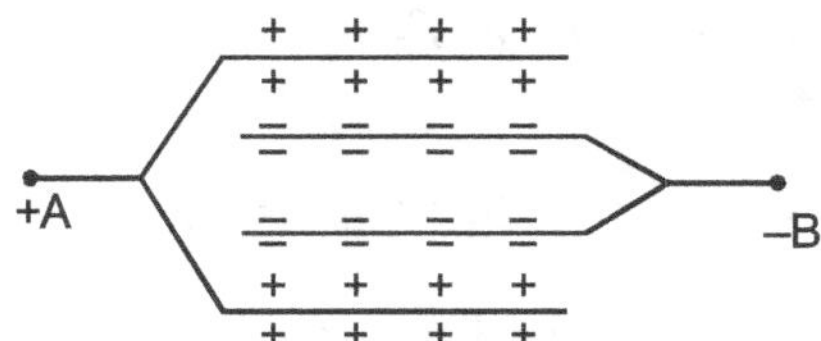

(The plates of B, having negative charge do not constitute a capacitor).

8. **(a)** The potential energy of a charged capacitor is given by $U = \dfrac{Q^2}{2C}$.

If a dielectric slab is inserted between the plates, the energy is given by $\dfrac{Q^2}{2KC}$, where K is the dielectric constant.

Again, when the dielectric slab is removed slowly its energy increases to initial potential energy. Thus, work done is zero.

9. **(a)** As $x = t\left(1 - \dfrac{1}{K}\right)$, where x is the addition distance of plate, to restore the capacity of original value.

$\therefore \ 3.5 \times 10^{-5} = 4 \times 10^{-5}\left(1 - \dfrac{1}{K}\right)$.

Solving, we get, $K = 8$.

10. **(b)** At. equipotential surface, the potential is same at any point i.e., $V_A = V_B$ as shown in figure. Hence no work is required to move unit change from one point to another i.e.,

$$V_A - V_B = \frac{W}{\text{unit charge}} = 0 \Rightarrow W = 0$$

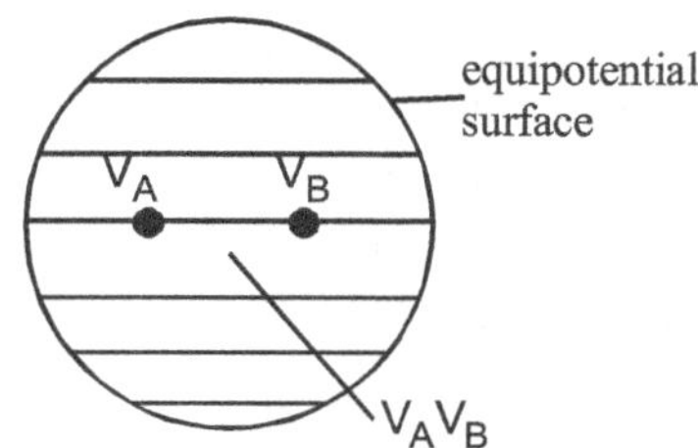

11. **(b)**
(i) Electrostatic field is zero inside a charged conductor or neutral conductor.
(ii) Electrostatic field at the surface of a charged conductor must be normal to the surface at every point.
(iii) There is no net charge at any point inside the conductor and any excess charge must reside at the surface.
(iv) Electrostatic potential is constant throughout the volume of the conductor and has the same value (as insde) on its surface.
(v) Electric field at the surface of a charged conductor is
$$\vec{E} = \frac{\sigma}{\varepsilon_0}\hat{n}$$

12. **(b)** In shell, q charge is uniformly distributed over its surface, it behaves as a conductor.

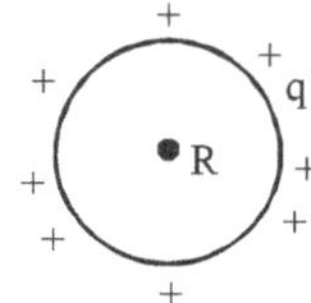

$V=$ potential at surface $= \dfrac{q}{4\pi\varepsilon_0 R}$ and inside

$$V = \frac{q}{4\pi\varepsilon_0 R}$$

Because of this it behaves as an equipotential surface.

13. **(c)** Volume of big drop = 1000 × volume of each small drop

$$\frac{4}{3}\pi R^3 = 1000 \times \frac{4}{3}\pi r^3 \Rightarrow R = 10r$$

$$\because \quad V = \frac{kq}{r} \text{ and } V' = \frac{kq}{R} \times 1000$$

Total charge on one small droplet is q and on the big drop is 1000q.

$$\Rightarrow \frac{V'}{V} = \frac{1000r}{R} = \frac{1000}{10} = 100$$

$$\therefore \quad V' = 100V$$

14. **(c)** In a round trip, displacement is zero. Hence, work done is zero.

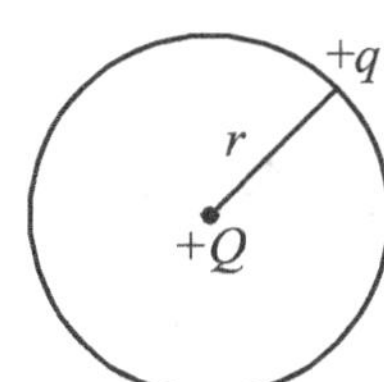

15. **(b)** The two capacitors are in parallel so

$$C = \frac{\varepsilon_0 A}{t \times 2}(k_1 + k_2)$$

16. **(d)** In equilibrium, $F = qE = (ne)\dfrac{V}{d} = mg$

$$n = \frac{mgd}{eV} = \frac{1.96 \times 10^{-15} \times 9.8 \times 0.02}{1.6 \times 10^{-19} \times 800} = 3$$

17. **(a)** $E = \dfrac{1}{2}CV^2 = \dfrac{1}{2} \times 1 \times 10^{-6} \times (4000)^2 = 8\,J.$

18. **(d)** As we know,

$$\text{Common potential} = \frac{\text{Total charge}}{\text{Total capacity}}$$

$Q_1 = C_0 V_1, Q_2 = 0$, therefore

$$V_2 = \frac{C_0 V_1 + 0}{C_0 + kC_0} = \frac{V_1}{1+k}$$

$$1 + k = \frac{V_1}{V_2} \text{ or } k = \frac{V_1}{V_2} - 1 = \frac{V_1 - V_2}{V_2}$$

19. **(b)** Potential difference across the branch de is 6 V. Net capacitance of de branch is 2.1 μF
So, q = CV
$\Rightarrow q = 2.1 \times 6\ \mu C$
$\Rightarrow q = 12.6\ \mu C$
Potential across 3 μF capacitance is

$$V = \frac{12.6}{3} = 4.2 \text{ volt}$$

Potential across 2 and 5 combination in parallel is 6 − 4.2 = 1.8 V
So, $q' = (1.8)(5) = 9\ \mu C$

20. **(c)**

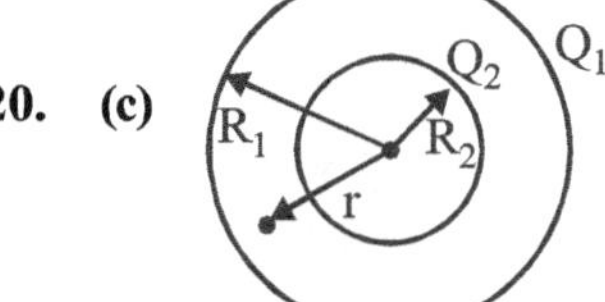

$$V_r = \frac{Q_2}{4\pi\varepsilon_0 r} + \frac{Q_1}{4\pi\varepsilon_0 R_1}$$

$$V_r = \frac{1}{4\pi\varepsilon_0}\left(\frac{Q_2}{r} + \frac{Q_1}{R_1}\right)$$

21. **(d)** $U = \dfrac{1}{2}QV = $ Area of triangle OAB

22. **(b)** Charge on α particle, q = 2 e.
K.E. = work done = q × V = 2e × 10^6 V = 2 MeV.

23. **(a)** Let the side length of square be 'a' then potential at centre O is

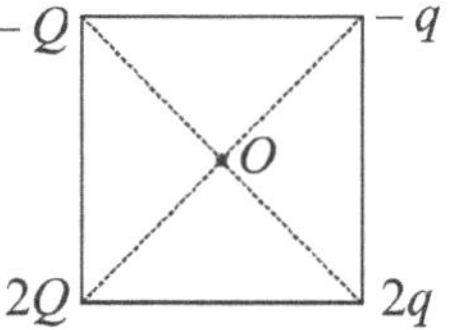

$$V = \frac{k(-Q)}{\left(\frac{a}{\sqrt{2}}\right)} + \frac{k(-q)}{\frac{a}{\sqrt{2}}} + \frac{k(2q)}{\frac{a}{\sqrt{2}}} + \frac{k(2Q)}{\frac{a}{\sqrt{2}}} = 0$$

(Given)
$$= -Q - q + 2q + 2Q = 0 = Q + q = 0$$
$$= Q = -q$$

24. (b) $C_0 = \dfrac{k \in_0 A}{d}$

$$C = \frac{k \in_0 2}{3d} + \frac{2k \in_0 A}{3d} = \frac{4}{3}\frac{k \in_0 A}{d}$$

$$\therefore \quad \frac{C}{C_0} = \frac{\frac{4}{3}\frac{k \in_0 A}{d}}{\frac{k \in_0 A}{d}} = \frac{4}{3}$$

25. (b) Work done = Change in energy

$$= \frac{1}{2}\left(C + \frac{C}{2}\right)V^2 = \frac{1}{2}\left(\frac{3C}{2}\right)V^2 = \frac{3CV^2}{4}$$

26. (a) Potential at B, V_B is maximum
$$V_B > V_C > V_A$$
As in the direction of electric field potential decreases.

27. (a) The equivalent circuit diagram as shown in the figure.

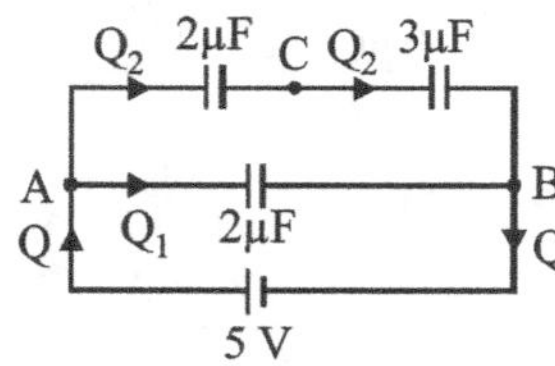

The equivalent capacitance between A and B is

$$C_{eq} = \frac{2\mu F \times 3\mu F}{2\mu F + 3\mu F} + 2\mu F = \frac{16}{5}\mu F$$

Total charge of the given circuit is

$$Q = \frac{16}{5}\mu F \times 5V = 16\mu C$$

$$Q_1 = (2\mu F) \times 5V = 10\mu C$$
$$\therefore \quad Q_2 = Q - Q_1 = 16\,\mu C - 10\,\mu C = 6\,\mu C$$
$$\therefore \quad \text{Voltage between B and C is}$$

$$V_{BC} = \frac{Q_2}{3\mu F} = \frac{6\mu C}{3\mu F} = 2V$$

28. (d) Electric field

$$E = \frac{\sigma}{\varepsilon} = \frac{Q}{A\varepsilon}$$

ε of kerosine oil is more than that of air.
As ε increases, E decreases.

29. (c) When a battery across the plates of capacitor is disconnected and dielectric slab is placed in between the plates, then
(i)   capacity C increases
(ii) charge q remains unchanged
(iii) potential V decreases
(iv) energy E decreases

30. (b) Electric lines of force are always perpendicular to an equipotential surface.

31. (c) All the charge given to inner sphere will pass on to the outer one. So capacitance that of outer one is $4\pi \in_0 b$.

32. (a) In Ist case when capacitor C attached with battery charged with the energy.

U_1 = U (stored energy on capacitor).

In IInd case after disconnect of battery similar capacitor is attached in parallel with Ist capacitor then

$C_{eq} = C' = 2C$.

$$\text{Now, } \frac{U_1}{U_2} = \frac{\frac{1}{2}\frac{q^2}{C}}{\frac{1}{2}\frac{q^2}{C'}} = \frac{C'}{C} = \frac{2C}{C} \quad (\because C' = 2C)$$

$$U_2 = \frac{U}{2}$$

33. (a) Here we have to findout the shape of equipotential surface, these surface are perpendicular to the field lines, so there must be electric field which can not be without charge.

So, the collection of charges, whose total sum is not zero, with regard to great distance can be considered as a point charge. The equipotentials due to point charge are spherical in shape as electric potential due to point charge q is given by

$$V = K_e \frac{q}{r}$$

This suggest that electric potentials due to point charge is same for all equidistant points. The locus of these equidistant points which are at same potential, form spherical surface.

The lines of field from point charge are radial. So the equipotential surface perpendicular to field lines from a sphere.

34. (c) Equipotential surfaces are normal to the electric field lines. The following figure shows the equipotential surfaces along with electric field lines for a system of two positive charges.

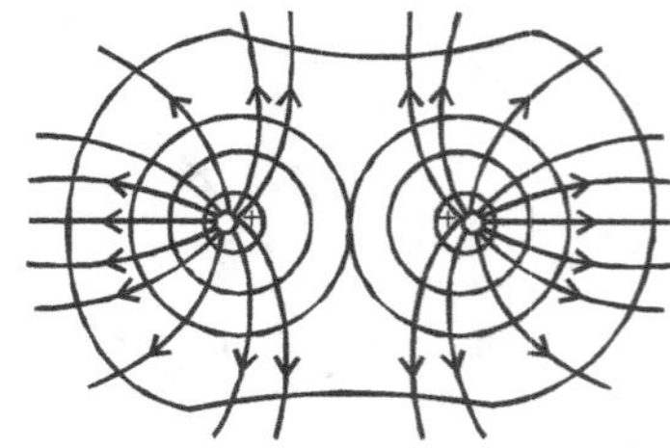

35. (c) Let plate A plate B be carrying charges Q_1 and Q_2 respectively. When they are brought closer, they induce equal and opposite charges on each other i.e. $-Q_2$ on plate A and $-Q_1$ on plate B. Therefore, net charge on plate A $= Q_1 - Q_2$ and net charge on plate B $= -(Q_1 - Q_2)$, so the charge on the capacitor $= Q_1 - Q_2$.

$\therefore$ Potential different between the plates

$$V = \frac{Q_1 - Q_2}{C}$$

36. **(d)** $C = \dfrac{\in_0 A}{d}$

A $\rightarrow$ common area, Here $A = A_1$

37. **(a)** The equivalent circuit is shown in figure.

$C_{AB} = 3\mu F$.

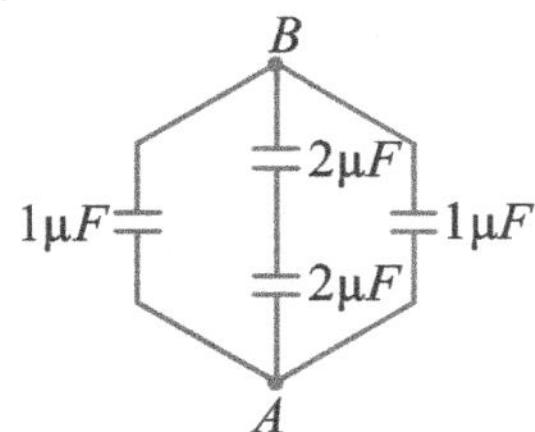

38. **(c)** If we increase the distance between the plates its capacity decreases resulting in higher potential as we know $Q = CV$. Since Q is constant (battery has been disconnected), on decreasing C, V will increase.

39. **(a)** $V = V_1 + V_2 + V_3 = \dfrac{1}{4\pi \in_0} \cdot \dfrac{Q}{R} + \dfrac{1}{4\pi \in_0}\left(\dfrac{-2Q}{R}\right)$

$\qquad + \dfrac{1}{4\pi \in_0}\left(\dfrac{3Q}{R}\right) = \dfrac{1}{4\pi \in_0}\left(\dfrac{2Q}{R}\right)$

40. **(a)** As we know, $E = -\dfrac{dV}{dx}$

Potential at the point $x = 2$m, $y = 2$m is given by :

$$\int_0^V dV = -\int_0^{2,2} (25dx + 30dy)$$

on solving we get,

$V = -110$ volt.

41. **(d)** On the equipotential surface, electric field is normal to the charged surface (where potential exists) so that no work will be done.

42. **(b)**

43. **(b)** Potential at the centre of the triangle,

$$V = \frac{\Sigma q}{4\pi\varepsilon_0 r} = \frac{2q - q - q}{4\pi\varepsilon_0 r} = 0$$

Obviously, $E \neq 0$

44. **(a)** Whenever a charge ($+50$ nC) is kept inside a hollow metallic spherical shell, it induces an equal and opposite charge on the inner surface and an equal and same type of charges on the outer surface.

$\therefore$ Inside, induced charge is -50 nC and outside, $+50$ nC -150 nC already present.

45. **(b)** In parallel, potential is same, say V

$$\frac{Q_1}{Q_2} = \frac{C_1 V}{C_2 V} = \frac{C_1}{C_2}$$

1. **(b)** $V = IR = (neAv_d)\rho\dfrac{\ell}{A}$

$\therefore \quad \rho = \dfrac{V}{V_d \, \text{lne}}$

Here V = potential difference

l = length of wire

n = no. of electrons per unit volume of conductor.

e = no. of electrons

Placing the value of above parameters we get resistivity

$\rho = \dfrac{5}{8\times10^{28}\times1.6\times10^{-19}\times2.5\times10^{-4}\times0.1}$

$= 1.6\times10^{-5}\,\Omega\text{m}$

2. **(d)** From the curve it is clear that slopes at points A, B, C, D have following order $A > B > C > D$.

And also resistance at any point equals to slope of the V-i curve.

So order of resistance at three points will be

$R_A > R_B > R_C > R_D$

3. **(d)** From the principle of potentiometer, $V \propto l$

$\Rightarrow \dfrac{V}{E} = \dfrac{l}{L}$; where

V = emf of battery, E = emf of standard cell.

L = length of potentiometer wire

$V = \dfrac{El}{L} = \dfrac{30E}{100}$

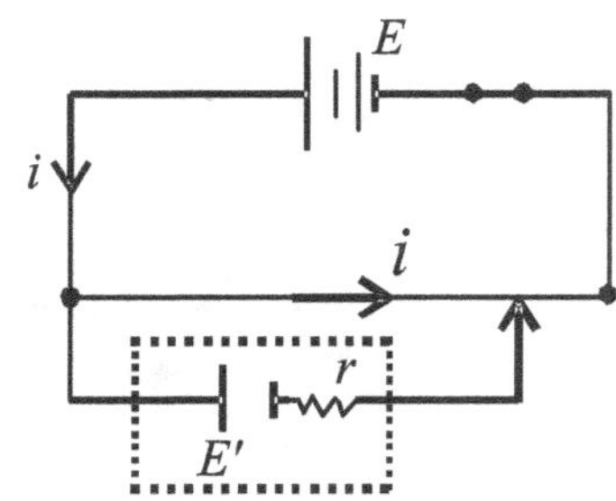

NOTE In this arrangement, the internal resistance of the battery E does not play any role as current is not passing through the battery.

4. **(d)** $R = \dfrac{\rho l}{\pi r^2}$. But $m = \pi r^2 \, ld \; \therefore \; \pi r^2 = \dfrac{m}{ld}$

$\therefore R = \dfrac{\rho l^2 d}{m}, \; R_1 = \dfrac{\rho l_1^{\,2} d}{m_1}, \; R_2 = \dfrac{\rho l_2^{\,2} d}{m_2}$

$R_3 = \dfrac{\rho l_3^{\,2} d}{m_3}$

$R_1 : R_2 : R_3 = \dfrac{l_1^{\,2}}{m_1} : \dfrac{l_2^{\,2}}{m_2} : \dfrac{l_3^{\,2}}{m_3}$

$R_1 : R_2 : R_3 = \dfrac{25}{1} : \dfrac{9}{3} : \dfrac{1}{5} = 125 : 15 : 1$

5. **(c)** In series, $R_s = nR$

In parallel, $\dfrac{1}{R_p} = \dfrac{1}{R} + \dfrac{1}{R} + \dots n \text{ terms}$

$\therefore R_s/R_p = n^2/1 = n^2$

6. **(a)** Efficiency is given by $\eta = \dfrac{\text{output}}{\text{input}}$

$= \dfrac{5\times15\times14}{10\times8\times15} = 0.875 \text{ or } 87.5\,\%$

7. **(b)** According to the condition of balancing

$\dfrac{55}{20} = \dfrac{R}{80} \Rightarrow R = 220\,\Omega$

8. **(a)** $J = \sigma E \Rightarrow J\rho = E$

J is current density, E is electric field

so $B = \rho$ = resistivity.

9. **(d)** Kirchhoff's first law is based on conservation of charge and Kirchhoff's second law is based on conservation of energy.

10. **(c)** $R = \dfrac{\rho\ell}{A}$

When wire is cut into 4 pieces and connected in parallel.

$R_{\text{eff.}} = \dfrac{R}{16} \Rightarrow P_C = 16P$

$P_A : P_B : P_C : P_D = \dfrac{V^2}{R} : \dfrac{V^2}{R/4} : \dfrac{V^2}{R/16} : \dfrac{V^2}{R/2}$

11. **(b)** $S = \dfrac{I_g R}{nI_g - I_g} \Rightarrow S = \dfrac{I_g}{(n-1)I_g} R$

12. **(d)** Resistance of a conductor, $R = \dfrac{m}{ne^2\tau} \dfrac{l}{A}$

As the temperature increases, the relaxation time τ decreases because the number of collisions of electrons per second increases due to increase in thermal energy of electrons.

13. **(b)**

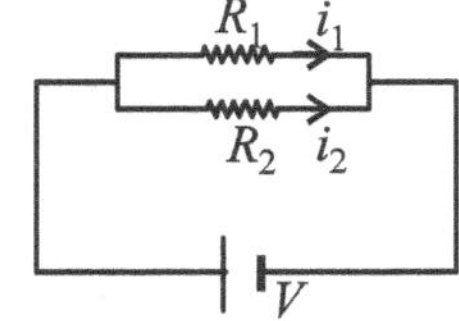

$$R_1 = \frac{\rho \ell_1}{\pi r_1^2} \; ; \; R_2 = \frac{\rho \ell_2}{\pi r_2^2}$$

$i_1 R_1 = i_2 R_2$ (same potential difference)

$$\therefore \; \frac{i_1}{i_2} = \frac{R_2}{R_1} = \frac{\ell_2}{\ell_1} \times \frac{r_1^2}{r_2^2} = \frac{3}{4} \times \frac{4}{9} = \frac{1}{3}$$

14. **(c)** $\dfrac{R_1}{R_2} = \dfrac{\ell_1}{\ell_2}$ where $\ell_2 = 100 - \ell_1$

In the first case $\dfrac{X}{Y} = \dfrac{20}{80}$

In the second case

$$\frac{4X}{Y} = \frac{\ell}{100 - \ell} \Rightarrow \ell = 50$$

15. **(c)** Before connecting E, the circuit diagram is

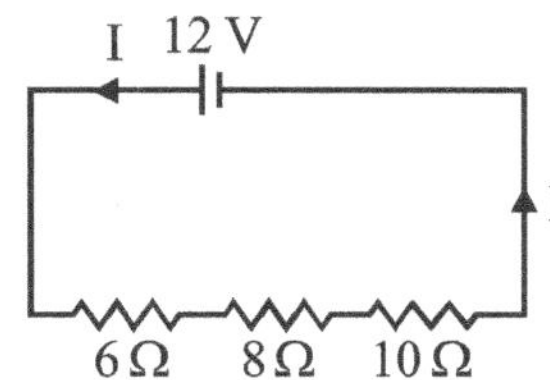

Then, $R_{eq} = 6\,\Omega + 8\,\Omega + 10\,\Omega = 24\,\Omega$

Current in the $8\,\Omega$ resistance, $I = \dfrac{12V}{24\Omega} = \dfrac{1}{2}A$

After connecting E, the current through $8\,\Omega$ is

$$I = \frac{1}{2}A$$

$$\therefore \quad E = \frac{1}{2}A \times 8\Omega = 4V$$

16. **(d)** By junction rule at point B

$-I + 1A + 2A = 0$

So, $I = 3A$

By Loop rule,

$-3 \times 2 - 1 \times 1 - E + 12 = 0$

$E = 5V$

17. **(d)** Resistance of bulb $R_b = \dfrac{(1.5)^2}{4.5} = 0.5\,\Omega$

Current drawn from battery $= \dfrac{E}{2.67 + 0.33} = \dfrac{E}{3}$

Share of bulb $= \dfrac{2}{3} \times \dfrac{E}{3} = \dfrac{2E}{9}$

$$\therefore \; \left(\frac{2E}{9}\right)^2 \times 0.5 = 4.5 \; \text{ or } E = 13.5\,V.$$

18. **(d)** The equivalent circuit is given below :

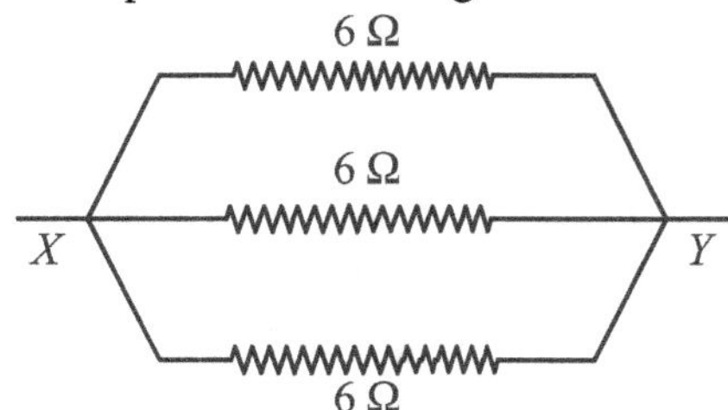

The equivalent resistance is given by

$$\frac{1}{R} = \frac{1}{6} + \frac{1}{6} + \frac{1}{6} = \frac{3}{6} = \frac{1}{2}$$

$$\Rightarrow R_{eq} = 2\Omega$$

19. **(a)** Since average drift velocity $= \dfrac{1}{2}\dfrac{eE}{m} \times (\tau)$

Now $I = NeA \times$ (avg. drift velocity)

$$= \frac{Ne^2 AE}{2m\ell} \times \tau = \frac{Ne^2 AV}{2m\ell} \times \tau$$

$$R = \frac{V}{I} = \frac{2m\ell}{Ne^2 \tau A}, \text{ where N is electron density.}$$

20. **(c)** The current through the resistance R

$$I = \left(\frac{\varepsilon}{R + r}\right)$$

The potential difference across R

$$V = IR = \left(\frac{\varepsilon}{R + r}\right) R$$

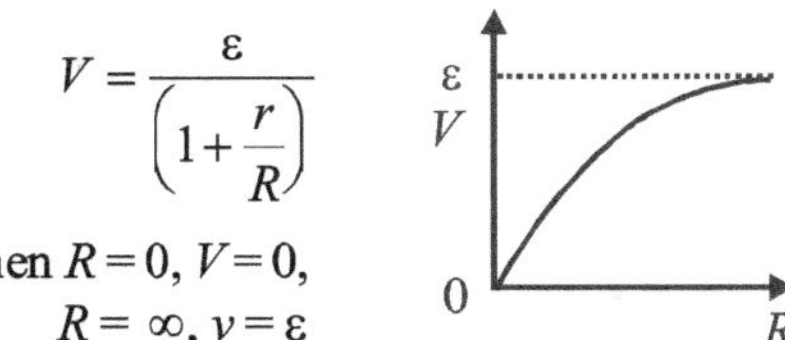

$$V = \frac{\varepsilon}{\left(1 + \dfrac{r}{R}\right)}$$

when $R = 0$, $V = 0$,

$R = \infty$, $v = \varepsilon$

Thus V increases as R increases upto certain limit, but it does not increase further.

21. **(c)** Resistance of bulb is constant

$$P = \frac{V^2}{R} \Rightarrow \frac{\Delta p}{p} = \frac{2\Delta V}{V} + \frac{\Delta R}{R}$$

$$\frac{\Delta p}{p} = 2 \times 2.5 + 0 = 5\%$$

22. **(a)** Potential gradient = Potential fall per unit length. In this case resistance of unit length.

$$R = \frac{\rho l}{A} = \frac{10^{-7} \times 1}{10^{-6}} = 10^{-1}\,\Omega$$

Potential fall across R is

$$V = I.R = 0.1 \times 10^{-1} = 0.01 \text{ volt/m.}$$

$$= 10^{-2} \text{ volt / m}$$

23. **(d)** $R_1 + R_2 = $ Constant, R_1 will increase, R_2 will decrease.

$R_1 \alpha \Delta T - R \beta \Delta T = 0 \Rightarrow R_1 \alpha \Delta T = R_2 \beta \Delta T$

$$\therefore \; \frac{R_1}{R_2} = \frac{\beta}{\alpha}$$

24. (d) Given : Number of cells, $n = 5$, emf of each cell $= E$
Internal resistance of each cell $= r$
In series, current through resistance R

$$I = \frac{nE}{nr + R} = \frac{5E}{5r + R}$$

In parallel, current through resistance R

$$I' = \frac{E}{\dfrac{r}{n} + R} = \frac{nE}{r + nR} = \frac{5E}{r + 5R}$$

According to question, $I = I'$

$$\therefore \ \frac{5E}{5r + 5R} = \frac{5E}{r + 5R} \Rightarrow 5r + R = r + 5R$$

or $R = r$ $\therefore \ \dfrac{R}{r} = 1$

25. (d) The total volume remains the same before and after stretching.

Therefore $A \times \ell = A' \times \ell'$

Here $\ell' = 2\ell$

$$\therefore \ A' = \frac{A \times \ell}{\ell'} = \frac{A \times \ell}{2\ell} = \frac{A}{2}$$

Percentage change in resistance

$$= \frac{R_f - R_i}{R_i} \times 100 = \frac{\rho\left(\dfrac{\ell'}{A'} - \dfrac{\ell}{A}\right)}{\rho\dfrac{\ell}{A}} \times 100$$

$$= \left[\left(\frac{\ell'}{A'} \times \frac{A}{\ell}\right) - 1\right] \times 100 = \left[\left(\frac{2\ell}{A/2} \times \frac{A}{\ell}\right) - 1\right] \times 100$$

$$= 300\%$$

26. (a) Pot. gradient $= 0.2\text{mV/cm}$

$$= \frac{0.2 \times 10^{-3}}{10^{-2}} = 2 \times 10^{-2} \text{V/m}$$

Emf of cell $= 2 \times 10^{-2} \times 1\text{m} = 2 \times 10^{-2} \text{V} = 0.02 \text{ V}$
As per the condition of potentiometer
$0.02 (R + 490) = 2 (R)$ or $1.98 R = 9.8$

$$\Rightarrow \quad R = \frac{9.8}{1.98} = 4.9 \ \Omega$$

27. (d) 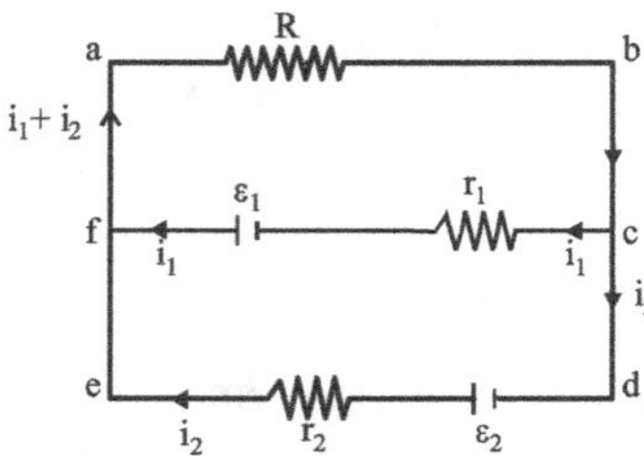

Applying Kirchhoff's rule in loop **abcfa**
$\varepsilon_1 - (i_1 + i_2) R - i_1 r_1 = 0$.

28. (c) Total power consumed by electrical appliances in the building, $P_{total} = 2500\text{W}$

Watt $=$ Volt $\times$ ampere

$\Rightarrow \quad 2500 = V \times I \Rightarrow 2500 = 220 \, I$

$\Rightarrow \quad I = \dfrac{2500}{220} = 11.36 \approx 12\text{A}$

(Minimum capacity of main fuse)

29. (a) 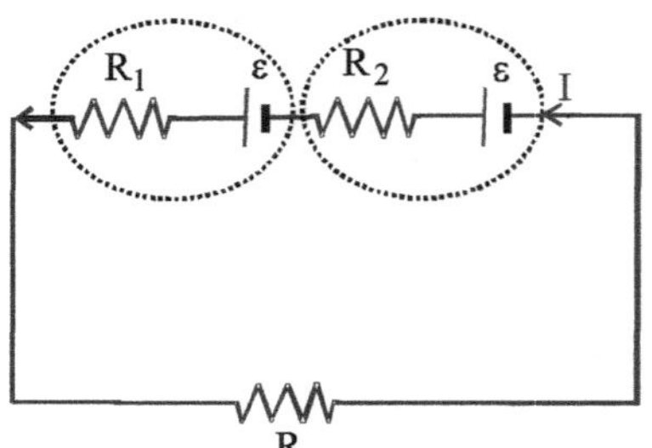

$$I = \frac{2\varepsilon}{R + R_1 + R_2}$$

Potential difference across second cell

$$= V = \varepsilon - iR_2 = 0$$

$$\varepsilon - \frac{2\varepsilon}{R + R_1 + R_2}.R_2 = 0$$

$$R + R_1 + R_2 - 2R_2 = 0$$

$$R + R_1 - R_2 = 0$$

$$\therefore \ R = R_2 - R_1$$

30. (c)

Resistance of the series combination,
$S = R_1 + R_2$
Resistance of the parallel combination,

$$P = \frac{R_1 R_2}{R_1 + R_2}$$

$$S = nP \Rightarrow R_1 + R_2 = \frac{n(R_1 R_2)}{(R_1 + R_2)}$$

$$\Rightarrow (R_1 + R_2)^2 = nR_1 R_2$$

Minimum value of n is 4 for that

$$(R_1 + R_2)^2 = 4R_1 R_2 \Rightarrow (R_1 - R_2)^2 = 0$$

31. (c) To convert a galvanometer into a voltmeter we connect a high resistance in series with the galvanometer. The same procedure needs to be done if ammeter is to be used as a voltmeter.

32. (c) Given, emf of cell $E = 200$ V
Internal resistance of cells $= 1 \ \Omega$
D. C. main supply voltage $V = 220$ V
External resistance $R = ?$

$$r = \left(\frac{E - V}{V}\right) R$$

$$1 = \left(\frac{20}{220}\right) \times R$$

$$\therefore \quad R = 11 \ \Omega.$$

33. **(a)** In steady state, flow fo current through capacitor will be zero.
Current through the circuit,

$$i = \dfrac{E}{r + r_2}$$

Potential difference through capacitor

$$V_c = \dfrac{Q}{C} = E - ir = E - \left(\dfrac{E}{r + r_2}\right)r$$

$$\therefore \quad Q = CE\,\dfrac{r_2}{r + r_2}$$

34. **(c)** $i = neAV_d$ and $V_d \propto \sqrt{E}$ (Given)

or, $i \propto \sqrt{E}$
$i^2 \propto E$
$i^2 \propto V$

Hence graph (c) correctly dipicts the V-I graph for a wire made of such type of material.

35. **(b)** Current, $I = (2.9 \times 10^{18} + 1.2 \times 10^{18}) \times 1.6 \times 10^{-19}$
$= 0.66A$ towards right.

36. **(a)** Copper rod and iron rod are joined in series.

$$\therefore R = R_{Cu} + R_{Fe} = (\rho_1 + \rho_2)\,\dfrac{\ell}{A}$$

$$\left(\because R = \rho\,\dfrac{\ell}{A}\right)$$

From ohm's law $V = RI$
$= (1.7 \times 10^{-6} \times 10^{-2} + 10^{-5} \times 10^{-2}) \div$
$$0.01 \times 10^{-4}\ \text{volt}$$
$= 0.117\ \text{volt}\,(\because I = 1A)$

37. **(d)** $I = \dfrac{E}{R + r}$, Internal resistance (r) is

zero, $I = \dfrac{E}{R} = $ constant.

38. **(b)** $R_t = R_0 (1 + \alpha t)$
Initially, $R_0 (1 + 30\alpha) = 10\,\Omega$
Finally, $R_0 (1 + \alpha t) = 11\,\Omega$

$$\therefore \dfrac{11}{10} = \dfrac{1 + \alpha t}{1 + 30\alpha}$$

or, $10 + (10 \times 0.002 \times t) = 11 + 330 \times 0.002$

or, $0.02t = 1 + 0.66 = 1.066$ or $t = \dfrac{1.66}{0.02} = 83°C.$

39. **(b)** As $P = I^2 R$, so $P_1 = (1.01\,I)^2 R = 1.02 I^2 R = 1.02\,P$.
It means % increase in power

$$= \left(\dfrac{P_1}{P} - 1\right) \times 100 = 2\%.$$

40. **(b)** Let I_1 be the current throug $5\,\Omega$ resistance, I_2 through $(6 + 9)\,\Omega$ resistance. Then as per question,

$I_1^2 \times 5 = 20$ or, $I_1 = 2A.$
Potential difference across C and D $= 2 \times 5 = 10V$

Current $I_2 = \dfrac{10}{6 + 9} = \dfrac{2}{3}A.$

Heat produced per second in $2\,\Omega$

$$= I^2 R \left(\dfrac{8}{3}\right)^2 \times 2 = 14.2\,\text{cal/s.}$$

41. **(b)** $\dfrac{P}{Q} = \dfrac{R}{S}$ where $S = \dfrac{S_1 S_2}{S_1 + S_2}$

42. **(c)** $R = \dfrac{\rho \ell_1}{A_1}$, now $\ell_2 = 2\ell_1$

$A_2 = \pi(r_2)^2 = \pi (2r_1)^2 = 4\pi r_1^2 = 4A_1$

$$\therefore \quad R_2 = \dfrac{\rho(2\ell_1)}{4A_1} = \dfrac{\rho \ell_1}{2A_1} = \dfrac{R}{2}$$

$\therefore$ Resistance is halved, but specific resistance remains the same.

43. **(d)** $E = V + Ir$
$V = 12 - 3 = 9\ \text{volt}$

44. **(c)** $I = neAV_d$

$$V_d = \dfrac{I}{neA} = 5 \times 10^{-3}\ \text{m/sec}$$

45. **(d)** Since due to wrong connection of each cell the total emf reduced to 2ε then for wrong connection of three cells the total emf will reduced to $(n\varepsilon - 6\varepsilon)$ whereas the total or equivalent resistance of cell combination will be *nr.*

1. **(a)** At a distance x consider small element of width dx.
Magnetic moment of the small element is

$$dm = \frac{\left(\frac{q}{\ell}dx\right)\omega}{2\pi}.\pi x^2$$

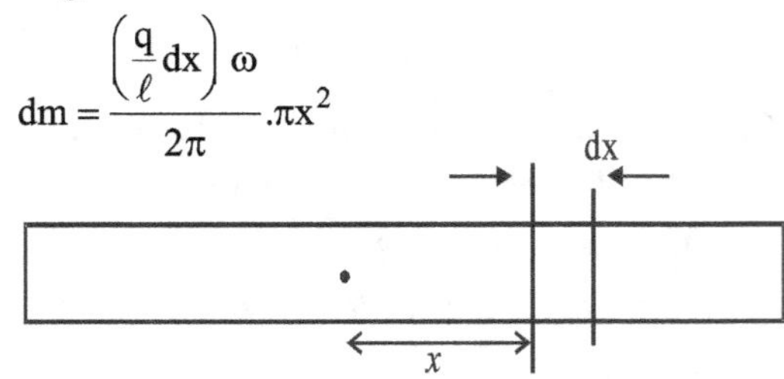

$$M = \int_{-\ell/2}^{\ell/2} \frac{q\omega}{2\ell}x^2 dx \ ; \ M = \frac{q\omega\ell^2}{24} = \frac{q\pi f\ell^2}{12}$$

2. **(d)** The straight part will not contribute magnetic field at the centre of the semicircle because every element of the straight part will be $0°$ or $180°$ with the line joining the centre and the element

Due to circular portion, the field is $\frac{1}{2}\frac{\mu_0 i}{2r} = \frac{\mu_0 i}{4r}$

Hence total field at $O = \frac{\mu_0 i}{4r}$ tesla

3. **(d)** Torque on the solenoid is given by
$\tau = MB\sin\theta$
where θ is the angle between the magnetic field and the axis of solenoid.
$M = niA$
$\therefore \ \tau = niA\,B\sin 30°$

$$= 2000 \times 2 \times 1.5 \times 10^{-4} \times 5 \times 10^{-2} \times \frac{1}{2}$$

$$= 1.5 \times 10^{-2} N - m$$

4. **(c)** Time period of cyclotron is

$$T = \frac{1}{\upsilon} = \frac{2\pi m}{eB} \ ; \ B = \frac{2\pi m}{e}\upsilon; \ R = \frac{m\upsilon}{eB} = \frac{p}{eB}$$

$$\Rightarrow \quad p = eBR = e \times \frac{2\pi m\upsilon}{e}R = 2\pi m\upsilon R$$

$$\text{K.E.} = \frac{p^2}{2m} = \frac{(2\pi m\upsilon R)^2}{2m} = 2\pi^2 m\upsilon^2 R^2$$

5. **(a)** $R_g = 50\Omega, I_g = 25 \times 4 \times 10^{-A}\Omega = 10^{-2} A$
Range of $V = 25$ volts
$V = I_g(R_e + R_g)$

$$\therefore R_e = \frac{V}{I_g} - R_g = 2450\Omega$$

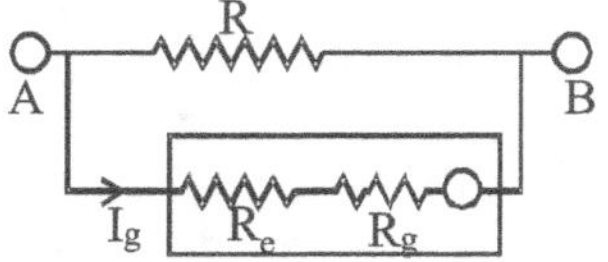

6. **(c)** $B_{axis} = \left(\frac{\mu_0 NI}{2x^3}\right)R^2$

$B \propto R^2$
So, when radius is doubled, magnetic field becomes four times.

7. **(c)** When a charged particle enters a transverse magnetic field it traverse a circular path. Its kinetic energy remains constant.

8. **(c)** K.E. of electron $= 10\,eV$

$$\Rightarrow \frac{1}{2}mv^2 = 10\,eV$$

$$\Rightarrow \frac{1}{2}(9.1 \times 10^{-31})v^2 = 10 \times 1.6 \times 10^{-19}$$

$$\Rightarrow v^2 = \frac{2 \times 10 \times 1.6 \times 10^{-19}}{9.1 \times 10^{-31}}$$

$$\Rightarrow v^2 = 3.52 \times 10^{12} \Rightarrow v = 1.88 \times 10^6\,m$$

Also we know that for circular motion

$$\frac{mv^2}{r} = Bev \Rightarrow r = \frac{mv}{Be} = 11\,cm$$

9. **(d)** No magnetic force acts on the electron and force due to electric field will act opposite to its initial direction of motion. Hence its velocity decreases in magnitude.

10. **(b)** $\frac{mv^2}{r} = qvB \Rightarrow r = \frac{mv}{qB}$

$$\Rightarrow r_p = \frac{m_p v_p}{q_p B} \ ;$$

$$r_d = \frac{m_d v_d}{q_d B} \ ; \quad r_\alpha = \frac{m_\alpha v_\alpha}{q_\alpha B}$$

$$m_\alpha = 4m_p, \ m_d = 2m_p$$

$$q_\alpha = 2q_p, \ q_d = q_p$$

From the problem

$$E_p = E_d = E_\alpha = \frac{1}{2}m_p v_p^2$$

$$= \frac{1}{2}m_d v_d^2 = \frac{1}{2}m_\alpha v_\alpha^2$$

$$\Rightarrow v_p^2 = 2v_d^2 = 4mv_2^2$$

Thus we have, $r_\alpha = r_p < r_d$

11. **(c)** Resistance of Galvanometer,

$$G = \frac{\text{Current sensitivity}}{\text{Voltage sensitivity}} \Rightarrow G = \frac{10}{2} = 5\Omega$$

Here i_g = Full scale deflection current

$$= \frac{150}{10} = 15\,\text{mA}$$

V = voltage to be measured = 150 volts
(such that each division reads 1 volt)

$$\Rightarrow \ R = \frac{150}{15\times10^{-3}} - 5 = 9995\,\Omega$$

12. (d) Magnetic field at the centre of the current loop is

$$B = \frac{\mu_0\,2\pi I}{4\pi R}$$

or, $B = \dfrac{\mu_0\,2\pi q\upsilon}{4\pi R}, \quad R = \dfrac{\mu_0\,2\pi q\upsilon}{4\pi B}$

Substituting the given values, we get

$$R = \frac{4\pi\times10^{-7}\times2\pi\times2\times10^{-6}\times6.25\times10^{12}}{4\pi\times6.28} = 1.25\,\text{m}$$

13. (b) Here, $\vec{E}$ and $\vec{B}$ are perpendicular to each other and the velocity $\vec{v}$ does not change; therefore

$qE = qvB \ \Rightarrow \ v = \dfrac{E}{B}$

Also,

$$\left|\frac{\vec{E}\times\vec{B}}{B^2}\right| = \frac{E\,B\sin\theta}{B^2} = \frac{E\,B\sin90^\circ}{B^2} = \frac{E}{B} = |\vec{v}| = v$$

14. (b) The force on the two arms parallel to the field is zero.

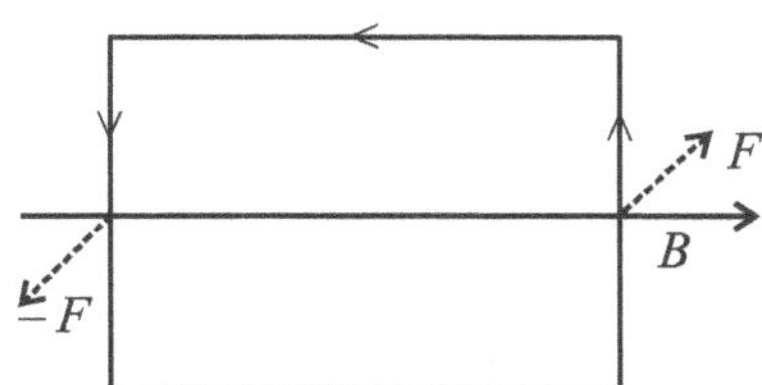

15. (d) Magnetic field at a point on the axis of a current carrying wire is always zero.

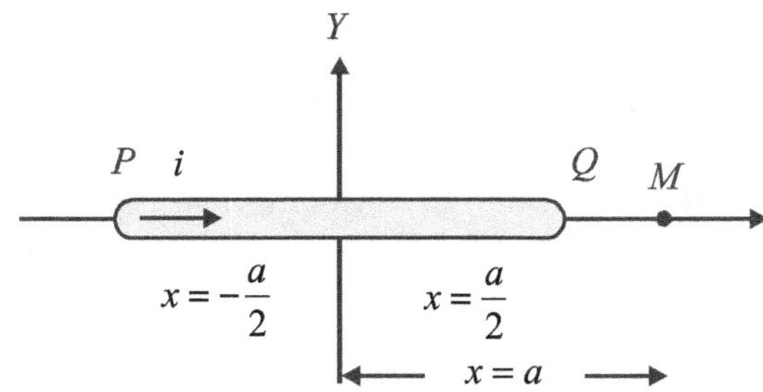

16. (b) Current carrying conductors will attract each other, while electron beams will repel each other.

17. (c) To keep the main current in the circuit unchanged, the resistance of the galvanometer should be equal to the net resistance.

$$\therefore G = \left(\frac{GS}{G+S}\right) + S'$$

$$\Rightarrow G - \frac{GS}{G+S} = S'$$

$$\therefore S' = \frac{G^2}{G+S}.$$

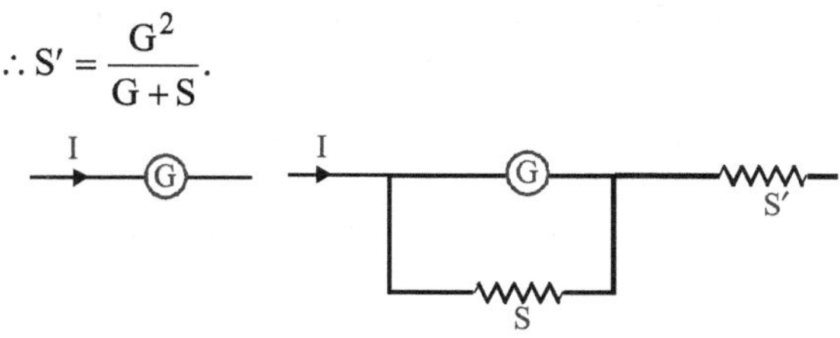

18. (d) Current in a small element, $dI = \dfrac{d\theta}{\pi}I$

Magnetic field due to the element

$$dB = \frac{\mu_0}{4\pi}\frac{2dI}{R}$$

The component $dB\cos\theta$, of the field is cancelled by another opposite component.
Therefore,

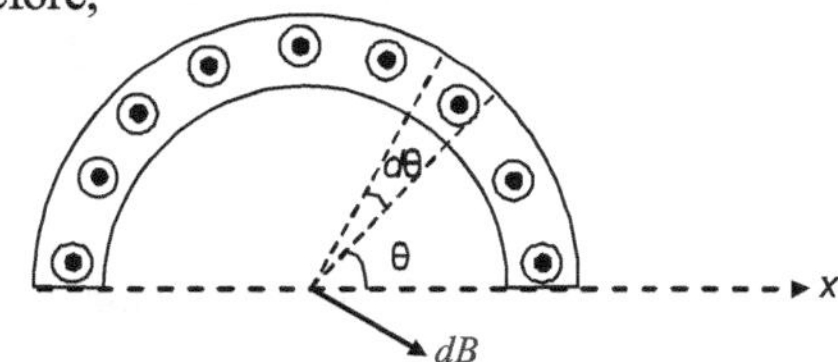

$$B_{net} = \int dB\sin\theta = \frac{\mu_0 I}{2\pi^2 R}\int_0^\pi \sin\theta\,d\theta = \frac{\mu_0 I}{\pi^2 R}$$

19. (a)

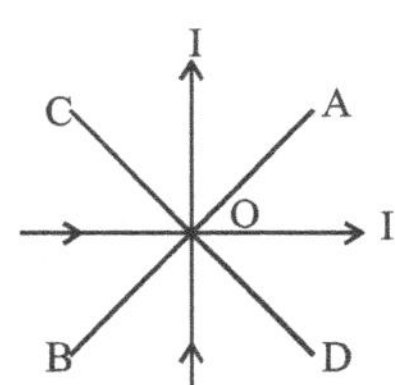

Net magnetic field on AB is zero because magnetic field due to both current carrying wires is equal in magnitude but opposite in direction.

20. (b) According to the figure the magnitude of force on the segment QM is $F_3 - F_1$ and PM is F_2.

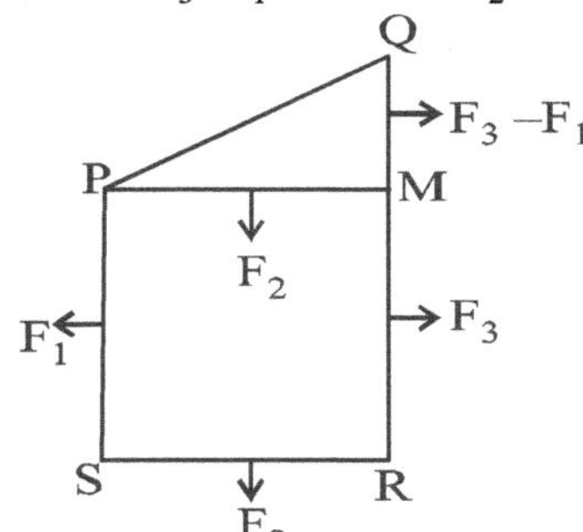

Therefore, the magnitude of the force on

segment PQ is $\sqrt{\left(F_3 - F_1\right)^2 + F_2^2}$

21. (c) $B = \mu_0 ni$

$$B_1 = (\mu_0)\left(\frac{n}{2}\right)(2\,i) = \mu_0 ni = B$$

$$\Rightarrow B_1 = B$$

22. **(c)** The angular momentum L of the particle is given by
$L = mr^2\omega$ where $\omega = 2\pi n$.

$\therefore$ Frequency $n = \dfrac{\omega}{2\pi}$; Further $i = q \times n = \dfrac{\omega q}{2\pi}$

Magnetic moment, $M = iA = \dfrac{\omega q}{2\pi} \times \pi r^2$;

$\therefore M = \dfrac{\omega q r^2}{2}$ So, $\dfrac{M}{L} = \dfrac{\omega q r^2}{2mr^2\omega} = \dfrac{q}{2m}$

23. **(c)** A current loop in a magnetic field is in equilibrium in two orientations one is stable and another unstable.

$\because \quad \vec{\tau} = \vec{M} \times \vec{B} = M\,B \sin\theta$
If $\theta = 0° \Rightarrow \tau = 0$ (stable)
If $\theta = \pi \Rightarrow \tau = 0$ (unstable)

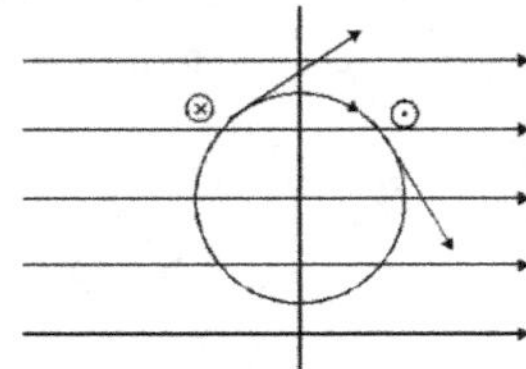

Do not experience a torque in some orientations
Hence option (c) is correct.

24. **(c)** $B = \dfrac{\mu_0}{4\pi} \dfrac{2i_2}{(r/2)} - \dfrac{\mu_0}{4\pi} \dfrac{2i_1}{(r/2)} = \dfrac{\mu_0}{4\pi} \dfrac{4}{r}(i_2 - i_1)$

$= \dfrac{\mu_0}{4\pi} \dfrac{4}{5}(5 - 2.5) = \dfrac{\mu_0}{2\pi}$.

25. **(a)** The direction of $\vec{B}$ is along $(-\hat{k})$
$\therefore$ The magnetic force

$\vec{F} = Q(\vec{v} \times \vec{B}) = Q(v\hat{i}) \times B(-\hat{k}) = QvB\hat{j}$

$\Rightarrow \vec{F}$ is along OY.

26. **(a)** According to Ampere's circuit law

$\oint \vec{B}.d\vec{l} = \mu_0 I_{enclosed} = \mu_0(2A - 1A) = \mu_0$

27. **(a)** We know that the magnetic field produced by a current carrying circular coil of radius r at its centre is

$B = \dfrac{\mu_0}{4\pi} \dfrac{I}{r} \times 2\pi$

Here $B_A = \dfrac{\mu_0}{4\pi} \dfrac{I}{R} \times 2\pi$

and $B_B = \dfrac{\mu_0}{4\pi} \dfrac{2I}{2R} \times 2\pi$

$\Rightarrow \dfrac{B_A}{B_B} = 1$

28. **(b)** When a charged particle enters a magnetic field at a direction perpendicular to the direction of motion, the path of the motion is circular. In circular motion the direction of velocity changes at every point (the magnitude remains constant).
Therefore, the tangential momentum will change at every point. But kinetic energy will remain constant as

it is given by $\dfrac{1}{2}mv^2$ and v^2 is the square of the magnitude of velocity which does not change.

29. **(a)** $I = 50$ k; $I_g = 20$k, where k is the figure of merit of galvanometer; $S = I_g R_g(I - I_g)$; so $12 = \dfrac{20\text{k}.R_g}{(50\text{k} - 20\text{k})}$

On solving we get $R_g = 18\,\Omega$.

30. **(d)** Let I be current and l be the length of the wire.

For Ist case : $B = \dfrac{\mu_0 In}{2r} = \dfrac{\mu_0 I \times \pi}{l}$ where $2\pi r = l$

and $n = 1$

For IInd case : $l = n(2\pi r') \Rightarrow r' = \dfrac{l}{2n\pi}$

$B' = \dfrac{\mu_0 nI}{2r'} = \dfrac{\mu_0 nI}{2\dfrac{l}{2n\pi}} = \dfrac{n^2\mu_0\pi I}{l} = n^2 B$

31. **(c)** $B = \dfrac{\mu_0 i\, a^2}{2(x^2 + a^2)^{3/2}}$

$B' = \dfrac{\mu_0 i}{2a} = \dfrac{\mu_0 i\, a^2}{2a(x^2 + a^2)^{3/2}}\left(\dfrac{(x^2 + a^2)^{3/2}}{a^2}\right)$

$B' = \dfrac{B.(x^2 + a^2)^{3/2}}{a^3}$

Put $x = 4$ & $a = 3 \Rightarrow B' = \dfrac{54(5^3)}{3 \times 3 \times 3} = 250\mu T$

32. **(a)** The force acting on a charged particle in magnetic field is given by

$F = q(\vec{v} \times \vec{B})$ or $F = qvB \sin\theta$

when angle between v and B is 180°,
$F = 0$

33. **(b)** The force acting on electron will be perpendicular to the direction of velocity till the electron remains in the magnetic field. So the electron will follow the path as given.

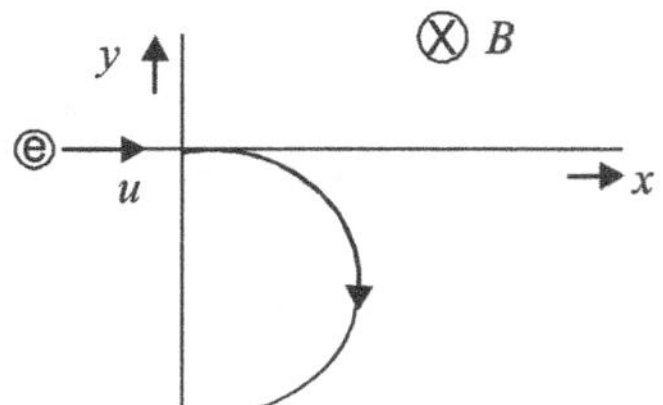

34. **(c)** A voltmeter is a high resistance galvanometer and is connected in parallel to circuit and ammeter is a low resistance galvanometer so if we connect high resistance in series with ammeter its resistance will be much high.

35. **(d)** Here, the wire does not produce any magnetic field at O because the conductor lies on the line of O. Also, the loop does not produce magnetic field at O.

36. **(d)** Magnetic field between the plates in this case is zero.

37. **(d)** For a given perimeter the area of circle is maximum. So magnetic moment of (S) is greatest.

38. **(a)** Lorentz force, $\vec{F} = q\{\vec{E} + (\vec{v} \times \vec{B})\}$

$$\vec{v} \times \vec{B} = \begin{vmatrix} \hat{i} & \hat{j} & \hat{k} \\ 1 & 2 & 0 \\ 5 & 3 & 4 \end{vmatrix} = 8\hat{i} - 4\hat{j} - 7\hat{k}$$

$$\vec{F} = 1(2\hat{i} - 3\hat{j} + 8\hat{i} - 4\hat{j} - 7\hat{k}) = (10\hat{i} - 7\hat{j} - 7\hat{k})$$

39. **(b)** Here, $R_g = 100\,\Omega$; $I_g = 10^{-5}\,A$; $I = 1A$; $S = ?$

$$S = \frac{I_g R_g}{I - I_g} = \frac{10^{-5} \times 100}{1 - 10^{-5}} = 10^{-3}\,\Omega \text{ in parallel}$$

40. **(d)**

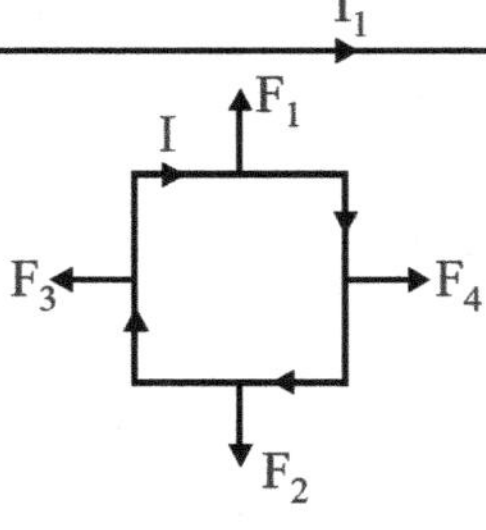

$F_1 > F_2$ as $F \propto \dfrac{1}{d}$, and F_3 and F_4 are equal and opposite.

Hence, the net attraction force will be towards the conductor.

41. **(c)** $\vec{F}_1 = \vec{F}_2 = 0$

because of action and reaction pair

42. **(c)** As electron move with constant velocity without deflection. Hence, force due to magnetic field is equal and opposite to force due to electric field.

$$qvB = qE \Rightarrow v = \frac{E}{B} = \frac{20}{0.5} = 40 \text{ m/s}$$

43. **(c)**

44. **(b)** To measure AC voltage across a resistance a moving coil galvanometer is used.

45. **(c)** As $\vec{F} = q\vec{V}\vec{B}\sin\theta$

F is zero for sin 0° or sin 180° and is non-zero for angle between $\vec{V}$ and $\vec{B}$ any value other than zero and 180°.

1. (b) As the axes are perpendicular, mid point lies on axial line of one magnet and on equatorial line of other magnet.

$$\therefore\ B_1 = \frac{\mu_0}{4\pi}\frac{2M}{d^3} = \frac{10^{-7}\times 2\times 1}{1^3} = 2\times 10^{-7}$$

and $B_2 = \dfrac{\mu_0}{4\pi}\dfrac{M}{d^3} = 10^{-7}$

$\therefore$ Resultant field $= \sqrt{B_1^2 + B_2^2} = \sqrt{5}\times 10^{-7}\,T$

2. (c) Initial magnetic moment of each magnet $= m\times \ell$.
As is clear from Fig., S_1 and N_2 neutralize each other.
Effective distance between

N_1 and $S_2 = \sqrt{\ell^2 + \ell^2} = \ell\sqrt{2}$

$\therefore\ M' = m\ell\sqrt{2}\cdot$

3. (d) As shown in the figure, the magnetic lines of force are directed from south to north inside a bar magnet.

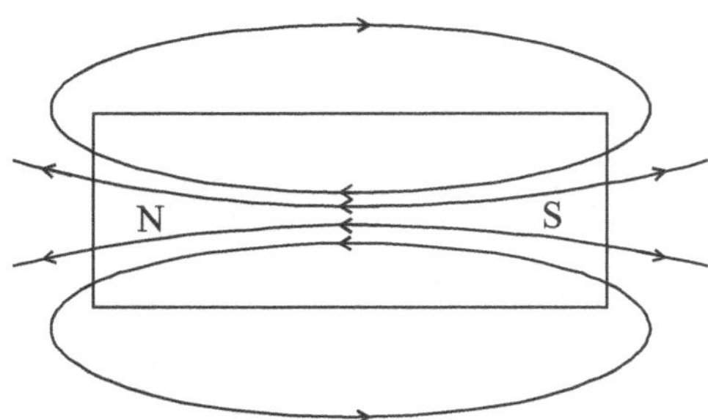

4. (b) For a diamagnetic material, the value of μ_r is less than one. For any material, the value of ϵ_r is always greater than 1.

5. (a) The time period of oscillation of a freely suspended magnet is given by

$$T = 2\pi\sqrt{\frac{I}{MH}}$$

Thus, $\dfrac{T}{T'} = \dfrac{2\pi\sqrt{\dfrac{I}{MH}}}{2\pi\sqrt{\dfrac{I}{MH'}}}$

Given, $T = 4\,\text{sec},\ T' = 2\,\text{sec}$,

So, $\dfrac{4}{2} = \sqrt{\dfrac{H'}{H}}$

or $\sqrt{\dfrac{H'}{H}} = 2$

or $H' = 4H$

6. (b) Diamagnetic materials are repelled in an external magnetic field.
Bar B represents diamagnetic materials.

7. (a) The temperature above which a ferromagnetic substance becomes paramagnetic is called Curie's temperature.

8. (a) Iron is ferromagnetic.

9. (b) $\tau = MB\sin\theta$
$\tau = iAB\sin 90°$

$\therefore\ A = \dfrac{\tau}{iB}$

Also, $A = 1/2\,(BC)\,(AD)$

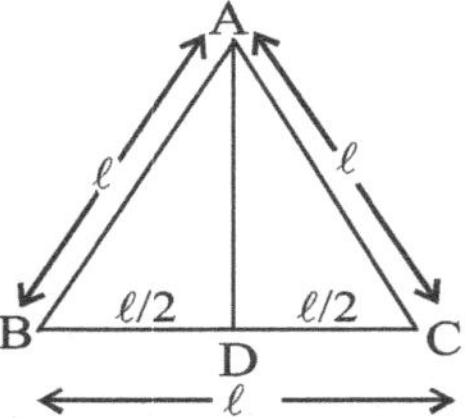

But $\dfrac{1}{2}(BC)(AD) = \dfrac{1}{2}(l)\sqrt{l^2 - \left(\dfrac{l}{2}\right)^2} = \dfrac{\sqrt{3}}{4}l^2$

$\Rightarrow\quad \dfrac{\sqrt{3}}{4}(l)^2 = \dfrac{\tau}{Bi}$

$\therefore\quad l = 2\left(\dfrac{\tau}{\sqrt{3}\ Bi}\right)^{\frac{1}{2}}$

10. (a) $M = 60\,\text{Am}^2$
$\bar{\tau} = 1.2\times 10^{-3}\,\text{Nm},\ B_H = 40\times 10^{-6}\,\text{Wb/m}^2$
$\vec{\tau} = \vec{M}\times \vec{B}_H \Rightarrow \tau = MB_H\sin\theta$
$\Rightarrow 1.2\times 10^{-3} = 60\times 40\times 10^{-6}\sin\theta$

$\Rightarrow\ \sin\theta = \dfrac{1.2\times 10^{-3}}{60\times 40\times 10^{-6}} = \dfrac{1}{2} = \sin 30°$

$\Rightarrow\ \theta = 30°$

11. (b) Electro magnet should be amenable to magnetisation and demagnetization.
$\therefore$ retentivity and coercivity should be low.

12. (b) $T = 2\pi\sqrt{\dfrac{I}{M\times B}} = 2\pi\sqrt{\dfrac{I}{MB}}$ where $I = \dfrac{1}{12}m\ell^2$

When the magnet is cut into three pieces the pole strength will remain the same and

M.I. $(I') = \dfrac{1}{12}\left(\dfrac{m}{3}\right)\left(\dfrac{\ell}{3}\right)^2 \times 3 = \dfrac{I}{9}$

We have, Magnetic moment (M)
$=$ Pole strength $(m)\times \ell$
$\therefore$ New magnetic moment,

$$M' = m\times\left(\dfrac{\ell}{3}\right)\times 3 = m\ell = M$$

$\therefore\ T' = \dfrac{T}{\sqrt{9}} = \dfrac{2}{3}s\,.$

13. (b) Graph [A] is for material used for making permanent magnets (high coercivity)
Graph [B] is for making electromagnets and transformers.

14. **(a)** The earth's core is hot and molten. Hence, convective current in earth's core is responsible for it's magnetic field.

15. **(b)** $T \propto \dfrac{1}{\sqrt{H}} \Rightarrow \dfrac{T_1}{T_2} = \sqrt{\dfrac{H_2}{H_1}} \Rightarrow \dfrac{2}{1} = \sqrt{\dfrac{H+F}{H}}$

$\Rightarrow F = 3H$ or $\dfrac{H}{F} = \dfrac{1}{3}$

16. **(a)** $H = B\cos\theta$, $V = B\sin\theta$
Here B = earth's magnetic field
θ = angle of dip = 90° at north pole
$\Rightarrow H = B\cos 90° = 0$
$V = B\sin 90° = B$
$\Rightarrow V \gg H$

17. **(d)** Initially for circular coil $L = 2\pi r$ and $M = i \times \pi r^2$

$= i \times \pi \left(\dfrac{L}{2\pi}\right)^2 = \dfrac{iL^2}{4\pi}$ ...(i)

Finally for square coil side $a = \dfrac{L}{4}$ and

$M' = i \times \left(\dfrac{L}{4}\right)^2 = \dfrac{iL^2}{16}$ ...(ii)

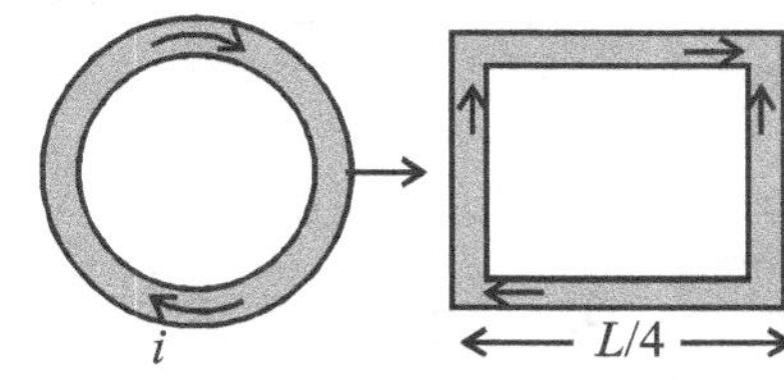

Solving equation (i) and (ii) $M' = \dfrac{\pi M}{4}$

18. **(b)** $FL = MB \ (= \text{Torque}) \Rightarrow L = \dfrac{MB}{F}$

19. **(a)** $\chi_d < \chi_p < \chi_f$
For diamagnetic substance χ_d is small and negative (10^{-5})
For paramagnetic substances χ_p is small and positive $(10^{-3}$ to $10^{-5})$
For ferromagnetic substanes χ_f is very large $(10^3$ to $10^5)$

20. **(b)** $B = \mu_0\mu_r H \Rightarrow \mu_r \propto \dfrac{B}{H} = $ slope of B-H curve

According to the given graph, slope of the graph is highest at point Q.

21. **(d)** On increasing the temperature by 700°C, the magnetic needle is demagnetised. Therefore, the needle stops vibrating.

22. **(b)** $\tau = MB\sin\theta$ $(\theta = 90°)$

$\tau = MB \Rightarrow \dfrac{B_1}{B_2} = \dfrac{\tau_1}{\tau_2}$ (since magnetic moment is same)

23. **(a)** Magnetic field due to a bar magnet in the broad-side on position is given by

$B = \dfrac{\mu_0}{4\pi} \dfrac{M}{\left[r^2 + \dfrac{\ell^2}{4}\right]^{3/2}} \; ; M = m\ell.$

After substituting the values and simplifying we get
$B = 6 \times 1^{-5}$ A-m

24. **(c)** Initially magnetic moment of system
$M_1 = \sqrt{M^2 + M^2} = \sqrt{2}M$ and moment of inertia
$I_1 = I + I = 2I.$
Finally when one of the magnet is removed then
$M_2 = M$ and $I_2 = I$

So, $T = 2\pi\sqrt{\dfrac{I}{M B_H}}$

$\dfrac{T_1}{T_2} = \sqrt{\dfrac{I_1}{I_2} \times \dfrac{M_2}{M_1}} = \sqrt{\dfrac{2I}{I} \times \dfrac{M}{\sqrt{2}M}}$

$\Rightarrow T_2 = \dfrac{2^{5/4}}{2^{1/4}} = 2\sec$

25. **(d)** A magnetic needle kept in non uniform magnetic field experience a force and torque due to unequal forces acting on poles.

26. **(d)** $\tan\delta = \dfrac{V}{H} = \dfrac{3}{4} \quad \left[\because \tan 37° = \dfrac{3}{4}\right]$

$\therefore \; V = \dfrac{3}{4}H$
$V = 6 \times 10^{-5}$ T

$H = \dfrac{4}{3} \times 6 \times 10^{-5}$ T $= 8 \times 10^{-5}$ T

$\therefore \; B_{total} = \sqrt{V^2 + H^2} = \sqrt{(36 + 64)} \times 10^{-5}$
$= 10 \times 10^{-5} = 10^{-4}$T.

27. **(b)** Ferromagnetic substance has magnetic domains whereas paramagnetic substances have magnetic dipoles which get attracted to a magnetic field.
Diamagnetic substances do not have magnetic dipole but in the presence of external magnetic field due to their orbital motion of electrons these substances are repelled.

28. **(d)** PQ_6 corresponds to the lowest potential energy among all the configurations shown.

29. **(a)** $\tan\theta = \dfrac{V}{H}, \tan\theta' = \dfrac{V}{H\cos x} \; ; \; \dfrac{\tan\theta'}{\tan\theta} = \dfrac{1}{\cos x}$

30. **(d)** In series, same current flows through two tangent galvanometers.

31. **(c)** Net magnetic dipole moment $= 2\,M\cos\dfrac{\theta}{2}$
As value of $\cos\dfrac{\theta}{2}$ is maximum in case (c) hence net magnetic dipole moment is maximum for option (c).

32. **(b)** Since magnetic field is in vertical direction and needle is free to totate in horizontal plane only so magnetic force cannot rotate the needle in horizontal plane so needle can stay in any position.

33. **(b)** Work done in rotating the magnetic dipole from position $\theta_1 = 0°$ to $\theta_2 = 180°$

$$\because W = MB (\cos\theta_1 - \cos\theta_2)$$
$$\therefore W = MB (\cos\theta° - \cos 180°) = 2MB$$

34. **(b)** The time period of a bar magnet in a magnetic field is given by.

$$T = 2\pi\sqrt{\frac{I}{MB}} \; ;$$

Here, I = moment of inertia $\propto m$, M = moment of magnet, B = magnetic field.

$T \propto \sqrt{I} \propto \sqrt{m}$; so, T becomes twice as mass becomes four times

35. **(a)** Given, $B = 4 \times 10^{-5}$ T
$R_E = 6.4 \times 10^6$ m
Dipole moment of the earth $M = ?$

$$B = \frac{\mu_0}{4\pi}\frac{M}{d^3}$$

$$4\times10^{-5} = \frac{4\pi\times10^{-7}\times M}{4\pi\times\left(6.4\times10^6\right)^3}$$

$$\therefore \quad M \cong 10^{23}\,\text{Am}^2$$

36. **(b)** From $\mu_r = 1 + \chi_m$;

Magnetic suscaptibility, $\chi_m = \mu_r - 1$

$\chi_m = 0.075 - 1 = -0.925$.

37. **(d)** $\delta_1 = 40°$, $\delta_2 = 30°$, $\delta = ?$

$$\cot\delta = \sqrt{\cot^2\delta_1 + \cot^2\delta_2} = \sqrt{\cot^2 40° + \cot^2 30°}$$

$$\cot\delta = \sqrt{1.19^2 + 3} = 2.1$$

$$\therefore \quad \delta = 25° \text{ i.e. } \delta < 40°.$$

38. **(d)** In magnetic dipole

Force $\propto \dfrac{1}{r^4}$

In the given question,
Force $\propto x^{-n}$
Hence, n = 4

39. **(b)** According to Curie's law, $\chi_m = \dfrac{\mu_0 C}{T}$

where C is Curie constant, T = temperature

$$\therefore \chi_m \alpha \frac{1}{T}$$

$$\frac{\chi_{m_1}}{\chi_{m_2}} = \frac{T_2}{T_1} = \frac{273+333}{273+30} = \frac{606}{303} = 2$$

$$\therefore \chi_{m_2} = \chi_{m_1}/2 = 0.5\chi_{m_1} = 0.5\chi\left(\because \chi_{m_1} = \chi\right)$$

40. **(a)** We know that
$$\mu_r = 1 + x$$
$$= 1 + 5500 = 5501$$
$$\therefore \quad \mu = \mu_r\mu_0 = (5501)\times(4\pi\times10^{-7})$$
$$= 6.9 \times 10^{-3}$$

41. **(a)** We know that
$$T_1 = 2\pi\sqrt{\frac{T}{MB_{H_1}}} \qquad \text{...(i)}$$

Where $B_{H_1} = 24\times10^{-6}$ T
The magnetic field produced by, wire

$$B = \frac{\mu_0}{2\pi}\cdot\frac{i}{r}$$
$$= (2\times10^{-7})\times\frac{(18)}{0.20}$$
$$= 1.8\times10^{-6}\text{ T}$$

Now $\quad B_{H_2} = B_{H_1} + B = 42 \times 10^{-6}$ T

$$T_2 = 2\pi\sqrt{\frac{I}{MBH_2}} \qquad \text{...(ii)}$$

Using equations (i) and (ii), and substituting the values, we get

$$T_2 = 0.076\,\text{s}$$

42. **(a)** As $BI = \mu_0 MI_M = \mu_0(I + I_M)$
Here, $I = 0$
Then $\mu_0 MI = \mu_0(I_M)$
$\Rightarrow I_M = MI = 10^5$ A

43. **(a)** Given $M = 8 \times 10^{22}$ Am^2
$d = R_e = 6.4 \times 10^6$ m

Earth's magnetic field, $B = \dfrac{\mu_0}{4\pi}\cdot\dfrac{2M}{d^3}$

$$= \frac{4\pi\times10^{-7}}{4\pi}\times\frac{2\times8\times10^{22}}{(6.4\times10^6)^3}$$

$$\cong 0.6 \text{ Gauss}$$

44. **(c)** Magnetic field in solenoid $B = \mu_0 n i$

$$\Rightarrow \frac{B}{\mu_0} = ni$$

(Where n = number of turns per unit length)

$$\Rightarrow \frac{B}{\mu_0} = \frac{Ni}{L}$$

$$\Rightarrow 3\times10^3 = \frac{100i}{10\times10^{-2}}$$

$$\Rightarrow i = 3\text{A}$$

45. **(a)** As length of each part also becomes half, therefore magnetic moment M = pole strength × length

$$\Rightarrow \frac{1}{2} \times \frac{1}{2} = \frac{1}{4}\text{th i.e. M/4.}$$

1. **(b)** Induced emf produced between the centre and a point on the disc is given by

$$e = \frac{1}{2}\omega BR^2$$

Putting the values,

$\omega = 60\,\text{rad/s},\ B = 0.05\,\text{Wb/m}^2$
and $R = 100\,\text{cm} = 1\,\text{m}$

We get $e = \frac{1}{2} \times 60 \times 0.05 \times (1)^2 = 1.5V$

2. **(a)** According to Faraday's law of electromagnetic induction, $\varepsilon = \dfrac{d\phi}{dt}$

Also, $\varepsilon = iR$

$\therefore iR = \dfrac{d\phi}{dt} \Rightarrow \int d\phi = R\int i\,dt$

Magnitude of change in flux $(d\phi) = R \times$ area under current vs time graph

or, $d\phi = 100 \times \dfrac{1}{2} \times \dfrac{1}{2} \times 10 = 250\,\text{Wb}$

3. **(a)** If a wire, ℓ meter in length, moves perpendicular to a magnetic field of B weber/meter^2 with a velocity of v meter/second, then the e.m.f. induced in the wire is given by
$V = B\,v\ell$ volt.
Here, $B = 0.30 \times 10^{-4}$ weber/meter^2,
$v = 5.0$ meter/second and $\ell = 10$ meter.
$\therefore\ B = 0.30 \times 10^{-4} \times 5.0 \times 10 = 0.0015$ volt.

4. **(d)** The magnetic field is increasing in the downward direction. Therefore, according to Lenz's law, the current I_1 will flow in the direction ab and I_2 in the direction dc.

5. **(a)** Self inductance of a solenoid,

$$L = \frac{\mu_0 N^2 A}{l} = \frac{\mu_0 N^2 \pi r^2}{l}$$

$\therefore\ \dfrac{L_1}{L_2} = \left(\dfrac{r_1}{r_2}\right)^2 \left(\dfrac{l_2}{l_1}\right) \qquad [\because\ N_1 = N_2]$

Here, $\dfrac{l_1}{l_2} = \dfrac{1}{2},\ \dfrac{r_1}{r_2} = \dfrac{1}{2}$

$\therefore\ \dfrac{L_1}{L_2} = \left(\dfrac{1}{2}\right)^2 \left(\dfrac{2}{1}\right) = \dfrac{1}{2}$

6. **(b)** $\ell = 1\text{m},\ \omega = 5\,\text{rad/s},\ B = 0.2 \times 10^{-4}T$

$$\varepsilon = \frac{B\omega\ell}{2} = \frac{0.2 \times 10^{-4} \times 5 \times 1}{2} = 50\mu V$$

7. **(c)**

8. **(c)** Emf induced in side 1 of frame $e_1 = B_1 V\ell$

$$B_1 = \frac{\mu_0 I}{2\pi\,(x - a/2)}$$

Emf induced in side 2 of frame $e_2 = B_2\,V\ell$

$$B_2 = \frac{\mu_0 I}{2\pi\,(x + a/2)}$$

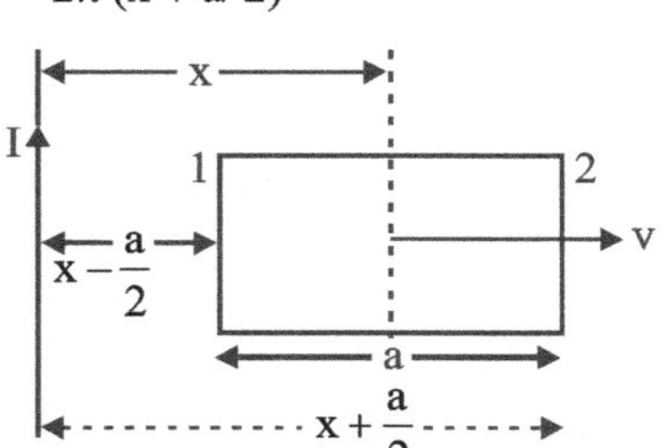

Emf induced in square frame
$e = B_1 V\ell - B_2 V\ell$

$$= \frac{\mu_0 I}{2\pi\,(x - a/2)}\,\ell v - \frac{\mu_0 I}{2\pi\,(x + a/2)}\,\ell v$$

or, $e \propto \dfrac{1}{(2x - a)(2x + a)}$

9. **(a)** When a north pole of a bar magnet moves towards the coil, the induced current in the coil flows in a direction such that the coil presents its north pole to the bar magnet as shown in figure (a). Therefore, the induced current flows in the coil in the anticlockwise direction. When a north pole of a bar magnet moves away from the coil, the induced current in the coil flows in a direction such that the coil presents its south pole to the bar magnet as shown in figure (b).

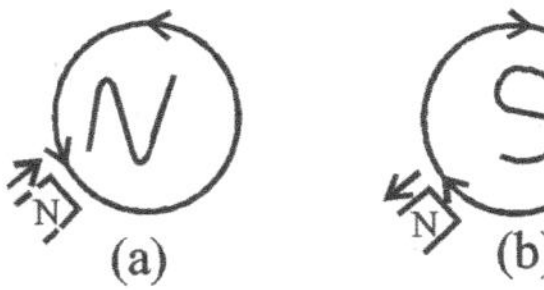

Therefore induced current flows in the coil in the clockwise direction.

10. **(d)** Given : $\phi = 4t^2 + 2t + 1$ wb

$\therefore\ \dfrac{d\phi}{dt} = \dfrac{d}{dt}(4t^2 + 2t + 1) = 8t + 2 = |\varepsilon|$

Induced current, $I = \dfrac{|\varepsilon|}{R} = \dfrac{8t + 2}{10\Omega} = \dfrac{8t + 2}{10}A$

At $t = 1$ s,

$$I = \frac{8 \times 1 + 2}{10}A = 1A$$

11. **(d)** $M = \dfrac{\mu_0 N_1 N_2 A}{\ell}$

$$= \frac{4\pi \times 10^{-7} \times 300 \times 400 \times 100 \times 10^{-4}}{0.2}$$

$$M = \frac{\mu_0 N_1 N_2 A}{\ell}$$
$$= 2.4\pi \times 10^{-4}\,H$$

12. **(d)** $\quad e = -\dfrac{\Delta\phi}{\Delta t} = \dfrac{-\Delta(LI)}{\Delta t} = -L\dfrac{\Delta I}{\Delta t}$

$$\therefore \; |e| = L\frac{\Delta I}{\Delta t} \Rightarrow 8 = L \times \frac{4}{0.05}$$

$$\Rightarrow L = \frac{8 \times 0.05}{4} = 0.1H$$

13. **(c)** Total number of turns in the solenoid, N = 500
Current, I = 2A.
Magnetic flux linked with each turn
$= 4 \times 10^{-3}$ Wb

As, $\phi = LI$ or $N\phi = LI \Rightarrow L = \dfrac{N\phi}{1}$

$$= \frac{500 \times 4 \times 10^{-3}}{2} \; \text{henry} = 1\,H.$$

14. **(d)** Electric field will be induced, as ABCD moves, in both
AD and *BC*. The metallic square loop moves in its own
plane with velocity *v*. A uniform magnetic field is
imposed perpendicular to the plane of the square loop.
AD and *BC* are perpendicular to the velocity as well as
perpendicular to applied field so an emf is induced in
both, this will cause electric fields in both.

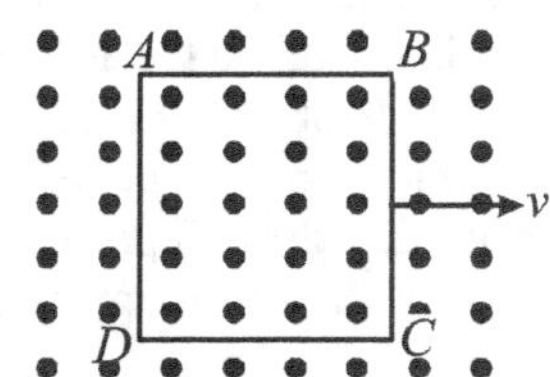

15. **(d)** E.M.F. generated, $\;e = -\dfrac{d\phi}{dt} = -\dfrac{d(N\vec{B}.\vec{A})}{dt}$

$$= -N\frac{d}{dt}(BA\cos\omega t) = NBA\omega\sin\omega t$$

$$\Rightarrow e_{max} = NBA\omega$$

16. **(c)** $L = 2mH, \; i = t^2 e^{-t}$

$$E = -L\frac{di}{dt} = -L[-t^2 e^{-t} + 2te^{-t}]$$

when $E = 0$,
$-e^{-t}t^2 + 2te^{-t} = 0$
or, $2t\,e^{-t} = e^{-t}t^2$
$\Rightarrow t = 2$ sec.

17. **(b)**

18. **(b)** $\dfrac{d\phi}{dt} = \dfrac{(W_2 - W_1)}{t}$ $\quad R_{tot} = (R + 4R)\Omega = 5R\;\Omega$

$$i = \frac{nd\varphi}{R_{tot}dt} = \frac{-n(W_2 - W_1)}{5Rt}.$$

($\because W_2$ & W_1 are magnetic flux)

19. **(b)** The individual emf produced in the coil $e = \dfrac{-d\phi}{dt}$

$$\therefore \text{ The current induced will be } i = \frac{|e|}{R} \Rightarrow i = \frac{1}{R}\frac{d\phi}{dt}$$

$$\text{But } i = \frac{dq}{dt} \Rightarrow \frac{dq}{dt} = \frac{1}{R}\frac{d\phi}{dt} \Rightarrow \int dq = \frac{1}{R}\int d\phi \Rightarrow q = \frac{BA}{R}$$

20. **(c)** Induced emf $= vB_H l = 1.5 \times 5 \times 10^{-5} \times 2$
$$= 15 \times 10^{-5}$$
$$= 0.15\,mV$$

21. **(b)** $\quad \varepsilon = \dfrac{d\phi}{dt} = n\,A\dfrac{dB}{dt}$

$$\therefore \; \varepsilon = 10 \times (10 \times 10^{-4})(10^4) \quad [10^8 \text{ Gauss/sec} = 10^4 \text{ T/s}]$$
$$= 100\,V.$$
$$I = (\varepsilon/R) = (100/20) = 5\,amp.$$

22. **(a)**

$$\text{W} \;\longrightarrow\bullet\longrightarrow\; \text{E}$$

$$\varepsilon_{ind} = Bv\ell$$

$$= 0.3 \times 10^{-4} \times 5 \times 20$$
$$= 3 \times 10^{-3}\,V = 3\,mV.$$

23. **(d)** The self inductance of a long solenoid is given by
$$L = \mu_r \mu_0 n^2 A l$$
Self inductance of a long solenoid is independent of
the current flowing through it.

24. **(d)** Here, induced e.m.f.

$$e = \int_{2\ell}^{3\ell} (\omega x)B dx$$

$$= B\omega\frac{[(3\ell)^2 - (2\ell)^2]}{2} = \frac{5B\ell^2\omega}{2}$$

25. **(b)**

26. **(b)** Induced e.m.f. in the ring opposes the motion of the
magnet.

27. **(a)**

28. **(b)**

29. **(d)** Magnetic flux, $\phi_B = BA\cos\theta$
Induced emf, $\varepsilon = BA\sin\theta$
Here, $\theta = 0^\circ$
$\therefore$ Magnetic flux is maximum and induced emf is zero.

30. **(c)** e.m.f. induced $= \dfrac{1}{2}BR^2\omega = \dfrac{1}{2}BR^2(2\pi n)$

$$= \frac{1}{2} \times (0.1) \times (0.1)^2 \times 2\pi \times 10 = (0.1)^2\,\pi \text{ volts}$$

31. **(a)** $\quad E = \dfrac{d}{dt}(NMI) \Rightarrow E = NM\dfrac{dI}{dt} \Rightarrow E = \dfrac{NMI}{t}$

$$\text{emf induced per unit turn} = \frac{E}{N} = \frac{MI}{t}$$

32. **(d)** According to Lenz's law, when switch is closed, the flux in the loop increases out of plane of paper, so induced current will be clockwise.

33. **(a)** Since $\varepsilon = -\dfrac{Nd\phi}{dt}$ if $\dfrac{d\phi}{dt}$ is fast, so ε is large.

34. **(d)** The e.m.f. is induced when there is change of flux. As in this case there is no change of flux, hence no e.m.f. will be induced in the wire.

35. **(b)** Given, $B = 0.01\ T, A = \pi R^2 = \pi \times (1\ \text{m})^2 = \pi\text{m}^2$
$$\omega = 100\ \text{rads}^{-1}$$
$\therefore$ The maximum induced emf $\varepsilon_{max} = BA\omega$
$$= 0.01 \times \pi \times 100\ \text{V} = \pi\text{V}$$

36. **(b)** $e = \dfrac{-(\phi_2 - \phi_1)}{t} = \dfrac{-(0 - NBA)}{t} = \dfrac{NBA}{t}$

$$t = \dfrac{NBA}{e} = \dfrac{50 \times 2 \times 10^{-2} \times 10^{-2}}{0.1} = 0.1\ \text{s}$$

37. **(c)** $\dfrac{\Delta\phi}{\Delta t} = \varepsilon = iR \Rightarrow \Delta\phi = (i\Delta t)R = QR$

$$\Rightarrow Q = \dfrac{\Delta\phi}{R}$$

38. **(d)** $\phi = BA\cos\theta = 2.0 \times 0.5 \times \cos 60°$

$$= \dfrac{2.0 \times 0.5}{2} = 0.5\ \text{weber.}$$

39. **(a)** $\xi = \dfrac{W}{Q} \Rightarrow V = \dfrac{W}{Q} \Rightarrow W = QV$

40. **(b)** Mutual inductance depends on the relative position and orientation of the two coils.

41. **(c)**

42. **(a)** As the magnetic field increases, its flux also increases into the page and so induced current in bigger loop will be anticlockwise. i.e., from D to C in bigger loop and then from B to A in smaller loop.

43. **(c)** As I increases, ϕ increases
$\therefore$ I_i is such that it opposes the increases in ϕ.
Hence, ϕ decreases (By Right Hand Rule). The induced current will be counterclockwise.

44. **(d)** According to Faraday's law of electromagnetic induction,

Induced emf, $e = \dfrac{Ldi}{dt}$

$$50 = L\left(\dfrac{5-2}{0.1\,\text{sec}}\right)$$

$$\Rightarrow \quad L = \dfrac{50 \times 0.1}{3} = \dfrac{5}{3} = 1.67\ \text{H}$$

45. **(d)** Mutual inductance between two coil in the same plane with their centers coinciding is given by

$$M = \dfrac{\mu_0}{4\pi}\left(\dfrac{2\pi^2 R_2^2 N_1 N_2}{R_1}\right) henry.$$

1. **(c)** Across resistor, $I = \dfrac{V}{R} = \dfrac{100}{1000} = 0.1\ A$

At resonance,

$$X_L = X_C = \dfrac{1}{\omega C} = \dfrac{1}{200 \times 2 \times 10^{-6}} = 2500$$

Voltage across L is

$$I\,X_L = 0.1 \times 2500 = 250\,\text{V}$$

2. **(a)** The phase angle between voltage V and current I is $\pi/2$. Therefore, power factor $\cos\phi = \cos(\pi/2) = 0$. Hence the power consumed is zero.

3. **(c)** The current drawn by inductor and capacitor will be in opposite phase. Hence net current drawn from generator $= I_L - I_C = 0.9 - 0.4 = 0.5$ amp.

4. **(c)** Capacitive reactance, $X = \dfrac{1}{\omega C} = \dfrac{1}{2\pi f C}$

$$\Rightarrow X \propto \dfrac{1}{f\,C}$$

$$\therefore \dfrac{X'}{X} = \dfrac{f}{f'} \times \dfrac{C}{C'} = \dfrac{f}{2f} \times \dfrac{C}{2C} = \dfrac{1}{4} \Rightarrow X' = \dfrac{X}{4}$$

5. **(a)** The charging of inductance given by,

$$i = i_0\left(1 - e^{-\frac{Rt}{L}}\right)$$

$$\dfrac{i_0}{2} = i_0(1 - e^{-\frac{Rt}{L}}) \Rightarrow e^{-\frac{Rt}{L}} = \dfrac{1}{2}$$

Taking log on both the sides,

$$-\dfrac{Rt}{L} = \log 1 - \log 2$$

$$\Rightarrow t = \dfrac{L}{R}\log 2 = \dfrac{300 \times 10^{-3}}{2} \times 0.69$$

$$\Rightarrow t = 0.1 \text{ sec.}$$

6. **(c)** $\tan\phi = \dfrac{\omega L}{R} = \dfrac{X_L}{R}$

Given $\phi = 45°$. Hence $X_L = R$.

7. **(d)**

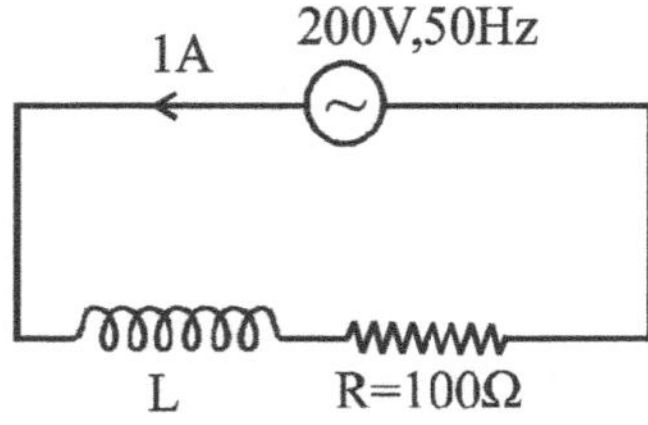

From the rating of the bulb, the resistance of the bulb can be calculated.

$$R = \dfrac{V_{rms}^2}{P} = 100\,\Omega$$

For the bulb to be operated at its rated value the rms current through it should be 1A

Also, $I_{rms} = \dfrac{V_{rms}}{Z}$

$$\therefore \quad 1 = \dfrac{200}{\sqrt{100^2 + (2\pi 50.L)^2}}$$

$$L = \dfrac{\sqrt{3}}{\pi}\,\text{H}$$

8. **(a)** At angular frequency ω, the current in RC circuit is given by

$$i_{max} = \dfrac{V_{max}}{\sqrt{R^2 + \left(\dfrac{1}{\omega C}\right)^2}} \qquad \text{.......(i)}$$

Also $\dfrac{i_{rms}}{2} = \dfrac{V_{rms}}{\sqrt{R^2 + \left(\dfrac{1}{\frac{\omega}{3}C}\right)^2}} = \dfrac{V_{max}}{\sqrt{R^2 + \dfrac{9}{\omega^2 C^2}}} \qquad \text{.....(ii)}$

From equation (i) and (ii) we get

$$3R^2 = \dfrac{5}{\omega^2 C^2} \Rightarrow \dfrac{\frac{1}{\omega C}}{R} = \sqrt{\dfrac{3}{5}} \Rightarrow \dfrac{X_C}{R} = \sqrt{\dfrac{3}{5}}$$

9. **(c)**

10. **(c)** Growth in current in LR_2 branch when switch is closed is given by

$$i = \dfrac{E}{R_2}[1 - e^{-R_2 t/L}]$$

$$\Rightarrow \dfrac{di}{dt} = \dfrac{E}{R_2}.\dfrac{R_2}{L}.e^{-R_2 t/L} = \dfrac{E}{L}e^{-\frac{R_2 t}{L}}$$

Hence, potential drop across L

$$= \left(\dfrac{E}{L}e^{-R_2 t/L}\right)L = Ee^{-R_2 t/L}$$

$$= 12e^{-\frac{2t}{400\times 10^{-3}}} = 12e^{-5t}\text{V}$$

11. **(a)** $I = I_o\left(1 - e^{-\frac{R}{L}t}\right)$

(When current is in growth in LR circuit)

$$= \dfrac{E}{R}\left(1 - e^{-\frac{R}{L}t}\right) = \dfrac{5}{5}\left(1 - e^{-\frac{5}{10}\times 2}\right)$$

$$= (1 - e^{-1})$$

12. **(d)** Power, $P = I_{r.m.s} \times V_{r.m.s} \times \cos\phi$

In the given problem, the phase difference between voltage and current is $\pi/2$. Hence

$$P = I_{r.m.s} \times V_{r.m.s} \times \cos(\pi/2) = 0.$$

13. (c) When the capacitor is completely charged, the total energy in the LC circuit is with the capacitor and that

energy is $E = \dfrac{1}{2}\dfrac{Q^2}{C}$

When half energy is with the capacitor in the form of electric field between the plates of the capacitor we get

$\dfrac{E}{2} = \dfrac{1}{2}\dfrac{Q'^2}{C}$ where Q' is the charge on one plate of the capacitor

$\therefore \dfrac{1}{2} \times \dfrac{1}{2}\dfrac{Q^2}{C} = \dfrac{1}{2}\dfrac{Q'^2}{C} \Rightarrow Q' = \dfrac{Q}{\sqrt{2}}$

14. (a) Energy stored in magnetic field $= \dfrac{1}{2}Li^2$

Energy stored in electric field $= \dfrac{1}{2}\dfrac{q^2}{C}$

$\therefore \dfrac{1}{2}Li^2 = \dfrac{1}{2}\dfrac{q^2}{C}$

Also $q = q_0 \cos \omega t$ and $\omega = \dfrac{1}{\sqrt{LC}}$

On solving $t = \dfrac{\pi}{4}\sqrt{LC}$

15. (c) The circuit will have inductive nature if

$\omega > \dfrac{1}{\sqrt{LC}} \quad \left(\omega L > \dfrac{1}{\sqrt{LC}} \right)$

Hence (a) is false. Also if circuit has inductive nature the current will lag behind voltage. Hence (d) is also false.

If $\omega = \dfrac{1}{\sqrt{LC}} \left(\omega L = \dfrac{1}{\omega C} \right)$ the circuit will have resistance nature. Hence (b) is false.

Power factor

$\cos\phi = \dfrac{R}{\sqrt{R^2 + \left(\omega L - \dfrac{1}{\omega C}\right)^2}} = 1$ if $\omega L = \dfrac{1}{\omega C}$

16. (b) $V_{rms} = \sqrt{\dfrac{(T/2)V_0^2 + 0}{T}} = \dfrac{V_0}{\sqrt{2}}$.

17. (d) Option (d) is false because the reason why the voltage leads the current is because $\dfrac{1}{C\omega} > L\omega$ and if the voltage lags, the inductive reactance is greater than the capacitive reactance.

18. (b) $P = \dfrac{1}{2}V_0 i_0 \cos\phi \Rightarrow P = P_{peak}\cdot\cos\phi$

$\Rightarrow \dfrac{1}{2}(P_{peak}) = P_{peak}\cos\phi \Rightarrow \cos\phi = \dfrac{1}{2} \Rightarrow \phi = \dfrac{\pi}{3}$

19. (c) $\eta = \dfrac{E_s I_s}{E_p I_p} \quad \therefore \eta = \dfrac{110 \times 9}{220 \times 5} = 0.9 \times 100\% = 90\%$

20. (d) $V = \dfrac{V_0}{T/4}t \Rightarrow V = \dfrac{4V_0}{T}t$

$\Rightarrow V_{rms} = \sqrt{<V^2>} = \dfrac{4V_0}{T}\sqrt{<t^2>} = \dfrac{4V_0}{T}\left\{ \dfrac{\displaystyle\int_0^{T/4} t^2 dt}{\displaystyle\int_0^{T/4} dt} \right\}^{1/2} = \dfrac{V_0}{\sqrt{3}}$

21. (a) $L = 10\,mHz = 10^{-2}\,Hz$
$f = 1MHz = 10^6\,Hz$

$f = \dfrac{1}{2\pi\sqrt{LC}}$

$f^2 = \dfrac{1}{4\pi^2 LC}$

$\Rightarrow C = \dfrac{1}{4\pi^2 f^2 L} = \dfrac{1}{4 \times 10 \times 10^{-2} \times 10^{12}} = \dfrac{10^{-12}}{0.4} = 2.5\,pF$

22. (d) Current is maximum when $X_L = X_C$

$\Rightarrow \omega L = \dfrac{1}{\omega C} \Rightarrow \omega = \dfrac{1}{\sqrt{LC}} = \dfrac{1}{\sqrt{0.5 \times 8 \times 10^{-6}}}$

$= \dfrac{1}{2 \times 10^{-3}} = 500\,\text{rad/s}.$

23. (a) If $\omega = 50 \times 2\pi$ then $\omega L = 20\Omega$
If $\omega' = 100 \times 2\pi$ then $\omega'L = 40\Omega$
Current flowing in the coil is

$I = \dfrac{200}{Z} = \dfrac{200}{\sqrt{R^2 + (\omega'L)^2}} = \dfrac{200}{\sqrt{(30)^2 + (40)^2}}$

$I = 4A.$

24. (a) At resonance impedance is minimum $(\because X_L = X_C)$ current is maximum, because V_L and V_C are equal in magnitude
$\therefore V_{LC} = V_L - V_C = 0$
Hence, voltmeter V_2 read 0 volt.

25. (b)

26. (d) As $E_p I_p = P_i \quad \therefore I_p = \dfrac{P_i}{E_p} = \dfrac{4000}{100} = 40\,A.$

27. (c) The phase angle is given by

$\tan\phi = \dfrac{\omega L}{R} = \dfrac{2\pi \times 50 \times 0.21}{12} = 5.5$

$\phi = \tan^{-1} 5.5 = 80°$

28. (c)

29. (a) Since $\dfrac{V_s}{V_p} = \dfrac{N_s}{N_p}$

Where
N_s = No. of turns across primary coil = 50
N_p = No. of turns across secondary coil = 1500

and $V_p = \dfrac{d\phi}{dt} = \dfrac{d}{dt}(\phi_0 + 4t) = 4$

$\Rightarrow V_s = \dfrac{1500}{50} \times 4 = 120\,V$

30. (a) $\dfrac{E_s}{E_p} = \dfrac{n_s}{n_p}$ or $E_s = E_p \times \left(\dfrac{n_s}{n_p}\right)$

$\therefore E_s = 120 \times \left(\dfrac{200}{100}\right) = 240\,V$

$\dfrac{I_p}{I_s} = \dfrac{n_s}{n_p}$ or $I_s = I_p\left(\dfrac{n_p}{n_s}\right)$ $\therefore I_s = 10\left(\dfrac{100}{200}\right) = 5\,amp$

31. (b) $R \uparrow \Rightarrow I \downarrow \Rightarrow \dfrac{dI}{dt} \to (-ve) \to e = (+ve)$

$\left[As\ e = -L\dfrac{dI}{dt}\right]$

Supporting $\to I_{net} \uparrow$

32. (b) We know that, $i = i_0(1 - e^{-t/\tau})$

or $\dfrac{3}{4}i_0 = i_0(1 - e^{-4/\tau})$

or $e^{-4/\tau} = \dfrac{1}{4}$

or $e^{4/\tau} = 4$

$\therefore \dfrac{4}{\tau} = \ln 4$

or $\tau = \dfrac{2}{\ln 2}s$

33. (d) At resonance, $\omega L = \dfrac{1}{\omega C}$. The circuit behaves as if it contains R only. So, phase difference $= 0$
At resonance, impedance is minimum $Z_{min} = R$ and current is maximum, given by

$$I_{max} = \dfrac{E}{Z_{min}} = \dfrac{E}{R}$$

It is interesting to note that before resonance the current leads the applied emf, at resonance it is in phase, and after resonance it lags behind the emf. LCR series circuit is also called as acceptor circuit and parallel LCR circuit is called rejector circuit.

34. (d) Condition for which the current is maximum in a series LCR circuit is,

$\omega = \dfrac{1}{\sqrt{LC}}$

$1000 = \dfrac{1}{\sqrt{L(10 \times 10^{-6})}}$

$\Rightarrow = L = 100\,mH$

35. (c) When a circuit is broken, the induced e.m.f. is largest. So the answer is (c).

36. (b) $V = 50 \times 2 \sin 100\,\pi \cos 100\,\pi t = 50 \sin 200\,\pi t$
$\Rightarrow V_0 = 50\,Volts$ and $\nu = 100\,Hz$

37. (d) $V = -L\dfrac{di}{dt}$

Here $\dfrac{di}{dt}$ is $+$ ve for $\dfrac{T}{2}$ time and

$\dfrac{di}{dt}$ is $-$ ve for next $\dfrac{T}{2}$ time

38. (b) $V = V_0 \sin \omega\,t$
Voltage in r.m.s. value

$V_0 = \sqrt{2} \times 234\,V = 331\,volt$

and $\omega t = 2\pi n t = 2\pi \times 50 \times t = 100\pi t$
Thus, the equation of line voltage is given by
$V = 331 \sin (100\,\pi\,t)$

39. (a) The resistance in the middle plays no part in the charging process of C, as it does not alter either the potential difference across the RC combination or the current through it.

40. (a) Here, $C = 100\ \mu F = 100 \times 10^{-6}\,F, R = 40\,\Omega$,
$V_{rms} = 110\,V, f = 60\,Hz$
Peak voltage,

$$V_0 = \sqrt{2}\ .\ V_{rms} = 100\sqrt{2} = 155.54\,V$$

Circuit impedance,

$Z = \sqrt{R^2 + \dfrac{1}{\omega^2 C^2}}$

$= \sqrt{40^2 + \dfrac{1}{(2 \times \pi \times 60 \times 100 \times 10^{-6})^2}}$

$= \sqrt{1600 + 703.60} = \sqrt{2303.60} = 48\,\Omega$

hence, maximum current in coil,

$I_0 = \dfrac{V_0}{Z} = \dfrac{155.54}{48} = 3.24\,A$

41. (a) Laminated core provide less area of cross-section for the current to flow. Because of this, resistance of the core increases and current decreases thereby decreasing the eddy current losses.

42. (b) $V = 200V;\ r = 10\,\Omega$
$R' = 10 + 100\,\Omega = 110\,\Omega$

$I = \dfrac{V}{R'} = \dfrac{220}{100} = 2A$

$P = I^2 R = 4 \times 100 = 400\,W$

43. (b) For step-down transformer,

$\dfrac{V_P}{V_S} = \dfrac{I_S}{I_P}$ $\quad \because V_P > V_S$ $\quad \therefore I_S > I_P$

44. (b) At $t = 0$, no current will flow through L and R_1

$\therefore$ Current through battery $= \dfrac{V}{R_2}$

At $t = \infty$,

effective resistance, $R_{eff} = \dfrac{R_1 R_2}{R_1 + R_2}$

$\therefore$ Current through battery $= \dfrac{V}{R_{eff}}$

$= \dfrac{V(R_1 + R_2)}{R_1 R_2}$

45. (d) These three inductors are connected in parallel. The equivalent inductance L_p is given by

$\dfrac{1}{L_p} = \dfrac{1}{L_1} + \dfrac{1}{L_2} + \dfrac{1}{L_3} = \dfrac{1}{3} + \dfrac{1}{3} + \dfrac{1}{3} = \dfrac{3}{3} = 1$

$\therefore L_p = 1$

1. **(b)** $\because$ The E.M. wave are transverse in nature i.e.,

$$= \frac{\vec{k} \times \vec{E}}{\mu\omega} = \vec{H} \qquad \ldots\text{(i)}$$

where $\vec{H} = \dfrac{\vec{B}}{\mu}$

and $\dfrac{\vec{k} \times \vec{H}}{\omega\varepsilon} = -\vec{E} \qquad \ldots\text{(ii)}$

$\vec{k}$ is $\perp \vec{H}$ and $\vec{k}$ is also $\perp$ to $\vec{E}$

or In other words $\vec{X} \parallel \vec{E}$ and $\vec{k} \parallel \vec{E} \times \vec{B}$

2. **(a)** $E_{rms} = 720$

The average total energy density

$$= \frac{1}{2} \epsilon_0 E_0^2 = \frac{1}{2} \epsilon_0 [\sqrt{2}E_{rms}]^2 = \epsilon_0 E_{rms}^2$$

$$= 8.85 \times 10^{-12} \times (720)^2$$

$$= 4.58 \times 10^{-6} \text{ J/m}^3$$

3. **(d)** $I_d = 1 \, mA = 10^{-3}$ A
$C = 2\mu F = 2 \times 10^{-6}$ F

$$I_D = I_C = \frac{d}{dt} (CV) = C \frac{dV}{dt}$$

Therefore, $\dfrac{dV}{dt} = \dfrac{I_D}{C} = \dfrac{10^{-3}}{2 \times 10^{-6}} = 500 \text{ Vs}^{-1}$

Therefore, applying a varying potential difference of 500 V s^{-1} would produce a displacement current of desired value.

4. **(c)** $E_0 = CB_0$ and $C = \dfrac{1}{\sqrt{\mu_0 \varepsilon_0}}$

Electric energy density $= \dfrac{1}{2} \varepsilon_0 E_0^{\,2} = \mu_E$

Magnetic energy density $= \dfrac{1}{2} \dfrac{Bo^2}{\mu_0} = \mu_B$

Thus, $\mu_E = \mu_B$

Energy is equally divided between electric and magnetic field

5. **(c)** In an electromagnetic wave electric field and magnetic field are perpendicular to the direction of propagation of wave. The vector equation for the electric field is

$$\vec{E} = E_0 \cos\left(\omega t - \frac{2\pi}{\lambda} y\right) \hat{z}$$

6. **(a)** Frequency remains constant during refraction

$$v_{med} = \frac{1}{\sqrt{\mu_0 \epsilon_0 \times 4}} = \frac{c}{2}$$

$$\frac{\lambda_{med}}{\lambda_{air}} = \frac{v_{med}}{v_{air}} = \frac{c/2}{c} = \frac{1}{2}$$

$\therefore$ wavelength is halved and frequency remains unchanged.

7. **(b)** For electromagnetic waves we know that,

$$\frac{E}{B} = c$$

$$\therefore \frac{9 \times 10^{-4}}{B} = 3 \times 10^8 \text{ ms}^{-1}$$

$$B = 3 \times 10^{-12} \text{ T}.$$

8. **(b)** Here, $k = \dfrac{2\pi}{\lambda}$, $\omega = 2\pi\upsilon$

$$\therefore \frac{k}{\omega} = \frac{2\pi/\lambda}{2\pi\upsilon} = \frac{1}{\pi\upsilon} = \frac{1}{c} \qquad (\because c = \upsilon\,\lambda)$$

where c is the speed of electromagnetic wave in vacuum. It is a constant whose value is $3 \times 10^6 \, m \, s^{-1}$

9. **(a)** E.M. wave always propagates in a direction perpendicular to both electric and magnetic fields. So, electric and magnetic fields should be along $+ X-$ and $+ Y-$directions respectively. Therefore, option (a) is the correct option.

10. **(d)** $\dfrac{1}{2}\varepsilon_0 E_0^2$ is electric energy density.

$\dfrac{B^2}{2\mu_0}$ is magnetic energy density.

So, total energy $= \dfrac{1}{2}\varepsilon_0 E_0^2 + \dfrac{B_0^2}{2\mu_0}$

11. **(c)** Incident momentum, $p = \dfrac{E}{c}$

For perfectly reflecting surface with normal incidence

$$\Delta p = 2p = \frac{2E}{c}$$

$$F = \frac{\Delta p}{\Delta t} = \frac{2E}{ct}$$

$$P = \frac{F}{A} = \frac{2E}{ctA}$$

12. **(a)** E_x and B_y would generate a plane EM wave travelling in z-direction, $\vec{E}$, $\vec{B}$ and $\vec{k}$ from a right handed system $\vec{k}$ is along z-axis. As $\hat{i} \times \hat{j} = \hat{k}$

$\Rightarrow E_x\hat{i} \times B_y\hat{j} = C\hat{k}$ i.e., E is along x-axis and B is along y-axis.

13. **(b)** From question,
$B_0 = 20 \text{ nT} = 20 \times 10^{-9}\text{T}$
($\because$ velocity of light in vacuum $C = 3 \times 10^8 \text{ ms}^{-1}$)

$$\vec{E}_0 = \vec{B}_0 \times \vec{C}$$

$$|\vec{E}_0| = |\vec{B}| \cdot |\vec{C}| = 20 \times 10^{-9} \times 3 \times 10^8$$

$$= 6 \text{ V/m}.$$

14. (c) Microwave oven acts on the principle of giving vibrational energy to water molecules.

15. (a) Displacement current is set up in a region where the electric field is changing with time.

16. (a) On comparing the given equation to

$$\vec{E} = a_0 \hat{i} \cos(\omega t - kz)$$
$$\omega = 6 \times 10^{8z},$$
$$k = \frac{2\pi}{r} = \frac{\omega}{c}$$
$$k = \frac{\omega}{c} = \frac{6 \times 10^8}{3 \times 10^8} = 2\,\mathrm{m}^{-1}$$

17. (b) Displacement current, I_D = conduction current, I_C

$$\therefore \quad \frac{dq}{dt} = \frac{d}{dt}[q_0 \cos 2\pi \upsilon t] = -q_0\, 2\pi \upsilon\, \sin 2\pi \upsilon t$$

18. (a) Momentum of light falling on reflecting surface $p = \dfrac{E}{C}$

As surface is perfectly reflecting so momentum reflect

$$p^1 = -\frac{E}{C}$$

So, momentum transferred

$$= P - P^1 = \frac{E}{C} - \left(-\frac{E}{C}\right) = \frac{2E}{C}$$

19. (d) (1) Infrared rays are used to treat muscular strain because these are heat rays.
(2) Radio waves are used for broadcasting because these waves have very long wavelength ranging from few centimeters to few hundred kilometers
(3) X-rays are used to detect fracture of bones because they have high penetrating power but they can't penetrate through denser medium like dones.
(4) Ultraviolet rays are absorbed by ozone of the atmosphere.

20. (d) Given : $\vec{B} = 1.2 \times 10^{-8}\hat{k}\,\mathrm{T}$

$$\vec{E} = ?$$
From formula,
$$E = Bc = (1.2 \times 10^{-8}\,\mathrm{T})(3 \times 10^8\,\mathrm{ms}^{-1}) = 3.6\,\mathrm{Vm}^{-1}$$

$\vec{B}$ is along Z-direction and the wave propagates along X-direction. Therefore $\vec{E}$ should be along Y-direction.

Thus, $\vec{E} = 3.6\hat{j}\,\mathrm{Vm}^{-1}$

21. (d)

22. (a) $E = \dfrac{hc}{\lambda} \Rightarrow \lambda = \dfrac{hc}{E}$

$$\Rightarrow \lambda = \frac{6.6 \times 10^{-34} \times 3 \times 10^8}{11 \times 1000 \times 1.6 \times 10^{-19}} = 12.4\,\text{Å}$$

Increasing order of frequency →

x-rays   u-v rays   visible   Infrared

23. (a) Velocity of light

$$C = \frac{E}{B} \Rightarrow B = \frac{E}{C} = \frac{9.3}{3 \times 10^8} = 3.1 \times 10^{-8}\,\mathrm{T}$$

24. (b) The average energy stored in the electric field

$$U_E = \frac{1}{2}\varepsilon_0 E^2$$

The average energy stored in the magnetic field $= U_B =$

$$\frac{1}{2}\frac{B^2}{\mu_0},$$

According to conservation of energy $U_E = U_B$

$$\varepsilon_0 \mu_0 = \frac{B^2}{E^2}$$

$$\frac{B}{E} = \sqrt{\varepsilon_0 \mu_0} = \frac{1}{c}$$

25. (b) EM waves carry momentum and hence can exert pressure on surfaces. They also transfer energy to the surface so $p \neq 0$ and $E \neq 0$.

26. (b)

27. (a) The decreasing order of the wavelengths is as given below :
microwave, infrared, ultraviolet, gamma rays.

28. (b) Infrared causes heating effect.

29. (c) Speed of EM waves in vacuum $= \dfrac{1}{\sqrt{\mu_0\, \epsilon_0}} = $ constant

30. (b)

31. (a) $I_D = \varepsilon_o\, d\phi_E / dt$.

32. (d) $\nu_{\gamma-\text{rays}} > \nu_{\text{visible radiation}} > \nu_{\text{infrared}} > \nu_{\text{Radio waves}}$

33. (b)

34. (d) Wave is uv rays.

35. (b)

36. (c) Electromagnetic waves are the combination of mutually perpendicular electric and magnetic fields.

37. (b) Audible waves are not electromagnetic wave.

38. (b) Wave impedance $= Z = \sqrt{\dfrac{\mu_0}{\varepsilon_0}} = 376.6\ \Omega$

39. (b)

40. (b) Depends on the magnitude of frequency

41. (d) $B_0 = \dfrac{E_0}{c} = \dfrac{9 \times 10^3}{3 \times 10^8} = 3 \times 10^{-5}\,\mathrm{T}.$

42. (d) To generate electromagnetic waves we need accelerating charge particle.

43. (d)

44. (d) For an E.M. wave power is transmitted in a direction perpendicular to both the fields.

45. (c) Speed of light of vacuum $c = \dfrac{1}{\sqrt{\mu_0 \varepsilon_0}}$ and in another

medium $v = \dfrac{1}{\sqrt{\mu\varepsilon}}$

$$\therefore \frac{c}{v} = \sqrt{\frac{\mu\varepsilon}{\mu_0\varepsilon_0}} = \sqrt{\mu_r K} \Rightarrow v = \frac{c}{\sqrt{\mu_r K}}.$$

1. **(b)** $\dfrac{1}{f_R} = (1.5 - 1)\left(\dfrac{1}{R_1} - \dfrac{1}{R_2}\right)$

$\dfrac{1}{f_v} = (1.45 - 1)\left(\dfrac{1}{R_1} - \dfrac{1}{R_2}\right)$

$\dfrac{f_v}{f_R} = \dfrac{0.5}{0.45} = \dfrac{10}{9}$

$f_R = \dfrac{9}{10} f_v = \dfrac{9}{10} \times 20 \text{ cm} = 18 \text{ cm}.$

2. **(a)** We have,

$\mu = \dfrac{\sin\left(\dfrac{A + \delta_m}{2}\right)}{\sin\left(\dfrac{A}{2}\right)}$

$\Rightarrow \cot\dfrac{A}{2} = \dfrac{\sin\left(\dfrac{A + \delta_m}{2}\right)}{\sin\left(\dfrac{A}{2}\right)}$

or $\sin\dfrac{A}{2} \cdot \cot\dfrac{A}{2} = \sin\left(\dfrac{A + \delta_m}{2}\right)$

or $\sin\dfrac{A}{2} \cdot \dfrac{\cos\dfrac{A}{2}}{\sin\dfrac{A}{2}} = \sin\left(\dfrac{A + \delta_m}{2}\right)$

or $\cos\dfrac{A}{2} = \cos\left[\dfrac{\pi}{2} - \left(\dfrac{A + \delta_m}{2}\right)\right]$

$\Rightarrow \dfrac{A}{2} = \dfrac{\pi}{2} - \left(\dfrac{A + \delta_m}{2}\right)$

or $A = \pi - A - \delta_m \Rightarrow \delta_m = \pi - 2A$.

3. **(a)** Let the distance between the lenses be d.

Then, equivalent power is

$P = P_1 + P_2 - d\,P_1\,P_2$

Given $P_1 = P_2 = +5\,D$

$\therefore P = (10 - 25d)\,D$

For P to be –ve,

$10 - 25d < 0 \Rightarrow d > \dfrac{2}{5}\,m$

or, $d > 0.4\,m$ or $d > 40\,cm$

4. **(b)** $^a\mu_g = \dfrac{\sin 60°}{\sin 35°}$ ... (i)

$^a\mu_w = \dfrac{\sin 60°}{\sin 41°}$ ... (ii)

$^w\mu_g = \dfrac{\sin 41°}{\sin \theta}$ ... (iii)

$^a\mu_w \times {}^w\mu_g = {}^a\mu_g$

$\dfrac{\sin 60°}{\sin 41°} \times \dfrac{\sin 41°}{\sin \theta} = \dfrac{\sin 60°}{\sin 35°}$

(Using (i), (ii) and (iii))

$= \sin\theta = \sin 35° \quad \theta = 35°$

5. **(d)** 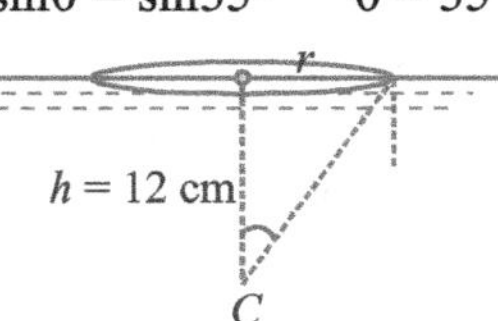

$\sin C = \dfrac{1}{\mu} = \dfrac{1}{4/3} = \dfrac{3}{4}.$

Now $\quad r = h \tan C$

$= 12 \times \dfrac{3}{\sqrt{7}} = \dfrac{36}{\sqrt{7}} \text{ cm}$

6. **(a)** $\dfrac{1}{f} = (\mu - 1)\left(\dfrac{1}{R_1} - \dfrac{1}{R_2}\right)$

According to Cauchy relation

$\mu = A + \dfrac{B}{\lambda^2} + \dfrac{C}{\lambda^4} \cdots$ Hence $f \propto \lambda$.

Hence, red light having maximum wavelength has maximum focal length.

$\therefore \quad f_v < f_r$ and also $F_v > F_r$ as focal length is negative for a concave lens.

7. **(c)** To minimise spherical aberration in a lens, the total deviation should be equally distributed over the two surfaces.

8. **(d)** 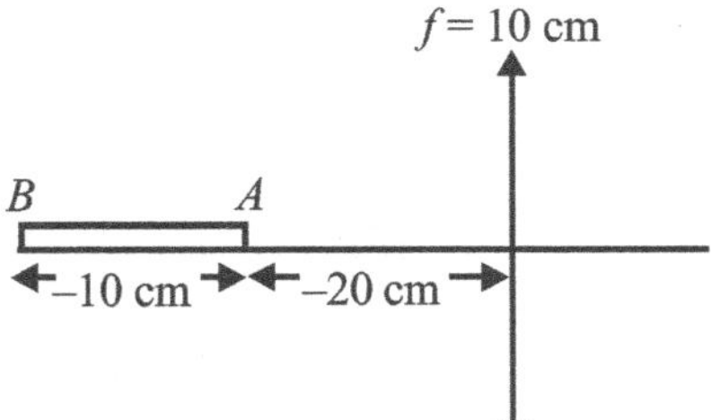

The focal length of the mirror

$-\dfrac{1}{f} = \dfrac{1}{v} + \dfrac{1}{u}$

For A end of the rod the image distance
When $u_1 = -20$ cm

$\Rightarrow \dfrac{-1}{10} = \dfrac{1}{v_1} - \dfrac{1}{20}$

$$\frac{1}{v_1} = \frac{-1}{10} + \frac{1}{20} = \frac{-2+1}{20}$$

$v_1 = -20\,\text{cm}$

For when $u_2 = -30\,\text{cm}$

$$\frac{1}{f} = \frac{1}{v_2} - \frac{1}{30}$$

$$\frac{1}{v_2} = \frac{-1}{10} + \frac{1}{30} = \frac{-30+10}{300} = \frac{-20}{300}$$

$$v_2 = -15\,\text{cm}$$
$$L = v_2 - v_1 = -15 - (-20)$$
$$L = 5\,\text{cm}$$

9. (a) Magnification

$$= \frac{f_0}{f_e} = \frac{\text{Angle subtended by final image on the eye}}{\text{Angle subtended by the object on eye (or objective)}}$$

$$\Rightarrow \frac{0.3\text{m}}{3\text{cm}} = \frac{\beta}{0.5°} \Rightarrow \frac{30\,\text{cm}}{3\text{cm}} = \frac{\beta}{0.5°}$$

$$\Rightarrow \beta = 5°$$

10. (b) Due to difference in refractive indices images obtained will be two. Two media will form images at two different points due to difference in focal lengths.

11. (c) For reading purposes :
$u = -25\,\text{cm}, \quad v = -50\,\text{cm}, f = ?$

$$\frac{1}{f} = \frac{1}{v} - \frac{1}{u} = -\frac{1}{50} + \frac{1}{25} = \frac{1}{50} \;;$$

$$P = \frac{100}{f} = +2\,\text{D}$$

For distant vision, f' = distance of far point = −3 m

$$P = \frac{1}{f'} = -\frac{1}{3}\text{D} = -0.33\,\text{D}$$

12. (a) Clearly,

$$i + r + 90° = 180°$$

$$\Rightarrow \quad i + r = 90° \qquad\qquad \ldots(i)$$

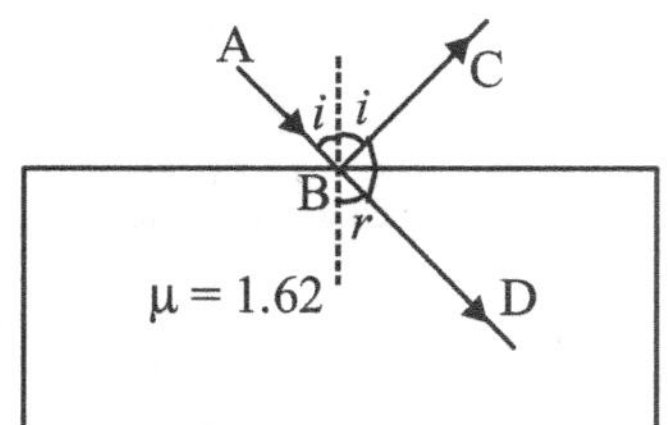

Now, $\dfrac{\sin i}{\sin r} = \mu$

$$\Rightarrow \quad \frac{\sin i}{\sin(90° - i)} = \mu, \text{ from (1)}$$

or $\dfrac{\sin i}{\cos i} = \mu \Rightarrow \tan i = \mu$

or $i = \tan^{-1}(\mu)$ i.e., $i = \tan^{-1}(1.62)$

13. (b) $f_0 = 100\,\text{cm}, f_e = 5\,\text{cm}$
When final image is formed at least distance of distinct vision (d), then

$$M = \frac{f_0}{f_e}\left(1 + \frac{f_e}{d}\right) = \frac{100}{5}\left(1 + \frac{5}{25}\right) \quad [\because D = 25\,\text{cm}]$$

$$M = 20 \times \frac{6}{5} = 24$$

14. (b) Secondary rainbow is formed by rays undergoing internal reflection twice inside the drop.

15. (b) $\tan 45° = \dfrac{h}{60} \Rightarrow h = 60m$

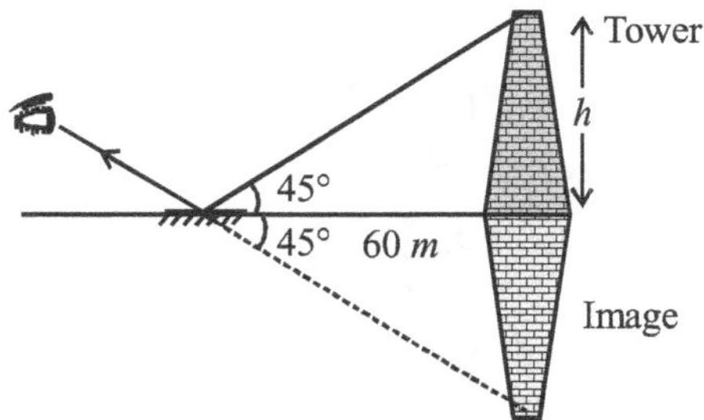

16. (c) Using, $\quad \dfrac{\mu}{v} - \dfrac{1}{u} = \dfrac{\mu-1}{R}$

or $\quad \dfrac{2}{v} - \dfrac{1}{\infty} = \dfrac{2-1}{R}$

$\therefore \qquad\qquad v = 2R$

17. (a) $_a n_\ell = 1.6, \; _a n_w = 1.33$
$f = 20\,\text{cm}$
We have,

$$\frac{1}{f} = \left(_a n_\ell - 1\right)\left(\frac{1}{R_1} - \frac{1}{R_2}\right)$$

$$\frac{1}{20} = (1.6 - 1)\left(\frac{1}{R_1} - \frac{1}{R_2}\right) \qquad\qquad \ldots(1)$$

Also, $\dfrac{1}{f'} = \left(_w n_\ell - 1\right)\left(\dfrac{1}{R_1} - \dfrac{1}{R_2}\right)$

$$= \left(\frac{_a n_\ell}{_a n_w} - 1\right)\left(\frac{1}{R_1} - \frac{1}{R_2}\right)$$

$$\frac{1}{f'} = \left(\frac{1.6}{1.33} - 1\right)\left(\frac{1}{R_1} - \frac{1}{R_2}\right) \qquad\qquad \ldots(2)$$

Dividing equation (1) by (2)

$$\Rightarrow \quad \frac{f'}{20} = \frac{0.6}{(1.2 - 1)}$$

$$f' = \frac{0.6 \times 20}{0.2} = 60\,\text{cm}.$$

Hence it's focal length is three times longer than in air.

18. (a) $m = \dfrac{v_0}{|u_0|}\left(1 + \dfrac{d}{f_e}\right) = \dfrac{20}{5}\left(1 + \dfrac{20}{10}\right)$

$= 4\left(\dfrac{10+20}{10}\right) = \dfrac{4 \times 30}{10} = 12$

19. (a) Given $\quad i = 60°$

$A = \delta = e$

$\delta = i + e - A \Rightarrow \delta = i \quad (\because e = A)$

$\mu = \dfrac{\sin\left(\dfrac{A + \delta_m}{2}\right)}{\sin\dfrac{A}{2}}$

Here angle of deviation is min. ($\because i = e$)

$\mu = \dfrac{\sin\left(\dfrac{60° + 60°}{2}\right)}{\sin\dfrac{60°}{2}} = 1.73$

20. (b) $u = -50\,cm = -0.5\,m$

$v = -30\,cm = -0.3\,m$

$P = \dfrac{1}{f} = \dfrac{1}{v} - \dfrac{1}{u} = \dfrac{-1}{0.3} + \dfrac{1}{0.5} = \dfrac{-0.2}{0.15} = -1.33\,D.$

21. (b) Object distance $u = -40\,cm$

Focal length $f = -20\,cm$

According to mirror formula

$\dfrac{1}{u} + \dfrac{1}{v} = \dfrac{1}{f}$ or $\dfrac{1}{v} = \dfrac{1}{f} - \dfrac{1}{u}$

or $\dfrac{1}{v} + \dfrac{1}{-20} - \dfrac{1}{(-40)} = \dfrac{1}{-20} + \dfrac{1}{40}$

$\dfrac{1}{v} = \dfrac{-2+1}{40} = -\dfrac{1}{40}$ or $v = -40\,cm.$

Negative sign shows that image is infront of concave mirror. The image is real.

Magnification, $m = \dfrac{-v}{u} = -\dfrac{(-40)}{(-40)} = -1$

The image is of the same size and inverted.

22. (a)

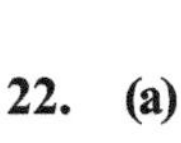

As refractive index, $\mu = \dfrac{\text{Real depth}}{\text{Apparent depth}}$

$\therefore$ Apparent depth of the vessel when viewed from above is

$d_{apparent} = \dfrac{x}{2\mu_1} + \dfrac{x}{2\mu_2} = \dfrac{x}{2}\left(\dfrac{1}{\mu_1} + \dfrac{1}{\mu_2}\right)$

$= \dfrac{x}{2}\left(\dfrac{\mu_2 + \mu_1}{\mu_1\mu_2}\right) = \dfrac{x(\mu_1 + \mu_2)}{2\mu_1\mu_2}$

23. (d) As $r_1 < i_1$ i.e., the incident ray bends towards the normal $\Rightarrow$ medium 2 is denser than medium 1. Or $r_2 < i_1 \Rightarrow$ medium 3 is denser than medium 1. Also, $r_2 > r_1 \Rightarrow$ medium 2 is denser than medium 3.

24. (d) Here, $v_A = 1.8 \times 10^8\,m\,s^{-1}$

$v_B = 2.4 \times 10^8\,m\,s^{-1}$

Light travels slower in denser medium. Hence medium A is a denser medium and medium B is a rarer medium. Here, Light travels from medium A to medium B. Let C be the critical angle between them.

$\therefore \quad \sin C = {}^A\mu_B = \dfrac{1}{{}^B\mu_A}$

Refractive index of medium B w.r.t. to medium A is

${}^A\mu_B = \dfrac{\text{Velocity of light in medium } A}{\text{Velocity of light in medium } B} = \dfrac{v_A}{v_B}$

$\therefore \quad \sin C = \dfrac{v_A}{v_B} = \dfrac{1.8 \times 10^8}{2.4 \times 10^8} = \dfrac{3}{4}$ or $C = \sin^{-1}\left(\dfrac{3}{4}\right)$

25. (a) For a thin prism, $D = (\mu - 1)A$

Since $\lambda_b < \lambda_r \Rightarrow \mu_r < \mu_b \Rightarrow D_1 < D_2$

26. (b) Difference between apparent and real depth of a pond is due to the refraction of light, not due to the total internal reflection. Other three phenomena are due to the total internal reflection.

27. (b) Using the lens formula $\dfrac{1}{f} = \dfrac{1}{v} - \dfrac{1}{u}$

Given $v = d$, for equal size image $|v| = |u| = d$

By sign convention $u = -d$

$\therefore \quad \dfrac{1}{f} = \dfrac{1}{d} + \dfrac{1}{d}$ or $f = \dfrac{d}{2}$

28. (a) Due to covering the reflection from lower part is not there so it makes the image less bright.

29. (b) From the fig.
Angle of deviation,

$\delta = i + e - A$

Here, $e = i$

and $e = \dfrac{3}{4}A$

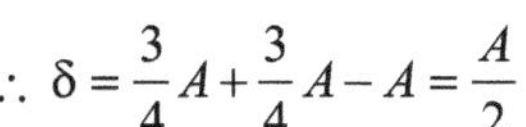

$\therefore \delta = \dfrac{3}{4}A + \dfrac{3}{4}A - A = \dfrac{A}{2}$

For equilateral prism, $A = 60°$

$\therefore \delta = \dfrac{60°}{2} = 30°$

30. (a) Power of lens, P (in dioptre)

$$= \frac{100}{\text{focal length } f \text{ (in cm)}}$$

$$\therefore \quad f = \frac{100}{10} = 10 \text{ cm}$$

By lens maker's formula, $\dfrac{1}{f} = (\mu - 1)\left(\dfrac{1}{R_1} - \dfrac{1}{R_2}\right)$

For biconvex lens, $R_1 = +R$, and $R_2 = -R$

$$\therefore \quad \frac{1}{f} = (\mu - 1)\left(\frac{1}{R} + \frac{1}{R}\right)$$

$$\frac{1}{f} = (\mu - 1)\left(\frac{2}{R}\right)$$

$$\frac{1}{10} = (\mu - 1)\left(\frac{2}{10}\right)$$

$$(\mu - 1) = \frac{1}{2} \quad \text{or} \quad \mu = \frac{1}{2} + 1 = \frac{3}{2}$$

31. (d) In the later case microscope will be focussed for O'. So, it is required to be lifted by distance OO'.

OO' = real depth of O – apparent depth of O.

Image $\longrightarrow$ $\cdot O'$
O

$$= 3 - \frac{3}{1.5} \qquad \left[\mu = \frac{\text{real depth}}{\text{apparent depth}}\right]$$

$$= 3\left[\frac{1.5 - 1}{1.5}\right] = \frac{3 \times .5}{1.5} = 1 \text{ cm}$$

32. (d) The cause of chromatic aberration is that lens focusses different colours at different points.

33. (c) For the prism as the angle of incidence (i) increases, the angle of deviation (δ) first decreases goes to minimum value and then increases.

34. (d) $d_A : d_B = 6 : 4$

$\because$ Time taken $\propto$ thickness

and time taken $\propto \dfrac{1}{\text{velocity}}$

$\therefore$ Thickness $\propto \dfrac{1}{\text{velocity}}$

$$\therefore \quad \frac{d_A}{d_B} = \frac{v_B}{v_A}$$

Also, $\mu = \dfrac{c}{v}$ $\therefore \dfrac{\mu_A}{\mu_B} = \dfrac{v_B}{v_A}$

$$\therefore \quad \frac{d_A}{d_B} = \frac{\mu_A}{\mu_B} = \frac{6}{4} = \frac{3}{2} = 1.5$$

$$\therefore \quad {}_B\mu_A = 1.5$$

35. (b) Since $\dfrac{\text{Apparent depth}}{\text{Real depth}} = \dfrac{1}{\mu}$

$\Rightarrow$ Apparent depth $= d/\mu$

So mark raised up = Real depth – Apparent depth

$$= d - \frac{d}{\mu} = d\left(1 - \frac{1}{\mu}\right) = \left(\frac{\mu - 1}{\mu}\right)d$$

36. (b) Dispersive power of a prism $\omega = \dfrac{\mu_V - \mu_R}{\mu_y - 1} = \dfrac{d\mu}{\mu - 1}$,

where $\mu = \mu_y = \dfrac{\mu_V + \mu_R}{2}$

37. (a) Considering refraction at the curved surface,

$$u = -20, \ \mu_2 = 1$$
$$\mu_1 = 3/2, \ R = +20$$

Applying $\dfrac{\mu_2}{v} - \dfrac{\mu_1}{u} = \dfrac{\mu_2 - \mu_1}{R}$

$$\Rightarrow \frac{1}{v} - \frac{3/2}{-20} = \frac{1 - 3/2}{20} \Rightarrow v = -10$$

i.e., 10 cm below the curved surface or 10 cm above the actual position of flower.

38. (b) When $\theta = 90°$ then $\dfrac{360}{\theta} = \dfrac{360}{90} = 4$

is an even number. The number of images formed is given by

$$n = \frac{360}{\theta} - 1 = \frac{360}{90} - 1 = 4 - 1 = 3$$

39. (b) The critical angle of incidence is that angle at which angle of refraction is 90°.

n_1, n_2, i_c

$\sin i_c = \dfrac{n_1}{n_2}$ where $n_2 > n_1$

As, refractive index $= \dfrac{\text{velocity (air)}}{\text{velocity (medium)}}$

$$\therefore \quad \sin i_c = \frac{2.2 \times 10^8 \, \text{m/sec}}{2.4 \times 10^8 \, \text{m/sec}} = \frac{11}{12}$$

$$\Rightarrow i_C = \sin^{-1}\left(\frac{11}{12}\right)$$

40. (b) $\dfrac{P_a}{P_1} = \dfrac{\left(\dfrac{\mu_g}{\mu_a} - 1\right)}{\left(\dfrac{\mu_g}{\mu_1} - 1\right)} = \dfrac{+5}{-100/100} = -5$

$$-5\left(\frac{\mu_g}{\mu_1} - 1\right) = \frac{\mu_g}{\mu_a} - 1$$

$$\frac{1.5}{\mu_1} - 1 = \frac{-1}{5}(1.5 - 1) = -0.1 \; ; \quad \mu_1 = \frac{1.5}{0.9} = \frac{5}{3}$$

41. (d) $\sin C = \frac{1}{\mu} = \frac{1}{\sqrt{2}} \quad \therefore C = \sin^{-1}\left(\frac{1}{\sqrt{2}}\right) = 45°$

Now $\dfrac{\sin C}{\sin r} = \dfrac{1}{\mu}$ or $\dfrac{\sin 45°}{\sin r} = \dfrac{1}{\sqrt{2}}$

$\sin r = 1$ or $r = 90°$

42. (d)

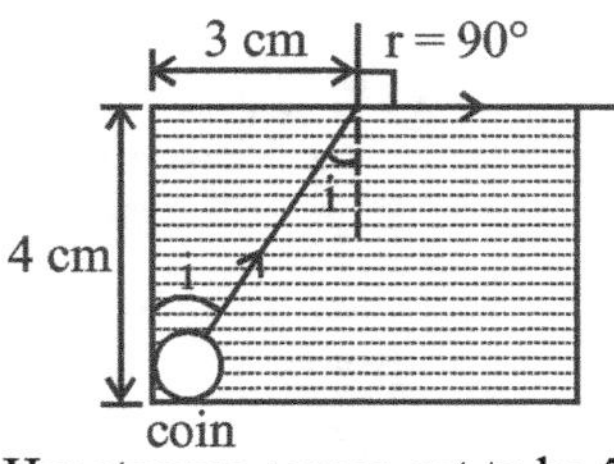

Hypotenuse comes out to be 5 cm.

Since, $\dfrac{1}{\mu} = \dfrac{\sin i}{\sin 90°}$

$\mu = \dfrac{1}{\sin i} = \dfrac{5}{3}$

Speed, $v = \dfrac{c}{\mu} = \dfrac{3 \times 10^8}{5/3} = 1.8 \times 10^8$ m/s

43. (a)

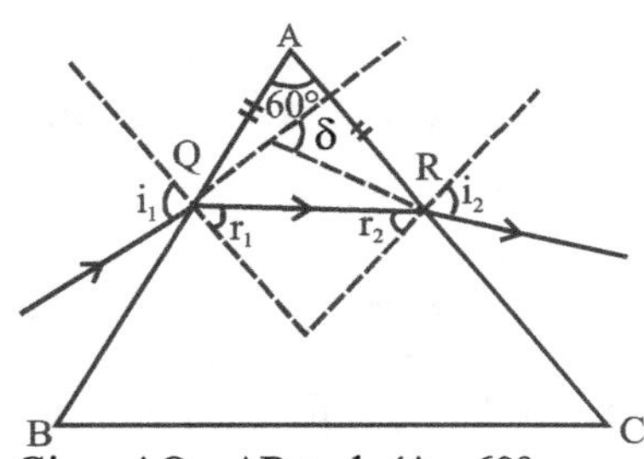

Given $AQ = AR$ and $\angle A = 60°$

$\therefore \quad \angle AQR = \angle ARQ = 60°$

$\therefore \quad r_1 = r_2 = 30°$

Applying Snell's law on face AB.

$\sin i_1 = \mu \sin r_1$

$\Rightarrow \sin i_1 = \sqrt{3} \sin 30° = \sqrt{3} \times \dfrac{1}{2} = \dfrac{\sqrt{3}}{2}$

$\therefore \quad i_1 = 60°$

Similarly, $i_2 = 60°$

In a prism, deviation

$\delta = i_1 + i_2 - A = 60° + 60° - 60° = 60°$

44. (a) $\dfrac{1}{f} = \left(\dfrac{\mu_g}{\mu_m} - 1\right)\left(\dfrac{1}{R_1} - \dfrac{1}{R_2}\right)$

If $\mu_g = \mu_m$, then $\dfrac{1}{f} = (1 - 1)\left(\dfrac{1}{R_1} - \dfrac{1}{R_2}\right)$

$\Rightarrow \quad \dfrac{1}{f} = 0$

$$\boxed{f = \dfrac{1}{0} = \infty}$$

This implies that the liquid must have refractive index equal to glass.

45. (b) Minimum deviation of the prism when it is dipped in water $= \delta_m' = (_w\mu_g - 1)A$

$= \left(\dfrac{_a\mu_g}{_a\mu_\omega} - 1\right)A = \left(\dfrac{\frac{3}{2}}{\frac{4}{3}} - 1\right)A = \dfrac{1}{8}A$

Minimum deviation of the prism with respect to air

$= \delta_m = (\mu - 1)A = \left(\dfrac{3}{2} - 1\right)A = \dfrac{1}{2}A$

$\dfrac{\delta_m'}{\delta_m} = \dfrac{\frac{1}{8}A}{\frac{1}{2}A} = \dfrac{1}{4}$

1. **(b)** For path difference λ, phase

difference $= 2\pi \left(Q = \dfrac{2\pi}{\lambda} x = \dfrac{2\pi}{\lambda}.\lambda = 2\pi \right)$

$\Rightarrow I = I_0 + I_0 + 2I_0 \cos 2\pi$

$\Rightarrow I = 4I_0 \qquad (\because \cos 2\pi = 1)$

For $x = \dfrac{\lambda}{4}$, phase difference $= \dfrac{\pi}{2}$

$\therefore I' = I_1 + I_2 + 2\sqrt{I_1}\sqrt{I_2} \cos \dfrac{\pi}{2}$

If $I_1 = I_2 = I_0$ then $I' = 2I_0 = 2.\dfrac{I}{4} = \dfrac{I}{2}$

2. **(c)** Here Angle of incidence, $i = 57$

tan $57° = 1.54$

$u_{glass} = \tan i$

It means, Here Brewster's law is followed and the reflected ray is completely polarised.

Now, when reflected ray is analysed through a polaroid then intensity of light is given by malus law.

i.e. $I = I_0 \cos^2 \theta$

on rotating polaroid 'θ' changes. Due to which intensity first decreases and then increases.

3. **(b)** Let nth fringe of 2500 Å coincide with (n – 2)th fringe of 3500Å.

$\therefore \quad 3500\,(n-2) = 2500 \times n$

$1000\,n = 7000, n = 7$

$\therefore \quad$ 7th order fringe of 1st source will coincide with 5th order fringe of 2nd source.

4. **(a)** When incident wavefronts passes through a prism, then lower portion of wavefront (B) is delayed resulting in a tilt. So, time taken by light to reach A' from A is equal to the time taken to reach B' from B.

5. **(b)** $^a\mu_g = \tan \theta_P$ where $\theta_P =$ polarising angle.

or, $^a\mu_g = \tan 60°$

or, $\dfrac{c}{v_g} = \sqrt{3}$

or, $v_g = \dfrac{c}{\sqrt{3}} = \dfrac{3 \times 10^8}{\sqrt{3}} = \sqrt{3} \times 10^8 \,\text{ms}^{-1}$

6. **(c)** Angular width $= \dfrac{\lambda}{d} = 10^{-3}$ (given)

$\therefore$ No. of fringes within $0.12°$ will be

$n = \dfrac{0.12 \times 2\pi}{360 \times 10^{-3}} = [2.09]$

$\therefore$ The number of bright spots will be two.

7. **(c)** Here $A^2 = a_1^2 + a_2^2 + 2a_1 a_2 \cos \delta$

$\because \quad a_1 = a_2 = a$

$\therefore \quad A^2 = 2a^2 (1 + \cos \delta) = 2a^2 \left(1 + 2\cos^2 \dfrac{\delta}{2} - 1 \right)$

$\Rightarrow A^2 \propto \cos^2 \dfrac{\delta}{2}$

Now, $I \propto A^2 \quad \therefore I \propto A^2 \propto \cos^2 \dfrac{\delta}{2}$

$\therefore I \propto \cos^2 \dfrac{\delta}{2}$.

8. **(b)** $\Delta x_1 = (\mu_1 - 1)t = (1.5 - 1)t = 0.5t$

and $\Delta x_2 = (\mu_2 - 1) \times 2t = \left(\dfrac{4}{3} - 1 \right) \times 2t = \dfrac{2}{3}t$.

As $\Delta x_2 > \Delta x_1$, so shift will be along $-ve$ y-axis.

9. **(d)** Given: $D = 2m; d = 1\,mm = 1 \times 10^{-3}\,m$

$\lambda = 600\,nm = 600 \times 10^{-6}\,m$

Width of central bright fringe $(= 2\beta)$

$= \dfrac{2\lambda D}{d} = \dfrac{2 \times 600 \times 10^{-6} \times 2}{1 \times 10^{-3}}\,m = 2.4\,mm$

10. **(d)** Conditions for diffraction minima are

Path diff. $\Delta x = n\lambda$ and Phase diff. $\delta\phi = 2n\pi$

Path diff. $= n\lambda = 2\lambda$

Phase diff. $= 2n\pi = 4\pi \ (\because n = 2)$

11. **(c)** When the wavelength of light used is comparable with the separation between two points, the image of the object will be a ϕ diffraction pattern whose size will be

$\theta = \dfrac{1.22\lambda}{D}$

where $\lambda =$ wavelength of light used

$D =$ diameter of the objective

Two objects whose images are closer than this distance, will not be resolved.

12. **(d)** The waves reflected from the top layer of oil interfere with the wave train reflected from the lower surface of thin oil film producing light and dark coloured pattern.

13. **(d)** Phase difference, $\phi = \dfrac{2\pi}{\lambda} \times$ Path difference

$\phi = \dfrac{2\pi}{\lambda} \times \dfrac{\lambda}{6} = \dfrac{\pi}{3} = 60°$

As, $I = I_{max} \cos^2 \dfrac{\phi}{2}$

$I = I_0 \cos^2 \dfrac{60°}{2} = I_0 \times \left(\dfrac{\sqrt{3}}{2} \right)^2 = \dfrac{3}{4} I_0 \quad \dfrac{I}{I_0} = \dfrac{3}{4}$

14. **(b)**

15. **(a)** We know that for maxima

$$b\sin\theta = (2n+1)\frac{\lambda}{2}$$

or $\sin\theta = \frac{2n+1}{2}\left(\frac{\lambda}{b}\right)$

So on decreasing the slit width, 'b', keeping λ same, $\sin\theta$ and hence θ increases.

16. **(b)** If the angular limit of resolution of human eye is R then

$$R = \frac{1.22\lambda}{a} = \frac{1.22\times5\times10^{-7}}{2\times10^{-3}}\ \text{rad}$$

$$= \frac{1.22\times5\times10^{-7}}{2\times10^{-3}}\times\frac{180}{\pi}\times60\ \text{minute} = 1\ \text{minute}$$

17. **(c)** $\mu = \tan i$

$$\Rightarrow i = \tan^{-1}(\mu) = \tan^{-1}(\sqrt{3}) = 60°.$$

18. **(d)** Order of the fringe can be counted on either side of the central maximum. For example, no. 3 is first order bright fringe.

$$\Delta X_C = \lambda,\ \Delta X_A = \frac{\lambda}{2}$$

$$\Delta X_C - \Delta X_A = \frac{\lambda}{2} = 300\text{nm}$$

19. **(a)** For a circularly polarised light electric field remains constant with time.

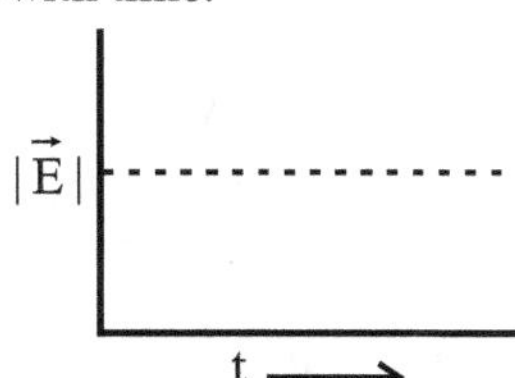

20. **(b)** $\beta' = \frac{\beta}{\mu} = \frac{0.133}{1.33} = 0.1\ \text{cm}$

21. **(b)**

22. **(d)** Let λ be wavelength of monochromatic light incident on slit S, then angular distance between two consecutive fringes, that is the angular fringe width is

$$\theta = \frac{\lambda}{d}$$

where d is distance between coherent sources.

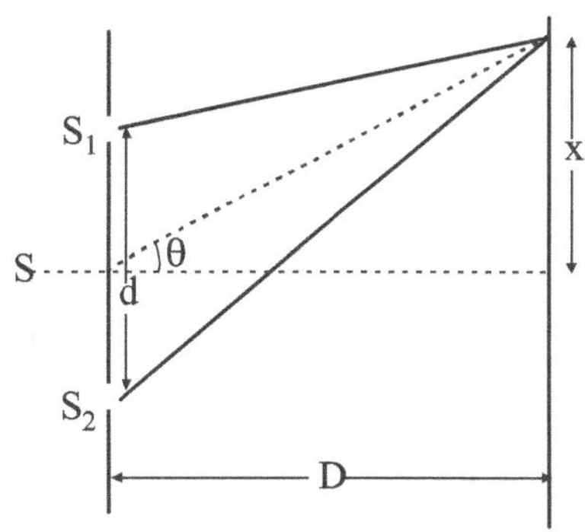

Give, $\dfrac{\Delta\theta}{\theta} = \dfrac{10}{100}$

So, from eq. (1),

$$\frac{\Delta\lambda}{\lambda} = \frac{\Delta\theta}{\theta} = \frac{10}{100} = 0.1$$

$$\Rightarrow \Delta\lambda = 0.1\lambda = 0.1\times5890\text{Å} = 589\text{Å}\ \ (\text{increases})$$

Note : Since, $\theta \propto \lambda$, as θ increases, λ increases.

23. **(c)** $\sin\theta = \dfrac{\lambda}{d} = \dfrac{589\times10^{-9}}{0.589\times10^{-3}} = 10^{-3} = \dfrac{1}{1000} = 0.001$

24. **(c)** In Fraunhoffer diffraction, for minimum intensity,

$$\Delta x = m\frac{\lambda}{2}$$

For first minimum, $m = 1$

$$\therefore\ \Delta x = \frac{\lambda}{2}$$

25. **(d)** Optical path difference

$$\Delta x = (\mu_2 - \mu_1)t\,.$$

26. **(b)** Separation between slits are $(r_1=)$ 16 cm and $(r_2=)$ 9 cm. Actual distance of separation

$$= \sqrt{r_1 r_2} = \sqrt{16\times9} = 12\text{cm}$$

27. **(b)** $\phi = \dfrac{\pi}{3}, a_1 = 4, a_2 = 3$

So, $A = \sqrt{a_1^2 + a_2^2 + 2a_1a_2\cos\phi} \approx 6$

28. **(c)** $\beta = \dfrac{D\lambda}{d}$, where D is the distance between the slits & screen and d is the separation between the slits.

$$\beta' = \frac{2D\lambda}{d/2} = \frac{4D\lambda}{d} = 4\beta$$

29. **(b)** For first minima at P

$$AP - BP = \lambda$$

$$AP - MP = \frac{\lambda}{2}$$

So phase difference, $\phi = \dfrac{2\pi}{\lambda}\times\dfrac{\lambda}{2} = \pi\ \text{radian}$

30. **(a)** Shift $= \dfrac{D}{d}(\mu-1)\,t = \dfrac{\beta}{\lambda}(\mu-1)\,t = 4\beta$

$$t = \dfrac{4\lambda}{\mu-1} = \dfrac{4\times 6000\times 10^{-10}}{1.5-1} = 4.8\,\mu m$$

31. **(c)** The fringe width is given by, $\beta = \dfrac{\lambda D}{d}$

The angular width of fringe is given by

$$\dfrac{d}{D} = \dfrac{\lambda}{\beta} = \dfrac{6\times 10^{-7}}{0.12\times 10^{-3}} = 5\times 10^{-3}\,\text{rad.}$$

32. **(c)** Distance of nth maxima, $x = n\lambda\dfrac{D}{d} \propto \lambda$

As $\lambda_b < \lambda_g$ $\therefore$ $x_{\text{blue}} < x_{\text{green}}$

33. **(a)** As $\beta = \dfrac{\lambda D}{d}$ and $\lambda_b < \lambda_y$,

$\therefore$ fringe width β will decrease

34. **(c)** At Brewster's angle, only the reflected light is plane polarised, but transmitted light is partially polarised.

35. **(b)** $\Delta x_{\text{max}} = 2\lambda$.

So there are five maxima.

These are for $\Delta x = 0, \pm\lambda, \pm 2\lambda$.

36. **(c)** The nearest white spot will be at P, the central maxima.

$$\therefore\ y = \dfrac{2d}{3} - \dfrac{d}{2} = \dfrac{d}{6}$$

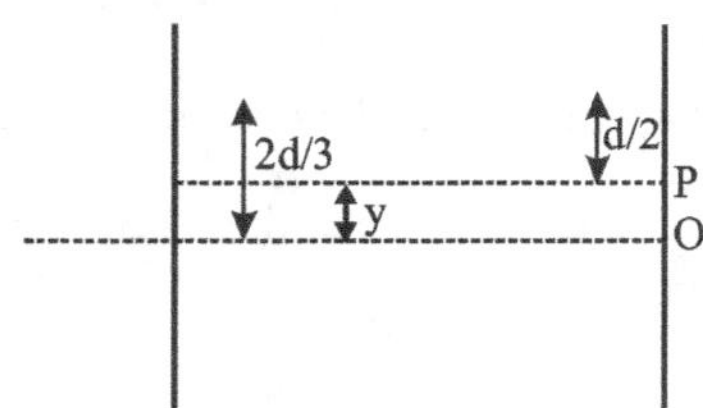

37. **(d)** : Resultant amplitude,

$$A = \sqrt{\left(A_1\right)^2 + \left(A_2\right)^2 + 2A_1 A_2\cos\theta}$$

Here, $A_1 = A_2 = 1$ cm, $\phi = 3\pi$ rad

$\therefore$ $A = \sqrt{1^2 + 1^2 + 2\times 1\times 1\times \cos 3\pi}$

$ = \sqrt{2 + 2\times(-1)} = 0$

38. **(c)**
39. **(c)**
40. **(c)**

41. **(b)** (Light bends upwards)
Refracted WF

42. **(a)** $I = I_0\left(\dfrac{\sin\phi}{\phi}\right)^2$ and $\phi = \dfrac{\pi}{\lambda}(b\sin\theta\ )$

When the slit width is doubled, the amplitude of the wave at the centre of the screen is doubled, so the intensity at the centre is increased by a factor 4.

43. **(a)**
44. **(a)** Where n is equivalent number of fringe by which the centre fringe is shifted due to mica sheet

$$\lambda = \dfrac{(\mu-1)\,t}{n} = \dfrac{(1.5-1)\,6\times 10^{-6}}{5}$$

$$= 6\times 10^{-7}\,m = 6000\ \text{Å}$$

45. **(c)** Suppose intensity of unpolarised light $= 100$.
$\therefore$ Intensity of polarised light from first nicol prism

$$= \dfrac{I_0}{2} = \dfrac{1}{2}\times 100 = 50$$

According to law of Malus,

$$I = I_0\cos^2\theta = 50\,(\cos 60°)^2 = 50\times\left(\dfrac{1}{2}\right)^2 = 12.5$$

1. **(d)** Wavelength of particle $(\lambda_1) = \dfrac{h}{mv} = \dfrac{h}{(1\times10^{-3})\times v}$

where v is the velocity of the particle.

Wavelength of electron

$(\lambda_2) = \dfrac{h}{\left(9.1\times10^{-31}\right)\times\left(3\times10^{6}\right)}$

But $\lambda_1 = \lambda_2$

$\therefore \dfrac{h}{\left(1\times10^{-3}\times v\right)} = \dfrac{h}{(9.1\times10^{-31})\times(3\times10^{6})}$

$\Rightarrow v = \dfrac{9.1\times10^{-31}\times3\times10^{6}}{10^{-3}}$

$= 2.73\times10^{-21}\,\text{ms}^{-1}$

2. **(a)** For electron De-Broglie wavelength,

$\lambda_e = \dfrac{h}{\sqrt{2mE}}$

For photon $E = pc$

$\Rightarrow$ De-Broglie wavelength, $\lambda_{Ph} = \dfrac{hc}{E}$

$\therefore \quad \dfrac{\lambda_e}{\lambda_{Ph}} = \dfrac{h}{\sqrt{2mE}}\times\dfrac{E}{hc} = \left(\dfrac{E}{2m}\right)^{1/2}\dfrac{1}{c}$

3. **(d)** The electron ejected with maximum speed v_{max} are stopped by electric field E = 4N/C after travelling a distance d = 1m

$\dfrac{1}{2}mv_{max}^{2} = eEd = 4eV$

The energy of incident photon $= \dfrac{1240}{200} = 6.2$ eV

From equation of photo electric effect

$\dfrac{1}{2}mv_{max}^{2} = hv - \phi_0$

$\therefore \phi_0 = 6.2 - 4 = 2.2$ eV

4. **(b)** $\lambda_{min} = 1$ Å (given)

$\because \lambda_{min} = \dfrac{1240}{E}$ (eV) (nm)

Thus, $E = \dfrac{1240(\text{eV})(\text{nm})}{0.01(\text{nm})} = 12400$ eV

$E = 12.4\,\text{KeV}$

5. **(a)** The maximum kinetic energy of an electron accelerated through a potential difference of V volt is $\dfrac{1}{2}mv^{2} = eV$

$\therefore$ maximum velocity $v = \sqrt{\dfrac{2eV}{m}}$

$v = \sqrt{\dfrac{2\times1.6\times10^{-19}\times15000}{9.1\times10^{-31}}}$

$v = 7.26\times10^{7}$ m/s

6. **(b)** Photoelectrons are emitted in A alone. Energy of electron needed if emitted from $A = \dfrac{hv}{e}\text{eV}$

$\therefore E_A = \dfrac{\left(6.6\times10^{-34}\right)\times\left(1.8\times10^{14}\right)}{1.6\times10^{-19}} = 0.74\,\text{eV}$

$E_B = \dfrac{\left(6.6\times10^{-34}\right)\times\left(2.2\times10^{14}\right)}{1.6\times10^{-19}} = 0.91$ eV

Incident energy 0.825 eV is greater than E_A (0.74 eV) but less than E_B (0.91 eV).

7. **(a)** According to relation, $E = \dfrac{1}{2}mv^{2}$

$\sqrt{\dfrac{2E}{m}} = v$

$\lambda = \dfrac{h}{\sqrt{2mE}}$

Because $m_1 < m_3 < m_2$

So for same λ, $E_1 > E_3 > E_2$.

8. **(a)** Emission of electron from a substance under the action of light is photoelectric effect. Light must be at a sufficiently high frequency. It may be visible light, U.V, X-rays. So U.V. cause electron emission.

9. **(b)** $\lambda_0 = \dfrac{c}{v_0} = \dfrac{3 \times 10^8}{5 \times 10^{14}} = 6 \times 10^{-7}\,\text{m} = 6000\text{Å}$

10. **(c)** $\lambda = \dfrac{h}{mv}$, $v = \dfrac{m_0}{\sqrt{1 - \left(\dfrac{v}{c}\right)^2}}$, $v \to c$, $m \to \infty$

hence, $\lambda \to 0$.

11. **(a)** Give that, only 25% of 200W converter electrical energy into light of yellow colour

$\left(\dfrac{hc}{\lambda}\right) \times N = 200 \times \dfrac{25}{100}$

Where N is the No. of photons emitted per second, h is planck's constant and c is speed of light.

$N = \dfrac{200 \times 25}{100} \times \dfrac{\lambda}{hc}$

$= \dfrac{200 \times 25 \times 0.6 \times 10^{-6}}{100 \times 6.2 \times 10^{-34} \times 3 \times 10^8} = 1.5 \times 10^{20}$

12. **(d)** For photon $E = hv$

$E = \dfrac{hc}{\lambda} \Rightarrow \lambda_2 = \dfrac{hc}{E}$ ...(i)

for proton $E = \dfrac{1}{2} m_p v_p^2$

$E = \dfrac{1}{2} \dfrac{m_p^2 v_p^2}{m} \Rightarrow p = \sqrt{2mE}$

From De Broglie Eqn.

$p = \dfrac{h}{\lambda_1} \Rightarrow \lambda_1 = \dfrac{h}{p} = \dfrac{h}{\sqrt{2mE}}$ ...(ii)

$\dfrac{\lambda_2}{\lambda_1} = \dfrac{\dfrac{hc}{E}}{E \times \dfrac{h}{\sqrt{2mE}}} \infty E^{-1/2}$

13. **(a)** $hv = W_0 + E_k = 3.5 + 1.2 = 4.7\,\text{eV}$

14. **(a)** $\phi = 6.2\,\text{eV} = 6.2 \times 1.6 \times 10^{-19}\,\text{J}$

$V = 5\,\text{volt}$

$\dfrac{hc}{\lambda} - \phi = eV_0$

$\Rightarrow \lambda = \dfrac{hc}{\phi + eV_0}$

$= \dfrac{6.6 \times 10^{-34} \times 3 \times 10^8}{1.6 \times 10^{-19}(6.2 + 5)} \approx 10^{-7}\,\text{m}$

This range lies in ultra violet range.

15. **(c)** Applying Einstein's formula for photo-electricity

$hv = \phi + \dfrac{1}{2} mv^2$; $hv = \phi + K$

$\phi = hv - K$

If we use $2v$ frequency then let the kinetic energy becomes K'

So, $h \cdot 2v = \phi + K'$

          $2hv = hv - K + K'$

          $K' = hv + K$

16. **(a)** $\because \lambda_0 = \dfrac{hc}{\phi}$

$\therefore (\lambda_0)_{\text{sodium}} = \dfrac{6.6 \times 10^{-34} \times 3 \times 10^8}{2 \times 1.6 \times 10^{-19}} = 6188\,\text{Å}$

$\because \lambda_0 \propto \dfrac{1}{\phi} \Rightarrow \dfrac{(\lambda_0)_{\text{sodium}}}{(\lambda_0)_{\text{copper}}} = \dfrac{(\phi)_{\text{copper}}}{(\phi)_{\text{sodium}}}$

$\Rightarrow (\lambda_0)_{\text{copper}} = \dfrac{2}{4} \times 6188 = 3094\,\text{Å}$

To eject photo-electrons from sodium the longest wavelength is 6188 Å and that for copper is 3094 Å.

Hence for light of wavelength 4000 Å, sodium is suitable.

17. **(c)** $\dfrac{1}{2} mv^2 = \dfrac{hc}{\lambda} - \phi \Rightarrow v = \sqrt{\dfrac{2(hc - \lambda\phi)}{\lambda m}}$

18. **(d)** de-Broglie wavelength,

$\lambda = \dfrac{h}{p} = \dfrac{h}{\sqrt{2.m.(K.E)}}$

$\therefore \lambda \propto \dfrac{1}{\sqrt{K.E}}$

If K.E is doubled, wavelength becomes $\dfrac{\lambda}{\sqrt{2}}$

19. **(b)** $\dfrac{1}{2} m v_1^2 = 2\,W_0 - W_0 = W_0$ and

$\dfrac{1}{2} m v_2^2 = 10\,W_0 - W_0 = 9W_0$

$\therefore \quad \dfrac{v_1}{v_2} = \sqrt{\dfrac{W_0}{9\,W_0}} = \dfrac{1}{3}$

20. **(a)** The work function has no effect on photoelectric current so long as $hv > W_0$. The photoelectric current is proportional to the intensity of incident light. Since there is no change in the intensity of light, hence $I_1 = I_2$.

21. **(c)** $n \to 2 - 1$

    $E = 10.2\,\text{eV}$

    $kE = E - \phi$

    $Q = 10.20 - 3.57$

    $h\upsilon_0 = 6.63\,\text{eV}$

$$v_0 = \frac{6.63 \times 1.6 \times 10^{-19}}{6.67 \times 10^{-34}} = 1.6 \times 10^{15} \text{ Hz}$$

22. **(d)** $h\nu = W + \frac{1}{2}mv^2$ or $\frac{hc}{\lambda} = W + \frac{1}{2}mv^2$

Here $\lambda = 3000\ \text{Å} = 3000 \times 10^{-10}$ m
and $W = 1\ eV = 1.6 \times 10^{-19}$ joule

$$\therefore \frac{(6.6 \times 10^{-34})(3 \times 10^8)}{3000 \times 10^{-10}}$$

$$= (1.6 \times 10^{-19}) + \frac{1}{2} \times (9.1 \times 10^{-31})v^2$$

Solving we get, $v \cong 10^6$ m/s

23. **(b)** According to Einstein's photoelectric equation, $h\nu = \phi_0 + K_{max}$
We have

$$h\nu = \phi_0 + 0.5 \qquad \text{...(i)}$$
and $1.2 h\nu = \phi_0 + 0.8 \qquad \text{...(ii)}$

Therefore, from above two equations $\phi_0 = 1.0$ eV.

24. **(c)** $\lambda_{max.} = \frac{2d\sin\theta}{n_{min.}} = \frac{2 \times 15 \times \sin 90^\circ}{1} = 30\text{Å}$

25. **(d)** $W_0 = h\nu_1 - eV_1$
$\qquad = h\,\nu_2 - eV_2$
$eV_2 = h(\nu_2 - \nu_1) + eV_1$

$$V_2 = \frac{h(n_2 - n_1)}{e} + V_1$$

26. **(b)** $KE_{max} = h\nu - \phi$
$1eV = h\nu - 1.9eV \Rightarrow h\nu = 2.9$ eV

Now threshold wavelength (maximum wavelength), $\lambda_0 = \frac{hc}{E}$

$$\Rightarrow \lambda_0 = \frac{6.6 \times 10^{-34} \times 3 \times 10^8}{1.9 \times 1.6 \times 10^{-19}} = 6513\ \text{Å}$$

And threshold frequency

$$\nu_0 = \frac{c}{\lambda_0} = \frac{3 \times 10^8}{6513 \times 10^{-10}} = 4.6 \times 10^{14} \text{Hz}$$

27. **(b)** $E = W_0 + K_{max} \qquad \text{...(i)}$
$\Rightarrow hf = W_A + K_A \qquad \text{...(ii)}$

and $2hf = W_B + K_B = 2W_A + K_B \left(\because \frac{W_A}{W_B} = \frac{1}{2} \right)$

Dividing equation (i) by (ii)

$$\frac{1}{2} = \frac{W_A + K_A}{2W_A + K_B} \Rightarrow \frac{K_A}{K_B} = \frac{1}{2}$$

28. **(d)** $h\upsilon - h\upsilon_0 = E_K$, according to photoelectric equation, when $\upsilon = \upsilon_0$, $E_K = 0$.
Graph (d) represents $E_K - \upsilon$ relationship.

29. **(d)** $K_{max} = \frac{hc}{\lambda} - W = \frac{hc}{\lambda} - 5.01$

$$= \frac{12375}{\lambda(\text{in Å})} - 5.01$$

$$= \frac{12375}{2000} - 5.01 = 6.1875 - 5.01 = 1.17775$$

$$\simeq 1.2 \text{ V}$$

30. **(b)**

31. **(b)** $\lambda \propto \frac{1}{\sqrt{V}}$

$$\Rightarrow \frac{\lambda_1}{\lambda_2} = \sqrt{\frac{V_2}{V_1}} = \sqrt{\frac{100\text{keV}}{25\text{keV}}} = 2$$

$$\Rightarrow \lambda_2 = \frac{\lambda_1}{2}$$

32. **(a)** In the Davisson and Germer experiment, the velocity of electrons emitted from the electron gun can be increased by increasing the potential difference between the anode and filament.

33. **(b)** According to Einsten's photoelectric effect, the K.E. of the radiated electrons
$K.E_{max} = E - W$

$$\frac{1}{2}mv_1^2 = (1 - 0.5)\ eV = 0.5 \text{ eV}$$

$$\frac{1}{2}mv_2^2 = (2.5 - 0.5)\ eV = 2 \text{ eV}$$

$$\frac{v_1}{v_2} = \sqrt{\frac{0.5}{2}} = \frac{1}{\sqrt{4}} = 1/2$$

34. **(b)** By using $h\nu - h\nu_0 = K_{max}$
$\Rightarrow h(v_1 - v_0) = K_1 \qquad \text{..... (i)}$
And $h(v_2 - v_0) = K_2 \qquad \text{..... (ii)}$

$$\Rightarrow \frac{v_1 - v_0}{v_2 - v_0} = \frac{K_1}{K_2} = \frac{1}{K}, \text{ Hence } v_0 = \frac{kv_1 - v_2}{K - 1}.$$

35. **(b)** Cathode rays get deflected in the electric field.

36. **(c)** As we know

$$\lambda \propto \frac{1}{\sqrt{V}}$$

$$\therefore \frac{1}{\sqrt{100}} : \frac{1}{\sqrt{200}} : \frac{1}{\sqrt{300}} = 1 : \frac{1}{\sqrt{2}} : \frac{1}{\sqrt{3}}$$

37. **(d)** Number of emitted electrons N_E
$\propto$ Intensity

$$\propto \frac{1}{(\text{Distance})^2}$$

Therefore, as distance is doubled, N_E decreases by $(1/4)$ times.

38. **(d)** Photoelectrons are emitted if the frequency of incident light is greater than the threshold frequency.

39. **(a)** K.E. $= h\nu - h\nu_{th} = eV_0$ (V_0 = cut off voltage)

$$\Rightarrow V_0 = \frac{h}{e}(8.2 \times 10^{14} - 3.3 \times 10^{14})$$

$$= \frac{6.6 \times 10^{-34} \times 4.9 \times 10^{14}}{1.6 \times 10^{-19}} \approx 2V.$$

40. **(d)** $\dfrac{hc}{\lambda} - \phi = eV_0$

$$v_0 = \frac{hc}{e\lambda} - \frac{\phi}{e}$$

For metal A   For metal B

$$\frac{\phi_A}{hc} = \frac{1}{\lambda} \qquad\qquad \frac{\phi_B}{hc} = \frac{1}{\lambda}$$

As the value of $\dfrac{1}{\lambda}$ (increasing and decreasing) is not specified hence we cannot say that which metal has comparatively greater or lesser work function (ϕ).

41. **(c)**

42. **(d)** Potential difference $= 100$ V

K.E. acquired by electron $= e\,(100)$

$$\frac{1}{2}mv^2 = e(100) \;\; \Rightarrow v = \sqrt{\frac{2e(100)}{m}}$$

According to de Broglie's concept

$$\lambda = \frac{h}{mv}$$

$$\Rightarrow \lambda = \frac{h}{m\sqrt{\dfrac{2e(100)}{m}}}$$

$$= \frac{h}{\sqrt{2me(100)}} = 1.2 \times 10^{-10} = 1.2\text{Å}$$

43. **(d)** Since $p = nh\nu$

$$\Rightarrow n = \frac{p}{h\nu} = \frac{2 \times 10^{-3}}{6.6 \times 10^{-34} \times 6 \times 10^{14}} = 5 \times 10^{15}$$

44. **(a)** From formula

$$\lambda = \frac{h}{\sqrt{2mKT}}$$

$$= \frac{6.63 \times 10^{-34}}{\sqrt{2 \times 1.67 \times 10^{-27} \times 1.38 \times 10^{-23}T}} m$$

[By placing value of h, m and k)

$$= \frac{30.8}{\sqrt{T}}\text{Å}$$

45. **(c)** The photoelectric equation
$K_{max} = h\nu - \phi_0$
Explains that the intensity of incident radiation will increase photocurrent only beyond the threshold frequency.

1. **(b)** $P.E. = \dfrac{-Ze^2}{4\pi\varepsilon_0 r}$. Negative sign indicates that revolving electron is bound to the positive nucleus.
So, it decreases with increase in radii of orbit.

2. **(b)** $E = Rhc\left[\dfrac{1}{n_1^2} - \dfrac{1}{n_2^2}\right]$

E will be maximum for the transition for which

$\left[\dfrac{1}{n_1^2} - \dfrac{1}{n_2^2}\right]$ is maximum. Here n_2 is the higher energy level.

Clearly, $\left[\dfrac{1}{n_1^2} - \dfrac{1}{n_2^2}\right]$ is maximum for the third transition,

i.e. $2 \rightarrow 1$. I transition represents the absorption of energy.

3. **(a)** Number of emission spectral lines

$N = \dfrac{n(n-1)}{2}$

$\therefore 3 = \dfrac{n_1(n_1 - 1)}{2}$, in first case.

Or $n_1^2 - n_1 - 6 = 0$ or $(n_1 - 3)(n_1 + 2) = 0$
Take positive root.
$\therefore n_1 = 3$

Again, $6 = \dfrac{n_2(n_2 - 1)}{2}$, in second case.

Or $n_2^2 - n_2 - 12 = 0$ or $(n_2 - 4)(n_2 + 3) = 0$.
Take positive root, or $n_2 = 4$

Now velocity of electron $\upsilon = \dfrac{2\pi KZe^2}{nh}$

$\therefore \dfrac{\upsilon_1}{\upsilon_2} = \dfrac{n_2}{n_1} = \dfrac{4}{3}$.

4. **(c)** $N \propto \dfrac{1}{\sin^4\theta/2}$; $\dfrac{N_2}{N_1} = \dfrac{\sin^4(\theta_1/2)}{\sin^4(\theta_2/2)}$

or $\dfrac{N_2}{5\times10^6} = \dfrac{\sin^4(60°/2)}{\sin^4(120°/2)}$

or $\dfrac{N_2}{5\times10^6} = \dfrac{\sin^4 30°}{\sin^4 60°}$

or $N_2 = 5\times10^6 \times \left(\dfrac{1}{2}\right)^4 \left(\dfrac{2}{\sqrt{3}}\right)^4 = \dfrac{5}{9}\times10^6$

5. **(c)** Magnetic moment of the hydrogen atom, when the electron is in n^{th} excited state, i.e., $n' = (n + 1)$
As magnetic moment $M_n = I_n A = i_n(\pi r_n^2)$

$i_n = eV_n = \dfrac{mz^2e^5}{4\varepsilon_0^2 n^3 h^3}$

$r_n = \dfrac{n^2 h^2}{4\pi^2 kzme^2}\left(k = \dfrac{1}{4\pi\varepsilon_0}\right)$

Solving we get magnetic moment of the hydrogen atom for n^{th} excited state

$M_{n'} = \left(\dfrac{e}{2m}\right)\dfrac{nh}{2\pi}$

6. **(a)** $E = \dfrac{hc}{\lambda} \Rightarrow \lambda = \dfrac{hc}{E} = \dfrac{6.62\times10^{-34} \times 3\times10^8}{12.5\times1.6\times10^{-19}}$
$= 993\,A°$

$\dfrac{1}{\lambda} = R\left(\dfrac{1}{n_1^2} - \dfrac{1}{n_2^2}\right)$

(where Rydberg constant , $R = 1.097 \times 10^7$)

or, $\dfrac{1}{993\times10^{-10}} = 1.097\times10^7 \left(\dfrac{1}{1^2} - \dfrac{1}{n_2^2}\right)$

Solving we get $n_2 = 3$
Spectral lines
Total number of spectral lines $= 3$
Two lines in Lyman series for $n_1 = 1, n_2 = 2$ and $n_1 = 1$, $n_2 = 3$ and one in Balmer series for $n_1 = 2$, $n_2 = 3$

n = 3
n = 2 — Balmer
Lyman   Lyman
n = 1

7. **(b)** $l = \dfrac{nh}{2\pi}, |E| \propto Z^2/n^2 ; n = 3$

$\Rightarrow l_H = l_{Li}$ and $|E_H| < |E_{Li}|$

8. **(b)** $r \propto n^2$

$\therefore \dfrac{\text{radius of final state}}{\text{radius of initial state}} = n^2$

$\dfrac{21.2\times10^{-11}}{5.3\times10^{-11}} = n^2$

$\therefore n^2 = 4$ or $n = 2$

9. **(a)** $R = \dfrac{R_0 n^2}{Z}$

Radius in ground state $= \dfrac{R_0}{Z}$

Radius in first excited state $= \dfrac{R_0 \times 4}{Z}$ $(\because n = 2)$

Hence, radius of first excited state is four times the radius in ground state.

10. **(a)** Speed of electron in nth orbit

$$V_n = \frac{2\pi\,KZe^2}{nh}$$

$$V = (2.19 \times 10^6\,\text{m/s})\,\frac{Z}{n}$$

$$V = (2.19 \times 10^6)\,\frac{2}{3}\ (Z = 2\ \&\ n = 3)$$

$$V = 1.46 \times 10^6\ \text{m/s}$$

11. **(b)** $KE_{max} = 10\,eV$

$\phi = 2.75\,eV$

Total incident energy

$E = \phi + KE_{max} = 12.75\,eV$

∴ Energy is released when electron jumps from the excited state n to the ground state.

∵ $E_4 - E_1 = \{-0.85 - (-13.6)\,ev\}$

$\qquad\qquad = 12.75\,eV$

∴ value of n = 4

12. **(a)** As the electron comes nearer to the nucleus the potential energy decreases

$$\left(\because \frac{-k.Ze^2}{r} = \text{P.E. and } r \text{ decreases}\right)$$

The K.E. will increase $\left[\because K.E. = \frac{1}{2}\,|\,P.E.\,| = \frac{1}{2}\frac{kZe^2}{r}\right]$

The total energy decreases $\left[T.E. = -\frac{1}{2}\frac{kZe^2}{r}\right]$

13. **(d)** When one e^- is removed from neutral helium atom, it becomes a one e^- species.

For one e^- species we know

$$E_n = \frac{-13.6Z^2}{n^2}\ \text{eV/atom}$$

For helium ion, $Z = 2$ and for first orbit $n = 1$.

∴ $E_1 = \frac{-13.6}{(1)^2} \times 2^2 = -54.4\,eV$

∴ Energy required to remove this $e^- = +54.4\,eV$

∴ Total energy required $= 54.4 + 24.6 = 79\,eV$

14. **(b)** For 2nd line of Balmer series in hydrogen spectrum

$$\frac{1}{\lambda} = R\,(1)\left(\frac{1}{2^2} - \frac{1}{4^2}\right) = \frac{3}{16}R$$

For Li^{2+} $\left[\frac{1}{\lambda} = R \times 9\left(\frac{1}{x^2} - \frac{1}{12^2}\right) = \frac{3R}{16}\right]$

which is satisfied by n = 12 → n = 6.

15. **(d)** For an atom following Bohr's model, the radius is given by

$$r_m = \frac{r_0 m^2}{Z}\ \text{where } r_0 = \text{Bohr's radius and } m = \text{orbit number.}$$

For Fm, $m = 5$ (Fifth orbit in which the outermost electron is present)

∴ $r_m = \frac{r_0 5^2}{100} = nr_0$ (given) $\Rightarrow n = \frac{1}{4}$

16. **(a)** Energy of electron in n^{th} orbit is

$$E_n = -(Rch)\,\frac{Z^2}{n^2} = -54.4\ \text{eV}$$

For He^+ is ground state

$$E_1 = -(Rch)\,\frac{(2)^2}{(1)^2} = -54.4 \Rightarrow Rch = 13.6$$

∴ For Li^{++} in first excited state (n = 2)

$$E' = -13.6 \times \frac{(3)^2}{(2)^2} = -30.6\ \text{eV}$$

17. **(a)** Angular momentum $= mrv = J$

∴ $v = \frac{J}{mr}$

K. E. of electron $= \frac{1}{2}mv^2 = \frac{1}{2}m\left(\frac{J}{mr}\right)^2$

$$= \frac{J^2}{2mr^2}$$

18. **(b)** When $F = \frac{k}{r} = $ centripetal force, then $\frac{k}{r} = \frac{mv^2}{r}$

$\Rightarrow mv^2 = $ constant $\quad\Rightarrow$ kinetic energy is constant

$\Rightarrow T$ is independent of n.

19. **(b)** $\dfrac{1}{\lambda'} = \dfrac{1}{\lambda}\sqrt{\dfrac{c-v}{c+v}}$

Here, $\lambda' = 706\,nm$, $\lambda = 656\,nm$

∴ $\dfrac{c-v}{c+v} = \left(\dfrac{\lambda}{\lambda'}\right)^2 = \left(\dfrac{656}{706}\right)^2 = 0.86$

$\Rightarrow \dfrac{v}{c} = \dfrac{0.14}{1.86}$

$\Rightarrow v = 0.075 \times 3 \times 10^8 = 2.25 \times 10^7\,\text{m/s}$

20. **(d)** ∵ $B = \dfrac{\mu_0 I}{2r}$ and $I = \dfrac{e}{T}$

$$B = \frac{\mu_0 e}{2rT}\ [\,r \propto n^2, T \propto n^5\,];\quad B \propto \frac{1}{n^5}$$

21. **(a)** 53 electrons in iodine atom are distributed as 2, 8, 18, 18, 7

∴ $n = 5$

$$r_n = (0.53 \times 10^{-10})\frac{n^2}{Z}$$

$$= \frac{0.53 \times 10^{-10} \times 5^2}{53} = 2.5 \times 10^{-11}\,m$$

22. **(a)** At closest distance of approach, the kinetic energy of the particle will convert completely into electrostatic potential energy.

Kinetic energy K.E. $= \frac{1}{2}mv^2$

Potential energy $P.E. = \dfrac{KQq}{r}$

$\dfrac{1}{2}mv^2 = \dfrac{KQq}{r} \quad \Rightarrow \quad r \propto \dfrac{1}{m}$

23. (c) $\dfrac{n(n-1)}{2} = 6$

$$
\begin{array}{l}
\rule{6cm}{0.4pt}\ 4 \\[2pt]
\rule{6cm}{0.4pt}\ 3 \\[2pt]
\rule{6cm}{0.4pt}\ 2 \\[2pt]
\rule{6cm}{0.4pt}\ 1
\end{array}
$$

$n^2 - n - 12 = 0$

$(n-4)(n+3) = 0 \quad$ or $\quad n = 4$

24. (c) The wavelength of spectrum is given by

$\dfrac{1}{\lambda} = Rz^2\left(\dfrac{1}{n_1^2} - \dfrac{1}{n_2^2}\right) \quad$ where $R = \dfrac{1.097 \times 10^7}{1 + \dfrac{m}{M}}$

where m = mass of electron

M = mass of nucleus.

For different M, R is different and therefore λ is different.

25. (a) $\because T \propto n^3$

$Tn_1 = 8\, Tn_2$ (given)

Hence, $n_1 = 2n_2$

26. (d) $\Delta E = h\nu$

$\nu = \dfrac{\Delta E}{h} = k\left[\dfrac{1}{(n-1)^2} - \dfrac{1}{n^2}\right] = \dfrac{k(2n-1)}{n^2(n-1)^2}$

$\approx \dfrac{2k}{n^3} \quad$ or $\quad \nu \propto \dfrac{1}{n^3}$

27. (c) A spectrum is observed, when light coming directly from a source is examined with a spectroscope. Therefore spectrum obtained from a sodium vapour lamp is emission spectrum.

28. (a) Energy of ground state 13.6 eV

Energy of first excited state

$= -\dfrac{13.6}{4} = -3.4$ eV

Energy of second excited state

$= -\dfrac{13.6}{9} = -1.5$ eV

Difference between ground state and 2nd excited state

$= 13.6 - 1.5 = 12.1$ eV

So, electron can be excited upto 3rd orbit

No. of possible transition

$1 \to 2, 1 \to 3, 2 \to 3$

So, three lines are possible.

29. (b) In Bohr's model, angular momentum is quantised i.e

$\ell = n\left(\dfrac{h}{2\pi}\right)$

30. (b) The smallest frequency and largest wavelength in ultraviolet region will be for transition of electron from orbit 2 to orbit 1.

$\therefore \quad \dfrac{1}{\lambda} = R\left(\dfrac{1}{n_1^2} - \dfrac{1}{n_2^2}\right)$

$\Rightarrow \dfrac{1}{122 \times 10^{-9}\,m} = R\left[\dfrac{1}{1^2} - \dfrac{1}{2^2}\right] = R\left[1 - \dfrac{1}{4}\right] = \dfrac{3R}{4}$

$\Rightarrow R = \dfrac{4}{3 \times 122 \times 10^{-9}}\,m^{-1}$

The highest frequency and smallest wavelength for infrared region will be for transition of electron from ∞ to 3rd orbit.

$\therefore \quad \dfrac{1}{\lambda} = R\left(\dfrac{1}{n_1^2} - \dfrac{1}{n_2^2}\right) \Rightarrow \dfrac{1}{\lambda} = \dfrac{4}{3 \times 122 \times 10^{-9}}\left(\dfrac{1}{3^2} - \dfrac{1}{\infty}\right)$

$\therefore \lambda = \dfrac{3 \times 122 \times 9 \times 10^{-9}}{4} = 823.5\,\text{nm}$

31. (c) $\dfrac{1}{\lambda} = R\left(\dfrac{1}{n_1^2} - \dfrac{1}{n_2^2}\right)$ where R = Rydberg constant

$\dfrac{1}{\lambda_{32}} = \left(\dfrac{1}{4} - \dfrac{1}{9}\right) = \dfrac{5}{36}$

$\Rightarrow \lambda_{32} = \dfrac{36}{5}$

Similarly solving for λ_{31} and λ_{21}

$\lambda_{31} = \dfrac{9}{8}$ and $\lambda_{21} = \dfrac{4}{3}$

$\therefore \quad \dfrac{\lambda_{32}}{\lambda_{31}} = 6.4$ and $\dfrac{\lambda_{21}}{\lambda_{31}} \simeq 1.2$

32. (d) $b = \dfrac{Ze^2 \cot\left(\dfrac{\theta}{2}\right)}{4\pi \in_0 k_i} = 0 \Rightarrow \cot\left(\dfrac{\theta}{2}\right) = 0$

$\Rightarrow \dfrac{\theta}{2} = 90° \text{ or } \theta = 180°$

33. (a) Speed of electron in nth orbit

$V_n = \dfrac{2\pi\, KZe^2}{nh}$

$V = (2.19 \times 10^6\,\text{m/s})\,\dfrac{Z}{n}$

$V = (2.19 \times 10^6)\,\dfrac{2}{3}\ (Z = 2\ \&\ n = 3)$

$V = 1.46 \times 10^6$ m/s

34. (d) $E = E_4 - E_3$

$= -\dfrac{13.6}{4^2} - \left(-\dfrac{13.6}{3^2}\right) = -0.85 + 1.51$

$= 0.66$ eV

35. (d) $\because$ The frequency of the transition $\nu \propto \dfrac{1}{n^2}$, when

$n = 1, 2, 3.$

36. **(c)** According to Bohr's theory, the wave number of the last line of the Balmer series in hydrogen spectrum,

For hydrogen atom $z = 1$

$$\frac{1}{\lambda} = RZ^2\left(\frac{1}{n_2^2} - \frac{1}{n_1^2}\right)$$

$$= 10^7 \times 1^2 \left(\frac{1}{2^2} - \frac{1}{\infty^2}\right)$$

$\Rightarrow$ wave number $\dfrac{1}{\lambda} = 0.25 \times 10^7 \, \text{m}^{-1}$

37. **(a)** Velocity of electron in n^{th} orbit of hydrogen atom is given by :

$$V_n = \frac{2\pi K Z e^2}{nh}$$

Substituting the values we get,

$$V_n = \frac{2.2 \times 10^6}{n} \, \text{m/s} \quad \text{or} \quad V_n \propto \frac{1}{n}$$

As principal quantum number increases, velocity decreases.

38. **(c)** $\dfrac{1}{\lambda} = R\left[\dfrac{1}{n_1^2} - \dfrac{1}{n_2^2}\right]$

$$\Rightarrow \frac{1}{970.6 \times 10^{-10}} = 1.097 \times 10^7 \left[\frac{1}{1^2} - \frac{1}{n_2^2}\right] \Rightarrow n_2 = 4$$

$\therefore$ Number of emission line $N = \dfrac{n(n-1)}{2} = \dfrac{4 \times 3}{2} = 6$

39. **(a)** We have $E_n = \dfrac{-2\pi^2 m K^2 Z^2 e^4}{n^2 h^2}$. For helium $Z = 2$. Hence requisite answer is $4E_n$

40. **(c)** As α-particles are doubly ionised helium He^{++} i.e. Positively charged and nucleus is also positively charged and we know that like charges repel each other.

41. **(b)** $\bar{v} = R\left(\dfrac{1}{n_1^2} - \dfrac{1}{n_2^2}\right)$, where $n_1 = 2, n_2 = 4$

$$\bar{v} = R\left(\frac{1}{4} - \frac{1}{16}\right)$$

$$\frac{1}{\lambda} = R\left(\frac{12}{4 \times 16}\right) \quad \Rightarrow \quad \lambda = \frac{16}{3R}$$

42. **(a)** The kinetic energy of the projectile is given by

$$\frac{1}{2}mv^2 = \frac{Ze\,(2e)}{4\pi\varepsilon_0 r_0}$$

$$= \frac{Z_1\,Z_2}{4\pi\varepsilon_0 r_0}$$

Thus energy of the projectile is directly proportional to Z_1, Z_2

43. **(a)** We know that $\dfrac{1}{\lambda} = RZ^2\left[\dfrac{1}{n_1^2} - \dfrac{1}{n_2^2}\right]$

The wave length of first spectral line in the Balmer series of hydrogen atom is 6561Å . Here $n_2 = 3$ and $n_1 = 2$

$$\therefore \quad \frac{1}{6561} = R(1)^2\left(\frac{1}{4} - \frac{1}{9}\right) = \frac{5R}{36} \qquad \text{...(i)}$$

For the second spectral line in the Balmer series of singly ionised helium ion $n_2 = 4$ and $n_1 = 2$; $Z = 2$

$$\therefore \quad \frac{1}{\lambda} = R(2)^2\left[\frac{1}{4} - \frac{1}{16}\right] = \frac{3R}{4} \qquad \text{...(ii)}$$

Dividing equation (i) and equation (ii) we get

$$\frac{\lambda}{6561} = \frac{5R}{36} \times \frac{4}{3R} = \frac{5}{27}$$

$$\therefore \quad \lambda = 1215 \, \text{Å}$$

44. **(a)** For Lyman series

$$\upsilon = R_C\left[\frac{1}{1^2} - \frac{1}{n^2}\right]$$

where $n = 2, 3, 4, \dots\dots$

For the series limit of Lyman series, $n = \infty$

$$\therefore \quad \upsilon_1 = R_C\left[\frac{1}{1^2} - \frac{1}{\infty^2}\right] = R_C \qquad \text{...(i)}$$

For the first line of Lyman series, $n = 2$

$$\therefore \quad \upsilon_2 = R_C\left[\frac{1}{1^2} - \frac{1}{2^2}\right] = \frac{3}{4}R_C \qquad \text{...(ii)}$$

For Balmer series

$$\upsilon = R_C\left[\frac{1}{2^2} - \frac{1}{n^2}\right]$$

where $n = 3, 4, 5 \dots$

For the series limit of Balmer series, $n = \infty$

$$\therefore \quad \upsilon_3 = R_C\left[\frac{1}{2^2} - \frac{1}{\infty^2}\right] = \frac{R_C}{4} \qquad \text{...(iii)}$$

From equation (i), (ii) and (iii), we get

$$\upsilon_1 = \upsilon_2 + \upsilon_3 \qquad \text{or} \qquad \upsilon_1 - \upsilon_2 = \upsilon_3$$

45. **(d)** As $r \propto \dfrac{1}{m}$ $\qquad \therefore \ r_0' = \dfrac{1}{2}r_0$

As $E \propto m$ $\qquad \therefore \ E_0' = 2(-13.6) = -27.2 \, \text{eV}$

1. **(b)** $B.E. = 0.042 \times 931 \simeq 42\,MeV$

Number of nucleons in ^7_3Li is 7.

$\therefore \quad B.E./\text{nucleon} = \dfrac{42}{7} = 6\,MeV \simeq 5.6\,MeV$

2. **(d)** $^A_Z X \longrightarrow \,^A_{Z+1}Y : \beta, \quad ^A_{Z+1}Y \longrightarrow \,^{A-4}_{Z-1}B^* : \alpha$

$^{A-4}_{Z-1}B^* \longrightarrow \,^{A-4}_{Z-1}B : \gamma$

$(\beta, \alpha, \gamma)\ (\because \beta = \,^0_{-1}e,\ \alpha = \,^4_2 He,$ mass number and charge number of a nucleus remains unchanged during γ decay)

3. **(c)** The radius of the nuclears is directly proportional to cube root of atomic number i.e. $R \propto A^{1/3}$

$\Rightarrow \quad R = R_0 A^{1/3}$, where R_0 is a constant of proportionality

$\dfrac{R_2}{R_1} = \left(\dfrac{A_2}{A_1}\right)^{1/3} \left(\dfrac{64}{27}\right)^{1/3} = \dfrac{4}{3}$

where R_1 = the radius of ^{27}Al, and A_1 = Atomic mass number of Al
R_2 = the radius of ^{64}Cu and A_2 = Atomic mass number of C4

$R_2 = 3.6 \times \dfrac{4}{3} = 4.8\,m$

4. **(c)** Nuclear forces are short range attractive forces which balance the repulsive forces between the protons inside the nucleus.

5. **(a)** $\lambda = \dfrac{1}{t}\log_e \dfrac{A_o}{A} = \dfrac{1}{5}\log_e \dfrac{5000}{1250}$

$= \dfrac{2}{5}\log_e 2 = 0.4\log_e 2$

6. **(d)** Radioactivity at T_1, $R_1 = \lambda N_1$

Radioactivity at T_2, $R_2 = \lambda N_2$

$\therefore$ Number of atoms decayed in time

$(T_1 - T_2) = (N_1 - N_2)$

$= \dfrac{(R_1 - R_2)}{\lambda} = \dfrac{(R_1 - R_2)T}{0.693} \propto (R_1 - R_2)T$

7. **(c)** ^2_1H and ^3_1H requires a and b amount of energies for their nucleons to be separated.

^4_2He releases c amount of energy in its formation i.e., in assembling the nucleons as nucleus.
Hence, Energy released $= c - (a + b) = c - a - b$

8. **(a)** Mass defect $= ZM_p + (A - Z)M_n - M(A,Z)$

or, $\dfrac{B.E.}{c^2} = ZM_p + (A - Z)M_n - M(A,Z)$

$\therefore M(A, Z) = ZM_p + (A - Z)M_n - \dfrac{B.E.}{c^2}$

9. **(d)**

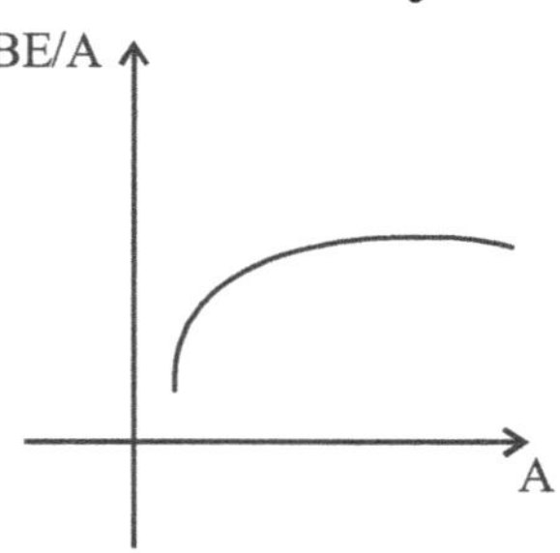

From the graph of BE/A versus mass number A it is clear that, BE/A first increases and then decreases with increase in mass number.

10. **(c)** The range of energy of β-particles is from zero to some maximum value.

11. **(a)** $_{72}A^{180} \xrightarrow{\ \alpha\ } _{70}A_1^{176} \xrightarrow{\ \beta\ } _{71}A_2^{176}$

$\xrightarrow{\ \alpha\ } _{69}A_3^{172} \xrightarrow{\ \gamma\ } _{69}A_4^{172}$

12. **(c)** $\dfrac{dN}{dt} = KN$

$9750 = KN_0 \qquad\qquad\qquad .... (1)$
$975 = KN \qquad\qquad\qquad\ ..... (2)$

Dividing (1) by (2)

$\dfrac{N}{N_0} = \dfrac{1}{10}$

$K = \dfrac{2.303}{t}\log \dfrac{N_0}{N} = \dfrac{2.303}{5}\log 10$

$= 0.4606 = 0.461$ per minute

13. **(d)**

14. **(d)** Extremely high temps needed for fusion make K.E. large enough to overcome repulsion between nuclei.

15. **(c)** Binding energy
$= [ZM_P + (A - Z)M_N - M]c^2$
$= [8M_P + (17 - 8)M_N - M]c^2$
$= [8M_P + 9M_N - M]c^2$
$= [8M_P + 9M_N - M_o]c^2$

16. **(c)** In this reaction mass is not conserved.

17. **(a)** $T_{1/2} = \dfrac{\ln 2}{\lambda} \therefore \lambda = \dfrac{\ln 2}{T_{1/2}}$

$\Rightarrow \lambda_A = \dfrac{\ln 2}{T_A}, \lambda_B = \dfrac{\ln 2}{T_B} \Rightarrow \dfrac{\lambda_A}{\lambda_B} = \dfrac{T_B}{T_A}.$

18. **(d)** $N_1 = N_0 e^{-10\lambda t}$, $N_2 = N_0 e^{-\lambda t}$

$$\frac{N_1}{N_2} = e^{-9\lambda t} = e^{-1} \; ; \; 9\lambda t = 1 \Rightarrow t = \frac{1}{9\lambda}$$

19. **(d)** Let at time t_1 & t_2, number of particles be N_1 & N_2. So,

$$R_1 = \frac{dN_1}{dt} = -\lambda N_1; \quad R_2 = \frac{dN_2}{dt} = -\lambda N_2$$

$$\frac{R_1}{R_2} = \frac{\lambda N_1}{\lambda N_2} = \frac{N_1}{N_1 e^{-\lambda(t_2-t_1)}} = e^{\lambda(t_2-t_1)}$$

$$R_1 = R_2 e^{\lambda(t_2-t_1)} = R_2 e^{-\lambda(t_1-t_2)}$$

20. **(c)** Average life of the nuclei is

$$t_{av} = \frac{1}{\lambda} \qquad\qquad ....(i)$$

Half life of the nuclei

$$t_{1/2} = \frac{0.693}{\lambda} \qquad\qquad ....(ii)$$

from (i) and (ii)

$$t_{av} = \frac{t_{1/2}}{0.693}$$

21. **(d)** Nuclear force is not the same between any two nucleons.

22. **(a)**

23. **(a)** $P = n\left(\dfrac{E}{t}\right) \Rightarrow 1000 = \dfrac{n \times 200 \times 10^6 \times 1.6 \times 10^{-19}}{t}$

$$\Rightarrow \frac{n}{t} = 3.125 \times 10^{13}.$$

24. **(c)** Binding energy per nucleon for fission products is higher relative to Binding energy per nucleon for parent nucleus, i.e., more masses are lost and are obtained as kinetic energy of fission products. So, the given ratio <1.

25. **(b)** We have $K_\alpha = \dfrac{m_y}{m_y + m_\alpha} \cdot Q$

$$\Rightarrow K_\alpha = \frac{A-4}{A} \cdot Q \Rightarrow 48 = \frac{A-4}{A} \cdot 50 \Rightarrow A = 100$$

26. **(b)** Using the relation for mean life.

Given : $t = 2\tau = 2\left(\dfrac{1}{\lambda}\right) \quad \left(\because \tau = \dfrac{1}{\lambda}\right)$

Then from $M = M_0 e^{-\lambda t} = 10 e^{-\lambda \times \frac{2}{\lambda}}$

$$= 10\left(\frac{1}{e}\right)^2 = 1.35g$$

27. **(d)** Because radioactivity is a spontaneous phenomenon.

28. **(a)** α-particle $= {}_2He^4$. It contains 2 p and 2 n. As some mass is converted into B.E., therefore, mass of α particle is slightly less than the sum of the masses of 2 p and 2 n.

29. **(c)** $T_{av} = \dfrac{T_\alpha T_\beta}{T_\alpha + T_\beta}$

If α and B are emitted simultaneously.

30. **(a)** Due to irradiation of α-rays on end A will make it (positive) and irradiation of β-rays on end B will make it (negative) hence current will flow from A to B (or from positive to negative).

31. **(b)** Momentum

$$Mu = \frac{E}{c} = \frac{hv}{c}$$

Recoil energy

$$\frac{1}{2}Mu^2 = \frac{1}{2}\frac{M^2 u^2}{M} = \frac{1}{2M}\left(\frac{hv}{c}\right)^2$$

$$= \frac{h^2 v^2}{2Mc^2}$$

32. **(c)** No. of nuclide at time t is given by $N = N_o e^{-\lambda t}$
Where N_o = initial nuclide
This equation is equivalent to $y = a e^{-kx}$
Thus correct graph is

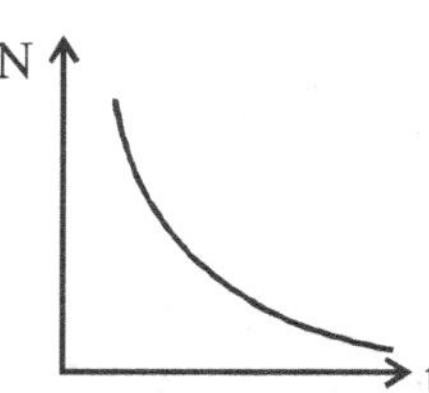

33. **(b)** By conservation of energy,

$$\left(M + \Delta m\right) c^2 \neq \frac{2.M}{2}c^2 + \frac{1}{2} \cdot \frac{2M}{2} v^2,$$

where v is the speed of the daughter nuclei

$$\Rightarrow \Delta mc^2 = \frac{M}{2}v^2 \qquad\qquad \therefore v = c\sqrt{\frac{2\Delta m}{M}}$$

34. **(a)** Suppose that,
The number of ^{10}B type atoms $= x$
and the number of ^{11}B type atoms $= y$
Weight of ^{10}B type atoms $= 10x$
Weight of ^{11}B type atoms $= 11y$
Total number of atoms $= x + y$

$$\therefore \quad \text{Atomic weight} = \frac{10x + 11y}{x + y} = 10.81$$

$$\Rightarrow \quad 10x + 11y = 10.81x + 10.81y$$

$$\Rightarrow \quad 0.81x = 0.19y \Rightarrow \frac{x}{y} = \frac{19}{81}$$

35. **(b)** Applying law of conservation of momentum,
$$m_1 v_1 = m_2 v_2$$

$$\frac{v_1}{v_2} = \frac{m_2}{m_1}$$

As $m = \dfrac{4}{3}\pi r^3 \rho \Rightarrow m \propto r^3$

Hence, $\dfrac{m_2}{m_1} = \dfrac{r_2^3}{r_1^3}$

$\therefore \dfrac{v_1}{v_2} = \dfrac{r_2^3}{r_1^3} \quad \Rightarrow \quad \dfrac{r_2}{r_1} = \left(\dfrac{1}{2}\right)^{\frac{1}{3}}$

36. (d) In an explosion a body breaks up into two pieces of unequal masses both part will have numerically equal momentum and lighter part will have more velocity.

$U \rightarrow Th + He$

$KE_{Th} = \dfrac{P^2}{2m_{Th}} , KE_{He} = \dfrac{P^2}{2m_{He}}$

since m_{He} is less so KE_{He} will be more.

37. (a) As we know, $R = R_0 (A)^{1/3}$

where A = mass number

$R_{Al} = R_0 (27)^{1/3} = 3R_0$

$R_{Te} = R_0 (125)^{1/3} = 5R_0 = \dfrac{5}{3} R_{Al}$

38. (a) Given : Mass of neutron $= M_n$

Mass of proton $= M_p$; Atomic mass of the element $= M$; Number of neutrons in the element $= N$ and number of protons in the element $= Z$. We know that the atomic mass (M) of any stable nucleus is always less than the sum of the masses of the constituent particles.

Therefore, $M < [NM_n + ZM_p]$.

X is a neutrino, when β-particle is emitted.

39. (a) Activity decreases

5000 dps to 2500 dps in 150 days

$\therefore$ Half life period $T_{1/2} = 150$ days

$\therefore 300$ days $= 2T_{1/2}$

Therefore, initial activity $= 5000 \times 2T_{1/2} = 5000 \times 2 \times 2$
$= 20000$ dps

40. (b) The order of density of uranium nucleus is 10^{17} kg/m^2.

41. (b)

42. (a) $B.E_H = \dfrac{2.22}{2} = 1.11$

$B.E_{He} = \dfrac{28.3}{4} = 7.08$

$B.E_{Fe} = \dfrac{492}{56} = 8.78 = $ maximum

$B.E_U = \dfrac{1786}{235} = 7.6$

$^{56}_{26}Fe$ is most stable as it has maximum binding energy per nucleon.

43. (d) Neutrons can't be deflected by a magnetic field.

44. (b) $_{-1}e^0$ is known as β-particle & $\bar{v}$ is known as antineutrino. Since in this reaction $\bar{v}$ is emitted with $_{-1}e^0$ (β-particle or electron), so it is known as β-decay.

45. (a) Given, $\lambda_A = 8\lambda$, $\lambda_B = \lambda$

$N_B = \dfrac{N_A}{e}$

$\Rightarrow N_o e^{-\lambda_B t} = N_o \dfrac{e^{-\lambda_A t}}{e}$

$e^{-\lambda t} = e^{-8\lambda t} e^{-1}$

$e^{-\lambda t} = e^{-8\lambda t - 1}$

Comparing both side powers

$-\lambda t = -8\lambda t - 1$

$-1 = 7\lambda t$

$t = -\dfrac{1}{7\lambda}$

The best possible answer is $t = \dfrac{1}{7\lambda}$

1. **(d)** $\Delta I_E = 8.0\,\text{mA}$
$\Delta I_C = 7.9\,\text{mA}$

$$\alpha = \frac{\Delta I_C}{\Delta I_E} = \frac{7.9}{8.0} = 0.9875 \approx 0.99$$

Also, $\beta = \dfrac{\alpha}{1-\alpha} = \dfrac{0.9875}{(1-0.9875)} = 79$

2. **(d)** Here, $n_i = 10^{16}\,\text{m}^{-3}$, $n_h = 5 \times 10^{22}\,\text{m}^{-3}$
As $n_e n_h = n_i^2$

$$\therefore\ n_e = \frac{n_i^2}{n_h} = \frac{(10^{16}\,\text{m}^{-3})^2}{5 \times 10^{22}\,\text{m}^{-3}} = 2 \times 10^9\,\text{m}^{-3}$$

3. **(d)** Energy band gap range is given by,

$$E_g = \frac{hc}{\lambda}$$

For visible region $\lambda = (4 \times 10^{-7} \sim 7 \times 10^{-7})\text{m}$

$$E_g = \frac{6.6 \times 10^{-34} \times 3 \times 10^8}{7 \times 10^{-7}}$$

$$= \frac{19.8 \times 10^{-26}}{7 \times 10^{-7}}$$

$$= \frac{2.8 \times 10^{-19}}{1.6 \times 10^{-19}}$$

$E_g = 1.75\,\text{eV}$

4. **(b)** Voltage gain $= \beta \times$ Impedance gain

$$50 = \beta \times \frac{200}{100} = 2\beta \implies \beta = 25$$

and power gain $= \beta^2 \times \dfrac{200}{100} = 1250.$

5. **(b)** When either of A or B is 1 i.e. closed then lamp will glow.
In this case, Truth table

Inputs		Output
A	B	Y
0	0	0
0	1	1
1	0	1
1	1	1

This represents OR gate.

6. **(c)** In p-region of p-n junction holes concentration > electrons concentration and in n-region electrons concentration > holes concentration.

7. **(c)** Peak value of rectified output voltage
= peak value of input voltage – barrier voltage
$= 2 - 0.7 = 1.3\,\text{V}.$

8. **(a)** Current gain $(\alpha) = 0.96$
$I_e = 7.2\,\text{mA}$

$$\frac{I_c}{I_e} = \alpha = 0.96$$

$$I_c = 0.96 \times 7.2\,\text{mA} = 6.91\,\text{mA}$$

$I_e = I_c + I_b$
$\Rightarrow I_b = I_e - I_c = 7.2 - 6.91 = 0.29\,\text{mA}$

9. **(c)** No. of electrons reaching the collector,

$$n_C = \frac{96}{100} \times 10^{10} = 0.96 \times 10^{10}$$

Emitter current, $I_E = \dfrac{n_E \times e}{t}$

Collector current, $I_C = \dfrac{n_C \times e}{t}$

$\therefore$ Current transfer ratio,

$$\alpha = \frac{I_C}{I_E} = \frac{n_C}{n_E} = \frac{0.96 \times 10^{10}}{10^{10}} = 0.96$$

10. **(c)** Here diode is forward biased with voltage $= 2 - 0 = 2\,\text{V}.$
$V_B = V_{knee} + IR$
$2 = 0.7 + I \times 200$
$(\therefore$ Total resistance $= 180 + 20 = 200\Omega)$

$$\therefore\ I = \frac{1.3}{200} = 6.5\,\text{mA}$$

11. **(b)** $\text{I} \to \text{ON}$
$\text{II} \to \text{OFF}$
In IInd state it is used as a amplifier it is active region.

12. **(b)** In half wave rectifier only half of the wave is rectified.

13. **(c)** $V' = V + IR = 0.5 + 0.1 \times 20 = 2.5\,\text{V}$

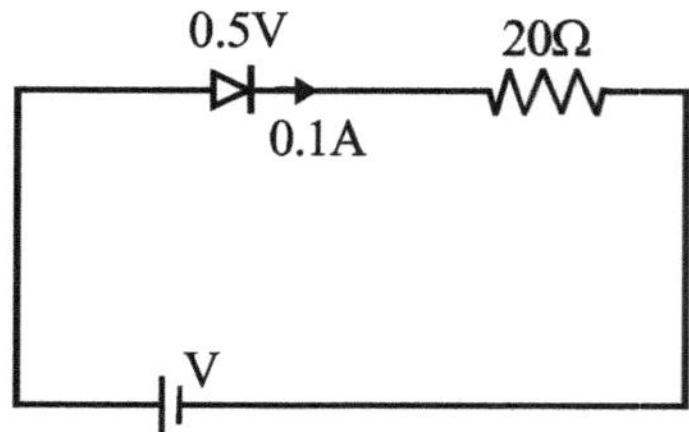

14. **(b)** $\dfrac{V_o}{V_{in}} = \dfrac{R_o}{R_{in}} \times \beta = \dfrac{5 \times 10^3 \times 62}{500} = 10 \times 62 = 620$

$V_o = 620 \times V_{in} = 620 \times 0.01 = 6.2\,\text{V}$
$\therefore V_o = 6.2\,\text{volt}.$

15. **(b)** Conductivity $\sigma = n_i e \mu_e = 10^{17} \times (1.6 \times 10^{-19}) \times 3800$
$= 60.8\,\text{mho/cm}$

16. (d) Negative feedback is applied to reduce the output voltage of an amplifier. If there is no negative feedback, the value of output voltage could be very high. In the options given, the maximum value of voltage gain is 100. Hence it is the correct option.

17. (a) In the given system all four gate is NOR gate

Truth Table

A	B	$(y' = \overline{A+B})$	$y'' = \overline{(A+y')}$	$y''' = \overline{(A+y'')}$	$y = \overline{y''+y'''}$
0	0	1	0	0	1
0	1	0	1	0	0
1	0	0	0	1	0
1	1	0	0	0	1

i.e.,

A	B	y
0	0	1
0	1	0
1	0	0
1	1	1

18. (a) Conductivity, $\sigma = \dfrac{1}{\rho} = e(n_e\mu_e + n_h\mu_h)$

$2.13 = 1.6 \times 10^{-19}(0.38 + 0.18)\,n_i$

(Since in intrinsic semi-conductor, $n_e = n_h = n_i$)

∴ density of charge carriers, n_i

$= \dfrac{2.13}{1.6 \times 10^{-19} \times 0.56} = 2.37 \times 10^{19}\,\text{m}^{-3}$

19. (d) Here $Y = \overline{(\overline{A}+\overline{B})} = \overline{\overline{A}}.\overline{\overline{B}} = A \cdot B$. Thus, it is an AND gate for which truth table is

A	B	Y
0	0	0
0	1	0
1	0	0
1	1	1

20. (d) $n_i^2 = n_e n_h$

$(1.5 \times 10^{16})^2 = n_e(4.5 \times 10^{22})$

$\Rightarrow \qquad n_e = 0.5 \times 10^{10}$

or $\qquad n_e = 5 \times 10^9$

Given $\quad n_h = 4.5 \times 10^{22}$

$\Rightarrow n_h \gg n_e$

∴ Semiconductor is p-type and

$n_e = 5 \times 10^9\,\text{m}^{-3}$.

21. (c) In n-type semiconductors, electrons are the majority charge carriers.

22. (d) For semiconductor, $n = AT^{3/2}e^{-\dfrac{E_g}{2KT}}$;

so $n \propto T^{3/2}$

23. (d) When PN junction diode is forward biased both depletion layer width W and barrier height V_0 decrease and current due to molarity carrier increases.

24. (b) D_2 is forward biased whereas D_1 is reversed biased. So effective resistance of the circuit

$R = 4 + 2 = 6\,\Omega$

$\therefore i = \dfrac{12}{6} = 2\,\text{A}$.

25. (d) In common emitter configuration current gain

$A_i = \dfrac{-hf_e}{1+h_{oe}R_L} = \dfrac{-50}{1+25\times10^{-6}\times1\times10^3} = -48.78$

26. (c)

27. (b) It is a p-n-p transistor with R as base.

28. (c) Here P-N junction diode rectifies half of the ac wave i.e., acts as half wave rectifier. During + ve half cycle Diode → forward biased output across will be

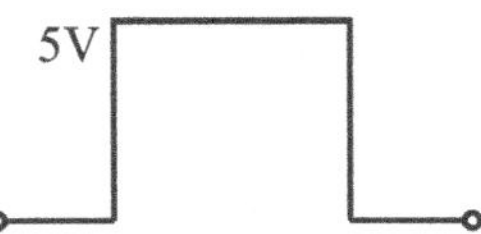

During −ve half cycle Diode → reverse biased output will not obtained.

29. (d) Due to heating, when a free electron is produced then simultaneously a hole is also produced.

30. (b) $I = nA\,ev_d$ or $I \propto nv_d$

$\therefore \quad \dfrac{I_e}{I_h} = \dfrac{n_e v_e}{n_h v_h}$ or $\dfrac{n_e}{n_h} = \dfrac{I_e}{I_h} \times \dfrac{v_h}{v_e} = \dfrac{7}{4} \times \dfrac{4}{5} = \dfrac{7}{5}$

31. (c) Electronic configuration of ^{6}C

^{6}C $= 1s^2, 2s^2\,2p^2$

The electronic configuration of ^{14}Si

^{14}Si $= 1s^2,\,2s^2\,2p^6,\,3s^2\,3p^2$

As they are away from Nucleus, so effect of nucleus is low for Si even for Sn and Pb are almost mettalic.

32. (d)

In forward bias, $V_1 > V_2$ i.e., in figure (d) p-type semiconductor is at higher potential w.r.t. n-type semiconductor.

33. (a) A positive feed back from output to input in an amplifier provides oscillations of constant amplitude.

34. (b) The power gain in case of CE amplifier,

Power gain $= \beta^2 \times$ Resistance gain

$= \beta^2 \times \dfrac{R_o}{R_i}$

$= (10)^2 \times 5 = 500$.

35. (c) Given : Voltage gain $A_V = 150$

$V_i = 2\cos\left(15t + \dfrac{\pi}{3}\right); V_0 = ?$

For CE transistor phase difference between input and output signal is $\pi = 180°$

Using formula, $A_V = \dfrac{V_0}{V_i}$

$\Rightarrow V_0 = A_V \times V_i$

$= 150 \times 2\cos\left(15t + \dfrac{\pi}{3}\right)$

or $V_0 = 300 \cos\left(15t + \dfrac{\pi}{3} + \pi\right)$

$V_0 = 300 \cos\left(15t + \dfrac{4}{3}\pi\right)$

36. **(a)** To use a transistor as an amplifier the emitter base junction is forward biased while the collector base junction is reverse biased.

37. **(d)** Copper is a conductor, so its resistance decreases on decreasing temperature as thermal agitation decreases; whereas germanium is semiconductor therefore on decreasing temperature resistance increases.

38. **(b)** In forward biasing, the diode conducts. For ideal junction diode, the forward resistance is zero; therefore, entire applied voltage occurs across external resistance R i.e., there occurs no potential drop, so potential across R is V in forward biased.

39. **(a)** Current gain $(\alpha) = 0.96$

$I_e = 7.2\,\text{mA}$

$\dfrac{I_c}{I_e} = \alpha = 0.96$

$I_c = 0.96 \times 7.2\,\text{mA} = 6.91\ \text{mA}$

$I_e = I_c + I_b$

$\Rightarrow I_b = I_e - I_c = 7.2 - 6.91 = 0.29\,\text{mA}$

40. **(d)**

The truth table for the above logic gate is :

A	B	C
1	1	1
1	0	1
0	1	1
0	0	0

This truth table follows the boolean algebra $C = A + B$ which is for OR gate

41. **(b)** $R = \dfrac{\Delta V}{\Delta I} = \dfrac{2.1 - 2}{(800 - 400) \times 10^{-3}} = \dfrac{1}{4} = 0.25\ \Omega$

42. **(c)**

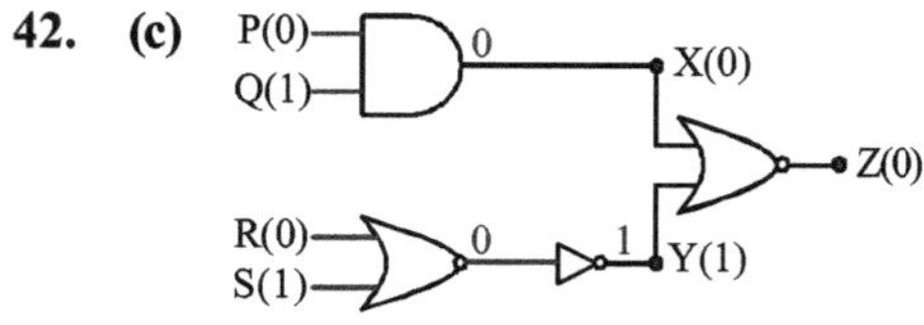

43. **(b)**

$Y_1 = A + B,\ Y_2 = \overline{A.B}$

$Y = (A + B)\cdot\overline{AB} = A\cdot\overline{A} + A\cdot\overline{B} + B\cdot\overline{A} + B\cdot\overline{B}$

$\qquad = 0 + A\cdot\overline{B} + B\cdot\overline{A} + 0 = A\cdot\overline{B} + B\cdot\overline{A}$ (XOR gate)

44. **(b)** $E_g = 2.0\,\text{eV} = 2 \times 1.6 \times 10^{-19}\ \text{J}$

$E_g = h\nu$

$\therefore\ \nu = \dfrac{E_g}{h} = \dfrac{2 \times 1.6 \times 10^{-19}\,\text{J}}{6.62 \times 10^{-34}\,\text{Js}}$

$= 0.4833 \times 10^{15}\ \text{s}^{-1} = 4.833 \times 10^{14}\ \text{Hz}$

$\simeq 5 \times 10^{14}\ \text{Hz}$

45. **(d)** The average value of output direct current in a full wave rectifier = (average value of current over a cycle)

$= (2I_0/\pi) = \dfrac{2I_0}{\pi}$

Mock Test Full Syllabus Physics

1. The resistance R of a wire is given by the relation $R = \dfrac{\rho \ell}{\pi r^2}$. Percentage error in the measurement of r, ℓ and r is 1%, 2% and 3% respectively. Then the percentage error in the measurement of R is
   (a) 6   (b) 9
   (c) 8   (d) 10

2. Figure shows the v-t graph for two particles P and Q. Which of the following statements regarding their relative motion is true?
   Their relative velocity

   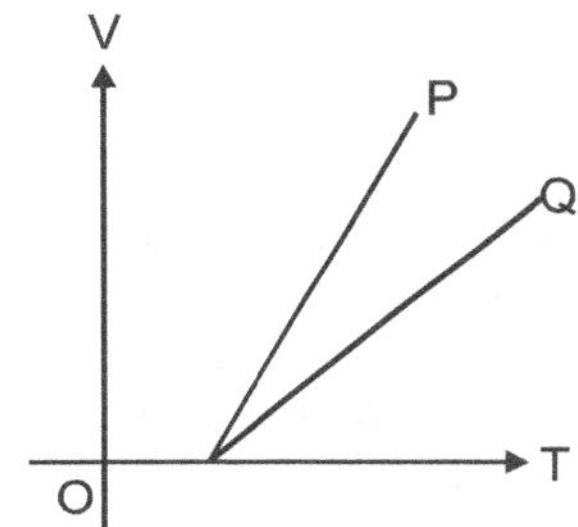

   (a) is zero
   (b) is non-zero but constant
   (c) continuously decreases
   (d) continuously increases

3. Time required to boil 2 litres of water initially at $20°C$ by a heater coil which works at 80% efficiency spending 500 joule/s is
   (a) 82 minutes   (b) 50 minutes
   (c) 28 minutes   (d) 37 minutes

4. A mass is tied to a string and rotated in a vertical circle, the minimum velocity of the body at the top is
   (a) $\sqrt{gr}$ (b) g/r
   (c) $\left(\dfrac{g}{r}\right)^{3/2}$ (d) gr

5. A man projects a coin upwards from the gate of a uniformly moving train. The path of coin for the man will be
   (a) parabolic
   (b) inclined straight line
   (c) vertical straight line
   (d) horizontal straight line

6. What is the disintegration constant of radon, if the number of its atoms diminishes by 18% in 24 h?
   (a) $2.1 \times 10^{-3}\,s^{-1}$ (b) $2.1 \times 10^{-4}\,s^{-1}$
   (c) $2.1 \times 10^{-5}\,s^{-1}$ (d) $2.1 \times 10^{-6}\,s^{-1}$

7. The frequencies of X-rays, γ-rays and ultraviolet rays are respectively a, b, and c. Then
   (a) $a < b, b < c$ (b) $a < b, b > c$
   (c) $a > b, b > c$ (d) $a > b, b < c$

8. A galvanometer can be changed into an ammeter by using
   (a) low resistance shunt in series
   (b) low resistance shunt in parallel
   (c) high resistance shunt in series
   (d) high resistance shunt in parallel

9. Which of the following statements is **FALSE** for a particle moving in a circle with a constant angular speed ?
   (a) The acceleration vector points to the centre of the circle
   (b) The acceleration vector is tangent to the circle
   (c) The velocity vector is tangent to the circle
   (d) The velocity and acceleration vectors are perpendicular to each other.

10. A monoatomic gas at $27°C$ is compressed adiabatically to $\dfrac{8}{27}$ of its original volume. The rise in temperature will be
    (a) $300°C$ (b) $350°C$
    (c) $375°C$ (d) $400°C$

11. Each of the resistance in the network shown is equal to R. The resistance between the terminals A and B is

    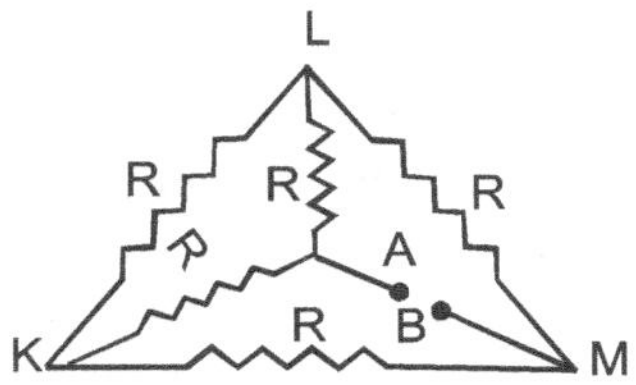

  (a) R   (b) 5R

  (c) 3R   (d) 6R

12. The energy of hydrogen atom in the nth orbit is E_n, then the energy in the nth orbit of single ionised helium atom is

  (a) $\dfrac{E_n}{2}$ (b) $2E_n$

  (c) $4E_n$ (d) $\dfrac{E_n}{4}$

13. Two identical particles move towards each other with velocity $2v$ and v respectively. The velocity of centre of mass is

  (a) v   (b) v/3

  (c) v/2   (d) zero.

14. The mass number of He is 4 and that for sulphur is 32. The radius of sulphur nuclei is larger than that of helium by

  (a) $\sqrt{8}$ (b) 4

  (c) 2   (d) 8

15. According to Newton's law of cooling, the rate of cooling of a body is proportional to $(\Delta\theta)^n$, where $\Delta\theta$ is the difference of the temperature of the body and the surroundings, then n is equal to

  (a) two   (b) three

  (c) four   (d) one

16. A body having initial velocity of 10 m/s moving on a rough surface comes to rest after moving 50 m. What is coefficient of friction between the body and surface? (g = 10 m/s^2)

  (a) 0.5   (b) 0.2

  (c) 0.3   (d) 0.1

17. The separation between successive fringes in a double slit arrangement is x. If the whole arrangement is dipped under water what will be the new fringe separation? [The wavelenght of light being used is 5000 Å]

  (a) 1.5x   (b) x

  (c) 0.75x   (d) 2x

18. A thin, metallic spherical shell contains a charge Q on it. A point charge q is placed at the cente of the shell and another charge q_1 is placed outside it as shown in figure. All the three charges are positive. The force on the charge at the centre is

  (a) towards left   (b) towards right

  (c) upward   (d) zero

19. A charge q is moving with a velocity v parallel to a magnetic field B. Force on the charge due to magnetic field is

  (a) $q\,v\,B$ (b) $q\,B/v$

  (c) zero   (d) $B\,v/q$

20. A bucket full of hot water is kept in a room and it cools from 75°C to 70°C in T_1 minutes, from 70°C to 65°C in T_2 minutes and from 65°C to 60°C in T_3 minutes. Then

  (a) $T_1 = T_2 = T_3$ (b) $T_1 < T_2 < T_3$

  (c) $T_1 > T_2 > T_3$ (d) $T_1 < T_2 > T_3$

21. In uniform circular motion, the velocity vector and acceleration vector are

  (a) perpendicular to each other

  (b) in same direction

  (c) in opposite direction

  (d) not related to each other

22. The current in a coil of L = 40 mH is to be increased uniformly from 1A to 11A in 4 milli sec. The induced e.m.f. will be

  (a) 100 V   (b) 0.4 V

  (c) 440 V   (d) 40 V

23. Two capacitors when connected in series have a capacitance of 3 μF, and when connected in parallel have a capacitance of 16 μF. Their individual capacities are

  (a) 1 μF, 2 μF   (b) 6 μF, 2 μF

  (c) 12 μF, 4 μF   (d) 3 μF, 16 μF

24. The weight of a body will be the least at

  (a) poles

  (b) equator

  (c) at height equal to R

  (d) centre of the earth

25. When a tuning fork produces sound waves in air, which one of the following is same in the material of tuning fork as well as in air?

  (a) Wavelength   (b) Frequency

  (c) Velocity   (d) Amplitude

26. The fermi energy for a substance is

  (a) independent of T

  (b) directly proportional to $\sqrt{T}$

  (c) directly proportional to T

  (d) directly proportional to T^2

27. ABC is a triangular plate of uniform thickness. The sides are in the ratio shown in the figure. I_{AB}, I_{BC} and I_{CA} are the moments of inertia of the plate about AB, BC and CA as axes respectively. Which one of the following relations is correct?

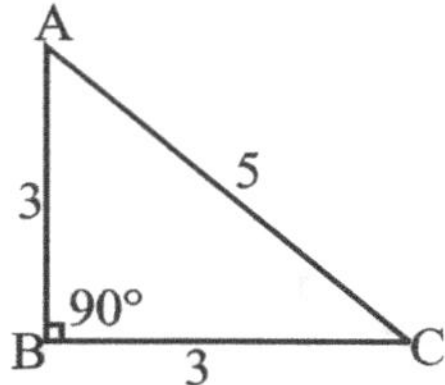

   (a) $I_{AB} > I_{BC}$ (b) $I_{BC} > I_{AB}$

   (c) $I_{AB} + I_{BC} = I_{CA}$ (d) I_{CA} is maximum

28. Consider the following statement:
    When jumping from some height, you should bend your knees as you come to rest, instead of keeping your legs stiff. Which of the following relations can be useful in explaining the statement? Where symbols have their usual meanings.

   (a) $\Delta\vec{p_1} = -\Delta\vec{p_2}$ (b) $\Delta E = \Delta(PE + KE) = 0$

   (c) $\vec{F}\Delta t = m\Delta\vec{v}$ (d) $\Delta x \propto \Delta F$

29. The amplitude of magnetic field of an electromagnetic wave is 2×10^{-7}T. It's electric field amplitude if the wave is travelling in free space is
      (a) $6\,Vm^{-1}$ (b) $60\,Vm^{-1}$
      (c) $10/6\,Vm^{-1}$ (d) None of these

30. The magnetic flux density B at a distance r from a long straight wire carrying a steady current varies with distance r as

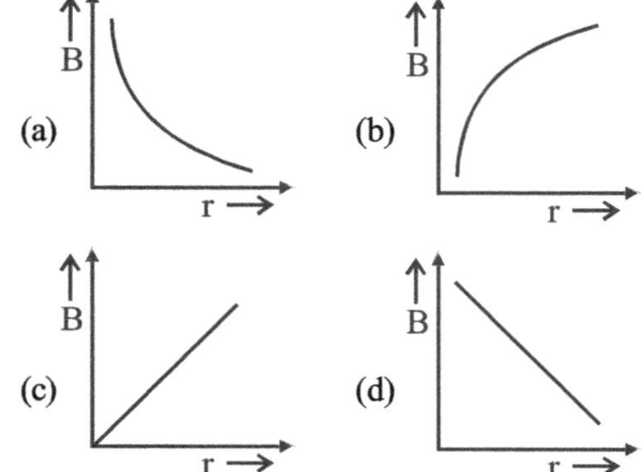

31. A metal piece is heated upto T° abs. The temperature of the surrounding is t° abs. The heat in the surrounding due to radiation is proportional to

   (a) $(T - T)^4$ (b) $T^4 - t^4$
   (c) $(T - t)^{1/4}$ (d) $T^2 - t^2$

32. Given, $_a\mu_g = \dfrac{3}{2}$, $_a\mu_w = \dfrac{4}{3}$, if a convex lens of focal length 10 cm is placed in water, then its focal length in water is
      (a) equal to 40 cm   (b) equal to 20 cm
      (c) equal to 10 cm   (d) None of these

33. If an alternating current is flowing in a spring, then the spring will be changing
      (a) in a straight line (b) periodically
      (c) elliptically   (d) first (c) then (a)

34. The unit vector along $2i - 3j + k$ is

   (a) $\dfrac{2i - 3j + k}{\sqrt{14}}$ (b) $\dfrac{2i - 3j + k}{5}$

   (c) $\dfrac{2i - 3j + k}{\sqrt{15}}$ (d) None of these

35. An iron rod of length 2m and cross-sectional area of 50 mm^2 is stretched by 0.5 mm, when a mass of 250 kg is hung from its lower end. Young's modulus of iron rod is

   (a) $19.6 \times 10^{20}\,N/m^2$ (b) $19.6 \times 10^{18}\,N/m^2$

   (c) $19.6 \times 10^{10}\,N/m^2$ (d) $19.6 \times 10^{15}\,N/m^2$

36. A particle of mass 1 kg is moving in S.H.M. with an amplitude 0.02 and a frequency of 60 Hz. The maximum force acting on the particle is
      (a) $144\,\pi^2$ (b) $188\,\pi^2$
      (c) $288\,\pi^2$ (d) None of these

37. According to Maxwell's hypothesis, a changing electirc field gives rise to
      (a) an e.m.f   (b) magnetic field
      (c) electric current   (d) pressure gradient.

38. The load versus elongation graph for four wires has been shown in the figure. The thinest wire is

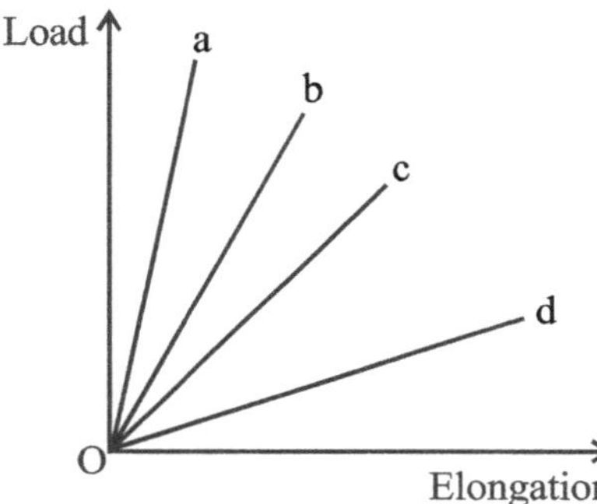

(a) a   (b) b
(c) c   (d) d

39. A ray of light is incident on the surface of separation of a medium with the velocity of light at an angle $45°$ and is refracted in the medium at an angle $30°$. Velocity of light in the medium will be (velocity of light in air $= 3 \times 10^8$ m/s)

(a) 3.8×10^8 m/s   (b) 3.38×10^8 m/s

(c) 2.12×10^8 m/s   (d) 1.56×10^8 m/s

40. The rain drops are in spherical shape due to
(a) residual pressure   (b) thrust on drop
(c) surface tension   (d) viscosity

41. A dip circle is so set that its needle moves freely in the magnetic meridian. In this position, the angle of dip is $40°$. Now the dip circle is rotated so that the plane in which the needle moves makes an angle of $30°$ with the magnetic meridian. In this position, the needle will dip by an angle
(a) $40°$ (b) $30°$
(c) more than $40°$ (d) less than $40°$

42. If the critical angle for total internal reflection from a medium to vacuum is $30°$. Then velocity of light in the medium is

(a) 1.5×10^8 m/s   (b) 2×10^8 m/s

(c) 3×10^8 m/s   (d) 0.75×10^8 m/s

43. An oscillator is nothing but an amplifier with
(a) positive feedback
(b) large gain
(c) no feedback
(d) negative feedback

44. For an AM-system the total power of modulated signal is 600 W and that of carrier is 400 W, the modulation index is
(a) 0.25   (b) 0.36
(c) 0.54   (d) 1

45. The drift current in a p-n junction is
(a) from the n-side to the p-side
(b) from the p-side to the n-side
(c) from the n-side to the p-side if the junction is forward-baised and in the opposite direction if it is reverse biased
(d) from the p-side to the n-side if the junction is forward-baised and in the opposite direction if it is reverse-baised

<table>
<tr><td colspan="18" align="center">ANSWER KEY</td></tr>
<tr><td>1</td><td>(b)</td><td>6</td><td>(d)</td><td>11</td><td>(a)</td><td>16</td><td>(d)</td><td>21</td><td>(a)</td><td>26</td><td>(a)</td><td>31</td><td>(b)</td><td>36</td><td>(c)</td><td>41</td><td>(d)</td></tr>
<tr><td>2</td><td>(d)</td><td>7</td><td>(b)</td><td>12</td><td>(c)</td><td>17</td><td>(c)</td><td>22</td><td>(a)</td><td>27</td><td>(b)</td><td>32</td><td>(a)</td><td>37</td><td>(b)</td><td>42</td><td>(a)</td></tr>
<tr><td>3</td><td>(c)</td><td>8</td><td>(b)</td><td>13</td><td>(c)</td><td>18</td><td>(d)</td><td>23</td><td>(c)</td><td>28</td><td>(c)</td><td>33</td><td>(b)</td><td>38</td><td>(d)</td><td>43</td><td>(a)</td></tr>
<tr><td>4</td><td>(a)</td><td>9</td><td>(b)</td><td>14</td><td>(c)</td><td>19</td><td>(c)</td><td>24</td><td>(d)</td><td>29</td><td>(b)</td><td>34</td><td>(a)</td><td>39</td><td>(c)</td><td>44</td><td>(d)</td></tr>
<tr><td>5</td><td>(b)</td><td>10</td><td>(c)</td><td>15</td><td>(d)</td><td>20</td><td>(b)</td><td>25</td><td>(b)</td><td>30</td><td>(a)</td><td>35</td><td>(c)</td><td>40</td><td>(c)</td><td>45</td><td>(a)</td></tr>
</table>

HINTS & SOLUTIONS

1. (b) Given $= R = \dfrac{\rho \ell}{\pi r^2}$, then

$$\frac{\Delta R}{R} \times 100$$

$$= \frac{\Delta \rho}{\rho} \times 100 + \frac{\Delta \ell}{\ell} \times 100 + 2\frac{\Delta r}{r} \times 100$$

$$= 1\% + 2\% + 2 \times 3\% = 9\%$$

2. (d) The difference in velocities is increasing with time as both of them have more constant but different acceleration.

3. (c) Heat required to boil water $= mc\Delta\theta$
$$= 2 \times 4200 \times (100 - 20)$$
$$= 6.72 \times 10^3 \, J$$

If t be the time of boil then
$$\eta \times 500 \times t = 6.72 \times 10^3$$

or $\quad t = \dfrac{6.72 \times 10^3}{0.8 \times 500} = 28$ minutes.

4. (a) Let velocity at $A = v_A$ and velocity at $B = v_B$

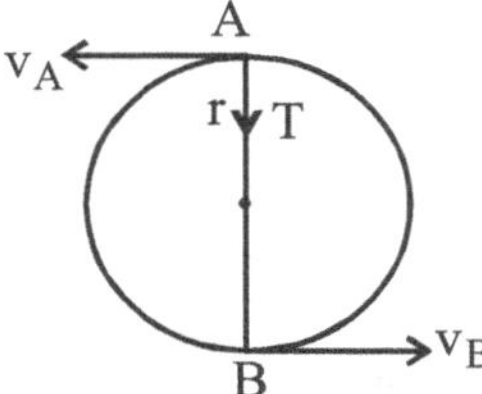

Applying conservation of energy at A & B

$$\frac{1}{2}mv_A^2 + 2gmr = \frac{1}{2}mv_B^2$$

$$v_B^2 = v_A^2 + 4gr \ldots\ldots\ldots(i)$$

Now as it is moving in circular path it has centripetal force.

At point $A \Rightarrow T + mg = \dfrac{mv_A^2}{r}$

for minimum velocity $T \geq 0$

or $\dfrac{mv_A^2}{r} \geq mg \Rightarrow v_A^2 \geq gr \Rightarrow v_A \geq \sqrt{gr}$

6. (d) For nuclear disintegration

$$\lambda = \frac{2.303}{t} \log \frac{N_o}{N_o - N}$$

$$= \frac{2.303}{24 \times 60 \times 60} \log \frac{100}{82} = 2.1 \times 10^{-6} \sec^{-1}$$

7. (b) γ rays has lowest wavelength and highest frequency among them while ultraviolet ray has highest wavelength and lowest frequency.

Order of frequency : $b > a > c$

8. (b) A galvanometer can be changed into an ammeter by the use of low resistance in parallel. So that ammeter does not draw much current which may change the magnitude of main current.

9. (b) Acceleration vector is always radial (i.e. towards the center) for uniform circular motion.

10. (c) $T_1 = 27ºC = 300 \, K$

$$V_1 = V \text{ and } V_2 = \frac{8V}{27}$$

Ratio of specific heats for monoatomic gas,

$$\gamma = \frac{5}{3}$$

In an adiabatic process,
$$T_1 V_1^{\gamma-1} = T_2 V_2^{\gamma-1}$$

or $\quad T_2 = \left(\dfrac{V_1}{V_2}\right)^{\gamma-1} \times T_1$

$$T_2 = 300 \times \left(\frac{1}{8/27}\right)^{(5/3)-1}$$

$$= 300 \times \left(\frac{27}{8}\right) = 300 \times \left(\frac{9}{4}\right) = 675\,K$$

$$= 402°C$$

Hence, rise in temperature
$$= T_2 - T_1 = 402 - 27 = 375°C$$

11. (a) The equivalent circuit is shown in fig. Since the Wheatstone's bridge is balanced, therefore no current will flow through the arm KL. Equivalent resistance between
$AKM = R + R = 2R$

Equivalent resistance between $ALM = R + R = 2R$

The two resistances are in parallel. Hence equivalent resistance between A and B is given by

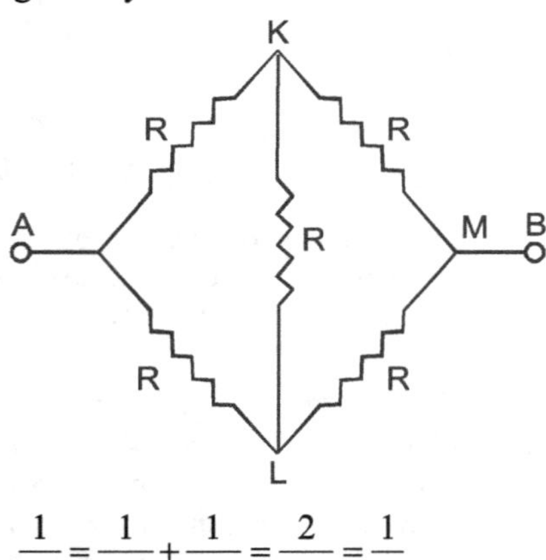

$$\frac{1}{R'} = \frac{1}{2R} + \frac{1}{2R} = \frac{2}{2R} = \frac{1}{R}$$

i.e., $R' = R$

12. (c) For n^{th} orbit, energy, $E_n = \dfrac{2\pi^2 em^4 z^2}{n^2 h^2}$

For hydrogen $(z = 1)$, $E_n = \dfrac{2\pi^2 em^4}{n^2 h^2}$

For helium $(z = 2)$,

So, $E = \dfrac{2\pi^2 em^4 \times 4}{n^2 h^2}$

$$\frac{E}{E_n} = \frac{4}{1} \Rightarrow E = 4E_n$$

13. (c) Conserving Linear Momentum
$$2Mv_c = 2Mv - Mv \Rightarrow v_c = v/2.$$

14. (c) $\dfrac{R_s}{R_\alpha} = \left(\dfrac{A_s}{A_\alpha}\right)^{1/3} = \left(\dfrac{32}{4}\right)^{1/3} = 2$

15. (d) $\dfrac{dH}{dt} \propto (\theta_2 - \theta_1) = (\Delta\theta)^n \Rightarrow n = 1$

16. (d) Use $a = \mu g$ and $v^2 = u^2 + 2as$

17. (c) When the arrangement is dipped in water;
$$\beta' = \beta/\mu = \frac{x}{4/3} = \frac{3}{4}x = 0.75x$$

18. (d) The charge q, which is kept at the centre of metallic spherical shell transfered to the outer surface of shell & inside the shell the electric field is zero & hence force is also zero.

19. (c) $F_n = q(\vec{v} \times \vec{B})$

$$= qvB\sin\theta = 0 \text{ (because } \theta = 0°)$$

20. (b) The time of cooling increases as the difference between the temperature of body & surrounding is reduced. So $T_1 < T_2 < T_3$ (according to Newton's law of cooling).

21. (a) In uniform circular motion speed is constant. So, no tangential acceleration.
It has only radial acceleration

$$a_R = \frac{v^2}{R} \text{ [directed towards center]}$$

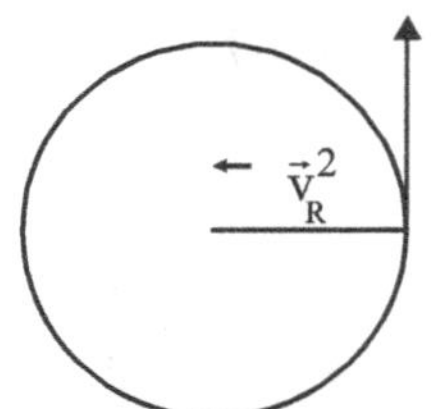

and its velocity is always in tangential direction. So these two are perpendicular to each other.

22. (a) $e = \dfrac{LdI}{dt} = \dfrac{40 \times 10^{-3}(11-1)}{4 \times 10^{-3}} = 100V$

23. (c) $C_s = \dfrac{C_1 C_2}{C_1 + C_2} = 3$

$C_p = C_1 + C_2 = 16$ $\therefore$ $C_1 C_2 = 48$

$$C_1 - C_2 = \sqrt{(C_1 + C_2)^2 - 4C_1 C_2}$$

$$= \sqrt{16^2 - 4 \times 48} = \sqrt{64} = 8$$

$\therefore \quad C_1 = 12\,\mu F$ and $C_2 = 4\,\mu F$

24. (d) At the centre of the earth gravity is zero.

25. (b) Frequency does not depend upon the medium, so, it will remain same in the material of the tuning fork and in air.

26. (a) The highest energy level occupied by an electron in the energy band at zero kelvin is called Fermi level and the energy associated is known as Fermi energy. So, it is independent of T.

27. (b) The intersection of medians is the centre of mass of the triangle. Since distances of centre of mass from the sides are related as : $x_{BC} < x_{AB} < x_{AC}$ therefore $I_{BC} > I_{AB} > I_{AC}$ or $I_{BC} > I_{AB}$.

28. (c) If $\vec{F}$ force acts for short interval Δt, then

$$\vec{F}\,\Delta T = m \Delta \vec{v}.$$

29. (b) For electromagnetic wave,

$$F_E = F_M \Rightarrow eE = BeC \Rightarrow E = B.C$$

$$= 2 \times 10^{-7} \times 3 \times 10^8 = 60 \text{ V/m}$$

30. (a) According to Biot Savart's law

$$dB = \frac{\mu_0}{4\pi} \cdot \frac{Id\ell \sin\theta}{r^2}$$

$$dB \propto \frac{1}{r^2}$$

So, graph (a) is correct.

31. (b) According to Stefan' law heat emitted per second per unit area $\alpha(T_1^4 - T_2^4)$ where T_1 is the temperature of body & T_2 is the temperature of surrounding (T_1 & T_2 are on Kelvin scale).

32. (a) $\dfrac{1}{f_\omega} = \left(^\omega \mu_g - 1\right)\left(\dfrac{1}{r_1} - \dfrac{1}{r_2}\right)$

[f_ω is focal length of lens in water]

$\dfrac{1}{f} = (^a\mu_g - 1)\left(\dfrac{1}{r_1} - \dfrac{1}{r_2}\right)$

[f is focal length of lens in air]
Dividing,

$\dfrac{f}{f_\omega} = \dfrac{(^\omega\mu_g - 1)}{(^a\mu_g - 1)}; {}^\omega\mu_g = \dfrac{^a\mu_g}{^a\mu_w}$

$$= \frac{3/2}{4/3} = \frac{3}{2} \times \frac{3}{4} = \frac{9}{8}$$

$$\frac{f}{f_w} = \frac{9/8 - 1}{\dfrac{3}{2} - 1} = \frac{1/8}{1/2} = \frac{1}{4}$$

$$f_w = 4 \times f = 4 \times 10 = 40 \text{ cm.}$$

33. (b) If current passes through a spring, it shrinks as in two adjacent wire, current is flowing in the same direction. Even if direction of current is reversed still the spring will shrink. As AC current is a periodically changing current, the process of shrinking will also be periodic in nature.

35. (c) $Y = \dfrac{F/A}{\Delta\ell/\ell} = \dfrac{\dfrac{250 \times 10}{50 \times 10^{-6}}}{\dfrac{0.5 \times 10^{-3}}{2}}$

$$= \frac{250 \times 9.8}{50 \times 10^{-6}} \times \frac{2}{0.5 \times 10^{-3}}$$

$$\Rightarrow 19.6 \times 10^{10}\,\text{N/m}^2$$

36. (c) Max. force = mass × max. acceleration
$= m\,4\pi^2 v^2 a = 1 \times 4 \times \pi^2 \times (60)^2 \times 0.02$
$= 288\,\pi^2$

37. (b) Changing electric field gives rise to displacement current which creates magnetic field around it.

39. (c)

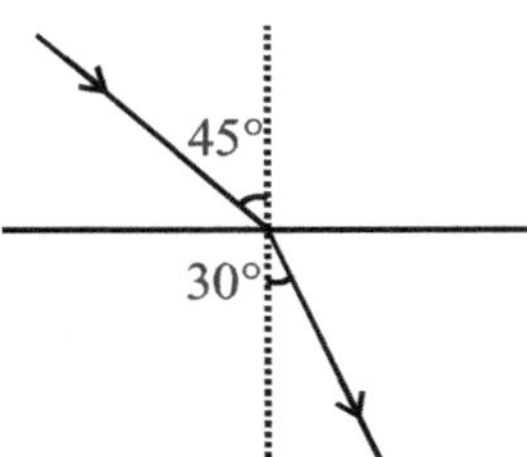

Refractive index, $\mu = \dfrac{\sin 45°}{\sin 30°}$

$$\mu = \frac{1}{\sqrt{2}} \times 2 = \sqrt{2}$$

Now, $\mu = \dfrac{\text{Velocity of light in air}}{\text{Velocity of light in medium}} = \sqrt{2}$

Velocity of light in medium

$$= 3 \times 10^8 \times \frac{1}{\sqrt{2}} = 2.12 \times 10^8\,\text{m/sec}$$

40. (c) Rain drops are in spherical shape due to surface tension.

41. (d) $\delta_1 = 40°, \delta_2 = 30°, \delta = ?$

$$\cot\delta = \sqrt{\cot^2\delta_1 + \cot^2\delta_2}$$

$$= \sqrt{\cot^2 40° + \cot^2 30°}$$

$$\cot\delta = \sqrt{1.19^2 + 3} = 2.1$$

$$\therefore \quad \delta = 25° \quad \text{i.e.} \quad \delta < 40°.$$

42. (a) $\mu = \dfrac{1}{\sin C} = \dfrac{1}{\sin 30°} = \dfrac{1}{1/2} = 2$

Velocity of light in the medium

$$= \frac{3 \times 10^8}{2} = 1.5 \times 10^8 \, \text{m/sec}$$

44. (d) $P_T = P_C\left(1 + \dfrac{m_a^2}{2}\right)$

$$\therefore \quad 600 = 400\left(1 + \frac{m_a^2}{2}\right) \Rightarrow \frac{3}{2} = 1 + \frac{m_a^2}{2}$$

$$\text{or} \quad \frac{m_a^2}{2} = \frac{1}{2} \Rightarrow m_a = 1$$

www.ingramcontent.com/pod-product-compliance
Lightning Source LLC
La Vergne TN
LVHW080540200726
843508LV00008B/1485